About the Author

A.N. Wilson was born in 1950 and educated at Rugby and New College, Oxford. A Fellow of the Royal Society of Literature, he has held a prominent position in the world of literature and journalism. He has written lives of Sir Walter Scott (John Llewellyn Rhys Prize), Tolstoy (Whitbread Award for Biography), C.S. Lewis, Hilaire Belloc, Iris Murdoch and John Betjeman. His novels include *The Healing Art* (Somerset Maugham Award), *Wise Virgin* (W H Smith Award), *The Sweets of Pimlico* (John Llewellyn Rhys Prize), *My Name Is Legion*, *A Jealous Ghost* and the five books in the Lampitt Chronicles. In 1992 he caused a sensation with his bestselling *Jesus* and this he followed up with his equally controversial *Paul*. His study of the Victorian age, *The Victorians*, was published by Hutchinson in 2002 to massive critical acclaim. He lives in North London.

AFTER THE VICTORIANS

A. N. WILSON

arrow books

Published by Arrow in 2006

12

First published by Hutchinson in 2005

Arrow Books
The Random House Group Limited
20 Vauxhall Bridge Road, London SW1V 2SA

Addresses for companies within The Random House Group Limited can be found at:
www.randomhouse.co.uk/offices.htm

The Random House Group Limited Reg. No. 954009

Grateful acknowledgement is made for permission to reproduce lines from the following:
'On a General Election' from *Sonnets and Verse* by Hilaire Belloc (Copyright © The Estate
of Hilaire Belloc 1938) by permission of PFD on behalf of the Estate of Hilaire Belloc
Collected Poems, John Betjeman, John Murray
The Complete Lyrics, Noël Coward, Methuen Publishing Ltd, Copyright © The Estate of Noël Coward
Winston Churchill Biography by Randolph S. Churchill and Martin Gilbert
reproduced with permission of Curtis Brown Ltd, London, on behalf of C&T Publications.
Copyright C&T Publications
The World Crisis, Liberalism and the Social Problem, and from various speeches by Sir Winston
Churchill reproduced with permission of Curtis Brown Ltd, London,
on behalf of The Estate of Sir Winston Churchill. Copyright Winston S. Churchill
The Complete Verse, Rudyard Kipling, Kylie Cathie Ltd, by permission of
A. P. Watt Ltd on behalf of the National Trust
Collected Poems of Henry Reed (1991) by Henry Reed, edited by Jon Stallworthy,
Oxford University Press
The Poems, W. B. Yeats, Macmillan, by permission of A. P. Watt Ltd on behalf of Michael B. Yeats.

A CIP catalogue record for this book is available
from the British Library

ISBN 9780099451877

Typeset by Palimpsest Book Production Limited, Polmont, Stirlingshire
Printed and bound in Great Britain by Clays Ltd, St Ives plc

Contents

List of Illustrations

Second section

Radclyffe Hall with Una Lady Troubridge (© *Getty Images*)
Margaret Wintringham and Nancy Astor (© *Getty Images*)
Marie Stopes (*Science & Society Picture Library*)
Lawrence of Arabia (© *Getty Images*)
Mohandas Karamchand Gandhi (© *Getty Images*)
Gandhi fasting as a protest against British rule in India (© *Getty Images*)
Max Aitken (© *Getty Images*)
Alfred Charles William Harmsworth (© *Getty Images*)
Agatha Christie (© *Getty Images*)
Edith and Osbert Sitwell (© *Getty Images*)
Noël Coward with Gertrude Stein (*Science & Society Picture Library*)
David Lloyd George and Winston Churchill (© *Getty Images*)
James Ramsay MacDonald (© *Getty Images*)
Stanley Baldwin (© *Getty Images*)
Neville Chamberlain (*Science & Society Picture Library*)
London slums (*Science & Society Picture Library*)
Basil Jellicoe (© *Popperfoto*)
Beatrice and Sidney Webb (© *Getty Images*)
Albert Einstein (© *Getty Images*)
Ernest Walton, Ernest Rutherford and John Cockcroft (© *Getty Images*)
John Maynard Keynes (*Private Collection, Roger-Viollet, Paris/Bridgeman Art Library*)
Poster for Ramsey MacDonald's Government of National Unity (© *Getty Images*)
Welwyn Garden City (© *Getty Images*)

Third section

Men queuing outside a London Labour Exchange (*Science & Society Picture Library*)
Jarrow Hunger March (*Science & Society Picture Library*)
Adolf Hitler (© *Getty Images*)
Ezra Pound (© *Getty Images*)
Sir Oswald Mosley (*Science & Society Picture Library*)
John Cowper Powys (© *Corbis*)
Stanley Spencer (© *Getty Images*)
Cosmo Gordon Lang, Archbishop of Canterbury (© *Getty Images*)

Poster advertising the Pageant of Empire, Wembley, 1924, by Gerald Spencer Pryse (*Victoria & Albert Museum, London, UK/Bridgeman Art Library*)

Guernica (1937) by Pablo Picasso (*Museo Nacional Centro de Arte Reina Sofia, Madrid, Spain/Bridgeman Art Library © Succession Picasso/DACS 2005*)

Recruiting poster for the Spanish Civil War (*Bibliothèque Nationale, Paris, France, Archives Charmet/Bridgeman Art Library*)

Poster advertising the Festival of Britain (*© Museum of London, UK/Bridgeman Art Library*)

Poster advertising the Exhibition of Science, part of the Festival of Britain, by Robin Day (*Private Collection, The Stapleton Collection/Bridgeman Art Library*)

Festival of Britain weather vane (*Private Collection/Bridgeman Art Library*)

Mushroom cloud from Ivy Mike (*© Corbis*)

Foreword and Acknowledgements

Like its predecessor, *The Victorians*, this book is a portrait of an age, rather than a formal history. It takes the story of Britain, and her place in the world, from 1901 to the Coronation of Queen Elizabeth II in 1953. Though it is as long a book as the last one, I am even more conscious as I finish it of the omissions. Yet, enough is enough, and a volume must be light enough to hold without the aid of a lectern.

As I wrote, it became more and more clear to me that what I was painting was a portrait of my parents' generation. It is the story of Britain in the five decades preceding my own birth. I grew up with this history as an oral tradition, as we all did. 'Before the war' . . . How many sentences on their lips began with that phrase. In this oral history different family members were associated, however private their lives, and however insignificant in terms of great public events, with those events themselves. Both grandfathers were said to have been ruined by the Slump. My father was just too young, by a few months, to have served in the Great War, but his elder sister, my beloved and favourite aunt Elizabeth, had served as a nurse in France during that war. Every Christmas, as some of us in the family went to church, we waited for the moment (no churchgoer she) for her to light her cigarette and say: 'The last time I attended a Midnight Mass was at Amiens Cathedral in 1917.'

There was the General Strike, in which my father had enjoyed himself as a mounted policeman. There was the extraordinary story of Germany, deeply linked to my mother's destiny as she recalled her two happy years in Koblenz from 1929 to 1931, and the clouds which fell over the household there when the father denounced his teenaged sons for enjoying a book called *Mein Kampf*. And of course there was the war itself, during which my brother and sister were born, and in which my father served as a colonel in the Royal Artillery. All these things went on before my arrival in the family, but they were constantly rehearsed and discussed, as were the subsequent excitements of the Great Winter of 1947. I suspect that the picture of the twentieth century in the following pages would not be the story that any of the rest of the family would have told. But it could not have been written without them.

Then again, as on previous occasions, I owe much to the libraries which I have visited. In the Bodleian Library, I have been guided skilfully to manuscript sources. In the British Library, I have also had kind help in the Manuscript Room, though I have chiefly worked from printed sources in the Humanities One Reading Room, where, as always, the staff have been exemplary for their courtesy and friendly helpfulness during a period of the library's history which has not been easy. I have also consulted the London Library, and am grateful to the staff who have always noticed, but not always objected, when I have borrowed more books than my ticket allowed. The Marylebone Public Library is also an excellent reference library and its staff are always helpful.

I have been extraordinarily lucky in my publishers. Sue Freestone is as good an editor as she is a friend. James Nightingale, an ever-reassuring presence, has been an unflappable co-midwife and has done hard work with picture research. Steve Cox has edited a long and difficult typescript with welcome rigour. On the other side of the Atlantic, the enthusiasm of Jonathan Galassi and Eric Chinski has been inspiring. Grateful thanks to Douglas Matthews who made the index.

None of my books would get written without the patient support, friendship and advice of Gillon Aitken, king among agents, who encouraged me at the beginning and helped me to the end. In initial stages he used to refer to the book as *Edward, George, Edward, George*, and in some ways I wish that I had kept this title, even though it suggests too exclusive an interest in the Royal Family – and this book is supposed to be about Britain in its politics, its changing social mores, its art and literature, its scientific achievements, its wars, its victories, its losses.

When I had written the book, Amy Boyle typed it, and then when I had scribbled on her typescript, she typed it again. My professional life would be impossible without her. Her speed and skill are phenomenal. Since she is always the first person to read what I write, her merry voice on the telephone reporting the completion of another chapter is always a tonic.

I feel very fortunate that five writers whose work I esteem much more highly than I do my own have found time to read this book in typescript and to make countless, often very detailed sugestions: Richard Aldous, Hugh Cecil, A. D. Harvey, Lawrence James and Hugh Massingberd. The oft-repeated formula is true, that any mistakes remaining are my own; but these friends have done their best to make this a better book.

After the Victorians

Oedipus Rex, Oedipus Kaiser

In 1900 there was published in Vienna one of the most extraordinary
and revolutionary texts ever to come from a human brain. *Die
Traumdeutung* (*The Interpretation of Dreams*) expounded the theory on
which all subsequent psychoanalysis was based, even or especially those
psychoanalytical theories which reacted most violently against it: namely,
that the human mind consists of what might be described as two layers.
With the outer layer, of our conscious mind, we reason and form judgements. In reasonable, well-balanced individuals, the pains and sorrows
of childhood have been worked through, put behind them. With the
unhealthy, however, neurotic or hysterical individuals, there is beneath
the surface of life a swirling cauldron of suppressed memories in which
lurk the traumas (the Greek word for wounds) of early experiences. Under
hypnosis, or in dreams, we re-enter the world of the subconscious and
with the care of a helpful analyst we can sometimes revisit the scenes of
our early miseries and locate the origins of our psychological difficulties. The author of this world-changing book, Dr Sigmund Freud
(1856–1939), was a happily married neurologist, born in the Moravian
town of Freiberg, but for most of his life resident in Vienna, hub of the
Austro-Hungarian Empire, where his consulting room in Berggasse 19,
Vienna IX (from 1931), and his celebrated couch, on which patients lay
to recite their sorrows, became a totemic emblem of the century which
was to unfold. The need to return to some forgotten, irrational, dark
place of our lost past became compelling, personal and collective, as the
hysteria of the twentieth century reached its crescendo-point and as Dr
Freud, a Jew, though a non-believing one, packed his belongings and took
his family to live in London for the last year of his life, following the
Anschluss, the joining together of Germany and Austria into a Great
Germany, *Grossdeutschland*. He had already had the honour of having
his books burned in Berlin in 1933, and in 1938 they were burned in
Vienna.

On the publication of *Die Traumdeutung*, there were many people
who, if not actually tempted to burn the book, must have found its
contents shocking.

If *Oedipus the King* is able to move modern man no less deeply than
the Greeks who were Sophocles' contemporaries, the solution can only

be that the effect of Greek tragedy does not depend on the contrast between fate and human will, but is to be sought in the distinctive nature of the subject-matter exemplifying this contrast. There must be a voice within us that is ready to acknowledge the compelling force of fate in *Oedipus* . . . His fate moves us only because it could have been our own as well, because at our birth the oracle pronounced the same curse upon us as it did on him. It was perhaps ordained that we should all of us turn our first sexual impulses towards our mother, our first hatred and violent wishes against our father. Our dreams convince us of it. King Oedipus, who killed his father Laius and married his mother Jocasta, is only the fulfilment of our childhood wish. But, more fortunate than he, we have since succeeded, at least insofar as we have not become psychoneurotics, in detaching our sexual impulses from our mothers, and forgetting our jealousy of our fathers.[1]

Dr Freud, further, told his Vienna lecture audiences: 'The dream of having sexual intercourse with the mother is dreamed by many today as it was then, and they recount it with the same indignation and amazement [as Oedipus].'[2]

Albert Edward, Prince of Wales, succeeded his mother Queen Victoria upon her death at half-past six in the evening on 22 January 1901, and became King Edward VII. He had waited a long time. 'Most people pray to the Eternal Father,' he had quipped, 'but I am the only one afflicted with an Eternal Mother.' If he ever had dreams about his mother of the kind believed by Dr Freud to be so usual, he did not record them for posterity. Queen Victoria did, however, believe that Bertie, as he was always known in his own family, in effect achieved half of the Oedipal destiny by killing his father, Prince Albert.

An indiscretion with an actress, Nellie Clifden, at the Curragh Camp near Dublin had brought Bertie's name into the newspapers, and his serious German father, embarrassed, angry and distressed, had gone to Cambridge, where Bertie was an undergraduate, to remonstrate with him during a wet evening in November 1861. A bad cold had turned to fever, and within a few weeks the doctors had diagnosed typhoid, almost certainly caused by the drains at Windsor Castle, one of the Prince Consort's obsessions, and hardly to be blamed on poor Bertie. Nevertheless, it was, from the very first moment of her widow's grief, one of the Queen's obsessions that Bertie's 'fall' had caused 'beloved Papa's demise', aged forty-two.

'Poor unhappy Bertie,' wrote the distraught mother a few weeks after Albert died, to Bertie's elder sister, the Crown Princess of Prussia, 'much as I pity I never can or shall look at him without a shudder as you may

4

imagine'.³ And again: 'If you had seen [your husband] struck down, day by day get worse and finally die, I doubt whether you could bear the sight of the one who was the cause.'⁴

By the time he inherited his kingdom, Edward VII was fifty-nine years old; at 67 inches high, he weighed 225 pounds. In some outward terms, he was not an obvious case of a man who bore any resentment of his upbringing by parents who had clearly deplored in equal measure his limitations of intellect and his lack of morals. For example, at a public dinner, when mentioning his father, he had burst into tears.

The speed with which he dismantled any physical reminders of his parents, however, tells its own story. In Windsor Castle, and in Buckingham Palace, the new monarch walked about cheerfully with a cigar stuck between his lips, Caesar, his long-haired white fox terrier,⁵ trotting at his heels, his hat still on his head as he cleared out and destroyed his father's and mother's memory. In these rooms, where smoking had always been forbidden, the obese, bronchitic king coughed, puffed smoke and gave orders that hundreds of 'rubbishy old coloured photographs' be destroyed. Busts and statues of John Brown, his mother's faithful Highlander, were smashed; the papers of the Munshi, Queen Victoria's beloved Indian servant, were burned. The huge collection of relics of the Prince Consort, undisturbed since his untimely death forty years earlier, was sent to the muniment room in Windsor's Round Tower. While getting rid of his parents' old rubbish, he also took the opportunity to extend the telephone networks, install new bathrooms and lavatories, and to convert coach houses into garages for the cars of his nouveaux riches friends. 'Alas!' Queen Alexandra wrote to Edward VII's sister, now the Empress Frederick, in Berlin. 'During my absence, Bertie has had all your beloved Mother's rooms dismantled and all her precious things removed.'

The most significant of the new king's anti-parental gestures was his decision to close Osborne House on the Isle of Wight, and make it, jointly, a Royal Naval College for young cadets and a convalescent home for retired officers. There is an apocryphal story told at Osborne of a visitor coming down the drive in the 1920s and seeing twenty or thirty elderly gentlemen of military or naval deportment, some in bath chairs and covered with plaid rugs, some strolling on the lawn. The visitor was waggishly told: 'Those are the Prince Consort's illegitimate children!' It would not be funny if, instead of referring to the priggishly monogamous Albert, the joker had claimed the old gentlemen to be children of the notoriously lecherous Edward VII. What the joke points up is the fact that the Prince Consort's real children were no longer there in the Italian palazzo which he had so lovingly built in the 1840s. It was where the distraught queen had spent the greater part of her long widowhood, and it was where she had died.

As the old queen lay dying in January 1901, Henry James, wisest of commentators, had written from his London club, the Reform, to American friends:

I feel as if her death will have consequences in and for this country that no man can foresee. The Prince of Wales is an arch-vulgarian (don't *repeat* this from me); the wretched little 'Yorks' are less than nothing; the Queen's magnificent duration had held things magnificently – beneficently – together and prevented all sorts of accidents. Her death, in short, will let loose incalculable forces for possible ill. I am very pessimistic.[6]

To another American, when the queen had actually died, he wrote:

We grovel before fat Edward – E. The Caresser, as he is privately named . . . But I mourn the safe and motherly old middle-class queen, who held the nation warm under the fold of her big, hideous, Scotch-plaid shawl and whose duration had been so extraordinarily convenient and beneficent. I fear her death much more than I should have expected; she was a sustaining symbol – and the wild waters are upon us now.[7]

James bids his compatriots to mourn Victoria, 'for she was always nice to us'.[8] His novelistic antennae caught, as political commentary might have failed to do, the vulnerability of the most powerful nation upon Earth, at the apogee of its pre-eminence.

From the perspective of over one hundred years, we look back to the early years of the twentieth century and see the Edwardian world through the mayhem of slaughters and revolutions which followed. Knowing what is to come will influence two quite different approaches. Some will look back on the period before the First World War as a Golden Age of peace and prosperity, of long afternoons and country house parties. Others will see in the troubled situation in the Empire, the terrible living conditions of the urban poor, the twin growth of nationalism and military technology, a terrifying howl of ancestral voices prophesying war. Both those opposing polarities will focus some of their thoughts upon the monarchy. After all, it was in the aim of ridding the world of the tyrannies and injustices with which a monarchical system is associated that the revolutions in Russia, Germany, Bulgaria, Italy, Spain, were to be driven forward. Some readers of history will continue to see that upturning of thrones to be, in the Cromwellian phrase, a cruel necessity. Others will note that in the years when other countries of the world had their civil wars, their Gulags, their Dachaus and their Kristallnachts, it was the conservative, monarchical, aristocratic Britain which maintained a political ideal of personal freedom, not merely for its own citizens, but also for foreign refugees to its shores and those in other lands who fought for freedom.

Those who lean towards the latter view, as I do myself, need to be clear in their minds what they are saying. While it might be true that the evolved monarchical system and a liberalized aristocracy in Britain undoubtedly did help to maintain a rule of law, a continuity with stabler days, in a way that revolutionary wars did not, it would be absurd to suggest that the monarchs themselves had very much to do with it. Faced with the military or economic disasters which befell some other European countries, it is unlikely that any of the four British monarchs of the first half of the twentieth century would have been able to withstand the rise of a British Lenin or a British Mussolini. It was often what they did not do, rather than what they did, which strengthened the monarchs' roles. The notion that beneath a deceptive appearance there lurked profound political acumen in the monarchs who reigned from 1901 to 1952, in Edward, George, Edward or George, is to be resisted. It is to overlook the truth of what Henry James intuited as he witnessed the passing of Victoria, the removal of 'a sustaining symbol'. This is not to say that Edward VII, who was personally amiable, did not have some aptitude for oiling diplomacy. His chief virtue, politically, however, was that he allowed that side of things, almost exclusively, to be handled by professional politicians.

'He subscribes to his cripples, rewards his sailors, reviews his soldiers and opens bridges, bazaars, hospitals and railway tunnels with enviable sweetness,' said Mrs Asquith, the wife of his Liberal prime minister. Lord Fisher said of him: 'He wasn't clever, but he always did the right thing, which is better than brains.'[9] No one would have said this of the king's Prussian nephew Willy.

If genial, self-indulgent and in many respects well-adjusted Edward VII would have been a disappointing subject for a psychoanalyst, the same could not be said for his nephew, the German Emperor Wilhelm II. Nor is this simply a matter of interest to doctors or to royal obsessives. It is now generally recognized that the Kaiser, an autocratic ruler with immense power over his 68 million subjects,* was governed in his foreign policy by the profound psychological complexity of his attitude to his mother. There is first the very matter of his birth, in 1858, to Queen Victoria's eldest child – herself named Victoria – and Prince

* The population of Germany rose from around 50 million in 1888 to 68 million in 1914.

Friedrich Wilhelm of Prussia. Princess Victoria insisted upon English doctors, and only English doctors, being present at the birth, which took place in Berlin. She always blamed herself for the fact that his arm was deformed, apparently as a result of clumsy midwifery. For the first few years of his life she was in denial about the withered arm, and throughout his youth she feared that it would warp his manliness or his independence. When he was eight and a half his tutor, Hinzpeter, was instructed by Princess Victoria to make sure that the disabled little boy could retain his balance on a horse. In Hinzpeter's words:

> The tutor, using a moral authority over his pupil that had now become absolute, set the weeping prince on his horse without stirrups and compelled him to go through the various paces. He fell off continually: every time, despite his prayers and tears, he was lifted up and set upon its back again. After weeks of torture, the difficult feat was accomplished: he had got his balance.[10]

Princess Victoria's anxiety for the moral and intellectual development of her son was no less demanding. She hero-worshipped her father Prince Albert, whose liberal politics were greatly at odds with the autocratic militarism of the Prussian Junkers. She abominated Bismarck, who rallied the conservative and militaristic elements of the country, with triumphant effect, to unify the German states under Prussia and with their victory over France in 1870 to create the unified Reich of modern Germany. Wilhelm was just twelve when Germany was born – the existence of the Reich was proclaimed in the Hall of Mirrors at Versailles as a triumphant gesture at the end of the Franco-Prussian war – and just thirty when in June 1888 his father, who had only been Emperor for ninety-nine days, died of throat cancer.

Vicky was quite as savage and violent towards her son the future Kaiser as Queen Victoria had been to Bertie. When the teachers at the horrible gymnasium at Kassel, which the boy was compelled to attend, humiliated and criticized him, Vicky redoubled their attacks by letter. 'I am so sorry to hear that you are so bad at your mathematics & so behindhand compared with other boys! I fear you fancy yourself far more perfect in many things than you really are, and you will have to find out by experience how little you really *do* know . . .' But it is one thing to find out from experience and another to hear no praise from a parent, no positive response to any effort.

Willy responded with heart-rending letters from the gymnasium about his somewhat disturbing dreams:

I dreamt last night that I was walking with you & another lady ... you were discussing who had the finest hands, whereupon the lady produced a most ungraceful hand, declaring it was the prettiest and turned us her back. I in my rage broke her parasol; but you put your dear arm round my waist, led me aside, pulled your glove off ... & showed me your dear beautiful hand which I instantly covered with kisses.[11]

Is it too fanciful to see in this fourteen-year-old's dream an insight into the psyche which commanded the later Kaiser's political and foreign policy? Unable with a part of himself to confront or accept his mother's coldness and downright callousness, he divides her into two beings: a beautiful lady who accepts his physical adoration and allows him to make innocent love to her by unpeeling her gloves and kissing her hands, and a harsh, ugly-handed woman who needs to be treated with violence? The lovely lady who responds to his love is the Germany whom his mother married, the cruel lady whose parasol deserves to be broken is the England who gave his hated mother birth.

Willy, as the parents called him, did everything possible to defy his liberal father and his English mother. He befriended the most extreme conservative Junker army officers. He married the fervently anti-English and anti-Danish Princess Augusta Victoria of Schleswig-Holstein-Sonderburg-Augustenburg. He was openly and vulgarly anti-Semitic, much to his parents' distress. His anti-English fanaticism could be so uncontrolled that when he suffered from a nosebleed he would do nothing to stanch the flow, exclaiming that he would be happy if he lost every drop of his English blood.

In other moods, the all but schizophrenic Wilhelm would tell his closest confidant Graf Philip Eulenburg-Hertefeld (1847–1921) that Britain was, for him, a home from home (*Es ist mir eine Heimat*). 'It sounds ghastly to a German ear when I say,' wrote Eulenburg, 'that the German emperor is not a German at all, but actually an Englishman.' Opinion differed about the degree of his mother's success in wanting to make her Hohenzollern son into an English gentleman.[12]

In England, where the Kaiser delighted in his title as an Admiral of the Fleet, he loved to attend the Cowes Regatta and to be a guest at the great country houses. True, there were snobs who believed that 'in his checked suit and boater he looked more of an incongruous cad than most Bank Holiday trippers to Margate'.[13]

It was not because he was badly received in England that the Kaiser had such a profoundly ambivalent attitude towards his mother's country. There was something deep in his psyche which longed both to love and to destroy her. While Queen Victoria was still alive, he had denounced her as an 'old hag'. But he rushed to her deathbed at Osborne and behaved like a model mourning grandson. It was he who, in an emblematic gesture, had insisted upon closing the dead queen's eyes. During the Jameson raid against the Boers he had infuriated English public opinion by sending the Boer leader Kruger a congratulatory telegram at having kept the English predators at bay. Yet he advised his nephew Prince Bertie, later Edward VII, about how to deploy English troops in South Africa. He was in awe of the Royal Navy and rejoiced in its strength. He also wanted to build a German navy which could destroy it. 'One cannot have enough hatred for England. Caeterum censeo, Britannia esse delendam,' he could proclaim to Eulenburg, yet he could splutter to the Austro-Hungarian ambassador:

> In England one seems to want to treat me as a *quantité négligeable*. But I will not tolerate this . . . I will certainly never be an enemy of England, in spite of all the insults which I have continuously been paid on their part. One seems in England not always to understand, in spite of the fact that I have often made it clear, that *I* and not my ministers make German policy.[14]

There was some justice in the Kaiser's impatience. One of the abiding themes in the story of Britain's relations with Europe in the twentieth century is the assumption, or half-assumption, by British politicians and diplomats that European peoples would have benefited from arranging their internal political affairs on a British model. Their failure to do so has often provoked bafflement. Queen Victoria herself, and her daughter the Kaiser's mother, dreamed of the liberal Germany towards which 'dear Papa' had aspired. If Edward VII had said 'I and not my ministers make British policy', he would have found himself being invited to see a doctor, if not to abdicate. Wilhelm II, particularly under the influence of Eulenburg, was tempted to ride roughshod over the delicate alliances and balances which constituted 'Germany'. Edward VII was a constitutional monarch in a country which (excepting Ireland) was politically united, and confident in its parliamentary evolutions. It had huge social problems, vast injustices: it had not yet extended the franchise to all men, let alone to any women, nor solved any of the problems of urban poverty. But its system of evolved parliamentary representative government, administered by an impartial civil service, rested on a national history stretching back hundreds of years. Germany, when Queen Victoria died, was but thirty years old.

Eulenburg persuaded Kaiser Wilhelm II to aspire after personal rule, total autocracy. Though Eulenburg retired as a result of scandal in 1902, his political influence remained as an aftertaste from which Wilhelm could not cleanse his palate. He was appallingly shocked when he learned the things of which Eulenburg stood accused – a passion for a Munich boatman a quarter of a century before. It would seem that Eulenburg, and all his *Altedel* entourage, were decidedly Grecian in their erotic preferences, and no doubt Dr Freud would have noted that the same men who excited the newspapers with their homosexual antics were also urging the Kaiser to build larger and bigger guns, and to expand the German navy. Most of the evidence against Eulenburg in his trial was perjury. The Kaiser only knew real emotional intimacy with men, and undoubtedly fell in love with them, but without knowing he had done so. No one in his position who understood the impression he was conveying would, on a visit to Eton, ask if he could watch 'a boy being swished'. He needed his son to explain what 'such men' did – when he did so, he was incredulous. His reaction was comparable to that of his cousin, the future King George V, who said: 'I thought men like that shot themselves.' There could hardly be a greater contrast between two human characters than between uncle and nephew, a difference manifested in their courts – Wilhelm's stiffly Protestant, highly aristocratic, steaming with only half-articulated homosexuality, violent and militaristic; Edward's boozy, jolly, nouveau riche in atmosphere, the monarch's taste for horses, women and rich food being reflected in his raffish friends, and his political ambitions veering in the direction of Entente with France and peace in Europe.

The Kaiser's schizophrenia about Britain provided just the sort of technicolor tragicomedy which newspapers love. The British public, fed by the ambivalence of journalists, loved, hated, love-hated and laughed at the Kaiser.

'The German Emperor is . . . addicted to saying startling things to his own people and others, and our Government may safely be left to clear away any misconception on his part of the facts of this particular case [the Kruger telegram] unless, of course, he really wishes to force at once a quarrel with this country,' the Liberal *Manchester Guardian* had written when Willy sent his tactless telegram congratulating Kruger for repulsing the Jameson raid in 1897. But the newspaper editors could have echoed the mood of the band in Portsmouth Harbour on 22 November 1899, when the Kaiser made one of his frequent visits: they played the old melody 'Oh, Willie, We Have Missed You'.[15]

He was such good copy. 'We welcome the Kaiser as one of the most remarkable personalities of the day,' gushed the *Daily Chronicle* – 'as a War Lord who has never created or invited a war, and as a Divine Right autocrat in an age when scarcely one man in a thousand believes in monarchy by divine right.'[16]

At the time of Queen Victoria's funeral, Willy made a deep impression. 'We have never lost our secret pride in the fact that the most striking and gifted personality born to any European throne since Frederick The Great was largely of our own blood.'[17] Even if the newspaper really believed Willy was more gifted than Napoleon, Metternich or Bismarck, it is difficult to see how with three wholly German grandparents and one who was half German, he could have been 'largely of our own blood'.

The *Daily Telegraph* was the most pro-German of the British newspapers, and in 1908 it was rewarded with one of the most prodigious scoops in the history of journalism. Its correspondent Colonel Stuart-Wortley managed to secure an interview with the Kaiser. It occurred at the height of fears of German aggression and the most delicate negotiations in which the English king was being used by the diplomats and politicians to try to get an agreement by both nations to a joint reduction in naval expenditure.

'You English are mad, mad as March hares,' said the Kaiser. 'What has come over you that you are so completely given over to suspicions quite unworthy of a great nation? What more can I do than I have done? Have I ever been false to my word? Falsehood and prevarication are alien to my nature.'[18]

Although he convinced Colonel Stuart-Wortley, the Kaiser persuaded few English readers. The speaker at a miners' rally in Swansea on 17 August 1908 was unusual:

I have been astonished and grieved to read much of the wild language which has been used lately by people who ought to know better about our relations with Germany. I think it is greatly to be deprecated that persons should try to spread the belief in this country that war between Great Britain and Germany is inevitable . . . There is no collision of primary interests – big, important interests – between Great Britain and Germany in any quarter of the globe. Why, they are among our very best customers . . . Although there may be some snapping and snarling in the newspapers and in the London Clubs, these two great peoples have nothing to fight for, and have no place to fight in.

This was the 33-year-old President of the Board of Trade in Asquith's Liberal government: Winston Churchill. ('As for Mr Churchill,' wrote the king to the Prince of Wales, 'he is *almost more* of a cad in office than he was in opposition.')[19]

In Germany, the hawks disliked the Kaiser's conciliatory tone to the

Daily Telegraph and the Social Democrats viewed it with as much incredulity as did the English king. While the English still saw him as a Hunnish warlord, his potential supporters in the Fatherland, the belligerent militarists, disliked his self-portrait in the English paper as an Anglophile leader of an Anglophobe nation. He was violently attacked in the Reichstag and questions were even asked about his fitness to continue as Kaiser. His chancellor, Bülow, who had egged him on to his most extreme positions of nationalism in earlier days, now did all in his power to undermine his royal master. After the exciting adrenalin of publicity, Willy felt such a corresponding let-down that Prince Fürstenburg, who had taken over the role of imperial best friend after the unfortunate 'outing' of Prince Eulenburg, decided to put on a little light-hearted entertainment at Court. Like so many things, especially farcical things, in Wilhelm II's life, this piece of fun was destined to end in macabre fashion. The Kaiser was being entertained in Prince Fürstenburg's Schloss. The orchestra was to play in the hall while General Dietrich von Hüber-Huseler, head of the military cabinet and a crucial figure in the armaments negotiations between Germany and Great Britain, appeared in one of Princess Fürstenburg's voluminous ball gowns, complete with feathered hat and fan. He executed a graceful dance to the music, described by those who had seen him enact the turn on earlier occasions as a beautiful performance, if a little too dainty for a man in his position. The general acknowledged the applause gratefully, blew kisses to his audience, and exited to a passage off the improvised stage. The audience then heard a loud crash, and calls for a doctor. Two medics were summoned, but too late. The 56-year-old general had died of heart failure. While everyone panicked and wondered what to do, rigor mortis began to set in. His Imperial Majesty was terrified, in the light of the Eulenburg debacle, that the public, let alone the international press, should learn that one of his most trusted associates and military advisers had died in drag. An unseemly scene ensued in which Princess Fürstenburg's ball gown was wrenched from the dead general, whose rapidly stiffening limbs were inserted into the breeches and epauletted tunic of his dress uniform.[20]

The general had died too soon to be given a copy of an English book which the Kaiser presented to all his general staff and to his Admiralty to analyse. It was a futuristic novel entitled *The Invasion of 1910*, by William le Queux. The German translator changed the ending of the story so that instead of the Kaiser's invasion being repulsed, the yarn ends with a triumphant German army marching through the shattered remains of a smoking London.[21] Only nine years had passed since Queen Victoria's funeral, when the English newspapers had heaped extravagant praises on his head. In 1901 the *Daily Mail* said, 'it would be impossible to find in the records of our history a foreign Sovereign who has so much endeared himself to the British People as has the Kaiser'.[22] By 1910 the *Daily Mail* had not only bought serial rights for le Queux's anti-German invasion fantasy, but was advertising it with sandwich men in spiked helmets and Prussian military uniform goose-stepping along Oxford Street.[23]

To those who know how the story will unfold – an assassination by a Serbian terrorist in Sarajevo of the heir to the Emperor Franz-Joseph leading to war between the Austro-Hungarian and the Russian empires; Germany entering the war on Austria's side and invading Belgium; Britain, committed to an alliance with France, sending an expeditionary force to the Continent in late summer 1914 and hoping they would return by Christmas – there is something all but intolerable about reading the diplomatic history of King Edward's reign. The tragedy is absolute. But so is the complexity, which is why so many books concentrate on the king's role in it all. With his fluent French and German, his kinship with so many European monarchs, and his geniality, he did play a role in the story. But the thing is much more than a story of how Uncle Bertie got on with mad nephew Willy, or how King Edward charmed Delcassé, the French president, or the old Austrian emperor or his nephew Nicholas, last emperor of Russia. Behind each individual diplomatic triumph, or setback, behind each example of one European nation or another jockeying for position or threatening another, there is one quite simple demographic fact. It is summarized in one of those German compound words which in a later decade would resonate so sinisterly in European minds: *Lebensraum*. The industrialization of the Western world was accompanied by huge population growth. Industrialized capitalism did not know how to cope with its vast urban proletariat, either politically or physically. The increase of huge numbers of overworked and unhappy people was both the industrial world's greatest problem and its greatest need – witness the scandal of Chinese labour being imported into Natal.

When, in 1904, there was found to be a shortage of labour on the Rand, the mine-owners decided that they should import workers. It was the direct responsibility of the Balfour government that Chinese labourers were enlisted. By the end of 1904, 20,000 of these workers had been sent to the mines in the Rand, and 47,000 nine months later. The mine-owners had what they desired: cheap labour. The political consequences, not only for Arthur Balfour's government but for Britain in the eyes of the world, were disastrous. The young Chinese were separated from their families.

They worked long hours for minimal wages and were cooped up constantly with no society but their own. 'The workmen spoke of it as slavery, and at least by Aristotle's definition of slavery they were right.'[24] Vice and rough punishment ruled the compounds where the young men lived, and when they broke their bounds, they terrorized the surrounding veldt farms. It was an ugly demonstration of how little the governing classes cared for human rights. Although the Liberals made capital out of it, and the notoriety of the 'Chinese slavery' issue harmed Balfour in the election of 1906, it was far from being a party issue. The Liberals, when they came to power, could end the 'slavery' of the Chinese in South African mines, but they could not end the wretched conditions of their own working class at home.

Behind all the sabre-rattling, the military parades, the boastful phallic rivalries about whose navy was bigger than whose, lay the fear that the factories and mines which needed the Nibelungs to produce the national wealth would not be able to house them, or feed them, or appease their discontents. Hindsight may very well suggest to us that Britain, with its Empire, did not need *Lebensraum* in the way it was so desperately needed in, let us say, the Rhinelands, in Bohemia, in the Balkans. Britain, it might be argued, could go on shipping coolies and slaves as required to different parts of the world. The idea has a grisly attractiveness no doubt to some imperialists, but it was always questionable, both economically and morally, whether the British Empire could survive, once its subject peoples rejected its *raison d'être*.

The French and the Germans, the Dutch and the Belgians, all had colonies too, of course, but it was never a realistic proposition that surplus population, to use a cruel Malthusian phrase, could be exported, as the British had so calmly, and without international protest, exported millions of their indigenous populations in Scotland and Ireland in the 1840s.

When the prime minister of the only significant European republic, Georges Clemenceau (1841–1929), went to Marienbad to meet King Edward at the Hotel Weimar he had more on his mind than the superficial annoyance of Caesar the wire-haired terrier being present at the dinner table. (Wasn't it illegal to bring a dog for short visits to the Continent? asked that canny, brave, cynical man. What about the quarantine laws? *Mais puisque c'est moi qui les fais,*' said the king.)[25] What Clemenceau wanted to know, after a couple of years of tiptoeing round the matter with talk of Entente Cordiale, was, quite simply, what would Britain do if Germany repeated its destructive war of 1870–1? What was to stop the German army marching into France once again? The Kaiser and the newspapers were obsessed by the size of the British navy, but frigates and battleships were not much use in Alsace-Lorraine, or cruising down the Meuse. '*Ce n'est pas à Trafalgar, qui était une bien brillante victoire navale, mais à Waterloo, qui était une bien petite bataille, que l'Angleterre à cassé le cou de Napoleon.*' When Clemenceau parted from the king he once again reiterated: '*Surtout, Sire, soignez notre Armée.*'[26]

The advice was not heeded. A policy which might, conceivably, have acted as a deterrent to an invading German army in Belgium and France – namely the commitment of a colossal Anglo-French army, with the most up-to-date artillery – was never even considered in London. Instead, the obsession continued with the navy.

Edward VII, who enjoyed travelling, and who had an easy conversational manner, came to be known as the Peacemaker after his performance as figurehead in the Entente Cordiale. On his first official visit to Paris, the royal entourage was booed, and the crowds cried '*Vivent les Boers!*'[27] By the end of his reign there had been a genuine rapprochement between Britain and France. When the Russian chief minister Stolypin met Edward VII he was fascinated. 'It was not only what he said but his manner bore the impression of an artist in international politics whom Europe regarded as the first statesman in Europe.' But however great an impression Edward made on the Russian diplomatists, and although it was Edward who summoned an international conference in 1908 to discuss the crisis in Bosnia and Hercegovina, he could do nothing to calm the tension there, nor the rival claims of Serbian nationalism and Austro-Hungarian imperialism. The Dogger Bank dispute of a few years earlier showed the true Russian indifference to British feeling or interest – when Admiral Rozhdestvensky, en route for the Far East in October 1904 with about twenty warships, encountered some Hull trawlers fishing off the Dogger Bank and, fearing them to be Japanese torpedo vessels, opened fire. Several ships were seriously damaged, one was sunk with its captain on board. Even when their mistake had been made clear to them the Russians steamed on eastwards, only themselves to be sunk off Japan in May 1905.[28]

Many of the political classes in England actually doubted the wisdom or helpfulness of Edward VII's 'hobnobbing'[29] with a 'blood-stained' creature such as the Tsar, whose regime was so oppressive. And a more accurate picture of Edward VII's diplomatic skills than Stolypin's 'artist in international politics' is probably to be found in the rather cruel reflections of Count Zedlitz Trützschler, controller of the Kaiser's household, who watched the king during his last visit to Berlin in 1909. It was a sad, nearly fatal visit. Edward was so bronchitic that at various moments he nearly passed out, and his attempts to reduce the growth of the German navy were vain.[30]

'The King of England,' wrote Trützschler,

is so stout that he completely loses his breath when he has to climb upstairs, and has to save himself in many ways. The Emperor told us that at the first family dinner he fell asleep. At the lunch at the British Embassy he was indisposed for a few minutes, but he eats, drinks, and smokes enormously. He has an amiable, pleasant manner, and looks very shrewd. But I fancy the part he plays in the affairs of his country is smaller than we have imagined. He allows a great deal of independence to the persons who have been carefully chosen for their duties, and only takes a hand when there is something of special importance to call for his intervention, and then with his age and experience and thorough knowledge of the world he acts very adroitly. I can imagine that a sly and amiable smile steals over his face, when he thinks how the whole world looks upon him as the guiding spirit of all the solid and brilliant achievements of British diplomacy.[31]

2

Rupees and Virgins

On 31 March 1904, a small army of some 1,200 men, accompanied by 10,000 bearers and 20,000 animals – mules, bullocks, buffaloes, ponies, yaks and camels – were making their way through the snowy, windswept terrain of southern Tibet. The military members of the expedition included Gurkha infantry, some Sikh pioneers, and British gunners of the Norfolk Regiment, who brought with them the comparatively new-fangled machine gun invented by Sir Hiram Maxim and adopted into the British army in 1889.[1]

The Maxim gun was sighted to 2,500 yards, and could fire about 450 rounds per minute. It was trundled along on a wheeled carriage.[2] In Tibet, in 1904, they had never seen a wheeled carriage, let alone a machine gun.[3]

The expedition as a whole was led by a short mustachioed figure called Colonel Francis Younghusband, of the King's Dragoon Guards. The troops were commanded by Brigadier-General James Macdonald of the Royal Engineers. Their aim was to reach Lhasa, the monkish capital of that mountainous land. There, it was believed, they would find evidence of Russian weapon-emplacements, Russian spies and possibly even a Russian governor. It was to counteract this danger to the British Empire in India that Younghusband's expeditionary force had set out, upon the instruction of the viceroy, to establish a British presence in the Tibetan mountains. A hundred miles inwards and upwards, they approached a hamlet called Guru.

They had climbed to a height of 15,000 feet and were making their way down a track between an escarpment and a dry salt lake. On the gravel flats through which they went, the Tibetans had barred their progress by constructing a rough stone rampart. A group of Tibetan horsemen rode out to meet the invaders. Colonel Younghusband told the Tibetans that they had fifteen minutes to clear the road. They failed to do so. Everyone waited. Younghusband gave orders that no one should fire unless fired upon. In complete silence, the infantry advanced towards the barricade. On high ground to the east of this spot, the Norfolk Regiment had dragged up the Maxim guns and placed them strategically to look down on the thousands of Tibetans who milled about beneath them.

The aim of the Gurkhas and the Sikhs was simple: to climb the escarpment and to manhandle the few Tibetan troops who were armed with antiquated muskets, matchlocks and swords. Having disarmed the enemy, they would then dismantle the roadblock and Younghusband would make his progress to Gyangtse, and then to Lhasa. Unfortunately, the Tibetan commander rode into the confused crowd, a Sikh attempted to grab his bridle, and he loosed off a pistol shot. The Tibetan commander shot an Indian soldier through the jaw – not fatally.

Colonel Younghusband had never seen a war at close quarters. He was as much an explorer as he was a soldier, and he watched with horror as the Maxim guns, on the orders of Brigadier-General Macdonald, began their rapid mechanical chatter. Tseten Wangchuk, one of the Tibetans in the valley, recalled: 'While we were waiting at the wall during the discussions, a hail of bullets came down on us from the surrounding hills. We had no time to draw our swords. I lay down beside a dead body and pretended I had been killed. The sound of firing continued for the length of time it would take six successive cups of hot tea to cool.'[4]

The next morning, in a confidential memo to the viceroy of India, General Macdonald gave an account of what happened. His men had used 50 shrapnel shells, 1,400 machine-gun rounds, and 14,351 rounds of rifle ammunition. Their casualties were: six lightly wounded, six badly wounded, none killed. Some 628 Tibetans were killed in that very short space of time, with, as he reckoned, some 222 wounded.[5]

Macdonald was a clumsy man, not a sadist. Neither the viceroy of India, Lord Curzon, who had authorized the expedition, nor Younghusband himself were by nature men of blood. On 4 April, Curzon wrote to Younghusband covering sixteen sides of paper.

I know that you will have been rather miserable over the recent encounter, just as sickened and distressed as I was. For carnage is a horrible thing, even when justified by every law of necessity – and with the bulk of the poor wretches who were shot down we had no sort of quarrel. At the same time in so far as I know the facts – in the main from newspaper correspondents, I do not feel that there is ground to blame anybody except the Lhasa general and his men.

In fact, when the killing-field was cleared, only three Russian rifles were found among the Tibetan dead and wounded.

'I dare say,' Lord Curzon continued, 'the soldiers may have been slow to seize the provocation given: and the appetite for slaughter, once aroused, is not easily slaked.'[6]

In spite of Younghusband's disquiet at the killings, the expedition continued, now divided into two, with Macdonald leading one party, Younghusband the other. On 8 April a further 200 Tibetans were killed at Kala Tso, defending their position with ancient matchlocks.[7] By 11 April the British had reached Gyangtse, and on 3 August they eventually got to Lhasa, the 'forbidden city' on the 'roof of the world'. They were not the first Europeans to do so. Jesuit missionaries had arrived there in 1625 and kept a presence there for a century.[8] What was new was the underlying political rationale for a British presence in this all but impenetrable place. Lord Curzon, antiquarian, linguist and historian, blanched at the prospect of British soldiers, at his behest, galumphing through historic sites. Writing to Younghusband from England from Walmer Castle, his official residence as Lord Warden of the Cinque Ports, Curzon urged:

> When you come to Lhasa or while you are there, please be very careful to stop any pillaging of the temples or Monasteries. Any other country would strip them bare. But let us set an example as at Peking. Of course enormously important discoveries may be made in respect of manuscripts. But let there be no burning or wanton destruction.[9]

Neither Curzon nor Younghusband had any doubts, however, not merely that the British had every right to be invading Tibet, but that they had a duty to do so. Younghusband wrote: 'I hope His Majesty's Government will never lose sight of the central fact that British interest in Lhasa is positive, legitimate and inevitable, and that Russian interest is factitious, ulterior, and pursued with unfriendly designs.'[10]

One Russian, a Siberian named Buriat Dorjieff, was active in Tibet, and was seen by British intelligence as a grave danger to British interests. He was a Buddhist convert, and his conversations with the Dalai Lama were of a largely spiritual character, but Lord Curzon and Younghusband had persuaded themselves that Dorjieff had 'taught the Tibetans to rely as trustingly on Russian support as Dr Leyds induced President Kruger' – of the South African Republic, the instigator of Boer resistance to British domination in South Africa, and so the key figure in promoting the Boer War – 'to rely upon the Germans'.[11]

Even when the British had entered Lhasa and found no evidence for their intelligence reports, no Russian presence, no plans for the Russian Tsar to convert to Tibetan Buddhism (which was one of the rumours), they could still persuade themselves that their very arrival was a blessing. 'The Tibetans', Younghusband believed, 'are not a people fit to be left to themselves between two great Empires . . . They are nothing but slaves in the power of the selfish and ignorant monks . . . To force ourselves into personal contact with the leading Lhasa men means no oppression of a harmless people: it means rather the emancipation of a people most willing to be friendly with us, who are held in bondage now by a cruel, self-seeking oligarchy of monks.'[12] The Communist Chinese offered similar justification for their invasion of Tibet in October 1950.

When they eventually arrived in Lhasa, Younghusband gave orders for full-dress uniform to be worn as he marched his troops through the muddy streets. He was delighted by the warm Tibetan welcome. A Tibetan eyewitness recorded: 'When the British officers marched to the Tsuglakhang [Jokhang] and other places, the inhabitants of Lhasa were displeased. They shouted and chanted to bring down rain, and made clapping gestures to repulse them. In the foreigners' custom these were seen as signs of welcome, so they took off their hats and said thank you.'[13]

By September, the British had withdrawn from Tibet. The secretary of state for war, Lord Lansdowne – Curzon's predecessor as viceroy of India – rather delighted in a diplomatic coup in which he received Russian reassurance that Russia would not occupy Tibet. The Younghusband expedition had divided opinion in Britain, and not just among cabinet colleagues and bigwigs who disliked Curzon.

Rudyard Kipling, 'that little black demon of a Kipling' as Henry James called him,[14] the poet of the Empire, was one of the very many English in the pages which follow to have married an American. (Henry James was best man, on 18 January 1892, when Kipling married Carrie Balestier at All Souls', Langham Place, in London with only five other people present – Edmund Gosse, his wife and son, the publisher William Heinemann and the clergyman who performed the ceremony.)[15] It was in 1899 that Kipling paid his final visit to the United States and apostrophized them upon their taking possession of the Philippine Islands.

> Take up the White Man's burden –
> The savage wars of peace –
> Fill full the mouth of Famine
> And bid the sickness cease;
> And when your goal is nearest
> The end for others sought,
> Watch Sloth and heathen Folly
> Bring all your hope to nought.[16]

Kipling's perspective of Empire was shaped by his childhood in India. His parents were artists and designers, he was a journalist. They were observers of those he most admired, the engineers, the administrators, the builders and soldiers. With his intuitive artistic antennae, Kipling, ardent British imperialist as he was, could sense, at the very acme of success for the Raj, that America was one day to supersede Britain as the world's policeman, emperor and banker.

Kipling's version of the imperial role was entirely shared by Curzon the viceroy, who said in a speech delivered at Bombay: 'Since this country first laid its spell upon me, I have always regarded it as the land not only of romance, but of obligation. India to me is "Duty" written in five letters instead of four. All the servants of Government, European or native, are also the servants of duty. The Viceroy himself is the slave of duty as well as its captain.'[17]

George Nathaniel Curzon had become the viceroy of India, aged only thirty-nine. In Washington, on 22 April 1895, he had married the beautiful Mary Leiter, the daughter of Levi Z. Leiter, who had made a fortune, partly out of his partnership in the Chicago store, Field, Leiter and Co., partly by successful real estate investments. (He did very well out of the great Chicago fire of 1871.) The family, German Swiss in origin, Mennonite, subsequently Lutheran, in religion, sprang from Pennsylvania, but after old Levi made his money they moved to the American capital. Young Mary captivated the president's wife, Mrs Cleveland, as she subsequently captivated British aristocratic society in the London season and at country house parties.[18]

Curzon, heir to his father the Reverend Lord Scarsdale's Derbyshire estate at Kedleston, was a person of flair and brilliance, but he had an income of merely £1,500 per annum. Though it may very well be true that he did nothing so crude as to marry for money, the Leiter fortune helped to establish him at a palatial London address, Carlton House Terrace, and there is no doubt at all that such an improvement in circumstances made it possible for him to live as a viceroy should. Upon their marriage, Mary and her descendants were offered immediately the annual income from $700,000 (£140,000) worth of bonds, which totalled $33,500 (£6,700), while on her father's death her marriage settlement would receive a further million dollars. In the event of Mary predeceasing him (an event to occur when she was aged only thirty-six), Curzon was to be allowed as much of the £6,700 as he desired.[19]

It certainly enabled them to keep up a princely style. And they were able, when the old queen died and was succeeded by her son Edward VII, whom Mary had befriended during her own version of 'The Siege of London', to represent their monarch at the splendid celebrations held in India, at the Delhi Durbar. On 12 January 1903 she wrote back to old Levi in Washington:

From the day we entered Delhi on elephants to the day we left it in a state procession, one pageant was grander than another and the State Ball in the palace of Akbar was a thing to dream of – The Duke of Connaught and the Grand Duke of Hesse who had both been to the Coronation in Russia said that nothing there could compare with the positively bewildering beauty of the scene – Halls of alabaster inlaid with precious stones dazzling in the glow of electric light, Indian chiefs covered with jewels – officers in full dress – women in jewels, and as a background the jewelled throne of the old Empress of Delhi towering in lofty beauty as a setting to British rule. People were perfectly speechless with admiration and there were no words to describe the beauty of it. I think that Mamma and Daisy [the youngest sister] enjoyed everything. I had them blessedly looked after, and they had the best places.[20]

Mary Curzon saw the superb pageantry of the Delhi Durbar as the outward and visible sign of an extraordinary political phenomenon, namely British rule in India. The subcontinent's 1,802,629 square miles were equal in size to Europe minus Russia. Its population of nearly 300 million (294,361,056 in 1900) was administered by a Civil Service of fewer than 1,000 people, almost all of whom were British. The Indian army of 150,000 troops was the mightiest in the East, and India also bore the cost of a further 75,000 British army men garrisoned *in situ*.[21] By an elaborate system of tariffs and controls, India was self-supporting, but it was also used to shore up the British economy, for example in its obligation to import cheap Lancashire-made cottons.

The daughter of the Chicago department-store millionaire Levi Leiter was, like the teeming millions of the Indian subcontinent, helping to bankroll an extraordinarily successful political oligarchy. Later generations came to believe that elitism and privilege were bad because they were based on inequity, because by allowing a family such as the Curzons a large estate in Derbyshire, and encouraging them to be the ruling class, you were depriving others, no less able perhaps but less fortunate, of the chance to share some of their wealth, or to exercise political power. Why should power be exercised by the few on behalf of the many?

This was to be the deepest political question of the twentieth century: Lenin's great question of *Who, whom?* Who has the power to do what to whom? Wherever the British held sway, or wherever they felt constrained to bring their influence, the question is going to arise. In national terms, it will lead to the question why the Indians, the Irish, the Africans, cannot throw off colonialism and govern themselves. In terms of class and personal politics, it will lead to individuals, in Britain and elsewhere, at length achieving political franchise, the vote, regardless of gender or class. In other parts of Europe political solutions, collectivist or corporatist, would be attempted which quickly became far more authoritarian, and certainly more murderous, than the apparently indefensible systems of empire and oligarchy which were in place at the beginning of the century – with much of the Balkans and the Middle East still under the increasingly shaky suzerainty of the Turkish sultans, and much of Africa and the Far East under the colonial rule of European powers – Germany, France, Belgium, Holland, Britain.

Of these world empires, the British was the richest, and the most powerful. George Nathaniel Curzon saw India as the key factor in that power. His reason for the greatest diplomatic blunder of his career, authorizing Younghusband's invasion of Tibet, was the simple fear that the Russian Empire would extend itself into Afghanistan, Tibet and India itself. The Russian Foreign Ministry in 1900 saw India as 'representing Great Britain's most vulnerable point'.[22] Curzon was voicing the same idea, from an opposite point of view, when he said that: 'As long as we rule in India, we are the greatest power in the world. If we lose it we shall drop straight away to a third-rate power.'[23]

Hindsight tells us that such a drop was bound to happen, that a small north European trading nation whose East India Company from the sixteenth to the eighteenth centuries was commercially so successful in its dealings with maharajahs and merchants in the subcontinent could never for long sustain a pseudo-Roman empire based on military control. For one thing, that control could never be sustained, without frequent massacre, if the indigenous population chose to rebel against the governing power.

In the year that Queen Victoria died, 1901, the British Empire was in the midst of its greatest trial to date, namely the Boer War. That war ended in 1902 with a British victory of sorts, but there had been some terrible setbacks, military defeats and psychological humiliations. The other great powers in the world, and many of the smaller nations too, had enjoyed these humiliations very much indeed, rather as the enemies of the United States enjoyed the Vietnam war, or some of President George W. Bush's Middle Eastern adventures. Two tiny anarchic states of Dutch Bible-bashing farmers had formed themselves into an amateur army which did not even possess uniforms. These Boers had seemed to many other people in the world, in their struggle against the British, to demonstrate what damage could be inflicted upon imperial power if a proud people had sufficient grit and faith. It took a British army of a quarter of a million men three years to defeat the Boers, and it cost not only £270 million, exclusive of postwar reconstruction,[24] but also the

British reputation for decency and fair play. General Kitchener's concentration camps, in which women and children suffered and died, have never been forgotten in South Africa.

In 1894, Curzon had written a book called *Problems of the Far East* and dedicated it 'to those who believe that the British Empire is, under Providence, the greatest instrument for good the world has seen'.[25] After Kitchener's genocidal murder and torture of Boer families, or Younghusband's misguided expedition in Tibet, this belief, unshakeable in Curzon's mind, was harder to maintain. Kipling, in one of his more awful poems, 'The Lesson', wanted to admit:

> It was our fault, and our very great fault – and now we must
> turn it to use.
> We have forty million reasons for failure, but not a single
> excuse.
> So the more we work and the less we talk the better results we
> shall get.
> We have had an Imperial lesson. It may make us an Empire
> yet![26]

The South African situation had demonstrated the weakness in the imperial idea, and the potential weakness of the Empire. One of the Indian orderlies, a member of the Indian Ambulance Corps, at the battle of Spion Kop in 1900 had been a young barrister, born in Porbandar, western India, trained as a lawyer at the Middle Temple in London, named Mohandas Karamchand Gandhi. He had gone to South Africa in 1893 to work on a single case, and he little by little found himself drawn into politics, defending the interests of Indians in Natal. The Boers had told the Indians: 'You are the descendants of Ishmael and, therefore, from your very birth bound to slave for the descendants of Esau.' Things did not much improve for Indians in South Africa when the British had won their war. Every Indian was a 'coolie'. Indian schoolmasters were 'coolie schoolmasters'. Gandhi was a 'coolie barrister'. One of the British officials in the Transvaal said many years later to Gandhi that it was the virtues rather than the vices of the Indians which had aroused the jealousy of the Europeans and exposed them to political persecution. Gandhi stayed on in South Africa to fight for basic political rights for the Indian people of Natal and the Transvaal, but these years were to have the profoundest effect upon India.[27]

The power of Gandhi's remarkable career stemmed from the fact that it could be seen as, and in some aspects actually was, apolitical. Gandhi's interests were genuinely religious and spiritual. One of the greatest influences upon him was Tolstoy's *The Kingdom of God Is Within You*, a pacifist classic which argues for the anarchic idea of following the precepts of Jesus not to resist violence violently. Gandhi drew his inspiration from the *Bhagavad Gita*, from the Gospels, from Tolstoy and from Ruskin. It was on a railway journey from Johannesburg to Durban that he first read Ruskin's *Unto This Last*. With money made as a barrister, Gandhi purchased a 100-acre estate near Durban where the ideals of Tolstoy and Ruskin, manual work and prayer, could be practised. At the same time he and his followers found themselves being arrested by the British authorities for defying such rules as those which forbade Indians to enter the Transvaal without permits. He developed the notion of *satyagraha* (Sanskrit: firmness in truth), a word which derives from *sadagraha*, firmness in good conduct – and which became the foundation stone of his policy of passive resistance.

I remember how one verse of a Gujarati poem, which, as a child I learned at school, clung to me. In substance, it was this: If a man gives you a drink of water and you give him a drink in return, that is nothing. Real beauty consists in doing good against evil . . . Then came the Sermon on the Mount. It was the New Testament which really awakened me to the rightness and value of Passive Resistance. When I read the Sermon on the Mount, such passages as 'Resist not him that is evil, but whoever smiteth thee on thy right cheek turn to him the other also.' . . . I was simply overjoyed and found my own opinion confirmed where I least expected it.[28]

The factors which were to undermine British imperial power were multiple and complex. Though more and more Britons, and Asians, came to doubt the Empire's *raison d'être* in the early decades of the twentieth century, there was only one nation in the world that could see it as a serious political or economic rival. This was the United States. Though Curzon feared the incursions of Russia in India, and though the Germans, French, Dutch and Belgians might regard the British as rivals for control of individual slices of African territory, the existence of a British Empire did not in itself cramp Russian, French, Dutch or Belgian style; it did not prevent them from being world dominators because it was never their ambition to be the supreme power over the rest of the world – what we now call the Third World. As Kipling half saw, in 'The White Man's Burden', the crucial political development for the British was to be their relationship with the United States, and further, the crucial fact in British imperial history would be whether, post-1900, the Americans would choose to emulate Britain in carrying imperial responsibilities.

When history began to show that American ambitions were rather different from Kipling's imaginings – that for some American statesmen and politicians at least, the expansion of their power seemed to depend on the diminution of the British – then the United States would be forced to make specific decisions, and take specific steps, to undermine and destroy British hegemony. But for a large, rich, patient nation like the United States of America, ready to bide its time, there were very many factors which could help their purposes. Sometimes it would be necessary to shake the branches, sometimes ripe fruit would simply fall of its own accord.

Gandhi's strength in helping to undermine British power lay in the spiritual simplicity of his appeal. British justification for their Indian Empire, their belief that they were in India to 'improve' it, derived largely from a strange alliance between Utilitarian economists and evangelical missionaries. The extent to which practical economics, or Christian piety, predominated varied from decade to decade and from administrator to administrator, but both were evident. The extremist Christians in the early to mid-nineteenth century had dreamed of converting India, but Utilitarian common sense made it clear that Hindus, Jains, Muslims, Sikhs and Buddhists were unlikely ever to become Anglican en masse, however clean British drains, however excellent British schools, however extensive British railway systems might turn out to be.

Although Curzon, to choose a colourful example, did not appear, as he and his wife rode into the Delhi Durbar on elephants in the full grandeur of his dress uniform, to be a man who believed that the meek would inherit the Earth, he was nominally a Christian, capable if confronted by the actual precepts of the Gospel of feeling shame. He believed that there was a providence in the British being given India to control. Gandhi's campaigns of civil disobedience in India, and the growth of the nationalist movement, belong to decades after Curzon's resignation as viceroy, and return to England in 1905. (His wife Mary, her health seriously undermined by the Indian climate, died in 1906.)

Curzon's resignation, angry and bitter, had come about after a dispute which ultimately arose from the Younghusband expedition. Lord Kitchener, hero or butcher, depending upon your viewpoint, of the Sudan and South Africa, condemned the system of dual control, whereby the Indian army possessed, in effect, two heads: the military member in the viceroy's council and the commander-in-chief. Kitchener had been made commander-in-chief in India on Curzon's recommendation, but the two fell out, and the viceroy remained in India only long enough to receive a royal visit, that of the Prince and Princess of Wales, on 9 November 1905.

Curzon's achievements as an autocratic viceroy had been immense. Not only had he, from a position of deep knowledge, restored and preserved many works of art and architecture – notably the Taj Mahal – he had also given India the basic infrastructure and political institutions which would enable it to become a modern nation. Not only, in his last year in India, did investments in railways increase by 56 per cent, savings banks deposits by 43 per cent, and exports by 48 per cent. Not only had he, in the tradition of British administrators, defended India's borders, provided her with access to the London money market, and modernized methods of irrigation and transport. He had developed India as a free-trade area the size of Europe, and continued the refinement of a civil service, the rule of law and the notion of individual freedom. All these things were acknowledged by Jawaharlal Nehru when he looked back on the British Raj of which Curzon was so proud and efficient an exemplar.

Yet Curzon was intensely reluctant to see any of the implications of his modernization. Though it was obvious that making India a modern free-trading nation would eventually lead it to require its own elected parliament, Curzon could retort:

> Remember . . . that to these people, representative government and electoral institutions are nothing whatever . . . The good government that appeals to them is the government which protects them from the rapacious money-lender and landlord and all the other sharks in human disguise . . . I have a misgiving that this class will not fare much better under these changes than they do now . . . I am under the strong opinion that as government in India becomes more and more Parliamentary – as will be the inevitable result – so will it become less paternal and less beneficent to the poorer classes of the population.[29]

Certainly, the emergence of India as an independent and in economic terms liberal democracy only forty-two years after Curzon left the viceroyalty was not achieved without hundreds of thousands of deaths, the price paid by most peoples of the world in the twentieth century for political change and development. Gandhi, whose career and achievements will form an important part of our story, sounded an early warning note by asking rather simply whether the Christian gentlemen who had taken it upon themselves to administer his native land actually believed in the words of their Lord and Saviour when He had walked the Earth, or whether they preferred to be guided by Jeremy Bentham.

It was a difficult question to answer. One of the most touching of the items in the Younghusband Collection in the Library of the India Office in London is the tiny copy of *Hymns Ancient and Modern*, which bears two inscriptions on its flyleaf. First, 'F. E. Younghusband from his loving sister Emmie. "Endure hardness as a good soldier of Christ."' There is then added in Francis Younghusband's own hand: 'This was carried with me through Manchuria, the Gobi Desert and over the Himalayas and was returned to my dear old sister Emmie as a remembrance of me. F. E. Younghusband, June 14 1888.' The two hymns which Younghusband has underscored heavily with pencil are Newman's 'Lead Kindly Light' (number 266) and one which is less well known, number 264.

> My God, my Father, while I stray
> Far from my home on life's rough way,
> O teach me from my heart to say,
> 'Thy Will be done'.

The dominant historical idea of the nineteenth century, popularized by Hegel, was determinism. Things must be as they are, history was moving in an ineluctable, inescapable progression. The Spirit of the Age cannot be gainsaid; nations and cultures have their day; once passed, the ascendancy is given to another. Hegel was a complicated thinker and he can be seen as the godfather of two quite contradictory movements, despotism, especially Prussian despotism, and freedom and liberalism. In his *Philosophy of Right (Grundlinien der Philosophie des Rechts)* he saw the established order of the Prussian state as the beginning of political stability and wisdom; but for rather similar reasons to Curzon's later defence of British domination. Democracy would be wasted on primitive or underdeveloped peoples. At the same time, Hegel, a profoundly influential philosopher in Britain among the political classes, saw history as 'none other than the progress of the consciousness of freedom'. This strand of essentially liberal thinking would persuade you in a different direction. Rather than thinking that order was the essential ingredient in political salvation, you might think that freedom is most important; and in collective terms, this means you would support nationalistic aspirations against the big collective ideal of an empire.

This is the big question, politically and diplomatically, at the start of the twentieth century. The old Ottoman Empire, the 'sick man of Europe', is crumbling away, and the lands over which it presides – Mesopotamia, Palestine, Syria, as well as the Islamic Balkan peoples – all aspire to self-determination. Liberals of all nations tend to be selective in the extent to which they support nationalist endeavour. The British in Ireland are a case in point. Gladstone, the Liberal leader, took several decades of evolution from being the rising hope of the stern unbending Tories to being the Grand Old Man of British Liberalism, before he could support Irish Home Rule. In his youth he had supported 'rebel' Italians against the Bourbon or Austrian hegemony. It took a long time to see parallels between the desire of continentals for freedom and the Irish aspirations on his own doorstep. His championing of Irish Home Rule split the Liberal party and as we start the story, with the reign of King Edward VII, the matter is still unresolved.

On the whole, English liberals (of both the Unionist and Liberal parties) supported nationalism as an idea when it suited them, and not when it did not. British nationalism was obviously as commendable a virtue as Prussian nationalism was an international menace. The aspirations of the Serbs to expel the Austro-Hungarians, who had annexed Bosnia-Hercegovina in 1878, or of the Bosnian Muslims to be independent of the Ottoman Porte, were good things, whereas the desire of the Irish or the Indians to manage their own affairs was a nuisance, or plain crazy.

We are at the beginning of the twentieth century, a period of history in which human beings massacred one another in numbers without historical parallel. The sheer number of deaths is actually impossible to comprehend or to absorb with the imagination, however often we might recite the actual numbers of those killed. Added to the prodigious numbers killed in war is that grisly and peculiarly twentieth-century phenomenon, the mass slaughter of civilians: the Turkish killing of one million Christian Armenians in 1915, the incalculable numbers who died, first in the Russian Civil War, but also in the famines in the Ukraine, which Stalin used as a method of deliberate elimination; the 6 million Jews who were killed during the Nazi period.

In an important essay, Robert Skidelsky[30] linked the growth of mass slaughter with the growth of those distinctive twentieth-century ideals, nationalism and democracy. 'Hitler and Stalin were not democrats, but they killed for the sake of the people – to secure them a Thousand Year Reich or the communist millennium. Genocide in Bosnia in the early 1990s started with the onset of democracy.' Skidelsky argues that without some limit to the idea of democracy it easily slides into despotism. And if you 'believe in "rule by the people" you have first to select the people'. In an Imperium, different racial and religious groups have to coexist in order to survive. Not so for the democratic nationalist, who actually asserts his 'freedom' by claiming the right to be a fully independent Hindu or Muslim, Indian or Pakistani. The inevitable concomitant is that the 'alien' in the nationalist's midst will, by the democratic will of the majority, be expunged.

Skidelsky concludes his essay:

We have not yet overcome the idea that the world should be divided into national units, exercising their sovereign right of self-government. Yet they are not the only, or necessarily the highest, principles of political life. Empires at their best stood for multiracialism and religious tolerance. They also allowed a great deal of devolution in practice. They foundered in the 20th century because no way could be found of making their rule acceptable to their subject peoples.

Indian nationalists would legitimately resent Curzon's lordly comment that 'to these people representative government and electoral institutions are nothing whatever'. His was one of the loftiest and most patronizing of all the grand imperialist attitudes, but it could have been echoed, for example, in the life's work and world view of Lord Cromer in Egypt, of the British in South Africa and Burma and Malaya. Cromer's latest biographer tells of some young modern Egyptian students who made the pilgrimage all the way to North Norfolk to find Lord Cromer's grave in order that they might spit upon it.[31]

We began this chapter with an account of Younghusband's ill-starred invasion of Tibet, the killing of hundreds of Tibetans, and the thick-skinned insensitivity of the British imperialists' attitude to the affair. But it would be unfair to leave the incident without setting it within a context of what came later. The massacre of 628 people in a mountain pass is a terrible thing, especially when the man who ultimately sanctioned the incident, the viceroy of India, can write: 'there is no ground to blame anybody except the Lhasa general'. But fairness compels us to add that the moments when the British behaved with brutality in India, during the 1857–9 troubles, and in 1919 in Amritsar, are bloody interludes in a general story of containment and good order. The numbers slain are tiny compared with the numbers of those slaughtered by Indians and Pakistanis when they achieved their yearned-for independence. Likewise, it was in the aftermath of the overthrow of the Sultans that the Young Turks massacred the Armenians; the oppression of the Russian people by the Tsars would seem mild by comparison with the mass murders perpetrated by Lenin and Stalin. No Hohenzollern or Habsburg autocrat brought about killings on the scale of the populist Hitler.

Hegelian or predestinarian historians would see the end of the British Empire as doomed, foreordained to self-destruct. Certainly such incidents as the Younghusband fiasco did not strengthen the imperialist position. At the time of the disaster, there were many flag-waving jingoists who supposed that the Empire would go on for ever; and it is easy to see why. The Empire was still growing, reaching its maximum extent in 1921. But for many readers of H. G. Wells's *The New Machiavelli* (published 1911) there must have been more than a hint of prophecy in its summary:

> The English rule in India is surely one of the most extraordinary accidents that has ever happened in history. We are there like a man who has fallen off a ladder on to the neck of an elephant, and does not know what to do or how to get down. Until something happens he remains . . . No one dare bring the average English voter face to face with the reality of India, or let the Indian native have a glimpse of the English voter. In my time I have talked to English statesmen, Indian officials and ex-officials, viceroys, soldiers, everyone who might be supposed to know what India signifies, and I have prayed them to tell me what they thought we were up to there . . . And beyond a phrase or so about 'even-handed justice' – and look at our sedition trials! – they told me nothing. Time after time I heard of that apocryphal native ruler in the north-west, who, when asked what would happen if we left India, replied that in a week his men would be in the saddle, and in six months not a rupee or a virgin would be left in Lower Bengal. That is always given as our conclusive justification. But is it our business to preserve the rupees and virgins of Lower Bengal in a sort of magic inconclusiveness? Better plunder than paralysis, better fire and sword than futility . . . The sum total of our policy is to arrest any discussion, any conferences that would enable the Indians to work out a tolerable scheme of the future for themselves . . . In some manner we shall have to come out of India.[32]

It is a chilling passage in what is supposed to be a novel, published thirty-six years before Wells's fellow socialists abruptly withdrew from India, on a 'better fire and sword than futility' ticket, leading to well over a million deaths during partition. The sort of dull district administrator so admired by Kipling saw rather more value than Wells did in preserving the rupees and virgins of Lower Bengal. But for British imperialists, as for Bengali virgins, dangerous days lay ahead.

3

The Land

It was the age of bicycling and the great outdoors. The Victorian enthusiasts for pedalling into the countryside had been obliged to wobble precariously on pennyfarthings, or on the well-named bone-shaker. It was in the manufacturing towns of the West Midlands – Coventry, Wolverhampton, Redditch, Bromsgrove – that the modern safety bicycle was pioneered, with its chain drive to the rear wheel, its diamond frame, pneumatic tyres and effective brakes. The Danish engineer Mikael Pedersen worked for many years in the Gloucestershire village of Dursley and developed the Dursley-Pedersen, by Victorian standards a dazzlingly lightweight machine with a hammock-like wooden seat, a bicycle which could achieve unheard-of speeds.

Cycling at this speed and distance naturally led its enthusiasts to discard superfluous costume. *Cycling Magazine*, in its issue of 10 May 1911, shows a photograph of 'the late Lady Harberton, attired in the cycling costume that led to her being refused admission to the coffee-room of an inn'. She looks a splendid figure, and would certainly be considered over-dressed if she appeared either at a cycling rally or an inn today in her high feathered hat, her waisted riding coat with a very full cravat at her neck, her bloomers which are calf-length and her dark hose and shoes. These bloomers, or baggy pantaloons, were an American import.

From the European Continent had come many ideas which inspired the Rational Dress Society in the 1880s when figures such as Mrs Oscar Wilde and Marie Stopes campaigned for women to be released from their heavy bone corsets, and tight stays which displaced the internal organs and led to curvature of the spine. Chief among the 'scientific' principles of rational dressers was that of the beneficence of wool. Dr Gustav Jaeger of Stuttgart was a professor of physiology who insisted:

It is most important to bear in mind that it is not enough to wear wool next to the skin and any other material over it. If at any point underclothing or lining, or padding or stiffening of vegetable fibre, or of silk, intervene between the body and the outer atmosphere, an obstacle is set up to the free passage of the exhalation from the skin, with the result that the noxious portion of the exhalation settles in the vegetable fibre, which consequently becomes mal-odorous; and everything mal-odorous is prejudicial to the health.[1]

An early convert to Dr Jaeger's ideas had been George Bernard Shaw, who had his first all-in-one woollen suit made with money inherited from a despised father. Other forms of 'rational' dress included the sandal. The dress reformist W. A. Macdonald had been turned away from the British Museum Reading Room for wearing sandals.[2]

Rational or rebellious dress, however, was by no means universal. The composer Edward Elgar, for example, went cycling in bowler hat, tweed suiting with display handkerchief in his top pocket, and highly polished boots. Arnold Bax, meeting Elgar once in the Malvern Hills, 'expected him to sling a gun from his back and drop a brace of pheasants to the ground'.[3] One of his most cherished possessions was his Royal Sunbeam, a fixed-wheel, 27-inch framed bicycle with a front plunger brake and a Bowden (calliper) rim brake for the rear wheel. It was manufactured by the Wolverhampton firm of John Marston Ltd and cost £21.10s. On such a machine as this you could ride across a country. Elgar christened the bike Mr Phoebus, partly as a pun on the name Sunbeam (Phoebus is the sun-god), partly after a character in Disraeli's *Lothair*, a favourite novel. Elgar wrote to his friend: 'I hate coming to town – shall miss the hay making I fear. Had 50 miles ride yesterday amongst the Avon country.'[4]

Like many a self-conscious embodiment of national *Geist,* Elgar was an outsider. In spite of the grand, even forbidding, appearance – in later life he was often mistaken for Arthur, Duke of Connaught[5] – he was the son of a Roman Catholic church organist and vendor of musical instruments. To be musical at all in Victorian England – seriously musical as opposed to being able to play 'The Lost Chord' on the pianoforte – marked you out. It was almost as if the practical, Benthamite, down-to-earth values of the Utilitarian economists and capitalist factory-owners had silenced English music itself. After the centuries of Dowland, Tallis, Byrd, Purcell, Handel, came an eerie silence as if the very birds had stopped singing. German propaganda in 1914 dubbed Britain *Das Land ohne Musik.* In the mid-nineteenth century it would have been almost a fair comment. Then, largely inspired by visits to Germany, the English musicians revived – the Royal School of Church Music and symphony orchestras flourished again.

Elgar, who left school at fifteen in Worcester, worked for a while as a clerk in a lawyer's office, and eventually went to London 'living on two bags of nuts a day', and was taught the violin by Adolf Pollitzer. There followed a brief, inspirational visit to Leipzig (1882). Then in the late 1880s he was bowled over by Dvorak's visit to England, and in the 1890s he discovered Wagner, and sat through two performances of *Parsifal* at Bayreuth.

Yet for all the Continental influences which enabled Elgar to become

a composer of very near greatness, all these models led him to a point
of inspirational psychological release in which he seemed to be tapping
a collective mood, annotating the very landscape of England, and its
soul. His feeling for the landscape of the Malvern Hills and the valleys
of Avon is reflected in his programme music the *Enigma Variations*, which
became immediately popular at its first performance – conductor Hans
Richter – in 1899. The following year Richter conducted, in Birmingham,
Elgar's oratorio, based on Cardinal Newman's poem about a man dying
and going to purgatory, *The Dream of Gerontius*. As with *Enigma*, you
can hear all the echoes of greater composers whom Elgar is imitating.
The anguished chromatics of Part I are all but a quotation from the first
act of *Parsifal*. Yet mysteriously something new has been created. In
Gerontius and in his other oratorio *The Apostles* Elgar's passionate
emotional commitment to his Roman Catholic faith is surely one of the
ingredients which explain why these works immediately hold and move.
They have the compulsiveness of pure sincerity.

This strange, melancholic dog-lover belonged to no 'in' set. He had
not been to a public school or a university: he did not belong to the
national Church. But it was he who set the Edwardian Age to an unforgettable music.

Parking Mr Phoebus outside the New Inn, a 'little roadside pub' near
Stretton Grandison, on 24 June 1902, he was about to hear some dramatic
news. The new King had appendicitis. The Coronation, at which Elgar's
Coronation Ode was to be performed, was delayed. 'Don't for heaven's
sake *sympathise* with me – I don't care a tinker's damn. It gives me three
blessed sunny days in my own country,' he wrote to the 'Nimrod' of
Enigma. Hearing the news for the first time in the New Inn he had said:
'Give me another pint of cider. I'm deadly sorry for the King, but that's
all.' The heads of state were all assembled in London for the ceremony,
and at first the king was adamant that it should proceed despite his
illness. Only when he developed peritonitis did the doctors persuade
him to postpone. To everyone's amazement the king was fit enough for
the Coronation to take place on 9 August. By any standards, the
Coronation – with Elgar's *Ode* and Parry's anthem, 'I was glad when
they said unto me' – was a musical feast. But it was at a concert performance of the *Coronation Ode* by Clara Butt that the extraordinary qualities
of the *Ode* were made clear to its composer.

The words had been written by a melancholic schoolmaster turned
don, fellow of Magdalene, Cambridge, compulsive diarist and prolific
belletrist, Arthur Benson. Although an Eton master and the son of an
archbishop of Canterbury, Benson's copious diaries are a chronicle of
feeling outside as well as in, crushed by insecurity, mental illness and

suppressed – to the point of being barely recognized – homosexuality. He was not an especially political being, certainly not a jingo. Yet he and Elgar, these two mustachioed introverts, managed to do in one evening for the British Empire what Leni Riefenstahl did for the Third Reich. Elgar made the tonic key E flat rising at the end to C minor. He asked Benson to rewrite several times to fit his rhythms, receiving disarming replies such as: 'I will try & [sic] write a finale on the lines you indicate – though the metre is a hard one – if you could string a few nonsense words just to show me how you would like them to run I would construct it, following the air closely.'

So, when Clara Butt stood up in the Royal Opera House, Elgar had arranged Benson's hastily composed doggerel into a high imperial theme accompanied by military brass, an organ and full orchestra. It had an amazing effect. Arthur Benson wrote in his diary: 'The Ode did both please and impress me very much; it is wizard-like music – I like the softer portions best'.[6] For the large audience, the wizardry did its magic.

From the instantaneous frenzy of the audience, Elgar knew that he had touched an extraordinary nerve. 'Land of Hope and Glory' became immediately a second national anthem. In spite of the fact, perhaps in part because of it, that its imperialistic sentiments are so shocking to the *bien pensants*, it remains a hugely popular song, bellowed enthusiastically by any British crowd if the opportunity arises. (It was not meant to be bellowed. Elgar introduced the tune *dolce* and *pianissimo* into the *Coronation Ode*, played by the orchestra alone.) Next to Beethoven's setting of Schiller's 'An die Freude', it must be the most compulsive of all open-air crowd-songs ever composed. For every one who is offended by the imperialist expansionism of its last lines, there must be a thousand who still believe the first two. Nor have the years since Benson wrote them, the years of refugees from every kind of tyranny, and the years of political emancipation and economic libertarianism, made the opening words of the *Ode* totally absurd. Of course, when Benson wrote the lyric, women (and nearly half of all men) were still not politically emancipated. Homosexual activity was illegal. Plays all had to meet with the approval of the Lord Chamberlain and press censorship was strong. The lives of the greater part of the population were circumscribed by the grinding demands of work. Ireland was held in an uneasy union with Westminster. The peoples of the Empire, especially in India, were beginning to wish for independence, or if not total independence the desire to have political rights equivalent to those enjoyed in the mother country. And yet, count the numbers of British people in the years covered by the ensuing pages of this present volume who voluntarily chose to go and live in the Ottoman Empire; Tsarist or Communist Russia;

Wilhelmine or Nazi Germany; socialist or Fascist Spain, Fascist Italy, the Irish Free State or Republic, and compare it with the number from those places who clamoured to get on a boat to Britain. Certain freedoms, of the right to trial by jury, for example, had been inviolate in England for ages, and some – a far greater freedom of thought and expression than existed in the rest of the world – had been fought for by Victorian radicals.

One of the things which redeems both the lyric and the music of the *Coronation Ode* is the elegiac note – which is also to be found in Kipling's hymn 'Recessional', which was also sung at Edward VII's Coronation.

> Far call'd, our navies melt away;
> On dune and headland sinks the fire:
> Lo, all our pomp of yesterday
> Is one with Nineveh and Tyre!
> Judge of the Nations, spare us yet,
> Lest we forget, lest we forget.

The Edwardian lyricists love a land which feels threatened less by enemies without than by a sense that it contains the seeds of its own dissolution.

Behind the music of Elgar is a lost music: not that of concert halls but of fields, pubs and kitchens. Contemporaneous with Elgar's most creative period, the Folk Song Society, guided by its formidable Hon. Secretary Mrs Kate Lee, began to collect up the living oral traditions of song before they were lost. At the inaugural meeting of the Society, Sir Hubert Parry saw the enemy of authentic folk music as the growth of industrial towns, 'our terribly overgrown towns' with their 'pawnshops and flaming gin palaces' where 'miserable piles of Covent Garden refuse which pass for vegetables are offered for food'. With the illness (and in 1904 the death) of Kate Lee, Cecil Sharp became the leading exponent of folk song, claiming to have collected over 500 tunes, of which 125 were modal tunes. 'I'm Seventeen Come Sunday', 'Blow Away the Morning Dew', 'Hares on the Mountains', 'The Trees They Do Grow High', they are all rural, and those who sang them belonged to the diminishing band of men and women who earned their living from the land, or from the sea.[7] If he had not collected them, their memory would have faded. Yet the very act of gathering them up was, it could be said, a way of changing or destroying them, and when they had been arranged by Cecil Sharp for piano, or for use in songs, and printed with sheet music, they had ceased to be folk songs. (In 1907, Sharp persuaded the music publisher Novello to sell cheap folk song collections for 2d. each.) Just as cyclists and ramblers helped to destroy the thing they went out for to see – unvisited and unspoilt country – so Cecil Sharp's musical version of Merrie England suburbanized an organic tradition.

For generations after they had become urbanized, however, the British continued not only to hanker after the country but to carry along and within them a sense of its rhythms and sounds. The commonest determinant factor in the shape of most English towns is the shape of the old fields on which they were built. Modern Liverpool owes its layout to the fields and farms which were there before the streets. Almost every block of nineteenth-century terraced houses in Leeds, especially in its suburbs of Hunslet and Armley, is rigidly controlled by pre-existing fields and their ownership. In some industrial towns, such as Nottingham, the common fields still existed in the early nineteenth century, so that expansion and building speculation on land which was available was all the more crowded and squalid.[8] The great Victorian slums, whose jerry-building made them, by the twentieth century, intolerable for their ever-expanding populations, sing their own bleak requiem for rural England, and of no city could this be truer than London, whose population had swollen to millions more than the limits which Thomas Malthus or Cobbett or Dickens would have deemed unendurable.

No wonder that in such circumstances the country, especially the country within easy reach of the great cities, seemed ever more poignantly attractive. *Country Life Illustrated* was a magazine which had been started in 1897 not by a countryman but by Edward Hudson, a tall fish-faced man, 'a kind of bourgeois gentilhomme' a friend called him, a bachelor who lived in north London with an invalid brother and two stiff spinster sisters who looked like old-fashioned dolls waiting to be wound up.[9] He had started work as a solicitor's clerk, and inherited a printing works from his father. The idea of *Country Life* struck him while playing golf with a solicitor friend on the golf course at Walton Heath: an illustrated magazine which would feed the townsman's appetite for country houses, and pay for itself with the advertising revenue from estate agents.

The best gardening articles were written by Gertrude Jekyll, pronounced to rhyme with Treacle. Born in 1843, she belonged to the first generation of women to receive a formal artistic training. She attended the School of Art in South Kensington with Helen Paterson (later Allingham) and Barbara Leigh-Smith. She knew most of the late Victorian painters and artists – G. F. Watts, Frederick Leighton, William Holman Hunt, William de Morgan – and her witty conversation compensated for staggering plainness of feature. Her passions were Surrey and gardens. 'To Munstead for good', she wrote in her diary on 26 September 1878 when she and her mother had moved into a large, somewhat Scottish-seeming house built for them by J. J. Stevenson in the splendid Surrey heathland south of Godalming.[10] She did stay in Munstead for good, dying in 1932, but she did not always reside with her mother at Munstead House.

Partly driven by poor eyesight and the fear of blindness, partly obsessed by the fact that rural Surrey was already beginning to be spoilt, Jekyll spent the 1880s chronicling the country she loved and building up a huge photographic archive, of flowers, trees, landscapes, old Surrey landscapes, cottages and their weather-beaten peasant inhabitants in their smocks and bonnets. It was on 17 May 1889 that she met a budding young architect, Ned Lutyens, born in 1869, who shared her love of old Surrey. Lutyens, the impoverished son of a painter, was taken up by Jekyll and introduced to the work of the great Arts and Crafts architect, Philip Webb.

Lutyens is to English architecture what Elgar is to English music, an amalgam of styles and influences fused into something entirely idiosyncratic, individual. His head was filled with vernacular details from Surrey cottage eaves, barns, swooping roofs and latticed windows. Shapes and motifs from his endless cycling and walking trips through these villages were to stay in his mind, often reappearing even after he developed into an imperial classicist. In his early Arts and Crafts phase, after meeting Gertrude Jekyll, he was much influenced by Webb and his school – but Jekyll herself gave him his first major commission and her specifications were to influence him in designing dozens of other country houses. Her mother died in 1895, her brother inherited Munstead House, and she commissioned Lutyens to build on adjoining land at Munstead Wood.[11]

It was all to be built in a vernacular manner out of dressed Bargate stone, with exposed oak beams (treated with hot lime to look greyish and powdery), oak mullions, oak window boards. No two door or window fittings were the same. Lutyens was to follow many of her directions into other commissions – for example, the very low treads on the oak staircase. Some hallmark details – the raked tile roof swooping down to the tops of the ground-floor windows – were very much his own. Munstead Wood, as far as its owner was concerned, was not simply a house, it was the setting for a garden. Lutyens knew nothing of gardens until he met Jekyll; she had been fully engaged with the cultivation of the gardens at Munstead House before designing her own at Munstead Wood. Her garden plans show her a meticulous colourist with an encyclopedic knowledge of plants. The paths and nooks and garden seats in any Jekyll garden give you the chance to see the abundance of plants at close hand. She wanted gardens to be abundant and colourful at all seasons, so for example to counteract the 'temporary look' of spring, bulbs would be planted in a setting in which clumps of *Myrrhis odorata*, *Veratrum nigrum* and *Euphorbia wulfonii* could flourish even when daffodils wilted. She liked enclosed gardens, with thick unclipped hedges of yew, holly and *Quercus ilex*. She liked rough sandy paths, and stone steps, and beds banked up so that the tall plants at the back of a bed were as visible as the tumbling drifts of colour in the middle and the trailing smaller flowers and leaves at the edge.

The combination of Gertrude Jekyll's gardening skills and Edwin Lutyens's architecture became extremely popular among the classes rich enough to patronize them. After Munstead Wood he built Orchards, for the Chance family, who had made their money in Smethwick in the West Midlands making lenses for lighthouses. The success of Orchards inspired Frederick and Margaret Mirrielees to spend money made exporting department stores to Moscow creating Goddards, near Abinger – the courtyard with its well, the low walls drowned in aubrietia, the swooping roofs – and indoors, the old fire irons and bedwarmers made by the local blacksmith created an atmosphere of a lost past, a new home for which one felt instantly nostalgic. There followed dozens of commissions, of increasing grandeur. Chinthurst Hill was built for Maggie Guthrie, a feminist medic who hated it and sold it at once to Lord Rendel. Fulbrook, another magnificent Surrey house, at Elsted, was for another client who was 'modern', Gerard Streithfield, a gentleman of leisure, and his wife who was a keen motorist.[12] John Galsworthy rightly noted in *The Forsyte Saga* that the status of the upper middle classes was confirmed by new building. The bohemian wife of Soames Forsyte, Irene, has an affair with Bosinney, the slightly Lutyensesque architect of their new-built house at Robin Hill. Soames was the solicitor for the impoverished estate, which is how he acquired the land. Going to view it, 'Soames, the pioneer leader of a great Forsyte army advancing to the civilisation of this wilderness, felt his spirit daunted by the loneliness, by the invisible singing, and the hot sweet air'.[13] Nevertheless, he is enraptured both by the beauty of the scene and, Man of Property as he is, by the notion of owning, mastering, making his mark by new building.

A long, soft ripple of wind flowed over the corn, and brought a puff of warm air into their faces.

'I could build you a teaser here,' said Bosinney, breaking the silence at last.

'I dare say,' replied Soames drily. 'You haven't got to pay for it.'

'For about eight thousand I could build you a palace.'[14]

The popularity of *Country Life*, as *Country Life Illustrated* became in 1901, cannot be blamed for the growth of the suburbs, but to some extent it determined their shape. As you turned its pages, if you were a stockbroker or a lawyer's wife, you would know that you could not afford to have a house on the same scale of grandeur as Deanery Garden, Sonning, built for Edward Hudson the proprietor by Sir Edwin Lutyens, with a garden planting by Miss Gertrude Jekyll.[15] But you could perhaps afford a new Tudorbethan mansion, with an oak staircase and mullioned windows and half-timbered gables, in Godalming or Esher, or Amersham or Penn. Such places were within easy reach of London now that suburban railways had been built. Comparable dormitory villages sprang up near Manchester (Altrincham, Cheshire, is the Esher of the North), Birmingham, Leeds. By the end of Edward VII's reign the country in between was being bought up by speculative builders. For, if you could not afford stockbroker Tudor in Godalming or Esher, you could at least get out of town and have a semi-detached in Surbiton. Thus the English, in pursuit of a bit of peace and quiet, destroyed it, and in preferring country to town merely ended up by creating an endless ribbon between the two, a ribbon of suburbs which were not perhaps either town or country. The process had begun decades before King Edward came to the throne, and would continue long after he died.

In flight from the ugliness and disease of the big industrial cities, and from the diseased values which had built them, was a wide variety of high-minded seekers. As early as 1891 'General' William Booth, leader of the Salvation Army which sought to bring spiritual and physical relief to the sufferings of the urban poor, had established a Farm Colony at Hadleigh, Essex, far from the temptations of East End pubs and music halls, where the working classes made bricks, kept a chicken farm and tended fruit. There were about 300 colonists in this 100 acres of farm which by the time of 1905 had grown to 500. John Ruskin would have approved. Adjoining was a settlement for recovering alcoholics. At Sternthwaite Mill, Cumbria, the Colonization Society had a colony for unemployed city workers. And perhaps the strangest of all, Whiteway Colony in Gloucestershire attempted to put into practice a home-concocted blend of the simple-lifer ideals of Count Tolstoy with the consolations of Free Love. It was hard to know what was the more shocking to the indigenous rural community: the knickerbockers and sandals with no socks[16] sported by the men, or the stories of their amorous goings-on.

All these movements – the colonists who saw the country as therapy, the folk song collectors who saw it as a musical trove – idealized the country, as did the essentially urban Lutyens, Jekyll and *Country Life*.

The Edwardian countryside was in seemingly irreversible decline. Edward VII was the first monarch of a predominantly urban Britain, most of whose population lived in towns. It was, in the words of the Liberal politician C. F. G. Masterman, 'the largest secular change of a thousand years: from the life of the field to the life of the city'.[17] The drift to the towns which had been a feature of the first thirty-five years of his mother's reign became a stampede during the agricultural depression of the 1870s. Land rents went into steady decline over the next quarter-century.

It is true that some of the worst reverses, during the worst periods of Victorian depression, were arrested during Edward VII's reign. Grain prices had begun to rise again from the mid-1890s and as American beef imports diminished, after 1908 – something which reflected the fall in cattle sales from American ranches – the price of British beef rose. But the bulk of the meat market was imported. Edwardian Britain imported three-fifths of its beef, mutton and lamb, three-quarters of its wheat and cheese. Britain was harder hit than other European countries because so many farms specialized in wheat and other grains.[18] Many Edwardian farmers had to take on secondary occupations. A survey of thirty-four farmers listed in Corsley, Wiltshire, in 1905–6, including five who held over 100 acres of land, showed that twelve had taken on secondary work – running a bakery, hauling coal, or a carrier's business. Ellis Rhodes, farming at Shelley in Yorkshire, combined running the farm with carting coal for the local gas-works, and working in the brewery. He was a part-time manager in the colliery where he was killed in 1907 in an accident. Thereafter his family left the farm. Not much Merrie England here. As for the labourers, their hours were long. They were ill- or . . . even non-educated. While the cost of living rose 10 per cent between 1900 and 1910 the labourer's wage rose by only 3 per cent. Prices increased by an average of 5 per cent, so the poverty of agricultural labourers was worsened during this reign.[19]

Real countrymen and countrywomen saw the rise of 'week-end' or golfing cottages. The villages within reach of London all found the old places scarred with new buildings, new roads. George Sturt, writing of The Bourne, near Farnham, Surrey, said his hamlet 'had ceased to be a country place, and had been turned instead into a suburb of the town in the next valley . . . The once quiet high-road is noisy with the motor-cars of the richer residents and all the town traffic that wails upon the less wealthy'. The toiling labourer could hear, drifting towards him over the fields, the sounds 'of piano playing coming to him, or of the affected excitement of a tennis-party; or the braying of a motor-car informs him that the rich who are his masters are on the road'.[20]

*

The motor-car was introduced to the English public at a Crystal Palace exhibition in 1896. In 1900, 800 cars were purchased in Britain; by 1913 the figure had risen to 33,800. (Fatal accidents involving cars exceeded those involving horse-drawn vehicles for the first time in 1910.) Edward VII, who as Prince of Wales was photographed taking his first ride in one in 1898, stated, truthfully: 'The motor-car will become a necessity for every English gentleman.'[21] This would have revolutionary consequences not merely for the English countryside but for the world. Areas of the globe which possessed oil reserves, some of them previously poor, began to assume an overwhelming importance in the scheme of things.

In ancient Mesopotamia, present-day Iraq, the Babylonians knew of an inflammable material which they called 'naphtha' or 'the thing that blazes', using what was probably a loan-word from Greek. This seepage from rock asphalt could be used for bitumen, but it had no other very obvious use. Though medicinal purposes were found for it in sixteenth-century Europe, and though in late seventeenth-century Shropshire, at Pitchford-on-Severn, a variety of turpentine was patented, made from boiling sandstone shale and water, the human race remained innocent of any need for what a sixteenth-century German philologist, Georg Bauer (Georgius Agricola), had nicknamed, in Latin, rock oil, *petra-oleum*.[22]

It was Edwin L. Drake, in 1859, who had first drilled for oil in north-western Pennsylvania, and thereby established the groundwork for the modern petroleum industry. But Drake and his followers – he drilled 69.5 feet or 21.18 m through bedrock – saw the fossil fuel as an illuminant. Within fifteen years, production in the Pennsylvania field had reached 10 million 360-lb (163.3-kg) barrels a year. The Russians had drilled at Baku in 1873. These early pioneers boiled the crude oil at 160°–250°C to produce paraffin (kerosene) for lamps, but the greater fraction of the crude thus processed became a highly flammable substance known as petroleum or gasoline, for which no obvious use could be found.[23]

By the time kerosene lighting had been made obsolete by the advent of electric lighting (four manufacturers had filament lamps on display at the first International Electrical Exhibition in Paris in 1881, and by the end of the decade there were several electrical power stations in Britain illuminating houses and streets in Brighton, London, Glasgow and elsewhere[24]), the petrol-fuelled internal combustion engine had been developed.[25]

Almost simultaneously in 1886 Karl Benz, Gottlieb Daimler and Wilhelm Maybach produced single-cylinder Otto-cycle engines using petrol and a carburettor, and by the end of the Nineties, Daimler had converted from the perilous flame-heated hot tube to electric spark ignition. Rudolf Diesel invented the compression ignition engine, pioneered in 1892–3.[26]

These inventions which were to change the story of land transport were also destined to have the most extraordinary effect on aeronautics. In 1893–4 Sir Hiram Maxim, he of the machine gun, had built a huge steam-fuelled carriage which, it was calculated, would need a mounted wing surface of 400 sq. m to make it fly. A Yorkshire landowner, Sir George Cayley, during the Regency period, had tried to work out a system of propelling flying machines by clockwork. Otto Lilienthal in the 1890s in Germany had pioneered the design of small gliders. They were really little more than aerodynamic hang-gliders. Lilienthal died while trying to fly one. Until the arrival of petroleum, and a suitably small engine, there was no practical possibility of heavier-than-air flying machines.

Wilbur and Orville Wright of Dayton, Ohio, powered a glider with a light four-cylindered petrol engine and made the first powered flight with a heavier-than-air machine on 17 December 1903 near Kill Devil Hill in North Carolina. By October 1905 they had so perfected the machine (after an heroic 120 unstable flights) as to remain in the air for half an hour. The Voisin brothers in France built a biplane which they developed in 1908–9, and Louis Blériot in his Type XI aircraft, fuelled by a three-cylinder Anzani engine and a wooden propeller (designed by Raymond Saulnier), flew the English Channel on 25 July 1909. All aircraft propellers were wooden until the 1920s.

The uses to which petrol-fuelled vehicles on land and in the air, and petrol-fuelled ships at sea, might be put was something which history was all too soon to reveal. The extent to which the human race would try to become the lords of petroleum, instantly thereby becoming its slaves, would change the subsequent map of the world. In a steam- and coal-powered world, Britain and Germany would remain triumphant, rivalled only in the East by an emergent industrialized Japan. Trade depended, as Alfred Tennyson wrote in *Locksley Hall* (published 1842), 'In the steamships in the railroad in the thoughts that shake mankind', but there were many factors involved in the story of Britain, a trading nation transforming itself and the Asian and African countries it occupied into an Empire. From 1910 onwards, as the world became dependent on oil, for its motor cars, motor-buses, motorized military vehicles, petroleum-fuelled aircraft and ships and submarines, and petroleum-fuelled industrial machinery, the oil-producing nations acquired new strengths, new vulnerabilities. The United States has appreciable oil reserves; it has always, historically, had the largest cumulative production in the world.[27] Russia has the third-largest cumulative production and a much larger oil reserve. But apart from the considerable amounts of oil in Mexico and Venezuela, the major oilfields of the world were to be discovered in the Arabian–Iranian basin. Add up the oil reserves of present-day Saudi Arabia

(261.2 billion barrels), Iraq (100 billion barrels), Iran (93 billion barrels), Kuwait (97.5 billion barrels) and the United Arab Emirates (98.2 billion barrels) and you have a present-day total of 649.9 billion barrels of oil possessed by the Arab world, compared with a mere 50 billion barrels of oil reserves beneath American rock or soil. The implications of this were not to strike the European nations immediately, but we cannot be blind to them. The flying machines and motor cars of the Edwardian era look like toys built for the amusement of Mr Toad, but they are harbingers of a new world order. Moreover, the Mr Toad at the wheel would be unlikely to have owned Toad Hall for more than a generation.

Disraeli, a London-born man of letters of Jewish origin, saw more clearly than any Victorian statesman that Britain was effectively owned and governed by the same people. That was until the collapse in agriculture, land values and rents. He extolled those squires who had, many of them, held land for generations, since the Middle Ages. As Justices of the Peace, and Members of Parliament and landlords, they had been the primary frame in the social structure of pre-industrial England. By the flexible laws of inheritance in Britain, and by its comparative social fluidity, it was possible to hold on to the aristocratic principle even in an industrial age.

'England', Disraeli had written in *Lord George Bentinck*, 'is the only important European community governed by traditionary influences, and amid the shameless wreck of nations she alone has maintained her honour, her authority and her wealth . . . But it is said that it is contrary to the spirit of the age that a great nation like England, a community of enlightened millions long accustomed to public liberty, should be governed by an aristocracy. It is not true that England is governed by an aristocracy in the common acceptation of the term. England is governed by an aristocratic principle. The aristocracy of England absorbs all aristocracies, and receives every man in every order and every class who defers to the principle of our society, which is to aspire and to excel.'[28] Those words were published in 1852, and they were, to a quite prodigious degree, true for many decades later. Yet, as Disraeli's own life showed, the very conservative fluidity which was the strength of what he termed an 'aristocracy which absorbs all aristocracies' meant in fact that money counted for more than lineage or status, or than land itself.

When he started out on his political career, he could not appeal to the Tory voters without being landed. His supporters simply bought him an estate and made him into the country gentleman of Hughenden Manor. He loved his country neighbours – rather more than they loved him, alas.[29] He enjoyed his visits to the squires and farmers who returned him as their Tory member of Parliament – 'the Pauncefort Duncombes of

Brickhill Manor . . . Colonel Hanmer of Stockgrove Park, the Chesters of Chicheley, the Lovetts of Liscombe, the Dayrells of Lillingstone Dayrell . . .'³⁰ Within fifty years of Disraeli's death, none of these families were still in possession of their estates.

The very 'aristocratic' principle which Disraeli so extolled was partially responsible for the change. In order for the new rich to rise, and to enter the political classes, they in turn bought estates and land from the impoverished squirearchy. Whereas the squires, so many of them, had held on through good times and bad for centuries, the *nouveaux riches* were the first to get rid of land, and to break up estates, when times were hard again, which accounts for the quite speedy ruination of so many old houses and estates in Britain after the First World War.

The palaces of the New Rich, both urban and rural, told their own crowing Toad-like tale. The Victorian and Edwardian millionaires liked to flaunt their money. Scotland sprouted spanking new baronial castles. Glen, Peeblesshire, proclaimed the greatness of the Tennants, and the money they had made from chemicals. Tennant's industrial empire stretched from the ironworks of Lanarkshire to the gold fields of Mysore. His factory at St Rollocks polluted the air of Glasgow with clouds of hydrochloric acid, but at Glen, with its 'pepper-pot turrets, high-pitched roofs like a French chateau . . . all was spick and span, superbly groomed and appointed. The gravel was meticulously combed . . . the lawns as smoothly ironed . . . only the hills were rugged and unkempt. Everything was new. "Each pineapple we eat costs us five pounds", Sir Charles Tennant would say as the desert was handed round.'³¹

Ballikinrain Castle in Stirlingshire was a vast pile built from a Glasgow dyer's fortune; Rosehaugh in Ross-shire was J. D. Fletcher's, who had made his money in Liverpool as a Peruvian alpaca merchant. Ardkinglas, Argyll, was built for Sir Andrew Noble, whose fortune was in armaments – as was Lord Armstrong's, for whom Norman Shaw built Craigside, the first electrically lit house in Britain.

The Rothschild Chateau at Waddesdon, built for Baron Ferdinand de Rothschild, is a dream of French opulence in the midst of the Buckinghamshire countryside, as to a smaller extent was Chateau Impney in Worcestershire, built for a local salt manufacturer named John Corbett.

London caught the Parisian fever to hideous effect. To match the palaces put up by financiers and South African diamond magnates, heavy with gilt and festooned with palms, Buckingham Palace was 'done up'. The Victorian ballroom was remodelled in French style by Frank Verity. The thrones themselves, from which purchased peerages and knighthoods were dispensed, were made in Paris in 1902.

In the time that Dr Johnson, Burke and Gibbon lived in London, the king of England spent much of his time living in a modest and beautifully proportioned house in Kew Gardens, not much bigger than those of his subjects. In the time of Edward the Caresser, the Palace had to outshine those of his new friends the Beits and the Rothschilds. Such grandiose efforts as Sir Aston Webb's Admiralty Arch (1911, but designed earlier) reflect that very short period of London's history when, rather than being a commercial and political capital of a vigorous, small trading nation, it took into its head vulgar imperial notions. Admiralty Arch, and Webb's other efforts – the splashy new façade to Buckingham Palace, the wedding-cake memorial opposite to the memory of Queen Victoria – now, like a collective hangover, serve as hideous reminders of the brief imperialist aberration. Webb was Napoleonic in inspiration, but it was Napoleon III and the Baron Haussmann who inspired him. What a pity the Luftwaffe never scored any hits against his work. When they bombed Buckingham Palace, they missed Webb's façade.

Snobs, at the time and since, have objected that King Edward VII spent so much of his time with the *nouveaux riches*, but this is to overlook the rather obvious fact that he was a *nouveau riche* himself. He was not slumming it, he was mixing with his own kind. When Queen Victoria and Prince Albert built Osborne House on the Isle of Wight they did so on the cheap, and they possessed no private fortunes. It was her long years of widowhood, when she carefully squirrelled away her huge Civil List allowances, which enabled her to pass on vast wealth to her son. He squandered it on race horses, women, cigars, which was why he was always pleased to borrow more. But he was not moving out of his class to do so. On the contrary. He was the vulgarian to end all *nouveau riche* vulgarians, and it was this which dominated not only his private views, but the politics of the age.

4

The Accursed Power

A narrowly political, in the sense of party and parliamentary, history of Edwardian Britain would see the year 1906, and the great Liberal landslide which it brought in, as the crucial moment of change. At the beginning of the reign until the Coronation, the prime minister was the 3rd Marquess of Salisbury, High Tory of High Tories, one of the cleverest and most enigmatic men ever to have held the office. He was succeeded by his nephew, Arthur Balfour, tall, languid, cynical, curiously detached from the world over which he exercised such influence. (He once asked one of his female relations to explain to him what a trade union was.) Balfour's cabinet was composed largely of landed aristocrats or their relations. Exceptions were the rich Birmingham tycoons Joseph Chamberlain, colonial secretary, who was an imperialist radical Liberal who had split with Gladstone over Ireland, and Austen Chamberlain, one of the few men (until the twenty-first century) destined to lead the Conservative party without being prime minister.

The 1906 election produced the greatest poll victory on record. The Liberals obtained 400 seats, a majority of 130 over all other parties combined.[1] They established the precedent, followed by the Labour governments of Ramsay MacDonald, Harold Wilson and Tony Blair, of a supposedly radical party coming in to a fanfare of excitement from its more optimistic or leftist supporters, only to adopt a broadly conservative set of policies. Though historians of party might see 1906 as a watermark, the incoming government could look at the problems of Britain and the world and quickly learn a policy of indifference which Lord Salisbury would have envied.

What were the major problems? What of the unresolved question of Women's Suffrage? You might have supposed that a Liberal party would have been pro-feminist, but it wasn't particularly. Its natural 'grass-roots' support came from the petite bourgeoisie, which was just as anxious as any Tory to keep the little woman in her place. The Liberal government passed the Qualification of Women Act, 1907, which allowed women to sit as councillors, aldermen, mayors or chairmen on county or borough councils; in the GLC election of 1907 there were 600,000 women householders, of whom over 100,000 voted. But the hot potato of women's suffrage, women's rights to a parliamentary vote, let alone to stand for parliamentary election, was given no time in the Liberal Parliaments.

The 1906 landslide happened just a decade before the Easter Rising in Dublin. The outgoing Tory chief secretary for Ireland, George Wyndham, did more to help small Irish landowners – with his Irish Land Purchase Act of 1903, enabling peasant and yeoman farmers to have a stake in their land – than any subsequent Liberal. This was the case in spite of the fact that the home secretary in the first Liberal administration was Herbert J. Gladstone, son of the Grand Old Man himself, the passionate advocate of Irish Home Rule.

Matters of arguably greater moment faced the new foreign secretary, Sir Edward Grey, the new secretary for India, John Morley, and the new colonial secretary, Lord Elgin. They were admirable Victorian Liberals, and it should not be said that they did nothing. They tried to reduce the ridiculous arms race with Germany, by having a conference on limitation at The Hague, in their first year of government. Though Grey wanted to reduce the number of dreadnoughts, one was launched just before the Hague Conference. Morley was destined forlornly to resign his cabinet seat when war eventually came. He had been powerless, and most of the Liberal party entirely unwilling, to stop it.

In South Africa, however, their record is rather better. As soon as the election was over, the new cabinet vetoed the further recruitment of Chinese slaves. The new liberal prime minister, Henry Campbell-Bannerman, had announced, at a rally in the Albert Hall, that his government would 'stop forthwith the recruitment and embarkation of coolies in China and their importation into South Africa'. The Liberal imperialist chancellor of the Exchequer, however, H. H. Asquith, reminded the prime minister that licences for the importation of 14,000 coolies, granted the previous November, had not yet been used. The cabinet immediately backed down and prohibited merely the future issuance of licences, rather than bringing the Chinese labour to an end forthwith. It was not legally in its power to do so, and so it was not until 1910 that the last Chinese labourers left the Rand compounds.[2]

For the Radical wing of the Liberal party, this was not enough. The new member of Parliament for South Salford, for example, in his maiden speech, demanded that the government begin deporting the Chinese labourers within three months, and at a set rate of, say, 5,000 per month. The man who made this suggestion was Hilaire Belloc, journalist, historian and poet, better known to posterity for his comic rhymes for children than for his parliamentary career. He was a colourful presence in the House, who very quickly came to tire of the compromises which the party system forced upon people. It was not enough for Belloc and his friends that the Liberals had made a step in the right direction. Like all Radicals he was impatient for the career politicians to act upon their promises, to do what they said they would do. It was not enough that Campbell-Bannerman's government did, in a number of significant ways, undermine the high imperialism of the previous administration. For example, in South Africa, the Liberals replaced the Tory system of complete British hegemony with self-government for the Orange River Colony (homogeneously Boer) and by 1908 they had drafted a constitution for a politically united South Africa which allowed universal suffrage among the white populace. The black majority, one need hardly say at this date, were not given the vote. No one offered it to them. Only the High Tory imperialist John Buchan in his thriller *Prester John* saw the potency of a black Africa as a political ideal. When the Scottish hero overhears the black clergyman, Laputa, urging the blacks to throw off white oppression ('a bastard civilization which has sapped your manhood') Davie cannot fail to be impressed. 'By rights, I suppose, my blood should have been boiling at this treason. I am ashamed to confess that it did nothing of the sort. My mind was mesmerized by this amazing man.'[3]

So quickly had the imperial idea, mooted as an experiment in the mid- to late nineteenth century, been fixed in the British mind! When Frederick Lugard colonized West Africa he had seen it as a temporary measure, a matter of two or three generations to teach the Africans civilization, before the Europeans went home again. Post Boer War, for an African to speak of self-government was 'treason'.[4]

On 13 June 1906 there was a riot in the Nile Delta village of Denshawui in which a British officer died. It had been precipitated by British officers shooting pigeons against the wishes of the inhabitants. Lord Cromer, the British consul general in Egypt, ordered a summary tribunal. There were floggings of great severity performed in front of the victims' families, four villagers were condemned to death and twelve imprisoned. Radicals like Belloc protested that there was no chance of an inquiry since Cromer had conveniently destroyed the evidence.[5] Belloc's Sussex neighbour Wilfrid Scawen Blunt, the foremost British defender of Egyptian rights, published a pamphlet condemning the atrocities. The case, with the fudging of the issue of Chinese labour in the Natal, 'together ought to shut English mouths forever about Russia and the Congo'.[6]

The British had gone into Egypt to tidy up after a local war. Gladstone ordered the occupation of the country in 1882 to help put down a mutiny against the Turks. The British fleet was sent to Alexandria but had been unable to prevent a riot in which the consul was killed. So they sent troops to support the Turkish Khedive. Before another year was up, General Gordon was making his fateful visit to Khartoum, and in the aftermath of that war, Evelyn Baring, financial adviser to the viceroy's council in India, arranged a loan of £9 million in aid to the 'Egyptian', in fact Turkish, government. Baring became Lord Cromer, the virtual ruler of Egypt from 1883 to 1907, and the British did not leave Egypt until they were forced to do so by Colonel Nasser in 1956 after the Suez fiasco. 'In the twenty-five years from 1882 to 1907 England is said to have made nearly 120 promises to evacuate Egypt while at the same time . pursuing policies which confirmed her hold over the country.'[7]

It was the Suez Canal, in which Disraeli had arranged that the British government should buy a majority shareholding, which had led Britain into this disastrous imperialist position in Egypt. And why was the canal so important? Because it was the quickest trade route to India, with whose fortunes in the narrow financial as well as the destinal sense Britain's were so intimately entwined. The new Liberal secretary for India, John Morley – patient Gladstonian and biographer of the Grand Old Man – put into place reforms in the subcontinent which matched what Britain had done in South Africa. Curzon's successor as viceroy, Lord Minto, saw his role less as a proconsul than a civil servant, and together with Morley he attempted to extend legislative and administrative powers to Indians. Not much headway was made, partly because these well-intentioned Liberal gradualists met opposition both from Indian nationalists and from Tory British diehards.

Behind all the public debate about the Empire, which the new government occasioned, there remained the economic issues which had haunted Balfour's government, and which would continue to dominate British life until the Second World War. These were the related questions of how the Empire enriched the mother country, how the domestic economy of Britain was managed, where British wealth came from, and how sustainable it was politically, given the huge growth of an urban industrialized and at times discontented working class. None of these questions can be studied or answered in isolation. They interrelate.

The Victorian success story had been entitled Free Trade. The old Corn Laws, by which Tory landowners could guarantee an income by fixing the price of grain, had been swept away by the radicals of the 1840s. The prophets of Free Trade like Cobden and Bright believed not only that it would make Britain rich, but that it would make the world peaceful. They entirely failed to predict that as other nations raced to catch up with Britain in industrial expertise and production they would see one another as deadly rivals, and that among the commodities they would perfect and develop and sell would be armaments.

Moreover Free Trade could impoverish as well as enrich. The most conspicuous example of this perhaps was the Lancashire cotton trade,

Britain's largest source of export. In the last thirty years of the nineteenth century, British cotton manufactures lost their European and American markets. The Europeans and the Americans developed means to produce and sell cotton goods of their own which were cheaper than the British products. So the British relied almost exclusively by 1900 on the markets of India, China and the Levant. It only needed the Indians to develop the means of industrial cotton-production, or actively to boycott British goods – both things were beginning to happen – for the working classes of Lancashire to face starvation, as they had done when cotton supplies gave up during the American Civil War.

This large single example will suffice as a paradigm for the whole debate which dominated Edwardian politics between those who clung to the Victorian belief in Free Trade and those who supported tariffs, artificially to shore up the British economy. This debate is related, economically and politically, to two other matters which would dominate the world in the decades following the First World War: namely currency and its fluctuations, and the question, never even considered in Britain until too late, of whether governments themselves could, or should, intervene to tackle employment problems. Carlyle could dismiss economics as the dismal science. In the century which followed Carlyle, economics were central.

It explains, for example, how a figure such as Joseph Chamberlain, the Radical mayor of Birmingham, through his advocacy of Empire and his belief in social harmony, should have undergone a total volte-face over the matter of Free Trade. It was Free Trade which made a great city such as Birmingham or Manchester, and which therefore made a successful entrepreneur such as Chamberlain. Equally, he discovered, Free Trade could unmake such places. In 1888 a dire new word entered the English language: unemployment.[8] 'Tariff Reform means work for all' was Chamberlain's boastful hope in 1903.[9] The Empire became the means of saving 'dying British industry'. The issue split the Conservative party: it was one of the reasons why they lost the 1906 election, and why Churchill, a keen Free Trader, left the Tories and joined the Liberal party.

The disparities between rich and poor in Edwardian Britain were by our standards grotesque. You would have to go to South America to find modern parallels. Vast population growth during the Victorian heyday was the essential ingredient in the story: it explained the prodigious wealth of the new plutocracy, and the abject poverty of those who, in an overcrowded market and in overcrowded cities, were pushed out of the possibilities either of work or decent housing. Add to that the fact that much of the rapid building in the mid- to late nineteenth century was of unsatisfactory quality and you have, above the level of the destitute, a large group of badly housed, unhealthy people.

The booming economy of the mid-nineteenth century needed an expanding population to match. Yet the rub was, when the economy contracted, that there would be a working population surplus to requirements in Malthusian terms. The situation would call for desperate remedies. If the ultimate Malthusian solution were not sought – a reduction of the population by war, massacre, plague, starvation, emigration – then some new, collective form of politics would have to be devised to contain an otherwise anarchic social situation. Yet how could such a solution not destroy the very wealth-creation which fuelled the economic boom in the first instance?

Had the population simply continued to swell, with no adequate means to increase the amount of food being imported into Britain, then a situation of Malthusian bleakness would have ensued. Indeed, Britain would have been starving. As it happened, however, food imports (while crippling British farmers) provided cheap grain, and meat, from America. And there was a further strange fact. At the moment when some improvement was brought to public health, and the death rate fell, so too did the birth rate. Death rates declined by 18.5 per cent between 1901 and 1913, while birth rates declined by 15.5 per cent.[10]

This did not stop the life of the urban poor being hard, nor did it prevent it from feeling overcrowded, wretched. Nor did the population actually decline, so the opportunities for wealth-creation remained prodigious.[11] In the closing decades of the Victorian era, vast amounts of money could be made by those selling or making those commodities which the newly expanded population needed. The brewers of eighteenth-century London were among its richest men because no sane person would in those days have drunk the fetid water. So the Whitbreads and the Thrales became rich in a world of well over half a million thirsty Londoners. In the world of a hundred years later the brewer who could use modern technology to make the drink and railways and ships to transport it could be well over thousands of times richer, as was demonstrated by the Guinness fortune.

Many in the lifetime of Charles Dickens used soap. Some perhaps not. When William Hesketh Lever, however, bought a modest Warrington soap works in Cheshire (output 20 tons a week) in 1885 he rightly reckoned on a world where all respectable persons would like to buy soap. In his second year of ownership production had risen to 450 tons. By 1894 Lever Brothers became a public company valued at £1.5 million. With the fortune he made from Sunlight Soap, 'Lifebuoy' (made from surplus oil

left over from Sunlight) and 'Lux' Flakes he built a model town, a pater-
nalistic fantasy where he was king: Port Sunlight. By the time he died in
1925 he had factories in twenty-five countries, 85,000 employees and a
capital of over £56 million.

The growth of Thomas Lipton, grocer of Stobcross Street, Glasgow,
was no less simple and in a sense demographically inevitable. Lipton was
said to feel unhappy if he did not open a shop every week. Having started
out aged twenty-one on borrowed capital of £100 he was able to use his
rapidly expanding chain of shops more or less to take over the Irish dairy,
egg and ham market, and to corner the market in American pork. (His
Chicago slaughterhouse alone killed and dressed 300–400 pigs a day.) 'If
you stick to business, business will stick to you,' he liked to say. When
Lipton's became a public company in 1898 applications for £40 million
of stock were received.

> No one seems to care anything but about money today. Nothing is
> held of account except the bank accounts. Quality education, civic
> distinction, public virtue seem each year to be valued less and less.
> Riches unadorned seem each year to be valued more and more. We
> have in London an important section of the people who go about
> preaching the gospel of Mammon, advocating the 10% command-
> ments, who raise each day the inspiring prayer, 'Give cash in our time,
> O Lord'.[12]

Money was not merely important in Edwardian England, it was para-
mount. Lord Bryce, British ambassador to the United States from 1907
to 1912, believed that Britain was more money-obsessed than America,
and in that sense less class-bound. In *The American Commonwealth*, he
wrote:

> It may seem a paradox to observe that a millionaire has a better and
> easier social career open to him in England than in America
> . . . In America, if his private character be bad, if he be mean or openly
> immoral, or personally vulgar, or dishonest, the best society may keep
> its doors closed against him. In England, great wealth, skilfully
> employed, will more readily force these doors open. For in England
> great wealth can practically buy rank from those who bestow it . . .

This was visibly the case, with honours and titles being on sale by all
prime ministers from Gladstone onwards, and with a new monarch who
needed money and liked the company of rich vulgarians more than that
of impoverished old aristocrats. 'My uncle has gone sailing with his

grocer' was the Kaiser's amused comment at Cowes, when King Edward spent the day with his friend Sir Thomas Lipton.

Chiazza Money, a Fellow of the Royal Statistical Society, who became a Liberal MP in 1906, had in the previous year published a survey of Britain which would shock any reader of a remotely egalitarian frame of mind. In the financial year 1903–4, Money reckoned that the national income was £1,710m. Of this sum £830m was taken by 5 million people. The rest of the nation, some 38 million persons, lived on £880m.[13]

Money's survey reveals a large prosperous middle class, and a prodigiously rich, mega-rich apogee at the top of Edwardian society. In this prosperous class Money reckoned 250,000 men supported about 1 million dependants.

Charles Booth, in his ground-breaking sociological researches into the lives of East Enders in London, *Life and Labour of the People in London* (1891–1903), reckoned that 30 per cent of those living in the capital did so in poverty. It was the capital city of the greatest Empire and the richest industrial power the world had ever seen. Well over a million Londoners lived beneath the poverty line and 37,610 (according to Booth) depended on a breadwinner whose income was less than 18 shillings a week. B. S. Rowntree and M. Kendall in their survey of 1913 reckoned that a family of two adults and three children could barely survive on £1.0s. 6d., and then only if they ate no butcher's meat, no butter, no eggs and almost no tea.[14]

Although surveys of the wages of labourers and unskilled factory workers suggest that real income was on the increase, it did not necessarily feel like this. If industrial action is any indication of discontent and fear among the working classes then the very modest efforts of the Liberal government to improve the lot of the workers and their families did not prevent a prodigious growth in strikes. In 1907 the total trades union membership in Britain and Ireland was 2,513,000. After six years that had risen to 4,135,000. Whereas in 1907 there were a little over 2 million working days lost through strikes, by 1912 this had risen to a mind-boggling 40,890,000 working days.

Winston Churchill, in the Christmas holiday of 1905, read Seebohm Rowntree's study of urban poverty in York which, as he said, 'has fairly made my hair stand on end . . . It is found that the poverty of the people extends to nearly one fifth of the population; nearly one fifth had something between one and a half and three fourths as much food to each as the paupers in the York Union. That I call a terrible and shocking thing, people who have only the workhouse or the prison as the only avenues to change from their present situation.'[15]

The very fact that Churchill himself was recklessly extravagant, and enjoyed the finest wines, the most expensive cigars and the patronage and company of the rich only increased his bewilderment when he allowed himself to be confronted by the cruel reality of other lives. Walking around the streets of Manchester with his friend Edward Marsh as they awaited the results of the 1906 poll, Churchill exclaimed: 'Fancy living in one of these streets – never seeing anything beautiful – never eating anything savoury – *never saying anything clever.*'[16] It is hardly communism. But it is an indication of why electors voted in the new Liberal government, which Churchill served – as assistant to David Lloyd George at the Board of Trade in 1906, becoming president of the Board of Trade under Asquith's premiership in 1908, and home secretary in 1910.

Lloyd George's brand of radicalism was very different from Churchill's Whiggery. He was only forty-three when he became President of the Board of Trade. His initial political concerns had appeared to be local, a passionate advocacy of the rights of self-determination of the Welsh. It was during the Boer War, which he opposed, that David Lloyd George had come to people's notice as an orator of genius and as a self-created thorn in the side of the English Establishment. He was neither left-wing nor right-wing by any recognizable standards. He was a solicitor by training, and he had the lawyer's knack of taking each case as it came along, and arguing with more passion and wit, sometimes, than consistency. He was against the Boer War, for example, but he was not markedly anti-imperialist. He approved of the British running South Africa, he merely disliked the idea of them fighting, and wasting public money in so doing.

After Asquith had succeeded Campbell-Bannerman as prime minister in 1908, Lloyd George had the opportunity, as Chancellor of the Exchequer, to demonstrate his social and economic preferences. The budget gave him the chance to bring in a very few measures which would introduce some extremely modest social benefits, and to pay for four dreadnought battleships for which the MPs were clamouring. (Lloyd George ignored their mantra of *We want eight and we won't wait.*) He founded a system of labour exchanges, which enabled the unemployed to look for work. (It cost £100,000.) He introduced a tax break for parents, giving them a £10 tax allowance for every child under sixteen. Asquith had already introduced Old Age Pensions in 1908, to start on 1 January 1909. By no stretch of the imagination could Lloyd George's 1909 budget be regarded as socialist or revolutionary, but he was raising public spending by 11 per cent – £16 million had to be found. Some of it he could get from levies on petrol and a newly introduced scheme of motor licences. That would bring in £600,000. Death duties, a measure which cut at the very heart and notion of family stability and property owner-ship, were raised to yield £4.4 million a year. Income tax was raised from a shilling to 1s. 2d. in the pound. Duty on liquor was put up. But the real sticking point, the red rag offered to the landowning classes, was a tax on land value – unearned increment in the value of land would be taxed at 20 per cent.

We shall probably never know whether Lloyd George introduced this measure as a purely economic solution to his difficulties in raising the necessary shortfall for his budget, or whether he did so in order to bait the big landowners. Certainly he enjoyed doing this very much indeed, and he was brilliant at it.

The aristocrats rose to the bait, and the House of Lords responded in a way which put their very political life in jeopardy. They threatened to reject the budget, and in November 1909 they did so. Asquith moved and carried a motion in the Commons on 2 December 1909: 'That the action of the House of Lords in refusing to pass into law the financial provi-sions made by this House for the service of the year is a breach of the Constitution and a usurpation of the rights of the Commons.'

In the January election, the Liberal vote slipped away: the figures were Liberals 275, Labour 40, Irish Nationalists 82 and Unionists, i.e. Conservatives, 273. It was assumed by Asquith's supporters that he had told the king, if the Lords rejected the budget in the new Parliament, that the Liberals would create 500 peers of their own political persua-sion. In fact, Edward VII, with some canniness, had not given any undertaking to do this. He had insisted that if the new peers were appointed, this would require a second General Election. As it happened, the matter was not to concern the king for much longer. King Edward died at Buckingham Palace on 6 May 1910, with the archbishop of Canterbury, Randall Davidson, on one side of the bed and Queen Alexandra on the other.

The constitutional crisis which had been precipitated by the Lloyd George budget was to be of interest to future historians. In terms of the status quo it left nothing changed. It was not surprising that a disillu-sioned Hillaire Belloc chose not to stand for re-election during the second election of 1910, which had been caused by the king's death.

> The accursed power which stands on Privilege
> (And goes with Women, and Champagne, and Bridge)
> Broke – and Democracy resumed her reign:
> (Which goes with Bridge, and Women and Champagne).[17]

Giving very minimal social welfare such as the Old Age Pension was considerably cheaper than keeping more and more urban indigents in workhouses where food and bedding, no matter how grudging, had to be provided. Lloyd George and his allies knew this, as did the many canny Liberal capitalists who supported him. This is not to decry these first steps towards using the tax system for the purposes of charity. But it is to doubt whether the measures considered were as revolutionary either as the Tory diehard peers dreaded in 1909, or as subsequent advocates of full-scale State Benefits might have wanted to suppose.

To many in 1909–10 it must have seemed as if the debates in Westminster about the budget, or about the relative power of the Commons versus the Lords, were a galanty show, a distraction from the really searching issues of the day – an unwieldy and perhaps untenable British Empire not facing up to the realities of, for instance, Indian aspirations to independence; a desperately unstable European situation, in which the national leaders and their diplomats appeared to be sleepwalking towards disaster; a tinderbox in Ireland, waiting to explode; a potentially revolutionary situation in British factories and slums, where hundreds of thousands of people felt themselves to be trapped by poverty, bad housing and uncongenial work, which was preferable to no work at all. And there was, in addition, the quiet revolution which had, in the country at large, though not in the political sphere, already taken place: the change in the position of women.

To say that women's position had changed is not to say that late Victorian or Edwardian women were 'liberated' in the sense of the word which would be meaningful in the mid- to late twentieth century. Women, in houses without servants, still did all the domestic drudgery; and in houses with servants it was left to the females on the staff to sweep the stairs, lay the grates, empty the chamber pots and peel the potatoes. Except for a tiny handful of privileged (not necessarily rich, but privileged) young women who attended the newly formed university colleges in London, Cambridge and Oxford, women still lacked the educational opportunities given to males. But things had, during the mid- to late Victorian years, altered. Women now were educated. They had achieved some significant parliamentary victories and changes in the law. The Married Women's Property Act of 1882, for example, had abolished a husband's absolute control over his wife's property. Women were now technically independent under the law. It was a huge advance, though many might not have felt its immediate benefit.

Thanks to the pioneering bravery of Elizabeth Garrett (Anderson) (1836–1917) – who qualified as a doctor in 1865 – and to Dr Sophia Jex-Blake, who founded the London School of Medicine for Women in 1874, it was now possible for women to aspire to the same professional careers as their brothers. When Christabel Pankhurst (1880–1958) applied to study law at Lincoln's Inn, her father's old Inn of Court, she was turned down because she was a woman, but she studied law at Manchester University. Very many women lower down the social scale had worked in mines and factories and mills and the Matchmakers' Union (not a dating agency, but a trade union based around Bryant and May's match factory in the East End of London) was founded by a woman (Annie Besant) for an almost entirely female membership. Their successful strike for slightly better pay and conditions in 1888 gave male workers the courage to start strikes of their own, and it was a key moment in British labour history.

The story of the political emancipation of British women, like the story of Ireland, is one which is still being written, and it poses important questions, beyond itself, about the nature of democratic change. In his smug history of this decade, *The Edwardians*, J. B. Priestley says that the 'militant' wing of the feminist movement, by their 'extreme' behaviour, actually delayed the arrival of Votes for Women. In a somewhat similar vein, it is suggested that if only the blacks, or the Irish, had been patient enough to trust their lords and masters, they would have been given their independence all in good time.

Others, whatever their view of trouble, by whomsoever it is made, will rather doubt this. For every male member of Parliament who was enlightened, there were dozens who were not. Take the example of Hilaire Belloc. Hardly a typical backbencher, you would say, and you would be right. But his mother, Bessie Parkes, had been a pioneering feminist radical, a friend of Barbara Bodichon, George Eliot and others. Yet he grew up with views which seemed to reflect none of this. He opposed female suffrage. Winston Churchill claimed, as a Liberal MP, to support female suffrage, and did once vote in its favour during a division in the House of Commons which was never going to bring the vote to pass. Using the militancy of suffrage activists, or 'Suffragettes', as his excuse for dragging his heels, he said: 'I am not going to be henpecked on a question of such grave importance' – a sentence which might have been echoed by many males who considered themselves enlightened so much as to consider the matter. As Home Secretary in 1910 he allowed the straitjacketing and force-feeding of suffragette political prisoners – though another Home Secretary, Roy Jenkins, in his biography of Churchill says that he did not demonstrate 'heavy-handedness' in this respect.

The truth is, we cannot know how quickly the all-male Parliament and the male monarch would have decided to give women the vote in Britain had they not been 'hen-pecked'. The historical evidence, which belongs later in this book, is that, as in the case of Ireland, and as in the slightly different case of India, political action became evident in the chamber of Parliament only after very disruptive action was taken on the ground by the 'militants'.

As with the Chartist movement, there were two broad strands of female suffragists: the 'moderates' who hoped to achieve their ends merely by argument, and those who favoured demonstrations of force. The most distinguished advocate of the former path was Millicent Fawcett (1847–1929), who at eighteen had married the blind professor of economics at Cambridge. She took part in the foundation of Newnham College, and knew all the grandees of Victorian radical thought – above all John Stuart Mill. Like many women who supported the suffragette cause, Millicent Fawcett was naturally conservative in other areas of political life. For instance, when the South African War broke out in 1899, she made many patriotic speeches, much to the horror of some of her suffragette supporters, and she even went to South Africa in an attempt to play down the stories coming out about British concentration camps, and the maltreatment and starvation of Boer women and children. She was president of the National Union of Women's Suffrage Societies, whose sole aim was the obtaining of votes for women 'on the same terms as it is or may be granted to men'.[18]

Emmeline Pankhurst (1858–1928) favoured the militant approach. Like Millicent Fawcett, she was married to a much older man, and when he died in 1898 she was left in very reduced circumstances in Manchester. She became the registrar of births and deaths at Rusholme in an attempt to make ends meet for herself and four young children (her eldest son having died). She tried to juggle this tedious job with her work for the cause, but by 1907 it was impossible, and she gave up work, and the hope of a pension. In 1903, with her fiery daughter Christabel, she founded the Women's Social and Political Union. During an election meeting in October 1905, when Sir Edward Grey was speaking (a moderate Liberal supporter of female emancipation), Christabel asked Sir Edward what would be the new government's policy on votes for women. She and Annie Kenney unfurled a large banner reading VOTES FOR WOMEN, upon which the two friends were expelled from the meeting. There were some highly satisfactory scuffles in the street outside and the Manchester newspapers devoted considerably more space to the women's issue than they would have done had they accepted Sir Edward's brush-off with demure silence.

Christabel and Annie Kenney made a splendid pair. Christabel had a marvellous speaking voice and beautiful skin. Annie, more abrasive and Yorkshire, had fair hair and blazing blue eyes. After their triumph of disruption at Sir Edward Grey's meeting, Annie went to the Albert Hall and disrupted a rally by the new prime minister, Henry Campbell-Bannerman, and by 1906 her rowdy attempt to force a meeting upon the then new home secretary, H. H. Asquith, landed her with two months in Holloway Prison – a place to which she would return. After the activity of these two spirited young women, women all over England flocked to the cause. As the heroines of the movement chained themselves to railings, broke shop windows, waved flags in the faces of pompous politicians, thousands of women, in quiet homes and provincial towns, joined Mrs Pankhurst's Women's Social and Political Union. When Emmeline Pankhurst herself was jailed in Holloway Prison in 1908, the women of Britain did not feel that they should accept what the males told them. Women had been given the vote in Australia in 1902. The obfuscations and delays of an all-male Parliament, and the resort where necessary to brutal suppression of the rebels, backfired badly.

The self-confidently male Liberals in their frock-coats and top hats were sending out dangerous parables to the world which could now read of such matters in the newspapers and see it in M. Pathé's newsreels. Indian nationalists, would-be communists or anti-communist revolutionaries could watch and see how a Liberal government could treat its women when it felt 'hen-pecked'. They could see that for all the rough handling by the police and the prison wardresses, this policy of government restraint, and everything passing through the due processes in the lobbies of Parliament, was not working. The Pankhursts and Annie Kenney sent out messages to the world which the Liberal government of Messrs Campbell-Bannerman and Asquith would much rather had not been heard.

But as the testimony of countless families in Britain shows, the government had completely lost touch with 'ordinary' or 'decent' opinion over this question. Look at the diaries of Emily Blathwayt, daughter of an Indian army colonel who had retired to Eagle House, Batheaston, and related to the nearby landowners at Dryham Park. The colonel was not a revolutionary; but he and his daughter's house became a centre of suffragette fervour, as did the house of a neighbour, a Mrs Tollemache. These, and not the seedy backstreet revolutionaries of Conrad's *Secret Agent*, were the sort who organized meetings all over the country, and took delegations of the Bristol WSPU to march on Holloway Prison when Mrs Pankhurst was arrested. When they shouted down a Liberal cabinet minister during a political meeting in Bristol, Emily Blathwayt wrote in her diary: 'Our women are justified as they have no legal voice as men have.'[19]

For as long as women were excluded from Parliament, and from parliamentary elections, the essential redundancy of Parliament was demonstrated. This redundancy would continue, even after the short-term battle was won and women were allowed, together with men, to take part in the sham of 'democracy'. It was the signal of their exclusion which was objectionable.

This makes all the more striking the position of those educated and privileged women who opposed Female Suffrage. In the liberal periodical the *Nineteenth Century*, the issue for June 1889, the popular novelist Mrs Humphry Ward had written an 'anti-suffrage appeal'. Ward was a strange woman, father-, son- and uncle-obsessed, as well might be the granddaughter of Dr Arnold of Rugby, the niece of Matthew, daughter of Tom Arnold, and mother of a ne'er-do-well whose gambling habit mopped up most of the profits from such high-minded bestsellers as *Helbeck of Bannisdale* and *Robert Elsmere*, books which popularized for a mass market the religio-ethical torments of doubters who had read John Henry Newman and T. H. Green.

What is so striking is the presence among Mrs Ward's co-signatories of the name of Beatrice Potter – not Beatrix Potter, the chronicler of clothed rabbits and hedgehogs in the Lake District, but Beatrice, daughter of the railway and timber millionaire Richard Potter, later to be famous by her married name, Beatrice Webb. As a young woman, she had been obsessively in love with Joseph Chamberlain, his brusque atheism and thrusting imperialism both alike wounding to her essentially mystical and religious temperament. Unhappiness drove her into the East End of London, where with such feminists as Octavia Hill she began her life's work, the accumulation of information (she called it gradgrinding) about the lives of the working classes. The conditions of women and children working in the sweatshops, and the mass misery of slum-dwellers, fashioned her political vision. As one of several researchers for Charles Booth, she worked on *The Life and Labour of the People in London*, and her study of the Co-operative Movement led her slowly but inexorably towards socialism.

It was in 1892 that Beatrice Potter married Sidney Webb, the political and economic thinker who was the driving force behind the foundation of the Fabian Society. Together with his friend George Bernard Shaw, Webb believed in state socialism brought about not by revolution but by gradualism (hence Fabian – after Fabius Maximus Cunctator (the Delayer) (d. 203 BC), the Roman general who wore down Hannibal and the Carthagiman invaders of Italy by a policy of slow caution and delay). Not for the Webbs the armed struggle on the barricade, but rather the hours spent in committee getting their supporters elected to the London

County Council and the various wards of other cities, to bring about 'municipal socialism'. In 1898, in two rented rooms of the Adelphi, the Webbs founded the London School of Economics, and just as after a long communion with the God of Israel, Moses descended from the mountain top with the Law inscribed on tablets of stone, so, after twenty years of earnest discussion with their fellow Fabians, the Webbs, in 1913, founded the weekly organ of leftist opinion in Britain, *The New Statesman*.

They are the godparents of the Labour party – and yet Beatrice had signed Mrs Humphry Ward's petition. Her comments about it in her autobiography, *My Apprenticeship*, are almost more baffling than the signature itself:

> In the spring of 1889, I took what afterwards seemed to me a false step in joining with others in signing the then notorious manifesto, drafted by Mrs Humphry Ward and some other distinguished ladies, against the political enfranchisement of women, thereby arousing the hostility of ardent women brain-workers, and, in the eyes of the general public, undermining my reputation as an impartial investigator of women's questions.

There are many very strange things about this sentence. First, she does not tell us why she signed the petition in the first place. Then, there is the curious use of the word 'brain-workers': as the woman who drafted the constitution of the Labour party, she made the notorious distinction, displeasing to later socialists, between those who worked with their hands and those who did so with their brains, implying – what she no doubt believed – that such a distinction existed, and that whatever passed through the 'brains' of the toilers need not be considered too carefully by the intellectuals of the party. Then again, there is the curious egotism of the idea of herself, in 1889 aged thirty and almost unknown, having a public reputation which either could or could not be damaged. She goes on in *My Apprenticeship* to say that Millicent Fawcett protested against Mrs Ward's anti-suffragist manifesto, and that the magazine editors then asked her, Beatrice, to pen the riposte to Mrs Fawcett. It was then 'I realised my mistake. Though I delayed my public recantation for nearly twenty years, I immediately and resolutely withdrew from that particular controversy.'[20]

Odder and odder. No explanation is given for her silence, until the period of the struggles, both of Fawcett-inspired moderates and Pankhurstian railing-chainers, for women's votes shamed her into writing a formal recantation of her previous position. ('I shall be thought, by some, to be a pompous prig,' she told her diary.) Perhaps she feared that the very unpopularity of feminism would put off likely male converts to 'municipal socialism'? The early Chartists had wanted the vote for women but had been dissuaded in the 1840s from making it part of their public platform for similar reasons. Perhaps it happened to be low down on Beatrice Webb's political agenda, though if so, this is strange. The painstaking cataloguing work she did for Charles Booth – the number of rooms occupied in tenement buildings, the number of persons per room, the sanitary arrangements of over a million dwellings, the working hours of women (and children) – all suggested a world where not merely the poor but the females especially of the species were downtrodden in part because they were not considered, by the system, to exist on the same level as the male. Yet, she was right to see it as a peripheral issue. Unless or until the egalitarian party she was helping to create had actual political power – and in spite of two Labour governments in 1924 and 1929, that would not happen until 1945 – it did not much matter who was elected to the House of Commons.

Behind Beatrice Webb's signature, though, there surely also lurked that attitude so commonly displayed by power-obsessed females, a dislike of her own sex. Witness the exclusion of women from positions of power by Golda Meir, or Margaret Thatcher.

When H. G. Wells (1866–1946) felt drawn towards the Fabians, Mrs Webb felt some misgivings. This was partly because she disapproved of his sexual morals, but chiefly because she feared he might have ideas of his own which did not conform to the carefully formulated diktats of the two-person Webb Politburo. 'It is more for "copy" than for reform that he has stepped out of his study,' she remarked sniffily of the popular novelist. 'When he has got his "copy" he will step back again.'[21] She found his Cockney accent and his general commonness hard to cope with, noting: 'It is a case of "Kipps" in matters more important than table manners.'[22] (*Kipps* was one of Wells's many autobiographical novels about a perky, intellectually curious, emotionally chaotic young man.)

In July 1906 Mrs Webb was especially disconcerted by Wells's fondness for the United States. 'Two months rushing about from New York to Washington, Philadelphia to Chicago, has convinced him that America is much nearer the promised land of economic equality than we in England are: that ideas are understood by a great number of people and that all else is unimportant.'[23] She seems, however, more concerned that Wells, by his conversion to American democracy, will try to foist these ideas on the Fabian Society. 'He seems confident that Sidney [Webb] and GBS will also have to retire if they do not fall in with his schemes,' she writes with the irony of one confident of her unshakeable position, 'and is constantly apologizing to us in advance for this sad necessity.'[24] After one of their quarrels with him Beatrice told her diary: 'Sidney had long had a settled aversion to H. G. Wells.'[25] They object to his being 'a sensualist', 'blown out with self-conceit'. 'He began to look on Webb and Shaw as back numbers.' This was bad enough, but one suspects that one of the things about Wells which the Webbs found hardest to stomach was his expressed belief in 'votes, votes, votes'.

'The Webbs were elitists,' the editors of her diaries write, 'with a conventional belief in the superiority of the civilized races and especially the educated classes which emerges in many thoughtless asides.'[26] The charge that the Webb scheme for reform of the Poor Law was 'undemocratic as well as bureaucratically complex and expensive was to be made repeatedly'.[27]

Novelists or poets, particularly of a leftist disposition, who fancy themselves as political pundits are so thick on the ground in the history of the twentieth century that the reader may wonder why we pause to consider Wells. It is because, although very little he wrote after the age of forty is worth reading (and he lived to be eighty), he was a genuine artist, and his response to his times is often memorable, instructive, reflective of something bigger than Wells and his own life, even when he is not on top form. It is a mistake to think that artists respond to the world intuitively, in contrast to scientists, economists, political theorists or statisticians who somehow 'gradgrind' into existence a more accurate world of 'fact'. On the contrary, all human impressions of a general character are intuitions, programmed by the character and circumstances of that very imperfect instrument the human consciousness. One reviewer of my book *The Victorians* complained that it was too 'literary', implying that a vision of the world compiled from Hansard or Bradshaw's Railway Timetable or Smiley's *Lives of the Engineers* might have given a truer impression of what was happening in Britain than the poetry of Tennyson, the novels of Dickens, the reflections of Carlyle and Ruskin.

H. G. Wells had the humiliating kind of early life that Dickens might have written about. His hopeless father, an unsuccessful shopkeeper in Bromley, Kent, specializing in cricket goods – bats, balls, pads, etc. – was no role model. At the earliest juncture, the mother returned to her favoured avocation, that of a housekeeper at Uppark, the Fetherstonhaugh seat where in her girlhood 120 years earlier Emma Hart – one day to be Nelson's mistress – had danced on the table. Bertie – H.G. – was sent to be a draper's assistant, but escaped through cleverness, and studied science under T. H. Huxley, Darwin's representative on Earth, at the Normal School. 'I had come,' he wrote later, 'from beginnings of an elementary sort to the fountainhead of knowledge.'

Wells shared most of the late Victorian illusions about science – believing that it had disproved religion, and so forth – but his intuitive response was much more double-edged than that of some Victorian apologist like Huxley. In his scientific fantasies and romances – the first, and the best, things he published – Wells could see not only that science was the religion of his own, and the coming, age, but that it was a greedy Moloch of a god which would need to be fed children to remain satisfied. It is hard, reading *The Island of Doctor Moreau* (1896), to realize it was written years before Nazi doctors experimented with just such cross-species unions between human and bestial.

In his scientific fables, Wells was able to see that the optimism of Victorian progressives was thoroughly misplaced. *The Time Machine*, in the story of the title, takes the traveller so far into the future that he has left the comforts of a cosy Victorian dinner party in Richmond and ended in an impersonal Darwinian horror. The Eloi are not, as the traveller at first supposes, cultivated persons like ourselves. They are being farmed as cattle to feed the machine-minders, the Morlocks, children of darkness and earth who live underground, only emerging to feed on human flesh. The cannibalistic theme is repeated in *The War of the Worlds*, in which the Martians invade and 'all those damned little clerks . . . The bar-loafers and mashers and singers' are to be turned into food for the voracious Martians, barbecued by heat-rays. In *The First Men in the Moon* the human race has in effect come to an end, since those who survive are the Selenites, a little like the Morlocks, subterranean and completely amoral. Wells's stories, dashed off at tremendous speed when he was a young man, place into grisly perspective his worthier, more optimistic political and historical writings. They are in the best sense catastrophic. He could feel, know almost, the destructive effects which science was going to have in the new century.

In a book which already enjoys something of classic status, *The Intellectuals and the Masses* by John Carey, the Merton Professor of English at Oxford notes with some horror the response by those he terms 'intellectuals' to the population explosion at the close of the Edwardian period. He quotes, and evidently enjoys quoting, a letter written by D. H. Lawrence from Croydon in 1908 after a woman, Daisy Lord, had been sentenced to death for the murder of her illegitimate child, a sentence which was later commuted to life imprisonment. (Women's suffragists campaigned unsuccessfully for her complete release.)

'Concerning Daisy Lord, I am entirely in accord with you', he wrote to Blanche Jennings, one of those young women with whom he enjoyed platonic and intense conversations. 'If I had my way, I would build a

lethal chamber as big as the Crystal Palace, with a military band
playing softly, and a Cinematograph working brightly; then I'd go out
in the back streets and main streets and bring them in, all the sick,
the halt, and the maimed; I would lead them gently, and they would
smile me a weary thanks; and the band would softly bubble out the
"Hallelujah Chorus"!'[28]

'What else would softly bubble out in order to make the lethal chamber
lethal, Lawrence even here does not specify, but maybe his later interest
in poison gas gives a clue to the direction of his imaginings,' writes
Professor Carey. He finds many comparable sentiments in the works of
H. G. Wells, concentrating especially upon Wells's notorious *Antici-
pations of the Reaction of Mechanical and Scientific Progress upon
Human Life and Thought*, which was published in 1901. In that chilling
book, Wells had prophesied: 'for a multitude of contemptible and silly
creatures, fear-driven and helpless and useless, unhappy or hatefully
happy in the midst of squalid dishonour, feeble, ugly, inefficient, born
of unrestrained lusts, and increasing and multiplying through sheer incon-
tinence and stupidity, the men of the New Republic will have little pity
and less benevolence'. Carey goes on to say that for Wells, genocide is
the only answer to the problems of world overpopulation, especially in
Africa and Asia, where the 'swarms of black, and brown, and dirty-white,
and yellow people' will 'have to go'.[29]

You can't fail to be shocked by these passages, but there are two
shocking things about them. The first, naturally, is that those who were
intelligent enough to write books which we have all admired and enjoyed
should have such very 'unenlightened' views. This, one suspects, is
Professor Carey's chief area of concern in his hilarious book. Had Wells
and D. H. Lawrence and the other writers excoriated by Professor Carey
lived in Dean Swift's time, we should merely be able to enjoy the luxury
of condemning their poor taste. The doubly shocking thing about such
ideas is that we know that within a few short decades of these science-
fiction fantasies being expounded the human race was actually to
encounter real Dr Moreaus, real genocidal tyrants. One of the scientists
who worked on the bomb dropped on Hiroshima, Leo Szilard, said that
the idea of nuclear chain reaction first came to him when reading Wells's
The World Set Free (1914), in which atom bombs falling on world cities
during the 1950s kill millions of people. These things were not possible
when Wells wrote about them. We know that the twentieth century would
see them happen. And the horrors were so often perpetrated by just such
small-town suburban types, nonentities, as H. G. Wells made the subject
of his comedies such as *Kipps* and *Mr Britling Sees It Through*. It was

not some Napoleonic tyrant who authorized the bombing of Hiroshima but a small-town lawyer, President Harry S. Truman, whose face could easily have been used to adorn the jacket of an H. G. Wells suburban comedy.

5

Love in the Suburbs

The spread of suburbs brought perhaps unforeseen emotional restrictions. Human beings have, historically, devised strict rules for sexual conduct. Whether these rules derive from the utilitarian requirements of protecting children, and women of child-bearing age, from neglect; or whether they have some more spiritual origin, is not to the purpose here. The fact remains that the existence in all societies of variations on these rules – a suspicion of sexual deviancy, a condemnation of same-sex relationships, the moral (or even actual) outlawing of adultery – points to a near-universal moral chaos, which human beings, as individuals and as societies, have felt the need to correct. It is because the sexual impulse is so strong that the rules, whether of churches, mosques, senates or parliaments, have been so fierce.

Sociological research would suggest that where the possibility exists of sexual errancy, it will be vigorously pursued. The sexual licence of the coal miners in Zola's *Germinal* would seem to have been widespread among the European proletariat, with men and women seizing gratification in the unlikeliest settings, as opportunity arose. Only a proportion of the English working class married during the Victorian and early twentieth-century periods. Many cohabited, and changes of partnership were commonplace. Likewise the upper classes, with large houses and boundless leisure time, hardly knew habits of restraint, as Henry James's shocked novels subsequent on the Dilke scandal – *What Maisie Knew* and *The Awkward Age* – suggest. Winston Churchill's mother Jennie was twenty when he was born. The daughter of a New York financier called Leonard Jerome, she brought £50,000 as a marriage dowry to the impoverished family of the Duke of Marlborough. (Winston's father, the Tory politician Lord Randolph Churchill, was the Duke's second son.) This produced £2,000 per annum. It was perhaps, even by the standards of the time, an extreme case, their marriage. The Anglo-Irish novelist George Moore guessed that Jennie had over 200 lovers, including, it was thought, King Milan of Serbia and the French novelist Paul Bourget.[1] When Lord Randolph died in 1895 aged forty-six, Jennie Churchill married a Scots Guard subaltern twenty years her junior, George Cornwallis West. After fourteen years, the marriage ended in divorce and he married Mrs Patrick Campbell. Churchill's mother married a West Country gentleman named Montague Porch who lived until 1964.

It might have been very unlike the home life of Queen Victoria, but adultery was regarded as the norm by Bertie as Prince of Wales, and continued being so after he had become head of the Church of England in 1901. His favourite mistresses as a young married man had been Lillie Langtry, the actress, and Daisy, Countess of Warwick. But in 1898, when he was fifty-six, Bertie met the enchanting 29-year-old Mrs George Keppel, the 'delectable Alice'. She was stylish and stunningly sexy. Petite, fleshy, when she lifted the veil on one of her ostrich-feathered hats, men gasped. Like her great-granddaughter Camilla Parker-Bowles, she smoked, and had a husky voice. Her lustrous chestnut hair was piled on her head. There was something almost Mediterranean about her appearance (she had a Greek grandmother) and she had a vivacious and delightful manner.

Her husband was the handsome son of the 7th Earl of Albemarle. His hopelessness with money was one of the factors which probably led to his acquiescence, quite early in their marriage, in her adulteries with very rich men who paid the bills. One of these, the future Lord Grimthorpe, Ernest William Beckett, almost certainly fathered her daughter Violet. As Mrs Trefusis, Violet was destined herself to have a celebrated love affair with Vita Sackville-West; before that, the two had been childhood friends. Vita would recollect returning to the Keppel house in Portman Square after an afternoon's walk. Papa – the Hon. George – would discreetly have retreated to his club. A little one-horse brougham would be waiting by the kerbstone. When the little Vita walked into the hall, she was hustled by the butler, Mr Rolfe, into a darkened corner of the hall. 'One minute, miss, a gentleman is coming downstairs.' Trailing a whiff of unguents and cigars the gentleman would come downstairs, collect his hat, gloves and cane from the butler and be shown to the waiting brougham.

To Violet and Sonia Keppel, their mother's lover was known as 'Kingy'. Violet remembered that he was 'very kind to us children. He had a rich German accent and smelt deliciously of cigars and eau de Portugal. He wore several rings set with small cabochon rubies and a cigarette case made of ribbed gold, no doubt by Fabergé.' Sonia, the younger sister, liked to play a game with 'Kingy'. Two pieces of bread and butter, buttered side down, would be placed on his check trouser legs, and bets would then be placed to see which piece slithered down fastest.[2]

Was marriage, as an institution, on the way out? H. G. Wells, who had a sexual career which was to say the least mouvementé, certainly hoped so. On 18 October 1906 he read a paper for the Fabian Society advocating Free Love. Mrs Webb was not impressed.

There remains the question whether, with all the perturbation caused by such intimacies, you would have any brain left to think with? I know that I should not, and I fancy that other women would be even worse off in this particular. Moreover, it would mean a great increase in sexual emotion for its own sake and not for the sake of bearing children. And that way madness lies?

So, the childless Mrs Webb tantalizingly confided in her diary:

H. G. Wells is, I believe, merely gambling with the idea of free love. Throwing it out to see what sort of reception it gets, without responsibility for its effect on the character of hearers.[3]

Years later, in 1922, when H.G. was proposed as parliamentary Labour candidate for London University, she noted:

To refuse such an obviously eligible candidate, except for his scandalous exploits (none of which however have come to the courts), seemed an unjustifiable insult, so Sidney and I acquiesced and he accepted the candidature. Whereupon R.H. Tawney resigns from the chairmanship of the University Labour Party, but before doing so, proposes as the alternative Bertrand Russell! He declares that Bertrand Russell is a gentleman and H.G. a cad, which is hardly relevant if it is sexual morality which is to be the test.[4]

In today's media-dominated, intrusive climate, an aspirant politician with Wells's erotic track record would be seen as more a vote-loser than an asset by party selection boards. The morality of the times was what later ages would deem hypocritical. Lloyd George and Asquith were both rampant adulterers, but nothing of this ever reached the newspapers. It was Wells's absence of hypocrisy which made him a political liability. Advocates of Free Love still belonged to the eccentric edges of society.

Augustus John, the son of a solicitor in the West Welsh small town of Haverfordwest, threw off the restraints of his conventional upbringing and became a by-word for the Bohemian way of life, with strings of mistresses, a fascination with gipsies, and self-conscious desire to live on the fringes. At the same time, and not just because he needed the cash, he became a portrait-painter of huge popular appeal, immortalizing many of his contemporaries, from Lloyd George to Lawrence of Arabia, in splashily coloured, exuberantly 'painterly' canvases. Some of his female sitters, most notably Lady Ottoline Morrell, stare at him, and at us, with a mixture of rapture and wariness. It does not surprise us to discover that they were among the great company who shared his bed.

His sister Gwen John's trajectory is altogether more muted. As the canvases of Augustus became brighter and splashier, Gwen's became ever more etiolated and pale, resembling fabric whose colour has been bleached out by too bright sunshine. Her exile in France, her besotted love for the sculptor Rodin, its frustration, and her subsequent nunlike devotion to Catholic simplicities reflect another side of the attempts by women, at this date, to defy the conventions. There were rules, and if you defied them, you paid the consequence.

Otto Gross, a pupil of Dr Freud's, was a great success with women although or perhaps because he was suffering from *dementia praecox*. It was heady stuff for one of his mistresses, Frieda Weekley, to receive his assurance:

I *know* now what people will be like who keep themselves unpolluted by all the things that I hate and fight against – I know it through *you*, the only human being who *already, today*, has remained free from the code of chastity, from Christianity, from democracy and all that accumulated filth – remained free through her own strength – how on earth have you brought this about, you golden child – how with your laughter and your loving have you kept your soul free from the curse and the dirt of two gloomy millennia.

Frieda, born von Richthofen in 1879 outside Metz, was a voluptuous, blonde, highly sexed girl who had married an English professor fourteen years older than herself who had taken her to live in a dark, miserable middle-class house on the outskirts of Nottingham. They had three children in close succession, but the marriage was sexually unsatisfying to her. On her wedding night she had waited by the bedroom door for her Mr Casaubon. 'When Ernest came in, I threw myself naked into his arms. He was horrified and told me to put my night-dress on at once.'[5] It is not surprising that she found Otto Gross such an exciting companion. In March 1912, a former pupil of her husband's from Nottingham University College, David Herbert Lawrence, came to lunch at the Weekleys' house, and within twenty minutes she had Lawrence in bed.[6]

D. H. Lawrence, known in the title of a film about him as The Priest of Love, was one of the twentieth century's most celebrated exponents of erotic freedom. Born the son of a coal miner at Eastwood, Nottingham, on 11 September 1885, the fourth of five children, he was totally overshadowed by his diminutive, intense, puritanical mother, Lydia. The nature of their relationship was made public by his third – and perhaps best – novel *Sons and Lovers*, which tells of the agonizing rivalry between the girl he loves and his mother.

This girl in real life, Jessie Chambers, told a friend that she had had the following exchange with Lawrence – David as she called him, Bert to his family:

'You know, Jessie, I've always loved mother.'

'I know you have,' I replied.

'I don't mean that,' he answered, 'I've loved her – like a lover – that's why I could never love you.'[7]

Lawrence had worked his way through Nottingham High School, became a junior clerk at Haywoods Surgical Appliances in Nottingham, and then, at his mother's urging, began a teaching apprenticeship, and won a place at Nottingham University College (founded by Boot, the local chemist). As a young teacher, he found work in the dreary London suburb of Croydon, teaching at Davidson Road School for £15 per year – less than a miner's pay.

Lawrence's eldest brother George had 'had to' marry – that was his mother's morality forcing him – because he got a girl pregnant. D.H., who disliked rough boys' games and preferred painting and flower-arranging, was timid in his sexual attitudes. When he was a clerk the voracious girls at the Surgical Appliances factory set on him and tried to debag him, a trauma he worked up in a powerful short story, 'Tickets Please', where six vengeful girls attack a young man on a tram. He was astounded, at college, when his friend George Neville told him that women have pubic hair. (Lawrence leapt from his chair and pummelled Neville crying: 'It's not true!') Thin, intense, slight, bisexual, timorous, Lawrence was as much of a windbag as Otto Gross, and every bit as demanding, from an emotional viewpoint, as the three children from whom Frieda was forcibly separated when they eloped.

The children are miserable, missing her so much. She lies on the floor in misery – and then is fearfully angry with me because I won't say 'stay for my sake'. I say 'decide what you want most, to live with me and share my rotten chances, or go back to security, and your children – decide for *yourself* – choose for yourself.' And then she almost hates me, because I won't say, 'I love you – stay with me whatever happens.' I *do* love her. If she left me, I do not think I should be alive six months hence. And she won't leave me, I think – God how I love her – and the agony of it.[7]

Lawrence's greatness as a writer, which coexists with the childishness and the windbaggery, could not find romance among the suburbs. Before Frieda, peculiar metaphors of frustration clog his letters. 'I've now got to digest a great lot of dissatisfied love in my veins,' he had written to Louie Burrows, to whom he was engaged. 'It's very damnable, to have slowly to drink back again into oneself all the lava and fire of a passionate eruption . . . The most of the things, that just heave red hot to be said, I shove back.'[8]

When he actually took the plunge with a woman and ran away with Frieda, D.H. seems to have required exotic backgrounds for the romance – Cornwall, Tasmania, Mexico – as though the molten lava of passion was chilled by the kind of suburban residences in which most people led their lives.

Only two years before Lawrence wrote that letter, Arnold Bennett had stood in the chill of an exceptionally cold April evening outside the non-descript semi-detached villa of The Pines, Putney, where Algernon Charles Swinburne, Victorian advocate of Baudelairean erotic wickedness, lay dying in suburban respectability. His hectic alcoholic youth, enlivened – he was tiny – by visits to Amazonian prostitutes who inspired his wonderful poem to 'Dolores', 'Our Lady of Pain', had led to collapse. He had been rescued by one of the dullest men who ever lived, a literary-minded lawyer, dear to the Pre-Raphaelite circle, called Theodore Watts-Dunton, and there Swinburne had lived, allowed his one bottle of Bass each day, and a walk on Putney Common, where he could indulge his passion for looking in babies' prams. In The Pines he grew stone-deaf. Max Beerbohm and Arthur Benson made visits, largely in order to mock the silvery-haired squeaky-voiced poet. But Bennett perhaps came closest to the heart of The Pines and its tragicomedy, when he wrote: 'A few yards from where the autobuses turned was a certain house with lighted upper windows, and in that house the greatest lyric versifier that England has ever had, and one of the great poets of the whole world and of all ages, was dying. But nobody looked; nobody seemed to care; I doubt if anyone thought of it.'[9]

There is something very moving about Bennett, vulgar, successful, cocky, who had written so well about sexual love and its possibilities of tragedy, bothering to leave the West End of London and to seek out the lighted window where the tiny Victorian poet lay on his deathbed. (The night nurse thought he was muttering in a foreign language, perhaps Greek.) Bennett's novels – *Hilda Lessways, These Twain, Clayhanger, The Old Wives' Tale* – tell so well the story, of which Swinburne's death was a kind of parable, of the incompatibility of Romance with the humdrum aspirations of every day. Dire physical and emotional disappointments lay in store for those who married, and those who did not. As Edward VII canoodled with Mrs Keppel, the queen of England felt as spurned as any suburban wife would have done if betrayed. Being well born did not numb the pains of betrayal, disappointment or sheer disgust.

The shocking thing about Jane Ridley's book[10] about her great-grandparents Ned and Lady Emily Lutyens is not that their wretched marriage was unusual, merely that so much articulate evidence of anger and frustration from it survives. When Emily married, her mother Lady Lytton gave her only one piece of advice, which was never to refuse her husband, and to keep a jar of cold cream beside the bed.[11] She and Ned read Edward Carpenter's book *Love's Coming of Age*, which sought to elevate the 'sex passion', and which advocated the rhythm method of contraception. Emily was dissatisfied by Ned's rough and hasty lovemaking. With Pussy Webbe, a leading light of the Women's Movement, she attended the Lock Hospital for Venereal Disease and read aloud to the sick prostitutes. She went to conferences to hear eminent doctors lecturing 'on sex and family planning to a room packed with women and crackling with suppressed sexual anger'.[12] She yearned for a sexually satisfying love-match, and failing to get it, she brought her physical relations with her husband to an end when the children had been born. 'I have suffered intensely physically during all my married life,' she wrote to him.[13]

There must have been so many less articulate women in Edwardian Britain who could have echoed these words. In Edwardian Britain? In any age – but in that age of suburban restraints and middle-class rectitude it was possible to be trapped in a marital cage from which it seemed as if there was no escape but the death of one party or another.

Asked if she had ever contemplated divorce, the aged Elizabeth Longford, long married to a philanthropic peer, replied in the late twentieth century: 'Divorce never – murder often.' That was her choice. In the early twentieth century, the kind of scandals started by H. G. Wells or Frieda Weekley were not strictly imaginable. Each age finds in its favourite crimes images of what it would most love/hate to do. Our own generation of overworked, guilty, child-dominated couples makes of child-abduction the ultimate horror, perhaps because with a dark part of themselves they wish their children dead. The favourite Edwardian murder was undoubtedly centred upon adultery in the suburbs.

The prodigious popularity of the Crippen murder case, the mesmeric hold with which it possessed the newspaper-reading public, surely reflected some deep general preoccupations. Dr Crippen's 'ordinariness', his mildness, were harped on again and again in the reports of the case. His address, 39 Hilldrop Crescent, Holloway, North London, was in the same postal district as that charming fictitious address 'The Laurels',

Brickfield Terrace, where Carrie and Charles Pooter led their tedious existence in *The Diary of a Nobody*. 'There was something almost likeable about the mild little fellow who squinted through thick-lensed spectacles, and whose sandy moustache was out of all proportion to his build,' thought the detective who had led the Crippen investigation, Chief Inspector Walter Dew.[14] It was not sadism which attracted so many people to the story, so much as Romanticism, a sense that it was a lower-middle-class Héloïse and Abelard, a Tristan and Isolde played out behind lace curtains. It was not alone the fate of Crippen and his lover which fascinated the readers of the *Daily Mail* and the *Daily Mirror*. It was their own fates, their own lives, their own missed opportunities, stuck in unrewarding jobs, and poky, jerry-built houses, and stultifying conventional marriages.

That was what made the trial of this quiet, dull little man one of the most sensational London ever saw. W. S. Gilbert – 'always attuned to popular emotion'[15] – was assiduous in his attendance at the committal proceedings, and wrote a one-act play, *The Hooligan*, based on Crippen. At the trial itself at the Old Bailey theatrical impresarios as grand as Sir Herbert Beerbohm Tree and Sir John Hare joined the crowds in the public gallery. The demand for seats in Court Number 1 was so strong that a two-house-a-day system was inaugurated, Blue Tickets for one show, Red for the next.

Crippen was charged with the 'murder and mutilation'[16] of his wife, some of whose remains were found buried beneath the cellar of 39 Hilldrop Crescent. The head was never found, but there was plenty to excite the ghoulish, as when a piece of skin eight inches long, horseshoe-shaped and fringed by what appeared to be pubic hair was passed around the jury. The trial marked the debut of Bernard Spilsbury, then aged thirty-three, who was to become the most celebrated pathologist of his day. He gave evidence at every important murder trial for the next quarter-century.

It has never been established beyond question exactly how Mrs Crippen died. The senior Home Office analyst, Dr W. H. Wilcox, found two-fifths of a grain of hydrobromide of hyoscine in the organs submitted to him, and this drug, which had been used as a means of quelling the rage of mental patients in the London Bethlehem Hospital, the Bedlam, when Crippen worked there, was probably used to poison her. (There is also a theory that he shot her.)

The drama of the case was not how Mrs Crippen died but how she and her husband lived. In fact, no one could have been less like Carrie and Charles Pooter. Both Crippens were working-class Americans. Belle Crippen had been born Kunigunde Mackamotzki and was the daughter of a poor Polish grocer from Brooklyn. She had dreamed of being an opera diva. It was the age of such great divas as Adelina Patti, who earned $5,000 per performance at the Metropolitan Opera House in New York. Instead, she ended up, having married the ten-years-older widower Dr Crippen, a travelling salesman in quack medical cures, in London, as Belle Ellmore, a somewhat shrieky soprano whose speciality, when she found work at all in the music halls, was a ballad entitled 'Down Lovers' Walk'.

Being an American should have helped her career. English music hall turns at this date were changing their accents and appearing as 'The Knickerbocker Kut-ups' or 'The Madcaps from Manhattan'. Belle's trouble, from the musical point of view, was lack of talent. She blamed her failure on her husband, and, as they took in lodgers to pay for the brandy she consumed in great quantities, she lost no time in regaling everyone with accounts of his selfishness. It had been a shaky marriage from the start, made even less happy by brandy, and unfaithfulness. They had separate bedrooms at Hilldrop Crescent, and when Crippen found her in bed with one of the lodgers, a young German student, it was his signal of release.

Although he is always known as 'Doctor' Crippen, and although he left the University of Michigan's School of Homeopathic Medicine in 1883, he did so without graduating. His employment was on the edge of the medical world, selling first the notorious Munyon's homeopathic cures for piles. Millions of Americans hopefully bought the suppositories, which were advertised with a picture of Munyon himself, his arm upraised and one finger pointing suggestively upwards.

When Munyon fired Crippen as his London agent – Crippen had been spending too much time vainly trying to promote Belle's stage career – he found work at a questionable establishment called the Drouet Institute for the Deaf. Dr Drouet, representing himself as 'a respectable man of science', was an alcoholic Frenchman, operating first at 72 Regent's Park Road, then from premises near Marble Arch. He claimed to have discovered a cure for deafness. Evan Yellon, editor of the *Albion Magazine*, and stone-deaf, went along for an examination and was appalled to find himself being examined by a quack doctor, fantastically dressed in a bright shirt, cracked patent-leather shoes, and frock-coat. The doctor, with an American accent, put a filthy speculum into one ear, and then into another without disinfecting it. None of his instruments had a disinfectant bath. Two years after Crippen's death, the Royal College of Surgeons officially condemned the patent medicines being purveyed by the Drouet Institute.

Ethel Clara LeNeve was an archetypically respectable lower-middle-class girl, of just the class which was soon to be emancipated politically. When she was seventeen, she had gone to work at Drouet's as a shorthand typist, fresh from Pitman's School. She was highly intelligent, and by the time Crippen, eighteen years her senior, arrived at the Institute she was effectively running the administration of the place. She fell in love with him, and, using the sleazy hotels off Argyle Square near King's Cross Station, they became lovers.

It is clear that Crippen had persuaded himself, as well as Ethel, that they were already in some senses man and wife. He refers to her in his letters as 'wife' and it would seem that they went through some form of ritual or ceremony together, perhaps standing beside an iron bedstead one afternoon in King's Cross. Her respectability is a key ingredient in the murder story, and it is almost certainly true that, as Tom Cullen wrote in his excellent study of the case, 'she was holding out for marriage lines and a home of her own, an "Acacia Villa" in that row of suburban "Chez Nous" and "Bide-a-Wee" and "Mon Repos" villas that stretches to infinity'.[17]

> I make this defence and this acknowledgement – that the love of Ethel LeNeve has been the best thing in my life – my only happiness – and that in return for that great gift I have been inspired with a greater kindness towards my fellow human-beings and a greater desire to do good.
>
> We were as man and wife together, with an absolute communion of spirit. Perhaps God will pardon us because we were like two children in the great unkind world, who clung to one another and gave each other courage.[18]

We shall never know why Crippen made so many blunders – why for example, having in effect filleted his wife, removing not just the head but other bones, and effectively disposed of them, he did not simply dump the rest of her in a weighted bag in the nearby canal. If he had simply known the difference between slaked lime, which preserves human flesh, and quicklime which destroys it, Belle's remains would have disappeared beneath the cellar floor.

It is partly the inefficiency of Crippen which makes him a semi-endearing figure. The penultimate act of the drama, when he and Ethel thought to escape across the Atlantic in disguise, was, unknown to them, played out each day in the pages of the *Daily Mail*, thanks to the pioneering, by the Marchese Guglielmo Marconi, of wireless telegraph. Crippen and Ethel believed they had eluded the police, and at Antwerp they had boarded the 5,431-ton cargo vessel *Montrose*, bound for Canada, posing as John Philo Robinson, a merchant, and his sixteen-year-old son being taken abroad for his health. Captain Kendall noticed many strange things about the pair. One was that Mr Robinson, when his name was called, frequently forget that this was what he was supposedly called and did not turn. The boy, who spoke with an English accent quite unlike his father's, had beautifully manicured hands, strange curves beneath his waistcoat, and the back of his trousers had been split, and was held together with safety pins. Thus it was that Kendall was able, as the boat steamed 130 miles west of the Lizard in Cornwall, to telegraph the ship's owners in Liverpool: HAVE STRONG SUSPICIONS THAT CRIPPEN LONDON CELLAR MURDERER AND ACCOMPLICE ARE AMONG SALOON PASSENGERS. The dispatches he sent daily to the *Montreal Star* during the voyage were very dramatic.

'They have been kept under strict observation all the voyage, as, if they smelt a rat, he might do something rash. I have noticed a revolver in his hip pocket,' reported the captain. Ethel and Crippen had no idea that Kendall was in contact with the *Montreal Star* and that his words were being marconigrammed to the *Daily Mail*. Before they even reached Quebec, to be greeted by their nemesis Inspector Dew, their every move had been chronicled in the newspaper. Music hall artistes were singing, even before her arrest:

> Oh, Miss LeNeve, oh Miss LeNeve,
> Is it true that you are sittin'
> On the lap of Dr Crippen
> In your boy's clothes
> On the Montrose
> Miss LeNeve?[19]

Most modern readers would find more sadism in such jokes than in Crippen's desperate decision to dispose of his wife.

In his last letter from Pentonville Prison, written on 19 November 1910, Crippen said:

> As I face eternity, I say that Ethel LeNeve has loved me as few women love men, and that her innocence of any crime, save that of yielding to the dictates of the heart, is absolute.
>
> To her I pay this last tribute. It is of her that my last thoughts have been. My last prayer will be that God may protect her and keep her safe from harm and allow me to join her in eternity.[20]

Of how many wives or husbands would their spouse truthfully write this on the eve of death?

6

God – and the Americans

Our story occurs against the background of Europe's collective suicide. Its self-destruction. Its insane political convulsions. Its violent, self-punishing revolutions and civil wars. Its repeated blood-letting. Britain and its Empire, which occupies our centre stage, cannot hold aloof. The dissolution of its Empire, the diminution of its world status, its financial ruin are played out against the background of a war in South Africa, two wholly destructive European wars, the rise of the European dictatorships, the wholesale slaughter of Armenians, Ukrainians, Russians, Germans, Jews and Spaniards.

With all this happening during the fifty years of our story, we are concerned with a period unlike any other in human history, or at any rate unlike anything which had happened since the nomadic barbarian tribes began their inroads into an imperial Italy whose very gods and religious life had been insidiously undermined by the spread of Christianity.

That religion, which began as a cult within a cult, a sect of apocalyptically minded Jews eagerly awaiting the end of Time itself during the reign of the Emperor Nero, had, by the time of the nineteenth century, begun to stare at its own apocalypse. The biblical scholars of Tübingen had undermined the faith of the Protestant North in the infallibility of Scripture; while the painstaking lifetime of botanical and biological observations of Charles Darwin had shaken the faith of intellectuals in the Creator himself. By the end of the Victorian century, atheism had become the religion of the suburbs, as G. K. Chesterton observed.

There is no doubt that, as the career and popularity of H. G. Wells demonstrates, unbelief was rife among the masses. As far as Britain was concerned, however, there was not the wholesale abandonment of religion which might have been expected, given the devastations visited on the Faith, not only by biblical scholars and the Darwinians, but also by the general prosperity of Western life, its easy materialism, which sat oddly beside a religion which professed to believe in the Incarnation of a God who chose to be a poor man, asserting the very unVictorian sentiment that it was fruitless to lay up treasure on Earth.

In fact, as far as Britain was concerned, the half-century or so covered by the scope of this book was one in which religion prospered. In the Church of England alone, there were far more interesting scholars, admin-

GOD - AND THE AMERICANS

istrators, bishops and priests than in the Victorian age. Whereas nearly all the great Victorian writers and intellectuals had an ambivalent or actively hostile attitude to religion or positively disbelieved it, the era we are now entering was that of – to name but a few names – G. K. Chesterton, T. S. Eliot, Graham Greene, Evelyn Waugh, John Betjeman, C. S. Lewis. Many of the most popular writers, such as crime writers, were Christian. Church music flourished, and Church architecture.

Consider the career of Sir John Ninian Comper, an ecclesiastical obsessive, who had been articled to the architectural firm of Bodley and Garner, and who, from the 1890s onwards, and throughout a long career (he lived from 1864 to 1960), beautified and changed the interiors of countless churches and chapels, while creating an overpoweringly eclectic blend of Gothic and classical. Whether designing a church from scratch or beautifying an existing building, Comper creates the illusion that history itself has been transformed. Here is a Great Britain in which no Reformation happened. At St Mary's, Wellingborough, an undoubted masterpiece, there is an English medieval perpendicular nave, with Gothic side chapels. The whole is a blaze of colour and gilding, with Spanish screens and a glorious classical baldachin. Another striking creation of Comper's is the brick church of St Cyprian's, Clarence Gate, just round the corner from the house where the fictitious Mr Sherlock Holmes was investigating his mysteries. Comper created glorious mysteries of his own. Push open the door of this dull-looking brick building, and you find yourself in a clear white interior, with no pews to clutter it. The vast Gothic screen is what the Catholics of Southwold or Lavenham or Long Melford might have looked at in the fifteenth century – a blaze of gilding, with four-winged cherubim, and Christ on His Rood, attended by the gilded figures of Our Lady and St John. Beyond is the altar, above which can be seen Comper's very distinctive coloured glass window, against whose yellows and blues flit the silhouettes of London pigeons.

Here was an answer of a kind to Darwin and the materialists. When the church was opened in 1903, it is probably fair to say that no English congregation had ever seen anything quite like it. It has been cleverly observed by Peter Anson that 'The overpowering richness of Comper's ecclesiastical *décor*, even if late medieval in inspiration, was as opulent as the setting of Edwardian dinner-parties, where the masterpiece of decoration, usually of sweet peas, was saved for the centre of the dining-table, which would be dotted with olives, salted almonds, sugared green peppermints and chocolates in cut-glass bowls, or silver dishes.' Pious ladies would be conveyed to St Cyprian's on a Sunday morning in hansoms, or new motorized taxi-cabs or in their own electric broughams. They were 'laced into corsets that gave them pouter-pigeon bosoms and protruding posteriors'. The evening before, after they had withdrawn from their dining-rooms, their husbands had created a silvery fume of cigars. And now in the morning light of St Cyprian's, the incense wafted before the enchanted eyes of these women. 'Perched on their heads, and elevated by a little roll just inside the crown, were hats which had grown as frivolous as the milliner's trade could make them – enormous galleons of grey velvet with vast grey plumes of ostrich feathers sweeping upwards and outwards, or they would be trimmed with artificial flowers and fruit.'[1]

A more elegiac form of Anglicanism is to be found in the imagination of that unlikely armaments manufacturer John Meade Falkner (1858–1932), who, after Oxford, went to be the tutor to the sons of Sir Andrew Noble, the principal figure in the Messrs Armstrong, Newcastle-upon-Tyne. He eventually became Noble's private secretary, travelling on the Continent to negotiate the contracts for the sales of ships and guns, while privately pursuing his scholarly researches into heraldry, Oxfordshire churches, and ecclesiastical architecture generally. In 1901 he joined the board of Armstrong, eventually rising to become its chairman, while still pursuing his cycling holidays in pursuit of unusual fonts, rood lofts and stained glass. He was honorary librarian to the Dean and Chapter of Durham Cathedral and a reader in palaeography at Durham University.

Alan Bennett has memorably said that to be a fervent Anglican is a contradiction in terms; but Falkner almost was this embodied oxymoron. He attended church whenever he could, but he never took Holy Communion. Was this because scruples forbade him to approach the altar of Peace, knowing he had made his money from battleships and heavy artillery? Or was he a Doubting Thomas, with a sense that for all its beauty, the Church itself had become a house built on shifting sands, its creeds untenable, its high moral demands unsustainable in the new century? Or was there some buried emotional guilt? His only known love-letter, which survives in a fragment, was addressed to a woman, but his three novels, especially the ghost story *The Lost Stradivarius*, seem to hint at a post-Wildean notion of the essentially destructive nature of same-sex emotional involvement. A decade which produced the late masterpieces of Henry James, Conrad's *Nostromo* (1904), Wells's *Kipps* and Arnold Bennett's *The Old Wives' Tale* could surely claim to be one of the greatest ten years in the history of English fiction. With such mighty rivals, John Meade Falkner's *The Nebuly Coat* (1903) could strike the careless reader as no more than a curiosity, a bit of amateur work. This would be a mistake. What makes the story addictive is not its somewhat melodramatic plot, but its atmosphere, its whole perception of existence. It would be much too heavy to read it as an allegory of England, its ancient faith and its aristocracy on the verge, like the great Minster church at the heart of the story, of collapse. If not an allegory, however, it certainly is a mirror of such things. More an extended elegy than a novel, it is 'poetry in stone', as someone in the book defines architecture, an expression of the Anglican spirit, with the old seventeenth-century musical books still in use, the old clock bells chiming the hours to hymn tunes, and with nostalgia and suppressed emotion seeping through the very stones of the damp, precarious church. In an epilogue, a Royal Navy lieutenant sailing down the Channel in the corvette *Solebay* turns his spyglass towards the familiar landmark of Cullerne Tower, and finds it is not there any more. 'He rubbed his glass, and called some other officers to verify the absence of the ancient seamark, but all they could make out was a white cloud, that might be smoke or dust or mist hanging over the town.'[2]

The old order was fading, crumbling. Queen Victoria had predicted that the monarchy would not long outlast her demise. Her faithful laureate, Lord Tennyson, had made the same prediction about religion itself. Although in his greatest work, *In Memoriam*, he had appeared to hold on to some nebulous faith, 'believing where we cannot prove', he said before he died that within a century the forms of the old religion would have vanished from the Earth. It is just such a thought which must occur to any thoughtful reader of Falkner's masterpiece when the great tower of Cullerne Minster descends in a cloud of dust and rubble.

When religious certainties are generally undermined, the diehard instinct takes over those in the bunker, or the last ditch. Unbelief had swept across Europe from the middle of the nineteenth century, in part as a result of German biblical scholarship, which made it difficult to believe the Bible to be set apart from other ancient literature, different, infallible. Study it in the same way you would study Homer or Hesiod and you come across a body of texts written at different periods, composed for different purposes, and fashioned late into the shapes and patterns we now read. If this approach undermined Protestantism more than Catholicism at first, the great Western Church was affected: by the biblical revolution, as by the advance in scientific knowledge. Geology demonstrated that the universe was infinitely older than the Bible had taught. Evolutionary theory culminating in Darwin removed the necessity of positing a Creator, or a purpose, behind the automatic self-adaptations of the species as they made life safer for themselves, a predatory, mindless environment.

Yet the religious impulse is deep in humanity. No civilization has ever existed without temples, fanes, shrines or pilgrimages. Was there no chance for faithful and intelligent men and women to accept the March of Mind while holding on in some form or another to the rituals and stories which their ancestors had used to give shape to their deepest experiences of sin and loss? The great German Protestant scholar Adolf Harnack (1851–1930) in *Das Wesen des Christentums* and his huge *Lehrbuch der Dogmengeschichte – History of Dogma* – believed he had somehow unpicked the historical lock to Jesus's original mission. He found the 'kernel', which was that Jesus, all those years ago, had been a German Liberal Protestant. The rest – the apocalyptic teachings of the Jews, the mystery cults favoured by St Paul, and so on – had been added to the original simple message about the Fatherhood of God. Christian tradition was thereby dismissed.

The modernists, especially the French, believed this was approaching the problem from entirely the wrong way round. The Abbé Loisy was in his day the most famous modernist. In *L'Évangile et L'Église*, 1902, he reminded readers that it was only through tradition, through the Church, that we knew anything at all about Christ. His fellow modernist Marcel Hébert, in a book which knew some popularity in its English translation of 1899, described going to High Mass in the Duomo at Pisa.

I listened, and I heard these words –

> Sub diversis speciebus,
> Signis tantum et non rebus,
> Latent res eximiae!

[Wonderful things lie hidden under different species, which are not reality, merely signs].*

I started. It was a complete expression of my own thoughts. Appearances, signs, symbols, which veil the mysterious reality, but which nevertheless adapt us to it, so that it penetrates us and makes us live – is not this one of the essential elements of all faith and of all philosophy?[3]

Such figures on the English scene as Father George Tyrrell S.J. and Baron Friedrich von Hügel (1852–1925) – born in Italy of an Austrian father and Scottish mother but long resident in Hampstead – certainly took this approach. The first twentieth-century pope, who was also the first holder of that office in modern times not to be educated beyond seminaries,

---

* The lines come from a Eucharistic hymn by Thomas Aquinas (*c*.1225–74).

nor to be of noble birth, took a very different line.

On 8 September 1907, Pope Pius X released his encyclical condemning the modernists, *Pascendi Dominici Gregis*. He left no room for doubt: the attempt to reconcile modern or agnostic views of the tradition, while worshipping within it, was wholly unacceptable. This pope taught not merely that the existence of God could be proven but that it must be proven by every believer. He asserted that only a literal and fundamentalist reading of the Bible and Catholic doctrine could be accepted.

There followed an extraordinary witch-hunt within the Church. Not only were modernists driven out, but would-be modernists were spied upon, bullied and cajoled. Loisy was excommunicated in 1908. Parishioners were encouraged to report any suspicion that their priest might be a modernist. (Hilaire Belloc absurdly believed that any priest who took longer than twenty minutes to say Mass was, or might be, a modernist.) 'Pope Pius X approved, blessed and encouraged a secret espionage association outside and above the hierarchy itself, even on their Eminences the Cardinals.'[4] The communists, when they seized power in Russia and other parts of Europe a decade after *Pascendi*, learnt much from the techniques of the Vatican bully-boys. 'Rome is causing horrible suffering to the simple souls of my entourage,' moaned one excommunicate modernist, a scholar, J. Turmel. Father Tyrrell in England was forbidden a Christian burial by his Church; sensibly, his friends merely buried him in the Anglican graveyard, with a stirring address by the great modernist scholar the Abbé Henri Bremond at Storrington, Sussex.

Pius X's attempt to hold the pass was of comfort to timid bigots within the fold who believed, or feared, that thought, and intellectual journeyings, might destroy faith. To enemies of religion, and of Christianity in particular, it confirmed the sense that to be Christian was necessarily to be obscurantist, and it drove many half-believers out of the sphere of the Churches altogether into unbelief.

In *The Makers of Modern Europe* (1930) Count Carlo Sforza remarked upon the peasanty origins of the anti-modernist pope. Whereas 'the prejudices of the aristocrat are often counterbalanced by his scepticism, always by his laziness . . . those of the peasant have no counterpoise'. Characters such as Pope Pius are 'hard on the noblest minds whose doubts and misgivings they do not understand' and 'very often put their whole trust in fanatics who please them with certainties'.[5] There would be plenty of repetitions of this phenomenon in the coming century of the Common Man, when the political dogmas and simplicities of communism and fascism would have little time for noble minds with doubts and misgivings.

'Modernism' as narrowly understood in Church history refers to a movement within the Catholic Church which was suppressed in 1907. Many of the Catholic modernists were aesthetically conservative, as the liturgical taste of Marcel Hébert suggests. Yet there is a link between what Church historians call modernism and the same word as applied to what was happening in music, poetry, painting and sculpture. The old minster tower had crumbled. To rebuild in some pastiche of the old order, as the neo-Gothic architects or the Nazarene or Pre-Raphaelite painters might have done, was no longer an option.

In the United States, a young travelling musician named Scott Joplin (1868–1917) had begun, not just to perform but to compose and write down the music which he had evolved from the black Dixie traditions of Missouri, where he had settled in his early twenties. His opera based on his lifetime vision, *Treemonisha* (1911), was never performed while he was alive, but in many short piano pieces of Joplin's, ragtime had entered the popular consciousness, not merely of Europe but America. A palpably new sound had arrived, signalling a world which was mysteriously different from anything which had gone before.

This difference, an agonizing and baffling one in so many respects, was nowhere more obvious than in the heart of the most conservative of all the great European empires, the Austrian. It was in Vienna that Sigmund Freud revolutionized contemporary perceptions of the human mind. It was in Vienna that the leading analytical philosopher of the twentieth century, Ludwig Wittgenstein, had been born; just as it was in Vienna that, under the leadership of Moritz Schlick, a group of philosophers would develop the system of thought known as Logical Positivism.

But if there is any sphere of human achievement with which Vienna is immediately associated it is music. And in that city, where Joseph Haydn had composed and performed so many of his greatest works, where Mozart had first known independence and had written his greatest operas, where Beethoven had lived and died, and where Franz Schubert was born and died, another Viennese, Arnold Schoenberg (1874–1951), and his disciple Alban Berg (1885–1935), began to pioneer atonal music. It was as if the tradition of harmony itself had been taken, by Wagner, Debussy and Richard Strauss, as far as it could go, and the next stage was to step into a void, in which the shapes and patterns to which the European ear had been responding for centuries no longer reflected the music of soul or sphere. Schoenberg's in many ways agonized music, recognizable as belonging to the great Austro-German tradition, reflects a new horror, tension, anxiety, as if it had plumbed down, like Dr Freud listening to the outpourings of an hysteric patient, and heard rumours of the tragedies which the new century was bringing forth.

Something highly comparable was happening in literature, though you would not know it if you merely read the solid Edwardian novels of Galsworthy and Arnold Bennett, distinguished as these may be, or the lyrics of Belloc and A. E. Housman. There was a similar sense of things coming to an end, of the end of a civilization.

'Fin de siècle' was a phrase used of and in the 1890s to suggest not merely the decadent behaviour of some of the more exhibitionistic bohemians in London and Paris, but also the sense that an era had ended. A young American poet named Ezra Loomis Pound (1885–1972), who was obsessed by the Nineties and the 'characters' thrown up by that drug- and alcohol-fuelled decade, was also possessed by a sense that European culture, the story which had begun with Homer, and known some of its highest points in medieval Provence and Italy, had now reached the buffers. He looked like a Nineties eccentric dreamed up by Max Beerbohm, with a shirt of midnight blue, a satin sock worn as a cravat, trousers tailored from bright green felt used normally for billiard tables, and an old dinner jacket. The goatee beard and the sombrero were modelled loosely on the clothes Whistler had worn to take London by storm thirty years before. The spats and the pince-nez were equally conservative, as was the ebony cane carried as a bohemian sceptre. London to this twenty-three-year-old seemed 'the centre at least of Anglo-Saxon letters and presumably of intellectual action . . . There was more going on, and what did go on, went on sooner than in New York.' 'Deah old Lunnon,' he wrote. 'Seeking what giants and dragons I may devour.'[6]

Of course, Pound was on one level no more than a young poseur, coming to a capital city as a way of boosting his ego. But great artists intuit things, about themselves and about the civilizations in which they move. The first English periodical to publish one of his poems was the *Evening Standard*, whose readers could discover the idea this young American had of himself – 'Thus am I Dante for a space and am/One François Villon, ballad-lord and thief.' To eke out his living he gave lectures at the London Polytechnic in what he called in his Ezra-lingo 'The Devil upment of Literachoor in Southern Yourup' – followed up by a course on Romance Literature.[7]

England was to be resistant to literary modernism. No English poets matched Pound or his young American friend Eliot. The giant W. B. Yeats, a *sui generis* Irishman, had belonged to a shared English tradition in the 1890s, and still resided in London much of each year, but he self-consciously placed himself outside the English tradition. No English composer successfully followed the musical lead of Schoenberg or Berg, no English painters followed Braque or Picasso. The British cultural traditions of the fifty years covered by this book produced much in the way of charm, quiet elegiac or eccentric work. But one of the sure signs that Britain was finished as a civilization, long before two world wars had bankrupted the British economy and dismantled the British Empire, was the cultural emptiness of the years 1900–1950. That is not to say there was no one of any charm or talent painting or composing or writing a poem; but from now onwards, everything is transposed into a very minor key.

This test, which no doubt some would consider contentious, applies chiefly to poetry. The twentieth century produced a far wider range of excellent novelists in Britain than did the nineteenth. Though there is none to match Dickens, the list hardly needs to be made, starting with H. G. Wells, Conrad, Bennett and their generation, in a glorious line from D. H. Lawrence, John Cowper Powys, Elizabeth Bowen, Evelyn Waugh, Anthony Powell . . . it is obvious that this was a half-century in which the novel flourished, on the British mainland, while James Joyce, an Irishman in exile, towered above his contemporaries at home. It is the poets whom I am using as an acid-test of something amiss with a whole civilization. When Spenser and Shakespeare wrote, continuing through the lifetime of Milton, this coincided with a time when England felt itself almost literally possessed by a divine *afflatus*. Racine and Corneille matched the flowering not merely of French power, but of French self-possession, Goethe and Schiller flourished before the nightmare of nationalism or pseudo-imperialism clouded the German picture, when Germany, a group of federal states, was most itself. The explosion of Pushkin's career coincided with the birth of modern Russia. The etiolated lyrics of the English Edwardian poets, followed by the feeble poetic productions of the years which followed, should sound a warning note; something has gone out of the mixture. We are drinking a martini cocktail in which someone has forgotten to put the spirits. Yeats, speaking of the high horse in whose saddle Homer rode, found it in his day to be 'riderless'.

It was this fact which the young Ezra Pound, however tiresome he might seem to us, could feel. It was something much more than the mere coincidence, which happens every few decades in any literary culture, that apart from the Irishman Yeats and old Thomas Hardy there were so few poets of any stature writing in Britain in 1908. It was something much deeper than that. Something had died in the night, and no one had noticed. We are told that the Edwardian period was some kind of glory age, the last summer afternoon before the storm, the brightly lit house party before they all went to die in the mud. Of course one sees how such a perception can be formed. But it might be truer to say that the culture which could allow itself to move into the First World War was one which was already moribund, morbid.

Britain was poised to die, America was poised, half desperately, half unwillingly, to take over the world. It is entirely apt that those who sniff the putrescence in the London air in the Edwardian period should be Americans, just as it is entirely fitting that those Americans who are capable of keeping great literature alive should choose to do so off home territory. Pound, Henry James, T. S. Eliot did not merely have an ambivalent attitude to the land of their birth, they embodied and reflected a much more widespread American ambivalence about itself, either as imperial power or cultural standard-bearer.

In the decade of Edward VII, Henry James was analysing the European and American scenes with new eyes, and his brother William, the pioneer psychologist and pragmatist philosopher, had turned his generous intelligence towards the question of religious belief.

'Modernism' is a term applied to a particular phase of religious thought; and it is also used to describe what was happening in Europe and America in poetry, painting, architecture, sculpture. The young modernists in poetry, of whom Pound was pre-eminent, looked to Henry James as 'the Master'. Pound reread the complete works of James when he came to London. When he had been married two months and met James by chance in a Chelsea street, he came to feel there was an emblematic significance in the Master's question as they strolled along together – 'And is she a com-patriot?' The syllables spaced, the accented vowel short.[8]

The beginning of modernism was that perception, our means of perception, is all. It is no accident that so many modernists were conservative in temperament. For a transitory phase of the nineteenth century, some of the painters who thought themselves most old-fashioned, the English Pre-Raphaelites, had tried to imitate the most modern of inventions, the camera. The Impressionists, by contrast, returned to Turner's efforts to reproduce not what an impersonal camera-lens but a human eye actually saw. Artists after the Impressionists began to return to even older traditions, shown forth in Christian icon-painting or 'primitive' masks and fetishes of what human beings felt about their material surroundings.

While Henry chronicled, obliquely but surely, the transformations in human consciousness which were to change civilization itself, his brother William, psychologist and philosopher, probed the mystery of religious belief. Was it the case, as nineteenth-century literalists had believed, that Christianity depended upon the verifiability of a series of actual events or the provability – whatever that would mean – of the existence of God? Was there something in the human mind or personality which could explain why we are, or are not, religious? In his great book, *The Varieties of Religious Experience*, delivered as lectures at St Andrews University in 1902, William James found all but no 'evidence' which could justify belief, but he refused to be reductionist and suggest that piety was simply a matter of temperament, still less that religious feeling was a substitute for other sorts of feeling. He maintained the legitimacy of faith, and he did so on the robust grounds that faith, for many, worked. He quoted with approval another American psychologist, Professor Leuba, as saying:

> *God is not known, he is not understood; he is used* – sometimes as meat-purveyor; sometimes as moral support, sometimes as friend, sometimes as an object of love. If he proves himself useful, the religious impulse asks for no more than that. Does God really exist? How does he exist? What is he? are so many irrelevant questions. Not God, but life, more life, a larger, richer, more satisfying life, is, in the last analysis, the end of religion.[9]

Whether it is the end of religion or not, it is certainly a very similar attitude which informs both the humanism of Henry's late novels – 'Live all you can – it is a mistake not to,' urges Strether in *The Ambassadors* – and the warmth of William James's reflections on the spiritual dimension of human experience.

William James, who died aged sixty-eight in 1910, had sobbed, 'It's so good to get home,' when he finally reached Connecticut after the last of his European lecture tours. Their peripatetic childhood and youth, traipsing from one European city to the next, and living often in hotels, had made one brother, William, feel more intensely American and the other, Henry, ever a stranger, a wanderer upon Earth. They were extremely fond of one another while being in some ways polar opposites.

Staying with his brother at Lamb House, Rye, in 1908, William became fascinated by the figure of G. K. Chesterton (1874–1936), the vastly obese poet-journalist who happened to be in the area. Rye, the original of E. F. Benson's Tilling in the Mapp and Lucia stories (Benson moved into Lamb House when James vacated it), was a small town which enjoyed the joys of discreet neighbour-watching. On 27 July 1908, Henry James instructed his secretary, Miss Bosanquet, to 'peep through the curtain to see "the unspeakable Chesterton" pass by – a sort of elephant with a crimson face and oily curls. He [Henry James] thinks it is very tragic that his mind should be imprisoned in such a body.' Brother William was so excited by the phenomenon that when he heard that Chesterton was standing in a neighbour's garden, he borrowed the gardener's ladder to peer over the wall. Henry was appalled. By the small-town rules of British intrusiveness which he instinctively picked up, it was all right to peer at oddities through a curtain; quite another thing to gawp openly from the top of a ladder.[10]

Chesterton, in the reign of Edward VII, had written two books about religion which have not worn very well, in spite of being enlivened with some marvellous phrases and the occasional good paragraph: *Heretics* and *Orthodoxy*. His expertise was for instant journalism, for wonder-fully perceptive criticism – witness his books on Browning and Dickens, among the best on their subjects – and for rollicky versifying about the Rolling English Drunkard making the Rolling English Road. He had also in this period managed to fit in the time to write two very distinctive novels, *The Man Who Was Thursday* and *The Napoleon of Notting Hill*, and to have endless public debates, challenging the opinions of those with whom he disagreed, notably Shaw. The passion for opinions will strike us as one of the great curses of the twentieth century. Chesterton had it in advanced, but benign form. A philosopher or a theologian he was not, strictly speaking, but he has enjoyed more repu-tation as a thinker than many who were. Although at this stage of his life not much of a churchgoer, he had set up as Defender of the Faith against such comers as the neo-pagan Kipling, the scientific materialist H. G. Wells, the Nietzschean Bernard Shaw and others – the 'Heretics', in short, of his title. Neither of the books mentioned offers a scintilla of evidence or argument for his opinions. Their power, which is undoubted, depends upon their advancement of an idea in an attractive manner. Chesterton makes his reader feel that Christianity is a point of view more plausible, because more decent, than its rivals. He set himself up against 'motor-car civilization going its triumphant way'.[11] He saw Christianity as essentially democratic, decent, and on the side of the individual against the bosses and the collectives. 'The old tyrants had enough insolence to despoil the poor, but they had not enough inso-lence to preach to them' nicely skewers both the laissez-faire Benthamite liberals and the new Fabian socialists such as the Webbs. Although seeing himself as defending 'orthodoxy', and admired by many today who consider themselves thoroughgoing supernaturalists, Chesterton's given reasons for being a Christian and eventually for accepting Roman Catholicism were essentially pragmatic – that this view of the world 'fitted' with his experience.

Henry James never entered the church at Rye for solemn worship. 'For James the Christian religion . . . figures most frequently as a means of withdrawing unwanted members of a house-party from his scene on a Sunday morning.'[12] There is no doubt that James was personally an agnostic humanist. He had enough in him, however, of his old

Swedenborgian father to believe that human beings were essentially mysterious, in life and in death. There was nothing simple about being a humanist because there was nothing simple about being human.

The closing decades of the nineteenth, and early decades of the twentieth centuries, saw a deepening interest, among thinking people, in the occult and the dead. Yeats was obsessed with mediums, ouija boards and the like. He was far from being unusual. Arthur Balfour, philosopher and prime minister, was in constant touch with the Other Side, and was in receipt of over 20,000 letters from his dead sweetheart, penned by a spirit medium.

Henry James, who picked up on what was going on around him with what one might term a passionate obliquity, absorbed all this interest into his fiction. Indeed, he must have shared the interest himself. As we should expect, however, from a man who had more capacity than almost any other (except perhaps his brother William) to see 'round' a subject, to understand its implications, he never spelt out what he thought in simple terms. If forced to ask whether there was life after death Henry James would not perhaps have wished to answer this question directly, but one could imagine that his answer, were he forced to give one, would have been – as was his brother William's – a very, very cautious Yes.

As far as his fiction was concerned, he made use of the Other, and the Ghostly, in completely original ways. One of his most accomplished stories, 'The Jolly Corner', describes a man very much like himself returning to the New York house of his childhood after thirty years of European absence. He intends to set his affairs in order. One of his properties is being converted into 'a tall mass of flats', from whose rental he intends to live. The other, however, the old brownstone house of his family memories, he intends to keep as a sort of shrine, looked after by the redoubtable Irish housekeeper Mrs Muldoon.

New York appals Spencer Brydon, the hero of the tale:

> Proportions and values were upside-down; the ugly things he had expected, the ugly things of his far-away youth, when he had too promptly waked up to a sense of the ugly – these uncanny phenomena placed him rather, as it happened under the charm; whereas the 'swagger' things, the modern, the monstrous the famous things, those he had most particularly, like thousands of ingenious enquirers every year come over to see, were exactly his sources of dismay.

On his last visit to the States, James himself complained of 'the violence of the assault of this appalling country on almost every honourable sense'. Everything which Henry James stood for, as an artist, was summed up in the simple biographical fact that he was an American who chose to reside in Europe – in what he (unlike Mr Rumsfeld) would have been pleased to call old Europe. He was destined, so passionately attached was he to these values, which he saw Britain as defending in the Great War, to become a British subject in 1915. But what would have happened, had he not done so? That is really the theme of 'The Jolly Corner'. The ghost whom he is tracking down in the deserted old house near Washington Square is none other than his own. In an interesting variation on two other tales of the uncanny, Dickens's *A Christmas Carol* and Wilde's *The Picture of Dorian Grey*, James is on the prowl for a self who never came into being – his American self.

Readers of ghost stories, whatever they believe or 'believe' when they are not holding the volume in their hand, momentarily suppose that the spectre or haunting is real. It is quite an achievement on James's part that he turns us to gooseflesh, as he undoubtedly does in 'The Jolly Corner', by this pursuit of a phantom.

> It gloomed, it loomed, it was something, it was somebody, the prodigy of a personal presence. Rigid and conscious, spectral, yet human, a man of his own substance and stature, waited there to measure himself with his own power to dismay.

Spencer Brydon goes to New York to meet his old self, but also to renew acquaintance with an old female friend with whom, perhaps, he might have enjoyed an intimacy which was closer. When she shows, at the end, that she understands his quest – which is more, wholly, than the reader does – the two draw together in an embrace. Such overcoming of emotional stiffness was never to be James's in life. He lived in his imagination, and to a remarkable degree for a man so worldly-wise, in his boyhood, his prepubescent self.

The dark, shadowy house is frightening, and yet reassuring at the same time – just like childhood memories themselves. James, therefore, in this story penned in his mid-sixties, managed to expand the capacities of the Uncanny Tale, identifying, in our sense of the ghostly, something else – namely our feelings about childhood, children and, one of his favourite themes, innocence. To this extent, 'The Jolly Corner' is a companion piece, and in part a commentary, on James's most celebrated tale of the uncanny, *The Turn of the Screw*.

But it was in his late masterpiece *The Golden Bowl* that we feel James meditating on things larger than its supposed theme of an adultery, meditating upon the place of his old country in the world, and on its relation to his adopted country.

The Golden Bowl is a dense book, and there must have been many who have been repelled by its quite extraordinary style. The old joke was that Henry James's career moved through three phases – James the First wrote such early triumphs as *Washington Square*, James the Second, deemed by most admirers to be the best, wrote the majestic and psychologically brilliant *Portrait of a Lady*. The next phase was that of The Old Pretender. It was H. G. Wells, a protégé of Henry James, who so unkindly but memorably captured what this last phase was like:

> He splits his infinitives and fills them up with adverbial stuffing. He presses the passing colloquialism into his service. His vast paragraphs sweat and struggle; they could not sweat and elbow and struggle more if God himself was the processional meaning to which they sought to come. And all for tales of nothingness . . . It is leviathan retrieving pebbles. It is a magnificent but painful hippopotamus resolved at any cost, even at the cost of its dignity, upon picking up a pea which has got into a corner of its den. Most things, it insists, are beyond it, but it can, at any rate, modestly, and with an artistic singleness of mind, pick up that pea.[13]

And yet, for all the absurd prolixity and circumlocution, *The Golden Bowl* is one of the great books of the world – arguably the greatest novel in the English language.

There used to be a vogue for seeing it as some kind of religious allegory. I do not think it is an allegory at all, but the very title, and the cracked, flawed *objet* at the centre of the story, is suggestive – which is different. When Maggie's friend Fanny Assingham smashes the bowl – Maggie has been tricked into buying it even though it is flawed, and tricked into ignorance of an affair between her best friend and her husband – we sense that more is at work than a melodrama. Asked once how he thought of his stories, James once replied: 'It's all "about", it's about – it's in the air so to speak, it follows me and dogs me.' *The Golden Bowl* is 'about' more than it seems to be about.

Surely this extra 'about' is the special relationship between America and Britain. It is really the old theme of themes for James – it had been from the beginning, with such crystalline early masterpieces as *Daisy Miller* – the story of innocent Americans coming to dissipated 'Old Europe' and being ensnared. This is the central theme of *The Portrait of a Lady*, in which Isabel Archer is tricked by Madame Merle.

In *The Golden Bowl*, however, there is a dramatic reversal of the usual pattern. Whereas in most of James's stories the innocent Americans are duped and tricked by the Europeans, in this last masterpiece the simple, decent all-American girl beats the devious Italian Prince whom she has married.

The essential ingredient in the story is old Mr Verver's money. One says old, but he is forty-seven at the beginning of the story; such is the stately pace of the book that one thinks of all the characters as antique. As far as Prince Amerigo is aware, it is England which is the big, rich, powerful nation. He comes to London at the beginning of the book and finds 'by the Thames a more convincing image of the truth of the ancient state than any they have left by the Tiber'. In the superb central chapter, when Amerigo and Charlotte consummate their adultery, it is at the appropriately named Matcham – a country house weekend where Lady Castledean and her 'toy-boy' Mr Blint preside over a 'great house, full of people, of possible new combinations, of the quickened play of possible propinquity'. The Prince in his vulgar way sees that everything about the patterned day at Matcham – the walks, the billiards, the meals, 'the nightly climax over the "bottigliera", as he called it of the bristling tray' – costs money. Everywhere he senses 'a bottomless bag of solid shining British sovereigns'. But what James has sensed, surely, in this book, is that the bag is no longer bottomless. The Yankees have more verve, more energy. It is the Verver fortune which can be quietly manipulated to save both marriages – his own to Charlotte, his daughter's to the prince. Charlotte the adulteress is taken back to the United States by Mr Verver. Maggie sacrifices herself and stays in old Europe, but we sense in this strong moral choice of hers that she now remains, not as a pathetic exile – as so many previous Jamesian heroines had done – so much as an occupying power.

7

Nationalisms

On a wet June day in 1912, 13,000 Welshmen 'of all ranks'[1] assembled in Regent's Park in London, marched down Regent's Street and up Piccadilly to Hyde Park. The rain was so heavy by the time they reached their destination that the speeches were curtailed, but later in the day they repaired to the shelter of the Albert Hall, where the proceedings were chaired by the Archbishop of York, and speakers included the Duke of Devonshire and the Bishop of St Asaph. In spite of the ardour with which these speakers addressed an enthusiastic audience, we read that the general public remained 'apathetic'[2] to the subject which caused them so much concern, namely the possible disestablishment of the Welsh Church.

At this date, the bishops of the Welsh Church, in common with those of England, were appointed by the Crown – in effect by the prime minister in London. Eventually, after decades of debating the matter, Parliament would pass Welsh Disestablishment into law on 18 September 1914, by which time politicians in Britain and Europe had more pressing affairs on their minds. It was agreed that the operation of the Act would be suspended until after the war. It was only with the passage of the Welsh Church Temporalities Act, 1919, that the new ecclesiastical province was formed, with Bishop A. G. Edwards of St Asaph being formally invested as the first Archbishop of Wales on 1 June 1920.[3]

The issue is one of such esoteric obscurity that even today, many actual members of the Church in Wales, that is Anglicans, find it confusing. In the years before the Welsh Disestablishment Bill passed into law, however, feelings, or at any rate rhetoric, ran high. This was because like so many quarrels which seem obscure to outsiders, much more was at stake than the narrow issues in small print. It was a matter, in miniature, which reflected the great movements of events which would change the face of Europe, and which in other places would lead to violent conflict and Europe's near self-destruction. It was, apart from other things, a class issue. The Church was perceived, with some justice, as being part of the old feudal order. The parson and the bishop were at one with the squire and the mine-owner. In many minds, the matters of Church and Education were intimately linked. Lloyd George had been (very well) educated at a church school in Llanystumdwy, but he had asserted his Baptist credentials by refusing to say the Creed when a boy there. 'I hate a priest, Daniel, wherever I find him,' he confided in a friend. He was not very conspicuous in his Christian observance, but his hammy attacks on attempts to force Church catechisms on Baptist, Methodist or Congregationalist Welsh children went down very well with his audiences in the valleys.

> There was once a time when the people of this country had mastered the Bible, and at the same time there arose a monarch who taxed the people without their consent for purposes to which they objected. There also arose a State priesthood who wanted to exalt over all their extravagant pretensions. There was a famous Scripture reader with Welsh blood in his veins, of the name of Oliver Cromwell. He had mastered all the revolutionary and explosive texts in that Book, and the result was destructive to that State priesthood. The bench of bishops was blown up, the House of Lords disappeared, and the aristocracy of this land rocked as though an earthquake had shaken them.[4]

Even hammier, and even more memorable:*

> Give the children the Bible if you want to teach them the Christian faith. Let it be expounded to them by its Founder. Stop this brawling of priests in and around the schools, so that the children may hear Him speak to them in His own words. I appeal to the House of Commons now, at the eleventh hour, to use its great influence and lift its commanding voice and say, 'Pray, silence for the Master'.[5]

Those speeches refer not to disestablishment as such but to the influence of the Church in Welsh schools. They show, however, that, as in Ireland, the question of religion was deeply bound up with that of nationalism.

There were some 550,280 practising Nonconformists in Wales in 1906, against 193,081 communicants in the established Church.[6] The case for disestablishment could be seen, then, not only as a class-based, but as a nationalist issue. With some one and a half million people living in Wales,[7] the overwhelming majority were worshippers at some non-Anglican chapel. Gladstone, in 1891, speaking in favour of disestablishment, had declared in Parliament that 'the nonconformists of Wales were the people of Wales'.[8] The compulsory payment of 'tithes', that is a proportion (originally a tenth) of rent to the Church, was understandably resented by the Baptist smallholder, the Calvinistic Methodist shepherd or the Congregationalist coal miner. Here was a case not merely of one class

---

* Literally. As a boy in Wales in the 1960s I heard old men quote it with tears in their eyes.

exploiting another, but of Welsh national identity discovering and focusing itself in this comparatively esoteric question.

Dr John Clifford, a fiery bearded Baptist preacher, used the Welsh education bills and disestablishment bills to argue, not merely for a disestablished Bishop of Bangor, but for a different world, in which small nations and minorities within those nations had self-determination. On the other hand, the defenders of the status quo such as Lord Robert Cecil or the Duke of Devonshire knew that more was at stake than Welsh tithes. Lord Robert, 'who believed Welsh Disestablishmentarianism was "individualism gone mad" or else . . . an unconscious conviction that religion is of no serious importance',[9] resigned from the government on principle when the Bill was passed. F. E. Smith, during the second reading of the Bill in the Commons, said it had 'shocked the conscience of every Christian community in Europe', prompting Chesterton's 'Antichrist, or the Reunion of Christendom, an Ode':

> Russian peasants round their pope
> Huddled, Smith,
> Hear about it all, I hope,
> Don't they, Smith?
> In the mountain hamlets clothing
> Peaks beyond Caucasian pales,
> Where Establishment means nothing
> And they never heard of Wales,
> Do they read it all in Hansard
> With a crib to read it with –
> 'Welsh tithes: Dr Clifford Answered'
> Really, Smith?

Chesterton's *reductio ad absurdum* skewered F. E. Smith with brilliance, but, read nearly a century later, it reminds us that the various peoples and races evoked in the spoof – the Breton fishermen, the Turks – would all be encouraged by the dreams of nationalism and democracy. So would the Irish and the Serbs. The Jews, who had possessed no homeland since the Emperor Titus sacked Jerusalem in the year 70, would, such was the climate of the times, believe that the solution to their problems was the same as that for which many Irish and some Welsh, and most Balkan peoples, were yearning: Home Rule.

The Bible played a central role in the way that the Protestant peoples of northern Europe saw themselves. Just as Luther's Bible, as well as being the translation of Hebrew and Greek texts, is also a work of German literature; just as the Geneva, and to a smaller degree the

Authorized Version of the Bible shaped the political self-consciousness of Milton and Bunyan's Englishmen; so the Bible in Welsh became something much more than a version of Near Eastern culture transposed into a Celtic tongue. It became a template by which the Welsh read their own story, a beleaguered, proud, small, pious people maintaining their identity against the threats of powerful neighbours. If the Welsh Bible was important at the time of the Reformation, it became even more so at the time of the Nonconformist conversion of Wales in the eighteenth century and during the various Nonconformist revivals of the nineteenth century. Tens of thousands of Welsh bibles were in circulation. One eyewitness in July 1810 described the arrival in a remote rural spot of a new printing of the New Testament, selling for one shilling each:

When the arrival of the cart was announced, which carried the first sacred load, the Welsh peasants went out in crowds to meet it; welcomed it as the Israelites did the ark of old; drew it into the town; and eagerly bore off every copy, as rapidly as they could be dispersed. The young people were to be seen consuming the whole night in reading it. Labourers carried it with them to the field, that they might enjoy it during the intervals of their labour, and lose no opportunities of becoming acquainted with its sacred truths.[10]

At the beginning of the twentieth century it was 'quite a common thing to find in cottages three, four or more Bibles'.[11] Welsh identification with the Jews became, on an analogical level, all but complete. Their chapels – Bethel, Bethesda, Ephraim, Ebenezer – took their names from the Bible, as did many of their villages. (My English father liked to post his Christmas cards in the Carmarthenshire village of Bethlehem.) After the English effectively obliterated the right of the Welsh to possess family names, many Welsh families took Jewish names such as Aaron or Samuel. (By paradox, many Jewish immigrants took Welsh names such as Lewis or Davis as rationalizations of Levi or David.) The identification of Protestant Bible-readers with the People of God in the Bible was not uniquely Welsh. 'I think it is good to be brought up a Protestant', wrote D. H. Lawrence:

and among Protestants, a Nonconformist, and among Nonconformists, a Congregationalist, which sounds pharisaic. But I should have missed bitterly a direct knowledge of the Bible, and a direct relation to Galilee and Canaan, Moab and Kedron, those places that never existed on earth . . . To me the word Galilee has a wonderful sound. The Lake of Galilee! I don't want to know where it is. I never want to go to

Palestine. Galilee is one of those lovely, glamorous worlds, not places, that exist in the golden haze of a child's half-formed imagination.[12]

One of the most striking ways in which the British male of this date expressed a feeling of kinship with the Jews was in the popularity of circumcision. 'It is a curious fact,' wrote Ronald Hyam in his masterly *Empire and Sexuality*, 'that outside the traditional circumcising communities [Jewish, Muslim, Melanesian, Amerindian and some African] the only Westerners to adopt it as a common practice were the English-speaking peoples.'[13] The plot of George Eliot's last great novel, *Daniel Deronda*, published in 1876, had hinged upon the discovery by the central character that he was Jewish, a fact unknown until his mature years. An American critic of our own day remarked that 'Deronda had only to look'.[14] But not, in 1876, if he had been of Jewish origin, but brought up from birth as if gentile.

In the later generation, there would have been much greater opportunity for confusion. Circumcision became popular among the medical profession in the 1890s. Some attribute this fact to the pioneering skills of a Jewish doctor named Remondino.[15] Others think that circumcision became popular in army medical circles, especially in India. The periodical literature in the Edwardian period is extensive. For example, the *British Medical Journal* of 15 June 1907 contains a learned lecture on the subject by J. Bland Sutton, FRCS, who outlines the history of the custom among Jews, Muslims and the Masai and the Kavindondos of East Africa. Clearly, there were circumstances where British doctors had undertaken the operation for treatment of specific disorders. Dr Bland Sutton gives as an example: 'The Museum of Charing Cross Hospital contains a prepuce removed from a man of 35 years of age, with an orifice so narrow that when the urine escaped from the urethra it ballooned the prepuce to the size of an orange, and it was then expelled by squeezing. Micturition required fifteen minutes.'[16] But this was the consequence of congenital phimosis. The practice of circumcision upon males whose religion did not require it was, for Bland Sutton, a modern development. He notes that in 1906, 54 children were circumcised at his own London hospital, the Middlesex, while at the Hospital for Sick Children in Great Ormond Street in the same year a striking 874 patients were circumcised.

In our own day, once more, something like 1 per cent of the male population of Great Britain is circumcised, and this almost always for ritualistic reasons. In the period of the Empire's heyday, however, especially among the professional and officer classes, the proportion was high. In the 1930s, a survey suggested that two-thirds of public schoolboys in Britain were circumcised. As the Empire declined, so did the circumcisions. In 1946, a survey of boys born on 4 March found that 38.8 per cent of the professional and salaried families had circumcised their sons, with 29.9 per cent of manual and unskilled workers.[17] The separation of Cavaliers (uncircumcised) and Roundheads at private schools, from the Edwardian period to the early years of Elizabeth II, was something with which every privately educated British boy would have been jocularly familiar. Dr Remondino had believed that evolution would eventually lead to the disappearance of the prepuce altogether. Certainly, gentile doctors pointed to the much lower incidence among Jewish children of infant mortality, and there was a belief that circumcision was more hygienic. It is certainly remarkable that the British adoption of the habit coincided with the period, roughly from the 1890s to the 1950s, of the sand and heat of the Empire, though it is hard to see exactly why the popularity of this observance, hitherto in history of unambiguously religious significance, should be seen as 'primarily an imperial phenomenon'.[18] Lloyd George – presumably, born 1863, a Cavalier rather than a Roundhead – nevertheless identified as a Bible Welshman with the People of God in other respects.

Lloyd George himself said: 'I was taught in school far more about the history of the Jews than about the history of my own land. I could tell you all the kings of Israel. But I doubt whether I could have named half a dozen of the Kings of England and no more of the Kings of Wales.'[19] David Lloyd George, who, as prime minister, played a pivotal role in the promotion of Zionism, was actually employed as a solicitor for the Zionists between 1903 and 1905. He drew up the first documents submitted to the British government proposing a Jewish homeland, working on behalf of Theodor Herzl's – founder of the Zionist movement – London representative, Leopold J. Greenberg, later editor of the *Jewish Chronicle*.[20]

Perhaps it was the very fact that some Protestants make the Bible their own story, that they see Moab and Kidron – as D. H. Lawrence did – as 'those places that never existed on earth', which makes the presence of actual Jews on occasion disturbing. The Jewish population of Wales was tiny, but it experienced in the summer of 1911 what the Home Secretary, Winston Churchill, described as a 'pogrom'.[21]

It had been a hard summer. A strike in the coal-mining industry, lasting from September 1910 to August 1911, had been broken by police and military violence. (Churchill sent the Metropolitan Police to patrol strike areas in Cardiff. Two rioters were shot dead in Liverpool in August 1911.) A railway strike had given the chance for local shopkeepers to raise prices, which in the heightened tension of the strike caused widespread anger and hardship. The Jews of South Wales were not miners. They tended to be small shopkeepers or landlords. Their numbers were tiny – less than 1 per cent – about 1,800 – of the population of Cardiff; in small Glamorgan towns or villages, negligible. Some 135 in Brynmawr, 150 in Tredegar. Yet in that summer of 1911 Churchill had to send the Worcester regiment to break up anti-Semitic disturbances. In Tredegar a band of '200 young fellows' attacked Jewish shops while singing 'several favourite Welsh hymn tunes'. These outrages were followed by attacks on Jewish shops in Ebbw Vale and Rhymney, in Cwm, Abertysswg and Brynmawr. Two Jewish shops in Senghennydd were torched at the end of the week. The total financial damage exceeded £16,000.

Haute Juiverie in London tried to dismiss the incident as no more than the fisticuffs of hooligans. Alfred de Rothschild, Sir Edward Sassoon and the *Jewish World* tried to pass it off as mere 'lust of criminals: rioting would have taken place, Jews or no Jews'. Many of the Jews in South Wales had fled pogroms in Russia, and the prospect of the phenomenon extending even to remote valleys in Wales was no doubt intolerable. But the reports in *The Times* and the Welsh newspapers make it clear that the attacks were organized, that the rioters were not common criminals but 'respectable people to all appearances', 'respectable working men':[22] precisely the socio-economic types who would rally to the fascist banners thirty years later.

Some 120,000 Jews lived in Britain in 1911,[23] the huge proportion recent immigrants from Russia and Poland.* The Russian pogroms of 1905–6, savage even by the standards of Eastern Europe, had produced fresh refugees. It was the virulence of Continental anti-Semitism which led, inexorably, to the hope first by a few, then by many, Jews that they might form a nation. The founding father and inspiration of modern Zionism, Theodor Herzl, believed that anti-Semitism was endemic in European society. 'We are one people and subject to one fate.' This was his view. The only solution was for them to find a place on Earth which was their own, though even that, given the fact that Jews were scattered across the face of a hostile Earth, must perforce be on sufferance. 'Shall we choose Argentina or Palestine? We shall take what is given us.'[24]

Zionism as a plausible, viable idea came into being at the height of two mighty European political phenomena: British imperialism and small-nation nationalism. The British at various times supported the national aspirations of the Czechs, or the Serbs and the Greeks, since they wished to be independent of other imperialisms. The national aspirations of Indians, Irish or, later, Africans, who wanted to be rid of the

---

* 106,082 Russians and Poles in England and Wales with others uncounted in Scotland.

British Empire, as opposed to the Austro-Hungarian or Ottoman or Russian empires, were a rather different story.

Theodor Herzl, born in Budapest, was in adult life resident in Vienna. He was a sophisticate, an internationalist who had been led to his idea of *Der Judenstaat* by the horrors of contemporary anti-Semitism, especially the Russian pogroms and the Dreyfus Affair in France. As well as approaching the British with the idea of a Jewish homeland in their colony of Uganda, Herzl had dealings with Kaiser Wilhelm II, with Pope Pius X, with the Tsar of Russia's interior minister, and with the Ottoman Sultan in attempts to try out the possibility of establishing the homeland in Palestine. 'The salvation of Israel will be achieved by prophets and not by diplomats,' he had asserted.[25]

When Herzl died in 1904, Chaim Weizmann wrote to his fiancée that 'Africa' – the idea of a Jewish homeland in Uganda – 'can now without doubt be regarded as finished . . .'[26]

Weizmann has been called an historic hero in a well-defined sense – 'one who altered his people's history in a way that would have been impossible but for his extraordinary gifts and achievements'.[27] He was born in a ghetto, in poverty, in southern Russia in 1874 at a time when Zionism was little more than a dream, when spoken Hebrew was unknown outside rarefied rabbinic circles, and when Judaea was part of the Ottoman Empire, an underpopulated, picturesque but decayed region. When he died in 1952 in Rehovot, he was the president of the state of Israel. He had been the key figure in bringing that state into being.

He came to England from Russia – via Switzerland – becoming a demonstrator in chemistry at Victoria University, Manchester, in 1904. Winston Churchill, electioneering in Oldham, approached the Jewish leaders in Manchester, hoping for their support of the Liberal party. On the eve of the 1906 election, Weizmann met the Tory prime minister, Arthur Balfour, and they had the conversation which passed into legend.

Weizmann was concerned that many British assimilated Jews were extremely dubious about the Zionist idea.

I began to sweat blood to make my meaning clear through my English. At the very end I made an effort, I had an idea. I said 'Mr Balfour, if you were offered Paris instead of London, would you take it?' He looked surprised, 'But London is our own!' I said, 'Jerusalem was our own when London was a marsh!' He leaned back, continued to stare at me, and said two things which I remember vividly. The first was: 'Are there many Jews who think like you?' I answered, 'I believe I speak the mind of millions of Jews whom you will never see and who cannot speak for themselves, but with whom I could pave the streets of the country I come from.' To this he said, 'If this is so, you will one day be a force.' Shortly before I withdrew, Balfour said, 'It is curious. The Jews I meet are quite different.' I answered: 'Mr Balfour, you meet the wrong kind of Jews.'[28]

It was Weizmann's conviction that 'England will understand the Zionists better than anyone else'.[29] The models used by Weizmann, who was neither a prophet like Herzl, nor an historian, but a chemist, were, consciously or not, anachronistically contemporary. In seeking to 'recreate' the ancient homeland of the Jews, it was no accident that he found that England understood the idea 'better than anyone else'. Although the Ugandan proposal was ditched, Weizmann went on thinking of the new country as a colony on the British model. Soon after Turkey entered the First World War, he wrote:

Don't you think that the chance for the Jewish people is now within the limits of a discussion at least? . . . Should Palestine fall within the sphere of British influence and should Britain encourage a Jewish settlement there as a British dependency, we could have in 25–30 years about a million of Jews out there, perhaps more; they would develop the country, bring back civilization to it.[30]

In just the same way, Europeans appropriating African or Asian or South American territory considered themselves to be thereby bringing 'civilization'. Though he was always careful in his public utterances to express his respect for the rights of the indigenous population of Palestine – 'There is an Arab nation with a glorious past' – he was candidly colonialist in his language. He spoke of the Jewish settlers as 'colonialists' following his first visit to Palestine in 1907,[31] the Arabs were 'primitive people'.[32] The Jewish incomers would be 'bearers of the torch and the preparers of civilization'.[33] It is true that as his thinking developed Weizmann categorically stated and patently wished that '600,000 Arabs have just as much right to their life in Palestine as we have to our National Home.'[34] It was an optimistic aspiration. Like the British in India, the Zionists of Weizmann's generation could not entirely shake off the sense that when a European man set foot on non-European soil he did so as the superior of the native population. He came to conquer and to improve. In his more unguarded moments he suggested, in his thinking about the settlement of Palestine, that the fate of 'several hundred thousand negroes' was 'a matter of no consequence'.[35] Just as the British in South Africa could dehumanize the Indians by referring to them as coolies, so Weizmann could see the indigenous population of the Middle East as negroes.

*

The Liberals depended upon Irish support for their majority in the House of Commons at Westminster, so it was inevitable that they would try to appease the majority of Irish members who wanted Home Rule for Ireland. The passage of the Parliament Act* meant that opposition from the House of Lords could not impede the passage of the 1910 Home Rule Bill into law. But something much more damaging than a veto in the Lords stood in the way.

There were plenty of English Unionists dismayed by the notion of an independent, or quasi-independent, Ireland, but their fury was not to be compared with that of the Irish Unionists, above all those Protestants of the six counties of the North, Ulster. They chose as their leader and spokesman the solicitor general in the previous Conservative government, the lawyer who had prosecuted Oscar Wilde, Sir Edward Carson, member of Parliament for Dublin University. In January 1913 the Ulster Unionist Council raised the Ulster Volunteer Force: 100,000 men between the ages of seventeen and sixty-five. By summer, there was a march-past of 15,000 trained men at the Balmoral grounds near Belfast. F. E. Smith took the salute.[36]

These men were in the paradoxical position of preparing to take up arms against the British Crown, in protest against an Act passed in the British Parliament, in order to declare their loyalty to Britain. Asquith's Liberal government dithered, as British politicians always dither when faced by Irish violence, and suggested the hopeless solution – namely that Home Rule would come into being, with Ulster possessing an 'opt out' for six years. 'We do not want sentence of death with a stay of execution for six years' was Carson's contemptuous response. The Home Secretary, Winston Churchill, no Home Ruler he, denounced the Ulster Provisional Government as 'a self-elected body, composed of persons who, to put it plainly, are engaged in a treasonable conspiracy'.[37] There followed the so-called 'Mutiny at the Curragh' in which General Sir Hubert Gough, commander of the Cavalry Brigade at the Curragh, notified the commander in chief in Dublin, Sir Arthur Paget, that he and fifty-nine other officers would have no part in suppressing a Unionist revolt.

Ireland was on the edge of potential civil war, and the Westminster government could not now proceed without disaster. If they imposed Home Rule on the Protestants of the North, there would have almost certainly been the armed resistance threatened, with no opposition from the military. Equally, having passed the Home Rule Bill to the satisfaction of Irish members, Asquith's government could not renege on the

* See next chapter.

deal. To do so would be to invite the armed reaction of those Irish nationalists for whom Home Rule – that is, a measure of independence under
overall British hegemony – was never going to be enough.

It is not an exaggeration to say that the impasse over Ireland was one
of the factors which made Asquith and his Cabinet colleagues go to war
with Germany, Austria and Turkey in 1914, rather than to seek a negotiated settlement or declare Britain to be neutral in the conflict. Of the
awkward list of domestic problems which the Liberal government could
not solve – Welsh disestablishment, female suffrage – Irish independence
was much the most grave. Terrible as the prospect of a European war might
prove, politicians think in short terms. The war could rally the dissident
voices of the Welsh, the Women, the Irish, behind a common cause.

It certainly in the short term was an effective policy. Sir Edward Grey
had no sooner told the House of Commons on 3 August 1914 of the
government's decision to go to war, than John Redmond, leader of the
parliamentary Irish Nationalists, pledged his full support. British troops
could be withdrawn from Ireland. Irish Nationalists would work hand
in hand with the Ulster Volunteers in defending both Britain and Ireland.
'And today I honestly believe that the democracy of Ireland will turn
with the utmost anxiety and sympathy to this country in every trial and
every danger that may overtake it.'[38] It was in this atmosphere that the
Irish Home Rule Act received the royal assent on 18 September 1914.
(The entire Conservative opposition walked out of the House of
Commons in protest.)

Enormous numbers of Irishmen volunteered to fight in the First World
War. About 150,000 were in active service by April 1916 and over 200,000
had enlisted by the end.[39] (There was never conscription in Ireland.)
Hugely more Catholics than Protestants volunteered. No doubt patriotism played its part in Ireland, as everywhere else, in rallying men to
the colours, but so did poverty. A government report estimated that of a
Dublin population of 304,000, 63 per cent, some 194,000, were working-
class. Living conditions were among the most squalid and deprived in
the Empire. Thirty-seven per cent of Dubliners lived six to a room and
14 per cent of the houses were deemed 'unfit for human habitation'. In
such tenements, lavatories were unknown, and excreta lay scattered in
corridors. 'We cannot conceive,' wrote the committee presenting this
report, 'how any self-respecting male or female could be expected to use
the accommodation such as we have seen'.[40]

No doubt many of those who fought believed the wartime propaganda
that Britain, and Ireland with it, was going to war to defend the rights
of plucky little nations like themselves, Belgium or Serbia. Equally, there
were very many Irish men and women who were not at this juncture

politically or emotionally prepared for total independence. Many Irish people, until the London government played into the hands of Fenian out-and-out republicans, would have been content with devolved power to Dublin rather than full-blown independence.

This was not how it appeared to all Irishmen. Sir Roger Casement, in a letter of 17 January 1914 to the *Freeman's Journal*, wrote: 'As a matter of fact the people of Alsace-Lorraine today enjoy infinitely greater public liberties within the German Empire than we are ever likely to possess within the British Empire', adding praise for 'the extraordinary liberty German imperialism accords a lately conquered territory'.[41] Casement entitled one of his denunciations of Britain, published in America in 1914, *The Crime Against Europe*. 'Whereas the Triple Alliance' – that is Germany, Hungary and Austria – 'was formed thirty years ago, it has never declared war on anyone, while the *Triple Entente*' – that is the alliance of Britain, France and Russia – 'before it is eight years old has involved Europe, America, Africa, and Asia in a world conflict.'

Many ingenious psychological explanations have been sought for this Ulster Protestant's virulent hatred of the English. At some point of such investigations allusion is usually made to his notorious diaries which reveal a refreshingly shame-free attitude to his promiscuous homosexual compulsions. Alas, the simplest explanation for why a man who spent his grown-up life in government service, culminating in a knighthood, should have come to his hostile, anti-British opinions was that they were based on actual first-hand observation.

To see photographs of Casement in his British consular uniform – cocked hat, white gloves, sword, gleaming brass buttons on his tunic – is to see a tormented character from one of Joseph Conrad's novels. For looking out above the gold embroidery of the tunic collar is a man somehow at variance with the uniform. The bearded, half-humorous, quizzical face has looked into some morass: known, like Conrad's Jim or Nostromo, the complicated emotion of being loyal to a principle while betraying a cause; perhaps even, like Marlowe recounting the terrible tale of 'the heart of darkness', seen into 'the horror, the horror'. In 1904, Casement's diaries record 'a delightful day' spent at Conrad's house at Pent Farm, near Hythe,[42] and the two men had followed some of the same paths, both in South America and in Africa – Conrad a Pole who had served as a merchant marine officer, Casement as a British diplomat, both strangers upon the Earth and looking at the imperialist phenomenon with sceptical eyes. In 1907 Casement explained to a friend:

I was on the high road to being a regular imperialist jingo – although at heart underneath all and unsuspected almost by myself I had remained an Irishman. Well the [Boer] war gave me qualms at the end – the concentration camps bigger ones and finally when up in those lonely Congo forests where I found Leopold, I found myself also, the incorrigible Irishman . . . I was looking at the tragedy with the eyes of another race.[43]

The extent of Belgian atrocities in the Congo was not exaggerated by Conrad in 'Heart of Darkness'. Here was the horror, the horror indeed: Europeans behaving with unrestrained brutality towards the indigenous population. Africa cured Casement of any sense that imperialism was essentially, or even potentially, benign. The activities of the Ulster Unionists, his fellow Northern Irish Protestants, filled him with disgust on his return home. His stint of consular work in South America only confirmed his sense of alienation from the British Establishment of which he was a representative.

There is no doubt that Roger Casement was a traitor in the legal and technical sense of the term. While still serving in the British consulate, he enlisted in the Irish Volunteers, a quasi-military organization committed to securing 'the rights and liberties common to all the people of Ireland without distinction of creed, class or politics'. They were preparing to fight the Ulster Unionists and if necessary the British troops. He went to America, which he increasingly detested, to raise money for guns. When the European war broke out, he wrote to his fellow-revolutionary John H. Horgan: 'I feel for you my Catholic countrymen perhaps even more than you feel for yourselves – I feel for Ireland . . . – the shame and ignoring of our race – the white slave race of European peoples. But I don't despair – because I believe . . . that the manhood of Ireland will outlast the British Empire.' These fighting words turned out literally true.

'My country can only gain from my treason' was Casement's view.[44] Casement went to Germany, finally reaching Berlin, from America, on 31 October 1914, accompanied by the quasi-comic, slightly sleazy figure of Eivind Adler Christensen, a Norwegian sailor whom he appeared to have met casually in Times Square, New York. Casement's surely hare-brained scheme was to secure the promise of 25,000 German troops, with 50,000 extra guns. He formed an Irish Brigade from those Irish soldiers taken prisoner in Germany and he optimistically calculated that the 150,000 Irishmen enlisted in the British army would fight for an Irish Free State.

The Germans were prepared to offer weapons, but not troops. Casement realized too late that he and his German friends were talking at cross-purposes – 'Oh Ireland, Why did I ever trust in such a Govt [sic] as this – or think that such men would help thee! They have no sense of honour, chivalry, generosity . . . They are Cads . . . That is why they are hated by the world and why England will surely beat them.'[45]

Meanwhile, in Ireland, Casement's friends in the Irish Republican Brotherhood – the IRB – sent a message via the German embassy at Berne that they had fixed the Rising for Easter Sunday 1916, and that the arms ship should reach Tralee Bay, with its German officers, not later than Easter Monday. Casement, Robert Monteith and another conspirator named Bailey arrived from a submarine in a rubber dinghy on Banna Strand, County Kerry, on Good Friday. In vain had Casement tried to make contact with the conspirators, and tried to dissuade them from continuing with a doomed enterprise. He was arrested, hiding in an ancient fort, with a ticket from Berlin to Wilhelmshaven in his pocket. A priest visited him in Tralee gaol – though he was not yet a fully fledged convert to the Catholic faith – and thus it was that Patrick Pearse, leader of the rebels, received the message on Holy Saturday: 'Germany sending arms, but will not send men.'

British Naval Intelligence had broken the German diplomatic code as early as a year before. They knew of the planned Easter Rising. They knew of Casement's homosexuality – a fact they would use against him in the later propaganda war. They knew of a possible invasion of Ireland. The Irish Chief Secretary, Augustine Birrell, took the view that the rebels were extremists, fanatics. The mainstream Irish Nationalist leadership – John Redmond, John Dillon, Joe Devlin – were against the Irish Volunteers; so were the tens of thousands of Irishmen who had enlisted in the British army to fight the Germans. If the rebellion could be contained as a nuisance and not elevated into a revolution, the moderates could hold the pass. Sadly, this sensible approach on the part of the British only lasted until the Easter Rising itself.

On Easter Monday 1916, Sir Matthew Nathan, under-secretary of state, was sitting in his office in Dublin Castle when a shot rang out beneath his window.

An Irish policeman had been shot dead by the Citizen Army. The Rising had begun. For the rest of the day, all over Dublin, the rebel forces shot their fellow Irishmen, often quite arbitrarily. The writer James Stephens saw them shoot a civilian trying to extricate his cart from a barricade which they had erected on St Stephen's Green.[46] The next day an army officer of the Royal Irish Rifles arrested three non-combatant journalists, Thomas Dickson, Patrick MacIntyre and Francis Sheehy Skeffington, a well-known pacifist, and had them shot by firing squad. Two days later, on Wednesday, British reinforcements arrived at Kingstown. The rebels, particularly those led by the half Spanish, half

American Catholic enthusiast Eamon de Valera, kept up extremely effective sniper fire in central Dublin while the British guns bombarded rebel strongholds with heavy shells. The Post Office in O'Connell Street had been taken over by the rebels as their headquarters. It was emblazoned with the words IRISH REPUBLIC and flew the green flag for just a few days. By Thursday evening the flag had been scorched brown. By the following Monday, the GPO had been evacuated, 450 had been killed, 2,614 wounded, 116 soldiers and 16 policemen were dead.[47]

It was now rather harder than a week earlier to contain the rebellion as a 'nuisance'. Though the majority of Irish people still favoured a moderate political devolution, something had changed. Mythologizing the Easter Rising, W. B. Yeats could make of the men holed up in the GPO and subsequently shot by the English heroes of an Homeric status. He asked whether their sacrifice had been vain, given the fact that England was going to concede to Ireland a measure of self-government in any event.

> Too long a sacrifice
> Can make a stone of the heart . . .
> Was it needless death after all?
> For England may keep faith
> For all that is done and said.
> We know their dream; enough
> To know they dreamed and are dead;
> And what if excess of love
> Bewildered them till they died?
> I write it out in a verse—
> MacDonagh and MacBride
> And Connolly and Pearse
> Now and in time to be,
> Wherever green is worn,
> Are changed, changed utterly:
> A terrible beauty is born.[48]

This was to be the story, not only of Ireland, but of almost every European country at some stage of the early twentieth century. Russia was on the verge of evolving into a prosperous liberal democracy; instead it had the bloodiest revolution and civil war. Weimar Germany, in spite of overpowering political and economic problems, could have struggled towards manageable consensual politics, as Britain did during its economic travails. It voted in National Socialism. The twentieth century looked to solve its problems by violent means. It distrusted consensus, it preferred mayhem.

The British troops had brought stability to Dublin, and in spite of their initial blunder in shooting three journalists, they had the overall support of Dubliners, especially of the working class. Above all they had it in their power to be magnanimous, since the heroic rebels had been utterly routed.

John Redmond, moderate Irish Nationalist leader, saw the Prime Minister, Asquith, as early as he could to explain the delicate balance of Irish feeling. On 3 May 1916, Patrick Pearse, Thomas MacDonagh and Thomas Clarke were shot at dawn at Kilmainham gaol. Although they had been told they would be allowed a priest near them when they were shot, the soldiers in the event refused this. The next day four more executions – of Joseph Plunkett, Edward Daly, Michael O'Hanrahan and William Pearse – were carried out. The next day, John MacBride, briefly married to Maud Gonne in 1903, was shot. Asquith, with typical ambivalent weakness, told the War Office to 'go slowly' but did nothing personally to stop the shootings. The wounded James Connolly, taken on a stretcher from Dublin Castle to Kilmainham gaol, had to be propped in a chair to be shot. He held his head high. There were 3,000 arrests after the Rising, and although many were released almost at once, 1,867 were interred in criminal prisons in Ireland or Wales.

At the end of Easter week, the British ambassador in Washington had reported that Irish-American opinion was on the whole opposed to the rebels. Within three weeks all that had changed. A Home Ruler from Vermont wrote to Redmond: 'The present wave of fury sweeping through Irish America originated with the executions and not with the rising.' A similar reaction occurred in Ireland itself. British intransigence, and lack of willingness to take the broader view, paved the way for further bloodshed. Or so it was perceived. A Capuchin father in Dublin noticed his working-class flock became 'extremely bitter' after the executions, 'even amongst those who had no sympathy whatever with the Sinn Feiners, or with the rising'.[49]

In fairness it has to be said that the government was in the middle of the bloodiest and most damaging European war in history. A full-scale Irish rebellion, even a civil war, would undoubtedly have weakened the British position, which had been the reason the Germans had supported the Easter Rising. Was Irish-American feeling truly so moderate until the first rebel was shot, or did the executions provide Irish-Americans with the excuse to do what they had done since the famines of the 1840s, hate the English? What government in time of war in 1916 would *not* have shot those who led an armed rebellion against it?

Yeats, in another poem of magnificent myth-making, 'Sixteen Dead Men', said:

O but we talked at large before
The sixteen men were shot . . .[50]

But there were only fifteen rebels executed after the Easter Rising. Eamon de Valera is often said to have been spared because of American intervention – he lived in America until he was two – but there is no evidence for this.[51] It would seem as if this lucky, strange man owed his life to John Redmond, who intervened personally with Asquith. The sixteenth man of Yeats's poem, not shot, but hanged, was Sir Roger Casement. He was held in Brixton Prison, then in the Tower of London in miserable conditions, weak, but able to charm his guards. He greatly feared, once it became clear that the British authorities had got hold of his diaries, that he would be put on trial for sexual offences rather than treason. The Archbishop of Canterbury, Randall Davidson, petitioned to plead for clemency for Casement, was shown extracts of the diaries. 'Huge' – a favourite adjective in *The Black Diary* – sometimes refers to a club dinner but more often to the size of the male organs of strangers encountered in Hyde Park, or on his African and South American journeys. The notion that the diaries were a forgery, for long a theory entertained by Irish republican sympathizers, has been scotched forever by Jeffrey Dudgeon in his definitive edition of *The Black Diaries, with a study of [Casement's] background sexuality and Irish political life*. Archbishop Davidson, having seen evidence of Casement's hidden life, concluded: 'it may be taken as further evidence of his having become mentally unhinged.'[52]

Casement died, like that other vilified Irish Protestant homosexual, Oscar Wilde, having been received into the Roman Catholic Church. The hangman, John Ellis, a hairdresser from Rochdale, accurately computed the necessary drop for a 6 ft 2 in, man weighing 12 stone – 168 pounds. 'He is dead this Knight of the Flaming Heart, hanged by the neck with a rope manipulated by a Rochdale barber' was the reflection of the one-time secretary to Sir Horace Plunkett, Maurice Joy, in *The Irish Rebellion of 1916 and Its Martyrs*. Accompanied by the RC padre, Casement was calm and said: 'Lord Jesus, receive my soul' before he died. (The hangman later committed suicide.)

In 1965, after secret negotiations between the Dublin government and the recently elected Labour government of Harold Wilson in London, it was agreed to disinter Casement's body from Pentonville Prison. Black hair and an element of scalp were visible on a very white skull. The remains were placed in a lead-lined coffin. Casement's dream of being buried at Murlongs Bay was firmly rejected by the Northern Ireland government, so the body was taken to Dublin. The staggering figure of

665,000 people, all but the same figure as the population of Dublin itself, trooped past to pay their respects during the five days when the body lay in state at Arbour Hill. Two nieces who had never known Casement, and who were now in their seventies, came from Australia for the State funeral. There was a day of national mourning as the gun carriage draped with the tricolour was borne from the procathedral to Glasnevin cemetery. Eamon de Valera, eighty-two and blind, spoke at the graveside – 'I do not think it presumptuous on our part to believe that a man who was so unselfish, who worked so hard for the downtrodden and the oppressed and who died, that that man is in heaven.'[53]

Casement's position at the end of his life, in spite of the fact that the German government was composed of 'Cads', was simple: 'I am wholly pro-German always for the sake and cause of the German people. It is not my own honour at stake alone but the cause of Irish nationality in the extreme form I have stood for.'[54]

It is easy enough to see why Eamon de Valera revered Casement and believed him to be in heaven when he spoke in 1965. But there is another way of viewing, not merely the Irish Republican movements, but all small nationalisms that since the dissolutions of empires during the First World War have struggled to express their identity by violence. P. S. O'Hegarty (1879–1955), a member of the Supreme Council of the IRB and an historian of Sinn Fein, wrote towards the end of his life:

We adopted political assassination as a principle. We turned the whole thoughts and passions of a generation upon blood and revenge and death; we placed gunmen, mostly half-educated and totally inexperienced, as dictators with powers of life and death over large areas. We decided the moral law, and said there was no law but the law of force, and the moral law answered us. Every devilish thing we did against the British went full circle, and then boomeranged and smote us tenfold; and the cumulating effect of the whole of it was a general moral weakening and a general degradation, a general cynicism and disbelief in either virtue or decency, in goodness or uprightness or honesty.[55]

8

Shipwreck

It is said that the following verses, circulated among friends, but inevitably 'leaked' to a wider audience, delayed their author's knighthood 'for twenty years'.[1] Almost more fascinating, given the obvious truth of Max Beerbohm's gentle satire, is the fact that he could temporarily suspend his sense of humour to the point of being prepared to accept a knighthood. His 'Ballade Tragique in Double Refrain' is set in 'A room in Windsor Castle' and is a dialogue between a Lady-in-Waiting and a Lord-in-Waiting.

> SHE: Slow pass the hours, ah, passing slow;
> My doom is worse than anything
> Conceived by Edgar Allan Poe
> The Queen is duller than the King.
>
> HE: Lady, your mind is wandering,
> You babble what you do not mean;
> Remember to your heartening,
> The King is duller than the Queen.

Bearded, neat, five foot six inches in height, a naval officer and a countryman, King George V was within a few weeks of his forty-fifth birthday when he acceded to the throne in 1910. He would remain on the throne for a quarter of a century, during which he and his household changed hardly at all, and the world changed utterly. His chief preoccupations were shooting, when the season allowed it, his stamp collection, and clothes and uniforms. His one sartorial eccentricity was to wear his trousers pressed sideways, with no crease at the front. Otherwise he dressed like an Edwardian country gentleman – for formal occasions, a tall silk hat and a frock-coat; for race meetings or the Chelsea Flower Show, a well-cut brown or grey suit and a curly bowler hat. For shooting he often wore a Homburg, as had his father. But no one could have been less like King Edward.

George V was the reverse of a sensualist. He was socially shy and awkward. Like Queen Victoria, and like both his sons Edward VIII and George VI, he had uncontrollable temper tantrums. 'Stupid dog!' he unconvincingly exclaimed when he himself had farted, kicking out at the animal which, being unfortunately made of china, smashed to smithereens.

'Inquiries are being made as to whether Your Majesty is going to wear a tall hat at Epsom today,' wrote an equerry. At the bottom of the page the king wrote, 'Who are the damned fools? A tall hat is always worn at this meeting at Epsom.'[2] When a journalist asked him if it was true that Princess Margaret of Connaught was engaged to the crown prince of Sweden he replied: 'Young man, I regret to find that you are ignorant of the very alphabet of your calling. Members of royal houses are *not* engaged. They are betrothed. In similar manner we speak of the conjunction of elephants and the copulation of mice.'[3] When a footman, bringing him early morning tea, tripped and dropped the tray he heard a voice from the bed say: 'That's right, smash up the whole bloody Palace.'

The court, with its unvarying rituals, was hedged about with a discretion which was obsessional. Anyone who 'revealed' to an outsider talk with the king or queen was banished. Sir Philip Hunloke, the king's sailing master, confided to colleagues: 'There is a blackbird on the lawn. But for God's sake don't quote me.'[4]

The king's wife, known as Queen Mary, had been Princess Mary of Teck. King George, together with her intimate family, always called her May. Because of her ramrod-straight back and her habit of wearing a toque she appeared to tower over her husband, though they were in fact of identical height. She had a peripatetic childhood, divided between Kensington Palace, where her parents were sometimes allowed an apartment, and a variety of German dukedoms and principalities — Rumpenheim, Strelitz and Reinshal. Her mother was the grotesquely obese Princess Mary Adelaide, daughter of Adolphus, Duke of Cambridge, and Augusta, Princess of Hesse, and wife of Prince Franz of Teck. Princess Mary Adelaide was so large that she required two chairs if sitting out a dance. Her ample clothes usually contained a packet or two of Abernethy biscuits, of which she was a devotee.

Queen Mary's innumerable German relations were nearly all redundant royalties, with mixed nationality. Typical in that respect was her mother's sister, the Grand Duchess of Mecklenburg-Strelitz, who was in some ways closer to May in girlhood than her own mother. The Grand Duchess's life spanned five reigns, from George IV, whom she could remember at Windsor, to George V. She imparted her implacable Toryism to May. She always wore a primrose on the day of Disraeli's death and loathed Gladstone. ('How is it possible people can still be taken in by that wicked madman!') By the time she died, in Strelitz in 1916, Britain and Germany had been at war for two years. The last word she uttered was 'May'.[5]

Queen Mary brought to marriage with her cousin an acute consciousness of how vulnerable royalty was in a changing world – a belief shared
with the old Grand Duchess of Strelitz that 'people delight in a *monde
réversé*'.[6] It is difficult to exaggerate the extent to which the king and
queen of England at a moment in history when many believe the British
Empire was at the height of its power were insecure. They could always
hear the rattle of tumbrils over cobblestones.

Their way of life was simple by comparison with George's sybaritic
father. When Edward VII died, George and his wife allowed old Queen
Alexandra to continue to live in the big house at Sandringham. George
V and Queen Mary much preferred York Cottage on the Sandringham
estate. 'It was,' wrote the king's official biographer, 'and remains a glum
little villa, encompassed by thickets of laurel and rhododendron . . . The
rooms inside, with their fumed oak surrounds, their white overmantels
framing oval mirrors, their Doulton tiles and stained glass fanlights, are
indistinguishable from those of any Surbiton or Upper Norwood home.'
The king bought his furniture from Heal's in Tottenham Court Road.
From his unpretentious cottage, he managed the large Sandringham
estates, while continuing his work as a constitutional monarch, and
Emperor of India.

Sophisticates could sneer at the royal family, but there was a certain
beauty in their modest ways. On 18 April 1912, for example, at St Mary
Magdalene's church, Sandringham, the future George VI – then the Duke
of York, and always known in the family as Bertie – was confirmed by
the Rt Reverend Bishop Boyd Carpenter. The hymns were (from *Hymns
Ancient and Modern*) number 349 – 'My God, Accept my Heart this
Day'; number 280 – 'Thine for Ever!'; and number 27 – 'O Jesus I have
Promised'. Two years later, while serving aboard HMS *Collingwood*, 1st
Battle Squadron, and signing himself 'your most sincere friend Albert',
the young Bertie wrote to the bishop: 'It is just two years ago to-morrow
that you confirmed me in the small church at Sandringham. I have always
remembered that day as one on which I took a great step in life. I took
the Holy Sacrament on Easter Day alone with my father and mother, my
eldest brother and my sister. It was so very nice having a small service
quite alone, only the family.'[7]

When Bertie's gorgeous cousin, Victoria Louise, was confirmed as a
Lutheran in Berlin in 1909, her father the Kaiser marked the occasion by
making her Colonel-in-Chief of the Death's Head Hussars. When she
appeared for the first time in uniform, looking both powerful and erotic,
her father proudly declared that she could ride at the head of the first
regiment that invaded England.[8]

The dullness, or the modesty, of the English monarchy during the reign of George V was surely one of the ingredients not merely in its own survival but in the comparative political stability of Britain in the years 1910–1936, compared that is to say with the other nations of Europe. Lenin formed the central question of politics, but it is one which everyone asks who wishes to exercise power: Who? Whom? Who does what to whom? Who persuades, or frightens, or encourages the ever-growing masses to accept government, supervision, laws? Where does power lie? With control of money? With land-ownership? With ancient privilege or new brute force? The Whig, or Liberal aristocratic answers to these questions had always involved, since 1832, sleight of hand. The landed classes and the aristocracy wished to continue to exercise power and very broadly, during the nineteenth century, they continued to do so. Nearly all Queen Victoria's prime ministers were landed aristocrats, and the three who were not – Peel, Gladstone and Disraeli – all aspired to belong to, and mix with, the landed classes. With the coming of a new plutocracy, wealth based on finance, on manufacturing, not on land ownership, the importance of the old aristocracy was diminished, and with it, perhaps, that of the Crown.

Queen Mary, born in 1867, grew up with the complaints of her German relations echoing in her childish ears that the newly formed Prussian Empire had deprived them all – grand dukes, kings and princes – of power. 'Alas!' her grandmother the Duchess of Cambridge would exclaim. 'All the dearest countries that my heart loved best have been *stolen* (I can't give it another name) . . . Hanover, which is the cradle of our English family, Hesse is mine and Nassau was my dearest own mother's; so you may judge of my feelings at the moment; that is the moment of Germany becoming one nation.'9 In new Germany, moreover, there was an absolute division between the broadly Liberal and leftist Reichstag, Parliament, and the Junkers, the supporters of royal autocracy. It had required the political skill of Bismarck to hold together the warring factions of the newly created country, Germany. In Russia, the stubborn way in which Tsar Nicholas II, George V's cousin, held on to autocracy had led to the revolution of 1905, since when, as the hours ticked past, it remained to be seen whether Nicholas would learn how to become a constitutional monarch. As the examples of Germany and Russia show, it is by no means the case that countries who throw off the supposedly outdated trappings of monarchy and aristocracy move seamlessly into eras of political contentment.

George V's reign began with a constitutional crisis in which deep questions were being asked about how Britain was governed. The House of Lords had precipitated the crisis by rejecting Lloyd George's 1909 budget. Asquith, the prime minister, called an election, and a Parliament Bill was introduced which effectively removed the Lords' right to veto Commons measures either if the matters discussed were 'Money Bills', or if a bill had been passed three times by the lower house. Before this bill could become law, Edward VII died, and one of George V's first tasks was to summon Tories and Liberals together to agree the way forward. The Constitutional Conference[10] broke up with nothing resolved, but the Parliament Act passed eventually into law.

On the other hand, Lord Curzon could tell the electors of Oldham, a largely working-class northern constituency, that the House of Lords represented 'the permanent sentiment and temper of the English people'; 170 members of the House of Lords had previously served in the Commons, 200 in the army or the navy, 70 had seen service in South Africa. If there were no working men in the Lords – though he would not be averse to seeing them there – there were no great generals or ex-colonial governors in the Commons. Two hundred and twenty-five Liberal and 181 Conservative peers had been created since 1831. Ernest Renan had said that all civilizations had been the work of aristocracies. Curzon also pointed out that the movement to reform working conditions in the factories and to improve labour conditions had originated in the Lords. He argued that an unfettered second chamber would be dangerous.[11]

Curzon's Oldham speech is mentioned only to be dismissed by Roy Jenkins in his book on the constitutional crisis, *Mr Balfour's Poodle*,[12] written in 1954. But half a century would pass, after Jenkins published his book, before the legislative rights of hereditary peers were removed. Throughout the period of the present book, the first half of the twentieth century, Britain was at least partially governed by an aristocracy, and the Commons continued to be, as they are today, representative of geographical areas rather than political interest groups solely: that is people elected members for their own area to represent every person in the constituency regardless of their political persuasion. Though they took the party 'whip', MPs were the Honourable Member for such and such a place, *not*, as in parliaments where seats are allotted to party factions, the Socialist or the Liberal or the Conservative stooge.

The constitutional crisis was averted. The Parliament Act was passed in 1911. It had rocked the boat, but the monarchy and the House of Lords remained in place. Power, however, had shifted. Liberal optimists hoped and supposed that, because the power of the peers had been curtailed, that of the Commons had been strengthened. This is not how things work. 'As the English kingship became in the nineteenth century, so parliament's will became in the twentieth, a solemn and empty pageantry. As then sceptre and crown, so now people's rights are paraded for the multitude, and all the more punctiliously the less they really signify.'[13] The Commons might have become stronger than the Lords, but both were weakened. Real power was elsewhere, in industry, commerce, the Press.

The rank smell of corruption began to rise from a dying body politic. One obvious symptom was that titles and peerages were, when not blatantly for sale, then available to those with the money. Curzon saw that the demand for 'social preferment' on the part of the upstart plutocracy was 'insatiable'. One plutocrat offered the bishop of Peterborough £50,000 for his diocesan funds if he could obtain a baronetcy for the donor. Another offered to build a sea-wall at Cromer round Lord Suffield's estate in exchange for a peerage.[14] Mr Arthur du Cross, a Conservative MP, settled the debts of Lady Warwick – a talkative ex-mistress of Edward VII – and was rewarded with a baronetcy in 1916. William Waldorf Astor, the American millionaire, showed that if you had the dollars, no one would stand in the way of your joining the aristocracy. He bought huge houses in London and the country, he bought a newspaper, he was elected to Parliament. In 1911 he went to a fancy-dress ball dressed in peer's robes. He gave $100,000 to the Boer War effort, $250,000 to the universities of Oxford and Cambridge, $275,000 to hospitals. He achieved his barony in 1916. By the time Lloyd George was a triumphant warlord and prime minister, there was a recognized tariff: £10,000 for a knighthood, £30,000 for a baronetcy, and £50,000 upwards for a peerage. As Lloyd George's election funds dwindled in 1921–2 creations reached higher and higher levels, with 26 peerages, 74 baronetcies and 214 knighthoods.[15] So simple and so easily satisfied is snobbery as an appetite that within a very few years no one in England much notices whether a family is of old or new nobility. Romantic snobbery such as that of Proust's Baron de Charlus, caring about whether a family can trace itself back to Charlemagne, is a rarity. Most satisfy themselves with the thrill of a 'handle' to their names.

> For the hoary social curse
> Grows hoarier and hoarier,
> And it stinks a trifle worse
> Than in the reign of Queen Victoria.[16]

So wrote Hilaire Belloc, who left the Commons after the first, not bothering to contest the second, election of 1910. Belloc and his friend Cecil Chesterton, brother of G.K., were the journalists who did the most to expose the Marconi scandal which was another manifestation of political corruption.

In March 1912 the Postmaster General, Herbert Samuel, provisionally accepted a tender from the English Marconi Company for the construction of a chain of wireless stations across the Empire. The managing director of the English Marconi Company was Godfrey Isaacs, who was the brother of the Attorney General, Sir Rufus Isaacs. Godfrey Isaacs decided to expand the American Marconi Company – of which he was also managing director – and he floated a new issue of shares on the British market on 18 April 1912. Two of his brothers bought a block of new shares – his brother Harry bought 56,000 – nine days before public flotation. Rufus bought 10,000 shares at £2 a share and sold 1,000 to Lloyd George – Chancellor of the Exchequer – and 1,000 to the Liberal chief whip, the Master of Elibank. On 18 April the new issue was floated. The price of the shares bounced to £4, and all three ministers sold their shares at a handsome profit.

Cecil Chesterton and Belloc exposed the scandal – what would today be illegal insider trading – in their small-circulation magazine *The Eye Witness*. Their case was spoilt by minor inaccuracy and by ill-concealed anti-Semitism. This stung Samuel and Godfrey Isaacs to sue a French newspaper, *Le Matin*, which had repeated the supposed libels. On 11 October Samuel moved in the Commons to appoint a select committee to investigate the Marconi story. Both Rufus Isaacs and Lloyd George made statements to the House which were economical with the truth, since when they disclaimed any dealing in shares of 'the Marconi company' they could claim to have been speaking only of the *English* company.[17]

Lord Robert Cecil was almost the only member of the select committee to ask properly searching questions. 'The life of the nation,' he said, 'is bound up with our respect for our public men and their personal integrity. That must be preserved and unless it is, we are done for absolutely.'[18] In the event, the committee divided along party lines and the Liberals closed ranks. They were far too worried by the state of Ireland, by the instability caused by industrial unrest and by the Suffragettes, to allow themselves to be brought down by a corruption scandal. No doubt by the standard of corruption in other lands and at other periods, the British political scene in 1912 was only minimally corrupt. But there was a definite feeling of putrescence in the atmosphere, and, that very dangerous political thing, a sense of Parliament being an all-male club which did not represent the political interests or aspirations of growing masses of the population.

As we have already observed, strikes in the South Wales mining industry had been broken up by troops. In July 1910 there had been a four-day rail strike in Newcastle. There were strikes over a similar period in the Lancashire cotton industry, and among boilermakers in the northeast.

Iron workers in the vital shipping industry stayed out for fourteen weeks – crippling to the poor families of the workers, but desperately frightening to an established class which had convinced itself that it needed more and more ironclad battleships to maintain its supremacy over the seas, hence over the world. In June 1911 there were dock strikes in London, Liverpool and Manchester threatening to paralyse trade. These were followed in 1912 by more dock strikes, and by miners' strikes.[19]

It was by no means a time of stability, or general happiness. There is almost no truth in the cliché that 1914 brought to an end a seemingly endless, sunlit afternoon with Britain prosperous, peaceful, innocent. The strikes and industrial unrest heralded unease of a proportion unseen since 1848.

Immigration into Britain has always caused unease to the indigenous population, and the disturbed situation of Russia in particular had driven large numbers of refugees from that land and its satellites, Poland, Latvia, Lithuania. Many were Jews. Some, as is reflected in such fiction as Conrad's *Secret Agent* or G. K. Chesterton's *The Man Who Was Thursday*, belonged to dissident political sects. The customs at Dover, according to one political report, stopped one Russian and found forty-seven automatic pistols and nearly 5,000 rounds of ammunition. In 1907 a Social Democratic congress was held at the Brotherhood Church in Whitechapel. Addressed by Lenin, the three hundred or so delegates included Trotsky, Voroshilov (a future Soviet field marshal), Maxim Litvinov (a future Soviet ambassador) and Maxim Gorky. Hindsight would surely vindicate the suspicions of police and Home Office that some fairly dangerous characters were there assembled, even if you did not add that one of the minor delegates at the congress, from Georgia, was Joseph Vissarionovich Dzhugashvili, later known as Stalin. There was every reason for the authorities to be very wary indeed.

In 1909 two anarchists were involved with the murder of a policeman in Tottenham after an attempted ambush of the weekly wages arriving from the bank at Schurmann's rubber factory.[20] The two men fired over 400 rounds of ammunition and as well as two dead – a policeman and one of the criminals who shot himself – twenty-one were injured. 'Who are these fiends in human shape, who do not hesitate to turn their weapons on little boys and harmless women?' asked the *Daily Mirror*. 'The answer is: they are foreign Anarchists, men who have been expelled from Russia for their crimes, whose political creed and religion is that human life is of no value at all.'

Of course, most refugees came not as aggressors, but in flight from dreadful state brutality in Tsarist Russia. But there was enough truth in the *Daily Mirror*'s words to make them frightening. Dostoevsky's prophecy of social mayhem in *The Devils*, when just such an anarchist, nihilist cell, inspired by a charismatic, heartless leader, terrorizes a provincial Russian town, had been brought to the streets of London. Special Branch believed that the organizer of the Tottenham Outrages was a young Latvian named Jacob Fogel. His real name was Christian Jalmish, and he had helped a breakout of prisoners from Riga Central Prison in 1905 in which fifty-two armed fighters of the Latvian Social Democratic Workers Party escaped. They included one Peter Piatkov ('Peter the Painter'), who, together with some of his Latvian friends, was interrupted by police in January 1911 trying to tunnel into a jeweller's shop in Houndsditch, East London. There were rumours in the East End among the Russian and Latvian exiles that this shop in a very mean little slum-street was concealing the Tsarist Crown Jewels. The anarchists needed funds, and that was their motive for the burglary. When the police caught them in the act of burgling the shop, they opened fire and killed Sergeant Robert Bentley, as well as another officer, Sergeant Charles Tucker. When P.C. Choate wrestled one of the criminals – Gardstein – for his gun, he too was shot, many times, and eventually killed.[21] The criminals then retreated up the tunnel to their adjoining quarters in 100 Sidney Street, Mile End Road, and the house was soon under police siege. Unable to reach the criminals with their revolvers, the police sent for reinforcements from the Scots Guards in the Tower.[22]

This required the authority of the Home Secretary, Winston Churchill. He gave it. In addition he ordered up the Horse Artillery from St John's Wood Barracks, though they were not in the event required, and then, very characteristically, he hastened to the scene of the sieges, where bullets were flying in and out of the windows. The anarchists set fire to themselves in the house, and when it had been gutted by fire three corpses were found in the ruin, one of whom had been shot, the other two asphyxiated.

Churchill had gone down to witness the scene at first hand partly because he was excited by the whiff of grapeshot and partly because he was momentarily penitent at having attacked what he conceived as a mean-spirited Tory immigration law, the Aliens Bill of 1904. The king's Private Secretary was not slow to inform Churchill of His Majesty's hopes 'that these outrages by foreigners will lead you to consider whether the Aliens Act could not be amended so as to prevent London from being infested with men and women whose presence would not be tolerated in any other country'. Churchill felt there was a case for tightening the laws against aliens. One of his staunchest allies, however, the backbench radical Josiah Wedgwood, whose namesake and forebear had struck the anti-slavery medallion AM I NOT A MAN AND A BROTHER? in their

Staffordshire pottery, wrote memorably to Churchill: 'It is fatally easy to justify them [i.e. draconian anti-terrorist laws] but they lower the character of a whole nation. You know as well as I do that human life does not matter a rap in comparison with the death of ideas and the betrayal of English traditions. Rebelling against civilisation and society will go on anyhow and this is only a new form of the disease of '48; so let us have English rule not Bourbon.' In spite of these wise words Churchill drafted the outlines of the Aliens Act of 1911 which attempted to combat terrorism by forbidding aliens to carry firearms.[23]

As in the case of twenty-first-century paranoia against terrorism, some of the fears were justified – desperadoes with guns really were killing policemen – and some of the fears were expressions of unease about something else. Those who are confident in the idea of their own country, who truly believe in it and its values, do not believe that they can be brought down by a few fanatics with guns. Churchill at Sidney Street must have wondered as Conrad wondered when he wrote *The Secret Agent* and *Under Western Eyes* whether the values or institutions of the West really were that strong. Christianity, for Churchill's generation, was a thing of the past. He certainly did not believe in it.[24] As the Parliament Act made clear, you could remove power from the Lords at a stroke. (Churchill favoured at this date the total abolition of the House of Lords.[25]) Even before the collapse of the Prussian, Austrian and Russian monarchies at the end of the First World War, there were signs of change in the air. Portugal became a republic in 1910, and between 1901 and 1914 at least three monarchs and a number of Russian grand dukes were assassinated. Churchill had enough historical sense to know that it took very little to unseat a monarchy. And what would be left? Dear old Jos Wedgwood's 'ideas and English traditions'. What if these did not amount to very much against the more articulate forces of Marxism, or against nationalist expansionism, or anarchism, or Prussian militarism, or America?

There was a palpable sense in the early years of George V's reign that, prosperous and powerful as Britain was, all was not as it had been. The image of shipwreck came to mind, and in April 1912 there occurred one of those catastrophic events which possess, almost as soon as they happen, the qualities of a defining myth – what in the early twenty-first century could be seen as a 9/11 moment. It was an essential part of this myth, of the wreck of a luxury liner, that it was on its way to the United States of America.

A myth is a story by which people define themselves. No less than the peoples of pre-literate or semi-literate ages, the peoples of the Western world in the twentieth century projected myths about themselves in order to place themselves in the universe, to make sense of their predicament. The sinking of the RMS *Titanic* on its maiden voyage almost instantaneously took on a mythic dimension.[26] For example, one of the things which 'everyone' knows about the *Titanic* is that it was known as 'the unsinkable ship'. In his seminal book about the disaster, *A Night to Remember*, made into a film by the J. Arthur Rank Organisation in 1958, with Kenneth More, Walter Lord stated: 'The *Titanic* was unsinkable. Everybody said so.'[27] But when did everyone say so? Not *before* the voyage, as you might expect: but *after it*. It is true that in 1911 the small-circulation trade publication *The Shipbuilder*, describing the watertight doors that divided the bulkheads in the liner, stated that the capacity of the captain to close the doors by flicking an electric switch made 'the vessel practically unsinkable'.[28] Such language was not, however, used in any of the promotional literature to advertise the maiden voyage, nor by any of what we could call the journalistic hype beforehand. When Harland and Wolff, the Belfast shipbuilders, were commissioned to build the luxury liner for the Liverpool-based White Star Company it was recognized that to make the operation lucrative they would need to make weekly transatlantic crossings. This would require three ships of identical speed and capacity to provide a reliable 'ferry' service, one at each end and one on stand-by. The first two to be built were the *Olympic* and the *Titanic*, with the *Gigantic* ordered.

The *Olympic* and the *Titanic* were the biggest ships ever built. The White Star publicists put out brochures of one of the liners up-ended so that potential voyagers could see it outsoaring in height Cologne Cathedral, St Peter's in Rome, the Great Pyramid of Giza and even the New Woolworth Building, NYC.[29] At over 46,000 tons gross they were considerably larger than the existing record-holders, the liners *Lusitania* and *Mauretania*, which weighed in at a little less than 32,000 tons. The *Olympic* was launched on 20 October 1910, the *Titanic* on 31 May 1911. The two ships were identical in construction, with exactly similar hulls, construction and propulsion, and the advertising was for both ships – 'OLYMPIC and TITANIC'. Only an obsessive expert could spot differences between the first-class promenades on A-deck in the two ships. Indeed, in the sale catalogue for *Titanic* memorabilia at Christie's in 1992 the cover uses an illustration of the *Olympic*. The ships were built by the same yard, owned by the same company and captained on their maiden voyages by the same man, Captain Edward John Smith. Of the two, however, only the *Titanic* is remembered as the 'unsinkable' ship. The *Olympic* which did not in fact sink, and which stayed afloat until 1937, winning the sobriquet 'Old Reliable', until it was scrapped in Scotland, was never described as 'unsinkable'.

It was the collision of the *Titanic* with an iceberg during the night of 14–15 April 1912 which introduced the word unsinkable into the popular vocabulary and began the process of myth-making. On the morning of Monday 15 April, the vice-president of the White Star Line in New York, Philip A. S. Franklin, announced: 'We place absolute confidence in the *Titanic*. We believe the boat is unsinkable.' By then, the ship had sunk: 1,490 passengers were dead and the 711 survivors were bobbing about despondently in the icy waters of the North Atlantic. 'Manager of the Line Insisted *Titanic* was Unsinkable Even After She Had Gone Down' declared a sub-headline in the *New York Times*. 'Mr Franklin called her unsinkable' – the qualifier 'practically' has been lost – 'and last night when he knew at last that the pride of his line was beneath the ocean he could not seem to comprehend that the steamer had sunk. "I thought her unsinkable", he declared, "and I based by [*sic*] opinion on the best expert advice. I do not understand it."'[30]

The gigantic floating palace, hubristic in its self-image, cruising at speed towards disaster, was an obvious emblem of Europe on the edge of self-destruction. For Marxists, the shipwreck seemed a repulsive opportunity on behalf of the capitalist press to lament the death of the rich.

'Among the dead were millionaires,' wrote 'Virtus' in the Italian language Communist paper *La Fiaccola* (The Torch, Buffalo, NY), 'and our readers have been able to read in other papers long articles and sensational stories about the 200 rich people who with 1,400 poor, met their deaths, as if the heroism and the grief of the 1st, 2nd and 3rd classes unfolded in the same circumstances!' *La Fiaccola* shone its torch-rays on the fact that the 700 crew died like martyrs and went on to lament the deaths of 500,000 in American factories each year, deaths which went largely unreported.[31] The *Denver Post* was more biblical, more elemental, and saw the sea claiming rich and poor, famous and obscure figures alike. John Jacob Astor, worth two hundred million dollars: he 'would give all he possesses for the place of that woman and child in the lifeboat'.[32] Many[33] saw it as a Judgement, though quite what the Judgement signified was a trifle vague. 'The sixteen hundred who went down were typical of mankind . . .' opined the *Christian Century*. 'Manhood triumphed when the *Titanic* sank.'[34] George Bernard Shaw stirred up controversy by refusing to believe in the heroic tales of the Night to Remember. He pointed out that whereas pious newspapers claimed that the band played 'Nearer My God to Thee' as the ship sank, it had actually played popular Ragtime tunes to allay panic. Further, vital information about the disaster was withheld from passengers, especially those travelling 3rd class, and their supposedly unruly behaviour had been exaggerated so as to highlight the heroic and gentlemanlike behaviour of the richer passengers and the officers.[35]

To many, GBS's compulsion to debunk was in the lowest degree distasteful. Had not Benjamin Guggenheim, the American multi-millionaire, gone back to his cabin to change into evening dress and said to an amazed steward: 'If we have to die we will die like gentlemen'?

Arthur Conan Doyle[36] wrote to the *Daily News* to denounce Shaw's iconoclasm, furious at the implication that rich or pushing men found their way into the lifeboats, and that heroism was not displayed by the officers and their class. The conservative Doyle and the iconoclastically socialist Shaw took opposing views of the reporting of the *Titanic* disaster because they took radically different views of the nature of society. For one man, who was destined to become a spiritualist and who in later life was tricked into believing that some children had managed to photograph fairies, the disaster was heroic, the gentlemen behaved like gents, the officers like officers, while the poor piously praised their God. For Shaw the incident exemplified the unfairness of the social divide and the collaborative need shared by popular newspapers and their readership to invent consoling versions of intolerable truths.

At the Royal Opera House Covent Garden at a Titanic Disaster Fund Matinée, Thomas Hardy, the old Victorian agonistic pessimist, took the stage on 14 May 1912, the very day of Shaw's *Daily News* article, to read his interpretation of events, 'The Convergence of the Twain'. Hardy's poem saw it as a fatalistic moment. Now the ship, 'and the Pride of Life that planned her', lay at the bottom of the ocean. Even as the ship was being built, however:

> In stature grace, and hue,
> In shadowy silent distance grew the Iceberg too.

> Till the Spinner of the Years
> Said 'Now!' And each one hears,
> And consummation comes, and jars two hemispheres.[37]

Here is the true prophetic note, from the poet.

Alongside the arms race between the Great Powers, and the desire for the British and the Germans to have more and bigger battleships than one another, European and American companies vied with one another for larger, faster and speedier ocean liners. The British led the field with 17 vessels of 12,000 tons and upwards in June 1910 as against 14 Germans, but the German boats – the *George Washington*, *Kaiser Auguste Viktoria*, *Cleveland*, *Kaiser Wilhelm der Grosse* and others – were magnificent, luxurious boats.[38] You could say that the rivalry was one of the things which caused the disaster on the *Titanic*. Shaw scornfully wrote: 'the one thing positively known was that Captain Smith had lost his ship by deliberately and knowingly steaming into an ice field at the highest speed he had coal for'.[39] You could certainly see the *Titanic* as the very embodiment of the enterprise and ambition which created it. The entrepreneurial ambition of a Liverpool shipping company called on the combined skill of Scottish engineering – Harland – and Jewish finance – Wolff – to make a floating emblem of the Edwardian class structure. Everyone knew, didn't they – surely they did – that the British Empire was one on which the sun would never set? It was an unsinkable vessel . . . wasn't it? At its summit were gentlemen and officers who, even though they kept company with extravagant millionaires and vulgarian financiers, would behave like heroes – wouldn't they? When disaster struck? Wouldn't they? And if the unthinkable happened the disaster would not be accompanied, would it, by the airs of Ragtime and Dixie, but by the dignified melancholy of the old hymn, 'Nearer My God to Thee'?

Generations of American children have sung the song round campfires:

> O they sailed from England and were almost to the shore,
> When the rich refused to associate with the poor,
> So they put them down below, where they were the first to go.
> It was sad when that great ship went down.
> It was sad, it was sad,
> It was sad when that great ship went down.
> Husbands and wives, little children lost their lives –
> It was sad when that great ship went down.[40]

For those attentive enough to recognize it, Europe, and certainly Britain, had reached a crisis in its destiny. Something was about to change, or had changed, for ever. D. H. Lawrence's greatest novel, *The Rainbow*, which he was writing as the world sleep-walked into the most destructive war in its history, is full of this sense of loss, of elegy. So are Lawrence's letters which must rank among the greatest ever written in English. To his friend Lady Cynthia Asquith he wrote from an Oxfordshire manor house where he was staying in November 1915:

> When I drive across this country, with the autumn falling and rustling to pieces, I am so sad, for my country, for this great wave of civilisation, 200 years, which is now collapsing, that it is hard to live. So much beauty and pathos of old things passing away and no new things coming: this house of the Ottolines* – It is England – my God, it

---

* Ottoline and Philip Morrell lived at Garsington Manor, Oxfordshire.

breaks my soul – this England, these shafted windows, the elm-trees, the blue distance – the past, the great past, crumbling down, breaking down, not under the force of the coming buds, but under the weight of many exhausted, lovely yellow leaves, that drift over the lawn and over the pond, like the soldiers, passing away, into winter and the darkness of winter – no, I can't bear it. For the winter stretches ahead, where all vision is lost and all memory dies out.[41]

9

An Asiatic Power

Nearly all general histories of the First World War, especially if directed to British, American, French or German readers, concentrate upon the mass slaughter of young men in the trench warfare of the Western Front. Given the numbers who died, and the sufferings all combatants endured, this is hardly surprising; but it can make a puzzling war – just what did they think they were doing, committing mass murder in the mud *for four years*? Shift the geographical focus, and the war is perhaps easier to place in some kind of perspective.

It is possible that we shall fail to understand the First World War, and its development, if we forget Disraeli's quip that Britain was an Asiatic rather than a European power. George V was the first, and last, king-emperor of India to visit his Eastern Empire as monarch. The Delhi Durbar which saluted the beginning of his reign even outsoared the magnificence of that ceremony a decade earlier when Lord Curzon and the daughter of a Chicago department store-owner had wobbled into Delhi on the back of an elephant. The new king entered the city on a small brown horse in a field marshal's uniform and a sun helmet. George V had proposed to crown himself as the central act of the Durbar, but the Archbishop of Canterbury had vetoed any such Napoleonic gesture. In the event, he arrived wearing a crown, but since the Imperial Crown in London was far too heavy to be worn for three hours of a ceremony in blazing heat, they ordered a new lighter model from Garrard's, the Crown Jeweller, at a cost of £60,000, borne not by the royal family itself, still less by the British tax payer, but by the people of India. After the imperial visit, the crown was moved back to London, where it has been preserved ever since in the jewel house in the Tower of London. If ever there was a case for some London exhibit being returned to its rightful owners, it is surely not the Parthenon Marbles, for whose purchase Lord Elgin ruined himself, but the Indian crown jewels, for which no Britisher, royal or commoner, paid so much as one penny.

George V, unlike his father, did not feel at home in Europe. The Delhi Durbar, where a crowd of 100,000 had watched him being crowned, was a parable of how he, and so many of the governing class, saw his country as a great Asiatic Empire, having very little to do with his German cousins and their quarrels with the French. Flown with the success of the Durbar, George wanted to go the following year to South Africa, but this his

Cabinet refused on rather devastating grounds. 'We decided,' wrote the financial secretary to the Treasury, Sir Charles Hobhouse, 'he had much better stay at home, and not teach people how easily the machine worked without a King.'[2] But George V had returned from Delhi with a new confidence, unseen in his character before, and a new idea of himself as king-emperor. His wife, Queen Mary, felt almost drunk with it – 'I am still under the influence of the Imperialism it [the Durbar] inspired,' she wrote.[3]

Queen Mary was much more of a Continental European than her husband, and the First World War was a deep personal tragedy, separating her from her many relations. Her aunt, Augusta Caroline, Grand Duchess of Mecklenburg-Strelitz, could send her poignant message to King George V just before she died in her pine-girt Schloss in 1916: 'Tell the King it is a stout old English heart that is ceasing to beat!'[4] But she was an amazing survival, a granddaughter of George III who was able to advise her niece May of Teck on etiquette remembered from the court of Queen Adelaide. Her stout old English heart had begun to beat in Hanover, her birthplace, and she lived on German soil for most of her life. When she became the Grand Duchess, the alliance between Britain and the German duchies, kingdoms and principalities seemed natural. Only a few years before her birth, all Britons had rejoiced at the prospect of a Prussian army racing through Belgium to help Wellington defeat the French at Waterloo. (About a third of Wellington's own army were Germans, Hanoverians.) The Continental disruptions, leading eventually to war, were felt by no family so sharply as by the extended family of the king and queen. Perhaps this played its part in their choosing to concentrate so firmly on Britain's imperial rather than her European role. But perhaps in his way the new king had more wisdom than his father, or than the politicians? Belgium, France, Holland, Germany, Italy, were European countries with colonies in different parts of the world. Britain actually was an Asiatic power. Yet this was a power which was destined not to last. Indian nationalism, and the tensions within Indian society, between different castes, religions and regions, were phenomena from which the king could blind himself while he entered Delhi on his charger. But only a week after the Durbar, when the viceroy, Lord Hardinge, made a state entry into the new capital, a bomb was thrown at his elephant, seriously wounding the viceroy himself and killing his attendant.[5]

The Delhi Durbar 'marked perhaps the peak of British authority in India'.[6] It was also the occasion when three important administrative measures were introduced. The first was the raising of Bengal to the state of a province, with its own governor. The second was the undoing of the partition of Bengal. The third – 'one of the few secrets successfully kept in modern India'[7] – was the transfer of the capital from Calcutta to Delhi.

The coming of the First World War was to change India radically and deeply. As many as one-third of all the British forces in France in autumn 1914 were from India – Indian army troops or British army personnel drawn from Indian garrisons. The force used to enter Basra in November 1915, in an attempt to absorb Mesopotamia into the Raj, was Indian.[8] India provided a 'barrack in the Eastern seas'. The Indian army became a reserve army which could be redeployed in theatres as various as East Africa, Egypt and Palestine, as well, of course, as the Western Front.[9] Many of these troop movements were resisted by the Liberal viceroy, Lord Hardinge, whose own perceptions of Britain, India and their imperial relationships had been surprisingly expressed in November 1913, when he spoke up in a distinctly Gandhian voice for the beleaguered Indians in South Africa. He expressed 'the sympathy of India, deep and burning, and not only of Indians, but of all lovers of India like myself, for their compatriots in South Africa in their resistance to invidious and unjust laws'.[10]

Such words caused dismay in Britain, but they are a good example of the paradoxical quality of so much of the British attitude to India, where the desire to own and to dominate, violently apparent in some administrators and areas, was always balanced by a profound sympathy for India, its peoples and traditions. This was partly the sense, which breathes through all Kipling's work, for example, that Indian culture and civilization was older and in some ways more beautiful than the combination of Benthamism and Protestantism which the Raj had brought to Asia. It was partly the more brutal politico-economic consciousness that Curzon had been right in his analysis: without India, Britain would cease to be a first-rate, and become instantaneously a third-rate world power. The Delhi Durbar marked the high point of the Raj's strength. Within only three years, the Raj was confronted with the greatest drain on resources in its history. In the wake of economic hardship – India paid £146 million towards the war and suffered inflation and shortages in consequence – that strength waned. With the developing imperial recognition of the legitimacy of Indian political aspirations came the inevitable dissolution of the Raj, and with it the British Empire.[11]

The First World War was, therefore, a disaster as far as it concerned the British Raj. But to view things from another angle, it was British anxiety for the strength and preservation of the Raj – and with it British status as the supreme world superpower – which led to Britain's conduct of the war in the West, and in the Near East.

If one remembers all the time, as no British statesman in 1914 could forget, the primal importance of India and the Eastern Empire in the story, then the strategic centrality of Turkey will become plain. Britain's dominance of the East depended upon ease of access. She possessed Gibraltar and the Suez Canal, two conduits of the Mediterranean. So long as the Ottoman Empire remained, as it was known in the Victorian era, the 'sick man of Europe', the other powers could sniff around it hungrily hoping for economic, material, political advantages. As far as this great Islamic Empire was concerned, its history since the late seventeenth century had been one of shrinkage. In 1683 it had exercised dominion over all the territories from Budapest in the west to Baghdad in the east, from the River Dnieper in the north to the bulk of North Africa – Tunisia, Tripoli, Libya, Egypt. In the Crimean War, the Russians had made attempts to possess Constantinople, the old Byzantine patriarchate and centre of Eastern Christendom. They had been repulsed by an alliance of France and Britain. In later years of the nineteenth century, the Ottoman dominion over the Balkans shrank. It lost Bosnia-Hercegovina, Macedonia, Bulgaria, Romania, which had been, in effect, self-governing since the Crimean War. The Austro-Hungarian Empire, another sick man of Europe, with an emperor who had been on the throne since 1848, wanted to gain from Ottoman losses but had to face up to the phenomenon of modern nationalism, with Serbs, Albanians, Croats, Bulgarians and others all wishing to have independent nation-states rather than be satellites to an empire.

In an atmosphere where small states can make a romantic appeal for nationhood, logic cannot deny the same dream to large states. And this really is the nub of the twentieth-century political tragedy. Poor little Serbia, poor little Ireland, poor little Palestine or would-be Judaea can win sympathy. Hindsight very often suggests their people enjoyed more peace and in practical day-to-day terms independence when they lived under the umbrella of an Imperium than when threatened by the rival nationalisms of big countries such as Germany or Turkey. For Turkey now becomes a word in international vocabulary. Hitherto, in postclassical vocabulary, a Turk had been a synonym for a lout – just as the abusive word 'Arab' had been used for Bedouins in the eastern provinces.[12] Now, in the early years of the twentieth century, the word Turkish was used in newspapers, and Europeans referred to the Ottoman Empire as 'Turkistan' or 'Turkey'.

In 1908, a coup d'état gave power to the 'Young Turks'. They allowed the old Sultan, Abdulhamit II, to reign until his death in 1909, but from then on, this junta of modernizers and nationalists took control. In the major cities of Turkey happy mobs crowded into the streets,[13] embracing and swearing eternal brotherhood – Jews, Arabs, Greeks, Serbs, Bulgars, Armenians, Turks. But if you have ceased to define your state merely in terms of imperial authority and territory controlled, how do you define a nation? Ethnicity and religious allegiance take on a significance which they lacked before.

The Armenians were the first major victims of that distinctively twentieth-century phenomenon: genocide. From the late nineteenth century, they had been forbidden to carry arms, and they had been taxed at a higher rate than other Ottoman citizens. They were hated because many of them were successful merchants and financiers with contacts outside the empire. Many Armenians lived beyond Mount Ararat in the Russian Empire. In 1895, Armenian revolutionaries had seized a bank in Istanbul and the retaliations had been terrible. As many as 300,000 Armenians perished according to Armenian sources. Under the Young Turks, the Armenians fared even worse than under Sultan Abdulhamit, and in 1915, when they were suspected of siding with the enemy, a Final Solution was perpetrated. Able-bodied Armenian males were drafted into labour battalions, and having built roads or railways, bludgeoned to death or shot. Women and children were herded into 'orphanages' which turned out to be deep pits in which they were buried alive beneath heaps of stones. Rape was widespread; Armenian women were disembowelled, and had their breasts cut off. Thousands of Armenians fled over the border into Russia.

Turkish historians still speak of these movements of peoples as necessary 'evacuations' into enemy territory. They concede that as many as 40,000 may have perished in their flight to Russia.[14] The American ambassador to Turkey, Henry Morgenthau, provided refuge for Armenians in the United States where this was possible and supported the Armenian claim that the scale of slaughter had been much more extensive: namely, that one and a half million Armenians, out of a total of three million, were killed by the Turks.[15]

This is Turkey, this is the 'sick man' with which the European powers wished to get involved. And this is the part of the story which so often gets tagged on to accounts of the Great War in Flanders and France. Having described the devastation of trench warfare, historians then turn their attentions to the Gallipoli campaign almost as an interlude in the main business of the war. A. J. P. Taylor could airily write: 'It is a mystery why most people, then and since, assumed that the fall of Constantinople would lead to the defeat of Germany ... Turkey might have been knocked out of the war, but this would have lessened the burden on Germany. An army would have had no light task to march from Constantinople to Central Europe ...'[16] and so on. This is to look at everything from a Western perspective, with its talk of marching from Constantinople to Europe. What had been painfully obvious at the time, and an absolutely key factor in Britain's decision to fight a potentially suicidal war with Germany, was not the difficulty of *marching* from the Ottoman capital to Central Europe. It was the ease, after the completion of a German railway through the middle of Turkey in 1911, of travelling by steam-powered transport all the way from Berlin to the Persian Gulf.

Britain, to recap what was said earlier, was secure in the possession of Gibraltar and the Suez Canal, the conduits of the Mediterranean which gave her access to her Indian Empire, her source and ground, as she saw it, for world power. Furthermore, access to the oilfields of Persia and Mesopotamia had now become essential. Churchill, in *The World Crisis*, wrote of the 'formidable decision . . . to change the foundation of our Navy from British coal to foreign oil', adding that as First Lord of the Admiralty, 'during the whole of 1913 I was subjected to an ever-growing difficulty about the oil supply'.[17] The new German railway put all that in jeopardy by short-circuting British command of the seas. 'It was felt in England that if, as Napoleon is said to have remarked, Antwerp in the hands of a great continental power was a pistol levelled at the English coast, Bagdad and the Persian Gulf in the hands of Germany (or any other strong power) would be a 42-centimetre gun pointed at India.'[18]

La Société Impériale Ottomane du Chemin de Fer de Bagdad, a German syndicate, launched its agreement with the Ottomans in 1903, merging with a slightly different syndicate, the Société du Chemin de Fer Ottoman d'Anatolie, the Anatolian Railway Company. It received concessions to build not only a railway but roads, and it then mysteriously changed its name once more to the Bagdad Railway Company.[19] German engineers built and designed the roads and the railways. The two leading spirits of the project, Dr Siemens and Dr von Gwinner, actually offered English and French capitalists a share in the enterprise, but they were turned down on the illogical view that this threat to British trade and influence must not be pandered to. Better no cooperation than allowing a German toe in the door to India.

When the Kaiser visited Damascus in 1898 he had declared himself 'friend and protector of the three hundred millions of Mohammedans'. He had a vision glorious, extending his influence to the Holy Land – he entered Jerusalem helmeted and riding on a charger – and as far east as India. Although Dr von Gwinner and his syndicate of German busi-nessmen in fact did all they could to 'internationalize' their railway,[20] the politicians could not fail to see its importance. It began at Haidar-Pasha, adjacent to Scutari, where Florence Nightingale had nursed the sick of the Crimean War, and went down through Turkey to Konya, the Iconium of New Testament times, reaching Adana, Aleppo and Harran. This was where it stood by the outbreak of war, with a projected extension to

Mosul in northern Iraq, Tikrit, later famed as the birthplace of Saddam Hussein, Baghdad, and right down to oil-rich Basra, a vitally important place to control, now that modern warfare depended on petrol-fuelled planes, armoured cars, ships, and eventually tanks. Once in the Persian Gulf, you would indeed be pointing the gun at India.

When the railway had been started, in 1903, the Prime Minister, Arthur Balfour, had wondered 'whether it is or is not desirable that what will be undoubtedly the shortest route to Indian should be entirely in the hands of French and German capitalists to the exclusion of British capitalists'.[21] He had assured the House that the company was not owned by the German government, but for the next eleven years it was with German diplomats and the German Foreign Office that Britain was in constant negotiation about the railway.

Five large boxes in the India Office Records contain the story of Britain realizing, and trying not to admit, that she was exposed to potential disaster. Hitherto, in spite of Ententes drawn up with gritted teeth, Russia had been seen as the enemy – in Turkey, in Persia, in Tibet. Germany was just as much of a threat. As the Germans received the franchise to extend the railway to Kuwait in July 1912 the viceroy of India sent a desperate memo to the Foreign Office in London:

> News just received of German attempted intrigue with Sheikh (vide my telegram of 11 July) emphasizes the necessity for carefully avoiding any concessions that may estrange Sheikh and drive him into German hands, or which Turkey may be able to transfer to Germany to our detriment.[22]

If it did not grab the public imagination as a major threat, the railway obsessed the diplomats and politicians. They knew that access to the oilfields of Persia and to India were vital to their interests, and that this was no rumoured threat, such as the supposed Russian occupation of Tibet, which sent Younghusband on his fateful expedition to Lhasa. This was, as Perceval London wrote on 25 May 1912 in the *Daily Telegraph*, 'no mere light railway . . . The Germans have decided to carry out the construction in a solid and businesslike way from the beginning.'[23] In the very debate in the House of Commons after the assassination of the archduke and his wife in Sarajevo, Sir Edward Grey, the foreign secretary, having offered his personal sympathy, referred to a tragic loss, and spoken of the pleasure given by the visit to the king of the Archduke Francis Ferdinand and his consort, began almost immediately to speak of those things which most concerned British interests in a coming war. He said barely a word about France or Belgium. He used the question of a backbencher to allow him to revert to oil concessions in Persia and whether two brigades would be enough to protect them. Aubrey Herbert rose to speak of the appalling conflicts in the Balkans, giving graphic descriptions of Christian and Muslim atrocities against one another. Once again, the foreign secretary chose not to dwell on that, but to speak of the railway and of the concessions – which at that late hour in 1914 must have seemed somewhat flimsy – obtained by Britain from Turkey and Germany that the railway would not go further than Bussora. He admitted that 'this was a subject of great anxiety to this country'.[24] This was what was on the mind of the Foreign Office on the very eve of war.

'The European situation', wrote Morris Jastrow, professor in the University of Pennsylvania in 1917, 'would have assumed an entirely different colouring if England and Germany had not clashed in the East over the Bagdad railway, as happened immediately upon the announcement of the convention of 1902–3'.[25] Even if we do not go so far as Jastrow in his claim that 'the Bagdad railway will be found to be the largest single contributing factor in bringing on the war',[26] it would clearly be quite wrong to overlook its significance; wrong to see that, once Turkey had entered the war against Britain and on the side of Germany, Britain was fighting not just for France and the new-found Entente, but for its very imperial existence.

The war in France and Belgium, which will concern us in the next chapter, surprised all who took part in it by the speed with which it turned into a murderous deadlock. Within three months of the declaration of war, trenches extended all along the Allied line. The casualties were catastrophic, and the prospect of a swift victory for either side was non-existent. In such circumstances, the political and military leaderships were terrified of moving any troops from the immovable, bloody and pointless battles of the Western Front for fear of allowing a German breakthrough. Lord Kitchener, veteran of Khartoum and Omdurman, sat in the cabinet as Secretary of State for War. He saw the force of arguments put forward by Sir John Fisher, First Sea Lord, Winston Churchill, First Lord of the Admiralty, and Lloyd George that the war should be pursued on another front. Lloyd George favoured an attack on Austria with the aid of the Serbs, and an invasion of southeastern Turkey at Alexandretta. Fisher believed it would be possible to launch a joint operation against Turkey, using Greek, Bulgarian and Romanian forces to join a force of 75,000 British and 25,000 Indian troops. This was sheer fantasy. There simply were not 75,000 British troops to spare.

Churchill, however, liked Fisher's general ideas, perhaps because of all the cabinet, even including Kitchener, he had the keenest sense of Britain as an imperial or oriental power. Fisher himself quickly cooled, and by the time of the campaign itself he was adamantly opposed to it. But on 25 November 1914 Churchill proposed to the War Council that there should be a naval bombardment of Gallipoli, followed by a blockade of the Dardanelles, while Allied forces landed on the Gallipoli peninsula and made their way to Constantinople. There were no Dreadnoughts available for the task. Most of the Fleet was at Scapa Flow, waiting for the Germans to come out from Wilhelmshaven. Older battleships would have to be used in the Dardanelles, but, said Churchill, 'the importance of the result would justify severe loss'.[27]

The American ambassador in Constantinople, Henry Morgenthau Sr, who knew the parlous state of the Turkish economy and saw the Turkish war effort at a standstill, looked back at it all and said: 'It seems so strange now – this conviction in the minds of everyone then – that the success of the Allied Fleets against the Dardanelles was inevitable, and that the capture of Constantinople was a matter of only a few days.'[28]

The very words 'Gallipoli' and 'Dardanelles' still have the power to chill Australians, New Zealanders or British. The campaign is remembered as one of the great disasters of the First World War. Had it succeeded, however, it would almost certainly have led to the surrender of Turkey. The Ottoman Empire would have been in British hands. The command of Mesopotamia, Syria and Palestine, which came much later and after great hardship and loss of blood, would have given to Britain confident control of the Near East and the Mediterranean and greatly weakened both the Austro-Hungarians and the Germans. A British victory at Gallipoli would certainly have shortened the war and saved many lives. In the short term, however, it was a calamity. Churchill was pursued by its memory for years. It appeared to have ruined his career, since he was removed as first lord of the Admiralty when the remaining troops were withdrawn from the peninsula, and as late as the general election of 1923 his public speeches would be interrupted with cries of 'What about the Dardanelles?'[29]

From the start, the campaign was bedevilled by indecision. At first the war cabinet approved the whole scheme. Then they persuaded themselves that the peninsula could be captured by a naval offensive alone. Sir John de Robeck, an undistinguished admiral, was in charge of the ships, some French, some British, which sailed into the Strait on 18 March 1915. After further indecision on the part of Kitchener it was decided that troops would be sent, but too late and too few.

One French ship, the *Bouvet*, was sunk, and two British ships, *Inflexible* and *Irresistible*, mined and severely damaged. The admiral and his officers panicked. It never occurred to the Turks that the Allied ships would not resume their bombardments, which had, in spite of their own setbacks, been very effective. In fact the fleet withdrew from the Strait and lay at anchor around the outlying islands.

When de Robeck began his bombardment of Gallipoli the peninsula was scarcely populated, and with persistence he could have taken it easily. By the time the 75,000 troops under the command of Sir Ian Hamilton arrived from Egypt, to land on 25 April – the British at Cape Helles, the Australians and the New Zealanders, the French on the opposite shore at Kum Kale – the fleet was in chaos. Far from bombarding the Turks while the soldiers disembarked, the ships were occupied in attempts to get the troops ashore. There were some catastrophic mistakes, with ships pulling alongside sheer rock faces which men could not possibly scale. Heroic fighting on both sides continued in the peninsula until December. Against appalling odds, the Australians fought in the Anzac beachhead. They had been dumped by the navy on a tiny stretch of sand. Animals, guns, ammunition, stores were wedged in an area 1,000 yards long and 30 yards wide.[30] Fifteen thousand troops were crowded into this area. Staggering up the cliffs, the men dug themselves in, remaining there, many of them for heroic months, living in holes, eating scraps and fighting the vigorous assaults of the brilliant Turkish commander Mustafa Kemal – destined to be known not only as the 'Saviour of Gallipoli' but also as the father of his new nation, Ataturk.

All the battles were terrible, especially perhaps the last big one, the failed attempt to capture Ismail Ogha Hill in August. Churchill wrote: 'On this dark battlefield of fog and flame Brigadier-General Lord Longford, Brigadier-General Kenna, VC, Colonel Sir John Milbanke, VC, and other paladins fell.'[31]

The total casualties for the entire eight and a half months of the Gallipoli campaign are hard to assess. Official Turkish figures are of 86,692 deaths and 164,617 wounded or sick. Most historians think this is an underestimate. British and Dominion casualties vary from 198,340 to 215,000. Including French, there were probably 265,000 Allied casualties, with some 46,000 killed in action or dying of disease.[32]

These are terrible casualties, but they are smaller than those on the Western Front. Had Sir Ian Hamilton's request been granted by the War Office and he had been sent 50,000 more reinforcements, he might well have won. As it was, a much weakened Turkey was now free to attack Russia and to threaten Egypt, and the war in the Near East dragged on with infinitely more loss of life.

The aim, and atmosphere, of the campaign are captured vividly in Ernest Raymond's 1922 bestseller *Tell England*. The young men of the Cheshires have a pep talk from their colonel – 'He reminded us that the Dardanelles Straits were the Hellespont of the Ancient World, and the neighbouring Aegean Sea the most mystic of the "wine-dark seas of Greece", he retold stories of Jason and the Argonauts; of "Burning Sappho" in Lesbos; of Achilles in Scyros; of Poseidon sitting upon Samothrace to watch the fight of Troy.' But the colonel also told them: 'See this greater idea. For 500 years the Turk, by occupying Constantinople, has blocked the old Royal Road to India and the East . . . He oppresses and destroys the Arab world, which should be the natural junction of the great trunk railways that, tomorrow, shall join Asia, Africa, and Europe in one splendid spider's web.' The British Empire is seen as the link between the gods and heroes of Greek myth and the commercial advantages of a trunk railway. There are plenty of 'Grecian' movements in Raymond's novel, as when the padre, leaning over a ship's rail and looking at the troops, murmurs: 'Don't you love these big handsome boys, who will not come to church.'[33]

The golden 27-year-old Rupert Brooke was part of the army which set out for Gallipoli. Sir Ian Hamilton offered him a staff job in Egypt but he refused. He wanted to be at the landing on the peninsula with his men. Hamilton noted in his diary that 'he looked extraordinarily handsome, quite a knightly presence stretched out there on the sand with the only world that counts at his feet'. He used the description when he spoke at Brooke's memorial service in the chapel of his old school, Rugby.[34]

To part of that only world that counts, the Prime Minister's daughter, Violet Asquith, Brooke wrote:

Do you think [the Turks]'ll make a sortie and meet us on the plains of Troy? It seems to me strategically so possible. Shall we have a Hospital Base (and won't you manage it?) at Lesbos? Will Hero's Tower crumble under the 15 in guns? Will the sea be polyphloisbic and wine dark and unvintageable . . . ? Shall we be a Turning Point in History? Oh, God!

I have never been quite so happy in my life, I think. Not quite so pervasively happy . . . I suddenly realize that the ambition of my life has been – since I was two – to go on a military expedition to Constantinople.

In the event, Brooke was destined to die of septicaemia, after a gnat in Port Said bit him on the lip. He died on a French hospital ship, and was buried on Achilles' island, Skyros.

Almost before he died Brooke had become an Immortal of almost Olympian stature in the eyes of a whole generation. There was a lot of bad poetry written during the First World War. Perhaps the best poetry to emerge, written either during or after it, was work by Ezra Pound, T. S. Eliot, David Jones and W. B. Yeats. But among the bad poetry was some good-bad poetry, and the best of this was probably Rupert Brooke's, even if, at this juncture of time, it is impossible to recapture an atmosphere in which 'The Soldier' or 'Grantchester' could be unironically admired. Yet as Brooke was dying in the Mediterranean, Dean Inge, a highly intelligent man and a pacifist, was intoning to a huge congregation in St Paul's Cathedral that there's some corner of a foreign field that is for ever England.[35]

'Once in a generation,' Sir Ian Hamilton wrote in his diary, 'a mysterious wish for war passes through the people. Their instinct tells them that *there is no other way* of progress and of escape from habits that no longer fit them .·. . Only by intense sufferings can the nations grow, just as a snake once a year must with anguish slough off the once beautiful coat which has now become a strait jacket.'[36]

Such was the extraordinary mood, and played out against the Mediterranean and the Near East, public schoolboys reared on Homer and Herodotus and the Bible could see themselves in a heroic mould.

Colonel T. E. Lawrence (1888–1935) was the key figure who helped coordinate the Arab revolt in 1917–18 against the Turks. By the time this had got under way, and the Arabs, with their guerrilla raids, terrorist attacks on railways, camel rides and rifle-shots had provided crucial help to the conventional army of General Allenby's Egyptian Expeditionary Force, the war in Europe was all but over. By the time Turkey signed the Armistice on 30 October 1918, German armies were retreating across France and their generals had already decided to seek terms with the Allies. A Turkish defeat in the Dardanelles in 1915 might, arguably, have very much hastened the end of the war. The Turkish defeat in 1918 felt like a cleaning-up operation.

The part played by 'Lawrence of Arabia' was itself marginal. He later said that his campaign was a sideshow attached to a sideshow.[37] This was certainly true, if Lawrence's campaigns are viewed solely as part of the diplomatic and military history of the times. Indeed as the man who emerged, after the First World War was over, as the most eloquent champion of the Arab cause, Lawrence could very well have viewed 1918 not as 'a triumph' – his subtitle for his own account of the campaign, *Seven Pillars of Wisdom* – but as its opposite.

The fighting continued in Palestine until 1 October 1918, culminating in the Battle of Armageddon. But a decisive moment was reached when, after a spectacularly brilliant campaign, Allenby captured Palestine from the Turks and entered Jerusalem at midday on 11 December 1917. In English, French, Arabic, Hebrew, Russian and Greek, a proclamation was read expressing a desire for reconciliation and respect for the city's ancient shrines. The period of the British Mandate in Palestine had effectively begun. Yet only a month before, the Balfour Declaration had, by its support for a future Jewish homeland, effectively stymied any hope for an Arab hegemony in Palestine. So disastrous did Allenby consider it that he tried to censor news or distribution of the Balfour Declaration in Palestine itself.[38] Copies, however, were distributed by the Turks, whipping up fears of mass Jewish immigration into the area when the war ended. This was hardly the 'triumph' of Lawrence or his Arab friends' dreams.

When Lawrence and his Arabs helped Allenby's conventional forces to take Damascus in October 1918, there was once again bad news. It remains unclear to this day whether Lawrence knew the plans of the European powers all along or whether he was taken as much by surprise as his friend Faisal. But, once Damascus had been occupied by an army consisting of British, Egyptian, Australian, French and New Zealand units as well as Indian lancers, Lawrence had to break it to Faisal that there was no hope of an independent Arab state, with Faisal at its head, taking in the territories occupied by Lebanon, Palestine and Syria. The European politicians had already carved up the area and Faisal was offered the chance to administer Syria under a French mandate. No 'triumph' there either.[39]

Out of the 'sideshow attached to a sideshow', however, T. E. Lawrence concocted an heroic legend, one of the most enduring to come out of the First World War. *Seven Pillars of Wisdom* was originally the title of a book he planned to write as a young Oxford student on his first visit to the Middle East as an aspirant archaeologist in 1911. He referred to it as 'Seven Pillars of Wisdom or my monumental book on the Crusades'.[40] He was then aged twenty-two years. Ten years later he had become a warrior as famous as his own Crusader hero Richard the Lion-Heart. It is probably the sheer unlikeliness of Lawrence as a great national hero which helped to equip him for the role. He was in some ways much less of an 'establishment' figure than Sir Roger Casement, who ended on the hangman's rope. One can readily imagine that had Fate thrown either man a slightly different die, their roles could have been reversed.

Lawrence was proud of the fact that his father, Thomas Robert Chapman, was a gentleman, the son of an Irish baronet. But Chapman left his lawful wife for the nanny, Sarah Junner, a tormented Presbyterian puritan, and they lived together as man and wife with the assumed name of Lawrence, with their five children. Ned, the future Lawrence of Arabia, was their second. By the time he was eight they had settled in one of the newly built villas in Polstead Road, North Oxford. That was in 1896.

Not much more than a decade later the future leader of the Labour party, Hugh Gaitskell, was a pupil at the Dragon School in Oxford. His parents disliked him playing with a child named John Betjeman, since Betjeman, whose father was in trade, had friends in Polstead Road. This was not a smart address. T. E. Lawrence's father might have been born as a gentleman but by the time he and his common-law wife had settled in Oxford he could not afford to educate his sons as gentlemen. T.E. went to the Oxford High School where his contemporaries were the sons of tradesmen. He went on to the small, and largely Welsh, college of Jesus.

You could not grow up in late Victorian or Edwardian England without the ridiculous business of class marking and dogging you. Lawrence's illegitimacy and his having been brought up in lower-middle-class circumstances go a long way to explaining the satisfaction he derived, once he confronted the officer class, in upsetting it, teasing it, shocking it. When he encountered Colonel Cyril Wilson at Jiddah in 1917, Wilson cabled his commanding officer in Cairo, Colonel, later Brigadier General, Bertie Clayton:

> Lawrence wants kicking and kicking *hard* at that . . . I look on him as a bumptious young ass who spoils his undoubted knowledge of Syrian Arabs &c. by making himself out to be the only authority on war, engineering, H.M.'s ships and everything else. He put every single person's back up I've met from the Admiral [Wemyss] down to the most junior fellow on the Red Sea.[41]

Seven Pillars is, among other things, an extended catalogue of instances in which its author had the pleasure of setting off comparable wretchedness in stuffy personages. Indeed, he derived almost as much pleasure from igniting pompous rage in British colonels as he did in discharging dynamite along the Hejaz railway.

He had not gone to the Middle East as a soldier. The fighting men who had accompanied him on his early journeys had been inside his head: the Crusaders, certainly, but also the heroes of Malory and Homer. The two books which accompanied him on his campaigns with the Arabs were the *Odyssey*, which he was destined to translate, and *Morte d'Arthur*.[42]

Lawrence studied history at university, his favoured period being 918 to 1273, and his special subject the Crusades. 'Your matter is passable, but you write in the style of a two-penny-halfpenny newspaper,' said one of his tutors, R. L. Poole of Magdalen College. In spite of his readable prose manner, Lawrence was awarded a First Class degree. Dr David Hogarth, keeper of the Ashmolean Museum and, like Poole, a fellow of

Magdalen, became Lawrence's patron, sending him off to do fieldwork in Syria and Lebanon. Lawrence sketched, photographed and measured Crusader castles. At Hogarth's request, he also visited Jerablus on the Upper Euphrates, seat of the Hittite city of Carchemish, to buy Hittite clay cartouches. Until the outbreak of the First World War this place was to become his second home. As an archaeologist he toured the Middle East extensively, getting to know Sinai, Syria and Palestine, perfecting his Arabic, and forming his view of 'Arabia' not so much as a political entity as an imaginative concept.

It was during his first digging season at Carchemish that he developed close ties with Selim Ahmed, an Arab boy whom he nicknamed Dahoum, the dark one – a joke about the boy's light skin. *The Seven Pillars* is dedicated to S.A.

> I loved you, so I drew these tides of men into my hands
> and wrote my will across the sky in stars
> To earn you Freedom, the seven pillared worthy house,
> that your eyes might be shining for me
> When we came.[43]

Selim Ahmed was destined to die, not as a warrior, but of dysentery in 1918, at the very place where he met Lawrence. It was in the course of loving him that Lawrence developed all his high Victorian fantasies about the Arabs. He disliked those who had become urbanized or Westernized, or whose reading of Darwin or Herbert Spencer had made them modify the simplicity of their religious fanaticism. He saw the Arabs, as English dreamers before him had done – C. M. Doughty, Richard Burton, Lady Hester Stanhope, A. W. Kinglake – as primitives, untainted with 'doubt, our modern Crown of Thorns'. He was wrong about Doubt. It was the all-achieving Victorians who were mature enough to live with that. The self-destructive twentieth century craved scientific and dogmatic certainty, discarding Hegelian idealism in favour of a belief in physics; abandoning Liberalism in favour of Marxism or fascism. Religion, which most Victorian intellectuals questioned, enjoyed a vogue again in the early to mid-twentieth century so long as it expressed itself in certainties which Carlyle's generation had deemed obsolete. So T. E. Lawrence was never more modern than when he looked to the Islamic Near East and saw there the certainties others would find in communism or Catholicism. For this reason he saw the Bedouin, the wandering desert Arabs, as the *echt* Arabs, and there was something paradoxical, not to say self-contradictory, about espousing the desire, supposedly on their behalf – in fact on behalf of the Herbert Spencer-reading modernizers – for an independent Arab nation-state with all the paraphernalia of foreign embassies, finance ministers, and administrators.

Many read *Seven Pillars of Wisdom* as a fraudulent historical text, without realizing that it is intended to be read, as Malory, Homer or the Bible are intended to be read, as a mythological compendium whose stories interpret, as they describe, the world. As in the story of Samuel, seeking out the Lord's anointed and being guided to Saul, later David, by the Lord Himself; or of Merlin discovering 'the once and future King' Arthur/Lawrence describes himself as one entrusted to find the true Arab Leader. When he meets Faisal, 'I felt at first glance that this was the man I had come to Arabia to seek – the leader who would bring the Arab Revolt to full glory. Faisal looked very tall and pillar-like, very slender, in his long white silk robes and his brown head-cloth bound with a brilliant scarlet and gold cord . . .'

One of the reasons *Seven Pillars* has such an hypnotic effect on the reader is precisely its lack of realism. A prosaic reader will wish to protest that its whole political stance is based on a contradiction. It proclaims Arab freedom, but this freedom is something *given* to the Arabs by an English Deliverer as if it were his to give. It seems like a story of an Englishman becoming an Arab. It is really a story about Arabs willingly and devotedly rising up against their Turkish oppressors because they want to become – in some way – part of the British Empire. This is the fantasy subtext, politically. It is significant that in actual fact none of the Bedouin would fight the Turks without huge down-payments of gold sovereigns. Between August 1917 and January 1918 £320,000 in gold sovereigns was handed over to tribal sheikhs by Lawrence in return for attacks on the Hejaz railway and adherence to Faisal. In reality, they were mercenaries. In *Seven Pillars* all this is suppressed.[44]

Prosaic literalists furthermore object to the flagrant historical distortions and lies. Lawrence conveniently forgets that the first Allied troops to enter Damascus were the Australian cavalry, and he makes no mention of the Indian lancers, and Allenby's huge infantry divisions. In this version, the Syrian capital is taken by Lawrence and his Arabs on camels.

Then there is the celebrated episode of Lawrence being captured by the Turks at Deraa, tortured, and sodomized by a Turkish officer named in the book Nahi. ('He began to fawn on me, saying how white and fresh I was, how fine my hands and feet, and how he would let me off drills and duties, make me his orderly, even pay me wages, if I would love him.'[45]) Lawrence adds: 'I bore it for a little, till he got too beastly; and then jerked my knee into him.' The torture which follows, and the further sodomization, and the whipping, produced 'a delicious warmth, probably sexual'.[46]

The unreliability of the incident has been lengthily debated since the book was first published. Within days, hours even, of this ordeal, in which welts have supposedly appeared on his back, our hero is escaping, and riding hundreds of miles at high speed to Aqaba for more deeds of derring-do. The Deraa episode fulfils several functions in Lawrence's narrative. First, it serves, or is surely meant to serve, as justification for the bloodbath inflicted by Lawrence on the Turks. There are scenes in the tenth and final book of obscene (his own word) bloodiness, and enjoyment of cruelty.

Much is made of Lawrence's masochism, perhaps his sado-masochism. Modern biography perhaps tells us too much. We know that in later life, when he retired from the glare of publicity to try to live as an aircraftman under an assumed name – John Hume Ross – he got men to cane him until he achieved orgasm. Actual physical contact with human beings repelled him.

These are the private quirks of the man. He was famous, so he was a marked man. Our generation, unused to corporal punishment except as a form of sexual diversion, sees Lawrence's obsession with the whip, and with pain, as one of the features which make him odd. No doubt the side of his nature which enjoyed baiting and annoying Colonel Blimps relished placing a scene of invented homosexual rape in a book which was obviously going to become one of the major bestsellers about the war. But another of the bestsellers, Ernest Raymond's Gallipoli novel *Tell England*, penned by a happily married man who became a father and grandfather, is if anything even more obsessed by corporal punishment inflicted on boys than anything written by Lawrence. The second half of Raymond's book tells of three young men at Gallipoli. The first half is a loving reconstruction of their 'gay schooldays'. When it was published in 1922 *Tell England* was family reading. Respectable middle-class women enjoyed it. Today it seems to be directed to the specialist readership of pederastic flagellants. ('I bent over, resting my hands on my knees. Radley was a cricketer with a big reputation for cutting and driving; and three drives, right in the middle of the cane, convinced me what a first-class hitter he was . . . Then he put his cane away and issued his little ration of gentleness – "You're two plucky boys", he said.')

Reading *Tell England*, and other school stories of the period in which whippings, canings, thrashings and biffings are the regular manner in which masters or senior boys show their affection for, and dominance of, little boys, undoubtedly provides an insight into the First World War ethos. Why, and how, else can we begin to imagine why so many adolescent boys went, at first not merely with willingness, but with rapture, to their miserable deaths?

Seven Pillars and the subsequent legendary reputation of T. E. Lawrence in the postwar years leaves a deeper legacy. The book has been rightly described[47] as a Modernist appraisal of the First World War which has more in common with Pound's *Cantos* or Eliot's *Waste Land* than with conventional military history. By its carefully stage-managed effects, however, it is not simply making an aesthetic but a political statement. It leaves the Arab world in turmoil. Its warfare is accomplished but its political leadership is in dispute. After the blood comes the excrement. In the penultimate chapter an Australian doctor confronts Lawrence with the realities in the Turkish hospital in Damascus, with dead bodies outstretched on a stone floor in pools of 'liquid muck'. In this hell-hole there are still very many alive. We are left with the overpowering feeling that this metaphor for the Middle East, a place where political discourse ends in confused shouts, and with the wounded lying in diarrhoea, needs the cleansing power of a great leader. One of the most eloquent moments comes in chapter CXX when Lawrence hears and transcribes the Call to Prayer – 'The clamour hushed, as everyone seemed to obey the call to prayer on this their first night of perfect freedom. While my fancy, in the overwhelming pause, showed me my loneliness and lack of reason in their movement: since only for me, of all the hearers, was the event sorrowful and the phrase meaningless.' The necessary rhetoric comes full circle. The lonely scholar asks General Allenby for permission to leave the Arabian Nights tale he has conjured for us. 'In the end he agreed; and then at once I knew how much I was sorry.'

But the rhetoric is eloquent with what it does not say. It calls aloud with its silence for a leadership in the Arab world as clear and firm as that call to prayer. Who, alone in its hundreds of pages, has shown himself able to cleanse the ordure of the Augean stable, to provide the leadership so desperately needed? They need not just the puppet-king whom Destiny had shown to the author. They need too a modern prophet, a mage – they need the one who is walking sorrowfully away.

Seven Pillars of Wisdom is then not simply a book of reminiscences about the war, it is also a prophecy of what was to come, when not only the Arabs but the peoples of Europe would look for prophets. Not only Arabs but Germans, Italians, perhaps, (who knew?) the English themselves would hear the incantations from some political muezzin and, discarding the old, worn-out methods, find release in collective servitude to a Leader.

10

Barbarous Kings

Well over 9 million young men were killed in the First World War –
1,380,000 Frenchmen, 1,935,000 Germans, 1,700,000 Russian and 942,135
from the British Empire.

> War, one war after another,
> Men start 'em who couldn't put up a good hen-roost.

So wrote Ezra Pound in his *Cantos* in typically robust manner. Pound is
one of the great writers of the twentieth century, but as a political analyst
he, no less than the politicians and the historians, is shocked into incomprehension by the sheer insanity of what they called the Great War.

When Blücher's Prussian army of 116,000 men invaded Belgium in
the summer of 1815 and encamped at Namur, they were regarded by the
British as their comrades in arms. Those British regiments who, for the
next hundred years and more, celebrated 18 June as Waterloo Day could
be forgiven for playing down the Prussian contribution to the Duke of
Wellington's victory over the French. After all, Wellington was the last
British military leader of genius in history. All serious students of the
battle, however, would agree with the duke that his victory had been 'a
damned close-run thing', and that he would not have achieved it without
German help.

When, again, the Germans invaded northern France in 1870 and
achieved a devastating victory over the moribund empire of Napoleon
III, British public opinion was broadly in their favour, if less shrilly so
than the queen, who likened the siege of Paris to the downfall of Sodom
and Gomorrah.

Yet within a century of Waterloo, the British army in Belgium and
France was entrenched in the bloodiest war in history, fighting the
Germans. The strangeness of this will always haunt an intelligent
observer. When all the explanations have been tried, there remains an
element of mystery about how such a destructive war, so damaging to
all participants, can have engaged Europe for so long.

Some of the explanations for how Britain could have believed it was
in her interest to go to war were explored in the last chapter. It was feared
that a powerful Germany, with a navy almost as large as the British, and
control of a railway which stretched from Berlin to Baghdad, could, if it

chose, threaten Britain's imperial hegemony. It could threaten India. Even if it had no direct plans to take over India, it could make contact between Britain and India difficult, it could interrupt trade. Great powers always suffer from collective paranoia. Whether or not such fears were justified, they could not but arise as German strength grew, and as the militaristic Junkers who appeared to control foreign policy used their loud voices to drown out the moderates. This goes some way towards explaining why the British diplomats, when the crisis came, were prepared to go to war with such comparative recklessness.

There were other factors, which affected all the European powers. One was the comparative ease with which the Prussians had beaten the French in 1870. That was the only serious war on the European mainland since Waterloo. Although it was a bloody one, and followed by the torments of the Siege, and then the Commune of Paris, it was, by comparison with the wars of the Napoleonic era, short. All sides, as they went to war in the summer of 1914, believed that like the Franco-Prussian war of 1870, it would be over in months.

As far as Britain was concerned, there was almost no one in public life, in a position of real administrative authority, except Winston Churchill and Kitchener, who had any direct experience of warfare. Churchill had been at the battle of Omdurman in 1898 when a combination of British artillery machine-gun and rifle fire killed or wounded over 16,000 spear-carrying Sudanese in four and a half hours. One of those who witnessed this bloodbath was Douglas Haig, who would command the British Expeditionary Force in France between 1915 and 1918.[1]

Apart from small wars, such as Kitchener's massacre of the Sudanese, the British had not been noted for their military prowess in the days of their greatest political and economic prosperity. During the whole reign of Queen Victoria they had fought the Crimean War against the Russians – a pointless war which merely advertised to the world the levels of administrative and military incompetence in the British army – and the Boer War in which the British only just managed to beat an entirely amateur army of Bible-bashing farmers. Churchill had also been a witness to this war – as a journalist, prisoner of war, and as a cheerfully self-publicizing escapee and combatant. His older civilian colleagues in the cabinet – and above all Asquith, the Liberal prime minister – were disastrously ignorant of the art of war or its possible consequences. Alan Clark called his unforgettable indictment of the British generals *The Donkeys* because of the exchange in Falkenhayn's Memoirs – *Ludendorff*: The English soldiers fight like lions. *Hoffman*: True, but don't we know that they are lions led by donkeys. Clark described the first year of the war as 'the story of the destruction of an army – the old professional army of the United Kingdom that always won the last battle, whose regiments had fought at Quebec, Corunna, in the Indies, were trained in musketry at Hythe, drilled on the parched earth of Chuddapore, and were machine-gunned, gassed and finally buried in 1915'.[2]

This is a stirring paragraph; and no one can doubt that the incompetence of Sir John French, the first commander of the British Expeditionary Force, and that of his successor Haig, resulted in tens of thousands of avoidable deaths. It is not entirely to exonerate the generals, however, to add that they were being asked, on occasion, to achieve impossible aims; asked by politicians who had lost control of the situation.

The director of Military Operations was, like so many twentieth-century British generals, an Ulsterman, though he grew up in the south of Ireland: Major-General Sir Henry Wilson. It was in the Irish conflict, and not the World War, that he was doomed to die. He had seen service in India and in the Boer War, but most of his career had been as a staff officer, working at the War Office and as commandant of the Staff College. When he became director of Military Operations in 1910, Wilson travelled frequently to France, Russia and Germany, and kept the British politicians briefed about the likely outcome of military engagements. As early as September 1910 he was telephoning Winston Churchill at the Café Royal, where he was dining with the foreign secretary, Sir Edward Grey, and getting them round to his house, spreading out maps, and speaking of what would happen if Germany invaded France.[3] Wilson's predictions, and those of his fellow army officers, and their French and Russian colleagues, were reasonably accurate. Rather as in the 1930s, Churchill was much readier than his colleagues to pay attention to military intelligence from the Continent. The questions which occupied Wilson's mind did not concern the possibility of war – he regarded it as an inevitability. They were how the British would be equipped to meet war when it came. About the navy, he had no doubts – no one did. The questions which exercised Wilson's mind were whether the British could muster enough troops to put together a convincing expeditionary force without either introducing compulsory conscription or bringing in the, perhaps unwilling, Dominions. The second and much graver fear expressed in his diaries concerned the low quality of the politicians. At the end of May 1911, he attended a meeting of the Imperial Conference on Defence. The premier of New Zealand, Sir Joseph Ward, said that unless they pursued a common policy, agreeable to New Zealand, Canada, South Africa and Australia, the Empire would disintegrate.

'It is difficult to imagine Asquith taking a strong straight line,' wrote Wilson, 'and yet if someone does not catch hold of us, I think the Empire will go before long . . . The task of welding this Empire into one is the most difficult that any man was ever called upon to perform. Obvious, therefore, that we *must* get a great man such as Pitt, Bismarck, etc. I confess I see no sign of such a man in this country.'[4]

Three years later, when he attended the first War Council at Number 10 Downing Street, with the likes of Lord Kitchener, Churchill, Prince Louis of Battenberg and Sir Douglas Haig – as well of course as the prime minister, Asquith, and the foreign secretary, Sir Edward Grey – Wilson tersely noted, 'an historic meeting of men, mostly entirely ignorant of their subject'.[5]

The First World War was truly a world war, involving Russia, Japan, Africa, the East Near and Far, and ultimately the United States of America. Its central theatre, however, was Europe and its central issues were – Who controlled which bits of Europe? Whose national independence threatened whose hegemony? Questions of cause and effect can be discussed endlessly. By the end of the war, Russia had had a communist revolution and murdered its emperor; the Austro-Hungarian and Ottoman empires no longer existed; Kaiser Wilhelm II had abdicated and gone to live in Holland; the Middle East was notionally controlled by the French and the British; the Jews looked for a homeland, unfortunately in the same territory where Arabs sought to establish their own independent kingdom(s); Ireland was moving towards independence and/or civil war; British women received the parliamentary franchise and had a far greater measure of work opportunity; socialism, having conquered Russia, was seen as a viable political option in Italy, Germany, France, Spain, Britain. By the end of the war, America – not one of the old European powers and not Britain with her Empire but America – was seen not merely as the essential ingredient in the Allied victory over Germany, but also as the natural broker of the Peace. The world had made that crucial step towards becoming our world, the world we know today, in which America would one day become the supreme power, politically. (Already American industrial output had reached double Britain's.)

You could say that all these developments would have occurred anyway, war or no war. The war hastened and enabled them. To that extent even without entering contentious debates about cause and effect you could say that the war was a Before and After event like no other in history. The vanquished were the British Liberal party, though it was slow to realize this; the imperial idea of government; Islam as a cohesive international political force – the only Muslim power had been eliminated, and another would not appear until Pakistan tested its hydrogen bomb; the aristocratic militaristic Prussian empire of Bismarck. The beneficiaries were newspaper proprietors; speculative capitalists; communist revolutionaries, especially Lenin; Irish revolutionaries, especially Sinn Fein; feminists and, ultimately, fascists. None of these consequences formed part of the war aims of Russia, Austria-Hungary, Germany, France or Britain as their politicians and military top brass prepared for war in the hot summer of 1914.

It is all the more remarkable when you consider that the territories known since 1870 as Germany had almost no history of conflict with Britain: some of the troops defeated by Marlborough at Blenheim were Bavarian, Britain was at war with Prussia between 1807 and 1812, but there had been no serious conflict, ever, between the British and the Germans. They had supplied Britain with their monarchs for two centuries; with their greatest shared composer, Handel; with their religion since the sixteenth century; and since the early nineteenth with most of their philosophical ideas. For all the Kaiser's *talk*, when in his anti-British manias, and for all the rivalries between the two navies, there was no European clash of interest between Germany and Britain as there was between Britain and France. Prussia had formed itself, together with the old princedoms and duchies and the kingdom of Bavaria, into a mighty nation, and this was uncomfortable for the older mighty nation on their western border, France. But their disputed territories – Alsace-Lorraine – and their mutual distrust, and indeed hatred, were of no political threat to Britain – either to her trade abroad, or her way of life at home. The diplomatic commitments entered into when the Entente Cordiale was hatched were what shifted the balance of power in Europe and led to the length of the war and the extent of its slaughter. Had Britain remained neutral, the obviously sensible option, there would probably have been a repeat performance of 1870, and the Germans might have reached Paris long before Christmas. Lenin might well have ended his days as a disgruntled pamphleteer in Zurich cafés, while in their Viennese equivalents Adolf Hitler, after a brave army career, would have eked out his no less disgruntled living as a water-colourist. Well over 10 million lives would have been saved.

Bismarck had said that the plum trees and pigs of Serbia were not worth the bones of a single Pomeranian grenadier,[6] but it was the fate of Serbia, this belligerent little place, still baring its teeth at its equally belligerent Croat, Bosnian and Albanian neighbours in the twenty-first century, which led to the ruin of all the great European powers in 1914. The war began in the Balkans. Since 1912, Serbia had been fighting Turkey for more territory, and feeling aggrieved because Austria-Hungary would not allow it an Adriatic port. Bulgaria and Greece, also anxious to rid Europe of Turkish sovereignty, were allied with Serbia, and behind Serbia stood their fellow Orthodox Christians, the mighty empire of Russia, seen as a threat both by Austria-Hungary and by Germany.

There can be no doubt that Germany was in the grip at this period of an ultra-reactionary aristocratic–military clique, intent upon using some international crisis as an excuse for war. When the eminent Texan Colonel Edward M. House was sent by President Wilson to Europe to urge its governments to sign a peace pact, he found in control of German policy 'a military oligarchy', determined upon war, and ready if necessary to depose the Kaiser in favour of his son if he opposed their machinations.[7] What they did not know was what Britain would do if, for example, Germany invaded Belgium, to 'show who was their master'.

Then, at this very volatile juncture in European politics, the heir to the Austro-Hungarian Empire, the Archduke Franz Ferdinand, paying a visit with his wife Sophie to Sarajevo, in Bosnia-Hercegovina, was assassinated by a Serbian terrorist called Gavrilo Princip. A group of seven young Serbians had crossed the border into Bosnia specifically to kill the heir apparent. They called themselves Young Bosnia and wanted to detach Bosnia from Austria-Hungary. The first attempt to kill the archduke and his wife – a student called Nedeljko Cabrinovic hurled a bomb at their car – was unsuccessful. It rolled off the back of the car and injured some bystanders. After visiting the town hall, Franz Ferdinand decided to visit the injured in hospital. Their driver took a wrong turning at the junction of Appel Quay and Franzjosefstrasse. Gavrilo Princip was loitering on the corner. Amazed to see the archduke passing by, he stepped forward and shot both Franz Ferdinand and his wife at point-blank range. Sophie died instantly, Franz Ferdinand within half an hour.

The man Princip shot was, at the court of his eighty-four-year-old uncle the Emperor Franz Joseph, a restraining moderate diplomatic influence. It was decided in Vienna that Serbia must be taught a lesson. The chief of general staff, Franz Conrad von Hötzendorff, believed, as a social Darwinian, that war was a natural human condition, that the struggle for existence was the 'basic principle behind all the events on this earth'. Politics, he said, 'consists precisely of applying war as method'.[8]

By attacking Serbia, Austria risked antagonizing Russia, but Germany had offered her unstinting support, her famous 'blank cheque'. They delayed for about a month, largely so that the mainly peasant Austrian army could gather the harvest.[9]

By 28 July the Tsar of Russia had responded to the Balkan crisis by mobilizing four military regions, and two days later he ordered a general mobilization. In Vienna, enormous and enthusiastic crowds filled the streets. They imagined there would be a quick victory over a small, exhausted and vulnerable nation, Serbia. As it happened, while the crisis brewed, the French president Raymond Poincaré and his prime minister René Viviani had been making a state visit to Russia. He had affirmed his support for Russian policy in the Balkans, but this had been generally interpreted as a willingness if necessary to fight on Russia's side should the war extend beyond its localized Serbian confines.

The diplomatic exchanges between the British Foreign Secretary Sir Edward Grey and the German ambassador Lichnowsky were civilized, leisurely, but grave. Grey urged Germany to restrain Austria. He tried to organize a peace conference in London, but by the time he had proposed a date, Austria had already gone to war with Serbia. The Germans meanwhile were sabre-rattling. They demanded French reassurance that France would not intervene on the side of Russia, and they were asked to decide within eighteen hours of the afternoon of 1 August. The Germans also demanded that as a token of neutrality the French should hand over the fortresses of Toul and Verdun – with all their dreadful memories of 1870 – to Germany for the duration of the war.

The British Foreign Office now realized the seriousness of having entered into the Entente with France. If he could have remained neutral, Sir Edward Grey would have done. He saw nothing but ruin – financial, commercial, political – facing Britain if she got involved. The cabinet was about two-thirds in favour of remaining neutral. The City of London was broadly anti-war. Of all the major European governments, the British cabinet alone was taken by surprise at the sudden emergence of the crisis. This was no longer a war game discussed by military experts such as Sir Henry Wilson. Germany declared war on Russia on 1 August, and on France on 3 August. The British ultimatum to Germany was that they must respect Belgian neutrality. John Morley, the old Gladstonian Liberal, and John Burns the working-class bibliophile resigned from the cabinet. On 4 August Asquith told Parliament that Germany had invaded Belgium. What had been a cause of British rejoicing in 1815 was, in the summer of 1914, a *casus belli*.

Germany had not set out to conquer Belgium. Theobald von Bethmann Hollweg (1856–1921), their civilized old chancellor, recognized immediately that a violation of international law had been perpetrated. But France had declared war from the West, Russia from the East. 'We shall undo the wrong we are doing as soon as our military objective has been achieved,' he promised. 'Someone who is threatened, as we are, and fights for his all can think only of how to cut his way through.'[10]

Bethmann Hollweg's predecessor as chancellor, Bernhard von Bülow, saw the Kaiser during those days, bleary with sleeplessness and yet excited. In the chancellor's eyes he saw an 'incredibly helpless and sad expression. "How on earth do you think this happened?" he asked.

Bethmann raised his long arms to heaven and said in a dull voice, "Heaven knows".[11]

The German plans were based on war-games devised as long ago as 1905 by their chief of General Staff, General Schlieffen. They involved the invasion of Belgium, passing by Brussels on the right wing, then turning swiftly southwest and west to Paris. The invaders would then move eastward, and drive the French army towards Switzerland, or towards the rest of the German army posted in Lorraine. This plan was drawn up on the understanding that Britain would stay out of the war. It came unstuck when it found itself outflanked by an improvised French army supported by the BEF. The Germans crucially lost the initiative, and the chance of taking Paris, by early September 1914.

On the other hand, they did defeat the French in Lorraine, even if they failed to encircle the whole of the French army. So in the first month of the war neither French nor German plans went right. The German armies went into full retreat across the Marne.[12]

The French army, under the command of General Joseph Joffre, was a superbly well-organized fighting force, motivated at this stage of hostilities by a greater passion than could possibly have inspired either the Germans or the British: that passion was for France itself, on whose soil the dreadful war was being fought. Left wing and right wing, royalist and freethinker, Dreyfusard and anti-Dreyfusard Frenchmen were, during that late summer, united in a violent desire to prevent a repetition of the disasters of 1870. It was probably this collective spiritual resistance, as much as any tactical decision from one day to the next on the field of battle, which gave the French army such power against the invaders. The French casualties in the first five months of the war – 300,000 dead and 600,000 wounded, captured or missing – exceeded the total number of British casualties in the whole of the Second World War.[13]

In the First Battle of Ypres, which began on 30 October 1914, the British put into line almost their entire regular army. 'The B.E.F. fought the Germans to a standstill and itself out of existence.'[14] The generals, mostly old men who remembered old wars, were in a hurry to finish the fighting before the winter set in. They did not at first appreciate that with the conveniences of modern warfare, there was no need to discontinue the fighting when bad weather came. The twentieth-century soldier could be fed on tinned food. Winter quarters were unnecessary. To avoid further slaughter on the battlefield, both sides dug themselves in to trenches which now stretched from the Channel port of Nieuport through Artois and Picardy and Champagne to the Swiss border.

Much to the displeasure of the War Office in London, peace momentarily was observed on parts of the Western Front on Christmas Day 1914. German soldiers walked across the British wire into no man's land. British soldiers walked out to join them. The dead were buried. Plum puddings were given. Carols were sung. Football was played. This happened 'almost everywhere in British No Man's Land',[15] though not in the French. Bruce Bairnsfather, author of one of the most popular of wartime volumes, *Bullets and Billets*, recorded that: 'It all felt most curious: here were these sausage-eating wretches, who had elected to start this infernal European fracas, and in so doing had brought us all into the same muddy pickle as themselves ... There was not an atom of hate on either side that day; and yet, on our side not for a moment was the will to war and the will to beat them relaxed.'[16]

The next day, they resumed their mutual slaughter.

One of the hundreds of thousands of Frenchmen who died – in his case, in a charge at Neuville St Vaast on 15 June 1915 – was the 23-year-old sculptor Henri Gaudier-Brzeska. In the avant-garde periodical *Blast*, his English friend T. E. Hulme published what is in effect his last testament, his artistic and philosophical manifesto. In the previous November he had written from the trenches:

> I HAVE BEEN FIGHTING FOR TWO MONTHS and I can now gauge the intensity of Life.
> HUMAN MASSES teem and move, are destroyed and crop up again.
> HORSES are worn out in three weeks, die by the roadside.

You might have expected a young artist in the prime of life to see war as a supreme evil, but in common with huge numbers of Europeans, perhaps the majority, Gaudier-Brzeska was pleased to contemplate the destruction which war brought. It was not merely the opportunities for patriotism and glory which excited him. It was the mass slaughter itself. It would be convenient to lay all the blame for the First World War on incompetent politicians and generals. They played their part. But there is a palpable sense, in the poetry, music, sculpture and painting of the period, that many people actually welcomed the era of mechanized destruction. The sculptor's friend Percy Wyndham Lewis transcribed Gaudier-Brzeska's last letter in capitals to give it the quality of a motto inscribed on memorial stone.

> IT WOULD BE FOLLY TO SEEK ARTISTIC EMOTIONS AMID THESE LITTLE WORKS OF OURS. THIS PALTRY MECHANISM,

WHICH SERVES AS A PURGE TO OVERNUMEROUS HUMANITY.

THIS WAR IS A GREAT REMEDY.

IN THE INDIVIDUAL IT KILLS ARROGANCE, SELF-ESTEEM, PRIDE. IT TAKES AWAY FROM THE MASSES NUMBERS UPON NUMBERS OF UNIMPORTANT UNITS, WHOSE ECONOMIC ACTIVITIES BECOME NOXIOUS AS THE RECENT TRADE CRISES HAVE SHOWN US.

MY VIEWS ON SCULPTURE REMAIN ABSOLUTELY *THE SAME.*

IT IS *THE VORTEX* OF WILL, OF DECISION, THAT BEGINS.

I SHALL DERIVE MY EMOTIONS SOLELY FROM THE *ARRANGEMENT OF SURFACES*, I SHALL PRESENT MY EMOTIONS BY THE ARRANGEMENT OF MY SURFACES, THE PLANES AND LINES BY WHICH THEY ARE DEFINED.

Philistines fail to see that artists, even in their posturings, hold up mirrors to what is going on in societies, they take soundings of a society's cohesion, moral wellbeing, strength or lack of it. That is why totalitarian regimes persecute poets and composers with just as much rigour as they devote to silencing overtly political opposition. Stalin and Hitler both had violently strong views about art and music. One method of dealing with the troublesome messages by which poets or painters instinctually telegraph to the rest of society what has become of the human spirit was to send them to prison. Another way was the highly effective British system of education for its governing class, more or less successfully eliminating artistic or literary sensibility by the values of public school boorishness.

When Thomas Hardy's seventieth birthday approached in 1910, Asquith's private secretary telephoned Buckingham Palace to suggest that a telegram to 'old Hardy' would be appreciated. Mr Hardy of Alnwick, who made King George V's fishing rods, was astonished to receive royal congratulations on achieving an age he had not attained, on a day which in his life was an anniversary of nothing. At the opening of the Tate Gallery extension, the king stood before a French Impressionist picture and called out to the Queen: 'Here's something to make you laugh, May.' At a canvas of Cézanne's he shook his stick.[17]

The art critics in London were scarcely less Philistine than their king. In November 1910, when Roger Fry and Desmond MacCarthy organized an exhibition at the Grafton Galleries called *Manet and the Post Impressionists*, London had its first taste not only of Cézanne, Van Gogh and Gauguin but also of younger artists such as Matisse, Signac, Derain,

Vlaminck and Picasso. *The Times* decided that it was 'the rejection of all that civilisation has done, good or bad'. H. M. Bateman did cartoons mocking it, and hundreds of visitors recorded indignant complaints in a special book provided by the gallery for the purpose.[18]

There were very few English painters who really wanted to engage with the developments of painting in Europe, and this was symptomatic of something much greater than painting technique. Britain, partly by virtue of its geographical separation from the Continent, was slow to absorb the effects on the European soul of mechanization, secularization, politicization. Things had changed and would never be the same again. British historians, even now, tend to attribute the extraordinary changes to the war alone. Before 1914, they see an idyllic Britain of Flora Thompson peasantry, of factory workers with waistcoats and watch chains, of *Wind in the Willows* and Gertrude Jekyll: afterwards, jazz, short skirts, an independent Ireland and socialism – symptoms of a lost innocence, and an irreversible change. But the truth is otherwise. We have already seen that prewar Britain was far from tranquil. From the politicians' point of view the war was a way of postponing, or not directly facing, the most urgent domestic questions of the day, such as the demand for female suffrage and the near civil war in Ireland. But you only have to look at the movements in painting and sculpture to see that the world had already changed – as Yeats would say, changed utterly – before any shots were fired.

As far as Britain was concerned, it was the Vorticist movement, in the visual and plastic arts, which was the most dramatic visible sign of the change which had occurred. Percy Wyndham Lewis (1882–1957) was its noisiest exponent. Augustus John's 1905 portrait of him is of a Balzacian anti-hero of the 1840s – big, violent hands, a curling sardonic lip beneath the moustache, dark hair falling over ears and side-whiskers, dark eyes, hooked nose. Gertrude Stein, when she first met him in Paris, said he was 'tall and thin . . . rather like a young Frenchman on the rise'.[19]

Lewis was of American origin. Born on his father's yacht off the coast of Nova Scotia, he came, paternally, from a line of merchants and lawyers in New York State, though his mother's family were of Scottish and Irish descent. When the marriage failed, Percy was still a child of ten, and his mother brought him to England, where she tried and conspicuously failed to have him educated as a conventional middle-class Englishman. As a schoolboy at Rugby, he would probably have seen the child Rupert Brooke, whose father was a housemaster there, but he entered the school some years before Brooke. He converted his study into a studio, and was delighted, both when this provoked the predictable, George V-like response from one of the other boys – 'You frightful artist!' – and, even more, when his mother was informed by his housemaster that the school was unsuitable. He was enrolled at the Slade School in 1898, the year that Augustus John, already legendary for his skill as a painter and seducer, had left it. His teacher Fred Brown did not find it hard to imbue his pupil with a hatred and distrust of Academy painting. In so far as, domestically, Lewis was drawn towards a group it was to the modern New English Art Club, and to the Camden Town School of Sickert. But it was always in Europe that he would find his inspiration, philosophical and visual.

In Paris, he threw himself utterly into the role of a self-conscious and self-created Bohemian. He attended Henri Bergson's lectures at the Collège de France, and absorbed Bergson's doctrine that an understanding of reality could never be entirely rational, but always intuitive. He dabbled with the extreme right-wing writers who contributed to Charles Maurras's daily paper *L'Action française*, while having no desire to disown his friendship with the exiled Russian anarchist Prince Peter Kropotkin (1842–1921), whose company he enjoyed. Lewis was a man who was drawn to extremes. In later life, his admiring articles about National Socialism in *Time and Tide* magazine saw the 'Hitlerist dream as full of an imminent classical serenity'. Then he recognized the error of his ways and published an equally extreme denunciation in *The Hitler Cult* (1939). He was in many respects an archetypal twentieth-century artist–intellectual in that he wished to overthrow authority while worshipping power. He could see in the work of the Cubists not merely an attempt to break away from the formalism and decoration of nineteenth-century artistic traditions, but a desire actually to undermine the European cultural tradition, to take it to bits, to rebuild it in blocks. Picasso's *Les Demoiselles d'Avignon* was on one level an academic exercise, reworking a painting by El Greco which was by no means 'realistic' in the starkest terms. Augustus John, who first told Lewis about the painting, which he had seen in Paris, compared it to the 'strange moonlights of Easter Island'. One of Picasso's many revolutionary devices was to rework European themes through allusion to non-European styles. The fetishes of Africa or of other 'primitive' cultures could provide lessons in simplicity of form, of texture, of truth, ultimately, which the degraded fag-end of the classical tradition could no longer do. Lewis would also have enjoyed the tangible wickedness of Picasso's great canvas, the fact that the young women are obviously prostitutes lolling about shamelessly between shifts of work. The great picture, one of the most important turning-points in human sensibility, could not have failed to impress Lewis, a young man in search of an artistic style and a philosophy for living.

But Vorticism, as it evolved as a separate development in Britain, separate from continental Cubism, while obviously drawing on Picasso's inspiration, had distinctive features of its own. It is not whimsical to see the industrial machinery, and the instruments of war, developed since the 1880s as objects of far greater importance for the Vorticist artists than the academic art schools. David Bomberg's inspiration for early abstract or semi-abstract works came from the tiled staircases of Schevik's Steam Baths in Brick Lane, near his Whitechapel boyhood home. Jacob Epstein, who had come to London from America (the son of Polish refugees, escaping the pogroms in Tsarist Russia and Poland), made sculptures based closely on the rock drills used in the Rand gold mines. Bent over his *Rock Drill* is the semi-mechanized, semi-robotic figure of the miner himself, his torso metallic, his helmet dehumanizing. All that remains human of him is the phallus which both seems to merge with, and become, the backbone of the figure and to be a part of the drill itself. These powerful Vorticist sculptures of 1913–16[20] do not come accidentally into being. They speak just as eloquently as any military history of what was going on in Europe as, hidden in tanks, or wedged down in their trenches, European males, in their hundreds of thousands, subsumed their individuality into a common, mechanized, destructive force.

In his manifesto for *BLAST* No. 1, 1914, the Vorticist periodical, Lewis lashed out to right and left. His pronouncements in bold upper and lower case are the verbal equivalent of machine-gun fire, let off in a crowd of civilians by a maniac. BLAST years 1837 to 1900, he began, promising to WRING THE NECK of all sick inventions born in that progressive white wake, Victorian sculpture and poetry (Swinburne's last days are mocked as PURGATORY OF PUTNEY). And the whole GLOOMY VICTORIAN CIRCUS is gleefully consigned to history. LONDON IS NOT A PROVINCIAL TOWN, he thundered. Then, with heavy irony, but obvious admiration too, he wrote: 'BLESS ENGLAND! BLESS ENGLAND *FOR ITS SHIPS* which switchback on Blue, Green and Red Seas all around the pink EARTH-BALL . . .'

The ships themselves are, when we see them in the photographs, floating Vorticist sculptures, their large planes of gun-metal grey, their tubular gun barrels at semi-parallel angles to one another, highly reminiscent of an Epstein sculpture or a Wyndham Lewis canvas. Figures such as Admiral John Jellicoe and Admiral David Beatty, Victorians who had done all in their power during the previous fifteen years to persuade politicians to keep building battleships, presided over a collection of huge destructive engines. Yet more Vorticist in outline were the submarines, the Unterseeboten, or U-boats. From his retirement the old first sea lord, John Fisher, builder of the modern British navy, urged upon the first lord of the Admiralty, Winston Churchill, 'Build more submarines!'[21] 'BLESS ENGLAND', echoed Wyndham Lewis, 'industrial island machine, pyramidal.'[22]

Many of those, perhaps Lewis included, who had watched the naval arms race before the outbreak of war might have expected that war, when it came, would provide the spectacle of some great naval battles. But while the land armies within months reached a near stalemate on the battlefields of France, the ships played a strategic role, rather than taking the risk of a modern-day Trafalgar in which outright defeat might be very hastily encountered. Churchill once remarked to Admiral Jellicoe that he was the man who could lose the war in an afternoon.[23]

The Kaiser was obsessed by the navy, and proud, until the outbreak of war, of his being an admiral of the British Fleet. Alfred Mahan's *The Influence of Sea Power upon History* was a favourite book. To his American friend Bigelow, in 1894, Wilhelm II had telegraphed: 'I am just now not reading but devouring Captain Mahan's book and am trying to learn it by heart.'[24]

The Kaiser would have been ready to acknowledge, when it was over, that the war had effectively been won by the Royal Navy, and this not in spite, but because of the fact that there had only been one great naval engagement involving the German High Seas Fleet under Admiral Scheer fighting the Grand Fleet off the Danish coast on 31 May 1916 – the so-called Battle of Jutland. (The Germans sank fourteen British ships, and lost eleven of their own, but they were unable to budge the strategic superiority held by the Royal Navy.) After Jutland, the German High Seas Fleet was in effect stuck in harbour.

From the moment that the BEF embarked for France in 1914, the Royal Navy provided the army with its lifeline of supplies, its kit, its boots, its canned bully beef, its ammunition. It was British naval domination of the English Channel which enabled British troops in the trenches to have periods of home leave. It was the navy which enabled Britain, throughout the war, to draw on reserves from India and the dominions, and to deploy large armies in the Middle East and Africa. It was also the navy which imposed the greatest hardships not only on German ships but on the entire German population, by a repetition of the strategy, which had caused such vexation to Napoleon, of blockading Continental ports. So effective was the Royal Naval blockade that it cut off German financial trade, thereby causing tax rises in Germany to pay for the war effort. It also denied the Germans food imports, leading to the dreadful 'turnip winter' of 1916 to 1917, which greatly heightened social tension, and weakened the Kaiser's position in the eyes of his people.

In March 1916, 89,000 French and more than 81,000 Germans were killed at Verdun. By the conclusion of the battle of the Somme in autumn, Allied losses were at 600,000, with comparable numbers on the German side.[25]

By December 1916, the Germans were offering peace negotiations to the Allies. Apart from these unconscionable losses in France, the British naval blockades had deadly consequences for the Germans at home; 88,232 civilian German deaths were attributable to the blockade in 1915, and in 1916 the number of deaths by starvation rose to 121,114. There were food riots in thirty German cities. Karl Liebknecht, a member of the Reichstag who had urged soldiers not to fight, had been expelled from the German parliament and condemned to two years' hard labour, but there was overpowering political and social pressure on the Kaiser and his government to sue for peace. Instead, after a year in which tens of thousands of Europeans had been killed, for the sake of possessing thirty miles or so of French mud which had been pounded into a wilderness, both sides intensified their struggle, recruiting more troops, buying more machine guns.[26]

In such circumstances, with the possibility of revolution at home if the starvation continued, and a stalemate–slaughter in France, the Germans desperately stepped up submarine activity. For the English navy to starve 120,000 German civilians was fair tactics. For the Germans to attack British or American merchant vessels was a deadly war crime. The German torpedo attack on the Cunard liner *Lusitania* on 7 May 1915 had been a terrible tactical blunder. This supposedly civilian ship was thought by some to have been carrying American munitions to Britain, but it was also carrying passengers, and when the torpedo struck, exploding the munitions, 1,201 people drowned, including 35 babies and 128 Americans – among them the millionaire sportsman Alfred Gwynne Vanderbilt and the theatrical impresario Charles Frohman. The German embassy's press attaché in Washington, Dr Bernhard Dernburg, noted: 'The American people cannot visualize the spectacle of a hundred thousand, even a million, German children starving by slow degrees as a result of the British blockade, but they can visualize the pitiful face of a little child drowning amidst the wreckage caused by a German torpedo.'[27]

The Vorticist magazine-title, *BLAST*, had been taken up, it would seem, by the leaders of the free world. Sir Martin Gilbert, meditating upon the invention of the machine gun, wrote: 'Maxim's invention had become the means whereby those who shared the highest values of civilization, religion, science, culture, literature, art, music and a love of nature, were to continue to bleed each other to death or victory.'[28]

Vorticism had been one of the indications that such a convulsion was in the air, even before the war. The Vorticists flirted with another group, this one Italian, the Futurists, but they had much in common. The future envisaged by Futurists was a bleak one, dominated by noise, nonsense and belligerence. Their chief spokesman was the firebrand Filippo Marinetti. At a memorable dinner given in his honour at the Florence restaurant in London before the war, Marinetti had declaimed his violent free verse, while the band played, 'You made me love you, I didn't want to do it'.[29]

'A day of attack upon the Western Front,' said Lewis later with characteristic lack of charity or taste, 'with all the heavies hammering together right back to the horizon, was nothing in comparison with Marinetti's unaided voice.'[30]

The First World War is the most horrible demonstration of life imitating art, that phenomenon first anatomized by Oscar Wilde, whose strange tomb, completed for the Père Lachaise cemetery in 1912 by the Vorticist sculptor Epstein, massive and Assyrian in inspiration, pays tribute to Wilde's disruptive and revolutionary life-view rather than his whimsical capacity to amuse.

These were violent times, and art reflected the changes through which Europe was being torn. Marinetti, after one of his recitals, pummelled his own chest as sweat poured from his brow and exclaimed: *'Il faut une force de poumon épouvantable pour faire ça!'* (You need a dreadful lung-power to do that.) Force, power, strength, *Macht* – these were the qualities, in war, in life, and in art, which were called forth by the times. The vapid lyricism of 'Georgian' poets, the landscapes and portraits executed by the British artists who stood aside from modernism, seem faded, deathly. The works of early modernism, whether of Cubist pictures or modernist poetry, still have a brutal strength, nearly a century later. And the art form which requires the greatest brute force, and which as far as Britain was concerned had been all but asleep since the Middle Ages, was sculpture. 'Sculpture, which seems in one sense, peculiarly a thing of the twentieth century,' wrote Pound. 'No, acrimonious reader, do not seize that last clause by itself; let me explain what I mean. Sculpture of this new sort, Epstein's, Brzeska's, is perhaps more moving than painting simply because there has been for centuries no sculpture that one could take very seriously.'[31]

Gaudier-Brzeska himself called sculpture 'this virile art'. Gaudier died aged twenty-three, having read aloud to the thirty men under his command from Pound's rendition of Chinese verse, *Cathay*. 'I use the poems to put courage in my fellows.'

A British soldier sets up a light Maxim gun at Chilas Fort on the North-West Frontier. Younghusband's expedition to Tibet was based on the false belief that the Russians were infiltrating that country and threatening the British Raj. The ensuing massacre of Tibetans was widely criticized.

(*Above left*) George Nathaniel Curzon, Viceroy of India leaves Bombay on 18 November 1905. Becoming Viceroy was for this learned, arrogant man 'the dream of my childhood, the fulfilled ambition of my manhood'. (*Above right*) Rudyard Kipling, here painted by John Collier, was the greatest writer to embrace the Imperial Theme.

Winston Churchill, whose career
dominated the first half of the
twentieth-century, and to some
extent determined its course.
Here, as Liberal First Lord of the
Admiralty, he is seen arriving by air
at Portsmouth from Wiltshire in 1914.

(*Left*) Here Churchill is seen defending Lloyd George's
controversial Budget of 1909. At this stage of his career,
Churchill believed in the abolition of the House of Lords.
(*Above*) As Home Secretary, Churchill held the values of the
clubland heroes depicted by John Buchan and 'Sapper'. He
is seen at the head of the queue beseiging a house of violent
criminals in Sidney Street, Stepney, enjoying the prospect of
pitched battle with anarchists from Eastern Europe.

Sir Edward Elgar, a keen cyclist, was the greatest English orchestral composer since Purcell; his mingled themes of elegy and triumphalism caught the period's mood

(*Right*) Model 'T' Fords at the factory in Trafford Park Manchester, poised to destroy rural England

(*Below left*) Gertrude Jekyll (pronounced to rhyme with treacle) the inspired horticulturalist

(*Below right*) The Edwardian age was marked by fierce industrial unrest. London crowds are here seen swarming on to the overcrowded buses during a tube strike.

George V succeeded to the throne in 1910. Here he is seen with his wife, the former Princess Mary of Teck, on their way to India for the Durbar ceremony at Delhi, one of the most magnificent of all Imperial demonstrations of pomp and glory.

Two power maniacs meet on horseback – Kaiser Wilhelm II and President Theodore Roosevelt

A late photograph of King Edward VII (left in the carriage) being escorted through the streets of Berlin by his nephew Kaiser Wilhelm II (to the right of the picture)

The great American novelist Henry James who adopted British citizenship during the First World War

Gaudier-Brzeska's sculpture were craggy embodiments of the new modernism. He was destined to die fighting for France before his twenty-fifth birthday.

Percy Wyndham-Lewis, novelist, Vorticist painter, and controversialist

Lewis's Vorticist Review, *Blast*, sought to relate art to the forces of industry, machinery and the mechanized warfare which was the most sinister development of the age

H.G. Wells (1866–1946) depicted here with his mistress, the writer Rebecca West, and other friends. Wells's prophetic fictions saw the centrality of science in the new century's imaginative life.

Dr Hawley Crippen was an American and not really a doctor. His arrest for the murder of his wife was facilitated by the new Marconi telegraphy. Here he is seen in the dock with his mistress Ethel le Neve.

Women's struggle for political suffrage led to many scenes such as this in British cities

Ireland's political destiny haunted that of England and helped to bring it down. The poet W.B. Yeats, here photographed with his wife Georgie Hyde Lees, was a fervent nationalist.

(*Above left*) The strange career of Sir Roger Casement (1864–1916) took him from British consular service to the gallows where he was hanged for treason. British intelligence made unscrupulous but successful use of his homosexual diary-confessions to blacken his reputation.

(*Above right*) Eamon de Valera (1882–1975), ultimately the President of Ireland, seen here addressing a meeting in Los Angeles to drum up support from the American Irish whence he sprang

J'ai vu...

LES TROIS GRANDS OUVRIERS
DU MONDE NOUVEAU
LLOYD GEORGE – CLEMENCEAU – WILSON

Three Imperialisms. The Entente Cordiale between France and Britain could be said to have led ineluctably to the First World War. In a French cartoon, President Wilson of America helps David Lloyd-George, the Prime Minister of Great Britain, and Georges Clemenceau, the French leader, to carve up the world after the War.

Arthur Balfour, former Tory Prime Minister and Foreign Secretary in Lloyd-George's coalition Government made the famous Declaration giving support to the aspirations of the Jews for a political homeland. Here he is seen in Jerusalem laying the foundation stone of the Einstein Institute with Chaim Weizmann the Russian chemist and Zionist champion – later first President of Israel.

Who has brought the flaming imperial anger?
Who has brought the army with drums and with kettle-drums?
Barbarous Kings.[32]

All his work is juvenilia – the hieratic, phallic head of Pound himself completed in 1913, the erect birds, the dancers. He was all but self-taught, having come to England as a trainee shipping-broker, attending drawing lessons in his spare time. Henri Gaudier was eighteen when he met Zofia Zuzanna Brzeska in a Paris library. She was nearer forty than thirty, and it was not for some years that they became lovers; but almost at once she became his muse. They lived together in a succession of poor lodgings and hotel rooms. He called her Mother or Mamus, she called him Pik, and when they first began to meet London Bohemians, they tried to pass themselves off as brother and sister. Gaudier was a slight, boyish figure. Zofia took him for a (very dirty) Spaniard when she first met him.[33] His thin inquisitive face has in photographs the look of a fox which is not going to let the hounds have him. The great influences on him artistically were Brancusi and Epstein, but you can see and feel something quite new coming to birth in his few surviving works – now scattered through four continents. He could not afford materials. He had come from an ordinary French bourgeois family. Yet he seemed to feel and to confront the whole Western tradition with his fingertips and his chisel. 'He was the first sculptor in a thousand years to work in modes that had been all that Homer, Ptahotep, Confucius and Sappho knew as beauty in stone.'[34]

In Gaudier's work, we feel the Victorian curse lift. Art can cease to be decoration. Of course when an artist dies young there is a tendency to overpraise. Pound, however, was not given to that tendency. He saw in Gaudier 'the most absolute case of genius I've ever run into'. What makes this death so continuingly haunting is that Gaudier-Brzeska's vision of Europe, its art, its culture, and the moment it had reached, was not at variance with the war which killed him. Quite the contrary. The anti-war poets and artists of this period tended either to be of poor artistic capability or to be retrospective in their hatreds – or both. Gaudier-Brzeska, hideously in tune with his times, embraced the struggle and saluted the violence. The huge numbers being slaughtered reduced the sense of each and every person being of unique value. As in modernist sculptures, men became almost indistinguishable from the tanks or submarines in which they set out to destroy one another, bringing about deaths in numbers which had hitherto only been known in slaughterhouses. From the nameless cannon-fodder arose an inevitable vision of humanity as something less than what it had once been – of people as 'the masses', scarcely distinguishable from one another. They awaited men of genius to lead or inspire them – and they certainly were not finding them in the bumbling, indecisive generals in charge of the battles of the Western Front, nor in the old aristocrats or classically educated Liberal politicians who sent the men to war. Pound chose as an epigraph to his memoir of Gaudier-Brzeska an epigram from Machiavelli: 'There are very few real men, and the rest are sheep – "*Gli uomini vivono in pochi e gli altri son pecorelle*".'

11

Revolutions

Food shortages, which threatened the end of social order in Germany, were having their dire effect upon the Russians also. There were widespread strikes in all the Russian cities, and by March 1917 the discontents of the working class had become too widespread, too powerful, too acrimonious for the authorities to suppress. On International Women's Day, organized by the socialists, fifty factories – 90,000 workers approximately – stopped work. The next day, 9 March, 200,000 were on strike, and the crowds swelled into the streets. It was in vain that the authorities insisted that bread had now reached the shops at last. A change had come upon Russia, and upon the world. The hardships of the war, the whole accumulation of horrors which afflicted civilians and soldiers, men and women, were of a magnitude which made it impossible, in any country, to go back to the old ways. The Romanov dynasty was finished. Their bizarre guru, the religio-sex maniac Rasputin, had been assassinated the previous December. In the Duma, the Russian parliament, the liberal historian P. N. Milyukov listed the misdeeds of the government in a superb piece of rhetoric; after each clause asking – 'Is this stupidity, or treason?' Russia, and all its mighty empire, was on the verge of anarchy. There were rebellions in the Muslim provinces. Turkestan, Samarkand and the Steppe Region were preparing to rise against their Muscovite overlords. The working class at home, and more crucially in the field of battle, had lost their instinctive loyalty to a royal family which had ruled Russia for 300 years.

On 12 March four regiments – the Volhynian, the Lithuanian, the Pavlovsky, the Semyonovsky – mutinied. The Tsar abdicated, the liberals offered his throne to his brother, but this was declined. Russia became a republic, and a provisional government, with the liberal prime minister Kerensky, was formed.[1] There was a tremendous and generalized rejoicing. Soldiers at the front, and workers in the factories, believed peace would come almost at once. The Russian equivalents of Asquith and Lloyd George could, with the reins of power in their hands, lead their great country to a peaceful, democratic and prosperous future. In a Zurich boarding house, the exile Vladimir Ilyich Ulyanov was finishing his breakfast and preparing to go to the library, to complete another piece of prose, by turns turgid and inflammatory, on the Marxist inevitability of world revolution. A Polish comrade came bursting into the dining room

– 'Haven't you heard the news? There's been a revolution in Russia.' Ulyanov, whose *nom de guerre* was Lenin, abandoned his idea of a day in the library, and ran out to buy the newspapers.[2]

Paradoxically, it was in part the Russian military and strategic success, or at any rate courage, which contributed to the weakness of morale in 1917 previous to the Tsar's abdication. General Alexei Brusilov had led devastating attacks on the Galician front, taking over half a million Austrian prisoners, and doing irreparable damage to both Austrian strength and morale. But the cost was ruinously high – over a million Russian casualties. Terrible, unimaginably terrible, as the sufferings of the English, French, Germans and Belgians were on the Western Front, the numbers dead and the torments endured were eclipsed by what the Russians went through. Kerensky, after he became prime minister in July, was determined to fight on. The provisional government, which had come to power with a slogan of 'Bread and Peace', was determined not to be defeated in the war. It gave Trotsky and Lenin their chance, secretly negotiating with the Germans to allow them into Russia with safe conduct. By the terms of the treaty of Brest-Litovsk, signed on 3 March 1918 after the Bolsheviks had taken power in the previous October, Russia abandoned many of its Baltic and Eastern territories.

One of the Austrian soldiers fighting in the Ukraine in July 1917, receiving the silver medal for valour at Ldziany and recommended a little later for the Gold Medal, was an intense, raw-boned, wild-eyed Viennese named Ludwig Wittgenstein. 'His exceptionally courageous behaviour, calmness, sang-froid, and heroism', said one of his citations, 'won the total admiration of the troops.'

Ludwig Wittgenstein (1889–1951), the son of an immensely rich Viennese industrialist, was the youngest of eight children, three of whom were destined to commit suicide. (His brother Kurt shot himself at the end of the war when his troops refused to obey his orders.) Like many men of genius, Ludwig as a child was not deemed by schoolteachers to be especially bright. Indeed, rather than receiving a grammar school (gymnasium) education like some of his siblings, he was sent to the more technologically inclined *Realschule* in Linz, where for two years Adolf Hitler was his contemporary. The history master was Dr Leopold Pötsch. 'Even today', Hitler was to recollect in *Mein Kampf*, 'I think back with gentle emotion on this grey-haired man who, by the fire of his narratives, sometimes made us forget the present; who, as if by an enchantment, carried us back into past times, and out of the millennial veils of mist, moulded dry historical memories into living reality. On such occasions we sat there, often aflame with enthusiasm, and sometimes even moved to tears.'[3]

There is no evidence that Wittgenstein ever had much to do with Hitler, who, though the same age as Wittgenstein, was two years behind him (he was forced to leave the *Realschule* in 1904 because of his poor performance). Wittgenstein hated the place, largely for snobbish reasons. His lower-middle-class coevals teased him, which, if he was as odd in his schooldays as in later life, was not especially surprising. He then went on to the technical university, the *Hochschule*, at Berlin, where he read engineering for two years, before turning up to study aeronautics at the university of Manchester in the spring of 1908.

Wittgenstein's primary interest was in the very new business of aircraft engines. He had an idea that it would be possible to rotate the propeller by means of high-speed gases rushing from the combustion engine, a little as water pressure from a garden hose rotates a lawn-sprinkler. His plans, worked upon steadily for a couple of years at Manchester, were flawed, but the idea was adopted during the Second World War in the design of certain types of helicopter.[4] The modernity of Wittgenstein's interests was in marked contrast to the *völkisch* history lessons in his provincial *Realschule*. Vienna, the centre of the obsolescent Austro-Hungarian Empire, was the heart of a dying world. When Austria found itself on the losing side of the war, Vienna lost the *raison d'être* which had sustained it for centuries. No longer the centre of a polyglot and multicultural empire of 50 million subjects, it became overnight the capital of an impoverished Alpine republic of little more than 6 million Germans. When, in 1919, they voted for *Anschluss,* union with the rest of Germany, the victorious Allies refused their request.

Throughout Wittgenstein's youth, the head of state, Franz Joseph, presided over an autocracy which was in most respects unchanged since he had become Emperor in 1848. One of the reasons that Vienna became the centre of so much modern innovation was that its outer structures had become a chrysalis husk. In England and France, where reforms and changes had happened throughout the nineteenth century, there was an atmosphere much more conducive to gradualism. Vienna stepped directly from the eighteenth century to the twentieth, missing out the Victorian experiences of commercial success, bourgeois democracy, and Doubt. After the tired late rococo of late nineteenth-century decorative architecture it was Adolf Loos in Vienna who pioneered the still calm of pared-down modernist design. Whereas English Victorian novels darkly knew that boys were repressed by buried hatred of their fathers and unbelief in their Father-God, Sigmund Freud let them have it in one mouthful. Whereas Sir Arthur Sullivan could demonstrate that the traditions which bred Mendelssohn were going to hit the buffers, Alban Berg simply made the atonal revolution. Wittgenstein's musical tastes were in fact very old-fashioned. They stopped at Brahms. But his fascination with aircraft engines, in the very dawn of aeronautics studies, should not surprise us as the subject of interest in a young Viennese.

But it is not as an aeronautical engineer that Wittgenstein's name is known to us – nor as an architect, though he was to design a magnificent modernist house for his sister, a building of which Loos would have approved. Wittgenstein's name is synonymous with 'modern philosophy', even, or especially, among those who would find it difficult to put into words a single one of his ideas, and who know nothing of his work beyond a few aphorisms – such as 'If a lion could talk we could not understand him' (*Philosophical Investigations*) or 'The world of the happy is quite another than that of the unhappy' (*Tractatus Logico-Philosophicus*).

Among professional philosophers, there is disagreement about the significance, and influence, of his work.[5] For all that – perhaps partly because he distanced himself so resolutely from so many other professional philosophers – he was destined to be one of those twentieth-century figures of emblematic stature. Such figures, like characters in medieval legendaries, enter the public consciousness, resonate, 'stand for something'. (Machiavelli again – *Gli uomini vivono in pochi e gli altri son pecorelle*.) Wittgenstein stands like a lonely secular saint, a twentieth-century Mr Valiant-for-Truth, or perhaps more accurately, Mr-Irascible-and-Slightly-Mad-for-Truth. The very fact that most of his words (even or especially when translated into English) would seem unintelligible to ordinary mortals has served to enhance his reputation for profundity, just as James Joyce and Samuel Beckett are revered by their most ardent disciplines for those works of theirs which most people only partially understand.

In so far as it is possible to extrapolate simple influences from Wittgenstein's work, influences which have filtered into the general consciousness, it is probably true to say that they are influences which would make him distressed and angry. The popularity of the Verification Principle* espoused by the Vienna School is probably one reason why Wittgenstein, in the second half of his philosophical career, went so far to distance himself from it. In later life, his notion of 'Language Games',† his belief that all human utterance is imprisoned within its own linguistic frames of reference, has given birth to various types of 'postmodern' attitudes to ethics and aesthetics which Wittgenstein would equally have abominated.

---

* Which says that a statement is meaningful if, and only if, it is in principle verifiable. Whether the Verification Principle is itself verifiable, and what bearing it has on the *a priori* truths of mathematics, are two major problems encountered by its defenders.
† *Das Sprachspiel*, the language game, was Wittgenstein's coinage.

On 18 October 1911, Wittgenstein, an engineering student from Manchester University, had suddenly appeared at the rooms in Trinity College, Cambridge, of Bertrand Russell, who had just completed a monumental account of the foundations of mathematics, *Principia Mathematica*.

Russell (1872–1970), the diminutive grandson of the nineteenth-century statesman Lord John Russell, had a background which was different from Wittgenstein's in every respect other than this: both were born to privilege. Whereas Wittgenstein's family were *haute bourgeoisie*, Russell was a pure aristocrat. He grew up (his parents having died by the time he was four) at Pembroke Lodge in Richmond Park, a house given for life to his grandparents by Queen Victoria. His adolescent memories included being left, as the only male at the table apart from their guest, alone at the end of dinner with Mr Gladstone, after the ladies retired. 'He made only one remark: "This is very good port they have given me, but why have they given it me in a claret glass?" I did not know the answer and wished the earth would swallow me up.'[6] At the age of eleven, he began reading Euclid, and from that period until he was thirty-eight 'mathematics was my chief interest and my chief source of happiness'.[7]

On 13 December 1894, Russell, like so many English aristocrats of the period, had married an American, Alys Pearsall Smith. In this case, however, it would seem as if he married not for money (the Russells were rather richer than Alys's bookish, Quaker family) but for affection. At Cambridge, he began as a Hegelian Idealist like his tutor Ellis McTaggart, chiefly famed for having proved – to his own satisfaction if not that of others – that Time did not exist, and was then converted to a form of realism. Hegelians such as McTaggart taught that mathematics was true, not absolutely, but as an expression of our perception of the world. Russell believed that mathematics was true, it had an absolute reality, independent of those who perceive it: rather like Plato's Forms. Russell's abandonment of Idealism also sprang from his friendship with G. E. Moore, another Cambridge philosopher, whose essay *The Refutation of Idealism* (1903) brought to an end Cambridge's, or at any rate Russell's, belief in Hegel. Moore devoted much of his professional life to the analysis of propositions, and the defence of 'common sense' language against philosophical gobbledygook. His *Principia Ethica* (1903) was of huge influence in its day, taken by a whole generation, especially of the Cambridge-educated, as an agnostic guide to the Good Life – a 'philosophy', to use the word in its popular sense of life-view, which permeates, for example the novels of E. M. Forster, which had their unaccountable mid-twentieth-century vogue.

Russell and Moore were both perceived, in early twentieth-century

Cambridge, as having seen off Idealism and established a new approach to philosophical problems. The arrival of Wittgenstein altered this almost at once, as Russell was generous and clever enough to see. Wittgenstein was an Idealist, in the philosophical sense, as extreme as it was possible to be. Russell wrote to his new mistress, Lady Ottoline Morrell:

My German engineer very argumentative and tiresome. He wouldn't admit that it was certain that there was not a rhinoceros in the room . . . He came back and argued all the time I was dressing. [1 November 1911] . . . He admits that if there is no Matter then no one exists but himself, but he says it doesn't hurt, since physics and astronomy and all the other sciences could still be interpreted so as to be true.[8]

Moore took almost as great a shine to Wittgenstein as had Russell and gave him the rooms in Cambridge which he would occupy, with many absences, until he retired as professor of Philosophy. Being Wittgenstein, he wanted only the very simplest furnishings. Just as his philosophical task was to pare away mercilessly at error, leaving only the bare skeleton of what might truthfully be said, so he deplored unnecessary decoration or ornamentation in domestic furnishings. None of the shops in Cambridge had anything simple enough for his taste, so he had all his furniture especially made to his own designs.[9]

By the time he left Cambridge for a long period of contemplation in Norway in 1913, Wittgenstein had undermined Russell's beliefs in the Foundation of Mathematics, and in effect made him give up the pursuit of academic philosophy. Russell embarked upon his career thereafter as a public man, and political agitator.

While Wittgenstein joined the Austrian army, and fought with great gallantry for an imperial system in which he scarcely believed, Russell, against the personal background of professional and marital failure, threw himself into the role of public agitator for peace. The reaction of Russell's family doctor, on hearing he wished to be married, had been discouraging. He had unfolded to Russell the extent of madness in his family. One is sometimes reminded of this fact in the pages of Russell's autobiographical writings which have a chilly sprightliness that must be at variance with the author's intentions. There is the moment when, bicycling along a country road near Grantchester, he suddenly realizes he no longer loves his wife. He immediately told her. As he recalls the scene, he admits to finding his earlier self repulsive,[10] but one senses that even in old age he does not completely understand how strange, as well as repulsive, his behaviour seems to the reader. His subsequent love affairs are written up as affairs of the heart, but one feels no heart beating as he writes. Moreover, the logician seems entirely illogical. Not just a little, but totally illogical. 'One day in October 1914, I met T. S. Eliot in New Oxford Street. I did not know he was in Europe, but I found he had come to England from Berlin. I naturally asked him what he thought of the War. "I don't know," he replied, "I only know that I am not a pacifist". That is to say, he considered any excuse good enough for homicide.'[11] Anyone can see that this is hyperbole written for effect, but since it is so plainly untrue, it is hard to see the remark having any useful application. 'Any excuse good enough for homicide' is simply not the same as supporting the war, especially in its early stages when most pundits believed it would be short.

In January 1918, Russell published an article praising Lenin for having made peace with the Germans. 'Lenin, whom we have been invited to regard as a German Jew, is really a Russian aristocrat who has suffered many years of persecutions for his opinions,' he opined, making Lenin sound a little like a Russian version of Russell himself.

Russell went on: 'It is known that unless peace comes soon, there will be starvation throughout Europe. Mothers will be maddened by the spectacle of their children dying. Men will fight each other for the bare necessities of life.' But there was something even worse than starvation round the corner: that is, the domination of Europe by America. 'The American garrison which will by that time be occupying England and France, whether or not they will prove efficient against the Germans, will no doubt be capable of intimidating strikers, an occupation to which the American army is accustomed when at home . . .'[12]

This article, published in the No-Conscription Fellowship's periodical *The Tribunal*, had the desired effect of bringing Russell a very great deal of publicity and some 'persecution', albeit of a comparatively gentle kind. The military authorities interpreted the article as an incitation to British workers to strike and believed it was 'likely to prejudice His Majesty's relations with the United States of America'. Russell came up before the Bow Street magistrates and was sentenced to six months in prison. He was taken to Brixton gaol in a taxi. His sister-in-law Elizabeth von Arnim was allowed to furnish his cell, which was twice the normal size (he paid two and sixpence a week for the privilege). Lady Ottoline sent him fresh flowers from the garden at Garsington Manor each day. His friend Lytton Strachey sent him his debunking essays *Eminent Victorians*, which initially made him laugh aloud; but upon reflection, he was less sure of the book's merits. 'At the beginning of the Victorian era starvation and ignorance were almost universal,' he could write, the pardonable exaggeration of a man whose grandfather had single-handedly made the Irish Famine very much worse than it need have been. 'At the end there was little starvation and much education. Our age is pursuing the opposite, and we shall need a set of Victorians to put us right.'[13]

Russell looked and sounded very much like his famous prime minister grandfather: tiny, and with a very distinctive, rather ugly voice. It is astounding to think that this man who dined with Gladstone, and whose parents were friends of John Stuart Mill, should have survived into the age of the television chat show, still speaking in a rasping version of pre-1832 aristocratic English. Russell's standing, since a devastating two-volume biography by Ray Monk was published, has never been lower than it is today. As a husband, father, grandfather, he clearly had appalling defects. His decision, from time to time, to abandon serious academic philosophy and to indulge in popularizing, journalism and public campaigning was seen by fellow academics as impure. But for many, he will always be seen primarily as a campaigner for peace. As soon as he had visited Russia in 1920 and seen the evils which Lenin had unleashed, he lost no time in denouncing them.

The man who lived long enough to accuse the United States government of genocide for its intervention in Vietnam,[14] and who was a leading light in the Campaign for Nuclear Disarmament in the 1960s, was first inspired to anti-war protest in the earliest days of the First World War. Whatever his personal follies, there was a great nobility in this. Russell, for all his nineteenth-century appearance, was a quintessentially twentieth-century man. The evolution from philosopher to publicist, albeit in a good cause, would not have been possible other than in an age of mass media. Those of us who continue to revere the memory of the ancient Lord Russell, the removal of whose recumbent form into police vans formed an essential part of any peace ritual of the 1950s and early 1960s, believe his protests to be both sincere yet absurd; noble but theatrical.* The tainted century in which Russell gleefully played his totemic role allowed for little purity. Russell was not one of those rare beings – not like Einstein, Bonhoeffer, Gandhi or Wittgenstein – the pure in heart. He was a complex of impurities, whose very superficiality made him an increasingly appropriate mouthpiece for the age, as the decades unrolled. At the beginning of the First World War, he wrestled not only with the disagreement of many colleagues and friends, but with his own inner patriotism. He was 'tortured' by patriotism. 'I have at times been paralysed by scepticism, at times I have been cynical, at other times indifferent, but when War came I felt as if I heard the voice of God. I knew that it was my business to protest, however futile the protest might be.'[15] It cost him his academic job at Cambridge.

* Prison Warder: 'What do you do, then?' Russell, 'I think.' Warder: 'Well, do you think you can clean these toilets?' – *That Was The Week That Was.*

It would be frivolous not to see the importance of his discussions with Wittgenstein, esoteric as they must appear to nearly all of us. For much of the time, they disintegrate into near-farce. (Take, for instance, the moment when Wittgenstein paces up and down in Russell's room for three hours in silence. 'Once I said to him: "Are you thinking about logic or about your sins?" "Both", he replied and continued his pacing.')[16]

Yet of all the centuries, the twentieth was the most given to destructive ideas. Millions of Europeans were to be carried away with enthusiasm for movements whose ideas were based upon extravagant falsehoods. Beside Stalinist communism, or National Socialism, the wilder heresies of the past seem positively rational. The millenarian ravings of Anabaptists or Bohemian Brethren in the seventeenth century are the soul of reasonableness beside the ideas propounded by Himmler's SS; the most extreme superstitions of the Holy Orthodox censors in Tsarist Russia could not rival the thought-control of Stalin. In a century which could produce grotesque intellectual evils of this magnitude, it mattered very much that human beings should learn how to think clearly, and to determine what, if anything, could be seen as the truth.

While the philosophers returned to the very origins of Western thought and began to rethink the bases of logic and mathematics, science was undergoing profound revolutions. While Wittgenstein and Russell bothered their heads with the old chestnut of whether matter existed, and if so, how we can beyond doubt say that we know it exists, physicists were discovering that matter was not as had been previously described.

The second half of the nineteenth century had witnessed a burst of extraordinary scientific discoveries which would change the perspective with which human beings understood their planet, their place in the scheme of things, the manner in which matter cohered, moved, worked. James Clerk Maxwell (1831–1879), a Scottish physicist working in Cambridge, developed the theory of the electromagnetic field. It was working on his theories which enabled Hendrik Antoon Lorentz and Joseph Larmor to discover the properties of the electron. Wilhelm Conrad Röntgen, the son of a Dutchwoman and a German draper, discovered X-rays on 8 November 1895. Julius Plücker, William Crookes and Eugen Goldstein pioneered the discovery of cathode rays, which were to be the instrument of so much twentieth-century research in physics, as well as the eventual invention of television – 'seeing by electricity'. The existence of electromagnetic waves enabled physicists to develop wireless. Guglielmo Marconi was able to make commercial use of wireless telegraphy. During the First World War, scientists developed designs centred upon the thermionic valve, which enabled, for example, aeroplanes in flight to maintain radio contact with the ground. All these examples demonstrate what a short time elapsed between scientists having an idea in a laboratory and technologists applying those ideas with world-changing effect.

In 1900, in the scientific and secular equivalent of a papal conclave, the world's most eminent physicists gathered for a conference in Paris to discuss the progress being made in their subject. It seemed as if the electron was the unique building block between electricity and matter. It explained X-rays, the ion and radioactivity – the property identified in various elements, notably plutonium and uranium, by Marie Curie, her husband Pierre and her brother-in-law Jacques-Paul. What was lacking in 1900 was a theory which would explain atomic structure itself. The quantum theory was first propounded by Max Planck (1858–1947) at about the time of the Paris conference. Planck, working in the university of Berlin after 1889, was really the father of modern physics. His theoretical solution to the problem of radiation inside a closed cavity was to bring to an end 'classical' physics as it had existed since Newton's time. A humane, complicated man, Planck's life was an embodiment of Germany's tragedy. He represented all that was best about its high intellectual traditions. At the same time, he was a patriot, which is why his reputation took some knocks in the years after his death. As early as the mid-1890s, he was defending a Jewish physicist whom the government wished to expel from his laboratory for his socialist leanings. During the First World War, he prevented the German academy from expelling eminent foreign members. At the beginning of the war he was one of ninety-three German intellectuals who signed a manifesto defending the German invasion of Belgium. He was the only one of them brave enough to recant publicly, when the slaughterous consequences of that invasion became known. Later in life, he was to be faced with no less horrible personal choices. As a champion of intellectual freedom, he abominated National Socialism, but his act of defiance was to keep open his laboratories at the Kaiser Wilhelm Gesellschaft in Berlin – an act of collaboration in the eyes of those who had taken the, in some ways easier, path of exile. He was deprived of his teaching posts in 1938. One of his sons was killed in the First World War. During the second, another was executed for complicity in a plot to assassinate Hitler. When the war ended, his house destroyed by RAF bombardment, the aged Planck was found with his wife huddled in the woods.

It was against the background of the twentieth-century nightmare that Max Planck's scientific work was to be done. The crucial theory, the quantum theory, which emanated from Planck, was that radiation is emitted or received in energy 'packets' which he called quanta. The formula which works at all frequencies v was something which he worked out purely theoretically, and it was a number of years before other physicists could test its veracity. Energy $(E) = hv$, where h is the Planck constant – $h = 6.55 \times 10^{-27}$ (erg sec). Walking with his small son on the day that he formulated this theory, Planck told him in 1900 that the modern age had begun. Working on Planck's theory, Albert Einstein was able to account for the photoelectric effect. With amazing rapidity, Einstein was able to develop his theories of relativity – the special theory or SRT, which revised the notions of space and time, based on the idea of an equivalence between energy and mass – $E = mc^2$ – and general theory or GRT, which reinterpreted gravitation as an effect of the curvature of space-time. This opened the way to a so far unachieved unified field theory which would generalize all the interactions that operate on matter, both subatomic and electromagnetic.

It was as if the scientists and the philosophers, working along parallel lines, were worrying about comparable problems. The Enlightenment or empirical views of John Locke and Isaac Newton were fading before European eyes. In a celebrated speech in 1908 to assembled German scientists, the mathematician Hermann Minkowski declared that 'space by itself and time by itself are doomed to fade away into mere shadows, and only a kind of union of the two will preserve an independent reality'. Wittgenstein could not be sure that there was not a rhinoceros in Russell's room. Russell's old tutor McTaggart had worried about the existence of time. Albert Einstein's theory of relativity provided the kind of 'independent reality' which Minkowski had sensed evaporating. But the world was not fixed or composed in quite the way that the old classical physicists had supposed.

In 1919 a total solar eclipse was studied at two locations – at Principe Island off the West African coast and at Sobral in Brazil. Photographs were taken and they showed a deflection of light which supported Einstein's theory of general relativity – one of the most fundamental theories in the history of science.[17] It begins with a comparatively minor puzzle. Einstein himself expressed it often in this way. An observer on an embankment sees a light flash from the middle of a passing railroad carriage, equipped with a mirror at each end. An observer seated in the centre of the carriage would see the light returned from the mirrors simultaneously. The observer on the embankment would see the flash from the forward mirror after that from the rear. The speed of light is the same in both directions, but the light has farther to go to meet and return from the forward than from the rear mirror. From such a commonplace example, the genius of Einstein could extrapolate a principle about the nature of light, gravity, energy itself, a theory of such complexity that almost no one understood it, but which, in the photographic evidence of the sun's eclipse in 1919, was demonstrated to be valid.

Albert Einstein himself was to become one of those totemic or emblematic figures beloved of the twentieth century. As in the case of Bertrand Russell, it did not take much to transform him into a cartoon character. He was in some ways ready-made – small, heavily moustached, untidy and Bohemian in dress, the quintessential absent-minded professor. Physics from the later decades of the nineteenth century had gathered such momentum that some other scientist would surely have developed a theory of relativity without Einstein. But science, no less than ancient Greek epic, requires its heroes, and Einstein's very remarkable predictions about the nature of gravitational force, followed by photographic demonstration, confirmed his iconic status. Stephen Hawking in the late twentieth century became a bestselling author largely on the basis of having claimed in a new-fangled book to have seen into the mind of that old-fashioned phenomenon, God. Einstein had two lives, that of the serious academic, and of the media pundit. To a public who had very little idea what his theories were, Einstein seemed to have reasserted the existence of natural law.[18]

While Einstein developed a theory with widespread implications about the nature of the universe itself, other giants of physics were making their own micro-explorations about the structure of matter.

The career of Ernest Rutherford (1871–1937) was one of the most glittering examples of the scientific revolution which took place in the first two decades of the twentieth century. He was born in New Zealand, of Scottish stock, and had an outdoor boyhood on farms. Scholarships took him from Canterbury College, Christchurch, to Cambridge. He studied under Sir J. J. Thomson in the Cavendish Laboratory at a period when physics appeared to be making revolutionary strides every few years. A month after Rutherford's arrival in Cambridge came news of Röntgen's discovery of X-rays. In 1896, Antoine Henri Becquerel showed that uranium compounds emit radiations similar to X-rays. When he was only twenty-six, Rutherford became a professor at McGill University, Montreal, and it was there, with Frederick Soddy, that he discovered that radioactivity is a phenomenon accompanying the spontaneous transformation of the atoms of radioactive elements into different kinds of matter. What Rutherford discovered was that matter is not indestructible. The Nature of Things, as understood since the days of Lucretius, in some ways since the days of Aristotle, was now different.

Returning to England, Rutherford became Longworthy Professor of Physics at Manchester University in 1907. It was three years after Chaim Weizmann arrived in Manchester to work as a chemistry demonstrator, and a year before Wittgenstein arrived to work on aeronautics. Manchester was quite a place in those days. It was here that Rutherford was able to complete the work begun at McGill which demonstrated that helium is present in all radioactive minerals. He identified the alpha-particle as a positively charged atom of helium. By the use of a device pioneered by Professor Hans Geiger, he could count the number of alpha-particles produced in the disintegration of radium. It was for this work that he received the Nobel prize in 1908. It came as a surprise to Rutherford that he was awarded the prize for chemistry. He considered himself a physicist, and later in life he derided all scientific activity outside physics as stamp-collecting.

Something quite new about the very nature of atomic structure was on the point of being revealed to science. A discovery which would lead inexorably to the possibility among other things of a nuclear bomb.

Together with his team of researchers at Manchester, Rutherford conducted a series of experiments which determined what the atom looked like. It was not a solid thing, but an empty space, defined only by the movement of its outermost electrons. At its centre – this was the revolutionary discovery – lay the atomic nucleus. When an experiment by a young researcher named Ernest Marsden established this, on Rutherford's instructions and to his satisfaction, Rutherford was to say it was 'quite the most incredible event that ever happened to me in my life'. Inside the nucleus lay almost all the mass of a whole atom, packed to an incredible density.

When, in 1911, the Danish physicist Niels Bohr visited Rutherford's laboratory, he became convinced that the nuclear atom explained the whole mystery of atomic structure. Electrodynamics was now explained. A nuclear hydrogen atom with one electron could destroy itself instantly by radiation emitting the electron.

From now onwards, the universe was a different place. It was not a static or solid thing, or collection of things, all indestructible. It was an infinitude of little voids, each tiny nucleus of which was potentially destructive. Mass and energy were equivalents. Matter, whose very existence Idealist philosophers could still question, was charged with energy, an energy which could, with the right artificial adjustments, be tapped or controlled. Dust and stones were not lifeless. They were as energetic as tigers and much more potentially destructive.

It was a very long time before the implications of such ideas reached the public imagination, and could be adapted, with such terrifying consequence, for military or political purpose. But by the end of the First World War, scientists who had been away to fight returned to their laboratories to discover that they were literally in a different universe.

12

Chief

In February 1920, H. W. Wilson, leader-writer for the *Daily Mail*, and the 'mental backbone of the paper'[1] – according to its proprietor – delivered this judgement: 'As I write more and more clearly you appear as the force which won the war.'[2] He was not writing to President Wilson, nor to Lloyd George, nor to one of the Allied generals. He was writing to his proprietor Lord Northcliffe, one of the most energetic and colourful newspaper-owners who ever lived. The prime minister of Australia, W. M. (Billy) Hughes, spoke of Northcliffe as 'one of the great forces for the making of victory during the war'.[3]

One of the reasons Northcliffe regarded Wilson as the 'mental backbone' of his most popular newspaper was, no doubt, his underling's readiness to be His Master's Voice. 'I hear you are swanking about Fleet Street, being patted on the back for the excellent leaders which I write and don't get paid for,' the Chief once told Wilson.[4] Innumerable sycophantic letters from Wilson to his proprietor are preserved in the British Library, and they provide a reflection of the press chief's ascendancy. In October 1903, Wilson is writing to 'Dear Mr Harmsworth'; in 1905, he wrote, 'Dear Sir Alfred'; in 1906, 'My dear Lord'. Having dinner with Harmsworth after he had acquired his Northcliffe title was 'like translation to the Elsyian fields, where, according to the best authorities, the visitor banquets on the most superb comestibles, and is permitted to discourse with the wise and the great. The only trouble is that the return from such an existence to everyday life is like the descent into Purgatory of those who have tasted bliss complete.' One of Wilson's tasks was to supply Northcliffe with his expanding library of books about Napoleon. Soon 'My dear Lord' of the correspondence becomes simply 'My dear Chief'. It was as 'Chief' that Northcliffe was generally known. He signed his telegrams 'Chief'. When the Germans in February 1917 bombarded Broadstairs, Wilson wrote: 'I do beg you not to risk your life there. It is an unnecessary risk, and Napoleon condemned that. The Germans know perfectly well that you are the soul and the heart of this war, and that if you were out of the way, the various puppets now in office would probably run and make peace.'[5] In a later letter, thanking Chief for a cheque, Wilson grovellingly told Northcliffe that 'like that other N' he was 'under posterity's eye'.[6]

Many jokes were made about Northcliffe's power and influence. 'Have you heard? The Prime Minister has resigned and Northcliffe has sent for the King' was a familiar one.[7] There was no doubt in the politicians' minds that there was truth in the joke. The correspondence between Northcliffe and his leader-writers and his editors, both at the *Daily Mail* and at *The Times* (which put up slightly more resistance to his diktats and whims), makes it quite clear that he believed himself to have the power to remove or to instate British leaders, and possibly other world leaders too. He unquestionably played a role in unseating Asquith as Prime Minister in 1916; he saw himself (and so did Lloyd George) as the man who had put in Lloyd George, and three years later he mulled over the possibility of replacing Lloyd George with Winston Churchill. 'It is a question of whether Winston would not make a better Prime Minister than Lloyd George. He is untrustworthy but he knows more and has a clearer head; moreover in danger he has shown himself bold. His handling of the army question has certainly been a success. And slippery though he is, he is less slippery than Lloyd George whom no one trusts.'[8]

Important as the Fourth Estate became in Victorian England (and prime ministers from Gladstone to Salisbury saw nothing wrong with well-managed 'leaks', or favourable mentions in the influential newspapers), it is all but unimaginable that in any previous generation a British newspaper proprietor could have written in such terms, believing it to be within his power and his remit to appoint the government of the day. That he should be seen as having done so was partially a sign of the times and partially a tribute to the extraordinary personality of Sir Alfred Charles William Harmsworth, Bt., 1st Viscount Northcliffe and Baron Northcliffe of the Isle of Thanet (1865–1922). His appearance is electrifying, looking as he does like the most uncanny blend between Winston Churchill and Adolf Hitler. His hyper-energy and his dynamism still have the power to agitate as one reads his letters, or the transcripts of his speeches. One sees why he was loved – the subeditors and compositors on his papers were in tears as they made up the memorial issues of the *Daily Mail* and *The Times* on the day of his death. One sees why he was loathed. He fed off power, needed it as a vampire needs blood, and he was prepared to destroy in order to get it. Having failed to be elected as the Unionist candidate for Portsmouth at the age of thirty in 1895, he had a consistent loathing of elected politicians, and when they came to displease him he had no compunction about using any methods he could to displace them. Bonar Law and Asquith both lost sons on the Western Front. After Alfred Northcliffe lost a son, however, and after the cataclysm of the battle of the Somme – 60,000 British casualties, 19,000 of them dead *in one day* – the Prime Minister, Asquith, was finished as far as Northcliffe was concerned. ASQUITH A NATIONAL DANGER was one 'splash'.[9] 'Get a smiling picture of Lloyd George and underneath it put a caption "do it now" and get the worst possible picture of Asquith and label it "wait and see". Rough methods are needed if we are not going to lose this war.' Wilson, at the Chief's dictation, wrote the leader – 'A moment in our struggle for existence has now been reached when "Government" by some 23 men [that is, the cabinet] – who can never make up their minds has become a danger to the Empire.' Across the top of this piece, the Chief scrawled the headline: ASQUITH A LIMPET.[10]

Alfred Harmsworth came from Protestant Irish stock. At school his nickname was the 'Dodger'.[11] His parents were intelligent, genteel, but poor. His father was a sometime teacher and layabout, with an alcoholic weakness. Mrs Harmsworth, with a gesture which would acquire symbolic importance in Alfred's memory, wrapped her children in newspaper to keep them warm in the winters. From an early age, Harmsworth was hyper-active, gadget-obsessed. As a boy travelling from Grantham to London, he talked his way into being allowed to travel with the driver and fireman of the train, bombarding them with questions about how the steam locomotive functioned. He did not make much of a showing at conventional schoolwork, but he edited the school magazine, making arrangements with a local Kilburn printer to set it up in decent type. (At about the same time, he was caught poaching by the gamekeeper at Ken Wood on the edge of Hampstead Heath.)

Harmsworth was truly one of the geniuses of his age in the sense that he tapped all its potential. Inspired by the success of the magazine *Tit-Bits*, edited by George Newnes, Harmsworth started his own version, called *Answers*, when he was only twenty-three. With his younger brother Harold (the future Lord Rothermere), Alfred was soon running a mass-circulation paper. He understood the importance of technology. He understood the fact that there was now a huge, largely untapped, middle- to lower-middle-class market, who had never bought the expensive newspapers such as *The Times*. Within a year he was making an annual profit of over £30,000.[12] In 1892 he was selling over a million copies of his magazines in a year. By 1896 he had started the *Daily Mail*. Lord Salisbury the Prime Minister could sneer that it was a paper written by office boys for office boys, but in 1896 there were a very great number of office boys. The huge ranks of the lower middle class to which these 'office boys' belonged were not politically aligned. Northcliffe understood them better than did Salisbury; though it was Salisbury who helped promote the 'villa Conservatism' which offered the office boys protection against syndicalism. They voted Tory in 1895, and 1900; but it was office boys who would vote in the Liberals in 1906, office boys who supported Lloyd

George. Office boys cheered for war in 1914 and protested against it in 1916. Office boys, a little sheepishly but in the end determinedly, wanted Votes for Women, peace, old age pensions, modern household appliances, full employment. As the 3rd Marquess of Salisbury in his blackest moods knew only too clearly, there was but a handful of marquesses and the twentieth century was not very interested in their opinions. Ever since Harmsworth started the *Daily Mail*, British politicians have been obsessed by what the office boys wanted or thought they wanted, and they have been guided by such thoughts. He and his brother Harold reinvented the whole political landscape. In 1903 they started the *Daily Mirror*, a paper exclusively for women at first. By 1908, Alfred – now Lord Northcliffe – became the chief proprietor of *The Times*. There was a sense that the Harmsworths' millions of readers were voting with their pennies as they bought all these newspapers; a sense, therefore, in which popular journalism of this kind was genuinely democratic in a way that party politics, dominated by a governing class, did not intend to be.

Northcliffe's attitude to the war, therefore, was of huge importance and was deemed to be crucial, not just by the leader-writer on the *Daily Mail* but by public and political opinion in Germany. In the German *Cologne Gazette* in the summer of 1916, it was said that when Asquith and Lloyd George came to stand before the Judgement Seat, Christ would say: 'Father, forgive them, for they knew not what they did,' but that when Northcliffe came, 'Christ would look the other way'.[13]

Northcliffe was one of those who entered with enthusiasm into the arms race with Germany. Visiting German factories in 1909 he pointed at the chimneys and said, 'Every one of those factory chimneys is a gun pointing at England.'[14]

The *Daily Mail* with unambiguous enthusiasm, and *The Times* with slightly more muted reasoning, had urged the British government to go to war with Germany. On 5 August 1914, as the Chief wanted, there was a 'splash' on the front of the *Mail*: 'Great Britain declares war on Germany'. The streets of London were packed with people, and the crowds sang the National Anthem. The *Mail* editorial staff, and the compositors at Carmelite House, were denying themselves sleep as they planned the stories and decided who should join 'our army of war correspondents'. To their astonishment, however, the Chief was not pleased. In fact, he was furious. 'What is this I hear', he cried, 'about a British Expeditionary Force for France? It is nonsense. Not a single soldier shall leave this country. We have a superb Fleet, which shall give all the assistance in its power, but I will not support the sending out of this country of a single British soldier. What about invasion? What about our own country? Put that in the leader. Do you hear? Not a single soldier will go with my consent. Say so in the paper tomorrow.'[15]

Northcliffe, no doubt in common with most of the crowds who sang 'God Save the King' outside Buckingham Palace, thought – or 'thought' – you could have a war in which only foreigners got killed. Many of the minor wars in Queen Victoria's reign had been a little like this; and even the Boer War had casualties which, by the standards of twentieth-century wars, were remarkably small.

When war had been a matter of armchair politics, Harmsworth had been content to wage it. As long ago as 1900, he had dictated a leader – 'England must remember a fact with which Mr Churchill does not deal – that the Navy is a purely defensive force. We must be able to strike as well as to ward off blows, unless in the contests which the future may force upon us we are content to see hostilities languish on for an indefinite period.'[16]

As soon as it became clear, however, that the army was going to France, and that the war would be of long duration, Northcliffe seized the moment, and thought himself into a central position. Everything which happened from now onwards happened against a background of his whims and desires, and such was the strength of his solipsistic vision that not merely he and his newspaper employees but the wider political world came to believe it. He quickly arranged for the *Daily Mail* to be dispatched to the serving troops in the Western Front, so that it became their chief source of information about the war, their mirror on reality. As early as 18 August 1914 one of his staff was noting in his diary:

George Curnock, who, the Chief tells me, is the best reporter Fleet Street ever had, sent from France today his dispatch describing the arrival of the British Expeditionary Force. It came by courier from Boulogne. George made great play of the soldier's marching song, 'It's a long way to Tipperary', and the Chief has given us orders to boom it, to print the music so that everyone shall know it. He says, thanks to Curnock's genius, we shall soon have everybody singing it.[17]

Northcliffe, with his passion for detail, his bossiness, his obsession with military history and his close personal identification with Napoleon, was not alone in thinking that he would have made an ideal war leader. H. H. Asquith, by contrast, could scarcely have been a less suitable prime minister to lead an empire into the greatest conflict in history. When the war broke out, he was approaching his sixty-second birthday. He was the father of a large, clever, grown-up family which, thanks to his early snobbery and judicious marriages, belonged to a higher social notch than that of his middle-class parents in the North. He himself was languid, emotional, sexually obsessed and clever in a second-rate sort of way. He would have been fun as a dinner companion, unless, like some young women, you objected to his habit of seizing women's hands and thrusting them inside his trousers. He could quote Latin poetry and he 'knew everyone', but he was indecisive, vain and fundamentally idle. When he broke the news to his socialite second wife Margot that the country was drifting towards war, he did so in her boudoir while she was dressing for dinner. Her reaction was 'How thrilling! Oh! tell me you aren't excited, darling!' He was chiefly obsessed, that day, by his emotional need to talk about it to his young confidante Venetia Stanley, a friend of his daughter's with whom he was madly in love. The outbreak of the war forced him to cancel a visit to Venetia, and he wrote: 'I can honestly say that I have never had a more bitter disappointment. All these days . . . full of incident and for the most part anxious and worrying – I have been sustained by the thought that when to-day came I should once more see your darling face.'[18]

All this is personally attractive, but it is hardly the behaviour of a war leader. He was more than vaguely appalled when, at the first meeting of the war cabinet, 'Winston dashed into the room radiant, his face bright, his manner keen and he told us – one word pouring out on the other – how he was going to send telegrams to the Mediterranean, the North Sea and God knows where! You could see he was a really happy man. I wondered if this was the state of mind to be in at the opening of such a fearful war as this.'[19]

A year into the war, he admitted to himself that his preoccupation with Venetia had clouded his judgement, and not allowed him to think clearly enough about war strategy. And there are moments in his letters to her when the reader could be forgiven for thinking that her decision to get married and, horror or horrors, to marry a Jew, Edwin Montagu, weighed more on the Prime Minister's mind than the calamities being enacted in the Dardanelles. Montagu, a cabinet colleague of Asquith's, used to spend cabinet meetings writing love letters to Venetia, only half a dozen chairs away from Asquith who was doing the same thing.

Asquith formed a coalition government without consulting his Liberal backbenchers, on 26 May 1915. Nobody realized it at the time, but it brought to an end the political life of the Liberal party as the alternative party of government, which only eight years before had won so resounding a landslide victory in the General Election. There would never be a Liberal government again. Asquith's decision to rule with a group of the political elite – his old clubland cronies, combined with the rising stars – was an admission that for the first year the war had been conducted with culpable lack of efficiency, and terrible loss of life. The professional army had suffered terrible reduction at Ypres. Churchill's involvement with the Dardanelles venture had, it seemed, cost him his political fortune, as well as leading to the pointless death of tens of thousands of young men. No progress had been made towards the defeat of Germany. Asquith might have felt more politically safe with this government of national unity, surrounded by the Conservatives Lord Curzon as Lord Privy Seal and Arthur Balfour as First Lord of the Admiralty, but he had, as he half knew, begun his own walk down the plank.

Margot Asquith believed Churchill's assessment of David Lloyd George as 'the direct descendant of Judas Iscariot', who had 'blackmailed' Asquith into a coalition by threatening to resign.[20]

Lloyd George held one of the key positions in the new cabinet: minister of Munitions. This job had been created very largely because of the agitations in the Northcliffe Press. At the beginning of the war in August 1914 the *Mail* had seen Lord Kitchener as an essential architect of victory. 'The Nation' – by which it meant Lord Northcliffe – 'Calls for Lord Kitchener'. By the spring of 1915, it had changed its policy to 'Kitchener Must Go'.[21] A week before Asquith's decision to create a coalition, *The Times* had carried the message from a military expert, Colonel Repington, that the British advance at Ypres had been stopped by the lack of a high-explosive shell. 'The Tragedy of the Shells: Lord Kitchener's Grave Error' was the *Mail*'s splash on 20 May 1915. Kitchener had ordered tons of shrapnel, 'when any expert could have told him it was no good for breaking down wire and trenches'. At this point, the government began to censor the Harmsworth papers, and the police turned up each night to read the proofs of *The Times* and the *Daily Mail*. But this was in itself an admission of Northcliffe's power. He replied by sending uncensored proofs to Lloyd George at the Ministry of Munitions and to Curzon. 'We can get things done,' Northcliffe boasted. 'What these people in Downing Street loathe is publicity.'[22] When, inevitably, Asquith was ousted by a cabinet coup and Lloyd George became the Prime Minister on 7 December 1916, Lloyd George held a meeting with the national executive not of his own party, the Liberals, but of the Labour party, and told them: 'Politicians make one fundamental mistake when they have been in office. They think that the people who are in office, or who have been in office, are absolutely essential to the Government of the country, and that no one else is in the least able to carry on affairs. Well, we are a nation of 45 millions, and, really, if we cannot produce at least two or three alternative cabinets, we must really be what Carlyle once called us – "a nation of fools".'[23]

One of those who watched most carefully as Lloyd George

triumphantly seized the controls was a Canadian backbench MP named Max Aitken (1879–1964), with a face like a very amused monkey, and a bank account larger than anyone else's in the House of Commons. In those days, Canadians enjoyed full British citizenship. Aitken was the son of a Presbyterian minister of Scottish origin from Newcastle, New Brunswick. He made a fortune – with scrupulous Presbyterian honesty – by trading in bonds and was a multi-millionaire by the time he was in his mid-twenties. Apart from making money in prodigious quantities, his other genius was for political fixing, and he became the close confidant of another Canadian in British political life, Andrew Bonar Law (1858–1923). Aitken helped Law make a lot of money by his judicious financial advice. Law helped Aitken become the Unionist MP for Ashton-under-Lyme, a suburb of Manchester. Aitken had very light political baggage. He supported the Empire, and he believed in tariffs to protect imperial trade, but beyond that, it was largely a matter of chance that he was a Unionist rather than a Liberal. He quickly became Bonar Law's most intimate friend in the House of Commons,[24] at the time when Law became leader of his party.

While followers of Northcliffe attribute the collapse of Asquith and the advancement of Lloyd George to their hero's public trumpeting, the worshippers of Aitken see the coalition as the creation of the quiet Canadian.[25] At his country house in Surrey, Cherkley, Aitken brokered three secret meetings between Law and Asquith during the autumn of 1914, in which the Conservative leader promised his support for the government on condition that Asquith backed down from imposing Home Rule on Ulster. Certainly, by the time he had got his peerage, in 1917, and had become Lord Beaverbrook, Aitken saw himself as the sole architect of the new prime minister's career. 'It was not Mr Asquith's judgement that I distrusted; it was that of the kind of barnacles, especially in the general staff, which had affixed themselves to his administration. I believed with good reason as the event showed, that Mr Lloyd George's military opinions were better than those of Sir William Robertson and the War Office, and that the united command and all else was impossible unless the generals could be put under proper control by the Secretary of State for War and the Prime Minister.' That was what he told Mrs Asquith when the war was over.[26]

But Max Aitken had not been slow to see, during the first year of the war, that real power – as far as the politicians were concerned, terrifying power – was being exercised by Lord Northcliffe. In the autumn of 1916, as Asquith's career came to a close, and as Law began to look as if he might lose control of the Unionist party, Aitken bought controlling shares in the ailing *Daily Express*. His life as the greatest newspaper proprietor after Northcliffe belongs to a later period, but he could see clearly enough the way in which the wind was blowing. Fireside chats with political leaders would, for many a decade to come, and perhaps for ever, be one way in which political deals were brokered, and power wielded. But the days in which the political class met in clubs and country houses, and could conduct their nation's affairs without popular will or consultation, were over.

The fruitless slaughter of 1916 was leading to political upheaval all over Europe. In France agitation became so extreme that Clemenceau took all but dictatorial powers to himself. In Russia, in 1917, they went through two political revolutions. In Germany Bethmann-Hollweg, that gentle pessimist who played Beethoven on the piano each day, fell as Chancellor in July 1917. The collapse of Asquith's power must be seen against this background.[27] But the power of the Press in Britain was undoubtedly a key element in the story. It was the Age of the Journalist. George V could protest against the rise of Harmsworth and Aitken[28] but the creation of popular journalism was one of capitalism's most extraordinary developments. The hatefulness of the Press to aesthetes, aristocrats, dictators, poseurs, kings, poets, would grow and with reason. Its power without responsibility was to be likened to that of the harlot, in a phrase written for Stanley Baldwin, when Leader of the Opposition, by his journalist cousin Rudyard Kipling. The very phrase has such a journalistic ring to it. The truth is that the countries where such appalling vulgarians as Northcliffe and Beaverbrook flourished were, mysteriously, freer and better places to live than those where the Press was successfully bridled and stamped upon. Shortly before he became Prime Minister, Lloyd George received a visit from Monty Smith, one of Northcliffe's underlings, 'To present Lord Northcliffe's compliments and to say that he (L.G.) was too much in the company of Winston'.[29] There is something undoubtedly unpleasant about a bullying businessman writing in this way to an elected and royally appointed cabinet minister. But the twentieth century would witness countries where the bullies did not own newspapers – they suppressed them.

Churchill himself, who was one of Northcliffe's *bêtes noires*, was himself a keen popular journalist who was not ashamed to earn his crust from Northcliffe's brother Lord Rothermere, and indeed his many acts of populism show him, as well as being an aristocratic hero, to be a tabloid journalist with an eye to a good story. Churchill, however, had a divided attitude to popular journalism, as to so much else. He had risen to fame as a war correspondent in the Boer War; in his years of political exile during the 1930s he would use his friendship with Beaverbrook and Rothermere to propound his views. In power, he had an anti-libertarian attitude, however. As Prime Minister, in the Second World War he frequently tried to censor the BBC's news coverage, and in the First World War at the height of Northcliffe's anti-Asquith campaign, Churchill was urging his Prime Minister to close down *The Times*, or nationalize it and make it the official organ of public opinion.[30] Needless to say, Churchill's 'impudent desire to muzzle the press' – the phrase was that of a *Times* leader writer – came to nothing.

Clearly, if the war was to be won it needed new leadership and new initiative – and Lloyd George abetted by the Northcliffe Press could supply it. Common sense is obliged to say, however, that this begs a very big question. The great powers were locked in stalemate. Domestically they were on the edge of, or actually suffering, starvation, anarchy and revolution. If any demonstration was needed that the battles of Ypres, Mons, Verdun, the Somme had been lunatic, it was provided in summer 1917 at Passchendaele, when Sir Douglas Haig launched an attack against the Messines Ridge south of Ypres. It was a repeat performance of the other acts of mass-slaughter: 240,000 British casualties, 70,000 dead, with German losses around 200,000. By a second attack, in November 1917, on Cambrai, Haig took the Germans by surprise and gained about four miles of mud. Ten days later the German counter-attack regained all their lost ground. If ever there was an object lesson in the folly of war, the sheer pointlessness, here it was shown in all its bloodiness. This was how it began to seem to many Germans, including those in high command, who had tried to sue for peace in December 1916. It was, crucially, how it had seemed throughout 1916 to the President of the United States, the gentlemanly Princeton professor Thomas Woodrow Wilson (1856–1924).

Ramrod-straight, bespectacled, Woodrow Wilson was an old-fashioned Virginian, a child of the Enlightenment, but with a prim, even slightly puritanical manner. His heroes were Abraham Lincoln, Edmund Burke and W. E. Gladstone. For his Independent rival, Teddy Roosevelt, Wilson was 'as insincere and cold-blooded an opportunist as we have ever had in the Presidency', whereas admirers such as Ray Stannard Baker, his press aide, saw him as 'one of those rare idealists like Calvin or Cromwell, who from time to time have appeared upon the earth & for a moment, in a burst of strange power, have temporarily lifted erring mankind to a higher pitch of contentment than it was quite equal to'. He had his more genial aspects. He was good at imitating voices and accents. He liked women. When his first wife died he married a beautiful Washington widow seventeen years his junior. 'What did the new Mrs Wilson do when the President proposed?' was the joke circulating in Washington at the time. Answer: 'She fell out of bed with surprise.'[31]

To Wilson, as to any sensible outside observer, the best solution to the

European situation would surely be a negotiated peace. When he was re-elected president on 7 November 1916, Wilson had seen it as an opportunity for peace. On 18 November the eighty-five-year-old Emperor Franz Josef had died, to be succeeded by his twenty-nine-year-old great-nephew the Grand Duke Karl. On 12 December Bethmann-Hollweg made a speech in the Reichstag offering peace negotiations to the Entente, to be conducted in a neutral country. Wilson's letter to all warring powers suggesting that the United States were 'too proud to fight' caused profound offence. 'Did the President realize', asked a British diplomat, Lord Hardinge, 'that to support peace at that moment was to support militarism with all the horrors that it entailed?'[32] The Entente preferred to press on to Passchendaele, to mayhem and to slaughter.

For the governments of Britain and France, and for the political classes and groups which sustained them, a negotiated peace was too great a risk to take. They needed outright victory. Wilson did all he could to keep America out of the war. Had the German military, naval and diplomatic powers had their wits about them they would have moved and conciliated American opinion. Instead, they continued to threaten and torpedo passenger liners – the Cunard liner *Laconia* was sunk on 25 February 1917 without warning – and to make offers to Mexico to return their 'lost' territories in New Mexico, Texas and Arizona in the event of a German victory.[33] On 4 April the United States Senate voted in favour of war by 82 votes to 6. Two days later the House of Representatives also voted overwhelmingly for war (375 votes to 50). That day, 6 April, the United States declared war on Germany.[34]

Lloyd George sent Arthur Balfour to Washington that month. They could dress up the aim of the visit, but the real reason was basic: Britain had bankrupted itself and needed American money. America had very little military hardware, no modern aircraft, no hand grenades, no mortars, no poison gas. The US army remained 'a nineteenth century force and a very small one at that'.[35] Since the beginning of the war, however, the British had relied upon American money, and by 1917 the debt stood at $400 million. This was the material reality behind Lloyd George's marvellous rhetoric on America's entry into the war.

He said that America had at one bound become a world power in a sense she never was before. She had waited until she found a cause worthy of her traditions. The American people had held back until they were fully convinced the fight was not a sordid scrimmage for power and possessions, but an unselfish struggle to overthrow a sinister conspiracy against liberty and human rights. Once that conviction was reached, the great Republic of the West had leaped into the arena, and she stood now side by side with the European democracies who, bruised and bleeding after three years of grim conflict, were still fighting the most savage foe that ever menaced the freedom of the world.

The extent of British debt was actually difficult to assess, as Balfour discovered when he reached the American capital. He set up a British War Mission, with the aim of focusing the American mind and the American purse on British war needs. It was not in his area of skill – dreamy, aging philosopher as he was – to coordinate the different agencies. Balfour was not a money-and-propaganda man. Lloyd George had the Napoleonic brilliance to send Northcliffe in Balfour's place to become head of the British War Mission. The new Prime Minister had been Northcliffe's choice, but Lloyd George knew that it would only take a few setbacks in the European war for the *Daily Mail* to be clamouring: WELSH WIZARD MUST GO. L-G's Parliamentary Private Secretary, Major David Davies, said it was 'a damn bad appointment',[35] and called it 'a gratuitous insult to the Americans', but it removed from the British scene a potential troublemaker, and it had the effect of silencing the Northcliffe Press's instinctive anti-Americanism. Notice-boards in all *Daily Mail* departments soon fluttered with an urgent piece of information: 'I am leaving to take over Mr Balfour's American mission and it is essential that not one line of criticism of the United States, men, books, or anything else should appear in the *Daily Mail*, the *Continental Daily Mail*, the *Overseas Mail*, or any other publication associated with the *Daily Mail*.'

The British ambassador in Washington, Sir Cecil Spring-Rice, was utterly dismayed. This frock-coated Victorian, author of the hymn 'I Vow to Thee My Country', asked: 'Whatever induced the Government to send Northcliffe here?' 'To Spring-Rice, Northcliffe was the incarnation of all that he disliked in the twentieth century.' The Washington political class and the president's entourage in the White House looked forward to Northcliffe running 'amok', but he was much too astute for that. With his unconventional approach, his genuine understanding of money, the war situation, and America, he went down very well. He had been obsessed by America all his life and wanted to be the British Joseph Pulitzer. He generally wore a blue serge suit, soft white collar, red checked tie and soft grey hat. The American public liked him. He emphasized his Irish origins wherever he went. He was impatient of America. He was surrounded by detectives. They read his mail. He cabled:

NOT ONLY AM I WATCHED BUT EVERY PERSON CONNECTED WITH MISSION WATCHED GOVERNMENT THINK IT NECESSARY THAT I SHOULD NEVER MOVE UNLESS ACCOMPANIED BY SECRET SERVICE AGENTS WHO ARE WITH ME DAY AND

NIGHT THAT WILL GIVE YOU SOME IDEA OF THE DIFFER-
ENCE OF LIVING IN LONDON AND NEW YORK –
NORTHCLIFFE.

He missed his mother terribly. Northcliffe's marriage, and love life,
were tempestuous, but his love for Mrs Harmsworth was undying. He
wrote to her constantly. 'Most sweet and adored . . . I miss my cool
room at Poynters which I can see vividly as I write and I miss my darling,
darling Mother. Six o'clock is of course twelve o'clock with you. I keep
a clock and English time before me always. I cable every day, dear, and
I hope they arrive the same day.' Uncomfortable as Washington was
during a hot summer, however, he knew that he was doing good. In
New York he addressed a crowd of 14,000 and received a five-minute
standing ovation. The American papers proclaimed him 'the most
powerful man in Britain'. 'The American Govt', he told his mother, 'is
very nice to me. *They are a mighty people, these Americans, and will
end the war.*'

More than most British politicians, however, Northcliffe knew the price
which was being paid for the peace which was on its way. Having an
instinctual, journalistic intelligence, a *feel* (strong, though by no means
infallible) for the way the world was going, this newspaper man could
sense that debt lay at the heart of the story. What was not allowed in a
Northcliffe newspaper often speaks more eloquently than the headlines.
Northcliffe's months in America were devoted to begging – for tractors
'to keep starvation out' of Britain, for oil to fuel the Royal Navy, for
cheap food and clothes, for motor-cars, and motor parts. Although he
was received with personal adulation, he and his journalists saw enough
of American life to know that the American mood was not ecstatically
pro-British. Louis Tracy, formerly the manager of the *Evening News*, was
his correspondent in New York. There are some bright moments in Tracy's
picture, as when he tells the Chief that 'the American Army has suggested
that all the German-American Societies shall henceforth be grouped
together as one big organization, which shall be known as the Sons of
Botches'.[42] But Tracy was aware that the Great American Public resented
the deaths of American troops in an obscure French war. American
soldiers who returned home after being billeted in England were not
happy. When the war was over, Tracy told Northcliffe: 'There is a curious
anti-British propaganda going on among the troops returning from
abroad, especially those who have been stationed in England. It got to
such a pitch in the Garden City Camp that twenty men were placed under
arrest and may be court-martialled for sedition. These men could not
say anything bad enough about the treatment meted out to them while

in England, and it is a singular thing that they nearly all wore metal rings made by German prisoners.'[43]

There was nothing surprising about this. Just as many Americans are descended from German as from British stock, and the Irish-Americans in particular had every reason to loathe the British. 'There can be no question,' said Tracy, 'that some underground agency is spreading far and wide the United States, the belief that the next war is to be between England and in the United States.'[44]

When Northcliffe came back to England, however, no such talk was aired. He was offered the post of Minister of Aviation by the prime minister. He turned it down – not privately, but in an open letter in *The Times*: 'I feel that in present circumstances I can do better work if I maintain my independence and am not gagged by a loyalty that I do not feel towards the whole of your Administration.'[45]

There was something mad, as well as magnificent, about this. (In the event, Northcliffe's brother Lord Rothermere became the Air Minister.) Lloyd George did not ask Northcliffe to be an official part of the British delegation at the Paris Peace Conference when the war ended, and this put the seal on the enmity which Northcliffe felt for him. 'The break had to come', LG recalled, 'when he wanted to dictate to me. As Prime Minister I could not have it. Northcliffe thought he could run the country. I could not allow that.'[46]

Lloyd George said these words after Northcliffe's death in 1922, aged fifty-seven.

It was a terrible death, not less terrible for being, like his life, partially comic. The year before he died, he had made a world tour. It disconcerted him. He sensed that the Empire he loved was coming to an end, and he feared that newspapers would be supplanted by wireless. His tendency, when back in London, to send abusive and megalomaniac telegrams to underlings and government ministers became so uncontrollable that they had to be stopped, and his telephones disconnected – the equivalent in Northcliffe's case of disconnecting the valves of a lesser mortal's heart. He was suffering, not as his enemies averred from syphilis, but from endocarditis. Before they removed his telephone connection, he was heard whispering down the line to someone at the *Daily Mail*: 'I hear they are saying I am mad . . . Send down the best reporter for the story.'[47]

One of his last barked instructions was: 'Tell Mother she was the only one!'[48] Other scoops which he had vouchsafed to his staff included the intelligence that God was a homosexual.[49]

By then he had retreated to a hut on the roof of his house in 1 Carlton

House Gardens. The doctors believed that the cooling breezes would soothe his troubled mind. The roof was too weak to support the revolving shelter, and his neighbour the Duke of Devonshire gave permission for the roof of the adjoining house to be used. There, raving and sad, the father of modern British journalism died lonely beneath the modern sky of a London summer.

13

Peace

The Germans fought no less gallantly than the British or the French or the Russians. They nevertheless lost the war. There were a number of factors which could be said to explain this. One, undoubtedly, was the extent of socialist-inspired anti-war, anti-monarchical and anti-government feeling among the German people at home. Another was the effect on German morale of the American entry into the war, even though General Pershing's Expeditionary Force made little military impact at first. (By June 1918, when America had been a belligerent for over a year, 800 American troops had been killed in action, compared with the 1.8 million Germans, 1.7 million Russians and 1.384 million French who were killed in the entire war.) It was not so much the American army which helped to subdue Germany's hopes, as the thought of the world now being against the Fatherland. Austria-Hungary was collapsing, and the Ottoman Empire had failed to put up a resistance to the combined troops of the Entente. General Allenby entered Jerusalem as a conqueror, though humbly and on foot, on 9 December 1917. In these circumstances, with a feeling of the whole world being against them, only a supreme display of military strength, and a very good measure of luck, could have won the war for the Germans on the Western Front.

And it was here that the third, and principal, reason for their defeat was made clear to them. Munitions were the key. Lloyd George's decision to build more tanks, and more and bigger guns, than the enemy was the vital ingredient in the Allied victory. General Pershing's American forces had no tanks, and almost no artillery, but by the summer of 1918, 1.5 million US troops had arrived in Europe, to be issued with French and British equipment, particularly the 75-mm field gun and the Renault light tank. These young men who had arrived fresh and well-fed from the prairies, plains and cities of the New World made a powerful impact on the old world they had come to save or conquer. Vera Brittain, serving as a nurse in Etaples in the spring of 1918, saw a contingent of American soldiers march down the road: 'I pressed forward . . . to watch the United States physically entering the War, so godlike, so magnificent, so splendidly unimpaired in comparison with the tired, nerve-racked men of the British Army.'[1]

In the course of 1918, the Entente's production, possession and deployment of artillery at last began to outstrip that of the Germans. In

February 1917, Germany had 7,130 guns at the Front; by the spring of 1918, it had only 6,172. Whereas artillery regiments had composed only 18 per cent of the French army in 1915, by the end of the war it was 37 per cent. A quarter of the British army, that is half a million men, were in the Royal Artillery. By the end of the war, France's heavy artillery had risen from 300 big guns to 5,700. Britain manufactured 3,226 guns in 1915, but 10,680 in 1918, and shell production was always ahead of consumption. There was no repeat of the shell scandal which ruined Kitchener's career. In the last fights on European soil during 1918, therefore, the Allied generals Haig, Pétain and Pershing simply had more military hardware than their adversaries. They could go on pounding and shooting and killing for longer. At Amiens in March 1918 a British battalion would number 500 men and be in possession of 30 Lewis guns, eight mortars and six tanks, compared with a British battalion of 1,000 men on the Somme in 1916 with four Lewis light machine guns between them. The offensive at Amiens broke the German line, and broke their nerve. General Ludendorff suffered from violent mood swings, sometimes believing in the imminence of a victory, and sometimes in despair. The final attack on Amiens on 8 August 1918 was dubbed by Ludendorff 'the black day of the German army', with 27,000 casualties and 12,000 surrenders. By the end of September his nerve had cracked completely. He fell to the floor and foamed at the mouth, according to some accounts. By then, both the political and military leadership in Germany was weak. George von Hertling, the short-lived Chancellor, resigned, to be succeeded on 3 October by Prince Max of Baden. Both Crown Prince Wilhelm of Prussia and Crown Prince Rupprecht of Bavaria, military commanders as well as royal personages,* could see the writing on the wall not only for the German army but for the monarchy. By the end of October, their allies in Austria-Hungary were suffering from revolutions, in both Vienna and Budapest. Austria secured an armistice on 3 November, Germany on the 11th and Hungary on the 13th. Kaiser Wilhelm, whom many in the Entente regarded as a war criminal responsible for the conflict, abdicated, and fled to Holland. Kaiser Karl was merely driven from his throne, without abdicating. It was as a republic that Germany signed the Armistice, and it was to a republic, 'the greatest republic of the West', as Lloyd George called it, that Europe now looked to heal its wounds and pay its bills.

It is hard to think of anything in history which more tragically and clearly exemplifies the phenomenon of good political intentions achieving the precise opposite of their aim. On 11 November 1918, Lloyd George

*Wilhelm was the Kaiser's heir, Rupprecht heir to the now defunct kingdom of Bavaria.

told the House of Commons the conditions of the Armistice, and concluded: 'Thus at eleven o'clock this morning came to an end the cruellest and most terrible war that has ever scourged mankind. I hope we may say that thus, this fateful morning, came to an end all wars.'[2] At the beginning of the year, on 5 January 1918, he had addressed a conference of trade union leaders, and set out what he believed to be the aims of the war. 'We are not fighting a war of aggression against the German people . . . nor are we fighting to destroy Austria-Hungary or to deprive Turkey of its capital or of the rich and renowned lands of Asia Minor and Thrace.' Rather, said Lloyd George with a sleight of hand which could scarcely deny that the effects of the war would destroy the old empires and autocracies, they were fighting so that French democracy, and the national independence of other nations, above all Poland, could be established on true democratic principles.[3]

In fact, as could easily be seen before the war ended, the defeat of Turkey and Austria-Hungary would inevitably lead to a collapse of their hegemonies. What could be fairer, or more consonant with the ideas of human justice, than that the peoples of the world should, as far as was possible, be independent and self-determining, with their own languages, religions and cultures?

One of the grimmest consequences of nationalist aspiration in recent years had been the fate of the Armenians. On the Caucasus Front between Russia and Turkey, the Turks blamed their losses of men and land on the indigenous Armenian population, whom they accused of aiding and abetting the invader. On 8 April 1915, thousands of Armenian men were shot, and women and children, in hundreds of thousands, were deported southward to Cilicia and Syria. The Armenians appealed for help to the German ambassador in Constantinople, who was afraid of offending his Turkish allies. By 19 April 50,000 more Armenian civilians had been murdered. To this day, there is dispute about the numbers of Armenians massacred by the Turks, though few sources outside Turkish governments set the total figure of slaughtered Armenians at less than 800,000. The grisly precedent had been set, which would be repeated throughout the twentieth century, of whole categories of civilian populations, and ultimately whole races, being the target of programmes of obliteration. Hitler would ask: 'Who remembers the Armenians today?'[4]

Hindsight, the historians' parlour-game, can lead from false premise to false conclusion. Because we see the fateful consequences of our forebears' actions, we can wrongly suppose that, had they done differently, things would have been better. That is not necessarily the case. Yes – had Germany won the war speedily, as they supposed they would, and reached

Paris by the summer of 1914, there might have been no Russian Revolution. Certainly, the Armistice terms would not have punished Germany and there might, therefore, have been no economic crises in the 1920s, no disastrous unemployment, no rise of National Socialism. But there is no point in such speculations, since history deals not with what might have been, but what was. Even an outright German victory might not have prevented a German revolution at home, and a spread of social problems very similar to the ones which engulfed Europe in the postwar years.

Likewise, President Wilson's optimistic dream, of a peaceful world of independent, democratic nation-states, can be seen to be the fateful origin of German grievances in the 1930s. All hopeful and kindly minded people could cheer at the restoration of an independent Poland, but what would be the feelings of the German-speaking populations of Stettin or Danzig, that their fates should be determined? Lloyd George and President Wilson met together in a hotel in Paris, and unrealistically decided to make Danzig an 'independent city'. What of Upper Silesia, which until the war had provided Germany with a quarter of its output of coal, 81 per cent of its zinc, and 34 per cent of its lead? Poland's pianist-Prime Minister in waiting, Ignace Paderewski, with his great shock of red hair streaked with grey, could demand it all. The Germans could retort that in that case, there was no possibility of paying the heavy reparations extracted by France. A botched compromise would be the result, with bits owned by Germany, other territory by the new Poland, and both sides discontented. In the Baltic, similarly, the dreams of a Princeton professor needed to be examined bit by bit to see how wonderful they would be in practice. An independent Lithuania – who could quarrel with that? The answer, in 1919, was the Germans, the Poles and the Russians. Lloyd George warmed to the idea of Lithuanian independence; he saw it as a country the same size as his native Wales. Until the twenty-first century, when it enjoys the protective umbrella of NATO and the EU, a small country such as this could not survive in the wolf-pack.

The Bolsheviks drove the Poles out of Vilna in 1920, and to compensate for the trouble, Lithuania took over the Baltic port of Memel, with a 92 per cent German population. Sooner or later, some German leader was going to march in to take it back.

The Paris Peace Conference dispensed recipes for war. The powerful nations dished out independence: which meant it was not independence. Something which has been given you through the benevolence of a higher power is not true independence: it is a sign that you are not strong enough to stand on your own. Imperialism had had its day. But they were unable in 1919 to devise a system such as the present European Union, which has the imperial characteristic of 'diluting both the democratic and the nationalistic principles in the interest of a wider union of peoples'.[5]

The final peace treaty was signed at Versailles in July 1919, in that very Hall of Mirrors where in 1871 France had acknowledged her defeat, and where the German nation had at the selfsame moment been born. Perhaps if the treaty, and the negotiations which preceded it, had happened on neutral soil, there might have been happier consequences. But the fact of France's wounds, France's griefs, France's rage and France's fear for the future would not go away, wherever the treaty had been signed.

For half a year, Paris was 'the capital of the world',[6] its streets, hotels, restaurants teeming with foreign nationals hoping for a new political future, or to make a splash, or, like Lawrence of Arabia in his Arab costume, to do both. In our twenty-first century, some European writers whose first language is English have looked to America as to a culture more vivid, a linguistic tradition more vibrant than the moribund shell of old England, Wales, Ireland, Scotland. During the First World War, this was not so. American writers still looked towards Europe for their inspiration.

Henry James had been their beacon, their light, their Moses leading towards the Promised Land. He felt, on his visits back to the United States, that he was weighing '*prosperity* against posterity'. To his sister Alice he had confided: 'I could come back to America (could be carried back on a stretcher) *to die* – but never, never to live.'[7] When the war started, he was desolated. He visited wounded soldiers in hospital. He stayed with Asquith, when Prime Minister, at Walmer Castle in Kent. He became so emotionally caught up in the horror and tragedy of the war that he applied for British citizenship and was admitted by the king to the Order of Merit.

James had been worried all his life by the fact that two of his brothers had fought in the American Civil War, whereas he had been too ill to do so. Like many peace-loving men, he was haunted by an interest in war and had been a lifelong Napoleonic obsessive. As the war dragged on, he absorbed himself increasingly in reading Napoleonic memoirs. Theodora Bosanquet, his typist – or his typewriter as he would have said – still came regularly to take his dictation in his Chelsea apartment. Even when he suffered a series of strokes, in December 1915, he needed her presence, and she would note that, when he was in a coma, his hand passed to and fro over the bed-sheet as if it were writing. After one of these attacks, when he surfaced and resumed his dictation, Miss Bosanquet was aware that James had undergone a change of personality. The war was on his mind, but, like Lord Northcliffe, his character had been subsumed by that of Bonaparte. 'Wondrous enough certainly,'

Napoleon dictated to the typist, 'wondrous enough certainly to have a finger in such a concert and to feel ourselves touch the large old phrase into the right amplitude.' The French emperor was in some confusion, but he was evidently preparing for battle. Images of conflict and 'the grand air of gallantry' possessed him. 'They pluck in terror from the imperial eagle, and with no greater credit in consequence than that they face, keeping their equipoise, the awful bloody beak that he turns round upon them.' The next day, Napoleon was taken for a drive in 'some motor-car or other'. The statement he had to make was 'for all the world as if we had brought it on and given our push and our touch to great events. The Bonapartes have a kind of bronze distinction that extends to their finger-tips.' He also dictated messages to his 'dear and most esteemed brother and sister', about the decoration of various apartments in the Louvre and the Tuileries 'which you will find addressed in detail to artists and workmen who are to take them in hand'.[8]

The announcement of his OM came with the New Year, 1916. He received the news at his Chelsea flat in Carlyle Mansions. He had recovered from being Napoleon, but he lasted only until 23 February. His sister-in-law, Mrs William James, was with him, and it was she who arranged the funeral at Chelsea Old Church, followed by cremation at Golders Green. They sang 'For All the Saints' and 'O God Our Help in Ages Past'.

James, the greatest novelist of his age, was also a mirror of it, a parable. His later novels in particular had ceased merely to be stories of individuals trying to puzzle out one another's mysteries, and became reflections of the uneasy relationship which existed between the Old World and the New. To this extent, there was some parallel between the distinguished old American Man of Letters, dictating Napoleonic schemes for human improvement from his Chelsea deathbed, and the Princeton professor's blueprint for the postwar world settlement – President Wilson's Fourteen Points.

These Points, which had first been expounded to the Congress on 8 January 1918, were to be the underlying template of the Parisian Armistice, signed in July 1919. Their guiding principle, as we have seen, was self-determination. The peoples of the former Austria-Hungary, of the Ottoman Empire, should be given autonomy. The frontiers of Italy – a nation which, like Germany, had never really existed until modern times – were to be drawn 'along clearly recognizable lines of nationality'. Poland and Czechoslovakia and Yugoslavia were to be conjured out of the map.

Although the American president came from the state of Virginia, where everything from children's schooling to buying a tram ticket was determined along racial lines, his kindly liberal mind did not make any distinction, in his plans for a bright European future, between nationality and race. The fourteenth of his Points was that a 'general association of nations must be formed to guarantee political independence and territorial integrity to great and small states alike'. Hence was born the League of Nations.

The tragic flaw in the dream was the failure to distinguish between nations and ethnicity. Nation-states were not things of nature. In the case of France, and to a smaller extent Britain, they had grown up, and been defined, over many centuries, into the political entities which they were in 1918. Poland was an ancient kingdom which for years had been subsumed or threatened by greater kingdoms and empires. Germany and Italy, as we have seen, were not nation-states as France was a nation-state. They were very recent conglomerations: groups of states and kingdoms and duchies. As soon as the independent nation-state was seen, by kindly minded and well-intentioned liberals, as the ideal after which all peoples in the world should aspire, how were they expected to define their nationality? By language? As we have already seen, in Poland, Slovenia, the new Czechoslovakia and Austria there were many cities and territories where German-speakers were in the majority. When times grew hard – and they were destined to grow very hard indeed – such people would inevitably be drawn to the call for a Greater Germany – *Grossdeutschland*. In Turkey, it had already been demonstrated how you define nationality: in terms not of language alone, but of blood. The Armenian massacres of 1915 were not merely a harbinger of things to come because they showed no government could control civilian populations simply by culling. They were also a brutal answer to an intellectual question: what is a nation? The old world did not ask this question. The ploughman, the merchant, the young child and the grandmother went about their business in Damascus, Constantinople, Bucharest or Linz without needing to define themselves in national terms. Once the principle of their political existence was to be defined nationally, it was bound to be asked whether someone of Albanian ethnicity could really count as a true Bosnian, or an Armenian as a true Turk, or a Jew as a true Pole. Empires, and aristocratic hierarchies, had been half done away with in 1848, and 1918–19 finished the business. The new League of Nations was never going to possess the authority of the sultans in Constantinople, nor of the Habsburg emperors in Vienna. America had become 'repulsive and appalling' to Henry James,[9] and one reason for this was that it had become a racial mixture. The modern sensibility is shocked that so kindly and broad-visioned a man as James should be what we call racist, but we should fail to understand the past if we did not see that almost everyone in the past was.

Though the James family had an admirable Civil War record and had fought not merely for liberation but alongside the 'darks' in a negro regiment, Henry James could still feel America was spoilt by the recent influx of European flotsam and jetsam. Yet that was in some senses of its self-identity what America was and is: Irish, Italian, Dutch, Polish-Jewish, Indian – after a generation or two, you are American. In idea, you are American from the moment you collect your naturalization papers. Strong as this idea is, and not merely strong but admirable as it is, no American in 1919 would have believed that it had come to pass as a social reality except in theory. It was decades before racial segregation ended in the southern states. Recent immigrants lived in their own urban areas and retained much of their own identity. America was big enough, and untidy enough, and rich enough to live with the ideal, and work out the details piecemeal. Ironically, it was how the old empires got by, also – Jews, Armenians, Turks, Germans, Slavs and others knocked together in a multi-ethnic city such as Sarajevo because they had to, and because the umbrella of the imperium protected them rather as the Federal Laws of the United States, and their Constitution, remained the ultimate point of unity.

If President Wilson had been gifted with magical foresight, he might have devoted the six months of the Paris Peace Conference to re-establishing the Habsburgs in political power in Vienna, and helping the Turks undo the work of Young Turk modernizers in favour of a restored Sultanate. He could have urged upon the newly empowered Imperia a greater degree of liberalism and tolerance, and pumped money into all their more benign industries and enterprises. Instead, he supported nationalism. Every sort of nationalism, that is to say, except German nationalism. And he, together with Lloyd George, felt unable to resist all of France's demands.

The final treaty reflected the fear of France, with its 40 millions of inhabitants, that it would once again be threatened by Germany with its 65 millions. France took Alsace-Lorraine. It wanted the coal-rich Saar basin, which was under League of Nations trusteeship until 1935, when a plebiscite returned it to Germany. It failed to persuade America or Britain to agree to the creation of a new Rhineland state, but it insisted upon the Rhineland being occupied by French forces for fifteen years from the signature of the treaty. Heavy reparations were exacted from the German taxpayers, all payable to France.

If you were French, the treaty looked as if it had not gone far enough, though it was reasonable. If you were German, it must have seemed like an agenda for a new war. The reparation settlement in particular was seen by Clemenceau and the other French delegates as dependent upon having an international policeman to enforce it. But this was not to be. On 19 November 1919 the United States Senate rejected the treaty of Versailles. It came formally into force on 10 January 1920 without American endorsement. America, which in the person of the Princeton professor had come across the ocean with apparently evangelical zeal to impart its democratic values, retreated once more into isolationism. The League of Nations, which had been President Wilson's dream-child, was not an organization which the Americans ever went so far as to join. In 1920, the election year, the American people showed what they thought of President Wilson's foreign policy. The Republicans carried every state outside the South, and took Tennessee. The governor of Massachusetts, Calvin Coolidge, was Vice President, and the presidency passed from the hands of Woodrow Wilson to those of a nondescript, idle Ohio senator, Warren Gamaliel Harding. The American electorate had pulled down the shutters. The white man's burden, whether Asian, African or European, was not one it wished to carry.

Clemenceau could see where this would inevitably lead. Ten years after the war, he wrote rhetorically to the Americans:

Your intervention in the War, which you came out of lightly, since it cost you 56,000 lives* instead of our 1,364,000 killed, had appeared to you nevertheless, as an excessive display of solidarity. And either by organizing a League of Nations, which was to furnish the solution to all the problems of international security by magic, or by simply withdrawing from the European schemes, you found yourselves freed from all difficulties by means of a 'separate peace'. [Clemenceau is here referring to the fact that having rejected the Versailles Treaty, America drew up a separate peace treaty with Germany.] The nations of the world, although separated by natural or artificial frontiers, have but one planet at their disposal, a planet all the elements of which are in a state of solidarity, and far from man being the exception to the rule, he finds, even in his innermost activities, that he is the supreme witness to universal solidarity. Behind your barriers of ice, and of sun, you may be able perhaps for a time to isolate yourself from your planetary fellow-citizens, although I find you in the Philippines, where you do not belong geographically.[10]

The phrase about 'power without responsibility, the prerogative of the harlot throughout the ages' was one which, as we have seen, would be

---

* Michael Howard in *The First World War*, p. 146, gives American war dead as 115,000; Martin Gilbert in *The First World War*, p. 541, has the figure of 48,000. The *Encyclopaedia Americana* has 109,740 and the *Encyclopaedia Britannica* 116,516

written for use in Stanley Baldwin's rhetoric by his cousin Rudyard Kipling. It referred to the power of the Press, but it could be applied to American foreign policy in the decade after the First World War.

Like the Press, the USA did well out of the war. Every country in Europe emerged from the war financially ruined. The United States, however, was immeasurably enriched, not least by European debts, owing to various US institutions, to the tune of £2,000 million.[11]

Europe was to begin its new life of peace and democracy deeply in debt, and the fact was inevitably going to be muddled with the contentious matter of German reparations. By 1922, Arthur Balfour, Lord President of the Council, was delegated to send a polite note reminding the European allies of their debts – in all some £1,300 million to Britain from Russia and France, and £1,450 million owing from Germany in reparation. There was no hope of recovering this debt, of course, even though Britain was forced to honour its £850 million debt to the United States. When Balfour gingerly suggested cancelling all these debts in 'one great transaction', he received an abrupt response from the new president, Calvin Coolidge* – 'They hired the money, didn't they?'[12]

As the years rolled forward to 1929, and the Wall Street Crash, this uneasy and unsatisfactory relationship became a habit. European anti-Americanism and American unilateralism were in unholy alliance. But much as both wished to establish the difference between America and the rest of the world, the war had made the link. The debts were real. They hired the money. Wise old Henry James, as we saw when we closed the pages of *The Golden Bowl*, had seen it all in the relationship between the dissolute old European prince and the impassive financier Mr Verver.

There is something singularly appropriate in the fact that the greatest American poet should have found work in the colonial and foreign department of Lloyd's Bank in London. He took the post in March 1917 and occupied it until November 1925. When the peace treaty was signed, his job was specifically concerned with debts, and the claims of the bank on the Germans.[13]

Thomas Stearns Eliot (1888–1963) was born in St Louis, Missouri, the son of a businessman and a teacher. He was the youngest of seven children, and his family 'zealously guarded' its New England connections. It was his ambition, as a student, to become a professor of philosophy. He reacted against the pragmatists, such as Harvard's most famous philosopher William James, and went to Europe, first Paris, then Oxford, to study for his doctoral thesis on the work of an English Idealist. 'Experience and the Objects of Knowledge in the Philosophy of F. H.

---

* Coolidge became president upon Harding's death in 1923 and was re-elected in 1924.

Bradley' was its subject. Although this type of philosophy was precisely what Bertrand Russell had chosen to reject, he found the young graduate student charming when he himself was a visiting professor at Harvard. He described Eliot as 'the only one who was civilized'.[14]

Eliot himself rejected an academic career, Harvard, Boston and its bourgeois ways, and ultimately America. At the beginning of the war he found himself in London and decided to settle there. He married an Englishwoman, Vivien Haigh-Wood – and was disastrously unhappy. He taught in schools – first High Wycombe Grammar School, and then Highgate Junior School in North London, where one of his pupils was John Betjeman.

> I bound my verse into a book,
> *The Best of Betjeman*, and handed it
> To one who, I was told, liked poetry –
> The American master, Mr Eliot.
> That dear good man, with Prufrock in his head
> And Sweeney waiting to be agonized,
> I wonder what he thought? He never says
> When now we meet, across the port and cheese.[15]

Though Eliot never said, it is easy to guess what he thought.

When studying in Paris, he had told his friend Conrad Aiken that he hoped to find the 'truth of his time'.[16] His own poetry, as it evolved after that time, was to express this truth instinctually, as philosophy could not. At the Harvard Philosophical Society in 1913 or 1914, Eliot had complained that 'no radical is so radical as to be a conservative'.[17] He was a figure of profound paradox. No poet could have been more modern, or indeed revolutionary. When he arrived in London, he was writing Symbolist poetry which owed nothing to the English lyric tradition. His fellow American, Ezra Pound, naturally, took him up and paraded him as 'a kind of collector's piece',[18] but when in 1912 Aiken had shown Eliot's 'Love Song of J. Alfred Prufrock' to a London editor considered to be interested in new developments in literature, Harold Monro, he had dismissed it as absolutely insane, the morbid ravings of a madman.

Prufrock is partly based on the hesitant and uncertain figures in Henry James's late stories, holding back from the brink of life and terrified of experience. He is also Eliot himself. He is also, which is why Eliot became a pivotally central poet from the moment the poem was written, twentieth-century humankind. The blood-red sky at the poem's beginning is a sunset which recalls a patient on an operating table, torn open. Just such slits of red do occur at sunset, and on operating tables, but it is the mind of

Eliot which puts them together in his haunting hymn of loss. For the sun is setting, as the women talk of Michelangelo, on European civilization. Philosophy can draw no conclusions, it can only stammer and hesitate. Nor is there room or a place any longer for heroism. Even that most dithering and uncertain of heroes, Hamlet, has no place on this stage. In the age of Asquith, and Bonar Law, and Woodrow Wilson, there were only attendant lords. The poem has a hypnotic music. It says more than it seems to say, and it closes the door for ever on the tired old literary traditions of England.

There is much in common between Eliot's brand of modernism and Pound's. But there were deep divisions between the two men, even before Eliot formally embraced, what is implicit even in his blasphemous lyrics, the Christian religion. 'Christianity has become a sort of Prussianism and will have to go' was Pound's view. European culture, together with its creeds and churches, was in ruins, and it was the poets' task to pick around in it for images and melodies which they might be able to use, rather as contemporary artists such as Picasso might use pieces of old newspaper in a collage. But for Eliot, such an approach was never wholly satisfactory. He was a philosopher manqué, after all. 'I confess I am seldom interested in what Pound . . . is saying', he would write in 1928, 'but only in the way he says it.'[19]

Eliot saw the ruin, the desolation, the moral emptiness of Europe, as Pound did. His lyrics focus on a horrified vision of cities in which ugly, predatory people copulate, swindle and smell. It is a contemporary *Inferno* into which he gazed. But it was to the author of the *Inferno*, as much as to any of his contemporaries, that Eliot looked for a solution. Dante had provided a synthesis between his own personal sorrows and loves, the destructive wars of Europe, the collapse of Church and State, and a philosophy by which to live. He had done so in tight, formal verse which was entirely new, and yet resonated with classical literature and the liturgy of the Church. Dante was a poet who could hold up a mirror and tell 'the truth of his time'. Poets, in Eliot's belief, could still do that. He accepted Pound's friendship, and though he did not know it at the time, he benefited, as so many did, from Pound's generosity. Pound paid for Eliot's poetry to be published in Chicago in 1915. It was not published in England until 1917, by Harriet Shaw Weaver in *The Egoist*, and later by a small husband-and-wife publishing team called the Hogarth Press. The husband, Leonard Woolf, was a somewhat dry left-wing economist and progressive thinker. His bony, intense, beautiful wife Virginia was the daughter of the Victorian man of letters Sir Leslie Stephen, whose first wife was daughter of William Makepeace Thackeray. It was to the Woolfs and their friends that Eliot first read aloud 'The Love Song of

J. Alfred Prufrock'. They cautiously published 250 copies, at half a crown each. They were charmed by the young man, in his 'four piece suit'. Virginia Woolf's prose was as beautiful as her face, but like many twentieth-century English writers, she had nothing to write about. Their radicalism, which was surface radicalism, could not understand that here was someone 'so radical as to be a conservative' in the deepest sense – setting out to recover the coherence of Dante's vision from the devastations of European culture visited upon it by science and industry and the nineteenth century and the war.

14

Protons – Massacres – Bombs.
Ireland and Iraq

Nature is not static. The nature of things is not peace but agitation. Charles Darwin, drawing on the economic theories of Thomas Malthus, had constructed for his Victorian contemporaries an evolutionary theory of life itself being based on struggle, conflict, selfishness. Twentieth-century physics told an impersonal story, but it was no less disturbed, and disturbing. Matter itself was destabilized. Atoms, which were tiny specks of emptiness containing one energetic nucleus, were not the smallest constituent parts into which matter could be divided. Shortly after he became the Cavendish Professor of Physics at Cambridge in 1919, Ernest Rutherford would pursue his researches further into the nature of nitrogen atoms. By bombarding them with alpha particles, he discovered that the impact knocked out hydrogen nuclei, which he called protons. Barely a quarter of a century elapsed between this fascinating discovery and the nuclear obliteration of two Japanese cities. Even to Rutherford and his fellow physicists, the terrible implications of his discovery were not immediately apparent.[1] But they did not take place in a peaceful world. They took place in a world where the poet W. B. Yeats, as if he had peered through Rutherford's microscope, saw that 'Things fall apart; the centre cannot hold;/Mere anarchy is loosed upon the world'. Beyond the calm of the Cavendish laboratory, the world, though some of its nations had signed up to a so-called armistice, was very far from being at peace. The fighting men did not simply pack up their old kitbags and return to a stable homeland. All over the world, following the First World War, there was trouble.

The Islamic world had suffered a terrible blow with the defeat of the Ottoman Empire – a blow which to this day many Muslims regret and which the followers of al-Qaeda are still committed to avenge or reverse. In French, Italian and British African territories where there were Muslims, their mosques and clerics called for reprisals. They were labelled 'fanatics', of course, by the ruling authorities. What could be more fanat-ical than their objection to being ruled by Western secularists who had no sympathy with their culture, religion or history? There was a deep fear on the part of the British that there would be a united Islamic resist-ance to the British Empire. This had been the dream of the influential

Islamic thinker Jamaluddin al-Afghani (1839–97), whose followers hoped to throw the British out of Egypt, India and Nigeria. The Khalifat Movement in India was seen as the greatest threat to British rule since the uprising in 1857–9.[2] It fizzled out, but when it threatened to engulf India at the same time as unrest in Egypt, some of the elder statesmen felt cause for concern. Arthur Balfour, when Egypt appeared to be on the point of eruption in March 1919, wrote to the high commissioner:

> The Egyptian unrest is doubtless part of a world movement which takes different forms in different places, but is plainly discernible in every continent and in every country. We are only at the beginning of our troubles and it is doubtful whether, and how far, the forces of an orderly civilization are going to deal effectively with those of social and international disintegration.[3]

This was the central political problem of the postwar generation – chaos or order? And if order, order of what kind, and at what cost to human liberty? The ingredients for revolution – hunger, injustice, an unstable economy, and a much-weakened autocratic government – were present in almost all the nations of the world in 1918–19. Probably there was a degree of pure chance which determined which nations did or did not opt for outright civil war and revolution, and which chose to muddle along. And one element of chance was how ill the populations felt. As the war drew to an end, the world suffered 'the greatest single demographic shock mankind has ever experienced, the most deadly pestilence since the Black Death'.[4] Influenza swept round the world, greatly exacerbated by the unwonted movements of ships, troops, supplies, merchant vessels, politicians, refugees, which the war had occasioned. It probably killed 50 million worldwide. Two-thirds of Sierra Leone's population caught flu, with 1,000 dying in Freetown alone. At San Francisco Hospital in California, 3,509 cases were admitted, with 25 per cent mortality. It was a deadly viral pneumonia, soon wiping out soldiers and civilians at a rate which even General Haig and Clemenceau would have found difficult to match. Twenty-four thousand US soldiers died of flu, compared with the 34,000 who died in battle. In all, 675,000 Americans died of it, and 200,000 in Britain. Then, as quickly and mysteriously as it had come, the flu vanished, and the world was fit enough to resume death by violent means.

A month after Balfour wrote to the Egyptian high commissioner that he foresaw universal anarchy, there occurred the worst bloodshed in India for seventy years, and an event took place which hindsight can see quite clearly as the beginning of the end of British rule. Rioting broke out in

Amritsar, a glorious pilgrim-city in the Punjab, famed for its Sikh Golden Temple, in April 1919. At one point, 40,000 people were out on the streets. There was looting, and burning, and Christian churches were pulled down. Marcia Sherwood, a missionary doctor who had worked in Amritsar for fifteen years, mounted her bicycle and tried to ride to each of the five schools where she worked with the intention of sending her 600 female students (Muslim and Hindu) to their homes. She was set upon by a mob, and heard discordant cries of 'Kill her, she is English', and 'No, she is one of God's chosen who is educating our children.' She was badly beaten and left for dead as the crowd yelled: 'Victory to Gandhi.' (Gandhi was in Bombay at the time, totally unaware of what was happening in the Punjab.) Some Hindu shopkeepers rescued Dr Sherwood, and she would have been killed but for their courage. Very badly battered, she was taken to the Fort.

There were some other European deaths during the riots, many Indian injuries, and much wreckage of property. The response of the local British military commander, Brigadier General Reginald Dyer, was, first to proclaim a curfew, and to announce that any person found leaving their house after 8 pm would be shot. This announcement led to a furious riot, with thousands of people banging kerosene tins and shouting: 'An end to the British Raj.' A great crowd collected near the Temple in the enclosed square called the Jalianwala Bagh, for it was Baisakhi Day, the beginning of one of the most important Sikh festivals. With a mixed troop of Gurkhas, Sikhs and British soldiers, Dyer marched to the edge of the crowd and gave orders to fire. As the crowd panicked, and tried to escape the garden enclosure where they were such easy targets, the soldiers continued to fire with accuracy and determination. The superintendent of police, Mr R. Plomer, told Dyer that he was teaching the crowd a lesson it would not forget. From where Dyer was standing, on a platform of stamped-down earth looking down on the Temple gardens, he could see the corpses piling up like carcasses in an abattoir. By the time he ordered a ceasefire, 1,650 rounds of .303 ammunition had been fired, 379 had been killed, and many more injured.

The next day, Dyer grudgingly permitted the Indians to reclaim their dead and to begin burying them. When they went on strike and closed their shops, Dyer harangued them in bad Urdu: 'Speak up if you want war. In case there is to be peace, my order is to open all shops at once. Your people talk against the Government and persons educated in Germany and Bengal talk sedition. I shall uproot these all.' As a punishment for the attacks on Miss Sherwood, Dyer forced all the residents who had been living in the alley where she was assaulted to be punished – even though it was by no means clear that any of them had been responsible. He made every resident crawl along the alley on their stomachs, through the dust, the grit and the animal excrement. If any lifted a limb or their heads, they were prodded with rifle butts and bayonets. Conditions in the street only became worse, since street-cleaners were afraid to enter it, and anyone wanting to leave their house to buy food was obliged to crawl, in a street with no drainage and where the only way of getting rid of the human excrement was to throw it out of the window. The 'Crawling Order' as it was called was in force for about two weeks, until 24 April, when the viceroy, Lord Chelmsford, got to hear about it and insisted that it be revoked.

There were many other tortures and humiliations enforced by British officers upon the Indians. At Kasur, an entire wedding party, including the priest, were flogged because the wedding broke curfew regulations. Captain Doveton, an obvious sadist, ordered beatings and floggings of men found in a brothel; the prostitutes were forced to watch as their clients were punished. Women had their veils wrenched off while Mr Bosworth Smith, the district administrator, spat at them and called them 'flies, bitches, she-asses and swine'. Shopkeepers were taken out and flogged if they did not sell their goods cheap to British soldiers, and children were made to salute the Union Flag three times a day. An order was given that Indians should dismount from their vehicles and bow if a European approached. At Wazirabad a man who failed to salaam a British officer was forced to lick his boots.[5] Dyer's excuse was the same as that given throughout the twentieth century by brutal people inflicting death and injury on their fellow mortals – 'It was my duty – my horrible, dirty duty.'[6] Lord Stamfordham, the King's Private Secretary, gave an accurate picture of public opinion in Britain when he wrote to the Viceroy: 'On the one hand he [Dyer] is condemned for what is regarded as heartlessness, callousness and indifference to the value of human life; on the other hand, there are those who sum up their position in the words, "Dyer saved India".' History has shown that the latter view could not have been more wrong. The Amritsar massacre united Indians behind Gandhi's campaigns of civil disobedience, and destroyed any claims the British might try to advance that they were bringing values to the Indians which were more 'civilized' than what they could evolve for themselves.

Dyer was a child of Empire. He was born in the Punjab, where his father was a successful brewer. He had been educated at Simla – Bishop Cotton School – and almost his only experience of England was training at Sandhurst. After being commissioned into the Queen's Royal Regiment in 1885, his professional life had been spent in the Indian army, in which he had served with bravery and distinction in the Burma campaign of 1886–7, the relief of Chitral (1895), the Waziristan blockade and other examples of imperial derring-do from the pages of G. A. Henty. His India was not that of the early days of the East India Company, when Englishmen delighted in the exotic and alien civilization into which they had come as traders. It was post-Mutiny India, in which the white men were afraid of the brown men, and so asserted their invented superiority with racialistic slurs and military brutality.

It has been astutely observed that the Amritsar massacre had strong Irish overtones. Both Dyer and Sir Michael O'Dwyer (governor of the Punjab, who approved Dyer's actions and was assassinated in 1940) were ethnically Irish Protestants. In the Commons debate about Amritsar it was the Unionists and the Ulstermen who stuck up for Dyer, most notably Sir Edward Carson.[7]

Ireland had cascaded into violent anarchy almost before the end of the World War. The postwar election of December 1918 produced an overwhelming majority in Ireland for the Sinn Fein party. The old moderate Nationalists or Home Rulers had been ousted in favour of those who wanted complete independence of England, an Irish Republic with its own laws. The Irish Secretary in London said that 'the Irish question will be settled peaceably or bloodily within the next six months'. Four years were to elapse before the last British troops left Ireland. In the intervening period, both sides did their best to settle matters bloodily rather than peaceably, foolishly rather than wisely. During a dreadful Civil War, in which many were killed, the island of Ireland was split up. The Irish Free State came into being, one year after the signing of a treaty, on 6 December 1922, and the six counties of Ulster remained part of the United Kingdom. It was the worst possible solution, and certainly not one which either the Irish Nationalists or the English Unionist politicians had envisaged.

There was probably no way of solving the Irish question, but of one thing we can be certain. After the agitations and terrorist outrages began in Ireland, and on the British mainland, the government of Lloyd George made it far worse by attempting, Dyer-style, to intimidate the population by acts of state-sponsored terror.

Hear the words of Lieutenant-Colonel Smyth, DSO, a one-armed Great War hero who had been appointed divisional commissioner of the Royal Irish Constabulary for Munster after some Sinn Fein violence in June 1920:

> Now, men, Sinn Fein has had all the sport up to the present, and we are going to have the sport now. The police are not in sufficient strength to do anything to hold their barracks. This is not enough, for as long as we remain on the defensive, so long will Sinn Fein have the whip

hand. We must take the offensive and beat Sinn Fein with its own tactics ... If a police barracks is burned or if the barracks is already occupied, then the best house in the locality is to be commandeered, the occupants thrown into the gutter. Let them die there — the more the merrier. Police and military will patrol the country at least five nights a week. They are not to confine themselves to the main roads, but make across the country, lie in ambush and when civilians are seen approaching, shout 'Hands up!' Should the order be not immediately obeyed, shoot and shoot with effect. You may make mistakes occasionally and innocent people may be shot, but that cannot be helped, and you are bound to get the right parties some time. The more you shoot, the better I will like you, and I assure you that no policeman will get in trouble for shooting any man.[8]

Yes, this speech was written up in the *Irish Bulletin*, a Republican propaganda sheet, but the behaviour of the men whom Smyth was addressing showed that such orders were being carried out to the letter. These were the so-called Black and Tans, named after a pack of foxhounds which ran with a hunt in County Tipperary, but very far from being good sportsmen. They were not, as Irish propaganda liked to believe, the scourings of the British gaols, but out-of-work ex-servicemen recruited by Lloyd George as deliberate agents of terror to supplement the army and the regular police force. Sir Henry Wilson, himself destined to die by an IRA bullet in June 1922, discovered that Lloyd George believed that the Black and Tans were murdering 'two Sinn Feiners to every Loyalist the Sinn Feiners murdered. I told him, of course, that this was absolutely not so, but he seemed to be satisfied that a counter-murder association was the best answer to the Sinn Fein murders. A crude idea of statesmanship, and he will have a rude awakening.'[9]

After the election, the Sinn Fein members of Parliament, rather than assembling in Westminster, convened their own parliament, or Dail, in the Dublin Mansion House in 1919. Eamon de Valera, hero of the 1916 Easter Rising, escaped from Lincoln gaol in February 1919, was elected president of the Dail, and went to New York to rally support. He raised money, but no mainstream American politician at this date would recognize an Irish republic. On the very first day the Dail met in January 1919, two policemen were killed at point-blank range in County Tipperary and 'the Troubles' had begun.

Undoubtedly the mastermind behind the Sinn Fein operations was Michael Collins, who had joined the Fenian movement when working as a Post Office clerk in London. He was a natural organizer, and one of nature's spies, with agents in almost every big police station, a ruthless killer and fighter. All the most effective terrorist outrages had been planned by him. When the Irish Republican Brotherhood/Irish Republican Army began its offensives it had all the tricks up its sleeve. By contrast, the British were appallingly badly prepared. When General Sir Nevil Macready, commissioner of the Metropolitan Police, was put in charge of the forces in Ireland in March 1920, it was an appointment made by Lloyd George without consulting Churchill, the Secretary of State for War, or Sir Henry Wilson. Macready was appointed because Lloyd George could remember the vigour with which he had supervised the crushing of the Welsh miners' strikes in 1910. Arriving at Dublin, he recorded: 'Before I had been here three hours, I was honestly flabbergasted at the administrative chaos which seems to reign here.'[10] But if the British were in their usual muddle over Ireland and its affairs, they ultimately possessed more fire power, and more political clout. Michael Collins could outwit them by planting a bomb here, stealing some police papers there, but in the long term he was a pragmatist. After a hopeless struggle (hopeless both politically and militarily) to achieve a treaty with the English which allowed the Irish possession of the whole island, he compromised and went along with peace and the Free State. There was a certain illogic in his position. He gave as his reason for signing the treaty in 1922: 'To me it would have been a criminal act to refuse to allow the Irish nation to give its opinion whether it would accept this settlement or resume hostilities.' But he had not consulted the Irish nation as to whether it wanted to start the hostilities in the first place. The treaty was subsequently ratified by the Dail and passed overwhelmingly in a referendum. Collins, an official delegate in the peace negotiations, paid for the compromise with his life. He died in an ambush set up during the civil war in County Cork in August 1922.[11]

The carnage in Ireland has still, at the time of writing, not entirely ceased. When one contemplates the heroes of the Republican cause such as de Valera and Collins, it is hard to see them entirely as victims. They gloried in bloodshed and violence. The double standards applied were, admittedly, grotesque. If the English hanged an Irishman for sedition, there would be lachrymose scenes outside the prison, with crowds saying the rosary, followed by a huge funeral. When it came to Irishmen executing other Irishmen during the civil war the deaths were meted out with rather less ceremony. (Seventy-three Republicans were executed by their fellow Irish between November 1922 and May 1923.) But the Irish people whose shops and farms and houses were wrecked in the civil war were victims, both of Fenian terror and of English reprisals. It was very simple really. 'If we lose Ireland,' Sir Henry Wilson said, 'we've lost the Empire.'[12] If the British lost the Empire, what had been the point of fighting the Great War? How could the British define themselves?

Such an idea was, for most political and military Britons, unthinkable. That is why the *Morning Post*, the most Tory of the newspapers, was able to raise £26,371.4.10 for General Dyer as a token of its readers' high esteem for a man who in a later age would probably have been prosecuted. (Rudyard Kipling gave £10.) That is why readers of popular English newspapers are still encouraged to think of the Irish as potential troublemakers, and to see the British Empire as an essentially benign institution – which in some respects, compared with other empires in the world, it undoubtedly was.

The British Empire had in fact now passed its apogee, begun its decline. After the Irish treaty it ceased its expansion. Talk of the Empire being on the point of dissolution would have seemed complete insanity to the vast majority of its citizens in 1922. Far from being in retreat, the Empire was growing, and had been hugely expanded by the treaty of Versailles. In the postwar settlement it gained over 800,000 square miles, more than twice the area of Nigeria. Mesopotamia, now renamed Irak, with all its Mosul oilfields, became a British mandate. So did Palestine. Though Egypt became an independent kingdom in 1922, the British insisted on maintaining a military presence there in order to protect the Suez Canal. Much of Africa remained under British control, and the dominions of South Africa, Canada, New Zealand and Australia all owed allegiance to the Crown. There had never been a moment in history when, technically at least, Britain dominated a larger area of the planet. Yet for all its power, or perhaps because of it, it was not immune from the convulsions which upset less obviously fortunate countries, and the experience of Amritsar and of the Irish Troubles appears to offer a demonstration of the fact that the British government, no less than any other in the world, depended ultimately upon its willingness to use violence, not merely in war but against political enemies within its own state, and on its own civilian population.

The twenty-first-century world is that which was carved out by the diplomats and politicians after the First World War, and nowhere is this truer than in the Middle East. We are still, nearly a hundred years after its demise, living with the consequences of the collapse of the Ottoman Empire. The British saw themselves as the natural successors of the Ottomans in the Middle East. It was there that their natural imperial instincts were most clearly shown, and the essential precariousness and illogicality of the British imperial idea was demonstrated. The indigenous populations of the region had been offered self-determination when the war was over, but this generous dispensation was made by men who had no authority to make the offer, on behalf of governments who had other ideas. The big powers who took part in the Paris Peace Conference were committed to the idea of self-determination so long as it did not interfere with their own imperialism; and most Europeans felt uneasy about the idea of anyone with a brown face being left in charge of his own country or destiny. That was the one inherent contradiction in the post-Versailles thinking of the British: they supported a self-determining Hungary or Czechoslovakia, but were much less certain that an Arab or a Punjabi was really capable of managing his own affairs without the patronage of the white man. Attempts by such people to become self-governing were nearly always described by the British at this date as 'rebellions'. This is true in the newly established kingdom of Iraq. Glubb Pasha, a sympathetic and pro-Arab British soldier, for example, writes in his book *Britain and the Arabs*: 'In May 1920, the British government announced its acceptance of a mandate for Iraq, as decided' . . . not of course by the Iraqis, but 'by the San Remo conference' (which was composed entirely of Europeans). 'In June 1920, the Iraq tribes rose in revolt.'[13] You could as well speak of the Poles rising in 'revolt' when the Germans invaded in 1939. Throughout his exciting book, *War in the Desert*, about the part played by the RAF in establishing the kingdom of Iraq, Glubb talks about the Iraqis who fought against the British as 'rebels'.

As well as the political problems being stored up for the Empire, there was the economic contradiction of British imperialist dreams. The Empire which was begun for commercial reasons in the eighteenth century was becoming by the 1920s a drain on resources; but for that very reason it was seen by some imperialists as a duty which the British needed to continue. The very fact that it made no economic sense any more to have an Indian Empire, for example, was one of the reasons some of the British went on wishing to keep it. The fact that it was losing money seemed to demonstrate that the true motives for staying there were British altruism, and a desire to share with the Indians the superior administrative skills of the British.

If today the world has problems in Israel–Palestine, in Iran, in Iraq, these stem directly from decisions which the British did or did not make in the crucial period of the early 1920s. So many different factors come into play when describing the origins of Iraq that it would require book-length treatment to make sense of it. Crucial as it is to the world's concerns in the twenty-first century, we can see perhaps more clearly than we would have done a few years ago that Iraq was pivotal, not just for us today, but for them at the time. The British need to dominate and control this area, important in itself, was an early demonstration of so many factors which would colour the rest of the twentieth-century story, among them the British obsession with India, and dependency upon having an Indian Empire; the British need for oil; and the emerging importance of air power. In all these things, domination of the area now known as Iraq was vital. The population of the region was in some ways a secondary consideration as far as the British were concerned. Asquith's question in the House of Commons on 15 December 1920, when they were discussing the necessity of hanging Arab 'rebels' in Iraq, goes to the heart of the Middle Eastern question: 'Why are Arabs rebels? To whom traitors?'[14] Successive generations of imperialists or quasi-imperialists in the Middle East have failed to ask themselves that question, or to answer it satisfactorily. In the French Senate one senator got up one day in 1920 and asked: 'Why does not England take the mandate for Armenia since the U.S. have refused it?' Another replied: 'Because there are no oil wells there.'[15]

The Berlin–Baghdad Railway had been a major preoccupation of the British in the years before the First World War. The very existence of the railway prompted a British fear that Germany would block or dominate the route to India. Once the world's navies went over to fuelling themselves with oil, the oil-producing regions of the world, and especially Mesopotamia, or what we today call Iraq, assumed a consummate importance. After the First World War, the British would see it as crucial that they dominated the Middle East. Churchill was Colonial Secretary in the postwar Lloyd George administration. The ending of the war had left formidable problems all over the world, with many trouble-spots now requiring, either directly or indirectly, the attention of that office. Apart from the all-consuming problem of Ireland, there were troubles to be considered in the Middle East and India. In May 1920, Anglo-Indian troops were rushed to the shores of the Caspian after Russians seized Enzeli in support of the Persian nationalists who resisted British attempts to impose a new treaty on them. America and France resisted vigorously any attempts by Britain to dominate Persia. Apart from having to help provide garrisons in the Rhineland, British forces were waging war in the North West Frontier, suppressing an uprising in the Punjab. The British were also 'policing' Syria. Although the Anglo-Indian army there was due to evacuate whenever the French took up their mandate, in the years following the First World War, Syria alone was costing the British £9 million a year. In April 1920, Jerusalem was disturbed by violent riots protesting against Jewish immigration. Crowds brandished pictures of Faisal, yelling: 'Long live Faisal, our king!' Administering a reluctant Egypt was also ruinously expensive to the British.

The establishment of a kingdom of Iraq could satisfy almost every requirement of the self-contradictory imperialist dream. For such as T. E. Lawrence it could appear that the old adventures of 1917 in the desert might have a happy ending. Faisal could be rewarded, and the Arabs be offered 'self-determination' under the protection of the Crown. For the more hard-bitten mercantile realists, however, there was the fact that control of Iraq was of supreme tactical and economic advantage. By the establishment of a protected 'Jewish homeland', as opposed to Jewish state, in Palestine, a presence in Transjordan, as well as occupying and controlling Iraq, Britain could achieve its goal of keeping a land-bridge between the Mediterranean and the Persian Gulf, and guarding the shortest overland routes to India. In addition to this, Britain could build a pipeline to Haifa for the English-owned Iraq Petroleum Company.[16]

The situation in Iraq at the end of the First World War was a bloody mess. In July 1920 a young American diplomat, W. H. Gallaher, described in a letter sent care of the American consul the situation near Basra where 10,000 Arabs, instructed by German-trained Turkish officers, cut the railway line and blew up bridges. Gallaher foresaw the British losing Mosul, and possibly being driven out of Iraq before they established a presence there.

In my opinion the trouble all started from the bullheadedness of the British, first in persisting in the belief that the trouble out here is mainly religious whereas it is entirely political, and secondly in persisting in the belief that they can scare the Arab into submission. The average Englishman seems hurt and surprised, he can hardly believe that others do not like him, so he puts Arabian antipathy down to religion.[17]

It speaks volumes about the British mandate in Iraq that in 1940, despite the fact that the Iraqi Prime Minister General Nuri was broadly pro-British, the overwhelming majority of Iraqi public opinion supported either neutrality in the war, or open alliance with Nazi Germany. Herr Grobba, the German minister in Baghdad, was extremely popular among the ordinary Iraqis; German, Italian and Japanese investment in Iraq during the interwar years increased anti-British feeling. You find no explanation for this in Glubb Pasha's *Britain and the Arabs*, beyond a generalized suggestion that the Germans, Italians and Japanese, notoriously devious in their dealings, had mysteriously turned the Arabs against their natural friends. Glubb, a rather amiable soldier who had many friends in the Arab world and spent many years commanding the Jordanian army, gives a censored account of British involvement in Iraq from 1920 onwards, avoiding mention of the fact that, like the Anglo-American appointee and later enemy Saddam Hussein, in a subsequent generation, the British wished to subdue the rebellious population by dropping bombs of poison gas.

Churchill advocated the use of asphyxiating gases which would cause 'discomfort or illness but not death' in the dissident tribesmen. They were not in the event used in Iraq, since they were volatile and unpredictable in desert conditions. The so-called non-lethal gases, however, could 'even kill children and sickly persons, more especially as the people against whom we intend to use it have no medical knowledge with which to supply antidotes'.[18]

Churchill, at forty-six, chubby, loud, overconfident, treated the Cairo Conference at which the kingdom of Iraq was established as something of a holiday. He sailed on the French steamship *Sphinx* from Marseille to Alexandria, a six-day journey, in early March 1921. Having visited Aboukir Bay, scene of Nelson's victory over the French in 1798, he accompanied his wife by train to Cairo, where they motored to the Semiramis Hotel. Huge noisy aircraft circled ominously overhead, Bristol fighters and Handley Page bombers darkening the sky like metallic pterodactyls, while demonstrators gathered outside Shepheard's shouting: 'Down with Churchill.' The group assembled by the Colonial Secretary to decide the fate of Iraq did not contain a single Arab. The only Arabs at the Cairo Conference were serving Churchill with his drinks while he daubed at his canvases. The other members of the delegation were Sir Hugh Trenchard (1873–1956); Sir John Salmond (1881–1968), another air officer, who had been commander of the Royal Flying Corps in France at the end of the war; Sir Percy Cox (1864–1937), a veteran of the Indian army, acting minister in Teheran and due to become high commissioner in Mesopotamia; and Colonel T. E. Lawrence. Jessie Raven, wife of the civil servant who was accompanying Churchill, J. B. Crosland, noted that: 'When things were boring in the Hotel everyone would cheer up when Winston came in, followed by an Arab carrying a pail and a bottle of wine . . . he was unpopular with the Egyptians – many carriages had notices *à bas Churchill* – but he didn't care. He took his easel out and sat in the road painting – he also talked so loudly in the street that the generals got quite nervous . . . He didn't like the Arabs coming into the hotel, not even into the garden.'[19] While the Colonial Secretary painted and got blotto, the officers agreed to give Amir Faisal the newly created kingdom of Iraq, and make his brother the king of Jordan.

It was highly significant that the Cairo Conference contained two such senior Air Force officers, for it was here that a decision was made of profound consequence, not only in Mesopotamia but throughout the world in the twentieth century. The military on the spot in Iraq were constantly telling the government in London that they needed more troops. 'Whether we are to go or stay more troops are required' was the repeated message, sent in cypher from the civil commissioner in Baghdad to the secretary of state for India in London. The Colonial Secretary had other plans. Air power had been used in the First War, sometimes with great effect. But it was in the postwar situation of Iraq that Churchill was able to experiment with the use of air power to police an entire country.

The comparative cheapness of air power, versus manpower, had been demonstrated first in Somaliland, then in Afghanistan. In Somaliland, Mullah Mohammed bin Abdullah Hassan, inspired by memories of the Mahdi's holy war with the British in the times of General Gordon, excited a huge following. He claimed magical powers. His followers believed that he could push whole towns into the sea with his feet. No fewer than four British expeditions were mounted against him between 1904 and 1918, killing thousands of the mullah's men and expensively engaging thousands of British troops. On 21 January 1920 the first RAF bombing raid was sent against him at Medishe. A mere 36 officers of the RAF's Z Unit, with 189 enlisted men and one flight of six DH9 bombers, visited the mullah's fort twice daily. Within a month, the mullah had escaped to Abyssinia and the RAF men were back in Britain. The total of British casualties was two native soldiers. Churchill told the House of Commons that it would have cost £6 million to mount a conventional land assault on the mullah; the RAF campaign had cost £70,000.[20]

The emir of Afghanistan was the next to be subjected to RAF bombing raids. In 1919 he had declared jihad against British troops in the North West Frontier of India. The RAF shipped one Handley Page V/1500 bomber to Kabul, where it dropped four 112-pound and sixteen 20-pound bombs. 'Napoleon's presence was said to be worth an army corps, but this aeroplane seems to have achieved more than 60,000 men did,' wrote Basil Liddell Hart.[21]

Fired by the success of the RAF in Somaliland and Afghanistan, it was decided at the Cairo Conference that the defence of the new kingdom of Iraq would be conducted with air power.

In any case, as General Sir Aylmer Haldane (1862–1950) – he had been Churchill's fellow prisoner in Pretoria during the South African War – reported from Basra in 1922, when the temperature had reached 128 degrees Fahrenheit: 'This is not a white man's country and it is absurd to pretend it is. The British troops hate it and naturally so.' Churchill himself had noted in 1920 that keeping ground troops in Mesopotamia would have meant maintaining an enormous garrison simply in order to police 'a score of mud villages, sandwiched in between a swampy river and a blistering desert, inhabited by a few hundred half-starved native families, usually starving'.[22] By October 1922, all financial control from the War Office over Iraq ceased, and it was administered from the Colonial Office, saving millions of pounds. Iraq was to be administered by about 2,000 air force men.[23]

Faisal was installed as king, but Churchill made clear to Sir Percy Cox: 'You shd explain to Faisal that while we have to pay the piper we expect to be consulted about the tune whether under Mandatory or Treaty arrangements. If he wishes to be a sovereign with plenary powers, he must show that he is capable of maintaining peace and order in Iraq unaided.' He added: 'I am quite sure that if Faisal plays us false, & policy founded on him breaks down, Br[itain] will leave him to his fate & withdraw immediately all aid and military force.'[24] Churchill became edgy when his department was attacked in the press for wasting public money in Iraq. He was furious in the course of the year that there were still 21,632 Indian followers of the army in Iraq, and he wanted them all dispatched back to India.

The estimate was that £9 million would be required to finance Iraq in the coming year of 1922. 'Not one farthing more than 7 will be asked by me.' When he was asked for £150,000 to build a hospital in Baghdad, he refused. 'There is no military need.' Asked by Colonel Meinertzhagen (1878–1967), his Middle Eastern adviser, of Danish origin, mistakenly supposed by some to be Jewish, whether he realized that the air force was planning to use lethal gas bombs, which could damage eyesight or kill children and sick persons, Churchill replied: 'I am ready to authorize the construction of such bombs at once.'[25]

One RAF officer explained the strategy:

One objective must be selected – preferably the most inaccessible village of the most prominent tribe which it is desired to punish . . . The attack with bombs and machine-guns must be relentless and unremitting and carried on continuously by day and night, on houses, inhabitants, crops and cattle. No news travels like bad news. The news of the punishment will spread like wildfire . . . This sounds brutal, I know, but it must be made brutal to start with. The threat alone in the future will prove efficacious if the lesson is once properly learnt.[26]

Not everyone was convinced by the policy of, in the words of Field Marshal Henry Wilson, 'appearing from God knows where, dropping their bombs on God knows what, and going off again God knows where',[27] but the senior RAF officers in Iraq felt they had learnt valuable lessons, most notably Arthur Harris and Charles Portal, who would each head Bomber Command during the Second World War, and Edward Ellington, chief of Air Staff just before that war.[28]

In February 1922 the Prime Minister, Lloyd George, asked the cabinet 'warmly to congratulate' Churchill for having created a nation out of 'a mere collection of tribes'.[29] In July, Lawrence resigned from his advisory job at the Colonial Office, believing that he had done all he could to establish Faisal in his kingdom. In fact, very few of the optimistic predictions of the Cairo Conference came to pass. Because of the threat of Turkish invasion in the north, the British did in fact maintain ground troops in Mosul all the year round. Lloyd George complained that little had been done to exploit the oil. Churchill, after all his initial enthusiasm, was scared by all the bad publicity he was getting in the Press, and decided he would rather Britain withdrew from Iraq altogether. It was another of his bungles. 'We are paying eight millions a year for the privilege of living on an ungrateful volcano out of which we are in no circumstances to get anything worth having,' he wrote. 'If we leave,' Lloyd George complained, 'we may find a year or two after we have departed we have handed over to the French and the Americans some of the richest oilfields in the world.'[30] So Britain stayed until the 1950s, and must bear a heavy burden of responsibility for having created the 'kingdom of Iraq' in the first place, and then administered it so badly.

15

Communists and Fascism –
The Allure of Violence

Standing on a railway station in Belgium only a few days before he abdicated, Kaiser Wilhelm II was so troubled in mind by a dream which he had the previous night, that he bored the various adjutants and staff officers by telling it. Every royal personage in Europe was angry with him, except Queen Maud of Norway (George V's sister).

The Kaiser's dream touchingly suggests a longing for the European situation to return to the Victorian days when international disputes were seen as royal family squabbles. One minute, he was railing against the British, and saying that he would make peace with France or Russia, but never with Britain – 'Only amidst the ruins of London will I forgive Georgy.'[1] The next, he was saying that it was impossible so much as to speak to republicans in France or America. A peace settlement could only be formulated by kings, since war was 'a royal sport, to be indulged in by hereditary monarchs and concluded at their will'.[2]

In 1933, Lloyd George told the Kaiser's grandson Prince Louis Ferdinand that they had neither expected nor intended to overthrow the Hohenzollern dynasty. It was a disingenuous claim from a man who had at the time crowed that he was considering hanging or shooting the Kaiser, but in that year of omen, the Welsh radical could see that, had Germany retained its royal family, 'then we wouldn't need to give ourselves such headaches now about Herr Hitler'.[3]

It is easy to blame the British for their handling of the Amritsar massacre, or the Mandate in Iraq, or the settlement of the Irish question. But as the years unfold, and we see what happens in countries which had overthrown their aristocratic systems of government and their royal figureheads, it might be possible to find some virtue in constitutional monarchies.

Certainly the Hohenzollerns sank to a very low level. The Kaiser himself was just about all right, living sadly as a country squire in Holland. His sister married a Russian antiques dealer half her age. He spent all her money. They toyed with an offer from Hollywood to take part in a film playing themselves, but they could not decide, and in the course of the row they had about it, they separated. She died of depression in a bedsit in Bonn. He got a job as a waiter in Luxembourg. In vain did Wilhelm II, from his exile, try to persuade the restaurant to remove a poster from the window advertising the fact that diners would be served by the brother-in-law of the Kaiser.[4]

Heinrich Mann's just prewar satirical novel *Der Untertan* predicted the reversals which were to come upon the human race.

'I suppose you do not know whom history will designate as the representative type of this era?'

'The Emperor', said Dietrich.

'No', Buck replied. 'The actor'.[5]

The convulsions by which this transformation took place were not quiet, nor were they peaceful. While Ireland killed its hundreds, Russia killed its hundreds of thousands. Victorians of William Morris's era, seeing the grossness of inequality between rich and poor, the sheer hopelessness of the plight of the urban poor, the apparently unshakeable unfairness of things, could hardly fail, if they were sensitive human beings, to want some form of communist revolution. 'Horrible to say,' Gerard Manley Hopkins wrote to his friend Robert Bridges, 'I am a Communist.' How can it ever be known how many died as a consequence of Lenin's revolution, and the attempt to spread worldwide communism? A recent study in French called *The Black Book of Communism* calculates that at least a hundred million human beings have died as a result, first of the revolution itself, and its imitations in other lands, then in the concentration camps, the artificially contrived famines and the mass murders instituted by the communists.[6] That is what we see if we look backwards. Yet it isn't the way that Time works. History is peering the wrong way down a telescope. Our knowledge is greater than the actors' in the drama, but our understanding is not necessarily superior. The enthusiasm felt at the time for the Russian revolution is a case in point.

People were drawn to communism because of the obvious failure of the Tsars to bring a just or fair way of life; because of the huge disparity between rich and poor all over the Western world; because they believed that communism was a way of peace. Likewise, people were drawn to fascism because they could see the same injustices which drew people towards communism, but could also see the anarchy which resulted when communists actually took control. Many would have echoed the words of Trotsky's secretary, Evgenia Petrovna Shelepina, twenty-three years old at the time of the revolution, a beautiful, muscular, pipe-smoking girl who liked wearing sailor-suits. 'Arthur' – the English reporter whom she fell in love with and married – 'did not care in normal times one hoot for politics any more than I did, and it was only upheavals like the Revolution that stirred us up to taking sides. I have never been a communist or even a mild socialist but merely through starting reading the newspapers at the beginning of the war I gradually acquired a respect for socialists and when for a short period between the first or Duma revolution in March 1917 and the Bolsheviks' takeover in October, Russia enjoyed the real freedom of the press I was convinced the Bolsheviks were the only party which had the chance to extricate Russia from the chaos into which the war, entered so irresponsibly by the Tsarist Government, plunged the country.'[7]

The English Arthur with whom she fell in love was Arthur Ransome, one of the few foreign journalists to have close contacts with Trotsky during the Brest-Litovsk talks when revolutionary Russia made peace with Germany. His mentor when he went to Russia as an aspirant journalist had been Harold Williams, a gentle, intelligent man who had entertained high hopes of Kerensky's liberal revolution. Of Trotsky he believed: 'He is one of the most evil men I ever met. They want external peace for internal war. Remember my words, the Bolsheviks will fight no one except the Russians.'[8] Ransome was unwilling to believe Williams's pessimism. In common with the correspondent of the *Manchester Guardian*, Philip Price, Ransome wanted to believe that Lenin was bringing justice and prosperity to his people. His description of the Constituent Assembly, addressed by Trotsky, is reminiscent of the rapture felt by young Romantics such as Wordsworth at the time of the French Revolution:

My position was immediately behind and above the presidium, looking down on Trotsky's muscular shoulders and great head, and the occasional gestures of his curiously small hands. Beyond him was that sea of men: soldiers in green and grey shirts, workers in collarless ones, or jerseys, others dressed very like British workmen, peasants in belted red shirts and high top-boots: all picked men, not elected for this assembly alone but proved and tested in the local soviets that had chosen them as delegates. And as I watched that amazing crowd, that filled the huge hall and packed the galleries, following point by point Trotsky's exposition of the international and inter-class situation and the policy of the Revolution I felt I would willingly give the rest of my life if it could be divided into minutes and given to men in England and France so that those of little faith who say the Russian revolution is discredited could share for one minute each that wonderful experience.[9]

When Robert Bruce Lockhart, who had been sent by Lloyd George as an unofficial ambassador to the Bolsheviks, met Ransome he thought him 'a Don Quixote with a walrus moustache, a sentimentalist who could always be relied upon to champion the under-dog'.[10]

Ransome returned to England, with Evgenia, and published an account of the Russian Revolution which was meant as a corrective to the distortions of the right-wing press. His portrait of Lenin, with whom he once played chess, is of a ruthless man, but of a recognizable human being, rather than the villainous hobgoblin portrayed by the *Morning Post*. 'He was the most Russian of them. Time and again, after listening to speeches which might have been made in any language in any country by men of any nationality I have been suddenly, as it were, brought back to Russia when this urgent little figure stepped on to the tribune, stuck his thumbs in the armholes of his waistcoat, and mingled jest and argument in language that tasted of Russian tobacco and the life of the Russian peasantry.'[11] No wonder that Lenin wrote to the future author of *Swallows and Amazons*, offering him every assistance with his Russian history. He even got Ransome an interview with the second-in-command of the new secret police, the Cheka, forerunner of the KGB. Everything he said to justify the killings which had begun could have been said – and was said – by British government officials about the inhabitants of Dublin and Cork: namely, that although some innocents had been shot, for the most part, it had been necessary to kill people in order to maintain civil order.

At about the time that Arthur Ransome was having this conversation with the Cheka Commissariat, another Englishman, Sydney Gibbes, was in the Siberian town of Ekaterinburg. He had been the tutor to the Tsar's children, and he had come to the town, ten months after their murder, to see for himself what could be seen. Russia was now engulfed in civil war, and Whites, soldiers fighting the Bolsheviks, had found various items in the woods near a disused mineshaft known as Four Brothers – a pile of eggshells, some false teeth, six corsets. The eggshells had been ordered by the assassins. The Bolshevik guard had told the nuns who fed the royal family to boil fifty eggs, so that they should have something to eat. The false teeth belonged to the devoted family physician, Doctor Botkin, who tended the little haemophiliac prince, Alexis. The corsets had belonged to the empress, two elder grand duchesses and a faithful maid. Mr Gibbes went to the merchant's house which had been the last residence of the royal family and spent hours in the cellar, gathering up what relics he could find – coins, a blood-soaked handkerchief, scraps of paper. They would in time become sacred relics, just as Mr Gibbes, a bank manager's son from Yorkshire, would become Father Nicholas of the

Holy Orthodox Church. The only member of the royal household to survive was Joy, the King Charles spaniel, belonging to the haemophiliac Tsarevich Alexis.[12]

Only years later was it established what had happened to the royal family. In the middle of the night of 16–17 July 1918, Yakov Yurovsky, the local Cheka boss, and one of Lenin's most trusted lieutenants, roused the Tsar, now known as plain Nikolai Romanov, and told him to come to the basement with his family. At 2 am, dressed and ready, they came to the cellar. They were ordered to line up against the wall for a photograph. At their request, two chairs were brought for the empress, and for the haemophiliac Alexis, who had been suffering from one of his bleeding-attacks. Anastasia was holding her spaniel Jimmy. Yurovsky came into the room with five or six Hungarians (or Latvians in some accounts) and five Russians. He read out an order to shoot the Romanovs. Nikolai Romanov was baffled – 'What? What?' he asked. But the firing had begun. Yurovsky shot the Tsar at point-blank range. He and the empress died instantly. But the shooting continued for twenty minutes, partly because the bullets ricocheted off the jewels hidden in the corsets of the younger grand duchesses. Alexis, lying in a pool of blood, was still alive when the guard approached the slumped bodies on the cellar floor. Yurovsky shot him twice in the head. Anastasia was stabbed with bayonets to make sure she was dead.[13] The dog Joy survived the tragedy, but was blinded, said to have been traumatized.

There is no doubt that the orders for the murders came directly from Lenin. As Trotsky once said, 'We must put an end once and for all to the papist-Quaker babble about the sanctity of human life.' Felix Dzerzhinsky, who had the dubious distinction of having founded the Cheka, made an official statement to the press, confirming the death of the Tsar. 'The Cheka must defend the revolution and conquer the enemy even if its sword falls occasionally on the heads of the innocent.'[14]

The Bolsheviks had never made any secret of what they wished to do to their enemies. They were bound to have murdered the emperor sooner or later. There is no evidence that they ever contemplated the release of the Russian royal family. Some historians, however, have noted that King George V did not try very hard to rescue his cousins. When the Kerensky government forced the abdication of the Tsar, the foreign minister, Pavel Milyukov, was approached by the British ambassador, Sir George Buchanan, who asked if it might be possible for the imperial family to escape to England. Milyukov, Buchanan reported, 'was most anxious to get the Emperor out of Russia as soon as possible, the extremists having excited opinion against His Majesty'. This notion was viewed with approval by the British government, and on 22 March 1918, Lloyd George asked Lord Stamfordham, the king's secretary, to Downing Street to discuss the Tsar's future. They were joined by Bonar Law and Lord Hardinge, former viceroy of India. It was generally agreed that the Tsar should be offered asylum in Britain, but the King's Private Secretary immediately began to make difficulties. Where would the Romanovs live? They would have to be given a royal house, and Balmoral 'would certainly not be a suitable residence at this time of year'. The real reason was that the king feared the possibility of a socialist backlash if he offered his cousin refuge in England. The Tsarist regime had been much hated. Many of the Jews who had suffered persecution – with the full approval of the emperor – by 'good and simple Russian folk'[15] were now living in the East End of London, and many English liberals would have echoed the goodwill messages sent by Lloyd George to Kerensky, in which he had said that 'The Revolution whereby the Russian people have placed their destinies on the sure foundation of freedom is the greatest service they have yet made for the allied peoples.'

They were desperate times, and the king funked his duty. Although the politicians were going ahead with the proposal that the Tsar should be got out of Russia, on 30 March, Stamfordham approached Arthur Balfour, Foreign Secretary. 'The King has been thinking about the Government's proposal that the Emperor Nicholas and his family should come to England. As you are doubtless aware, the King has a strong personal friendship for the Emperor . . .' The friendship was not yet strong enough, however, to allow him to come to England. George V asked if the invitation could be rescinded. The latest, rather desperate excuse offered was that he worried about the 'dangers of the voyage'. The Foreign Secretary rebuffed the king and said that the invitation could not be withdrawn. But Stamfordham persisted. 'As you know, from the first the King has thought the presence of the Imperial family (especially of the Empress) [because she was German] in this country would raise all sorts of difficulties, and I feel sure you appreciate how awkward it will be for our Royal Family who are so closely connected with both the Emperor and the Empress.' This was followed by a letter, written on the same day, in which Stamfordham said the king 'must beg you to represent to the Prime Minister that from all he hears and reads in the press the residence in this country of the ex-Emperor and Empress would be strongly resented by the public'. The correspondence took place in April 1918. By the end of the month, the Romanovs had been moved to Ekaterinburg.

The king quickly forgot his own cowardice, and his (partial) responsibility for his cousins' deaths. 'May and I attended a service at the Russian Church in Welbeck Street in memory of dear Nicky, who I fear was shot last month by the Bolshevists,' he noted in his diary on 25 July 1918. In time, the British royal family had rewritten history. Louis Mountbatten, royal propagandist in chief, liked to put it about that George V had striven to rescue his poor cousin from the perils of the Russian Revolution, only to be thwarted by a heartless and opportunist Lloyd George.

Relations between Lloyd George and his sovereign were coloured by well-placed mistrust. Lloyd George's attack, made during one of his virulent assaults upon the House of Peers, on the principle of primogeniture ('You would not choose a *spaniel* on those principles'),[16] could hardly have recommended itself to an hereditary monarch.

Lloyd George had fought the election in December 1918 on a blatantly populist, 'Hang the Kaiser!' ticket. 'The men responsible for this outrage' – that is the World War – 'on the human race must not be let off because their heads were crowned when they perpetrated the deed.'[17]

The Kaiser had abdicated as emperor, though not as king of Prussia, and gone to live in exile in Holland. The idea of attempting his extradition was conveniently forgotten by the postwar government. The old gentleman was doing no harm to anyone. His first request, upon arrival in Holland, had been for a 'good strong cup of English tea', and his favourite reading became the novels of P. G. Wodehouse. In appearance and manner he came to resemble an old-fashioned English squire, and his disgruntlements with life were for the most part those of any other conservative-minded personage of comparable age. It worried him, for example, when Baden-Powell admitted 'Niggerboys' to join the Boy Scouts. 'It was the beginning of the treason to their race formerly only executed by the French negroids.'[18] Many a retired major in Cheltenham or Bath would have thought the same at that date. Only occasionally would glimpses of the old insane rage burst out to disturb the quiet routines of his secretaries and ADCs: then there would be furious denunciations by their royal master of the disloyalty of the army, the navy, the Prussian nobility, which had allowed him to come to such a pass. Sometimes, his bitterness was directed against the Jews. The Germans had, he ranted to Generalfeld-marschal August von Mackensen, been 'egged on and misled by the tribe of Judah whom they hate'. No German should be allowed to forget 'nor rest until these parasites have been wiped out from German soil and been exterminated! This poisonous mushroom on the German oak-tree!'[19]

George V had viewed with the greatest disquiet the possibility of his cousin Wilhelm being brought to England for trial. He firmly opposed all calls for retribution against the German emperor. He had done his best to wipe out his own German-ness, and that of his relations. He waited, significantly, until 1917 before he changed the name of the royal dynasty from Saxe-Coburg to Windsor, though everyone remains to this day in some doubt about their surname, or even whether they have one.

The Kaiser, when he heard of this decision, wondered whether there would now be performances of *The Merry Wives of Saxe-Coburg-Gotha*. Prince Louis of Battenberg was obliged to write to his family that George Rex felt vulnerable 'being attacked as half-German & surrounding himself by relatives with German names, &c.' He asked his Holstein, Teck and Battenberg relations to 'give up using in England our German titles & to assume English titles'. It was at this point in history that the Battenbergs became the Mountbattens.

Yet George V was a strange mixture of cowardice and bravery, the petty and the grand. Although his mean-spiritedness towards the Tsar could have cost the Romanovs their lives, he eventually showed great bravery in Ireland. When the king, in 1914, had expressed misgiving about his army shedding blood in Ireland, Asquith had bluntly retorted that the king was 'no more at its head than he was at the head of every Public Department, and any orders given to the troops was [*sic*] on the responsibility of Ministers'.[20] When the Troubles began after the World War, the king had once again had great disagreement with a prime minister, this time Lloyd George. 'The King is an old coward,' complained Lloyd George when Terence MacSwiney, mayor of Cork, went on hunger-strike in a British gaol in 1920, eventually dying, thereby enormously exacerbating anti-British feeling. 'He is frightened to death and is anxious to make it clear that he has nothing to do with it.' The king's attempts to remain distant from the hunger-strike were stridently attacked by his own equerry, Ponsonby. 'The King and I had a fierce argument on Ireland which ended in a yelling match,' Ponsonby told his wife.[21]

When George V stopped dithering, and eventually dared to be kingly, it had a powerful effect. When a Northern Ireland Parliament was convened in June 1921, he was told by his closest advisers not to go to open it. Such a gesture could only antagonize the Catholic South, and there was a strong danger that he would be assassinated. But in defiance of such caution, George V went to Belfast, rode through the streets in an open landau, and read an admirably conciliatory speech from the throne. The words were written by the former *Times* journalist Lord Altrincham.

The eyes of the Empire are on Ireland today – that Empire in which so many nations and races came together in spite of the ancient feuds, and in which new nations have come to birth within the lifetime of the youngest in this hall. I am emboldened by that thought to look beyond the sorrow and anxiety which have clouded of late my vision of Irish affairs. I speak from a full heart when I pray that my coming to Ireland today may prove to be the first step towards the end of strife amongst her people, whatever their race or creed . . .

With a balance of viewpoint which only a *Times* leader writer could have achieved, the monarch concluded:

> The future lies in the hands of my Irish people themselves. May this historic gathering be the prelude of the day in which the Irish people, north and south, under one Parliament or two, as those Parliaments may themselves decide, shall work together for a common love of Ireland upon the sure foundation of mutual justice and respect.[22]

Over eighty years later, the world is still waiting for the consummation of this devout wish. At the time, however, it made a great impression, and a period of virtual peace, until the mid-1960s, followed.

In 1924, Hilaire Belloc – poet, journalist, and sometime radical Liberal MP for Salford – 'made a sort of pilgrimage to see Mussolini . . . I had the honour of a long conversation with him alone, discovering and receiving his judgements. What a contrast with the sly and shifty talk of your parliamentarian! What a sense of decision, of sincerity, of serving the nation, and of serving it to a known end with a definite will! Meeting this man after talking to the parliamentarians in other countries was like meeting with some athletic friend of one's boyhood after an afternoon with racing touts; or it was like coming upon good wine in a Pyrenean village after compulsory draughts of marsh water in the mosses of the moors above, during some long day's travel over the range.'[23] Belloc was very far from being alone in his high estimation of *Il Duce*. Winston Churchill, when he had met Mussolini, wrote to him: 'If I were an Italian, I am sure I would have been with you from the beginning to the end in your struggle against the bestial appetites of Leninism.' In a speech in 1933, Churchill went further.

> The Roman genius impersonated in Mussolini, the greatest law-giver among living men, has shown to many nations how they can resist the pressures of Socialism and has indicated the path that a nation can follow when courageously led. With the Fascist regime, Mussolini has established a centre of orientation from which countries which are engaged in a hand-to-hand struggle with Socialism must not hesitate to be guided.[24]

Gandhi described him as a 'superman'. The archbishop of Canterbury, Randall Davidson, was sure that he was 'the one giant figure in Europe'.[25]

16

The Silly Generation – From Oswald Spengler to Noël Coward

'Dance, dance, dance, little lady,' sang Noël Coward in *This Year of Grace*, in 1928.

> Youth is fleeting – to the rhythm beating
> In your mind.
> Time and tide and trouble
> Never, never wait:
> Let the cauldron bubble –
> Justify your fate.
> Dance, dance, dance, little lady
> Leave tomorrow behind.[1]

It's a migraine of a song, whose speed and rhythm are doubly menacing when sung by Coward himself. It was a decade of wonderful songs – 'Ma, he's Making Eyes at Me' (1922), 'Yes We Have No Bananas' (1923), 'California, Here I Come' (1924), 'Tea for Two' (1925), 'Valencia', 'Five Foot Two, Eyes of Blue', 'Fascinating Rhythm' (1926), 'Chinatown', 'Ain't She Sweet' (1927), 'Ol' Man River', 'Sonny Boy', 'I Can't Give You Anything But Love, Baby' (1928), 'Ain't Misbehavin', 'Blue Moon', 'You're the Cream in My Coffee', 'Singin' in the Rain' (1929).[2] We are singing them still. This was because so many people had gramophones, and increasing numbers had wireless. (But gramophones remained expensive. A table gramophone with a pleated diaphragm instead of a sound-box or horn cost £22.10s. in 1924, when a stock-broker's senior clerk earned £4.15s. a week.) On 15 June 1920, Dame Nellie Melba sang from the Marconi station at Chelmsford, Essex, at the invitation of the *Daily Mail*, which paid the singer the colossal sum of £1,000. Her voice was clearly heard in Berlin and Paris. By the end of 1921 more than three thousand wireless amateurs had asked the Post Office, who controlled wireless telegraphy in Britain, to provide regular programmes. In America, over a million people now had receiving sets on which they could 'listen in', as the phrase went, to concerts, market prices, weather reports, sermons and speeches.

After considerable deliberation, the Post Office entrusted the task of entertaining the nation to a single company, the British Broadcasting Corporation. By December 1922 the BBC was broadcasting for forty hours a week. Listening in was a solemn ritual. Long poles for aerials had to be erected at the end of your garden. At first you had to listen on headphones to a crystal set, but soon devices were contrived in which the coils, wireless, loudspeaker and controls were contained within a single box or cabinet, and some advanced households even concealed their aerial in the attic. In 1924 the king acquired a set. 'How soon shall we be able to see by radio?' asked a newspaper correspondent in 1925. J. L. Baird had demonstrated that a still photograph could be transmitted and received by radio, and on 27 January 1926 in an upper room in Frith Street, Soho, he demonstrated 'television'.

But although serious-minded people hoped the wireless would be a means of improving the populace, it was inevitable that its most popular programmes should have been dance bands such as Jack Hylton's orchestra, playing the latest foxtrot, or comedians developing the unique opportunities for humour which radio offered: Tommy Handley, Stainless Stephen and Vivian Foster (the Vicar of Mirth) became household names, and more people listened in to them than to the real clergy, such as the bishop of London, who was cut off in mid-sentence from the Savoy Hill Studio, as listeners heard him remarking: 'I don't think that was too long, do you?'[3]

Cinema added a new imaginative dimension, not only to people's lives but to their shared inner lives. 1920–29 has been called the Golden Age of Hollywood. The truly remarkable thing about this was that, especially since it was also the last decade of the silent film, America for the first time became the centre of the cultural world. You did not need to know a language to sit enthralled by Mary Pickford, Douglas Fairbanks, Charlie Chaplin, Ronald Colman, Greta Garbo, Harold Lloyd and Clive Brook. Chaplin seems eerily unfunny today, as do back numbers of supposedly funny magazines like *Punch*. But what survives is his extraordinary mimetic, almost tragically mimetic, gift. Rudolph Valentino, born Rodolpho Alphonso Guglielmi di Valentino d'Antonguolla, settled in America in 1913. He began playing bit parts in Hollywood in 1918, but it was in the 1920s that he rose to glory. Perhaps aptly, his first big role was as one of the four horsemen of the Apocalypse in Rex Ingram's film of that name in 1921. His face, twice or thrice life size, stared over towns all over Europe from placards and posters. Animated, on the flickering black and white screen of darkened cinemas, he led men and women into realms of new fantasy in such popular works as *The Sheik* (1921), *Blood and Sand* (1922), *The Young Rajah* (1922) and *Monsieur Beaucaire* (1924). When he visited England in 1925 for the premiere of *The Eagle*, he was mobbed. The Second Coming could hardly have attracted more hysterical attention, and when he died the next year, thousands attended his funeral, openly weeping.

The politicians and aspirant politicians of the new era could not fail to notice the hypnotic effects of the new technology. The endearing amateurism of real bishops and politicians could only send listeners to sleep, but it did not take much imagination to see how demagogues could use radio and film. When the facetious *Punch* humorist and detective story-writer Father Ronald Knox broadcast in 1926 an account of an unemployment riot in London, hundreds telephoned Savoy Hill in alarm. They had believed his description of mobs attacking the Houses of Parliament and people being roasted alive in Trafalgar Square.[4] The mass media increased levels of public credulity. The world awaited leaders who could combine the bloodcurdling imagination of Knox and the hypnotic appearance of Valentino. No human being, even Napoleon, had been idolized as Valentino was. The new Napoleons could become faces staring from every cinema, voices yelling from every wireless set.

> I'm so ashamed of it,
> But I must admit
> The sleepless nights I've had about the boy.
> On the Silver Screen
> He melts my foolish heart in every single scene.[5]

One of the things which cinema and radio could accomplish was the illusion that purely passive viewers and listeners were somehow sharing in the action of a new age. Tuning in on the crystal set to the Savoy Orpheans, broadcast from 10.30 to 11.30 each night, you could imagine yourself a flapper in the heart of London, even though you were a factory girl in Bootle or a secretary in Wolverhampton. Purchasing the *Melody Maker* (founded 1926) you could read all about the latest jazz bands, and buy their records, even if you lived miles from anywhere that they might have been performing. The agitated sense that everyone was having, or meant to be having, a good time in the aftermath of war added, presumably, to the gloom of those who were not, and increased the frenzy of those who were. People became obsessed by speed. In 1926, the land speed record was gained by Parry Thomas on Pendine Sands, Carmarthenshire, at 178 mph. On 3 March of the following year, he was killed in his Thomas special when the driving chain broke and he was decapitated.[6] Pleasure itself had to be dangerous, and harder work than work. The nightclub, that self-punishing institution for the hedonist, flourished as never before. Alec

Waugh in his novel *Kept* (1925) described them as 'second-rate places for third-rate people'.

Queen of the third-raters, if this was true, was Kate or 'Ma' Meyrick, born in Dublin, who married a medical student in England, lived in Brighton and bore him four children. In 1919 the Meyricks separated, Ma Meyrick came up to London and her jollities began. After a police raid on Dalton's Club, next to the Alhambra Theatre in Leicester Square, Ma Meyrick protested strongly, both at having to pay £25 fine and at having her 'innocent venture' described by a magistrate as 'a den of iniquity'. She moved over the Charing Cross Road and started another club, Brett's, which she sold after only a year for £1,000. Then she started the '43 club, which was raided after only two months. Ma Meyrick was fined for selling drinks after closing hours. The '43 became a cult, with such illustrious clients as King Carol of Romania, the Crown Prince of Sweden, Rudolph Valentino and Tallulah Bankhead having been seen there at least once. Alas for Ma Meyrick, she was eventually sentenced to fifteen months' hard labour for bribing a policeman, Station-Sergeant George Goddard. His pay was £6 a week, but he was found by investigating officers with £12,000 in cash in one of his residences. He owned a house in Streatham, a car and two safe-deposit accounts, stuffed with notes. Several of the notes could be traced to Ma Meyrick and her girls. Goddard did eighteen months with hard labour. When Ma Meyrick was released, the Bright Young Things sang:

> Come all you birds
> And sing a roundelay.
> Now Mrs Meyrick's
> Out of Holloway.

They were a long way from the struggles of the working classes in the big industrial towns, from the growing pains of the incipient League of Nations, from the agonized inhabitants of the occupied Ruhr, from the warring Irish and the oppressed Indians. And yet, the noise of young people partying, dancing their Charlestons and singing their songs seemed emblematic of their times. There was a palpable sense of self-conscious decadence in the air, as on the airwaves; decadence in the most literal sense of things slithering downwards. When, in June 1922, the Leeds choral society gave a superb performance of Sir Edward Elgar's *The Apostles* at the Queen's Hall, according to George Bernard Shaw there were only Princess Mary, Viscount Lascelles and about four other people in the stalls. 'The occasion', said Shaw, 'was infinitely more important than the Derby, Goodwood, the Cup Finals, the Carpentier fights or any of the occasions on which the official leaders of society are photographed and cinematographed laboriously shaking hands with persons on whom Molière's patron, Louis XIV, and Bach's patron, Frederick the Great, would not have condescended to wipe their boots.'[7]

Shaw was giving expression to a widespread view among intellectuals that something had happened, not just to concert audiences in London, and not just to England, but to Western civilization in general. Whether the war had caused or promoted or only reflected this something was incidental to the fact that it had happened: Western civilization had gone down the drain. Shaw's invocation of Louis XIV and Frederick the Great resonates with the idea, which many of his contemporaries shared, that they had moved into a new era altogether. It was possible to imagine Frederick the Great holding a conversation with Tennyson or Carlyle, but not to imagine him (much as he might have enjoyed it for all sorts of reasons) sitting through Rudolph Valentino's *Monsieur Beaucaire*.

The arch-exponent of the idea that the twentieth century marked a new era, the end of a culture, was Oswald Spengler in his immensely long *Der Untergang des Abendlandes* – *The Decline of the West*.

One day in the early 1930s, after his return to Cambridge, Ludwig Wittgenstein arrived at the rooms of his friend Miles Drury looking distressed. 'I was walking about in Cambridge and passed a bookshop, and in the window were portraits of Russell, Freud and Einstein. A little further on, in a music shop, I saw portraits of Beethoven, Schubert and Chopin. Comparing these portraits I felt intensely the terrible degeneration that had come over the human spirit in the course of only a hundred years.' Wittgenstein's biographer, Ray Monk, sees the anecdote as what amounts to 'a pictorial representation' of one of Wittgenstein's favourite books, *The Decline of the West*.

Spengler does not offer any arguments to substantiate his vision of history. His book, rather like the lectures of Hegel on the *Philosophy of History*, which it copied, or Arnold Toynbee's *Study of History*, which it influenced, is one of those catch-all visions of human things which irritate the empirical, and delight a certain type of Idealist, mind. Using an analogy of Goethe's quasi-scientific work *Die Metamorphose der Pflanze*, Spengler saw cultures as evolving like plant-forms, flourishing and then atrophying. In a huge schema, he classified and categorized nine cultures, to which he gave arcane names – the Egyptian culture was 'Magian', the Russian culture 'Flat plane', the ancient Roman and Greek world the Apollonian. Modern culture was Faustian. Whereas the culture of Apollo conceived of man as living in an enclosed, finite space, the Faustian sees humanity as belonging to infinite space. So Western painting develops perspective, Gothic spires soar upward and Cecil Rhodes dreams of further dominions and conquests for the British Empire.

Each culture has a cycle of four seasons. In the spring, there is the time of seminal myths – for our culture this was the High Middle Ages, for the Apollonian it was the Homeric age. Then comes summer – for the Faustians, the growth of cities, the Renaissance, Shakespeare, Galileo and the triumphs of the uncorrupted intellect. Autumn is the time of ripening, with hints of exhaustion, heard by Spengler in the philosophy of Kant and the music of Mozart. Finally comes winter, the time of the world city, a rootless proletariat, plutocracy, imperialism, tyranny. Culture ceases to be culture and ossifies into mere 'civilization'. The highest works of the imagination are achieved not by artists but by scientists.

Spengler's book was enormously widely read and discussed on the European mainland, as well it might be after a destructive war. When he finished it before the war he could not find a publisher. In 1918, it exactly suited the pessimistic mood of the German-speaking world and it became a bestseller – not published in English until 1923. It was inevitable that Spengler was seen as a proto-Nazi, since, like Carlyle before him, he saw the only possibility of salvation in the rise of a new hero to visit and redeem his people. In fact, he did not see Hitler as that hero at all, his works were not admired by the Nazi ideologues, and when he died in 1936, Spengler was bitter and resentful that his work was not any longer appreciated in the land of his birth.

Certainly had he spent any time in England during the 1920s, and chosen for his company either the intellectuals or the supposedly Bright Young Things, Spengler might have found plenty of data for his note-books, and yet more people whose antics would have baffled or dismayed Frederick the Great or Louis XIV.

The war had been fought and concluded by old men, and the rising generation, looking back on what they had just missed, did not feel inclined to share the values of their fathers. If the Eminent Victorians had bred up mass murderers such as Kitchener, Haig, Asquith and Lloyd George, then Lytton Strachey was surely right to have guyed them? Logan Pearsall Smith saw in Strachey 'a sense equal I think to Voltaire's sense of the preposterousness of things, a shining sword of wit equal to or superior to his'.[8] Harold Acton, an eighteen-year-old Etonian aesthete about to go up to Oxford, saw Strachey as a literally iconic figure. His first glimpse of him had been at Garsington Manor, Lady Ottoline Morrell's house near Oxford. 'An Italian gate and avenue of ilexes led up to the house, an Elizabethan structure in stone which had once been a monastery. Behind it a bank sloped down to a pond with a sculptured group in the middle and statues along the side.' The pair who next enter the picture might themselves be statues in some pagan reredos, or, as Acton himself saw, figures depicted by Renaissance art. 'Lytton Strachey was standing beside the hostess, dressed, for all her high stature, in a Kate Greenaway costume of heliotrope silk with white stockings and I thought: What a fabulous couple! They should be painted together, hand in hand, like Van Eyke's [*sic*] portrait of John [*sic*] Arnolfini and his wife in the National Gallery. Lytton Strachey's beard and Lady Ottoline's hair seemed to have caught fire from the afternoon sun.'[9] Acton himself, when still a schoolboy, had achieved mythic status. One of his contemporaries described going to see one of Diaghilev's ballets at the Alhambra 'when Brian [Howard] and Harold [Acton] walked into the stalls, in full evening dress, with long white gloves draped over one arm, and carrying silver-topped canes and top-hats, looking perhaps like a couple of Oscar Wildes. My step-mother was astonished at the sight of them, and thought they must be foreigners. I was much too nervous, at about fifteen, to say that they were two of my very great friends from Eton.'[10]

Acton had been mortified, on that first visit to Garsington, when Lady Ottoline's husband, Colonel Morrell, had sat at a pianola, wearing riding-breeches, and rattling out 'a version of Scheherazade'. It was a blasphemy to attempt a honky-tonk rendition of the most memorable and romantic of Diaghilev's ballets. 'For many a young artist Scheherazade had been an inspiration equivalent to Gothic architecture for the Romantics or Quattrocento frescoes for the pre-Raphaelites. But now I put my hands to my ears and fled, as discreetly as I could.' Evidently not as discreetly as he had hoped, since, on another visit, when someone offered Acton a lift in their car, Ottoline Morrell sharply observed: 'Mr Acton prefers to hike.'[11] Unlike Englishmen of the period, Diaghilev was not in the least furtive about his homosexuality. It was part of his art. He was one of a whole group of gay artists and writers who led the rebellion against the nineteenth century, taking their revenge on the bourgeoisie for the perse-cution of Oscar Wilde. Proust had been present in 1910 at the opening night of *Scheherazade* in Paris in 1910, accompanied by his close friend Reynaldo Hahn.

Diaghilev was a sort of homosexual-aesthetic missionary, bringing to the new generation the message that Beauty and Love mattered more than the hateful values which had destroyed, and were destroying, bour-geois Europe. His ballets, choreographed by Michel Fokine, were a vehicle for his lover Nijinsky, and the sublime Pavlova. He also organized art exhibitions, and concert performances of great opera singers. It was Diaghilev who introduced the great Russian bass Feodor Chaliapin to the West. He came to London in 1911, the year of George V's coronation. Osbert Sitwell wrote in his autobiography that the Ballets Russes' performance of Stravinsky's *Firebird* changed his life. 'Now I knew where I stood. I would be for so long as I lived, on the side of the arts.'[12] It is a strange expression, suggesting that by liking ballet, Sitwell was taking sides – which of course he was. Stravinsky took sides when he composed *The Rite of Spring, The Firebird*, and his early symphonies, in two very courageous senses: he was on the one hand bravely innovative in orchestration, richly, flamboyantly demonstrating that Romanticism and Modernism need not be opposed; and he was forced to take sides politically. Stranded in Switzerland during the First World War, he made the tragic choice made by so many of his countrymen after the Revolution, not to return to Russia. So it is clear enough what 'sides' Stravinsky was forced to take.

For the English aesthetes, the battles were a little less dangerous, which perhaps explains why they so often resorted to silliness as a weapon against a disapproving bourgeoisie. You certainly could not get much sillier than the Sitwells. Indeed, they could be said to have taken silliness beyond the art form and made it a whole way of life. (When his colonel, in the 4th Battalion of the Grenadier Guards, suggested that the young Osbert Sitwell should smarten himself up by growing a moustache, Osbert replied: 'What colour sir?'[13])

Edith (1887–1964), Osbert (1892–1969) and Sacheverell (1897–1988) Sitwell were the children of an eccentric Yorkshire baronet. When travelling on the train in the 1860s, their father had been asked his identity and replied: 'I am four years old and the youngest baronet in England.'[14] 'Sir George is the strangest old bugger you ever met,' his butler, Henry Moat, told the composer Constant Lambert.[15]

The children made a career out of their father's and mother's 'strangeness', mocking and lampooning them to their friends and in their books. Their childhood was divided, enviably, between three splendid houses. Renishaw was Sir George's great seat near Sheffield, which served D. H. Lawrence as the model of Wragby in *Lady Chatterley's Lover*. Montegufoni was a villa in Tuscany with over a hundred rooms, which Sir George had bought at the beginning of the century. And Scarborough was the beautiful seaside resort where both sets of grandparents resided. 'What are you going to be when you grow up?' a friend of her mother's asked Edith, to receive the inevitable reply: 'A genius.'[16] Such is the human capacity for self-deception, that all three Sitwell siblings believed in their collective and individual genius, though neither Edith nor Sacheverell ('Sachie') left anything behind them in written form which was evidence of any particular talent. Edith wrote what she thought were poems, as did Sachie, who also indulged in travel-cum-art books in purple prose, of which *Southern Baroque Art* was the most popular. Osbert was no genius, but by contrast with his siblings he was a supremely gifted writer of autobiography, and his *Left Hand, Right Hand!* sequence is a wonderful, sub-Proustian compilation of anecdote and observation. Sir George is, of course, the hero of the story, with his desire to tell everyone their business – whether it was Sargent, painting their group portrait, or telling a knife-maker to soak the handles in condensed milk. 'Unless you learn to play ping-pong properly, you can never be a leader of men,' he once told his elder son. And, a good piece of advice for an artist, but of course ridiculed by his children: 'Such a mistake to have friends.'

Edith's greatest work of art was her Plantagenet-style appearance. Elizabeth Bowen once likened her to 'a high altar on the move'. Harold Acton saw her in 1922 as 'a rare jewel, a hieratic figure in Limoges enamel . . . Clamped in some tin biscuit box, but rarer, more hieratic against this background. The pale oval face with its almond eyes and long thin nose, had often been carved in ivory by true believers. Her entire figure possessed a distinction seldom to be seen outside the glass cases of certain museums. Physically, she was an extraordinary survival from the Age of Chivalry.'[17] Her most famous piece, Façade, was first put on in 1922, in the siblings' drawing room in Carlyle Square, Chelsea. It consisted in a series of her nonsensical 'poems', set to quite spirited music by Sachie's young protégé William Walton, and declaimed by Edith and her brothers through a mega-phone, or Sengerphone, a papier mâché instrument acquired from a singer called Senger. T. S. Eliot particularly cringed at the Sitwells' 'poems' since, somewhere in the minds of the public, or the Sitwells themselves, there existed a false syllogism. Deep, modern or high-falutin' verses which mean nothing at all are 'difficult'. Eliot's poetry is difficult. Therefore the Sitwells are in the avant garde with Eliot and Pound.

Eliot appears, in his 'four piece suit', at the parties of those who had friends – at Lady Ottoline's, Virginia Woolf's, the Sitwells'. But one senses him holding aloof. For Osbert, Edith and Sachie, as for Virginia and friends in the so-called Bloomsbury set, having the idea of oneself as an artist was an illusion which friends were perilously good at fostering and encouraging. That is the peril, for an artist, of 'sets'. When Tennyson read some of Maud aloud in Benjamin Jowett's drawing room at Oxford, the Master of Balliol said, in his high squeaky voice: 'I should not publish that if I were you, Tennyson.' No such voice in the early decades of the twentieth century was ever heard in the Sitwells' drawing-room, nor over the other side of London in Bloomsbury. Such a mistake to have friends. The second performance of Façade was held at the Aeolian Hall in the Chenil Galleries, King's Road. Harold Acton took a boyfriend, Evelyn Waugh, then an undergraduate at Hertford College. All the handpicked audience roared and cheered. On another occasion, Mrs Robert Mathias, patron of the Ballets Russes, had a performance in her drawing-room in the presence of Diaghilev. What can he have thought?

Of course, as soon as *Façade* appeared on a public stage it was lampooned and condemned by all the critics. The Sitwells took this as evidence of the philistinism of the bourgeoisie. The British tradition had been firmly established, of talentless 'arty' people convincing themselves that exhibitionism was a substitute for talent. It could be said that this had been going on in the nineteenth century to some extent, but in the twentieth century, there came a parting of the ways in England, especially in London, between good popular books, art and music, and 'highbrow' versions which only the initiated could appreciate. Within this veiled holy of holies, the initiates could learn to mouth the names of composers or artists they were supposed to admire, without actually possessing any discernment at all. True artists found themselves either alone, or being patronized by those who were 'on the side of the arts', a concept which would surely have been alien to Beethoven or Wordsworth.

One of the first to mock the Sitwells (as 'two wiseacres and a cow') was a truly brilliant young man called Noël Coward (1899–1973). A child prodigy, born in the suburb of Teddington to musical parents, Coward had started his professional career aged ten, playing Prince Mussel in *The Goldfish* alongside the infant Micheal Mac Liammoir (then Alfred Willmore) and Ninette de Valois (then Ninette Devalois). His favourite stage performer at the time was a stand-up comedian called Phil Ray ('I always abbreve, it's a hab'). At thirteen he played Slightly in *Peter Pan*, with Pauline Chase. The *Observer* noted: 'The immortal Slightly as acted by Master Noël Coward, is quite a young boy and his grave pretence at wisdom is all the funnier.' A voracious reader and playgoer, Coward wrote two novels by the time he was eighteen, as well as three plays, and some lyrics and songs. The first play of his own in which he appeared on the West End stage in London was *I'll Leave it to You*; it got good notices, but closed within five weeks. In 1922 he wrote a play called *The Young Idea*, and sent the script to GBS. Shaw wrote back a detailed critique, but concluded: 'unless you can get clean away from me you will begin as a back number, and be hopelessly out of it when you are forty'.

That was not part of Coward's ambition at all. Already he had developed his highly distinctive, clipped manner of utterance (he said it was to make his deaf mother hear what he said), but it was more brilliant than that. Cruel, cold and oddly toneless, the voice was the perfect vehicle for the words. He was the greatest cruel-verse genius in English since Alexander Pope. With his sleek, immaculately combed hair, bony face and sardonic mouth, he could have had an unkind expression, but there was a sense of the tragic in his large eyes. He was relentlessly ambitious, keen to improve his work, and to make contacts in the world. One of his earliest friends was Gladys Calthorn, who was to work with him as a designer for dozens of shows. Stranded in Naples together with no money in 1922, they had to go to the British consul, who agreed to cash them a cheque. 'Who shall I make it payable to?' Noël asked. 'Somers Cox.' 'And some 'asn't,' said Gladys.

The next year, 1923, Coward formed another of his great collaborations, this time with Gertrude Lawrence in a revue of which he was composer and part author called *London Calling*. Just as the show was in rehearsal, Coward was lunching at the Ivy Restaurant. It was a favourite haunt of his from the days when it had linoleum on the floor, two waitresses and paper napkins until, as happened rapidly in the early Twenties, it became a haunt of famous actors and of *le monde*. Its inspired owner Abel Giandolini hired an expert cook, and the tables soon filled up not only with famous theatre people, but with Winston Churchill, the Aga Khan, Duff and Diana Cooper (who came for the spaghetti) and Jacob Epstein, all to be seen there regularly. One day Osbert Sitwell stopped at young Coward's table and suggested he came to *Façade*. The invitation led to one of the Sitwells' silly carefully orchestrated feuds. Coward did come to *Façade*, and instantly added a sketch to *London Calling* about the Swiss Family Whittlebot. Miss Hernia Whittlebot, says the stage direction, 'should be effectively and charmingly dressed in undraped dyed sacking, a cross between blue and green, with a necklet of uncut amber beads in unconventional shapes. She must wear a gold band rather high up on her forehead from which hang a little clump of Bacchanalian fruit below each ear. Her face is white and weary, with a long chin and nose and bags under her eyes.'[18] 'Life is essentially a Curve,' says Hernia, 'and Art is an oblong within that Curve. My brothers and I have been brought up on Rhythm as other children are brought up on Glaxo.'[19] The Sitwells took umbrage and refused to speak to Coward for forty years.

In 1924 he staged his play *The Vortex*, about an embarrassing society lady who has much younger lovers, and her son, a drug addict. The first night, cleverly talked up by the fashionable, was in a tiny, hard-seated theatre in Hampstead, the Everyman, attended by Eddie Marsh, Edwina Mountbatten and others of comparable fame. Stella Gibbons wrote:

I was present at the very first performance of *The Vortex* in a little kind of converted drill-hall in Hampstead and I remember how shocked I was at the drug-addict boy (he would have been called a Drug Fiend in those days by ordinary people) and ever since I have had such enduring pleasure and laughter from his songs and jokes. He seems to me to incarnate the myth of the twenties (gaiety, courage, pain concealed, amusing malice) and that photograph . . . with poised fingertips held to hide the mouth, with the eyes delightfully smiling, is an incarnation in another form, even to the extreme elegance of the clothes.[20]

The Vortex still 'works' on the stage today, especially since they often now include in it his 1930s hit 'Mad about the Boy'.

But it is in his lyrics that Coward lives for ever. Throughout the Twenties, a series of revues and plays poured from him. He could be funny, harsh, naughty. He could also get away with being sentimental. 'I'll See You Again' from *Bitter Sweet* must be one of the most beautiful songs written in that song-filled decade. He could also, without heaviness or pretension, offer haunting commentaries on his times. 'What's going to happen to the children, when there aren't any more grown-ups?' seems as good a question as any to ask of the decade in which Harold Acton, Evelyn Waugh, Edith Sitwell, Brian Howard and Peter Quennell whooped and roared. 'It's very hard on nature when she's made a lot of plans/To have them all frustrated by a lot of Peter Pans.'[21]

Or, from the slightly later 'Bright Young People' (1931):

> Look at us three,
> Representative we
> Of a nation renowned for virility.
> We've formed a cult of puerility
> Just for fun.
> You may deplore
> The effects of war
> Which are causing the world to decay a bit.
> We've found our place and will play a bit
> In the sun.
> Though Waterloo was won upon the playing fields of Eton,
> The next war will be photographed, and lost, by Cecil Beaton.[22]

17

The Means of Grace and the
Hope of Glory

If some British observers believed absolutism to be all right for Italians
and Russians, the electorate at large was beginning to tire of Lloyd
George's rule by one party of coalition. And if democracy was a long
way off in India, it was felt to be time that they experimented with a
limited version of it once again in Britain. 'Lloyd George was the nearest
thing England has known to a Napoleon, a supreme ruler maintaining
himself by individual achievement.'[1] If that is true, then the electorate
in the early 1920s, such as it was, decided very firmly that it did not want
an English Napoleon, just as it would decide in later years that it wanted
neither an English Lenin nor an English Mussolini.

The very fact that twentieth-century English political history is blander
than its German, Italian, Spanish or Russian equivalent is perhaps
revealing. Only two political figures, post-Lloyd George, had the charismatic status which could, in differing circumstances, have led to a cult
of personality: Oswald Mosley and Winston Churchill. One of these men
ended up as a pariah, the other as a national hero. But from the resignation of Lloyd George until the appointment of Winston Churchill in
1940, the British prime ministers are a succession of nonentities. None
of the 'stars' in any of the three parties, in so far as they had stars, rose
to the heights of leadership. This tells us something if we are prepared
to watch closely. It would be gross sentimentality to deny the preparedness, in India, in Ireland, and in Britain itself, of the governing class to
look after its own interests by violent suppression of dissident groups,
races, classes. Equally, however, the refugees over the period 1918–39 have
a story to tell. True, some eccentric Britons emigrated to Russia or
Germany during these years, but overwhelmingly, the traffic was the other
way. Slowly and painfully, a democratic decency did evolve, and though
the British population underwent sore economic hardship during these
years, it also enjoyed far greater political stability and freedom than
almost any other country in Europe. This was partly because its economy
was, even at the worst of times, underwritten by US loans, or bolstered
by Empire trade. It must also have been, though, that British political
institutions, more flexible to change than their Continental equivalents,
were able to preserve some of the strengths they had possessed in times

past. There were a number of English revolutions and evolutions, but they did not involve, as they did in Russia, Germany, Spain, Italy, the wholesale dumping of the political classes, of the civil service, or of the Establishment.

During the Lloyd George-as-Napoleon era, the two major political parties, the Liberals and the Conservatives or Unionists, had been dormant, patients etherized upon a table. When they awoke, the Liberal party found itself divided into two. Asquith, still leader of the party, presided over only a few dozen members of Parliament. The Lloyd George Liberals were larger in number but in much greater political disarray. The Labour party, which before the war had been a fledgling, formed the new party of radical opposition to the new-found strength of the Conservatives. This is the story of the swift changes of party leadership and of governments between 1922 and 1924, which saw the resignation of Lloyd George and the formation of Bonar Law's Conservative government of October 1922; the succession of Baldwin's Conservative government of May 1923; the first Labour government of Ramsay MacDonald in January 1924; and Baldwin's second Conservative government in November that year.

David Lloyd George had come to England as an idealistic young Welshman determined to poke fun at the Establishment and to achieve a measure of justice for Wales and for the disadvantaged. He was at heart a radical, and he had done more than many politicians to help the poor. By introducing the Old Age Pension Act of 1908, and a National Insurance Act in 1911 he began the principle, ever since enshrined in British law, that provision would be made for the sick and the old out of the public purse. As a wartime leader, he had brio, and the gift of the gab. He had taken over the government at a woeful stage of the war, and although the slaughter had continued for another two years, he had some claim to be – as he'd claimed during the 1918 election – The Man Who Won The War. His later antics, ranging from the botched Versailles Treaty to the bloodbath in Ireland, were not made any more dignified by his cynical sale of peerages. It was time for Britain to resume party politics, an imperfect and in some respects farcical ritual, but one which at least allowed for the possibility of the electorate giving the government the sack and replacing it with another. It was a Triumph of the Will that Lloyd George kept his coalition going for as long as he did.

The coalition itself was maintained entirely by the Conservatives, but timidity had kept them from asserting independent political power. Then, in the summer of 1922, a crisis blew up in Greece. Mustafa Kemal, known to history as Ataturk, Father of the Turks (1881–1938), continued to fight the war against the Greeks. It was to be his ticket to popularity at home, and to enable him to abolish the Sultanate and unite Turkey behind him as a modern secular autocrat. In 1921 he had established a provisional government in Ankara, thus ending over a thousand years in which Constantinople was regarded as the imperial capital of the eastern Mediterranean. The military panache which had made him the hero of the Dardanelles led to a spectacular campaign against the Greeks when they invaded Anatolia. He massacred them by the thousand, took Smyrna, and by the end of the summer had advanced to the Straits and taken Chanak.

With memories of the Allied disaster in the Dardanelles still green, Lloyd George would have liked to resist Kemal's advance. Churchill and Birkenhead, his two allies in the coalition cabinet, forgot their earlier hostility to the Greeks and rallied to the cry of war, but they had misread the mood of the Empire and of their world allies. New Zealand, with prodigious heroism considering the numbers they had lost in Gallipoli, pledged support, but France and Italy were anxious to form alliances with Kemal, and most of the British Dominions were furious at not having been consulted about the policy. Australia and Canada were not going to provide Churchill and Lloyd George with more cannon fodder to be mown down by the Turks. Lloyd George decided to put the matter to the electorate. Still the timid Conservatives held back from breaking the coalition. Then there was a by-election in Newport and a candidate stood as a Conservative anti-Lloyd George candidate: that is, he broke away from the coalition, the mainstream Conservative line. He won the seat.

The leader of the Conservatives in the Commons was Austen Chamberlain (1863–1937), son of Joseph. 'He always played the game and always lost it,' as Churchill observed. In 1922, his losing tactic was to commit himself wholeheartedly to coalition with Lloyd George. He summoned a meeting of the Tory MPs at the Carlton Club on 19 October 1922 and they voted overwhelmingly to go it alone and break the coalition. Chamberlain could hardly do other than resign as leader of the Conservatives. They elected as their leader the mortally sick Bonar Law.

In French history, particular dates acquire a mythic status, so that streets can be named after them – Place du Dix-huit Juin, Rue du Quatre Septembre and so forth. The British have on the whole a less calendric approach to their historical mythologies. An exception is in the Conservative party, where their junta of back-bench members is known as the 1922 Committee in honour of the moment when they sacked one nonentity whom no one remembers, Austen Chamberlain, in favour of another, Bonar Law. The significance of Law, who was in any event dying of cancer, was that he was Beaverbrook's candidate – Beaverbrook's glove-puppet, as has been said. Now that he owned the *Daily Express*, and now that Northcliffe was dead, Beaverbrook's megalomaniac political fantasies need know no bounds. He could see most of Law's weaknesses, though he could not foresee quite how soon it would be before Law died. But Law would, for Beaverbrook's purposes, do. He was an easily malleable figure, who would do what he was told when Beaverbrook summoned him to one of his residences, either the intimate Tudor house the Vineyard, Fulham, where the drawing-room had space for four people at most, or Cherkley in Surrey on larger country weekends.[2]

Always with an eye, not merely to the present wielder of power, but to the man in the wings, Beaverbrook left an unforgettable image of Bonar Law's hour of triumph in the Carlton Club: 'Bonar Law came down the stairs of the Club alone. He was the man of the hour, the victor today, the premier tomorrow. His slight figure, with the deepest eyes and the lined features, held everyone's gaze. No one among the onlookers paid much attention to the stocky little man, five feet nine inches in height* with the florid, almost bucolic features, the face still unmarked by care, the gait yet unhindered by twinges of gout, who was following his leader.'[3] Not one of those present gave a thought to the possibility that in the guise of this unremarkable figure, this 'typical Englishman', destiny was stalking forward. Stanley Baldwin took, that morning, an obscure place on the stairway. But just the same he was a man of the future.[4]

Bonar Law duly formed his government. Among the coalition Conservatives the only one who consented to serve in the new adminis-tration was Lord Curzon. He certainly had not seen the significance of the bucolic figure of Baldwin.

Law's cabinet was overwhelmingly aristocratic. This was because the big Conservative guns of Lloyd George's coalition were still realigning themselves politically. F. E. Smith (Lord Birkenhead) was not ready to return and Churchill was still technically a Liberal. Law therefore assem-bled the most aristocratic cabinet there had been for a generation, with the Duke of Devonshire as colonial secretary, the Marquess of Salisbury as lord president, the Earl of Derby as secretary of state for War. Curzon continued as Foreign Secretary. The previous year, 1921, his earldom had been upgraded to a marquessate.

His tragicomic career was about to reach its most painful moment. He must have believed, as he looked around the cabinet table early in 1923, that in many respects the old aristocratic order remained in England, shaken but not fundamentally changed since prewar days. And

---

* Beaverbrook's height was also five foot nine inches in his socks, see A. J. P. Taylor, *Beaverbrook*, p. 252.

there were some respects in which this was true. The old order had been given a terrible pounding by the war. Twenty-nine thousand small country estates throughout Britain would come on the market in the decade 1920–30, and one reason for this was that the occupants had lost their sons; the village war-memorials throughout the British Isles, and the memorial plaques in the public schools, the London clubs and the Oxford and Cambridge colleges show the devastation visited upon the old aristocracy and squirearchy. Yet the class which had taken over the government of Britain in 1689 was remarkably resilient, partly because, unlike its Continental equivalents, it saw nothing wrong with injecting cash and talent from outside its ranks. Curzon himself exemplified this. His first wife was Mary Leiter, the daughter of a Chicago millionaire. When he was left devastated by her loss, he remarried, and to another American. Grace Duggan was a doll-like pretty woman in her thirties when Curzon began to woo her. She was the widow of an immensely wealthy Argentinian–Irish financier. When Curzon was denied the ultimate political prize of becoming the Prime Minister, Arthur Balfour remarked that 'even if he has lost the hope of Glory, he still has the means of Grace'.[5] It is a bore to explain jokes, but only a very small number of people now read the *Book of Common Prayer*, which in 1924 was still very familiar to a majority of the British, or at least to the English. In the General Thanksgiving in that book, Almighty God is thanked 'above all for thine inestimable love in the redemption of the world by our Lord Jesus Christ, for the means of grace, and for the hope of glory'.

Curzon was indeed to be disappointed. When Bonar Law was told by his doctors, in May 1923, that he had incurable cancer of the oesophagus, he resigned at once. He died on 30 October, and was the first prime minister after Gladstone to be buried in Westminster Abbey. It was a singular honour for so totally undistinguished a figure, but it allowed Asquith to make his joke about the Unknown Prime Minister being buried near the tomb of the Unknown Warrior. To George Nathaniel Curzon, marquess, former viceroy of India, there could have been no doubt about the monarch's choice for Bonar Law's successor. Law had hinted to Lord Stamfordham, the King's Private Secretary, that Curzon should succeed him, but when he heard of his impending death he stood aside from the political struggle and left matters in the hands of his own Parliamentary Private Secretary, a backroom fixer named John Colin (later Viscount) Davidson. He telephoned the king's secretary before Law announced his resignation to warn him of what was coming, recommending that the King, if he wished to make consultations, should speak to Salisbury or Balfour. Both these grandees disliked Curzon, and their dislike had been intensified by his breaking ranks to serve in Law's cabinet, rather than staying with the 'coalition Conservatives'. Salisbury, when asked his view of Curzon, gave the devastating opinion that the Foreign Secretary's 'faults were improving'. Balfour had a long meeting with the king in which he stressed that it was no longer easy to have a Prime Minister in the House of Lords. Davidson drafted a memorandum which began with the fateful words: 'Lord Curzon is regarded in the public eye as representing that section of privileged Conservatism which has its value but in this democratic age . . .'[6]

Poor George Nathaniel remained, aloof and unaware that any of this was going on, at Montacute, a great Elizabethan country house in Somerset whose lease he had taken while he waited, first for his father Lord Scarsdale to die, which he had done in 1916, and secondly to have the time and money to renovate his most beautiful house, Kedleston in Derbyshire, designed by Robert Adam. (He had also bought Bodiam Castle in Sussex and its estate in 1917.) Curzon's favourite great house was Hatfield, the Elizabethan stronghold of the Cecils, a powerhouse of the greatest political dynasty in Conservative history. Montacute was a house which allowed Curzon to imagine himself a Cecil, especially when it had been done up by his mistress, the novelist Elinor Glyn. (She had spent much time and energy on the task and referred to George Nathaniel as 'an ungrateful sneaking cad' when he dumped her for Grace.)[7] It was at Montacute that he awaited his sovereign's call – Montacute, that Elizabethan pile where he could imagine himself as a worthy successor to the greatest Victorian Tory Prime Minister, the 3rd Marquess of Salisbury. When one writes that Curzon awaited the call, he did not await anything so newfangled or so vulgar as a telephone. He regarded this as 'a disastrous invention'. It was on Whit Monday, as the Foreign Secretary was cutting the lawn at Montacute in his shirt sleeves, that he saw what he had been awaiting for several days, the uniformed figure of the village policeman cycling up the drive bearing a telegram from His Majesty's secretary. Curzon sent back his message that he would receive Lord Stamfordham the following afternoon at Carlton House Terrace.

On their way back to London, the Marquess and his American Marchioness sketched out their future together. They would not move into the poky Number 10 Downing Street, but would continue to reside at Carlton House Terrace. He would remain as Foreign Secretary as well as Prime Minister. What of ecclesiastical appointments? These too had their interest, and he spoke of them, as the train bore him towards the capital.

When they arrived at the front door Curzon was informed by his valet that Lord Stamfordham had been delayed. This was Curzon's first inkling that all was not well. At half-past three, Stamfordham arrived, stammering and embarrassed. He tried to tell him that the king had considered the merits of another candidate. Curzon expostulated. He had made no secret of the fact that he considered Baldwin 'a man of the utmost insignificance'.[8] If Baldwin were chosen, it would be necessary, said the former viceroy, for Curzon to withdraw from public life. Stamfordham was too cowardly to tell the marquess that the pipe-smoking ironmaster from the West Midlands had kissed his sovereign's hands and become the Prime Minister several hours earlier. It was a shattering blow to Curzon, and when he died, aged sixty-six, on 19 March 1925 it could be said that he died of a broken heart. Had he been less arrogant, perhaps Curzon might have stood a chance. But it is hard to doubt that it was not merely his aristocratic hauteur which was held against him; it was his cleverness. The Conservative party, with its horribly accurate political 'nose', could see that the country wanted 'a man of the utmost insignificance'.

Baldwin, who had persuaded his colleagues to see him as a safe pair of hands, almost immediately plunged his party into a self-destructive quarrel about the old question of tariff reform. It had been the issue which sundered the party under Arthur Balfour's premiership. Rather like British membership of the European Union in the post-1975 era, the matter of tariff reform called forth in Tory ranks all manner of deep doctrinal and atavistic divisions.

Law had fought the 1922 election with the pledge that he would not introduce tariffs without consulting the electorate, so Baldwin could claim he was duty-bound to call an election when he hitched the Conservative party to protectionism. It seemed a necessary measure at the time to fight rising unemployment. But Baldwin was before everything else a politician. He was watching his own party, and the Liberals, always edgy that they might outmanoeuvre him. This matter of Free Trade versus Tariff had divided the Tories since the beginning of the century. Lloyd George had gone to America, on a successful speaking-tour, and rumour reached Baldwin that 'the Goat' was about to announce the Liberal party's conversion to protection. If he did so, where would that leave the Tories?

If he needed to keep an eye on the Liberals, Baldwin was even more nervous about his enemies within his own party. There were grumbles from the moment of his selection. Some would have preferred to replace him with F. E. Smith (Lord Birkenhead), and they probably would have done so if Smith's private life had not been scandalous. He was clever – 'the cleverest man in the kingdom', Beaverbrook believed. He made a brilliant career at the Bar, and he was one of the best speakers in the House of Commons. His obsession with one of his friend's schoolgirl daughters was really what appalled the stuffier of his parliamentary colleagues. He seduced Mona Dunn when she was still in her teens. She was a great beauty, painted by Orpen. She would dance on the tables till dawn in the Criterion Restaurant. When she died, aged twenty-six, of peritonitis, Birkenhead wrote her a sonnet which he asked Beaverbrook to publish in the *Sunday Express*, but the request was refused. Such abandon did not suit the mood of the Conservative party. Although politicians could rely on the Press in those days not to print stories of their emotional lives – else, how would Lloyd George, or Asquith, or Curzon, have survived? – the new mood was for a party which espoused middle-class respectabilities. Baldwin, with his family business as an ironmaster, his pipe, his homely values, and his somewhat lugubrious mustachioed health minister, Neville Chamberlain, Austen's half-brother, made much more suitable images to present to the electorate at large. There was not yet television to reveal or distort the appearance and behaviour of politicians for the voters, but there was 'image', projected in part by the newspapers, in part by the number of public meetings which politicians underwent during electioneering campaigns.

The aristocrats had had their day when it came to providing leadership for the party, but Baldwin needed to keep the grandees happy – Lord Salisbury, Balfour and the rest. Apart from anything else, if he brought back the coalitionists who had sat in Lloyd George's cabinet, it would inevitably mean sacking some of the aristocrats whom Law had appointed in their stead. He needed to please both elements, and an election was a good way of doing this. After only six months in office, he gambled that if he went to the country he would 'dish the Goat', i.e. Lloyd George, and silence opposition from his own ranks. Conservatives dislike being in opposition, and will put up any show of unity in the face of a General Election. So Baldwin gambled, and he lost. Being consistently wrong is not nearly so dangerous a quality for politicians as being right. People will forgive a politician for being wrong. Baldwin was wrong in most of his economic predictions, most of his political judgements, most of his foreign policy. He would remain in office for much of the most crucial period of twentieth-century history. But, in this first instance of his wrongness, he lost an election – though his party remained the largest in the Commons.

It was a big poll – 74 per cent of the electorate voted. The Conservatives and their allied candidates secured 258 seats. The Liberals were now united again, with Asquithians and Lloyd George Liberals fighting on a single platform. They won 158 seats. But the Labour party won 191 seats. The Liberals were therefore in the position of holding a balance of power. As the party in third place, they could not expect office themselves, but they could, if they chose, support the Conservatives. Instead, they made an historic decision. They were caught up in a momentous political change. Anxious not to have a socialist Prime Minister, the king called Baldwin and asked him to form a government. Politically astute, Baldwin suggested he instead should invite Ramsay MacDonald to do so, thereby at one stroke bringing the Labour Party into the safety of the Establishment, and destroying the Liberals. They were never to hold office again – even though it was from their ranks that the biggest political innovations of the twentieth century in Britain would come: the advocacy of the economic theories of the Liberal John Maynard Keynes, and the report by the Liberal Sir William Beveridge which led, in the 1940s, to the establishment of a Welfare State.

The Liberal party has always been, historically, the Labour party's midwife, and so it was in its first electoral triumph. On 22 January 1924 the king called upon James Ramsay MacDonald to form a government.

The 1918 Representation of the People Act not only added women over thirty to the electorate, but also the poorer one-third of adult males who had remained unenfranchised by the 1884 Reform Act. This was what caused a surge in the Labour vote. The working classes made up the huge majority of the British population: 78.29 per cent of the population in 1921, and only very slightly less ten years later. This represented 30.2 million people in 1921, and nearly 32 million in 1931. From the moment they left school at fourteen, most British people were destined for a lifetime of hard and usually monotonous work in factories, mines, docks, distributive trades, agriculture, or as domestic servants. Yet if work was boring, and life-shortening, unemployment was worse, and the phenomenon of unemployment was a spectre which now haunted Europe and was to change entirely its political complexion. Unemployment in the close of the twentieth century and the beginning of the twenty-first is a risk that most people may run. In the 1920s it was almost entirely a working-class phenomenon.

Political ideologues would be tempted to assume that this represented a huge and potentially revolutionary movement of left or right. Nothing could have been further from the truth. The indifference of the British to religion is matched only by their indifference to politics; and in so far as they do have political interests, those have often defied expectation. It is the working classes in Britain who have consistently cheered on imperialism and warmongering, while the well-meaning middle classes tried to spoon-feed them with improvement.

Just as the national Church, formed from warring factions of Catholics and Puritans, had successfully managed to keep the religious temperature lukewarm for three hundred years, so the Labour Party, in many respects its secular equivalent, would manage to dissipate and dilute any tendencies within its ranks towards radical socialism. Zealots will always be scornful both of the Church of England and of the Labour Party. In fact both were institutions in which the British, and most specifically the English, learned the delicate art of living with contradictions and compromise, and became a mature political democracy. Whereas in other countries, social democrats, trade unionists, Marxists, state socialists who fell just short of Marxist, royalists, Christian socialists and advanced atheist secularists would have felt the need to form separate organizations of their own, in Britain they had somehow managed together to form the Labour Party. Like the Church in the reign of Queen Elizabeth I, the Labour Party, as it girded itself to take electoral power at the beginning of the 1920s, was really a coalition of mutually antagonistic, and indeed contradictory, sects.

There was the old Independent Labour Party, or ILP, which was the largest affiliated socialist society. It believed in state socialism, the nationalization of banks and major industries. Then there were the Trade Unions, who were very often much more right-wing than the ILP. Arthur Henderson, for example, who was the Home Secretary in the new government, was a representative of the Friendly Society of Ironfounders, but had never entertained any socialist beliefs at all. He merely wanted fair working conditions for his members. Then there were the Fabian socialists of whom the high priest was the new President of the Board of Trade, Sidney Webb. Together with his tall, elegant wife Beatrice, this tiny bulbous-headed figure, whom his wife likened to a tadpole, had founded the London School of Economics and the *New Statesman* to promote their doctrine of socialist gradualism. By means of education and persuasion, it would be possible for socialist ideas to 'permeate', and without immediate confiscation of personal property, the state could achieve the same result gradually by a rising scale of appropriation of middle-class savings and assets.

The new government was not in power for long enough to attempt any political changes, and it knew, in any event, that if it did try to be socialist, the Liberal Party would unite with the Tories to put it out of office. It had merely, as it were, sniffed the air.

It certainly tells us something about what had happened to England, that in the summer of 1923 the Marquess of Curzon supposed he was about to become Prime Minister, and six months later that office was handed to the illegitimate son of a female farmworker and a ploughman, from Lossiemouth, Morayshire. Malcolm Muggeridge, in his book on *The Thirties*, observed that:

it is impossible for one man, however determined and cunning he may be, to impose his will on other men for long unless they recognize themselves in him . . . Thus it was not chance or his own ambition merely which carried Ramsay MacDonald to the Premiership. He had his part to play, and that was the role in which he had been cast. Grounded in resentment against his obscure birth and childhood poverty, nurtured in the Fabian Society, the ILP and other offshoots of the late Victorian urge to improve the conditions of the poor without seriously incommoding the rich, brought to fruition in four and a half years of bloody warfare followed by a fraudulent peace and hysterical reaction against the strain and agony of war, his moment surely came.[9]

It was easy for Malcolm Muggeridge, whose father was a Labour MP, and who himself moved from a position of communism to disillusionment, to mock James Ramsay MacDonald, just as it was for him to mock the Labour Party as 'Marxists and nonconformist clergymen and pacifists and check-weighmen and Clydeside demagogues'. What these 'mugwumps' had in common, however, was the rather simple desire of wanting Britain to be a slightly more decent place, or in the case of some of the loftier radicals, such as Colonel Wedgwood, the desire to bring out England's inherent decency. 'Those who believe in human nature must above all seek to put an end to the present hideous exploitation of the working classes,' wrote this kindly factory-owner and pottery-manufacturer from North Staffordshire.

> The choice before us is obvious. There are just two roads. Those who will *not* believe that you can do away with exploitation – that is, those who do not want to do away with it – all those 'in the interests of Society' will regulate, inspect and convert the working man into a machine that shall like its servitude. And there are those who know that exploitation can be stopped, and that man can yet be free; they will take liberty and justice as their guides, and pin their faith to the perfectibility of human nature. Is our guide to be – Police or Freedom?[10]

Neither the Conservative Party nor Lords Beaverbrook or Rothermere much wanted to be around when this alarming alternative was seen as a realistic choice. Much to their relief, Ramsay MacDonald's government did not last out the year 1924. It attempted to do something to provide poor people with decent housing. The short life and career of Basil Jellicoe (1899–1935), nephew of the admiral who commanded the fleet at the battle of Jutland, demonstrated the desperate need for housing. He served briefly in the navy at the end of the war, and, as an Oxford undergraduate, he almost immediately went to work among the desperate slums in Somers Town, just north of Euston Station in London. Twenty-two thousand people lived in the parish of Somers Town, all sharing rooms, in damp, unhygienic houses with no adequate washing or lavatory facilities. He was ordained a priest in the Church of England, and with a capital of £250 founded the St Pancras Housing Improvement Society.

The squalid conditions in the district just north of Euston Station were noticed by Jellicoe, but he could have been speaking of Birmingham, Bristol, Bradford, Leeds, Manchester, Liverpool, Glasgow or any of the slums in the big Victorian cities, when he said that Somers Town houses were:

> the Devil's holiday, a kind of perpetual festival of All Sinners. It has been produced by selfishness, stupidity and sin, and only Love Incarnate can put it right. The slums produce something much more terrible than mere discomfort and discontent. They produce a kind of horrible excommunication; a fiendish plan on the part of the Powers of Evil to keep people from the happiness for which God made them, and from seeing the beauties of His world . . .[11]

In 1924 Basil Jellicoe, Percy Maryon-Wilson, Edith Neville and Miss I. N. Hill of the Charity Organization Society got together round Jellicoe's dining-table resolved to do something. It was not until a year later, July 1925, that the St Pancras Housing Improvement Society was inaugurated. They bought eight slum houses with money raised by subscription and began work reconditioning them. The next year, quite by surprise, sixty-nine houses and an open space of 16,000 square feet became available. They needed a substantial sum for the deposit and £25,000 for the remainder to be paid in five months. Maryon-Wilson managed, by engineering the public support of the Minister of Health, Neville Chamberlain, and such figures as John Galsworthy and Lord Cecil, to raise the money. The old houses in Sidney Street were finally dynamited in 1930, and two months later Admiral Jellicoe laid the first brick of the new blocks of flats.

Twenty-first-century aesthetes might flinch to read of these eighteenth-century houses being blown up and replaced with the tenement buildings which, seventy-five years later, wear a joyless air. Such purists would miss the heady atmosphere in which Jellicoe and his friends said farewell to the verminous Victorian legacy of urban poverty. They had a Solemn Burning in Sidney Street. 'We had previously built a large bonfire, ten feet high and on the top of this pyre had placed large models of a bug, a flea, a rat and a louse, all stuffed with fireworks, and these were solemnly burnt.'

People still remember Basil Jellicoe in North London. He was recently the subject of a spirited musical by Rob Inglis enacted at the Shaw Theatre, in his old parochial stamping-ground. His name survives in grateful families. A teacher I know in her thirties, of Irish Catholic stock, remembers her grandmother's fond memories of Father Jellicoe as the man who stood up for the poor. This woman's grandmother was struck in those intolerant days by how freely the Church of England parson Jellicoe gave himself for the Irish Catholics as well as for the Church of England people. The huge family of over a dozen children into which she had been born was rescued by Jellicoe from the foulest of slums and given a place to live which it was possible to clean, and where children could lead a healthy life.

Inspired partly by the example of Jellicoe, other areas of the country followed. In Leeds it was another Anglican priest, Charles Jenkinson, who led the campaign for better housing – though a very different sort of Anglican from Jellicoe's Anglo-Catholicism. Jenkinson was a member of the Modern Churchman's Union.[12]

Jellicoe died aged thirty-six. Archbishop Temple said: 'There are some with whom it seems to be a necessary quality that they should die young – Mozart among musicians; Keats and Shelley among poets; and among the saints, with many another, Basil Jellicoe.'[13]

Beyond its own modest housing schemes, the first Labour government made no attempt to make Britain socialist. It was hounded out of office by a press scare, designed to make everyone fear that Ramsay MacDonald was the mustachioed Caledonian mask of Leninism.

During the summer, Arthur Ponsonby, son of the royal courtier Fritz Ponsonby, and a Labour MP, was the chief negotiator on behalf of the British government with the Soviet Union, when it was proposed that Britain would give diplomatic recognition of the USSR and offer loans. Russia was in a bad way, in the aftermath of a civil war, with its agricultural system in chaos. From a humanitarian point of view, there was obviously a case for British loans. MacDonald and his party had welcomed the Kerensky government in March 1917 but had never given succour or encouragement to Bolshevism, nor indeed to any political acts of violence. But the two treaties drawn up, one for the settlement of diplomatic differences between Britain and the Soviet Union, and the other for loans, excited fierce opposition. 'No Money for Murderers' was the slogan behind which Lloyd George, the Conservatives and the press united to attack the Labour administration.

Then the Foreign Office got hold of a letter, dated 15 September, purporting to have been sent by one G. Zinoviev, president of the Communist International in Moscow, to the British Communist party, urging British Communists to do all they could to ratify the treaties. The letter reached Conservative Central Office, and the *Daily Mail*, which published it. MacDonald himself did not see a copy of the letter until 16 October, but by then the damage was done.[14] The public had been fed the idea that the Labour party was the deceptively benign face of International Communism. There was yet another election, and this time it was a triumph for the Conservatives. Stoked up by Lord Rothermere's *Daily Mail* and by Stanley Baldwin's Conservative Party, the electorate sent 419 Conservative members to Westminster, out of 615. Labour had 151 seats. The Liberals were reduced to 40 seats, and huddled behind Lloyd George's leadership. It was a mere eighteen years since their landslide victory, and only two years since Lloyd George, the Man Who Won The War, had been leading what looked like the natural party of government.

The fear of communism, rather than the charm of the Conservative party, was what lay behind the election result. Benign Colonel Wedgwood's rhetorical question backfired. 'Those who will *not* believe that you can do away with exploitation – that is, those who do not want to do away with it – all those "in the interests of Society" will regulate, inspect and convert the working man into a machine that shall like its servitude.' That, precisely, is what the early years of Baldwin's Second Government showed that the Conservative party wanted.

The word 'unemployment' had come into being during Gladstone's last government[15] to describe the mass effects of depression in capitalism. Since the 1880s at least, the capitalist world had suffered from cycles of unemployment, but in the post-world war era, it became much more acute. In 1921 there were 2 million British workers unemployed, the worst depression since the Industrial Revolution began. Then things picked up a little, but, in spite of an increase in the numbers in work, there were still 1 million unemployed. The export trades were continuing to produce goods for which there was no world market.[16]

It was at this stage of things that Baldwin returned for his second term in office and appointed as his Chancellor of the Exchequer a man who, for all his sterling qualities, was not noted for his skills as an economist: Winston Churchill.

The very last thing which should have happened at this stage of the economic cycle was for the British to so fix their currency that it became even more expensive for foreigners to buy British goods. John Maynard Keynes argued in a series of articles in the *Nation* that laissez-faire economics could not solve the unemployment crisis, and he also argued passionately for keeping Britain off the gold standard until the pound had found its level in the international currency markets.[17] Yet the new Conservative Chancellor – new in the sense of being new to the job, and new as a Conservative, having crossed over from the Liberal benches – was determined to fix the pound at its old prewar parity with the dollar: £1 = $4.86. Following the Conservative election victory, the pound rose against the dollar, reaching $4.80 in early 1925. Montagu Norman, the governor of the Bank of England, favoured Britain returning to the gold standard. Churchill was persuaded by the Treasury and by the Bank that it was worth while for Britain to go on to the gold standard at this rate, even if the short-term effects on the workforce were harsh. It was a 'sacrifice' worth making. Churchill was persuaded against his better judgement: he was half-persuaded by one of Keynes's articles: 'I would rather see Finance less proud and Industry more content,' he wrote in a memo to the Treasury.[18] But this mood did not last long.

With the inevitable dip in exports, Baldwin said in July 1925: 'All the workers of this country have got to take reductions in wages to help put industry on its feet.'[19]

As in 1848, when the government took very great precautions to prepare against a Chartist Revolution, so in 1926 Baldwin's Conservatives took highly effective steps to cripple the political power of the working class. The diplomatic settlement of the Ruhr occupation meant that there was now plentiful cheap coal available to be imported from Germany and Poland. It led to a reduction in the coal price, and the inevitable demand by mine-owners that the British coal miners should accept a cut in wages.

The miners were at the vanguard of the working-class struggle for fairly obvious and visible reasons. With their hard labour they had fuelled the industrial power and energy which had made Britain the supreme economic empire of the world. Until the arrival of oil-fuelled transport or industrial machinery, coal was visibly there, heaped in the factory yards, in the furnaces where Baldwin's ironworks melted the ore, in the bottle-kilns which fired Colonel Wedgwood's china: all over the industrial Midlands and North. Every railway station smelt of coal. It was smuts of coal which middle-class passengers wiped from their eyes if they leaned out of the express train window; it was slag heaps they saw, brooding like accursed mountains in a Dantean hellscape, as they steamed through the industrial heartlands. Coal, its dirt, energy and power, was the outward and visible sign of the contract which had been made since the Industrial Revolution began between the people who made and the people who owned the country's wealth. Those who mined it led short lives. They returned to small houses to be washed in front of the fire in tin baths, their faces grimy, their lungs thick with pneumoconiosis. While the idea of the Labour movement was that all workers were partners, in real terms there was not a great connection between, say, textile workers based in Lancashire and those making nails in Birmingham, between a railway stoker in Barnstaple and a docker on the Clyde. But coal and its visible dirt united them all. The dispute which developed between Herbert Smith and the National Union of Mineworkers and the owners escalated. The owners made a mean-spirited offer, and then threatened lockout if the men refused the terms. The government, and especially the Home Secretary, the evangelical Christian William Joynson-Hicks, believed that a Communist revolution was imminent, even though the Communists were not especially influential in any of the unions drawn into the dispute, certainly not in the TUC, which tried to mediate.

If the railwaymen came out on strike in solidarity with the dockers they had the capacity to cause damage, but no longer totally to immobilize the country. The government drew up emergency plans, with anyone who could drive being enlisted as lorry-drivers to take food to the main cities. There was some further attempt at mediation between the workers and the mine-owners, but the truth is that the government wanted this strike. On 1 May the dockers were locked out, and on 3 May 1926 a General Strike was called.

The middle classes responded with a whooping excitement to the challenge. Public-school-educated young men who had always dreamed of doing so drove trains. Those who for recreation rode to hounds now volunteered as mounted police. Millions of strikers were out, and in all major towns there were huge crowds, but they were on the whole peaceful. Four thousand at the end of a week were prosecuted for violence, but this was 4,000 out of crowds of millions. Much violence, on both sides, went unreported.[20] Churchill was in his element. He forgot that the job of Chancellor was merely to look after the nation's economy, and moved immediately into dictatorial mode. 'He thinks he is Napoleon,' J. C. Davidson complained to Baldwin. When the first convoy brought food into central London from the docks by volunteer drivers, Churchill wanted it to be escorted by tanks with machine guns tactically placed en route. He tried to commandeer the BBC, but Reith resisted. When the compositors at the *Daily Mail* went on strike rather than print an inflammatory and inaccurate article, and most of the other printers followed suit, Churchill decided to produce his own government propaganda sheet. The *British Gazette* was produced from the offices and printing plant of the *Morning Post*. He commandeered newsprint, paper and machines. By the last day of the strike, he had got the circulation up to 2.2 million.

His biographer Roy Jenkins calls this 'a formidable achievement', without mentioning that his own father, a Welsh miner who became a Labour MP, went to prison for his advocacy of the miners' cause.[21] Two months after the strike, when the House of Commons was debating it all, Churchill turned to a Labour member and said: 'I have no wish to make threats which would disturb the House and cause bad blood, but this I must say. Make your minds perfectly clear that if ever you let loose upon us again a General Strike, we will let loose upon you.' He paused. 'Another *British Gazette*.' There was laughter of course from both sides of the House. Churchill could not help being funny and charming, but his actual policy, and that of the government, was very far from charming or funny. He would certainly have been prepared to use machine guns and tanks on men who only eight years before were being asked to die for their country and who were rightly described by Lloyd George as heroes.

The General Strike lasted nine days. The miners held out for six months until starvation drove them back to accept worse conditions than before, lower wages and longer hours. Coal mines remained, until the Second World War, the largest employers of labour.[22] The behaviour of the owners was not forgotten, however, and this was one of the chief reasons why the coal-mining industry was nationalized as soon as there was a powerful and effective Labour government in 1945.

The King wrote in his diary: 'Our old country can well be proud of itself, as during the last nine days there has been a strike in which four million people have been affected, not a shot has been fired and no one killed. It shows what a wonderful people we are.'[23] But who needs to fire a gun if you have hunger and fear to drive people back to work?

The union leaders certainly did not want Britain to become communist. But for eight years since the end of the war, the working classes had waited for some of the promises of politicians to be fulfilled. Where was the Land Fit for Heroes to Live In which Lloyd George had promised? How did they live, in their back-to-back houses, and their tenements? How did they wash? How did they go to the lavatory? What happened to them when they were ill? What sort of schooling was offered to their children? Of course these were not the issues in the General Strike, but they were the circumstances which explained how and why so many people went out. It was a yelp of pain and anger, not an organized political programme. The Conservatives could capitalize on all the fears which the strike had aroused, by bringing in the Trade Unions Act of 1927. It greatly expanded the class of 'illegal strikes'. It banned all strikes 'designed or calculated to coerce the Government either directly or by inflicting hardship on the community'. Workers who refused to

Radclyffe Hall, the chronicler of Sapphic love, had the painful experience of seeing her novel *The Well of Loneliness* banned by law. Seen here with her lover Una Lady Troubridge.

The first two women MPs – Margaret Wintringham (Labour) and the American Nancy Astor (Conservative)

Marie Stopes's stormy and unhappy experiences of marriage helped drive forward her campaigns for a more open approach to family planning and sexual problems

Lawrence of Arabia was classically a man of the century where image outweighed substance. Though his campaigns in the First World War were of minimal strategic importance, he developed mythic status.

The early Mohandas Karamchand Gandhi was a successful radical lawyer working for human rights in South Africa

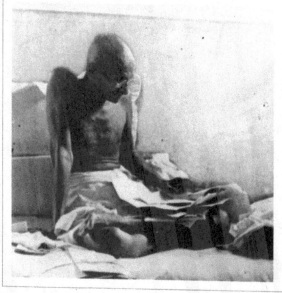

Gandhi's incarnation as an Indian national leader was as a holy man. Here he is seen fasting as a protest against British rule in India.

The Canadian-born Max Aitken, later Lord Beaverbrook, was one of the great newspaper proprietors

Alfred Charles William Harmsworth, the first Viscount Northcliffe, founder of the *Daily Mail*, proprietor of *The Times* and effectual inventor of modern journalism. He died on a rooftop in Mayfair, having tried to telephone through to his office the sensational scoops that he was going mad, and that God was homosexual.

In the Golden Age of the Detective Story, Agatha Christie was perhaps the most deft practitioner of the craft

The borderlines between silliness and art were explored by the Sitwell family. Edith (1887–1964) and her brother Osbert (1892–1969) both saw themselves as poets but they are remembered today not for their verses, which are completely forgotten, but for their exhibitionistic lives.

Noël Coward is photographed here with Gertrude Lawrence in a London theatre in 1935. He mocked the Sitwells, earning their eternal enmity. Behind their hostility must have lurked the knowledge that Coward was an authentic genius. His lyrics and music are the glory of the mid-twentieth-century in England.

SOME PRIME MINISTERS

(*Below*) David Lloyd George and Winston
Churchill, depicted in 1910 before either
of them attained that office

(*Right*) James Ramsay MacDonald, whose career
as Labour Leader was short, seen here after the
general election of 1931 which confirmed him
as Prime Minister of a National Government

(*Left*) Stanley Baldwin presided over cruel
economic conditions at home, and pursued
a policy of appeasement with the European
dictators. He remains a widely popular figure
in Conservative annals.

(*Below*) Neville Chamberlain succeeded
Baldwin as Prime Minister in 1937; after vainly
trying to appease Hitler, he took his country
to war with Germany, and died in 1940

These slums in Tooting Grove, photographed in 1935, were typical of the working-class homes of Baldwin's Britain

Basil Jellicoe, nephew of the admiral and an Anglican priest in Somers Town North London, did much to awaken the conscience of Britain to the consequences of poor housing. He founded the St Pancras Housing Trust and helped to rehouse thousands of poor people in sanitary conditions.

Beatrice and Sidney Webb, who helped to establish the *New Statesman* and the London School of Economics were key figures in the history of the British left

The greatest minds of the past were devoted to philosophy and art. In the twentieth-century they were scientists. Albert Einstein demonstrates here the theory of relativity to a no-doubt bemused lecture-audience.

Ernest Walton (1903–1995), Ernest Rutherford (1871–1937) and John Cockcroft (1897–1967) were all pioneers in the sphere of nuclear science, discovering the structure of the atom, and methods by which to split it

NO MORE SOCIALIST PROMISES FOR ME, I'M VOTING
FOR THE NATIONAL GOVERNMENT

John Maynard Keynes's economic perceptions might have saved millions from unemployment and poverty in the 1930s had they been adopted by British parties of government

This poster of the 1931 election urges the working classes to support Ramsay MacDonald's Government of National Unity. It destroyed the aspirations of the Labour Party for a generation.

The between-war years saw much new urban planning, including the growth of the Garden suburbs. Welwyn Garden City on a wet day in 1938.

accept changes in their working conditions were now deemed in the eyes of the law to be on strike. Peaceful picketing was banned. Civil servants were forbidden from joining a trade union. The comparative benignity of the Employers and Workmen Act of 1875 was swept away. Trade unions were limited in the extent to which they could fund political parties, so that the government was able, while limiting the power of the union, to ruin, financially, the Labour party, since trade unions were the principal sources of Labour party funding. Labour could now collect money only from trade union members who had specifically 'contracted in' to pay for party funding; this at a time when wages were being reduced and unemployment always threatened. Labour party membership fell from 3,388,000 in 1926 to a little over 1 million in 1927.[24]

There was now on the statute book a system of iron control over the disgruntled workforce, and the painstaking trade union movement, which had built up its rights and its power base over the previous century, was now firmly knocked into submission. In so doing, the Conservatives undoubtedly strengthened the Labour party in the long term, since many more individuals, as opposed to union people, joined the party over the coming decade, and for every one who joined there were ten who were sympathetic fellow travellers, and potential Labour voters when the next election came.

The General Strike had been an ugly episode. It did not show what a wonderful people the British were. It showed how selfish their middle classes were, and how strong was their monied power. On 28 October 1926, Hilaire Belloc wrote to his friend Katharine Asquith: 'We are in a state of permanent and sullen civil war, modified by general patriotism and terror of the police and the troopers. The rich are seeing to it that these divisions shall grow more acute. God has blinded them. I have not met one single gentleman or lady on the side of the poor in this crisis. That's ominous!'[25]

18

The Secrets of a Woman's Heart – Marie Stopes, Radclyffe Hall

If Belloc had not heard any rich people speaking up for the poor, in the sense of defending strike action on a national scale, it would have been wrong to say that it had no effect outside the immediate dispute between employers and union leaders. The strike did alert many people to the plight of the poor and of the unemployed. Immediately after the General Strike, the Conservative member of Parliament for the Sutton division of Plymouth, accompanied by Margaret Wintringham, MP for Louth, 1921–4, broadcast on behalf of the Save the Children Fund, a charity which had been started after the First World War. The MP and Mrs Wintringham also toured the mining districts of South Wales. 'We found such kindness and courage, and no bitterness among the miners and their wives . . . We returned with a longing to help, not only with milk and food, but in bringing about some method of settling disputes by some other way than war – for industrial disputes are war, in which women and children suffer most.' . . . 'Please send your gifts, remember that by doing this you will help to keep alive not only the bodies and spirits of those who are suffering, but, what is more important, their faith in their fellow men and women.'

The MP concerned represented a poor part of Plymouth, and was able, thanks to money from her husband's immensely rich family, to set up a housing trust on the model of those of Basil Jellicoe in Somers Town, and to establish, as well as cheap, healthy housing, a gymnasium, a carpenter's shop, a cinema, a printing-press and other facilities.[1] Many of the pioneers of women's suffrage must have been surprised by the fact that, when a woman first took her seat in the House of Commons, on 1 December 1919, it should have been as a Conservative. Others would have been surprised, too, that she was an American. A divorced and remarried American at that. (Fifteen years later such a biographical history would disqualify another American lady from an important role in British public life.)

Nancy Langhorne (1879–1964) had been born in Danville, Virginia. At the time of her parents' marriage her father, Chiswell Dabney Langhorne, had been an officer in the Confederate army. The reduced post-bellum circumstances in which they grew up gave credence to

Nancy's later claims that she knew about poverty. The family lived in a four-roomed wooden house. Nancy was the fifth child in a family of eleven. In 1897 she married a rich Bostonian named Robert Gould Shaw II, largely because she so admired his horsemanship. They were divorced in 1903, and she came almost at once to England, with her beautiful little son Bobbie Shaw, destined for a tragic, homosexual existence, her mother and a female friend. She had good introductions, and enjoyed hunting, and this beautiful, spirited woman did not lack for invitations. Her sometimes abrasive manner charmed people. When General Tom Holland offered to help her up on to her horse after a fall, she yelled: 'Do you think I would be such an ass to come out hunting if I couldn't mount from the ground?' They were friends for life. Soon she captured the heart of Lord Revelstoke, head of Barings' Bank. Nothing came of the relationship, however – he was too shy to speak out – and on a voyage back from America in 1905, she met Waldorf Astor.

Waldorf's father, William Waldorf Astor, had left the United States on the somewhat Jamesian grounds that 'America is not a fit place for a gentleman to live.' Having spent some of his fortune acquiring stupendous art works in Italy, and written a novel about the Borgias, he had settled in England. He lived in style in London, owning a house in Carlton House Terrace. His Tudorbethan offices on the Victoria Embankment had door handles which opened only on the inside, and the whole building – so obsessed was he by the possibility of kidnap – had centrally controlled security locks. He bought two stupendous country houses, Hever Castle in Kent, and Cliveden, Barry's Italian palazzo, in Buckinghamshire. He also became a newspaper proprietor, owning the *Pall Mall Gazette*, and later the *Observer*. When Nancy married Waldorf she wore a tiara containing the Sanci diamond, which had belonged to James I and Charles I and which had been worn by Louis XIV at his coronation. There could hardly have been a more eloquent demonstration of the conquest of Old Europe by American money.

Cliveden is one of the most beautifully situated houses in England. From its Italianate terraces, the lawns and gardens slope into a blue-green vista, through which snakes the silvery Thames. The statues and the balustrades come from the Villa Borghese in Rome. Nancy was a spirited hostess, and not consumed by guilt. She had a deep spiritual strength, enhanced in 1914 by her conversion to Christian Science – Mrs Baker Eddy's belief that evil was illusory being somehow suited to her brand of optimistic puritanism. She was a prig, a teetotaller, and as a mother, she was something out of Eugene O'Neill (Bobbie had four Astor half-siblings). But although many old suffragists must have been a little wistful about it being her, rather than Mrs Pankhurst or Ellen Wilkinson or some other feminist worthy, who first took her seat in Westminster, the important thing was, she had done it. One veteran suffragette pinned a badge on to her as she arrived at Westminster and touched her, as if she were semi-divine. 'It is the beginning of our era,' said the older woman. 'I am glad I have suffered for this.'

The First World War had changed the 'position of women' in very many ways. It was much more than simply the fact, important as this was, that women had worked in munitions factories, as medics, as administrators, and established their place alongside men in the workplace; much more, too, than that they had slowly forced upon a sluggish male establishment the notion that suffrage must one day come. Women over the age of thirty got the vote in 1918. It was not until 1928 that women aged twenty-one enjoyed the same parliamentary voting rights as men and over 5 million voters were added to the national registers. It was that the whole position of women in society, in the scheme of things, had ceased to be a subject discussed by a few enlightened, slightly earnest Victorian feminist friends of John Stuart Mill, heroic as these figures had been, and become rather something which now affected everyone. In 1925, in *The Right to Be Happy*, Dora Russell, Bertrand's second wife, spoke of the older feminists who could not 'see what sex had to do with political freedom'. Stella Browne, another pioneer socialist feminist of the new generation, would have agreed with this, and wrote that the 'incurably respectable tacticians' of the old Victorian suffragist institutions had neglected 'intimate liberation'.[2]

Marie Stopes's *Married Love* addresses questions more immediately important to people than whether to vote for the Asquithian or the Lloyd George Liberals or whether to come off the gold standard.

If Simone de Beauvoir was right that '*la liberté pour les femmes commence au ventre*'[3] (Freedom for women begins in the belly) then the story of female suffrage and votes for women was only part of the story of political life in the 1920s. Some time before he embarked on an unsuccessful mission to provide democratic self-determinations for the nations of Europe, President Woodrow Wilson was in receipt of a remarkable written question: 'Have you, Sir, visualised what it means to be a woman?' If the answer to this question was a negative, he had almost certainly not given his mind to her further question, whether he knew what '. . . it means to be a woman whose every muscle and blood-capillary is subtly poisoned by the secret ever-growing horror, more penetrating, more long-drawn than any nightmare, of an unwanted embryo developing beneath her heart? While men stand proudly and face the sun, boasting that they have quenched the wickedness of slavery, what chains of slavery are, have been, or ever could be so intimate a horror as the shackles on every limb, on every thought, on the very soul of an unwillingly pregnant woman?'

The author of this letter enclosed a petition signed, among others, by H. G. Wells, Arnold Bennett and Professor Gilbert Murray, none of whom had themselves been pregnant, though they had all – Wells and Bennett in their novels, Murray in his translations from Greek tragedy – made an imaginative stab at getting inside unhappy women's skins. The author herself, Marie Stopes, had in 1905 been the youngest Doctor of Science in Britain. (She never qualified as a medical doctor.) She had formed the ambition as a very young person to find herself 'a place with the Immortals'.[4] She wanted her life to fall into three phases. First, she would become a scientist. Next, she would devote herself to poetry and drama, and become a writer. Third, she would devote herself to helping the human race. In her way she did all three things, though rather than being first one thing, then another, and then the third, she was probably always all three at once: scientist, poet and missionary. Her archetypically Victorian idea that she should apply her scientific expertise to human betterment led inexorably to her turning into something else, a twentieth-century 'character', one who Stood for Something, a figure whose activities could be caricatured by the newspapers, and whose sometimes quite complicated range of responses to the universe could be summed up in a few shocking banner headlines.

Marie Stopes was beautiful, she had long flowing hair, she wrote short, compelling books and articles about subjects which obsess almost everyone. She addressed medical and scientific questions in the language of a tuppenny 'shocker'. Being a very quick-tempered exhibitionist who expressed herself in novelettish prose, she was a gift to journalists and the caricaturist school of history. She made some powerful enemies, and it is not surprising therefore that she should have been more than usually edgy about the exposure of her own private sorrows. In a sense, however, attempts to undermine Stopes's work by reference to these painful matters only rebound on the teller, since although she disputed the details of bedroom secrets in her two unhappy marriages, she never made any secret of the fact that her work as a sexologist, and her desire to spread a little happiness, sprang from her own private miseries.

Her first husband, Reginald Ruggles Gates, as late as 24 April 1962, bothered to write down: 'She got annulment 1915 or 1916 by swearing I was impotent. On my solicitor's advice I was examined by Sir Alfred Tripp and given a certificate of perfect normality. This stopped the slander for a time but it was destroyed by bombing in London in 1940. Recently, through a forgotten record, it is proved that I was fully fertile in 1947 at the age of 64.'[5] In 1938, when Marie was fifty-eight, her second marriage broke down. She made her then husband, a well-known aeroplane designer called Humphrey Roe, sign a paper which read:

> Five years ago, I told you I wanted no more sex union and that I should not object if you decided to have a lover to replace my deficiency. I wish to put it on record that, if you did, it would not alter our existing relations, and I should never reproach you or take any steps about it, as I have long considered a wife whose husband is incapable of coitus has every right to supplement his deficiency without breaking up the home.[6]

Marie was obsessed by the failure of her first marriage, and by the thought that her enemies, or posterity, would mock her. It was intolerable that the author of *Married Love* should have had not one, but two failed marriages, and she was as anxious to defend herself against charges of incompetence as any adolescent after an inadequate fumble had turned to mutual recrimination.[7] The first husband's testimony has a tragi-farcical plausibility. 'She says she endured misery, humiliation and frustration. Why – a man can not love an angry woman. Other men told me they could not have loved her.' Although bad temper turns some men on, in a great many cases it has the opposite effect, and poor Marie had the bad luck to have chosen two men as husbands who found her tantrums unappealing. Her character, which led to many a litigation, many a miso-gynistic newspaper headline, and many a family row, is subordinate to her achievement. That is, that on 17 March 1921 Marie Stopes founded the first Pioneer Birth Control Clinic. The patrons were Sir James Barr, Arnold Bennett, Dame Clara Butt, Aylmer Maude Esq., Miss Maude Royden and Admiral Sir Percy Scott.

'I loathe prudes and parsons: and the parsons are the worse because they make the prudes,' she wrote to one of her friends.[8] Perhaps this was what prompted one of her boldest pieces of socio-sexual research. In November 1920, Marie Stopes initiated what is probably the first statistical survey of human sexual habits. She sent a questionnaire to two thousand Church of England clergymen, chosen at random from *Crockford's Clerical Directory*, asking them about their married life, the number of children born, the dates and intervals between births and miscarriages, and whether any form of birth control was used. She listed:

(a) Total abstinence
(b) Safe period
(c) Use of withdrawal – coitus interruptus
(d) Use of quinine or other pessary

(e) Use of rubber cap or occlusive pessary
(f) Use of sheath
(g) Other means

Few of the replies were as prurient as that of the Yorkshire parson who described his method as 'rubbing out "stuff" out of erect penis by hand – self – wife – and middle-aged cook in absence of wife'; but there is no reason to suppose that this reply was fictitious. Some were answered by the wives – 'My husband', wrote a vicar's widow from Bath, 'would have considered all these suggestions absolutely criminal. He religiously confined himself to once-a-week unions but was quite rampant during the month of abstention during childbirth and I always thought, inclined to be "off his head" – I never felt any "orgasm" but he didn't seem to notice that.'[9]

Marie had opened a secret door into human life. Once her books became bestsellers, it was not merely the clergy who wrote to her. From all over the world, correspondents shared with her their most intimate sexual problems, fears and worries. When she died, she bequeathed her papers to the British Museum. They outnumber even the Gladstone papers, that is the archive of the most prolix and retentive of all Victorian statesmen. It took days and days for the removal vans to store all these letters in the National Library. For every correspondent who wrote 'disgusted with the filth', there were ten who felt deep gratitude to Marie for – to quote one correspondent – 'putting into words so beautifully the great message of help and hope to us poor mortals who strive to make married life a success and to place love in its right position'.[10]

Orgasms, happiness, tenderness, all the things D. H. Lawrence was writing about in *The Rainbow*, including the belief that the world might become a better place if men and women regarded one another a little more tenderly.

Women after the war looked different. They dressed differently. Ready-made frocks became cheaply available. Ankle-length skirts had risen to the calf by the end of the war and to the knee by the time of the fall of Lloyd George. Hair could be cut short. Veils had vanished. Young women no longer forced themselves into bone corsets. 'The freedom you have got with regard to dress is worth the vote a hundred times over,' said Sir Alfred Hopkinson, addressing the young women of Cheltenham Ladies College, among them my mother, in the early 1920s. Whatever their class, they were never going to go back to the lives of their heavily corseted mothers and grandmothers. By 1923 there were four thousand women serving as magistrates, mayors, councillors and guardians. In 1919 they were admitted to the legal profession, and Oxford University allowed them to take degrees. (Cambridge did not follow suit until after the Second World War.) Many middle-class women took jobs, and would wear light, simple clothes to the office. 'English women', said the couturier Norman Hartnell at the end of the 1920s, 'are dressing better each season; their preference is for simple, well-cut and well-made dresses; they avoid the bizarre and the conspicuous.'[11]

The washing-machine had been invented, though it was still cumbrous and big, and few could afford one. Vacuum cleaners were invented in 1901.

The first number of *Good Housekeeping* magazine, published in London in March 1924, said:

> Any keen observer of the times cannot have failed to notice that we are on the threshold of a great feminine awakening. Apathy and levity are giving place to a wholesome and intelligent interest in the affairs of life, and above all in the home. There should be no drudgery in the house . . . the house-proud woman in these days of servant shortage does not always know the best way to lessen her own burdens . . . The time spent on housework can be enormously reduced in every home without any loss of comfort, and often with a great increase in its wellbeing and its air of personal care and attention.[12]

And having watched the world being more than half destroyed by males, and macho politics, women were in many cases faced with the actual responsibility for rebuilding families, businesses, farms, institutions, in the absence of 'able-bodied' men. The intimate, biological facts of life could no longer be hidden away as something never to be spoken about, even though, for generations, in many individual families, this was precisely what people did continue to do, or try to do. As late as the 1940s, Mass Observation surveys showed that 'ordinary men and women have not even the vocabulary with which to frame enquiries and express their puzzlement. Husbands and wives are hampered in a discussion with one another. Parents, nowadays at least, are generally well-meaning, but are themselves too ignorant and inhibited to give reliable information to their children.'[13] Betty Tucker, a Stoke-on-Trent railwayman's daughter, recollected: 'My dear old dad told me nothing but in the taxi going to the church he gave me a tin of Vaseline because he said I might be a bit sore that night.' She did not tell him that she had already lost her virginity.[14]

Although such matters were still occasions of shyness in the 1920s, and presumably still are for many people in the twenty-first century, Marie Stopes's *Married Love* did alter the climate. And it could do so partly because so many stark physical facts confronted women in the years after the First World War. There was the fact that women still died in childbirth at a rate which by modern standards was 'Third World'. In the 1920s, around 39,000 women died in childbirth in England and Wales.[15] There was the fact that so many men had been killed in the war that for many women there would not be a chance of marriage. There was the fact of venereal disease.

Marie Stopes saw her birth-control mission as addressed to all, but much of her pioneer work had been done in poor districts of London. Margaret Sanger, American socialist and pioneer of birth control, was viewed by Stopes as a rival, and indeed Marie would enjoy one of her ridiculous public feuds with Sanger. But, like Stopes, Sanger had been radicalized, both as a socialist and as a pioneer of sexual revolution, in the poor districts of American cities. William Sanger, her husband, was imprisoned in the United States for sending her pamphlet *Family Limitation* by post, something which infringed the Comstock Obscenity Laws. And the pamphlet was impounded by the British police in 1922.

The poverty, degradation and disease to be encountered less than a hundred years ago in the slums of Europe and America is of a kind difficult for twenty-first century Western readers to envisage. Its scale was so vast that it is not surprising that it suggested desperate remedies to the minds which confronted it.

It is here that we enter the strange territory of eugenics, the notion that by breeding, and limitation of birth, the social problems caused by poverty and overpopulation could be eliminated.

Marie Stopes was early attracted to the Eugenics Society, which had been founded in 1908. Its first president was Francis Galton, the cousin of Charles Darwin, and its aim was the specifically Darwinian one of eliminating the 'unfit' from future generations of the human race. Its founder's purpose was to give 'the more suitable races or strains of blood a better chance of prevailing speedily over the less suitable'.[16] The Eugenics Society bore kinship to the much older Malthusian League, which Marie Stopes also supported. Charles Darwin had developed his idea of Evolution by Natural Selection after reading the economic theories of Thomas Malthus. It is obvious how the social Darwinists and the Malthusians should feed off one another's ideas. They both saw the fundamental problem of society as being overpopulation, with the further refinement on behalf of the eugenicists that it should now be possible to eliminate those strains from the human species which in Galton's word were 'unsuitable'.

The problem arises, for those who find, or place, themselves in a position where such social experimentation becomes possible: how do you define 'suitability'? Obviously, on one level this is a simple question. One of the phenomena which helped Darwin become sure of his evolutionary theory was pigeon-breeding. It would surely be possible to breed out undesirable physical defects from the human race in the same way that pigeon-fanciers mate healthier specimens to get faster, sleeker birds? When in the late 1940s her son Harry fell in love with the daughter of Barnes Wallis, the aeronautical genius, Marie saw it as a disaster, since not only was Mary Wallis 'plain and socially dreary': she wore specs. Harry Roe, Marie's son, was 'exceptionally fine and should marry his peer in looks, inheritance and health'. For him to marry Mary Wallis was to 'make a mock of our lives' work for Eugenic breeding and the race'. It was also a crime against '*his children* (and posterity) . . . it is cruel to burden children with defective sight and the handicap of goggles'. A footnote in the biography of Marie Stopes by Ruth Hall points out that of the four children born of Mary and Harry Stopes-Roe's marriage, two had slightly defective eyesight but all were useful and altruistic individuals. In other words, Marie's fears were exaggerated.[17]

Her belief in eugenics, however, was not some strange fad of her own. Although in the 1940s it became a discredited creed, because it was adopted with such enthusiasm by the German government, in the 1920s in England, nearly all *bien pensant* figures believed in it, and this from both left and right of the political spectrum. It was clear to the socialist Shaw as it was to the High Tory Dean Inge that eugenics was the Way Forward.

Some socialists, however, smelt a rat in the eugenicists' agenda. Stella Browne was not alone in finding a 'class-bias and sex-bias' in the eugenics programme. What Dean Inge candidly wanted was for the educated classes to breed, and the criminal and lower orders to be eliminated by Malthusian means. Great Britain would become an island populated by well-read, happy, well-behaved people who would not have swarms of proles threatening their stability. In 1922 the newspaper *The Communist* saw birth control as a capitalist quack remedy for unemployment which arose because 'the unemployed today are beginning dimly to be class-conscious'.[18] The controversy among the communists led to what one correspondent said was 'a timely reminder that we should be Marxians first and Malthusian after'.

Many women did not wish to be either. They merely wanted to live lives of less risk, and less circumscribed, wearying awfulness, than their mothers had done, which is why, in the 1920s, we see British families being so noticeably reduced in size. Following the opening of Marie Stopes's first clinic, birth-control clinics opened in various parts of London. They were followed in 1925 by one in Wolverhampton, in 1926 by clinics in Manchester, Salford, East London, Glasgow, Oxford and Aberdeen. Then came Birmingham in 1927, Rotherham in 1928, Newcastle upon Tyne in 1929, Exeter, Nottingham and Pontypridd in 1930 and Bristol and Ashington in Northumberland in 1931.[19] Women wanted and needed small families. Instinct, and the desire for a better life and for self-preservation, not theory, led them to it. In the last decade of Queen Victoria's reign, less than 20 per cent of all families in Britain had fewer than four children. By the 1930s, small families had become the norm, with only 19 per cent of families having more than three children.[20]

This is the demographic fact, showing that, by whatever means, women had made a quiet revolution, which no huffing and puffing by public moralists would ever change. Although they did it because they wanted to do it, and because they had to, much of the credit must go to noisy, exhibitionistic Marie Stopes, who tirelessly went on campaigning. Her poet's soul was never so carried away by romantic fancy that she shied away from the detail, prosaic as these often were. For example, the sale of the big Boots chemist empire – 'the only firm known to poor people' – to an American company allowed her to hope 'this will remove Lady Boot's influence, which was, in my opinion, the main factor in preventing them stocking any contraceptives'.[21] That was in October 1921. The matter of how contraceptives were sold, and indeed, whether they should be sold at all, went on being keenly debated in a manner which even at the time must have seemed bizarre.

Lord Dawson of Penn, the king's physician, saw it as his duty in 1934 to bring a Bill before the House of Lords which attempted to limit the sale of contraceptives. 'I venture to say,' he told Their Lordships, 'that no impartial observer of the events of today can doubt that birth control is here to stay and is part and parcel of our social fabric. I put it as a question of fact irrespective of whether we regret it or accept it. At the same time there is good cause for protecting young children and young persons from having contraceptives pushed at them by means of automatic machines in the public streets or by lurid displays in shops.'[22] Lord Banbury of Southam questioned the logic of Dawson's position. If it was right to have contraception, why restrict their sale? The answer was apparently supplied by the lord Bishop of London, whose imagination was inflamed by the use to which these objects were being put, not merely by the married but by the 'loose living among the unmarried'. 'I came back in my car late at night. Anybody who is doing that consistently, winter and summer, autumn and spring, and very often on by-roads and roads coming out of London, will know perfectly well what is going on in motor-cars held up at any hour of the evening or the night.'[23] 'Forgive me, my lords,' went on the bishop, 'if I speak hotly about it.' He did indeed speak hotly, and his speech showed how clearly class and race are always in people's minds when they discuss the matter of birth control.

'I regret greatly the passing of those old Victorian families. I am one of such a family and proud of the fact, and when I look round the British Empire, I should love to see far more of our British children filling up the empty spaces. I should like to see British families spread over the earth, multiplying abundantly.' (Dean Inge took the trouble to look up the forty diocesan bishops in *Who's Who* and found that one had five children, two had four each and the remaining thirty-seven had a mere twenty-eight children between them.)[24] The Bishop of London then wound up to a splendid peroration, asking whether 'it is really possible to think that there is no harm in these filthy things being sent as they are to every engaged couple in the country . . . I look upon the whole thing as downgrade. When I hear of 400,000 being manufactured every week, I would like to make a bonfire of them and dance round it.'[25] This must rank as one of the strangest speeches – and this is saying something – ever uttered in the House of Lords.

Not that the Lords had a monopoly of strange ideas when sex was being considered. In August 1928, a slightly sentimental novel by Radclyffe Hall called *The Well of Loneliness* was published, and the editor of the *Sunday Express*, James Douglas, published an article under the headline 'A Book That Must Be Suppressed'. The book was a celebration, in the chastest language imaginable, of love between women. 'I say deliberately,' wrote Douglas, 'that this novel is not fit to be sold by any bookseller or to be borrowed from any library.' He believed that it would encourage the growth of 'perversion', of which there was already far too much evidence. 'I have seen the plague stalking shamelessly through great social assemblies. I have heard it whispered about by young men and young women who do not and cannot grasp its unutterable putrefaction. Both aspects of it are thrust upon healthy and innocent minds. The contagion cannot be escaped. It pervades our social life.'

Many novel reviewers would feel they had exaggerated when they attributed this degree of influence to what was, after all, only a love story. But James Douglas still had more to say. In a final flourish, he managed: 'I would rather give a healthy boy or a healthy girl a phial of prussic acid than this novel. Poison kills the body, but moral poison kills the soul.'[26]

The Well of Loneliness was referred to the Director of Public Prosecutions by the Home Secretary, Joynson-Hicks. Poor Radclyffe Hall, John, as she liked to be called, with her slicked-back Eton crop hairstyle, her men's suits and bow ties, found her book described by the judge

as an obscene libel which would tend to corrupt those into whose hands
it fell. He ordered all copies to be impounded, and the publishers,
Jonathan Cape, had to pay costs of 20 guineas. The verdict shocked
sensible people, but none more than the author:

> I have been a Conservative all my life and have always hotly defended
> that Party. When people told me that they stemmed progress, that they
> hated reforms and were the enemies of Freedom, I, in my blindness,
> would not listen. I looked upon them as the educated class best calcu-
> lated to serve the interests of the country. And yet, who was the first
> to spring to my defence, to cry out against the outrage done to my
> book? Labour, my dear, and they have not ceased to let off their guns
> since.[27]

John still had her great love, Una, Lady Troubridge, and she could
still go on writing her books. She had not actually been sent to prison,
as male homosexuals were at this date (in 1931, Bobbie Shaw, Nancy
Astor's son, was arrested for an offence against public decency)'[28] but
she was right to have seen it as a political absurdity, a state intrusion into
private sensibility which was essentially at variance with a Conservative
point of view. In this sense, the prosecution of *The Well of Loneliness*
was a feminist concern, touching on that generalized issue of whether a
male-dominated state (or come to that any state) has the right to interfere with what a woman does with her own body, and what she feels in
her heart.

19

For the Benefit of Empire

On St George's Day 1924, in the presence of about one hundred thousand people, the King-Emperor had opened the British Empire Exhibition at Wembley. If the General Strike, two years later, was to make the British momentarily wonder whether they were on the verge of class war, the Empire Exhibition, and the abiding feelings about the Empire in the pre-1939 years, brought into play very different sensations: feelings of unity and pride, focused on the sovereign. Queen Victoria had never been an especially popular monarch until her old age, when love for her became bound up, especially at the times of her Golden and Diamond Jubilees, with feelings about the Empire. Monarchical feeling in Britain is still, in the twenty-first century, much stronger than any blasé or grown-up commentators would wish. When Queen Elizabeth II celebrated her Golden Jubilee, a crowd of a million gathered outside Buckingham Palace. It was easy to say that they were only tourists, or only this or only that. The fact is, they were there, and in far greater numbers than any politician could ever amass on British soil.

It is therefore glimmeringly possible for our generation to reconstruct what royalist feeling was like in the reign of Georges V and VI, but only glimmeringly, when we speak to the very, very old. Today's monarchists hold their faith with a measure of irony, and with a recognition that the stars of the royal show are far from being perfect individuals. They have all read or seen satirical journalism, TV shows, which mock the queen and her family, and they know that there are many people in the world, both in the former dominions and in Britain, who actually detest the royal family. In the 1920s, republican feelings were very unusual outside Ireland. Monarchism was serious stuff. When T. S. Eliot was converted to it, he was not simply being whimsical. Whereas the Victorians, those grown-up people who could live with doubt and contrarieties, could sing 'God Save the Queen', but at the same time recognize that there was something ridiculous and even on occasion scandalous about the queen and her son, the generation who had lived through the First World War had a much less quizzical viewpoint.

For the first time in history, on 23 April 1924, the King's voice was broadcast. Replying to his son, the Prince of Wales, who as president of the Exhibition had welcomed him, King George hoped that the Exhibition 'may be said to reveal to us the whole Empire in little, containing within its 220 acres of ground a vivid model of the architecture, art and industry of all the races which come under the British flag . . . We believe that this Exhibition will bring the peoples of the Empire to a better knowledge of how to meet their reciprocal wants and aspirations . . . And we hope further that the success of the Exhibition will bring lasting benefits not to the Empire only, but to mankind in general . . .'[1]

These words were heard by an estimated 10 million people.[2] The sovereign had become almost instantaneously something different. His personal dullness did not matter one jot. He was the centre of patriotic hope. There were recurring strikes on the Exhibition site as it was being built, and on the Whit Monday of 1924 there was an Underground strike. It did not stop the crowds pouring in. (The LNER, London and North Eastern Railway, could get you from Marylebone Station to Wembley in 12 minutes, as its posters gladly proclaimed. 'All trains non-stop'.)[3] During its first week, 321,232 attended the exhibition, exceeding the number who visited the Great Exhibition of 1851 in its first week by 75,000.[4]

Inside, the visitor was treated to a breathtaking array of pavilions and displays, representing the different parts of the Empire. Hard by the boating lake, and the dignified simplicities of the Australian pavilion, were the minarets and dome of the Malayan pavilion. A replica of Old London Bridge led to the Burmese pavilion, with its splendid pagodas. But the great centre of the exhibition, as of the Empire, was India. In its midst was a concrete replica of the Taj Mahal. In the courtyards, carpet-weavers from Baluchistan were at work, and in an ingenious model could be seen 25,000 miniature (inanimate) pilgrims to Hardwar. In the South African section, every industry of that country was represented, with gold and diamond mining, diamond cutting, as well as wine production and ostrich farming. At night, the whole Exhibition was electrically floodlit. The amusement park was still in action, with miniature trains whizzing through tunnels (there is an unforgettable newsreel of Queen Mary riding on it), and up the plaster mountains the small boats were carried by electric lifts to the chute which whooshed them down into the lake. On display in the Canadian pavilion was a life-size statue of the Prince of Wales carved out of butter. He said it made his legs look too fat.[5]

The butter has long since melted, and the Prince of Wales, as Duke of Windsor, sleeps in the churchyard at Frogmore. The royal exhibit which everyone remembers from the Wembley Exhibition and which is still on display at Windsor Castle, is Queen Mary's Doll's House, designed by Lutyens. On the walls hang original miniature royal portraits by Sir William Orpen. In the library are tiny books written in the very hands of their authors – Sir Arthur Conan Doyle, Rudyard Kipling, Max Beerbohm, Hilaire Belloc, Aldous Huxley. There are miniature stamps in the tiny stamp albums. Wisden made a tiny cricket ball and bat for the games cupboard. Brigg Umbrellas made a doll-sized working brolly. The jewel safe is by Chubb Locks. In the larder are real wines and jams. The beds have sheets and pillow cases. The housemaids' closet has the modern convenience of a vacuum cleaner. It still attracts the crowds who go to Windsor Castle, but although it is a splendid game, there is something slightly sad about it.

The British Empire Exhibition was a huge propaganda exercise, observed by the Soviet communists, by aspirant German demagogues, by the Vatican. The nineteenth century thought that a few thousand people were a great crowd. The twentieth century could create crowds of hundreds of thousands, and by means of broadcasting, such mass events could reach millions. It was not a medium by which very subtle messages could be delivered to individuals, but excitement, colour, noise and the distinctively twentieth-century phenomenon of crowd-emotion, or mass hysteria, could all be manipulated.

Wembley was designed with the very grandest motives of imperial propaganda. In its modernity, its efficiency, its blend of cheapness and grandiosity, it was an embodiment in concrete of those imperial ideals celebrated in Kipling's verse and tales. The firm engaged to build it was Sir Robert McAlpine and Sons. 'Sir Robert started life as a boy on railway construction works 68 years ago, and before he was 20 years of age had launched out in a small building business in Glasgow.' The catalogue informs us that he was responsible for building the huge Singer sewing machine works in Glasgow as well as 'the erection of the immense factories of British Dyes Ltd at Huddersfield; the Spondon factories and housing schemes of the British Cellulose and Chemical Manufacturing Company near Derby; the vast mechanical transport depot near Slough; and scores of other factories and works for the Government during the war, both in this country and in France'. Sir Robert, in short, proud to call himself 'the Concrete King', was one of those 'hard-faced men who had done well out of the war'. The architect was Maxwell Ayrton. The vast arena he constructed for the central stadium was Roman, the huge twin towers at the North Front Moghul in inspiration. The pamphlet begins:

When Titus of Ancient Rome built the vast Amphitheatre, known on account of its colossal size as the Colosseum, taking sixteen years to do the job, it probably did not enter his imperial mind that one day a stadium almost three times as large, and infinitely more enduring, would be constructed in less than a tithe of the time by a nation he and his forebears thought it scarcely worth while to conquer. Yet the task has been done, and in its accomplishment all records for speed of erection, size, beauty, accommodation and – in the opinion of experts – permanency – have been beaten.[6]

The claims to permanency are repeated throughout McAlpine's tract, and are very much part of the ethos which the Exhibition intended to convey. The everlasting British Empire which this concrete monster was supposed to represent had in fact only a quarter of a century to endure.

The Exhibition was deemed to be such a success in 1924 that it was repeated the following year, with the same ceremonies, even bigger massed bands, choirs and military displays. It was here that the Military Tattoo was first pioneered: that amalgam of gymnastics, son et lumière, and display of military hardware. The glorious story of the British army, from Waterloo to the present day, had become a show.

Readers of Nietzsche who attended such displays might have remembered the essay, written in 1873, in which he reminded his fellow countrymen that a victory in war can be more calamitous than defeat. 'It is capable of converting our victory into a complete defeat: the defeat, even the death, of German culture for the benefit of the German Empire.'[7] It was, and is, an essential part of the British self-image that whereas the patriotic and military displays of other countries are foolish, or even sinister, those held by Anglo-Saxons are essentially benign. Just as the British liked to believe that it was their moral superiority to the Germans, rather than their superior artillery and the assistance of over a million American servicemen, which won the war, so the displays of imperial might at Wembley, including an exhibition of fighter planes and 'a large bomb 12 feet in length; needless to state, the bomb is empty and is not fuzed [sic]', are essentially benign. The Empire Collect, read by the same Bishop of London whose ambition was to dance round a bonfire of flaming contraceptives, prayed that the Almighty would 'raise up generations of public men who will have the faith and daring of the Kingdom of God in them, and who will enlist for life in a holy warfare for the freedom and rights of all Thy children'.[8]

This aspiration could be interpreted in many ways. If 'freedom and rights' implied self-determination, or at least indigenous populations having a say in the running of their own affairs, then the words of the Collect must have sounded a little hollow to Asians and Africans. For example, the Government of India Act, 1919, was designed to appease left-wing opinion in Britain and India, but the pace of reform was very slow. By 1939 the Indian Civil Service was only about one-quarter Indian.

Beneath this British-dominated administrative structure, there were some million government workers doing what their masters told them to do. Although since 1858 admission to the ICS was 'race blind', the examinations were held in England, and the age limit of entrants was lowered to favour British candidates. In Nigeria, under Lugard's system of Indirect Rule, the plan was for the 'civilized' rulers to hand over eventually to the indigenous inhabitants. In practice, all the important administrative jobs were given to whites, and Lugard had a particular prejudice against educated Africans.[9] Enthusiastic imperialists were enchanted by the exoticism of the Exhibition. 'Dusky figures flit about the spot as if one was actually in Africa, instead of a few miles from Charing Cross.'[10] Black faces, today as numerous in Wembley as white ones, were a quaint oddity, though the writer felt the Exhibition area was so large that he could have done with a few Zulu rickshaw boys to assist the footsore. Actual Africans felt patronized. The Union of Students of Black Descent felt that their kinsmen were demeaned by being made into exhibits in a raree show, and wondered why it had been necessary to harp on African sorcery and witchcraft in the Exhibition catalogue.[11]

There were other Empire Exhibitions before the Second World War, most notably in Dunedin, New Zealand, in 1925–6, in Johannesburg in 1936–7, and in Glasgow in 1938, a more ambitious event even than Wembley, in a modern Art Deco stadium, which attracted over 12 million visitors.[12] In Wembley, there were considerably fewer visitors in 1925 than in 1924 and there was not the money to keep the Exhibition open at a loss. The Great Exhibition, which was in essence a trade exhibition, had made such a colossal profit that they had been able, with the proceeds, to build the Albert Hall, and the South Kensington museums. The Wembley Empire Exhibition, which was a political propaganda exercise, had made a loss. The stadium, which had cost £750,000 to build, was sold to the Wembley Stadium and Greyhound Racecourse Ltd for £150,000. They built a huge car park, capable of holding four thousand vehicles, opened a cocktail bar, a restaurant and a luxury smoking lounge. The Empire had literally gone to the dogs.

The Exhibition happened against a background of Indian discontent. The suave Harrow- and Cambridge-educated Jawaharlal Nehru, brought up as a Westernizing playboy lawyer, had had his political awakening after Amritsar, and been twice to prison for joining a picket-line in Allahabad to discourage Indians from buying British-made fabric. This well-groomed and beautifully attired young man made a surprising disciple of the Mahatma, and there were many features in Gandhi's campaigns which he found cringe-making, especially his repeated reference to the coming of Ram rajya, the rule of the Hindu god, Ram. Nehru also remained unconvinced by Gandhi's insistence upon non-violence as the only way forward to achieve their political goals. But there is nothing like prison for radicalizing the most unlikely persons, as the British had demonstrated again and again in Ireland. By putting this fastidious young man in a fetid Indian gaol in Nabha state, where he contracted typhoid fever, the British had found themselves another formidable adversary. In the late Twenties, the Nehrus moved to Geneva for a few years, where Jawaharlal focused his thoughts in writings such as 'The psychology of Indian nationalism'. He visited Britain, and was shocked by the changes since his undergraduate days, finding the miners and their families cowed by fear in the aftermath of the General Strike. The proximity to the League of Nations in Geneva offered a hope of a supportive international community outside the Empire.[13]

The first time Malcolm Muggeridge sailed to India on the P&O liner the SS *Morea*, bound for a stint as a teacher at a missionary college in Alwaye in Travancore, he was struck by a transformation in the passengers. 'They had come aboard as more or less ordinary middle- or lower-middle-class English, with perhaps, in the second class, the latter preponderating. Now they were changing, the men becoming more assertive, the ladies more la-di-da; as it were, moving farther and farther away from Bournemouth and Bexhill and nearer and nearer to Memsahib status and invitations to Government House. Luncheon was a tiffin, a whisky and soda, a chota peg, and instead of calling for a steward, the cry was: "Boy!"'[14] Muggeridge also noted the fact that when they had passed Port Said, these people brought out their sola topees, heavy, helmet-like items of headgear which, it was believed, protected them from the fateful glare of the sun. 'Now that the Raj is over,' he wrote in 1972, 'practically no one wears a topee, with no ill consequences. It is an interesting example of how medical lore, like trade, follows the flag.'[15]

The racialism and snobbery which the Raj appeared to need for its fuel were obviously a source of dismay to any intelligent observer. This is probably what accounts for the high status attributed to E. M. Forster's novel *A Passage to India*, published in the year of the British Empire Exhibition at Wembley. Forster fell in love with a young Muslim Indian, which is what occasioned his first visit to the subcontinent. The love was not consummated, or indeed returned, but its sentimentality colours his account of the British in India. With the perspective of time, we can see that Kipling, more than all the British writers who visited India, really had an instinctive feel for the place, and he was the only writer of first rank to emerge from the Raj. The Left found it intolerable that a great writer, as Kipling unquestionably is, should have been a reactionary who supported General Dyer and was the cousin of Stanley Baldwin. It needed a 'radical' work of genius to counteract the Kipling influence and seized on Forster's unsympathetic account of the petty snobberies, and sexual frigidities of a British local governor and his womenfolk. There is a little submysticism thrown in, with the old lady, Mrs Moore, having some kind of instinctive feeling for the wisdom of the East; and there is the rather lame conclusion in which the good Englishman, Fielding, by inference homosexual, wishes the Raj could end so that he could enjoy real 'friend-ships' with the Indians – especially, the reader is left to suppose, with the highly sexed but unfortunately heterosexual Dr Aziz, who has been wrongly accused of raping one of the Englishwomen in the Marabar caves. It is a much less sympathetic, and much less religious book than Kipling's *Kim*, the story of the half-caste Irish boy and the Guru, observing all castes, religions and types as they become embroiled in the Great Game. Perhaps political prejudices based upon sexual preference are, at base, just as racialist as those based on crude ideology. In any event, Forster's book might have seemed more charming to posterity if it had not had 'classic' status thrust upon it for political reasons. Perhaps it was the burden of this knowledge which silenced Forster; he never published any other fiction in his lifetime, and he lived forty-five years after the novel's publication.

Within twenty-two years of the British Empire Exhibition India had its independence and the dissolution of the Empire, predicted as inevitable once Ireland went, had effectively happened.

20

The ABC of Economics

It would be a bold person who predicted that any institution, or system, would last for ever. But capitalism has lasted much longer than its Victorian obituarists and their Marxian followers in the twentieth century would have predicted. The company, that Victorian creation,* has proved more flexible and in many ways more productive of human wealth and happiness than the empire or even in some cases than the nation-state. Today we live with the complexities and moral ambiguities of that. Global capitalism has its vociferous critics, and understandably so. But what cannot be denied, as we sit in the twenty-first century, is that the hopes and fears felt during the late 1920s and early 1930s about the actual survival of world capitalism were all groundless. We may hate capitalism. We may want to smash the windows of McDonald's and Starbucks when we find their branches in every corner of the Earth. But we know that the earlier fear of capitalism's extinction was simply ill-founded. This knowledge colours our perspective, and makes any memory of those years poignant, painful, at times unbearable. No student of the first hundred years of Christianity can fail to come to terms with the fact that St Paul and friends all believed that they were living in the last days, that Time itself was about to run out like sand in the hourglass, that the reckoning was coming. What happened after that is the fascinating thing called Christian history, but if the founding fathers of Christianity had been right in their predictions, there would not have been such a thing as Christian history or any other kind of history. There would have simply been a New Heaven and a New Earth.

The terrible fear felt by those running the world in the late 1920s was of a comparable order. Karl Marx was the Apocalypt. Capitalism would not work.

After the war, economics dominated all political considerations and debates. Some Europeans believed in Sound Money, based on the gold standard. In Britain, these individuals thought that if the pound could

---

* The 1862 Companies Act in England laid the foundations of modern shareholder capitalism. In May 1863 the French passed laws to allow business people to establish joint stock companies with full limited liability provided the capital did not exceed 20 million francs. When Germany was created in 1871, it was not long before it too became a country which encouraged the growth of companies, though German law, unlike America's Antitrust Act, was much more tolerant than other economies of monopolies.

be strong against the dollar, if its price could be fixed to the gold standard, then the social and political costs – potentially high unemployment and all its degradations, personal tragedies and real dangers to the stability of the state – would be worth paying. Others believed that the war had changed everything and that a non-interventionist state, a completely laissez-faire economic policy, was no longer a possibility. Political figures therefore had to make economic decisions, they had to be one thing or another.

But lurking behind many of their deliberations, and haunting all but the sanest minds, was the fear which hindsight knows to be completely false: namely that money itself, as had already happened to the weaker currencies, most notably to the mark in Weimar Germany, would lose its value, capitalism would implode, stock markets would crash beyond any hope of recovery and the world which had begun with such high hopes in the industrial revolution, and which had been speeded on its way by the abolition of the British Corn Laws, would come to an end. Modern civilization, its manufacturing bases, its large cities, its evolved democratic politics, its liberalism, its very culture, including a free and popular Press, had all grown directly out of capitalism. They would be unimaginable without it. Was the End in sight? The bourgeoisie and the rich, with savings and investments, obviously enough, dreaded this. Sane working-class people, knowing what such fluctuations and disasters did to jobs and prices, also dreaded it. Only apocalyptic Marxists and anarchist revolutionaries could look forward to it with rapture.

Some terrible fluctuations and disasters did indeed occur. It is hard for us, who know that the ultimate disaster was eventually averted, to remember this. We have to stretch our sympathies to recollect the anxieties which fed so many completely false notions of economics, notions which in turn led so many people into political stances which are grotesque to hindsight.

In T. S. Eliot's cryptic rhyme 'A Cooking Egg' we read:

> I shall not want Honour in Heaven
> For I shall meet Sir Philip Sidney
> And have talk with Coriolanus
> And other heroes of that kidney.

The words were published in 1920, and they reflected the fact that the old world, the world of the Hero, had been displaced in the aftermath of the war by the capitalist and the businessman.

I shall not want Capital in Heaven
For I shall meet Sir Alfred Mond.
We two shall lie together, lapt
In a five per cent. Exchequer Bond.[1]

Sir Alfred Mond (1868–1930) was one of the great industrialists and financiers of the early twentieth century, a pioneer of huge manufacturing corporations. The young son of a Jewish immigré from Kassel, he was educated at Cheltenham College and Cambridge, and then went into his father's business, the great chemical firm of Brunner, Mond and Co. Mond Junior was one of the great liberal pioneers of modern business. He believed that old laissez-faire was no longer the way to produce general prosperity, and he was an opponent of confrontational approaches to industrial relations. Economies, and businesses, needed planning. He believed that by expansion and conglomeration, businesses could realize more capital and provide better conditions for the workforce. He virulently opposed lockouts and strikes as methods of settling disputes, and thought there should be profit-sharing, employee shareholding and what would today be called a stakeholder economy. 'In the industry in which I am mainly interested,' he wrote in *Industry and Politics* (1927), 'we have succeeded in avoiding for a period of over fifty years any serious industrial dispute. This has been largely due to a liberal, far-seeing policy, which did not consist in waiting for claims to be made and then yielding to them reluctantly, but in foreseeing reasonable demands and in granting them even before they were asked.'

In 1926, the year of the General Strike, Mond was responsible for the consolidation of smaller firms under the umbrella of Imperial Chemical Industries (ICI), with £95 million of capital and a vast influence throughout the economy not only of Britain but of the Empire as a whole. He was also chairman of Amalgamated Anthracite Collieries, which effectively controlled most Welsh anthracite production from the late 1920s onwards; as well as the International Nickel Company of Canada, the Mond Nickel Company, South Staffordshire Mond Gas (Power and Heating) Company, the Westminster Bank, and the Industrial Financial Investment Corporation. The year after the strike, Mond formed a committee of employers to meet Ben Turner, the chairman of the Trade Union Congress. Observers such as Hilaire Belloc saw this agreement as the end of the working man's chance of freedom. The unions had thereby abandoned the struggle for joint ownership of business, and by denying themselves the right to negotiate wages except through the union they had in effect made their members into wage slaves. Years before, Belloc had written a book called *The Servile State*, in which he had tried to demonstrate that socialism and capitalism were both systems which enslaved men and women, reduced their very capacity to be independent. As Ezra Pound was to put it, 'The minute I cook my own dinner or nail four boards together into a chair, I escape from the whole cycle of Marxian economics. I know, not from theory but from practice, that you can live infinitely better with a very little money and a lot of spare time, than with more money and less time. Time is not money but it is almost everything else.'[2] Fine if you are a poet, living a Bohemian life in Rapallo, and can hope for a bit of money now and again from publishers, magazine editors, patrons and the like; less easy if you are an unskilled man with a family to support in an industrial town in the late 1920s.

There is no doubt that the 'Marxian cycle' imprisoned millions of lives in the Western world, but what practical alternative could Ruskin in the Victorian age or Belloc and his friend G. K. Chesterton or the radical fascism of Ezra Pound offer in the twentieth century? The idea that more freedom would result if everyone had three acres and a cow was not one which any existing political system would realistically promote. The Distributists, as the enthusiasts for this way of thinking called themselves, could think negatively: it was all right for a grocer to have one shop, but not when he wanted to own two shops, or a chain of a hundred.[3] But does money work like that?

As well as being a businessman, Sir Alfred Mond was also in the House of Commons, sitting as a Liberal representing Chester from 1906 to 1910, then as an MP for Swansea from 1910 to 1923. Finally, from 1924 to 1928 he represented the rural market constituency of Carmarthen in West Wales. His conversion to British Empire protectionism à la Beaverbrook led to his joining the Conservative party, but his constituents in Carmarthen asked him to continue as their MP, which he did until taking a peerage with the title Lord Melchett. In 1923, when Philip Snowden denounced the capitalist system in the House of Commons, Mond replied with what became in many people's eyes a classic defence of liberal capitalism. He spoke of his father's risk-taking and altruism, of the dangers they had endured to build up a huge business, and of the socially beneficial results. His father, his business partners and Mond himself had, he claimed, given work and prosperity to thousands, an enterprise which 'could never have been commenced under any Socialist system that I have ever known'.[4]

It is a curious feature of twentieth-century history that the businessmen who created what wealth there was for the majority of the population were automatically lumped together with the villains. Even when an enterprise produced as many jobs, and as much money for other people, as

ICI, a figure like Mond could still be written about as if he were Mr Melmotte, the cunning and entirely fraudulent capitalist of Trollope's *The Way We Live Now*. In his *English Journey*, a sort of sub-Cobbett ramble round the nation published in 1934, J. B. Priestley dismissed the 'shoddy, greedy, profit grabbing, joint-stock company industrial system'. C. S. Lewis, Oxford don and self-appointed Christian pundit, when speaking of Lord Nuffield, said: 'How I hate that man.'[5] Nuffield (1877–1963), who confusingly bore the same name as one of the most celebrated Victorian anti-industrialists and socialists, William Morris, started his own bicycle shop in Longwall, Oxford, with a capital of £4. He graduated to making motorcycles, and by 1910 he was a motor-car manufacturer and engineer, pioneering the Morris Oxford in the 1912 Motor Show. It was a fantastic car; the original 8.9 hp two-seater did 35–50 miles to the gallon and had speeds of up to 50 miles per hour. During the war, his Cowley factory concentrated upon making munitions, but he had already pioneered the 11.9 Morris Cowley, and in the postwar boom of 1919–20 he was selling 280 cars a month. He saw out the slump of 1921 by reducing his prices, and by 1923 Morris Motors were producing 20,000 cars a year; by 1926, 50,000, some one-third of the entire national output. He owned firms which made bodies, engines, radiators. During the Thirties, Morris Motors Ltd would expand to take over the MG Car Company and the Wolseley Company. He brought levels of prosperity to the working classes in Oxford which would have been unthinkable if they had all been living in the beautiful neomedieval pre-industrial world of his namesake the visionary William Morris. By 1926 he had endowed the King Alfonso XIII chair of Spanish studies at Oxford. During his lifetime he gave away some £30 million; he endowed a new medical school at Oxford, a residential Royal College of Surgeons, he was a benefactor to dozens of hospitals, and established major orthopaedic hospitals in Oxford, Australia, New Zealand and South Africa. He also endowed the Nuffield Provincial Hospitals Trust, as well as founding Nuffield College, with the primary aim of studying social, political and economic problems. The Nuffield Foundation continues to this day to finance research programmes and pioneering activities of all kinds.

It is to institutions founded by capitalistic benefactions from the likes of Mond and Nuffield that refugees from socialist states have gratefully come; not the other way around. Some British workers, especially coal miners, and dockers, were communists, but very few chose to seek work in the Soviet Union. Nuffield's car manufacturers at the Cowley works might have been a blight on the landscape as far as the nearby Oxford dons were concerned – and it is not difficult to guess what John Ruskin would have made of them. But they were not all clamouring at the first opportunity to go and find work in Stalin's Russia. And yet almost all intellectual people, from left such as Priestley or right such as T. S. Eliot, have regarded industrial capitalism as sinister.

In many areas, as at the very beginning of British expansion in the East India Company, it was not trade which followed the flag, but the other way about. British companies, circumscribed by the tariffs imposed by many of the European powers in the pre-First World War world, were not content to be exporters, but went abroad and became multinationals. William Lever, the British soap king, who died in 1925, was Britain's biggest manufacturing employer. At home he built Port Sunlight, a model town for his workers. He also got round protective tariffs in Germany, France and America by building factories in those places, as well as in Australasia. By 1914, roughly half Britain's largest companies had at least one factory abroad; Dunlop, Courtaulds and Vickers are only three famous examples. Like the Germans, the British established overseas trading companies in South America and the Far East. There was abuse and exploitation of cheap labour by many overseas firms, and imperialist despoiling, but there was also wealth creation. Hong Kong was the creation of Swire and Jardine Matheson as much as it was made by politicians.[6]

Clearly, the wealth created by these companies extended far beyond the immediate confines of their offices and factory gates. Investments of private individuals and corporations, and ultimately the stability of governments and whole societies, came to depend upon the health of international capital. 'We are in the presence of a new organization of society,' moaned President Wilson in 1919. 'Our life has broken away from the past.'[7] He was just as gloomy about the prospect of businessmen replacing statesmen as T. S. Eliot, or Belloc and Chesterton or Good Ole Ezra might have been.

But no matter whether they liked what had happened, or understood it, the men and women of the 1920s were in a new world, one where for many the Company, the Firm, was in effect the political and economic unit to which they belonged. This was as true of a Birmingham chocolate worker who lived in Bournville, the model village created by the Quaker cocoa kings the Cadbury family, as it was for the Welsh miner living in a valley where the only work was down the pits. When life was prosperous, it could be seen that ever-expanding industrial capitalism was the cause of that prosperity. But what protection existed for the victims of its voracious profit-appetite, its ruthless preparedness to strip assets, throw employees out of work, destroy commercial rivals? The wage-slaves, fearful of unemployment, crowd into the factories to work longer and longer hours for more and more limited wages, to produce quantities of stuff which perhaps the world does not need, in order to make money for the very few; and all, as Ezra says in *The ABC of Economics*, because 'some fool or skunk plays mean'. This was the nub of the fear which made the people of those times become Marxists and fascists, the fear that their lives were being controlled by a few cigar-smoking figures in panelled dining-rooms, manipulating the world for their own concealed and sinister ends. What could be seen, and what was freely admitted by the industrial magnates themselves, was that they were indeed the ones with power. When, for example, the second Labour government of 1929 tried to repeal the Eight Hours Act which had been passed after the General Strike, the colliery owners responded by saying they would introduce drastic wage reductions. The Miners Federation would not have had any power to resist, and nor could the politicians help them.[8]

If Stanley Baldwin and his Conservative government failed to see the Wall Street Crash coming in 1929, they had their ignorance in common with almost everyone else in the Western world. They were in any case thrown out of office before the crash happened. The electorate was shocked by Baldwin's claim that the unemployment problem was 'greatly exaggerated'. There were 1.1 million people unemployed when he called the election in May 1929. The previous year, Baldwin had brought in the Flappers' Bill, as it was nicknamed, to give women the same voting rights as men, that is the vote at twenty-one rather than thirty. One Conservative member suggested that once all women had the right to vote there would be no Conservatives returned to Parliament at all. The socialists would promise the working girl heaven on earth, and get all their votes. This was not necessarily the case. Mrs Pankhurst, the great suffrage leader, joined the Conservative party in 1926 and was adopted as a prospective candidate for Whitechapel and St George's in the East, one of the most deprived areas of London's East End. She was never elected to Parliament. She lived just long enough to see her lifetime's dreams for her fellow women come true. She died in June 1928 just a few weeks after 21-year-old women got the vote.

The Labour party won its second election victory outright. Ramsay MacDonald no longer depended upon the support of the Liberals when he took office in June 1929. They immediately brought in Unemployment Insurance Acts, and gave £25 million towards building up dole funds, and a further £25 million to schemes of public works. J. H. Thomas, as Lord Privy Seal, was given special responsibility to work on the problem of unemployment with the assistance of the leftist first commissioner of works, George Lansbury, and the non-cabinet member, the Chancellor of the Duchy of Lancaster, Sir Oswald Mosley, Bt, who had left the Conservatives in protest against the Black and Tans' thuggery in Ireland and was now a rising 'hopeful' of the Labour party. It was announced that the school leaving age would be raised to fifteen from 1931 onwards and the King's Speech, on 25 June, spoke of his government's intention to 'deal effectively' with unemployment.[9]

The all but incredible fact is that the second Labour government had come into power without any coherent policy on the central economic question of the day: that is, whether they supported a controlled economy – as for example Sidney Webb did, who as the newly ennobled Lord Passfield sat in the cabinet as Dominions and Colonial Secretary, or whether like the Chancellor of the Exchequer they 'believed fanatically in the Gold Standard'.[10] The most outstanding economic intelligence of the age was a man who was a member of neither the Conservative nor the Labour party, and who had left the employment of the government in 1919 in protest against the Versailles treaty.

Immensely tall, mustachioed, lofty in all senses, Cambridgey, John Maynard Keynes (1883–1946) is a name which still divides all who speak or think about twentieth-century British history. His heyday came decades after his death, when in the 1960s and 1970s the governments of the Western world appeared with disastrous results to put his most famous ideas into practice: namely that governments can borrow their way out of recessions, and that inflation, within limits, is good for economies. These are both distortions of what Keynes ever actually wrote or advised in his lifetime. But just as Marx was no Marxist, Keynes, who died in 1946, was no 1960s Keynesian.

As economic adviser to Lloyd George's government he had attended the Peace Conference and left in order to publish the damning indictment entitled *The Economic Consequences of the Peace*. His view was that the politicians had concentrated so myopically on political solutions that they had failed to see that the only way to build a lasting peace in Europe was by getting the economy right. The old days of laissez-faire were over, and some form of controlled economy was to be necessary to weather the vicissitudes ahead. The French would always see his book as a piece of troublemaking, if not a cause of the Second World War itself. By making the thinking classes in England believe that German war reparations were both unjust and economically unviable, he had weakened the case for resistance to German rearmament. That was the view, still aired from time to time, most vociferously expressed by Étienne Mantoux in *The Carthaginian Peace or the Economic Consequences of Mr Keynes*, published after Keynes's death. Keynes's book alerted the world to the fact that inter-Ally war debts and German reparations were a recipe not merely for economic but for political disaster. We can now see these factors to be the 'giant step in the descent' to totalitarianism and world war.[11]

It was Keynes who was the first economist to break the news to a world very unwilling to hear it, that unemployment was unavoidable in the current economic situation. It was bound to come, but there were solutions, or at least ways in which it could be drastically reduced. These were based on control of the interest rates, and a flexible currency not tied to the gold standard. The only party which had taken up his ideas with any enthusiasm in the 1929 General Election had been the Liberal party, and one could perhaps say that two of the greatest tragedies of British political life in this period were first that Lloyd George was the Prime Minister who negotiated the peace in 1919, and second that he was not the prime minister who oversaw the economic crises of the early 1930s. He was the only political leader with the stature and national following to have been followed, and the only one who had absorbed Keynes's new teachings. For whatever the rights and wrongs of the neo-Keynesians of the post-1960s era, Keynes in the 1930s was a figure of titanic importance.

Keynes's 1920s were a strange decade. A homosexual, he surprised all his friends by falling in love and making a very happy marriage to Lydia Lopokova, a Russian ballet dancer. His cleverer friends mocked her. 'What a beautiful tree!' she gaily remarked to Wittgenstein. When he glared at her and replied: 'What do you mean?' she burst into tears.[12] 'She hums in his wake, the great man's wife,' Virginia Woolf somewhat wistfully observed. Keynes adored her and loved her strange English usage. After a wedding, she once spoke of Jesus 'fomenting wine out of water at Cannes'. 'I had tea with Lady Grey,' she said on another occasion. 'She has an ovary which she likes to show everyone.'[13]

His life with Lydia was divided between Cambridge, where he enjoyed college business and college dinners at King's, and gave lectures on economics, and London and Charleston on the Sussex Downs, where he mixed with poets, painters and the clever and the clever-clever. The worst possible news which could come to this ballet-loving couple in the summer of 1929 was surely the death of Diaghilev – in Venice, in August. Lydia, that summer, was taking part in a filmed ballet, the first ballet ever to be inserted into a 'talkie' movie. *Dark Red Roses* was choreographed by George Balanchine with a score from Mussorgsky's *Khovanshchina*. The filming happened at Wembley, and when the news came of Diaghilev's death, the dancers 'crouched on a floor in a little group', as Keynes described it, 'talking memories of him hour after hour. It was an extraordinary scene.'

After this sad event, the summer vacation continued. The Cambridge term began as usual. Neither Keynes nor any other economic pundit in the Western world knew what was going to happen. Then, in October, he wrote from Cambridge to Lydia in London: 'Wall Street did have a go yesterday. Did you read about it? The biggest crash ever recorded.' Overnight, the certainty which underpinned millions of human lives in Europe and America was suddenly removed. The rich became poor. The poor became unemployable. The human race which had been lulled into feeling that everything since the war had been calming down, getting better, becoming more prosperous, had the experience of placing its foot on what it thought was solid earth and finding itself hurtling through the bottomless air.

21

Puzzles and Pastoral

On 16 January 1930, a letter appeared in *The Times* from Lieutenant-Commander A. C. Powell, Royal Navy:

> Sir, I am interested to see that you are including a cross-word [*sic*] puzzle in your *Weekly Edition*.
>
> Would it not be an additional attraction to your many readers – of whom I am pleased to be one – if the same cross-word puzzle were reproduced on one day of the week in your daily edition?[1]

The same page of the newspaper reported a service which had been organized the previous day at St Martin-in-the-Fields for the Howard League for Penal Reform, at which the Archbishop of York, Dr William Temple, had said in his sermon that 'it seemed to him quite plain that it would be for the benefit of society if the death penalty were abolished'.

The archbishop's suggestion fell on deaf ears among the governing classes, but the lieutenant-commander's idea took off. There were, inevitably, some voices of dissent. 'Let me entreat you to keep *The Times* from puzzles of all sorts. Space there is precious and prestige also,'[1] wrote M. Miller of 69 Warwick Square, SW1. M. Miller was either so pressed for space, or so jealous of prestige, or perhaps both, as not to be able to explain what she (or he) meant. The day that she (or he) wrote, *The Times* carried the news that Mr Patel had resigned as the president of the legislative assembly in India because the British had ratted on their assurance that India would be granted Dominion status – that is, treated like white countries in the Empire such as Australia and Canada and New Zealand. Sir Arthur Ponsonby became Baron Ponsonby of Shulbree, and Canon Spencer Carpenter became Master of the Temple.

Nearly all the subsequent correspondents, however, as a naval arms conference got under way between five great powers – Britain, France, Italy, Japan and America – clamoured for a cross-word.

The Times was the broadsheet newspaper with the largest circulation, and it had an importance in British public life which is difficult in these days to appreciate. It was the in-house journal of the Establishment, a term first used in 1923. Whereas Northcliffe had used it, in his days as proprietor, to scare and criticize the government, under the new proprietor, Major J. J. Astor,[2] who reappointed Geoffrey Dawson as editor,[3] it was a small-c conservative paper, intensely cautious in foreign policy, and stuffy in its attitude to change.

Over the matter of the crossword, Dawson commissioned his assistant R. M. Barrington-Ward, later to be editor of the paper (1941–48), to find a suitable crossword-setter. Barrington-Ward asked his friend Robert Bell, of the *Observer*, and Bell asked his son Adrian, then a thirty-year-old writer who had gone to live in the country to do a little farming and finish a novel. Adrian Bell had neither compiled nor completed a crossword puzzle in his life. He was offered three guineas per puzzle, and agreed to set two puzzles per week. (At this time, the small ads of the paper offered housemaids £40 per annum for full-time employment.) He was to be the paper's crossword editor and chief setter for the next forty years. He set puzzle number one, and he set puzzle number 10,000. 'I think you must be near dotty to spend your life setting crosswords,' he engagingly said in August 1970.[4] Bell made only a few mistakes, one of which was to misspell the surname Rossetti in one of his puzzles.

Before long the crossword lost its hyphen and became a regular feature of *The Times*. Like so many unmistakably British institutions, the crossword began in the United States. Evolving from other acrostic puzzles, the crossword proper first appeared in the Christmas edition of the *New York World* in 1913, set and edited by Arthur Wynne. By the 1920s crossword mania gripped America. Late in 1924 a man did a survey of all the passengers travelling between New York and Boston by train and found no fewer than 60 per cent engrossed in the puzzle. The *New York World* puzzle was one of the most popular, set by Gelett Burgess, author of

I never saw a Purple Cow
I never hope to see one;
But I can tell you, anyhow,
I'd rather see than be one.

Of his fans, addicts, victims, or whatever noun would be appropriate, he wrote:

The fans they chew their pencils,
The fans they beat their wives.
They look up words for extinct birds
They lead such puzzling lives.[5]

At this date, *The Times* in London had mocked the Americans for their crossword enthusiasm. AN ENSLAVED AMERICA was their headline[6]

to describe the 'menace' which was 'making devastating inroads on the working hours of every rank of society'.[7] Once the mania had crossed the Atlantic, of course, it became as English as, well, as female members of Parliament, as Winston Churchill and Agatha Christie,* as scrambled eggs and the briefcase and the ballot box, all of which had American origins or antecedents.

It was not long, however, after adopting the American pastime of doing crosswords, before readers of The Times were displaying a number of very genuinely British sophistications. It became the pastime of the Establishment classes. 'Do you think you could find me a copy in which the crossword puzzle has not been solved?' asked a weary bishop at the Lambeth Conference.[8]

To establish its élitist status, The Times included a Latin crossword on 1 March. It was not a cryptic crossword, it simply expected readers to be well-versed in those Latin authors read in public schools and at Oxford and Cambridge – especially Horace. Nearly all the poems cited are by Horace, and most of them the Odes. 'Horace calls Tarentum this' (ans. Lacedaemonium). 'Care rides behind me' was the only clue for equitem, a reference to the third book of Odes, Ode 1, line 40. 'One of the most remarkable results of this experiment in the crossword puzzle', crowed the editorial, 'is the overwhelming evidence it has brought us that the best brains in the country – Ministers of the Crown, Provosts of Colleges, King's Counsel and the rest – all engaged in the most arduous labour – find these little games the very thing to fill up odd moments'.[9] But they found them more than that. They found the little games the very thing about which to be aggressively competitive with one another. While Britain lagged behind in its serious attempts to solve the unemployment crisis, or to revive British industry, and while party politics went completely into quiescence, the 'best brains in the country' vied with one another to demonstrate trivial nimbleness of intellect combined with effortlessly worn classical erudition.

In the middle of the summer holidays, Sir Josiah Stamp wrote from St Jean-de-Luz the rather touching boast that he was able to complete the puzzle in just under an hour. Stamp (1880–1941) had been a civil servant with particular interest in tax. After the First World War, he had left the Civil Service and joined ICI, as well as becoming a director of the London Midland and Scottish Railway. As the son-in-law of the American General Dawes – he of the committee formed to make sense of the German reparations situation in 1925 – he was quietly pro-German and pro-American. A genial man, loaded with honorary degrees and

---

* Both, of course, half-American.

honorific titles – he became Baron Stamp in 1938 – he wrote in that pompous tone which was no doubt his natural idiom, but which seemed to be adopted by all but the best letter-writers to *The Times* until very recently. The letter-writers, especially when being archly facetious, adopted the orotund locutions of a butler in an Ivy Compton-Burnett novel. 'After a week's chequered but salutary acquaintance with the entertaining mind of your crossword puzzler, I correctly completed his effort of Wednesday last with – or in spite of – spasmodic and guerilla assistance, in 50 minutes,' wrote Sir Josiah.[10]

This was the month in which General Von Hindenburg died and Hitler became Leader of Germany. He did not need to take Hindenburg's place as Reichspräsident. Having been leader of his party, he was now leader of his nation. Simply, *der Führer*. *The Times* reported that Herr Hitler had flown in a monoplane to Hamburg. Thirty-eight thousand uniformed Nazis had saluted him on his way into town from Fuhlsbüttel aerodrome.

Sir Austen Chamberlain, now retired as cabinet minister, though still in the Commons, and not destined to have as much to do with Herr Hitler as his half-brother Neville,* wrote to tell Sir Josiah that he could beat his record. He himself had completed a puzzle in 41 minutes. But, 'Ask the Provost of Eton', i.e. M. R. James the ghost-story writer – who 'measures the time required for boiling his breakfast egg by that needed for the solution of your daily crossword – and he hates a hard-boiled egg'.[11]

Opposite Chamberlain's letter, *Times* readers could see that the Krupp factory on the Ruhr had started a youth training scheme and taken on 800 boys for skilled labour. After frequent visits to America, the German steel bosses had revolutionized means of production.

It was left to P. G. Wodehouse three days later to admit, along with the great majority, that he found crosswords – well, a puzzle. While the editorial piously intoned, 'every friend of Germany will hope that she will quickly recover from her present troubles and that as a strong, free and united nation, she may become a powerful factor in the maintenance of European peace'. R. Ruggles Gates – Marie Stopes's 'ex' – sent in to the letters page on the same day a contribution about the ethnicity of Jews. ('As regards the Jewish people through the world they are probably no more homogeneous than the Nordic, Alpine or Mediterranean races, but they have retained a racial consciousness which has long since been replaced in other peoples by the spirit of nationalism.') Wodehouse, however, was still on the crossword:

* Austen Chamberlain died in 1937.

Sir, on behalf of the great race of rabbits, those humble strivers who like myself have never yet succeeded in solving an entire *Times* crossword puzzle, I strongly resent these Austen Chamberlains and what not flaunting their skill in your columns. Rubbing salt in the wounds is what I call it. To a man who has been beating his head against the wall for twenty minutes over a single anagram it is g. and wormwood to read a statement like that one about the Provost of Eton and the eggs. In conclusion may I commend your public spirit in putting the good old emu back into circulation again as you did a few days ago? We of the *canaille* know that the Sun-God Ra has apparently retired from active work – are intensely grateful for the occasional emu.[12]

The cryptic crossword and the whodunnit mystery story were two distinctive products of their time, expressions no doubt of the belief that if one could only worry at a problem for long enough it would have a single simple solution: Keynesian or Marxist economic theory, Roman Catholic, communist or fascist doctrine. Many of the brightest minds of the age, if not necessarily the most analytic, while enjoying the mystery stories of Ellery Queen or Agatha Christie, and priding themselves on the speed with which they solved the crossword puzzle, were drawn fatefully towards ideologies, systems. Ronald Knox (1888–1957) was an addict of puzzles of all kinds, and the author of *A Book of Acrostics*. The book reeks almost heart-rendingly of late Victorian innocence, of parlour games in a large, intelligent, well-meaning upper-middle-class family. (Knox's father was a bishop.) 'To break off her engagement if she'd the intention/What place on the Thames would the young lady mention?' – answer Goring. 'If the Zoo were for a joy-ride through the streets of London hauled,/After what old-fashioned weapon might the vehicle be called?' Arquebus. You can almost hear the groans from the assembled company at the atrocious pun. He also wrote humorous articles for *Punch*, a magazine of which his brother E. V. (know variously as Eddie and Evoe) became the editor. Another brother, Wilfrid, was a distinguished New Testament scholar and Anglican holy man. Another brother, Dilly, a religious non-believer, was librarian of King's College, Cambridge. 'During the Thirties,' wrote his niece Penelope Fitzgerald, 'finding that smoking and patience [i.e. the card game] were not sufficient as alternative tranquilliser and counter-irritant to the active mind, Dilly suddenly produced a new way of writing poetry.'[13] Each line had to end with a word of the same form, but with a different vowel, the vowels 'of course' coming in their proper order, a, e, i, o, u or the equivalent sounds in English. On the death of A. E. Housman, Dilly wrote:

Sad though the news, how sad
Of thee the poet dead!
But still thy poems abide –
There Death, the unsparing god
Himself dare not intrude.[14]

Dilly would put his crossword mind to brilliant and patriotic use deciphering Enigma (the German electro-mechanical enciphering system) in the 1940s. In the Thirties he contented himself with doodles, and with an all but impenetrable translation of Herodas's all but impenetrable *Mimiambi* for the Loeb Classics. Ronald, known as Ronnie, was perhaps the most celebrated of the brothers in his lifetime, partly because he wrote detective stories. Of these, his niece wrote:

Between 1926 (*The Viaduct Murder*) and 1937 (*Double Cross Purposes*) he wrote six detective stories. All of them, even the earliest, were backward looking. To feel at home in them, you need to be familiar with *Bradshaw's Railway Timetables*, canoeing on the upper reaches of the Thames, vicarages, gas taps, and country house-parties in which the first duty is consideration for one's hostess . . . The solutions to the mysteries are most scrupulously set out, and page references are given, in case the reader has missed the clues. As a novelist, Ronnie was not strong on characterisation.[15]

His biographer and friend Evelyn Waugh tells us that 'at the time there was a limited but eager public for these puzzles . . . None was more ingenious than he, more scrupulous in the provision of clues, more logically complete in his solutions.'[16]

Ronald Knox belonged to that Etonian generation which had seen a whole generation blighted and in many cases destroyed by the First World War. Before the war, he was a wit, a president of the Oxford Union in the days when that institution was still a nursery of statesmen, and a scholar. His life was an elegy for the never-forgotten dead. In 1917 he became a Roman Catholic, and was ordained two years later, eventually becoming the Roman Catholic chaplain to his old university, Oxford. He always refused to have a telephone installed in his chaplaincy. ('I hate using the instrument; I hate being interrupted by bells; I hate enquiries from the editors of Sunday newspapers about the existence of a future life.')[17] The chaplaincy was only available for males, and what is more, males of a limited educational background – Eton and the larger Benedictine or Jesuit boarding schools. Roman Catholic women were directed to a convent in Cherwell Edge and grammar-school-educated

Roman Catholic men were advised to worship at one of the churches in the town.[18]

In Ronald Knox's own case, Roman Catholicism, like crossword puzzles and acrostics and detective stories, seems to have worked for him like a systematic exclusion of experience as much as one which sought to explore its complexities. To read his works of apologetics, such as a correspondence with the then agnostic, eventually Catholic, Arnold Lunn, *Difficulties*, is to be amazed by the breezy way in which Knox sees Roman Catholicism as a perfect solution. Subjects which must by definition be insoluble mysteries, such as a reason for supposing the Almighty to be omniscient, are rapped out on the typewriter, no doubt with pipe in mouth, in about as much time as it took to compose an acrostic. He is prepared to defend anything, even his Church's condemnation of Galileo – 'the congregations condemned his teaching while it was, in their view, still unproved'. Burning witches was not so much cruel as 'in accordance with the notions of the time'.[19] These strange letters were exchanged in 1932. In the Soviet Union, the five-year plan was resulting in widespread starvation and 'purges' of tens of thousands of people from the party. Japan had invaded Manchuria. In Germany, the Weimar Republic was teetering to its collapse, and in Britain, with no sign of the government knowing how to cope with the unemployment crisis, debts to the United States grew and grew. Every Western power lived with the perpetual fear that its currency would cease to have any value. As Roman Catholic chaplain at Oxford during the 1930s Ronald Knox not unnaturally found the conversations of the undergraduates about the European situation dismaying. 'Let me see: what country are you boring about now?'[20] Evoe, in the editorial chair at *Punch* in 1933, ran a drawing by Bernard Partridge of Hitler treading Jews underfoot. *Punch* in those days carried serious drawings each week illustrative of what was happening in the world, but even so, the proprietors thought the message of the drawing needed reinforcement with the words ANTI-JEWISH CAMPAIGN written across the sky. Sitting with his friend Beachcomber, J. B. Morton, in the Fleet Street Bar, El Vino, Evoe wondered whether humour had had its day, and the two men would agree that the state of the world had become such that nothing was too absurd or unpleasant to come true.[21]

No wonder the murder mystery was the most popular literary form of its age. Inevitably, when made, or more accurately remade, into successful films or TV serials in our times, the classics from the Golden Age of mystery-writing are made to seem like period pieces, and the directors and designers take pride in the whole visual background to their stories, in the authentic Art Deco furniture, wide-lapelled suits, trilby hats and fedoras, low-backed limousines, in the cloche hats of the ladies and the black dresses with white aprons of the housemaids, as actual or pastiche jazz or big band music plays in the credits. The popularity of such series on TV demonstrates that the 1930s have a glamorous appeal in themselves, but nearly always what gets lost in the adaptation is the actual nature of the stories.

If the revenge tragedy and the simplistic history play were the staple of the Elizabethan and Jacobean theatre audiences it was surely because they and their parents had just lived through a period of bloody civil war, and were holding at bay the thought that England might once again resemble the battlefield of Bosworth or the last scene of *Hamlet* with King, Queen, Prince and friends all corpses. The corpses in the Golden Age mystery stories play a similarly powerful but different role.

Murder on the Orient Express is one of the most perfect of Agatha Christie's stories. It is a very simple revenge story. The train leaves Stamboul for Europe. One of the passengers is murdered during the night, and the train is stuck in a snowdrift in the Balkans. Poirot, the Belgian detective, is conveniently on hand to solve the mystery. An American passenger is the victim, repeatedly stabbed during the night the train is unable to move. Known as Mr Ratchett, it turns out that he was really a gangster named Cassetti, who had kidnapped a baby, little Daisy Armstrong, the child of an English war hero and a famous American tragic actress. When the kidnapped child was delivered back to its parents dead, the mother had given birth to a stillborn child and her worthy husband had shot himself. Cassetti had escaped justice on some legal technicality. Now, twelve suspects are assembled on the train. Could it be, as Poirot eventually realizes, that this villainous figure has been dispatched by a self-appointed 'jury' of odd-balls – the nanny, the valet, the ex-actress, the soldier, the Russian princess, and so forth? Or could it be simply that he was killed by a stranger who has mysteriously escaped into the snows? Poirot, having established the truth of the story, which is indeed that they have all stabbed the villain, allows the second explanation to be offered to the Yugoslavian police when, eventually, the snow clears and the luxury train glides smoothly on its way towards Paris.

Simple as it is, and indeed transparently devoid of any symbolic intention on the author's part, the tale nevertheless shimmers with import. When Poirot meets the villainous Ratchett/Cassetti, 'I had a curious impression. It was as though a wild animal – an animal savage, but savage, you understand – had passed me by.' 'And yet he looked altogether of the most respectable.' 'Précisément! The body – the cage – is everything of the most respectable – but through the bars, the wild animal looks out . . .'[22]

Christie wrote stories which are a little like unpretentious versions of

Greek tragedy. Their elemental simplicities explain why they have survived when so much contemporary literature, more obviously ambitious and 'literary', has failed the test of time. A great wrong was done, and twelve people have conspired to avenge it. There will always be something satisfying at a profound level about that story. Yet it appeals to more than an archetypical moral response. We do not need to posit intention on the author's part when with the eyes of hindsight in the twenty-first century we find political echoes and meanings in this story, first published in 1934. The wrong which has been accomplished by the American, and which has to be avenged as they all pass through the Balkans by a multi-cultural and multinational group of individuals – what does it suggest? Not an allegory, of course, but can we quite dismiss the thought that this league of nationalities wishes to put its multifarious stab-wounds into the heart of the man who has brought disaster on them all? Are they the League of Nations taking revenge, in the very area of the world where their troubles began – the Balkans – upon the old gentleman, President Wilson, who . . . No, that is too neat an 'explanation'. But these stories, which have such a totally compulsive appeal, must be appealing to more than the human desire to solve a puzzle; or, to put it another way, the need to solve a puzzle, by the very fact of its being so obsessively important to so many crossword and mystery addicts, would appear to be something which goes deeper than its surface attractions.

One reason why it would be a mistake to offer any one simple explanation for the appeal of the mystery genre in the Golden Age is that the stories fall into many different categories. John Dickson Carr (1905–77, sometimes writing as Carter Dickson) and the two cousins Frederic Dannay (1905–82) and Manfred Bennington Lee (1905–71), who wrote as Ellery Queen, were masters of the brilliant puzzle. Julian Symons, in his definitive study of the genre, *Bloody Murder*, listing Queen's *The French Powder Mystery* (1930), *The Dutch Shoe Mystery* (1931), *The Greek Coffin Mystery* (1932) and *The Chinese Orange Mystery* (1934), opines that 'Judged as exercises in rational deduction, these are certainly among the best detective stories ever written.'[23] The ingenuity of Dickson Carr is nearly always exercised upon variations of the locked-room mystery, the kind of puzzle which would appeal to Freudians. The Queen books abound in deductive reasoning, which feels reasonable while you are reading it. They are among the best stories which derive from the ratiocinative side of Sherlock Holmes. Rex Stout's Nero Wolfe stories, with the portly Wolfe never leaving the old brownstone house on West Thirty-Fifth Street while Archie Goodwin paces the streets of New York in search of clues, are in their way a child of the Holmes–Watson relationship. There will always be those who cherish mystery stories more for their settings than their plots, and for such readers Wolfe's house, with his sophisticated tastes (orchids, the *Times* crossword) and unvarying routines, will be as comforting a place as the English villages and country houses of Dorothy L. Sayers in *The Nine Tailors* or Agatha Christie's St Mary Mead in her Miss Marple stories.

For W. H. Auden, whose poetry was first published in 1930, the mystery story was essentially a religious myth. 'The fantasy which the detective story addict indulges is the fantasy of being restored to the Garden of Eden, to a state of innocence, where he may know love as love and not as the law.'[24] The enclosed worlds of country-house parties or institutions which his favourite authors depicted were disturbed by the murder, but order and redemption were restored by the detective, who, like God, brought order and justice back into the tarnished garden.

The great critic W. Northrop Frye, another mystery-addict, believed that the amateur detectives – Poirot, Archie Goodwin, Miss Silver, and the rest – were recording angels. It is a striking fact that among the most successful practitioners of the genre, so many should have been Christians. Agatha Christie's only bedtime reading was Thomas à Kempis's *The Imitation of Christ*. Dorothy L. Sayers abandoned crime stories altogether to concentrate upon Dante and theology. Ngaio Marsh from New Zealand, one of the best of the Golden Age writers, was 'a High Church Anglican . . . never quite able to recover the faith she had as a child. It was one of her great regrets.'[25] Margery Allingham was religious. Much of this is reflected in her work, as it is in Christie's. Very many classics of detective fiction do actually involve vicarages, or clergy-detectives – from Chesterton's Father Brown to the parsonage in Sayers's best novel *The Nine Tailors* and to Agatha Christie's *Murder at the Vicarage*. But at a much deeper, more elemental level, these writers appear to be asserting, in the midst of a world which has come morally adrift, that the moral order can still be reclaimed by the angel/detective. Amy Leatheran, the common-sense English nurse who narrates *Murder in Mesopotamia*, concludes: 'Sometimes, I declare, I don't know what's become of the good strict principles my aunt brought me up with. A very religious woman she was . . .' She wonders whether she could end her story with 'a really good telling phrase. I must ask Dr Reilly for some Arab one. Like the one M. Poirot used. In the name of Allah, the Merciful, the Compassionate . . . Something like that.'[26]

The 1930s turn into a murder story on a grand scale. Old scores will be settled, old injustices avenged, new resentments expressed in murder. Of the dominant figures who cross the pages in the early years – Hitler, Laval, Mussolini, Ribbentrop – very many, like characters in Cluedo, were heading for violent ends.

Auden wrote that:

In the detective story, as in its mirror image, the Quest for the Grail, maps (the ritual of space) and timetables (the ritual of time) are desirable. Nature should reflect its human inhabitants, ie it should be the Great Good Place; for the more Eden-like it is, the greater the contradiction of murder. The country is preferable to the town, a well-to-do neighbourhood (but not too well-to-do – or there will be a suspicion of ill-gotten gains) better than a slum. The corpse must shock not only because it is a corpse but also because, even for a corpse, it is shockingly out of place, as when a dog makes a mess on a drawing-room carpet.[27]

It is noticeable that the idyllic Eden is often the English village or the English countryside, even when the author is far from England. John Dickson Carr was American but set his mysteries, most of them, in England. 'Michael Innes' (the pseudonym of J. I. M. Stewart) began his nostalgic evocations of an England of very old-fashioned Oxford colleges and country houses miles from the nearest remote railway halt while he was a lecturer in Australia. England, even for those who lived there, but perhaps even more acutely for those who did not, came to stand for something recognizable, if difficult without absurd sentimentality to define.

Exile intensified, for writers, a sense of 'Englishness'. One discerns this in the perfectly crafted short stories and novels of Somerset Maugham, whose characters never feel more English than when they are on liners crossing from Tahiti to San Francisco, or pursuing their expatriate lines of business in Rangoon, Singapore or Molucca. One feels it too in the four magnificent Wessex novels of John Cowper Powys (1872–1963) – *Wolf Solent* (1929), *A Glastonbury Romance* (1933), *Maiden Castle* (1936), and perhaps the greatest, *Weymouth Sands* (1934). These incomparable explorations of the hidden human psyche, of relations between the sexes, of the mysterious and occult quality of the landscape and archaeological history of England itself, have things in common with Hardy and with Lawrence but are much more ambitious achievements. They are the only novels in English to rival the great Russians, especially Dostoyevsky – one of Powys's great heroes. They were all composed in America where the need to earn his living forced him into the unstoppable and exhausting routines of the itinerant lecturer. Bard, show-off, mystic genius that this craggily built Celt was, these lectures were triumphant. His *Autobiography*, also a masterpiece, reveals the extent to which he is embedded in the Victorian traditions of a clerical family. Through the interstices of his family tree, he was related to the great mainstream of intellectual and literary life – from the eighteenth-century poet William Cowper to the Macaulays. His parsonage upbringing and boarding-school education were those of so many of the best minds of the nineteenth and early twentieth centuries. Strangely enough, the books which he wrote after he had come home lack the deeply felt and extraordinary quality of the novels he wrote in the period 1929–36. The reader opening one of these stories for the first time might suppose he was entering a purely idiosyncratic version of England. When the addiction grows, however, you realize that with his finely attuned intuitive antennae, Powys understood better than many political and religious analysts what was happening to his native country during his exile. He is infinitely old-fashioned, and yet more shockingly modern, not least in his portrayal of sexual feeling, than his younger contemporaries. Like many of the greatest English artists in any medium, Powys is hard to define against the backdrop of modernism which shapes the American or European scenes.

Modernism in poetry, painting, theology, had been attempted in Britain but with no notable native-born exponents. The poetry of Eliot knew many English imitators, but that is what they were. An English Joyce was unimaginable. After the war, Britain retreated into itself. Stanley Spencer's return to his childhood village of Cookham was emblematic, as the life-choices of great artists often are. So, in a very different way, was Ivy Compton-Burnett's decision to set all her novels in a period before the First World War. British Elegy, and most specifically English Elegy, is the overriding note of serious art and literature for the next twenty years. So much had been lost and destroyed in the war that it is as though the creative intelligences in Britain wanted to recover Eden, not to chart new lands. The most successful productions in music, painting and literature in the period all have a kindred *völkisch* feeling for a lost England, to be heralded in the strains of Britten's folk songs, in Betjeman's evocations of a Victorian world, in John Piper's switch from very weak imitations of continental Cubism and abstract collage to a quite distinctive representational style elegizing such apparently threatened phenomena as Welsh chapels or country houses. Whence came the threat? From industrial pollution, from the expansion of towns, from foreign enemies? No doubt some of these thoughts explain the appeal of English elegy. But is there not here a simple metaphysical perception, on the part of the elegists and of their admirers, that Britain had reached, if not the very end, a penultimate chapter?

Stanley Spencer's extraordinary confidence as a painter, his absolute at-homeness with the medium of oil paint, is as obvious as a poster. He was born the son of a piano teacher, the grandson of a builder, in the Thames Valley village of Cookham, a place he would mythologize, immortalize in rather the way that Samuel Palmer made Shoreham in Kent seem a gateway to the beyond. He went to the Slade School of Art. A photograph of Slade students on a summer outing in 1912 shows us David Bomberg, Dora Carrington, Edward Wadsworth and C. R. W. Nevinson. Gwen Raverat well might have been there – she too was a contemporary at the Slade. And there is the diminutive figure of Spencer, whom they nicknamed 'Cookham'. The condescension in the soubriquet hovered round Spencer for most of his life, when he must have been regarded as a primitive, an eccentric, a boy from a suburban village on the edge of Maidenhead, doing spiritually in his art what he did actually, for reasons of poverty, as a student: returning each night to Cookham and his 'Pa'.

In subject-matter, the paintings of Spencer follow the grand traditions of European art – stylishly executed landscapes of a highly traditional kind and, his hallmark, religious pictures, in which, for example, the villagers of Cookham experience a General Resurrection upon the Last Day. His experiences serving in the Royal Army Medical Corps during the First World War were poured into the haunting murals in the Sandham Memorial Chapel. There are scenes of life – soldiers frying rashers of bacon in a billycan in the Camp at Karasuli – and scenes of death and resurrection. There is sometimes grandeur in his perception of humanity, and sometimes low ribaldry, as in his low-life pictures, chiefly executed during the 1930s, between overweight women and randy, bewildered little men like himself.

Many English viewers of these grotesque paintings – the funny little man in trousers staring imploringly, but alarmedly, at the bulbous women bulging from their flowery frocks – will be transported into the world of Donald McGill's comic postcards. If Disraeli was – as he so inconsequentially once informed Queen Victoria – the blank leaf between the Old Testament and the New, then perhaps Stanley Spencer was the missing leaf between the art of the High Renaissance and the saucy postcard. As in the world of his contemporary John Cowper Powys, spirituality and ribaldry and self-conscious Englishness can be disconcerting until you get your eye in, learn how to overlook some of the tomfoolery. You feel 'important' themes are being given a lightness they can't bear – the exact opposite of the sort of thing going on in Europe at the time, where French or German writers and artists might take themselves more seriously.

Spencer's art was a continual stripping, self-revealing, self-lacerating. And it might be as well to mention, before exploring its overtly religious dimension, the autobiographical counterpoises to the Donald McGill–Maillol roly-poly joke-pictures. In 1950 Sir Alfred Munnings came across some of Spencer's 'couple' pictures and initiated a prosecution of the artist for obscenity. One always dislikes reading accounts of artists persecuting one another by means of the law – think of A. A. Milne acting the Pharisee over P. G. Wodehouse during the Second World War. As it happens, the whirligig of time brings its revenges. The scenes which Munnings depicted – harmless equestrian canvases, race meetings and the hunt – would probably be much more shocking to many people today than Stanley Spencer's searingly honest nudes – particularly the self-portraits with Patricia Preece.

Patricia Preece was Stanley Spencer's reason for returning to his childhood village in the early Thirties. Spencer divorced his wife Hilda, and made over his property to Patricia Preece, whom he married at the Maidenhead registrar's office on 29 May 1937. Patricia Preece went on loving, and wishing to live with, her lover Dorothy Hepworth, one of those pre-Second World War lesbians who look exactly like a man. Spencer wanted to have his ex-wife as a lover, not an idea which pleased either woman very much.

The Thirties were a time of sexual revolution, just as much as the 1960s – in some ways much more so.

See the advertisements of the period for new suburban housing, or drive out of any big British conurbation until you reach the mile upon mile of 1930s housing, the semi-detacheds, all aping larger houses, the stockbroker Tudorbethan of Edwardian Surrey and Middlesex and Altrincham and Edgbaston; all nagging the mortgage-slaves to aspire to something higher. An Englishman's home is his dungeon. These houses were supposed in every way to be better than the tenements and terraces of the Georgian and Victorian cities. Each had a scrap of garden behind its privet hedge. Many had a garage. Once inside them, though, and you find that the rooms are poky, just as small in many cases as those in a rotting Georgian rented terrace, but, unlike the town house, miles from anywhere or anything which could be described as interesting. What hopes these miserable little dwellings represent, what spiritual and emotional constriction they must have offered in reality, as hubby went off to the nearest station each morning from just such a dormitory village as Cookham, and the wife, half liberated and half slave, stayed behind wondering how many of the newly invented domestic appliances they could afford to purchase, and how long the man would hold on to his job in the Slump. No wonder, when war came, that so many of these suburban prisoners felt a sense of release.

Stanley Spencer, 'Cookham', used to the coming and going of the trains to Maidenhead and Slough and Reading, knew the soul of lower-middle-class, imprisoned British humanity during the years of the Slump and the preparation for war. His own life was deeply bizarre, but he made of it a parable of his times. His nude canvases of himself and Patricia Preece give off an overpowering atmosphere of sexual frustration. One of the most successful shows her lying on some crumpled sheets wearing the sort of black lacy 'lingerie' men are supposed to like to buy for their womenfolk. (She looks as if she ought to have a bubble coming out of her mouth saying to the figure leering at her from behind the easel: 'You silly bugger!') Spencer wrote her a poem at this time:

> I will buy my God a chemise
> To wear over her
> I embrace her with suspenders
> And worship her with drawers
> My adoration dresses her
> Covering her with loveclothes.

Spencer always, whether he is depicting sexual or religious themes, retained a very strong element of absurdity. The canvas now hanging in the Fitzwilliam Museum in Cambridge is a truly ghastly scene of crestfallen Spencer, naked from the front, gazing at Patricia as she leans with her hands behind her head and her legs splayed. It must be one of the most ridiculous, as well as the saddest, pictures of human non-meeting, non-love, incomprehension and depression. (When Spencer left his wife and child and married Patricia Preece, it was an unconsummated union.) The uncooked joint of mutton in the foreground with its perkily phallic leg-bone is in sad contrast with the drooping Spencer.

Companions to these terrible pictures are the self-portrait of Spencer alone, in tears, in a bedsit in Belsize Park, and the painting done two or three years earlier of his estranged wife Hilda, looking away from him with tight lips, his contemptuous daughter and her alarming death-like dolls, held like a father's broken promise in the arms of her summer frock. So all this lies behind and alongside the Stanley Spencer we all know and love: the potboiling evocations of the sunny Thames valley, and the overtly religious stuff – Christ carrying his cross down Cookham High Street, and the General Resurrection happening in Cookham Churchyard.

In all this there was a turning of the British back upon the rest of the world, a pulling up of the shutters. The troops had come back from the war. The politicians and the businessmen had conned everyone into thinking life would be different. It wasn't a land fit for heroes. It was still as unfair and as class-riven and as silly as before, simply less rich, and less certain of itself. The way that English art turns its back on the Continental traditions is emblematic. Piper stops being a pseudo-Braque and becomes a minor but distinctive figurative artist in his own right. A definitive article, explaining his position, is Piper's 'England's Early Sculptures', published in *Architectural Review* in 1936. He was struck by such wonders as the carvings of the Last Supper on the twelfth-century font at North Grimstone in Yorkshire. His work as an abstract artist had drawn him to 'an instinctive search for the everyday symbols of geometry'. A medieval Wiltshire wit in Peter Langtoft's *Chronicle* of 1307 is obliged, when studying the antiquities in Rome, to admit that he has never seen Stonehenge. He is kicked out of doors and told to go home and see the beauties of his own culture. Everyone, says Langtoft, should be treated thus 'who scrap for barley cornes of vanity on foreigne dung hills'.[28] Whether painting lighthouses or harbours, Welsh Nonconformist chapels or aristocratic houses (see his magnificent series of paintings of Renishaw), Piper appears to have been released by Langtoft's injunction into a series of powerful elegiac visions. It is as if he has seen a Britain which is about to destroy itself, and is determined to capture it in a series of rapid, haunted, almost tear-stained visions. When George VI saw Piper's series of Windsor Castle, he expressed commiseration with the artist for having struck such bad weather. It would be crazy to think of Piper as a great artist in the league of Picasso or Titian, but sometimes minor artists see a clear truth. His great friend John Betjeman, similarly, was never in the league of his old schoolmaster Eliot, but Betjeman's hymn-like verses about the strapping thighs of girls in tennis clubs, or the rattling tram-ride of his boyhood back to Parliament Hill Fields through poverty-stricken North London, have similar power to Piper's sad washes and sketches. Like Noël Coward's songs, they stay in the head for ever, indelibly recording

> Dear old, bloody old England
> Of telegraph poles and tin,
> Seemingly so indifferent
> And with so little soul to win.[29]

22

Two Thousand Whispered Voices

Today in the twenty-first century, the robust vernacular religious traditions of Anglicanism (the Church of Tranter Dewey from *Under the Greenwood Tree*) have been all but forgotten in these days of church being only for the devout. The Victorian High Churchmen, the so-called Tractarians, started the rot, of course – one sees that now. But as the novels of Hardy, George Eliot and E. F. Benson show, church as a place where communities gathered – partly for worship, partly for music, ribaldry, and gossip, partly for nebulous reasons which did not need to be defined – went on for a very long time, even after the box pews were removed, and the bewigged parish clerk reading the responses to the curate in the three-decker pulpit gave way to Kempe glass and 'piety'. Stanley Spencer in all likelihood is seen by modern secular gallery-goers as some kind of religious nutter. In fact, his canvases are the last flowering of normal English religion. On the surface you have the bright world that he painted so incomparably well – brick and flint-knapped houses, lush green countryside, a blacksmith's yard, boats and goldfish in a tank on the edge of the Thames, a goose-run where cherry blossom flowers in 1949. He is able to show how England retained its stubborn wish to be idyllic long into the post-Second World War years. Yet beneath this surface, and in these houses, men and women are looking for their God-in-suspenders, and there's more vigour in the Sunday joint than in their sex lives. It's a sad, silly world that Spencer depicts, and in this context the religion seems both part of the silliness, and a moving way of coming to terms with it.

If the Victorian sages – Darwin, Herbert Spencer, Marx, George Eliot – had returned to England after the First World War, they would have been astounded to discover that religion survived – that indeed Christianity, and the Church of England in particular, flourished as never before. This was not simply a matter of folk religion, nor of the Establishment wishing to decorate its power-base with religious trappings. In 1931 the Archbishop of York, William Temple, conducted a mission to the University of Oxford. It made an extraordinary impression. The vicar of the university church believed that it 'stopped the rot in the Christian life of post-war Oxford. There are large numbers of men and women rendering influential Christian service all over the world today who owe all that is best in them to that week. It was, indeed, a decisive moment in the history of that generation, and the influence still endures and spreads. It was when the tide began to come in . . .' The metaphor alludes to Matthew Arnold's great Victorian poem about the Sea of Faith ebbing away.

William Temple (1881–1944) was the son of the Victorian Archbishop of Canterbury Frederick Temple. His mother, Beatrice Lascelles, was a granddaughter of both the 2nd Earl of Harewood and the 6th Earl of Carlisle. He is a good example of how vigorously the hereditary principle continued to replenish the stock of British public life. A brilliant scholar of Balliol, and by training and temperament a philosopher, Temple delayed his ordination because of doubts about the Virgin Birth and the Bodily Resurrection of Christ – though not about God. One of the only 'dead' public performances of this corpulent, eloquent, attractive man was when asked to address the Student Christian Movement on 'Why I believe in God'. When asked by the warden of the Student Movement House in Bloomsbury why he had been off form he replied: 'You see, *I have never known what it is to doubt the existence of God*, and I felt I had no right to be speaking to that audience of young people.'[1]

His mission to the university of Oxford was based on his belief that the Christian world-view was a coherent one, which could be defended intellectually. The approach he adopted was the same as in his book *Christus Veritas* (1924), to acknowledge that 'the method of Philosophy is secure, but its result comparatively barren'. Theology, following a more 'precarious' method, accepts its doctrines from Religion. 'One day, perhaps, the two' – Theology and Philosophy – 'will probably co-incide: but that day is not yet.'[2]

The Oxford Mission was not disloyal to the intellectual requirements of the two disciplines, but in the end it was an appeal to the religious impulse. It climaxed, on the final evening, after a week's exposition of his 'philosophy of life', with the singing of the hymn 'When I Survey the Wondrous Cross'. A huge crowd roared out the words, and then Temple stopped the singing. 'I want you to read over this verse before you sing it. They are tremendous words. If you mean them with all your hearts, sing them as loud as you can. If you don't mean them at all, keep silent. If you mean them even a little, and want to mean them more, sing them very softly.' There was a dead silence while every eye was fastened on the printed hymn-sheet, and then – to hear Isaac Watt's words

> Were the whole realm of nature mine,
> That were an offering far too small
> Love so amazing, so divine
> Demands my soul, my life, my all

whispered by the voices of two thousand young men and women was (in the recollection of one of them) 'an experience never to be erased from my memory till the whole tablet is blotted'.[3]

The religious revival which took place at this time was welcomed by those who had been dismayed in 1928, when Parliament rejected a revision of the Book of Common Prayer which the Church's own Assembly had passed. By the standards of later liturgical revisions, the new book was moderate indeed. Extreme Protestants were offended by its provision for Reservation of the Sacrament for the use of the sick – that is, keeping back some of the bread consecrated in the Communion Service. They feared it would lead to Romish idolatry. Extreme Catholics within the Church of England, Anglo-Catholics, disliked the book because it was not Romish enough and specifically did not allow them to worship or to parade the sacred bread. It may seem strange that in a Britain which was still wrestling with poverty and disease, Parliament should have concerned itself with such matters, but the pages and pages devoted to the matter in Hansard show the bewildered twenty-first-century reader that old prejudices – still alive and well in Northern Ireland to this day – remain in a national bloodstream for much longer than reasonable people would expect. It might have been supposed that, whatever their individual views about God, the Trinity, the Communion Service or ecclesiastical ceremonial might have been, the members of Parliament would have thought these things were best left to the Church itself. Winston Churchill said in the debate:

> The Church stands at the Bar of the House of Commons and waits. That to me is a most surprising spectacle. Here you have the greatest surviving Protestant institution in the world patiently listening to Debates on its spiritual doctrines by twentieth century democratically-elected politicians who quite apart from their constitutional rights, have really no credentials except good will. It is a strange spectacle, and rather repellent . . . In the present age the State cannot control the Church in spiritual matters: it can only divorce it.[4]

This was the view of many churchmen. The Prayer Book controversy, for example, converted the arch-Tory, highly acerbic Bishop of Durham, Hensley Henson, one of the wittiest diarists in our language, to a belief in disestablishing the Church – making the Church of England into the Anglican or Episcopal Church, of equal status with the Roman Catholics, Christian Scientists, Jews and others. Had they done so, and had the monarch no longer been required to be titular head of the Church, then Edward VIII, instead of reigning for a mere ten months in 1936, would have been able to continue as king until his death.

So the Prayer Book debate, esoteric as it reads today, had wider implications than the individual quirks of these parliamentarians who were involved in throwing out the Revised, or Deposited, Book, as it was called. The Duchess of Atholl, a Scottish Episcopalian, made probably the most learned speech, pointing out that her own Church had Reserved the Sacrament for 200 years without lurching to Rome. She also pointed out that the new rite contained the *Epiklesis* or invocation of the Spirit over the Bread and Wine – and that hitherto the old Book of Common Prayer failed to do this. The new book 'appeals to the moderate Anglo-Catholics, to the Broad Church people and to the Low Church people, because it gives them all something for which they wish'.[5] This was not enough for the diehards. Old Colonel Wedgwood got up and said it was a matter of 'the eternal struggle between liberty and authority'. You would have supposed this was a reason for giving the Church freedom to govern its own affairs. Though, Unitarian that he was, he might not have liked the 'bells and smells' of High churches, might he not as a socialist have liked the fact that these churches were so often staffed and run by Christian Socialists who had found Christ in the poor and underprivileged? No – the matter sparked in Colonel Jos a gut-feeling of intolerant Protestantism:

> These symbols – the Reservation of the Sacrament, the chasubles and robes, prayers for the departed in purgatory – may all seem little things to us. They are symbols, mere symbols; but think what they meant to those people who went before. It was against those symbols that men fought in the field. It was for fear of those symbols that nations were driven across the sea. It was because of those symbols that men, women and even children were burnt at the stake.[6]

The Home Secretary, Joynson-Hicks, one of the most pompous and ridiculous people who ever exercised that office (and that is saying something), believed it was within the remit of the Home Office in 1928 to control the liturgy. 'Thirty years ago there were thirty churches where reservation was practised; today there are nearly 700,' he said, adding that the new book which allowed this regrettable practice could not 'bring peace to the Land'.[7] As for the authority of Parliament to interfere in how the English said their prayers: 'In the reign of Henry VIII, Parliament declared that the King's consent was requisite to all canons, and in 1534, it was not the Church, but Parliament, which abolished the jurisdiction of the Pope in this land. The First and Second Prayer Books of Edward

VI were established by Parliament in 1549 and 1552. The prayers and worship of the Church have all been settled by Acts of Parliament.'[8] So Joynson-Hicks with his frock-coat and striped trousers resembling one of the more orotund buffoons in Dickens, as it were a Tite Barnacle, could from his Conservative Evangelical position lead through the lobbies Colonel Wedgwood the Unitarian, Saklatvala the Parsee Communist, and a motley band of Jews, Methodists, agnostics and Presbyterians to defeat the Deposited Book. The divorce between Church and State which Churchill had said was inevitable happened, to the extent that actual churchgoers took no notice of the absurdity – even though at the time of writing, 2005, Church and State are still saddled with Establishment.

What kept the Church of England alive was not the deliberations of Parliament, as Joynson-Hicks seemed to think, but the imaginative and spiritual needs of its members. In 1937 was published a book, edited by Father A. G. Hebert, called *The Parish Communion*. Its motto was 'let your church be the church'. By making the Eucharist the chief service of the Church this book revolutionized Anglican worship for many who would never have called themselves Anglo-Catholic or worshipped in 'extreme' churches. It was also a time when the cathedrals of England came into their own. In Victorian England many cathedrals were only open to paying worshippers. Archibald Campbell Tait, later Archbishop of Canterbury, was when Bishop of London responsible for urging the Dean and Chapter of Westminster Abbey to allow in some non-paying worshippers at Evensong. As late as 1940 one dean of an English cathedral reminded the congregation that they were only allowed to worship in the choir at Christmas, and that at any other time of year the Dean and Chapter would turn them out.[9] One of the pioneers of giving the cathedrals back to the people, and of reviving their worship, was Frank Selwyn Macaulay Bennett, Dean of Chester. When he arrived in Chester in 1920, Bennett met many people who had lived their whole lives under the shadow of the cathedral and never been inside it.[10] He introduced mystery to the common worship – 'The best preparation for a great crowd in a cathedral is to burn some incense.'[11] Inspired by Bennett, other dioceses began to use their cathedrals and these great buildings became popular again. Hewlett Johnson, moon-faced Stalinist Dean of Canterbury, is nowadays derided for his politics, but he was a good dean, filling the cathedral. T. S. Eliot's *Murder in the Cathedral* made a sensation when it was first performed at the Canterbury Festival, organized by George Bell, in 1935. The self-confidence of the national Church was further expressed in its financing and building of two giant new cathedrals – Sir Giles Gilbert Scott's magnificent one at Liverpool consecrated in 1924, and in Guildford the cathedral designed by Edward Maufe in

1932, and towering above the town like a monastic mountain-top. Maufe is a figure like Betjeman, Britten and Piper in their different fields: not an architect of the first rank,[12] but one by paradox who can produce work that is more satisfying than those who are. His austere concrete cathedral, faced with brick and stone, is hauntingly atmospheric, within and without.

Bell, incidentally, when Dean of Canterbury, had been the first to allow Canterbury Cathedral to be open to visitors between services on Sundays, and to admit female sightseers or worshippers without hats. He also, with John Reith, then general manager of the BBC, pioneered broadcast services on the wireless. George Bell was one of the most impressive Englishmen of his age, a figure wholly of the Establishment, and yet when conscience required it, utterly subversive. He was the child of a parson. He was for many years the chaplain to Archbishop Randall Davidson, then Dean of Canterbury, and in 1929 Bishop of Chichester. He will always be remembered as the link between Britain and the very many whom some still think of as the 'good' Germans. The Athenaeum Club in London, a place of limitless dullness, seems hallowed when one remembers that this was the place, between 1933 and 1935, where Bishop Bell, small and smiling in his black frock-coat, breeches and gaiters, would give luncheon to the young German pastor Dietrich Bonhoeffer, who was at the time looking after the Lutheran parish in Forest Hill, South London. Bonhoeffer had first met Bell at a Church conference in Geneva in 1932. Perhaps one of the things the two men had in common was their normality. They were not religious maniacs. Bonhoeffer came from a clever, agnostic family; he was heterosexual, and far from puritanical. (He was to tell his family of his engagement to an aristocratic girl called Maria von Wedemeyer on the day of his arrest by the Nazis.) He liked spending money, having a good suit made, and, being tall and quite heavily built, he was very fond of his food. Bell, likewise, gentle and smiling, was a perfectly normal-seeming person, who belonged to neither of the 'extreme' wings of the national Church. Bell was probably a more or less orthodox Christian. Bonhoeffer was on a journey, moving from an admiration for Karl Barth's view – that faith must be above reason – to a more reasoned absorption of the theology of Rudolf Bultmann: namely, that the events described in the New Testament are mythology; that Christian faith consists in making them real to yourself in an existential way. Bonhoeffer himself, when he was waiting in prison to be killed by the Nazis, foresaw a time when institutional religion itself would die, but believed that what he called 'religionless Christianity' would be and was eternal.

From the very first, Bonhoeffer had seen that there could be no compromise whatever between Christianity and Hitlerism. He saw Christianity as the last, and in the end the only, bulwark against Nazism. Some Christians in Germany, as he foretold in a very early sermon in Berlin – before Hitler even rose to power – would be called to martyrdom. The one thing they could not do was to absorb the National Socialist creed, with its contempt for humanity and its discrimination between persons on grounds of race, into their own view of the world. So strongly did Bonhoeffer feel about racism, that he had turned down a good job at the Union Theological Seminary in New York because he could not in conscience live in the United States, which still practised segregation. (He and a black friend were not admitted to a New York restaurant, which was the incident which decided him.)

One of the most sinister of possibilities, for Bonhoeffer, was that Nazism might swallow up Christianity itself. Bishop Ludwig Muller was appointed head of the German Church by Hitler. Previously the Lutherans did not have a national hierarchy. Muller was confidential adviser to Hitler when he became Chancellor, and a full Nazi. It was clear to true Christians that they must leave Muller's Church and set up the Confessing Lutheran Church, which they did, so as not to be a party to – among other things – excluding those of Jewish or partially Jewish ancestry from their congregations. The Confessing Church was the object of particular opprobrium to the Bishop of Gloucester, Arthur Headlam, who often wrote letters to *The Times* praising the National Socialists, and the many supposed benefits which they were bringing to the Fatherland.

When the very end came, and he knew he was about to be hanged, it was to Bell that Bonhoeffer sent his last message. Bell recalled:

I knew him in London in the early days of the evil regime: and from him, more than any other German, I learned the true character of the conflict, in an intimate friendship. I have no doubt that he did fine work with his German congregation: but he taught many besides his fellow-countrymen while a pastor in England. He was crystal clear in his convictions; and young as he was, and humble-minded as he was, he saw the truth, and spoke it with a complete absence of fear.[13]

It was in the Athenaeum Club that Anthony Trollope wrote some of his novels of English cathedral life. It was there one day that, overhearing two old club bores talking of his fictional battleaxe, Mrs Proudie, the bishop's wife, he resolved to write her death scene in *The Last Chronicle of Barset*. Had he returned to Earth in 1934, Trollope would have seen the Athenaeum full of characters from his novels – bishops in frock-coats, their top hats adorned with rosettes and rigging; club servants in livery. So little had changed. Bonhoeffer knew that a fundamental conflict was about to engulf the world, as it had already engulfed his own country.

It was in this club, too, that so many of the Victorian intellectual giants – Huxley, Darwin, Lyell and others – could be seen raising silver soup spoons to whiskered mouths. Their vision of a universe, where unfit species were 'cast as rubbish to the void', had seemed to many of their contemporaries to put to death not merely the tradition of the Church but the very God whose existence had hitherto underpinned, not only the universe of matter, but also that of value. Tennyson had seen in the relentless evidence of Lyell's fossils a careless, heedless process at work. The 'dragons of the prime/That tore each other in their slime' mocked the old decencies. Now the sky was darkening outside the club windows. Just around the corner, in the stuccoed elegance of Carlton House Terrace, the German embassy was preparing for the arrival as ambassador of Joachim von Ribbentrop, whose smooth talking would bamboozle so many in London society. Bonhoeffer's conversations with Bishop Bell convinced at least one sane and influential Englishman – though alas, not influential enough – that there was an enormous opposition to Hitler in Germany, that most of the Catholic South had never voted for him, that decent Germans who were pleased by the reversals of the Versailles treaty and by full employment would soon wake from their dreams. If those of good will in both countries united against Nazism, was not this the best way of averting war?

So the two men spoke, in that atmosphere of Victorian clubland, where to all outward appearances the Church of England, by law established, was still a force of influence. And if Bonhoeffer had looked around the dining-room, and seen Lang, then Archbishop of Canterbury, or Henson of Durham in their episcopal attire, it might well have seemed to be true.

Of course the Church of England was not the whole story in the religious life of the 1930s. There was the growth of Christian Science, and the very fine churches which went with it, most notably the huge temple in Curzon Street, Mayfair. There was the phenomenon of Moral Rearmament, in which Frank Buchman's 'Oxford Group' persuaded his often rather athletic disciples to make public confession of their sins. Some who attended the meetings were embarrassed by the sight of Rugger 'Blues' weeping as they acknowledged impure thoughts. Others found Buchman inspiring, with his belief that by millions of individual conversions the Holy Spirit would transform the world. 'I thank heaven', Buchman declared after the 1936 Berlin Olympics, 'for a man like Adolf Hitler, who built a front line of defence against the anti-Christ of Communism.'

No less startling, to a twenty-first-century eye, is the support given to violent political causes by the British branches of the Roman Catholic Church. The monks of Downside held regular novenas of prayer for the IRA, as well as for the success of Franco's armies in the Spanish Civil War; indeed, prayers for a Franco victory were all but universal among British Catholics.[14] The Order of Preachers (Dominicans) stands out among fellow Catholics for taking a bigger and more daring view of world affairs, and some of the most impressive twentieth-century exponents of Christianity have come from within its ranks. Particularly notable was Bede Jarrett, OP, a learned, holy scholar, who opened Blackfriars at Oxford exactly seven hundred years after the first arrival of the Dominicans in that place, 15 August 1221. Jarrett died on 17 March 1934, aged fifty-two.[15] His mentor within the Order, Vincent McNabb (1868–1943), was a man with a wider sphere of influence. Born in a poor family in Northern Ireland, he combined the distinctive Dominican virtues of scholarship with eloquence. He was also a person of almost Tolstoyan simplicity of life, never taking public transport in London, where he chiefly worked, and where he tramped about in his medieval garb and hobnailed boots, an uncompromising soldier for Christ whose life makes some of the rather bizarre anti-Catholicism of the Parliamentary Prayer Book debate seem not merely misplaced but crazy.[16] Friends with such luminaries as Belloc and Chesterton, Father McNabb was nonetheless the reverse of a socialite or intellectuals' darling. That role was chiefly occupied by Father Martin d'Arcy, SJ, who managed to convert a number of well-known people to his faith, including Evelyn Waugh and the future Earl of Longford. 'Are you rich and nobly born?' asked Betjeman.

> Is your heart with sorrows torn?
> Come to me, I'll heal them all
> Martin d'Arcy. Campion Hall.

But in the event, it was his own sorrows which were poor Father d'Arcy's undoing. His life was clouded by a hidden tragedy. Not for nothing was he a Jesuit, so the matter was all hushed up, and the famous Master of Campion Hall was spirited away to the Jesuit house in Boston, Massachusetts. No one in his lifetime ever knew what had happened. A Jesuit scholastic, a very young man, little more than a boy, had committed suicide when d'Arcy had revealed, by propositioning the youth, a darker side to 'The Mind and Heart of Love'.[17]

While many Roman Catholics, especially converts, probably look back to the 1930s as a period of expansion and triumph, other nonconformist bodies suffered a decline in numbers at this time. The Baptists, for example, who numbered 434,741 in 1906, had lost nearly a quarter of their members over the next thirty years.[18] Almost certainly the three chief causes of this were Death; Doubt – very many nonconformists who learnt their left-wing politics in the chapel abandoned religion for politics when they grew up; and the unthreatening inclusiveness of modern Anglicanism, which meant that many whose Victorian forebears had been Baptists, Methodists, Congregationalists, found that Episcopalianism in one form or another answered their needs.

There was, however, another way in which the Church of England occupied a unique place in national life, and this had scarcely anything to do with religion, certainly nothing to do with belief. Drive round twenty-first-century England and in every village and small town you will pass a gateway or a drive to 'The Old Rectory' or 'The Old Vicarage'.

In the post-Second World War world when Church membership began to decline drastically, and with it Church money, the authorities made the decision to sell off the parsonages – some Victorian villas, but for the most part decent, sometimes large Georgian houses, with a few acres of garden and a glebe, that is a patch of land set aside for the parson to grow his own fruit and vegetables. The clergy were seldom rich, but they were treated as if they were gentlemen: very often they were. Nearly all of them had degrees. High Church, Low Church, Broad Church, they were disseminated throughout the land. If they were even half good at their jobs, they and their wives and families mixed with everyone in their parish. They were extraordinary agents of social communication. It meant that almost everyone in England was within five miles of a man who could read ancient Greek.

Their families, often impoverished but growing up with a certain set of shared values which could loosely be defined as decency, were notably more bookish, more self-reliant than other middle-class families who had more servants or moved in narrower social fields. It is no wonder that such a very high proportion of writers, creative men and women of other talent, teachers, civil servants, and of course clergy, came from 'clergy families'. Nowadays the clergy family is all but obsolete and only a few of the children of priests follow in father's (or nowadays mother's) footsteps. Much has been lost, not least some of the more wildly eccentric figures in British national life; for living in a small community where you were the only middle-class family, the only family who read books, the only family that was neither as rich as the squire nor as common as the shopkeeper, isolated people and intensified their tendency to oddness.

On Trafalgar Day, 21 October 1932, an extraordinary scene was enacted in Norwich Cathedral. At a quarter to twelve, the Bishop of Norwich, Dr Bertram Pollock, the Chancellor of the Diocese, the Registrar in a legal wig, the Dean and the canons, the Archdeacon and various other bewigged lawyers proceeded to the Beauchamp Chapel. Outside the building they could hear a car screeching to a halt, followed by the cheers of a crowd. Before the proceedings began, they saw, hurrying into the cathedral and clutching a silk hat, the diminutive (five foot three) figure of the Reverend Harold Francis Davidson, MA, accompanied by his sister and a female friend. The appointer called out: 'Oyez, Oyez, Oyez, all persons cited and admonished to appear at this court and answer to your names as you shall be called. God save the King.' The rector's name was called three times and he answered 'Here.' The bishop then proceeded with the melancholy ceremony of defrocking the rector, or depriving him of his holy orders. He had entered the cathedral a priest. He left it a yelling, furious layman, calling out that he would make an appeal to the Archbishop of Canterbury.

There was hardly an English newspaper, between March and July 1932, which did not contain daily references to the Rector of Stiffkey, the north Norfolk village pronounced Stewkey, whose parish priest Davidson became, aged thirty-one, in 1906.[19] For years, Mr Davidson had been conducting the services at Stiffkey each Sunday. As Monday dawned he would leave his wife and five children in the Rectory while he himself would catch the train (London-North-Eastern Line) from Wells-next-the-Sea to the capital, where he would spend the remainder of the week making a nuisance of himself with adolescent girls. At Marble Arch for example he met Barbara Harris, aged sixteen. Surely she was – she must be – Miss X – and he had named a famous film star. Barbara was no innocent, but she liked the chat-up line. At 2 am. not long afterwards the Rector called on her and found her sitting up in bed with an Indian lover – a policeman – who told the over-excited padre fascinating stories of temple prostitutes in his native land.

When Harold Davidson was prosecuted and brought to Church House in Westminster to answer charges of conduct unbecoming a clerk in Holy Orders, he was forced to go through one of those humiliating cross-examinations which seem designed for the sadistic amusement of lawyers and enrichment of cheap newspapers, but which are curiously difficult to see as advancements of civilization. When one of the girls, Rose Ellis, had given evidence, Roland Oliver, for the prosecution, asked the rector:

'Is it your view of decency to go to a flat and to get this pretty girl to dress your naked body?'

'You are making the most outrageous suggestion. I never said that.'

'Was the boil on the buttock of your body?'

Silence.

'Have you to think?' nagged Oliver.

'Yes. I do not know what the buttock is.'

'Do you not know?'

'Honestly, I do not.'

'Mr Davidson!'

'It is a phrase honestly I have never heard. So far as I remember, it is a little below the waist.'

Davidson was more interested in red lips and white teeth and cheeky smiles than in what could be found a little below the waist. In the weeks of trial no evidence was produced that he had made love to the girls whom he flattered and pestered. He had kissed and fondled and chatted. He had invited them down to the Rectory for pyjama parties. He had approached so many young girls in ABC tea shops and Lyons' Corner Houses that there were many such establishments where he was banned. He was unsavoury and a little mad, but the savage processes brought against him were unable to yield quite the results they wanted. Even Rose Ellis, most salacious of the witnesses, admitted under cross-examination that she had lied, having been bribed with port wine in a saloon bar by a private detective engaged on behalf of the Chancellor of the Diocese of Norwich.

The trial and defrocking of the Rector had revealed the extent to which upright bourgeois 'morals' were upheld more in the minds of leader-writers and suburban Sunday school teachers than in the actual lives of young people living in big cities. The girls Davidson befriended – whom he claimed by turns he wanted to rescue from the dangers of drink, prostitution, the Roman Catholic Church, or the Stage – were those who in a very few years would join the ATS, become Land Girls, Wrens, factory workers, the pillars of England. In 1932 they were bored teenagers, hanging around in cafés, easy in morals, and amused by the antics of funny little Harold who sometimes wore a collar and tie and pretended to be a theatrical impresario and sometimes wore a clerical collar – 'For years I have been known as the Prostitutes' Padre – to me the proudest title that a true priest of Christ can hold. I believe with all my soul that if He were born again in London in this present day He would be found constantly walking in Piccadilly. He suffered the cruellest slander, but this did not deflect Him from solicitude for the fallen, and His attitude to the woman taken in adultery and still more His close friendship with the notorious harlot of Magdalene . . . has always been my inspiration and comfort in the difficult work I have humbly undertaken in His name.'

'Hello you old thief,' called out one barman who, in spite of Davidson's being an undischarged bankrupt, allowed him to cash cheques. 'How are all the girls?'

So might Our Saviour have been greeted had He walked in England in the 1930s. Or so Davidson believed. His end was as dramatic as had been his vision of life. Unable to take his case to appeal, he raised money by performing stage re-enactments of his trial. When one of the vindictive landladies who gave evidence at his trial pursued him in law for £45 he was unable to pay. He spent nine days in a Liverpool gaol and upon his release he rode through the streets of Blackpool, with a young negress on either side of him, throwing flowers to a jubilant crowd of spectators. The Church had arrayed itself in the clothes of Caiaphas to condemn this mentally unbalanced figure. In its brutality towards Davidson there was some foreshadowing of the way it would destroy the new king in 1936. By then, Davidson's fate as Tragic Buffoon cum Early Christian Martyr was grotesquely sealed. He had begun to appear during the summer months at Skegness Amusement Park, in a lion's cage. In July 1937, from a cage measuring 14 feet by 8 feet, Davidson addressed the crowds on the iniquities of the Archbishop of Canterbury and the Bishop of Norwich. Freddie, the lion who shared the cage while these denunciations were in progress, reared up on his haunches and began to maul the little man. It was appropriate that the human being who came to his rescue, Freddie's tamer Irene Violet Sumner, should have been a sixteen-year-old girl. He never recovered consciousness when they took him from the cage. Perhaps, who knows, as he drifted towards death, his spirit saw Irene Violet and leaned smilingly towards her with the offer of a tea-cake, or help in getting a 'position', or with an exclamation of astonishment at her supposed resemblance to Miss Jean Harlow. As he died, he perhaps entered the Empyrean as Dante did, thinking of girls, or like Goethe's Faust, whose last gasp is an affirmation of belief in the Eternal Feminine Principle leading us on:

> Das Ewigweibliche
> Zieht uns hinan.

23

Politics

If you were an English Tory of the generation who voted for Disraeli and the 3rd Marquess of Salisbury, in the closing years of Queen Victoria, you would have seen the rising generation of socialists as the greatest possible threat to the old order. Such a figure as Philip Snowden (1864–1937) would have filled you with terror. He was a broad-shouldered, thin-lipped, intensely serious Yorkshireman, with blond hair, steely light blue eyes and the gift of the gab.[1] With the rise of the Independent Labour Party, Snowden was always seen as second only to Keir Hardie himself as a 'draw' of crowds. Malcolm Muggeridge, the disillusioned ex-socialist, used to say that had Keir Hardie lived – he died heartbroken by the failure of international socialism in 1915[2] – he would have ended his days on the right wing of the Conservative party. Muggeridge spoke satirically, but he also spoke whereof he knew. Snowden, who had been born as a weaver's son in a two-roomed cottage in the hamlet of Ickornshaw, Cowling, near Keighley in West Yorkshire, died as Viscount Snowden. He was one of those senior members of the Labour party who followed Ramsay MacDonald into the National Government of 1931, sitting in collaboration with Tories such as the iron-master Stanley Baldwin and the Liberal Rufus Isaacs, who was one of nine children of a Jewish fruit merchant from Spitalfields.

All three of these – Snowden the poor weaver's son, Isaacs the fruiterer and Baldwin the Bewdley ironmaster – ended up in the House of Lords: Viscount Snowden; Earl Baldwin of Bewdley; Rufus Isaacs was the Marquess of Reading, the British Ambassador to the United States and Viceroy of India.

Romantic snobs such as Proust's Baron de Charlus, who liked to trace his ancestry back to the Emperor Charlemagne, would perhaps have considered that this marquess, this viscount and this earl were not 'real' aristocracy. But there is not a single member of the British aristocracy whose family was not, once upon a time, doing something just as lowly as the forebears of these three noble lords. Britain's premier duke's surname, Howard, means harbourmaster, and that was the original avocation of the dukes of Norfolk.

There were many things about the political system in England which would have made, and did make, angry, thinking and discriminating people into communists, or, if they knew the nature of communism in

Russia, into fascists. The poor were still horribly poor, and the conservatism, small c, of the English system seemed relentlessly biased against them. As a political vehicle, the system of hereditary monarchy seemed, in 1936, as if it had run into the ground. The system of parliamentary democracy threw up some quite shockingly pedestrian and short-sighted political leaders. And the system of aristocracy, in a democratic world, might well have seemed untenable. Probably on any logical level it was. But it is important to recognize the kind of aristocratic system it was. It was not, like so many aristocratic castes on the Continent, one designed to keep people out of it. On the contrary, it evolved as a flexible system. If a weaver's son shook his fist at privilege, said this system, do not fight a class war with him. Create a viscountcy for him. This Gilbert and Sullivan and mildly, but not sensationally, corrupt method of doing things allowed for many of the things which warring factions on the Continent in their separate ways wanted. It allowed the old aristocracy, who had administered Britain since 1689, to remain in place. It also allowed the rising class, created by the industrial revolution and free trade and the repeal of the Corn Laws in 1840, to exercise the power of their own money. In many cases, at the top end of this class they intermarried with the 'old' families. It also allowed for Ramsay MacDonald and for Philip Snowden to be respectively Prime Minister and Chancellor of the Exchequer. What it did not appear to allow for, which is why so many of the Labour party saw MacDonald as a traitor, was true socialism, and the dismantling of the old order altogether. When the British looked at the countries with socialist leaders such as Lenin, Léon Blum or Hermann Müller, or those of the Spanish Republic, who guaranteed their liberal-socialist regime by sending the entire Spanish gold reserve to the Soviet Union, they might have felt happier with British muddle.

Philip Snowden, as Chancellor of the Exchequer, had economic ideas which were indistinguishable from those of Churchill, his Conservative predecessor. True, he put taxes up, increasing income tax by sixpence to four shillings and sixpence in the pound to pay for the worthy measures introduced immediately by the Labour government, such as the Widows' and Old Age Pensions Act, which greatly extended benefit to those in need. But over the two great economic questions of the age – whether to support tariffs or free trade, and whether to remain on the gold standard, Snowden was deeply unbudgeable. He was implacable in his devotion to free trade, in spite of what the downturn in the world economy was doing to British jobs. And he was a fanatical believer, as an eloquent and highly popular socialist, in the pound being tied to the gold standard. So it was that in Britain, in the opening years of Ramsay

MacDonald's government, the position of the working man grew more perilous than at any stage in history since the worst days just after the Napoleonic Wars. When Labour took office in June 1929, unemployment stood at 1,163,000 – that is 9.6 per cent of the insured population. A year later there were 1,912,000 unemployed, and by December the total was 2,500,000.[3] The withdrawal of American money following the Wall Street Crash threatened to plunge the economy of the West into ruin. Within the Labour cabinet there was complete confusion about what should be done. Snowden's policies would obviously prove unworkable – eventually. But in the meantime, how many more men would be thrown out of work, and what would be the social and political consequences of such a disaster?

Wisdom after the event does not help very much, though there is usually plenty of that in the histories of the 1929–31 government. It has been assumed that some form of New Deal would have saved the day. But, from an economic point of view, the New Deal was coming unstuck by 1937, when American unemployment climbed again to 10 million. What saved the US economy by the following spring was rearmament. The same was true in Germany. The mysterious disappearance of the German unemployed into useful labour as soon as the Nazis took control was seen by Hitler's admirers to have solved the crisis by means of building autobahns, holiday camps and schemes of public works. They overlooked the fact that from the beginning his aim was to have a war. He had written at length about it in *Mein Kampf*, and the only secret was the extent to which, in defiance of the Versailles treaty, he was rebuilding Germany as a military force *sans pareil*. Neither he nor Roosevelt adopted their policies as a result of reading J. M. Keynes. It could be said that Keynes in part developed his ideas during the 1930s as a consequence of seeing the apparent success of American and German national revivification programmes.

For the young Sir Oswald Mosley, it was intolerable that his party, the Labour party, should not be adopting a policy after the Wall Street Crash which got to grips with the soaring unemployment figures. Mosley had visited America in 1926 and gone for a fishing trip with Roosevelt off the coast of Florida. He wrote in his autobiography that he owed his economic ideas partly to reading Keynes and partly to the Federal Reserve Board, whose officials he had met in New York. Although they were speaking, in those days, to deaf ears when they tried to influence presidential policy they came into their own when Roosevelt became president.

Mosley, then, wanted a much more radical approach to the economic and political crisis. Above all, he wanted to use the Keynesian expedient of borrowing money to promote expansion – a notion which was anathema to Snowden, and incomprehensible to J. H. Thomas, Mosley's supposed colleague in dealing with the unemployment problem. His ideas were dismissed by Snowden as 'wild-cat finance', but they broadly coincided with those of Keynes and Lloyd George.[4]

In May 1930, Mosley impulsively resigned from the government, and from the Labour party. It was a dramatic, if small, event. Those who looked back on his career within the party saw Mosley as a future leader, in all likelihood the successor to MacDonald. 'Every prophet fixed on Sir Oswald as the next party leader,' said John Scanlon in *The Rise and Fall of the Labour Party*. Emanuel Shinwell, former Communist, who lived to be over 100 and to become the darling of the Labour party, said: 'Almost everyone expected that because of his popularity, he would replace Ramsay MacDonald.'[5] R. H. Crossman, a minister in Harold Wilson's Labour government of 1964–6 and subsequently editor of the *New Statesman*, said Mosley was 'the outstanding politician of his generation . . . spurned by Whitehall, Fleet Street and every party at Westminster simply and solely because he was right.'[6] Beatrice Webb, now Lady Passfield, saw Mosley as MacDonald's successor. 'MacDonald owes his pre-eminence largely to the fact that he is the only artist, the only aristocrat by temperament and talent, in a party of plebeians and plain men. Hitherto, he has had no competitor in personal charm and good looks, delightful voice and the gift of oratory. But Mosley has all these, with the élan of youth, wealth and social position added to them.'[7] But in May, incensed that he had not been listened to, Mosley walked. It was obvious to anyone with any political intelligence that he was walking into oblivion, doomed to become, in the words of his loyal second wife, a footnote in history. Beatrice Webb made some very astute observations in her diary:

An amazing act of arrogance, Oswald Mosley's melodramatic defection from the Labour Party, slamming the door with a bang to resound throughout the political world. His one remaining chance is to become the He-man of the newspaper lords in their campaign against Baldwin's leadership of the Conservative Party.[8]

Mosley and a few friends – notably John Strachey, a Labour MP, and Harold Nicolson, an ex-diplomat and writer married to the novelist and poet Vita Sackville-West, joined together and started what was called the New Party. Nicolson was at this stage – with very great self-pity since he felt it to be beneath his dignity – working for the Londoner's Diary gossip column on Beaverbrook's *Evening Standard*. There was tremendous enthusiasm for the New Party – but only among the enthusiasts.

The Sitwells asked Mosley to Renishaw, where 40,000 inhabitants of Sheffield came to hear him speak.[9]

It was quite clear to those with any political nous what Mosley was up to, and in what direction he was going. Even before he had left the Labour party, a foreign journalist at the Labour party conference nicknamed him the English Hitler. Beatrice Webb thought: 'the British electorate would not stand a Hitler. Mosley has bad health, a slight intelligence and an unstable character. He also lacks genuine fanaticism. Deep down in his heart he is a cynic. He will be beaten and retire.'[9] As an analysis of his character that is a bullseye, and as a prediction of what would happen to him politically it is all but true. When Virginia and Leonard Woolf came to stay with the Webbs, they were quizzed by Beatrice about their friend Harold Nicolson, and asked for gossip about the rising New Party. Mosley was already speaking of sweeping the constituencies, and becoming Prime Minister. Beatrice, who has been rightly blamed for her myopic reverence for the Soviet Union, nevertheless understood the British political system inside out. She thought it was 'passing strange that so clever a man [as Mosley] should be so completely ignorant of British political democracy, of its loyalty and solid judgment, of its incurable dullness and slowness of apprehension of any new thought'.[11]

People started to leave the New Party almost as soon as it was formed. Professor C. E. M. Joad, for example, had a conversation with Nicolson on 24 July 1931. Nicolson said: 'I have joined the Party since I felt it was the only party which gave to intelligence a position above possessions or the thoughts of Karl Marx. He says he left the Party because he felt it was about to subordinate intelligence to muscular bands of young men.'[12] Nicolson was slow to realize what this meant. One of his New Party candidates in the 1931 election was Kid Lewis, a welterweight boxing champion. (When asked why he had pulled his punches during one fight he had replied he was afraid of killing someone.) Lewis, a Jew, stood as a New Party candidate for the constituency of Whitechapel, where he came from. He lost his deposit. When the New Party achieved electoral disaster, and when Communist thugs tried to break up Mosley's meetings with razorblades, Mosley thought – again, Nicolson's diary tells us – that 'this forces us to be fascist and that we need no longer hesitate to create our trained and disciplined force. We discuss their uniforms. I suggest grey flannel trousers and shirts.'[13] This charming suggestion was not followed. Before long, Mosley had set up the British Union of Fascists, with its sinister, but also ludicrous, black shirts.

By then, Britain had passed through an economic and political storm which amounted to a mini-revolution. It was caused by the very same problem which had led to Mosley's 'amazing act of arrogance', the economic crisis of 1929–31.

For the next fourteen years in England, party politics were, as far as government was concerned, in suspension. MacDonald formed two national governments in 1931. In June 1935 he was succeeded by Stanley Baldwin, who himself gave way to Neville Chamberlain in May 1937. They were governments by coalition, governments by bores, and governments by men who were barely equipped to deal with the two great political issues of the time: poverty at home, and the rise of fascism abroad. In the face of both these threats, the successive British governments of the 1930s seemed to be governed by the 3rd Marquess of Salisbury's maxim: Leave Ill Alone.

Out of the Stock Market Crash of 1929 came the Depression. Out of that slump came the political leaders who would become the chief players in the century's drama. But not in Britain. Britain was affected by the Crash, but its political leadership was as nondescript before as after. In America, by contrast, there emerged the titanic figure of Franklin Delano Roosevelt – who was inaugurated as President in the same year, 1933, that Adolf Hitler became the Chancellor of Germany. Though utterly different, they both came forward as saviour-figures, while the Hollow Men of Britain drifted ineffectually. Or so it certainly seemed. Roosevelt made vigorous and semi-successful attempts to deal with the scourge of unemployment. Hitler appeared, within only two years in power, to have pulled off the miracle of curing it altogether. Britain retained its means test, its tough trade union law, its class system, more or less callously, more or less intact.

The very ingredients which made the great capitalists so prodigiously rich in the good times were those which caused the Crash and the subsequent Depression. The bigger the conglomerates, the greater the amounts of capital they were able, in times of prosperity, to raise on the stock markets. As shares boomed in the 1920s, the harder it was for anyone with spare cash to resist the urge to become a speculator. In fact, in 1929, at most 7 or 8 per cent of the American population actually owned stocks,[14] but many who did not own share certificates were indirectly affected by the stock market, in their insurance, mortgages and savings plans. The huge growth of gadgetry and domestic appliances, and modern 'convenience' ways – such as chain stores – had led to an explosion of companies after the war, with businesses making automobiles, radio sets, electric toasters, electric irons, telephones. Many of the little firms depended on larger ones for their business. Successful companies were always going to be gobbled up by the larger sharks in the ocean, but in the energy of the expanding market many very dubious concerns were in operation, and sound money was not what the investors were after. As the speculative craze took hold, they wanted, and seemed to be offered, a quick buck. As he left office in 1928 President Coolidge told the electorate that their prosperity was 'absolutely sound' and that stocks were 'cheap at current prices'.[15]

His successor was Herbert Hoover, born in the tiny Midwestern town of West Branch, Iowa, a devout Quaker, who had become a mining engineer in his twenties and amassed a fortune. His was an archetypical, virtuous American success story and he probably spoke with complete sincerity when, in his inaugural address in 1929, he said: 'We in America today are nearer to the final triumph over poverty than ever before in the history of any land. The poorhouse is vanishing from among us. We have not reached the goal, but, given a chance to go forward with the policies of the last eight years, we shall soon with the help of God be in sight of the day when poverty shall be banished from this nation.'[16]

Throughout the summer there were warning signals for anyone with the wit to notice them. Production was easing in all the major industries, unemployment was slowly but appreciably going up. Brokers' loans were rising steadily, from about $43.5 million in June 1927 to $48 million in September 1929. But the investors did not read the signs, and the New York Stock Exchange continued to rise.

It was in October that the crash came, and a wild scramble began to unload stocks which were tumbling in value. On 29 October the *New York Times* index of industrials fell 49 points, followed next trading day by another 43 points. The fall from high to low is awesome to consider. By 1 March 1933, the value of stocks on the New York Exchange was less than one-fifth of the market's peak. The *New York Times* stock average, which stood at 452 on 3 September 1929, bottomed at 52 in July 1932.[17]

The cost in human terms was terrible. Industrial production in the United States fell by 50 per cent, and by 1933 one-third or one-quarter of the labour force – no one could calculate exactly – were out of work. The Ford Motor Company, which in spring 1929 employed 128,000 workers, was down to 37,000 by August 1931. This was the era of the soup kitchens, semi-starvation in the cities, the mass exodus, described in Steinbeck's *The Grapes of Wrath*, of dispossessed migrants into California. Almost overnight, the richest country in the capitalist West had become what we would today call a Third World country, dominated by the basic need to eat and the fear of starvation itself. Twenty thousand took part in the Bonus March of 1932 – some from as far away as California. This was when war veterans, holding government bonus certificates which were due years in the future, marched on Washington demanding that Congress pay them off now. They came in battered old cars, on freight trains, or by hitch-hiking. Chief Running Wolf, a jobless Mescalero India from New Mexico, came in full Indian dress with a bow and arrow. The 20,000 were mostly encamped, when they reached Washington, on Anacostia Flats, on the far side of the Potomac River from the Capitol. President Hoover, the Quaker, ordered the army to evict them. He walled himself up in the White House guarded by four troops of cavalry, four companies of infantry, a machine-gun squadron and six tanks, commanded by General Douglas MacArthur and aided by Major Dwight Eisenhower.[18]

The words of the song by 'Yip' Harburg for the 1932 show *Americana* had terrible resonance.

> Once in khaki suits,
> Gee, we looked swell,
> Full of that Yankee Doodle-de-dum.
> Half a million boots went sloggin' through Hell,
> I was the kid with the drum.
> Say, don't you remember, they called me Al –
> I was Al all the time.
> Say, don't you remember I'm your pal –
> Brother, can you spare a dime.

It was inevitable that when the election came in 1932, the Republicans would finally be sent packing, and Franklin D. Roosevelt should come in.

The New Deal enjoyed a measure of success, in the short term, in making lives better for the unemployed. In the long term, it helped lift poorer Americans into the possibility of education, self-betterment, and economic opportunity, by a whole range of measures. Opinions will always differ about whether it 'worked' economically. The most striking feature of the times, after the 1929 debacle, was that all the major countries of the world except Britain appeared to be moving in the direction of powerfully controlled economies. Roosevelt rushed the National Recovery Act, handing over to himself and a small committee of big businessmen, trade associations and a few fledgling trade union leaders the power to take control of the economy.

The plight of the unemployed in Britain was brought to public attention by hunger marches. Groups of men from depressed areas would march through the country on the capital as visible demonstrations that capitalism had failed. The Communist Wal Hannington was a pioneer of the idea of the marches. They were enthusiastically adopted by Ellen

Wilkinson, who for four years was a member of the Communist party, but who was elected as MP for Jarrow in 1935. This tiny woman from Greater Manchester, who possessed her Irish mother's vivid colouring and high temper, was one of the livelier members of a dull, almost criminally dull, Parliament. It was she who organized the most famous of the hunger marches, that from her own constituency, in 1936. Charles Palmer's great shipyard closed in 1933. This great shipbuilding port in County Durham, which had supplied the Empire with so many of its trading vessels, was dead: it had become, in the title of Wilkinson's most famous book, *The Town That Was Murdered*.

Ellen Wilkinson would not have supported rearmament. Otherwise she might have been urging the government to put public money into reopening the shipyards of the North-East. Admiral of the Fleet Sir Frederick Field was warning as early as 1931 that naval power was dangerously depleted: 'The number of our capital ships is now so reduced that should the protection of our interests render it necessary to move our fleet to the East, insufficient vessels of this type would be left in Home Waters to ensure the security of our trade and territory in the event of any dispute arising with a world power.'[19]

In 1918 the Royal Navy had 433 destroyers. By 1936 there would be only 65 which were not over-age. There were no adequately defended ports in the entire British Empire, as the Japanese discovered in Singapore in February 1942.[20]

Successive governments – MacDonald, Baldwin, Chamberlain – were prepared to do little. Public opinion was against the war. They got away with it because towns such as Jarrow (where 68 per cent of the workforce were employed in just one industry, shipbuilding) were unusual. For most working-class people in Britain, unemployment was sporadic, and for the middle classes it was all but unknown. After 1932, unemployment levels began to fall.[21] Life was hard, but actual destitution, such as was suffered in Germany or America, was rare.

It was a century of disguises, and masks. If the war in the desert in 1917 was haunted by a middle-class Englishman disguised as an Arab, the dosshouses and dole-queues of the 1930s were to be most vividly chronicled by a tall Old Etonian with an upper-class drawly voice, who somehow believed that rolling his own cigarettes and wearing corduroy made him into an honorary proletarian. In his direct reportage, however, of what life was actually like for working-class people in the depressed industrial districts of Northern England, George Orwell has no rival. Who, having read *The Road to Wigan Pier*, first published in 1937, can ever forget his description of a coal miner's working day, in which he points out that in order to start a seven-and-a-half-hour shift, the miner has to make a subterranean journey of at least an hour, sometimes several hours, through dark, low, dripping passages? Or his observation that however squalid the housing, there is such a housing shortage that people are desperate to live in the jerry-built back-to-back terraces. Or the common sense of his observation that it was the small landlords who were the worst. 'Ideally, the worst type of slum landlord is a fat wicked man, preferably a bishop, who is drawing an immense income from extortionate rents. Actually, it is a poor old woman who has invested her life's savings in three slum houses, inhabits one of them and tries to live on the rent of the other two – never, in consequence, having any money for repairs.'[22]

All the observation has the ring of truth. So, too, does his vivid treatment of statistics. 'When you see the unemployment figures quoted at two millions, it is fatally easy to take this as meaning that two million people are out of work and the rest of the population is comparatively comfortable.' He reminds us that an unemployed man's dependants never appear on the list, and when you remember this, the figure of two million must immediately be multiplied to six. Then take in those who are not unemployed but are living on money which is less than a living wage, and you quickly come to a figure like 10 million people. Another calculation, quoted by Orwell, puts it as more like 20 million people living in the degraded and anxious conditions he describes in his first fifty masterly pages.

In the second half of the book there is a change of gear and Orwell the camera turns into Orwell the ranter. The fact that it is rant delivered in a quiet, grammatical parody of a sensible voice does not stop it being rant. Much of the rant is highly enjoyable. His hatred of literary London is congenial. 'In the highbrow world you "get on", if you "get on" at all, not so much by your literary ability as by being the life and soul of cocktail parties and kissing the bums of verminous little lions.' Even if it isn't true, it is satisfying to read. And his attacks on Roman Catholics are always funny. He has found some absurd passage of G. K. Chesterton where it is stated that true Catholics drink beer, and tea-drinking is pagan. The riposte is Orwell at his simple best: 'Tell an Irish dock-labourer in the slums of Liverpool that his cup of tea is "pagan", and he will call you a fool.'[23]

Orwell, like most English writers of the period, is class-obsessed. He writes that there are two types of clever working-class people. The first remains working-class, goes on being a mechanic or a dock-labourer, keeps his accent, and works for the ILP or the Communist party while improving his mind. The other type uses his cleverness to escape his class background. The only man to have done this without earning Orwell's disapproval is D. H. Lawrence. Orwell especially hates the ex-working-class types who have become writers or intellectuals. '[I]t is not easy to crash your way into the literary intelligentsia if you happen to be a decent human being.' The man who supposes that he has transcended the class barrier here in fact sounds perilously like an Old Etonian snob complaining about the literary equivalent of counter-jumpers. 'Literary London now teems with young men who are of proletarian origin and have been educated by means of scholarships. Many of them are very disagreeable people, quite unrepresentative of their class . . .' There is something of Marie Antoinette here, a disappointment that the sons and daughters of miners when they come to write a novel or train as a doctor do not go on speaking with an Oliver Mellors accent or tying their mole-skin trousers with pieces of string. At the end of the book, Orwell has a fantasy in which the poor middle classes, including himself, will in the future generation all sink down the social scale.

And then perhaps this misery of class-prejudice will fade away, and we of the sinking middle class – the private schoolmaster, the half-starved free-lance journalist, the colonel's spinster daughter with £75 a year, the jobless Cambridge graduate, the ship's officer without a ship, the clerks, the civil servants, the commercial travellers and the thrice-bankrupt drapers in the country towns – may sink without further struggles into the working class where we belong, and probably when we get there it will not be so dreadful as we feared, for after all, we have nothing to lose but our aitches.[24]

This ending, after the first half of the book, is bathos of the starkest kind. He has demonstrated that if anyone sank to the level of the poor in the industrial North in 1937 they would lose far more than their aitches. They would lose their health, their liberty, their chance to have a bath or read a book, in the relentless struggle to survive. Just such a slither awaited anyone who had the misfortune to live in a Marxist state. In Orwell's Britain, there were appalling austerities ahead over the next decade, but when that dreadful decade had passed, little by little the conditions of working-class people improved. Those who had the chance stopped being working-class because they were bored by their parents' way of life and because – gradually – technological advance rendered such activities as crawling for hours to reach a coal face mercifully unnecessary in order for a modern society to be lit, kept warm, and fuelled. Orwell shows no interest at all in technology, and never in the course of *The Road to Wigan Pier* does he reflect upon the possibilities of much of the industry he observes being something which technology will render obsolescent. It never occurs to him once that the future will be one in which business, and technology, will transform politics and family life, rather than the other way about. His reflections upon the attractions of fascism are also wide of the mark. It is no surprise that Sir Oswald Mosley and his wife regarded *The Road to Wigan Pier* as a treasured text, which fully justified all their political adventures.[25] Even by the time he wrote the book, the British Union of Fascists was losing support – largely because of its absurd uniforms, parodies of Mussolini, and its thuggery towards small Jewish shopkeepers. Although the National Government failed to bring in a New Deal, it was clear from the example of Roosevelt in America that you could bring in the kind of Keynesian solutions promised by Mosley without embracing the dangerous mythologies of fascism.

Within two years of Orwell's book being published, the war had broken out, and the English revolution had begun. This did not mean an end to the class system. That will probably be with the British always. But it meant that encounters between members of different classes, which Orwell describes as such an outlandish adventure, became commonplace with the coming of war. A form of benign state socialism of the kind he advocated in the closing pages of *The Road to Wigan Pier* was indeed brought in by the wartime government. (When it came, Orwell disliked it and used it as a model for the austere tyranny of *1984*.) So although Orwell is nowadays regarded as semi-divine by a certain type of journalist, especially the neo-conservatives who enjoy his digs at 'vegetarians with wilting beards ... earnest ladies in sandals ... birth-control fanatics and Labour Party backstairs-crawlers' (e.g.), it is hard to see him as an especially wise or coherent prophet of his times when he trained his lens on Britain. *Animal Farm* remains, and will always remain, a classic analysis of the Soviet experiment, but that was a different book, and belonged to a different era from his down-and-out phase.

24

The Abdication

1936, a year marked by a phenomenal lack of sunshine,[1] was when the roads divided. The divarication left the old Victorian world behind. Britain faced a great crisis and emerged almost unchanged, whereas in other lands violent confrontations both occasioned and heralded a new world. The Italian invasion of Abyssinia shocked observers by its gratuitous brutality. Mussolini from the balcony of the Palazzo di Venezia in Rome gave to the King of Italy the title Emperor of Ethiopia. It has to be said that while Rastafarians like to trace back the Ethiopian Emperor's ancestry to the Queen of Sheba and King Solomon, Haile Selassie was in fact only the second member of his family to be emperor. Vittorio Emanuele's family had been kings in Italy since the eighteenth century, and sovereign dukes before that. Although he appeared to be Mussolini's puppet, it was in the event the king who sacked the Duce, and not the other way about. In the short term, however, Western Europeans were shocked by the bombing of civilians and the use of poison gas to accomplish the political dream.[2]

In Spain, another ancient kingdom or pair of kingdoms, now a republic, the Left deposed the moderate President Niceto Alcalá Zamora. The architect of the republic, Manuel Azaña, held together an uneasy coalition of leftists, while the fascistic Falange Española of gunmen made it their business to save Spain from Bolshevism by thuggery. It was obvious that the country was moving towards civil war. In Germany, the Nuremberg Laws against Jews were being relentlessly enforced. The laws removed German citizenship from Jews, forbade sexual intercourse or marriage between Jews and Aryans, and banned Germans from employing female Jewish servants under the age of forty-five.[3] Innumerable cases of Race Debauchery were brought against Jewish men who had dared to love Gentile women. While the Olympic Games were held in Berlin during the summer, some of the more blatantly anti-Jewish laws – signs outside Jewish shops telling Gentiles to boycott them – were disguised or removed so as not to scandalize tourists. The ever-popular Führer had occupied the Rhineland on 7 March. On the whole this action caused much less indignation in Britain than did the Italian atrocities in Eritrea. From correspondence in the newspapers and other indications of public mood, it is clear that the majority of people in Britain thought the Germans were entitled to occupy the Rhineland, and even those who deplored the cavalier way in which Hitler had disregarded the Versailles treaty did not view it as a plausible reason for Britain to go to war.

This was the troubled world background to the dramas in Britain that year which focused upon the royal family and upon the truncated reign of King Edward VIII, who came to the throne on 20 January and abdicated on 10 December.

The weather that January was miserable: snow turning to cold drizzle and rain.[4] On 16 January died Shapurji Saklatvala (1874–1936), a rich Parsee merchant,[5] born in Bombay, who in 1924 had been elected as the Communist MP for Bermondsey. His political trajectory, from membership of the National Liberal Club, where he once resided, through the Independent Labour Party, to Communism was largely explained by his detestation of the British Empire, and his disgust at the living conditions of the London poor. Had Belloc met him, he would have found what he had sought in 1926 during the General Strike – 'one single gentleman or lady on the side of the poor'. Saklatvala was imprisoned for speaking on behalf of the strikers in Hyde Park – two months in Wormwood Scrubs.[6] He lost his seat in 1929 and thereafter came to the view, shared by Mosley on the opposite political extreme, that Parliament was no longer a suitable venue for serious political debate. He spoke tirelessly at meetings up and down Britain. 'Sak was a comrade who could have chosen the easy path to great riches, to a political career and to a high place in society, but who consciously chose the path of anti-imperialist struggle and revolutionary Communism' was the tribute of Harry Pollitt, the general secretary of the Communist party.[7]

Hundreds of admirers came to the funeral, and the road between the tube station and the crematorium at Golders Green was lined with people watching the cortege.[8] Nowhere so much as a crematorium in a large city emphasizes the inexorability of Death, wiping out the young and the old, the just and the unjust, in an unstoppable progression, and often providing incongruous conjunctions. At Golders Green crematorium, the funeral cars, the grieving families, the undertakers and their palaver form lines to wait their turn, so that each ceremony within the chapel, before the casket is confined to incineration, is of necessity brief, intense. Three Parsi priests conducted the final rites for Saklatvala, but the chapel was decked with red flags and Communist regalia as, outside, the crowd sang the Communist International.[9]

This hymn to human equality and anti-imperialism could not be heard inside the chapel, but on the tarmacadam outside it rang loud and clear as the next coffin was taken from its hearse, and borne, after a short but seemly interval, into the chapel. The new arrival, who had been carried through the drizzly courtyard only minutes since it echoed to cries for a death to imperialism and an end to British dominion in India, was Rudyard Kipling. Staying at Brown's Hotel, the great poet of imperialism and celebrant of the British Raj had suffered a burst ulcer and died in the Middlesex Hospital. It was decided to cremate him before the interment of his ashes in the national Valhalla, Westminster Abbey. Though his funeral proper would echo to his own hymn 'Recessional', his cremation came hard upon its polar opposite: though perhaps with its vision of empires, the British included, being 'one with Nineveh and Tyre', the pessimism of Kipling's hymn and the destructiveness of the revolutionary vision are not so different in our eyes as they would have seemed to his contemporaries on that miserable January day.

Kipling's ashes were attended by eight pall-bearers in the Abbey: the Prime Minister, Stanley Baldwin, Admiral of the Fleet Sir Roger Keyes, Field Marshal Sir Archibald Montgomery-Massingberd, Sir Fabian Ware, A. B. Ramsay, Howell Gwynne, A. S. Watt and Professor J. W. Mackail, representing Sir James Barrie.[10] Anyone seeing these men, the 'old men who never cheated, never doubted' of Betjeman's verses,[11] would know that they represented a world under threat. Unpleasing, downright repellent, as some features of imperialist, Conservative Britain would seem to a sensitive, rich Communist such as Sak, what worlds were being brought into being by those who shared his contempt for bourgeois capitalism and imperialist aristocracy? By the National Socialists in Germany? By the Communists in Spain, showing their enthusiasm for the Popular Front by shooting nuns, or by their brutal Falangist enemies? By Stalin, ponderously and murderously enacting his Five Year Plan, or by Signor Mussolini, making new emperors by unleashing mustard gas on the women and children of North Africa?

> The tumult and the shouting dies—
> The captains and the kings depart—
> Still stands Thine ancient Sacrifice,
> An humble and a contrite heart.
> Lord God of Hosts, be with us yet,
> Lest we forget—lest we forget!

Would the Lord God remain, as the kings departed? Kipling went as a herald before his king. George V died at Sandringham on 28 January, two days after the man who, though he had refused the Laureateship, and titles, was effectively the Laureate in verse and prose, as Elgar had been the musical accompanist, Lutyens the set designer, of late British imperial glory.

A number of amusing mythologies grew up about the death of George

V: for example that, when a courtier suggested he would benefit from a visit to his favourite seaside resort, Bognor, he received the characteristically robust reply, 'Bugger Bognor', or that, to avoid the indignity of the king's death being first read about in the *Evening Standard*, the announcement was delayed, so that it could be published next day in *The Times*. Some have averred that when he wrote on a menu card 'The King's life is moving peacefully towards its close' Lord Dawson, the royal physician, had already injected a lethal mixture of morphine and cocaine into his jugular vein,[12] an appropriate end for a monarch in the Golden Age of the murder mystery. After dinner, the queen and the royal family gathered round the bed while Cosmo Gordon Lang, archbishop of Canterbury, read the 23rd Psalm and the prayer beginning: 'Go forth, O Christian soul'. The king died at 11.55 pm, or so they said. M. Poirot not having been present, we must take their word for it.[13] Whether or not he had ever said 'Bugger Bognor', it was given out that one of his last inquiries from the deathbed had been How is the Empire? an interrogative which could have been answered in innumerable ways, though probably once again Kipling would have agreed with Saklatvala that it was in poor shape.

Even as his father lay dying, the Prince of Wales, impatient with the discrepancy between Sandringham time and Greenwich Mean Time, gave orders that all the clocks in the house should be altered (put back) to conform with the rest of the country ('I'll fix those bloody clocks'). It was a symbolic act of defiance, deliberately disrespectful to his parents. 'I wonder', sighed Archbishop Lang, 'what other customs will be put back also.'[14]

The new king was in his early forties. The Prime Minister, Mr Baldwin, was nearly seventy. Queen Mary was the same age. Cosmo Gordon Lang, who would be responsible for placing a crown on the new sovereign's head, was seventy-one. Of prominent members of the cabinet, Neville Chamberlain, the Chancellor of the Exchequer, was in his late sixties; Lord Halifax, the comparatively youthful Lord Privy Seal, was fifty-five when the new king succeeded. The only member of the government even close to him in age was Anthony Eden, the new Foreign Secretary, who was hardly sympathetic to him. He was a young(ish) man becoming the constitutional monarch of a country ruled by old men, and which would go on being ruled by old men for years to come. At a visceral level, the old men felt fear and resentment of the new man, who moved in a fast, rather spivvy set, and who visibly derided, or was bored by, the values of his parents. Above all, the Old Guard feared the new king's popularity. He was not particularly clever. By royal standards, though, he was a ball of fire, capable unlike his poor younger brother Bertie, Duke of York, the future George VI, of speaking two sentences without an appalling stammer; able, unlike his brother Harry, Duke of Gloucester, to drive a car without hitting a tree or a ditch; and, unlike his in many ways more charming brother George, Duke of Kent, heterosexual. He caused some confusion over this question in 1924 when on a private visit to the United States. He turned up at the Belmont Park races wearing suede shoes – always, in King George V's eyes, the sign of 'a cad', but in the America of the 1920s something which carried the connotations of homosexuality. Once he was told this, he never wore them again.[15]

For parallels in our own times for the public impact of a royal person, we must think of Diana, Princess of Wales. As with her, part of the ingredient in his widespread popularity was beauty – a beauty which in adolescence and young manhood had been breathtaking. Part of the magic, too, stemmed from a personal unhappiness which was palpable. Those who are happy within, happy in a fulfilled relationship, don't make very good idols. It is the unhappy, with their unsatisfied need to be loved projected on to the masses, who produce – a Valentino, a Marilyn Monroe, a Diana, an Edward VIII. His socialite bisexual American friend 'Chips' Channon did not exaggerate when he called the new king-emperor the 'adored Apollo' of the country and the Empire.[16] Another homosexual courtier, this time of Edwardian times, the second Viscount Esher, noted when the prince was twelve years old 'the look of *Weltschmerz* in his eyes' which he could not 'trace to any ancestor of the House of Hanover'. The same Esher, when David – as the prince was always known by his family – had served with bravery in the war in France, recorded meeting Queen Mary. 'She is proud of the Prince of Wales. I tried to make her see that after the war thrones might be at a discount, and that the Prince of Wales's popularity might be a great asset.'[17] It is revealing that even at such a moment, Esher felt he had to persuade the mother to see the son's good qualities. The *Weltschmerz* might have been something new in the prince as far as the House of Hanover was concerned, but the king and queen kept up the time-honoured tradition of that House of treating their children with distant contempt, and of fostering a positive loathing for their firstborn.

Towards the end of the war, David fell deeply in love with a married woman called Freda Dudley Ward. They met during an air raid, huddled in the cellar of a house belonging to one Mrs Kerr-Smiley – the sister, as Fate or Chance would have it, of that Ernest Simpson who would play so momentous a part in the royal story. So began a sixteen-year love affair between David and an attractive, discreet, pretty, affectionate and pleasure-loving woman.

Being Prince of Wales isn't a job, but David did his duty as heir to the throne with enough aplomb to make him a matinée idol on the world stage. He toured the Empire. He did his share of visiting different parts of Britain, making speeches, visiting ex-servicemen's clubs, and the like. He was a good horseman. Slight and thin as he was, he made a nimble polo-player; he enjoyed point-to-pointing. He liked smoking. He wore outrageous clothes, jazzy socks, turn-ups on Oxford bags, bright tweeds, all the garments which would have made Jeeves wince had Bertie Wooster insisted upon wearing them. There was (a bit) more sex in Edward VIII's world than in Bertie Wooster's, though not nearly so much as in Edward VII's, and the people among whom he moved were decidedly more *mondains* than Gussy Fink-Nottle or Catsmeat Potter-Pirbright. Among his best friends were Duff and Diana Cooper, Sibyl Colefax, Nancy Cunard, Henry 'Chips' Channon. Chips was born in Chicago, the son of a businessman, but like many Americans in exile, he loathed his native land. 'The more I know of American civilization,' he wrote when he was twenty-eight years old, 'the more I despise it. It is a menace to the peace and future of the world. If it triumphs, the old civilizations, which love beauty and peace and the arts and rank and privilege will pass from the picture. And all we will have left will be Fords and cinemas. Ugh!'

In Paris he had met Proust, and Chips's famous diaries reveal an obsession with high society which is Proustian in its intensity, if not its artistry. Like Proust, too, he was bisexual, with a distinct preference for young men. He was the lover among others of George, Duke of Kent, and of Terence Rattigan. In 1933 he married Lady Honor Guinness, the eldest daughter of the 2nd Earl of Iveagh. In 1935 Chips became MP for Southend-on-Sea, a seat which had been occupied before that by his mother-in-law, Lady Iveagh, and before that by his father-in-law. His friend, a fellow MP, Harold Nicolson, described their house, 5 Belgrave Square:

Oh my God, how rich and powerful Lord Channon has become! There is his house in Belgrave Square next to Prince George, Duke of Kent, and Duchess of ditto and little Prince Edward. The house is all Regency upstairs with very carefully draped curtains and Madame Récamier sofas and wall-paintings. Then the dining room is entered through an orange lobby and discloses itself suddenly as a copy of the blue room of the Amalienburg near Munich – baroque and rococo and what-ho and oh-no-no and all that. Very fine indeed![18]

Being king gave Edward less time than he would have wanted for his amusing friends, and much has been made of his bored expression during the grotesque summer ceremony when 600 debutantes were 'presented' at court, or his failure, during a summer holiday in Scotland, to turn up and open a hospital. But the truth is, he did far more than Queen Victoria had ever dreamed of doing in the way of public duties, and he performed some of them with imagination and aplomb. His occasional lapses are not to be compared with the temper-tantrums and awkward shyness of his brother Bertie throughout his public life both as Duke of York and as George VI. Nor did not ever commit a gaffe such as his sister-in-law Elizabeth Bowes-Lyon perpetrated when visiting South Africa as queen empress, when the whole fiasco was over, and, with her umbrella, she rapped the knuckles of the little children who dared to stretch out to her in her limousine as she glided past them. Edward would have made a perfectly satisfactory king had he been allowed to stay in place, but history, extraordinarily babyish in this respect, has to depict him as a selfish sybarite, a Nazi sympathizer, a man who would have 'brought down' the monarchy, and his brother – a decent enough person in his way for someone all but talentless – as a sort of saint. Of course, had Edward VIII been allowed to stay on the throne, he would, just as much as his brother, have been a devoted wartime leader to his people, and it would have been he, and his queen, who were the beloved icons, adored by their own generation for their unselfish touring of bombsites, their visiting of hospitals, and their plucky refusal to leave Buckingham Palace even when it was bombed. As it happened this script was handed to Edward's brother and his wife to enact. He was doomed instead to play another role, of exile, and oddball.

Quite how it happened, although or because it has been written about so often, is actually hard to explain. When one reads about the story, it really is as if none of the participants in the drama exactly knew what they were doing; as if they were being guided by completely irrational impulses.

If an ardent monarchist, yearning for the institution of kingship in a changing world to survive, had sat down and invented a person most likely to continue, while adapting, its historic role, they could hardly have found anyone more appropriate than the new king. He was handsome. The masses adored him. He was bright but not disconcertingly clever. He was weirdly willing to serve. On a private level at least, no Prince of Wales more completely lived out his motto, *Ich dien*.

At Fort Belvedere, the pretty little folly which he inhabited in Windsor Great Park, he was an affectionate and attentive host. When someone said they would prefer to drink white wine rather than champagne he did not bother a servant, he went and fetched it himself. This habit of pleasant courtesy continued throughout life. Once, lunching with a friend just outside Paris in his retirement years, David, by then demoted to being Duke of Windsor, saw that a minor crisis had occurred. It was hardly the Marriage Feast of Cana, but Daisy Fellowes wanted a glass of Coca-Cola and her hostess had none in the house. Immediately, the Duke of Windsor went to the telephone and rang his German butler. 'Fritz, hier ist der Herzog,' he was heard saying in his cockneyfied but fluent German. 'Können Sie eine Flasche hier schicken? . . . Nein, nein, nicht Wein. Koka-Kola. Bitte sehr.'

Some time in May 1934, the prince's mistress, Mrs Dudley Ward, was distracted by the illness of a daughter and remained out of touch with him for some weeks. When she rang the switchboard at St James's Palace she spoke to the telephonist whose voice she had heard on an almost daily basis for many years. 'I have something so terrible to tell you,' said the young woman, her voice trembling with emotion, 'that I don't know how to say it. I have orders not to put you through.'

That was how his friend and mistress of over fifteen years learnt that she had been dropped. It had been some time in January 1932 that the Prince of Wales had first met an animated American lady, married to Ernest Simpson – in whose sister's house he had met Mrs Dudley-Ward. The new woman in his life had been born on 19 July 1896 in Baltimore, and called by her parents Bessiewallis Warfield. She disliked the name Bessie and soon came to be known simply as Wallis. Though her own parents were not rich, she was born into a distinctly upper-class family, and her relations all lived in large houses with servants. After an unhappy marriage in America she had come to Europe, and in 1928 she had married Ernest Simpson. That marriage too was doomed to fail, largely through his unfaithfulness. The person who introduced her to Prince Edward was Lady Furness (Thelma), with whom he was having an affair, blighted, she was unkind enough to say, by his sexual incompetence. When Lady Furness had to leave England for a few months in the spring of 1934, she asked Wallis Simpson to 'look after the Prince while she was away'. It soon became clear to the prince's circle that he had fallen deeply in love with Mrs Simpson.

When Chips Channon first met Wallis Simpson on 23 January 1935 he found 'a nice, quiet, well-bred mouse of a woman with large, startled eyes and a huge mole. I think she is surprised and rather conscience-stricken by her present position.' By 11 May, he saw her rather as an adventuress in a Henry James story – his description would fit Mrs Headway in 'The Siege of London'. 'Never has he been so in love. She is madly anxious to storm society, while she still is his favourite, so that when he leaves her (as he leaves everyone in time) she will be secure.'[19] At cocktails in her 'little flat in Bryanston Court' Chips noted the Prince of Wales wearing a short black coat, soft collar, checked socks and a tie. 'He shook and passed the cocktails very much the "*jeune homme de la maison*".' Later, when the whole matter was over and the king had been driven into exile, Chips reflected:

> I really consider she would have been an excellent Queen. She is never embarrassed, ill at ease, and could in her engaging drawl charm anyone . . . Her reserve and discretion are famous, and proved by the fact that no one knew of her impending divorce, also by the fact that she never confided in anyone her hopes of becoming Queen. I think that the idea grew, gradually. She was encouraged by the King to believe that he could marry her, and indeed there was nothing legal to prevent him doing so. Perhaps at first the idea was a joke, which blossomed into a plan.[20]

Certainly, by the time he became the king, Mrs Simpson was a fixture in his heart. What by the standards of the twenty-first century is so extraordinary is that the very existence of Mrs Simpson was kept out of the British newspapers. This was largely because Lord Beaverbrook approved of her and was on the new king's side. But it was in part because no British newspaper would have considered it seemly to discuss the love life of the royal family, any more than it would have spilled the beans about the extramarital indiscretions of such well-known political philanderers as Lloyd George or Sir Oswald Mosley. Victorian double standards still ruled, and it was the king, not the newspapers, who broke the taboo. So, while the diaries of Chips Channon make it clear that London society, and political circles, gossiped constantly about the king and Mrs Simpson, the matter in general was unknown. Wallis had very openly accompanied the king on a Mediterranean cruise with a group of friends on board a large yacht called the *Nahlin*. Sailing along the Dalmatian coast they had been greeted by cries of *Zivila Ljubav!* (*Vive l'amour*), so it was no secret to the Yugoslavians – nor to the American press.[21] But it was a secret in Britain, where Queen Mary or Mr Baldwin were as likely to shout *Zivila Ljubav!* as *Allah akbar*.

On 27 October 1936 Wallis was granted a decree nisi, which meant she could be fully divorced (decree absolute) by 27 April 1937: in time for the Coronation. It was then that the old men, especially Baldwin and the Archbishop of Canterbury, started to panic and to devise the systematic destruction of their monarch. Friends of the king, such as Duff Cooper or Winston Churchill, pointed out that if – as became clear – he was intent upon marrying Wallis, he could have a morganatic marriage. The archduke who was shot in Sarajevo had a morganatic wife, which would have meant, had he lived to become the Austrian emperor, that she would still have been his wife but not an empress. Wallis, similarly, in deference to those who believed that the titular head of the Church should not marry a divorcee, could have become the king's wife, given any title they chose to invent, while he was crowned as king-emperor.

When this was put to the cabinet, only Duff Cooper approved it. Baldwin claimed he had sounded out the prime ministers of the Dominions and of the Empire. Those of Canada, Australia and South Africa were said to be definitely against Mrs Simpson marrying the king by any formulary whatever. The Prime Minister of New Zealand, who had never until that moment heard of Mrs Simpson, sat on the fence saying 'his country would not quarrel with anything the King did, nor with anything his Government did to restrain him'.[22]

By the beginning of December Baldwin had lined up the Church, the Dominions and the Labour party against the king. He had done so because he knew that when the Press eventually broke its silence it would inevitably become a matter of public debate. Such a thing could very well have created a King's Party in the country at large.

One part of the story, true but achieving almost instantaneously legendary status, was that the king went on a tour of the depressed mining villages of South Wales. He saw the Merthyr Tydfil Labour Exchange, and made a detour, not on his schedule, to see the Bessemer Steel Works at Dowlais. Where 9,000 men had been employed only a few years before was a desolate scene of wreckage, with hundreds of men sitting on piles of twisted metal and the rubble of demolished factory buildings. Seeing their king, they stood and sang hymns. The king stood bareheaded and said grimly: 'These works brought all these people here. Something must be done to find them work.'

It was deemed to be an 'inappropriate' political remark. The Conservatives and the mainstream Labour party were united in the need for bumbling, ineffectual means of getting the unemployed back to work. Efficient, Keynesian experiments were things to be left to such extremists as the Blackshirts, who while making no headway whatever in parliamentary elections, created a somewhat sinister parody of Continental fascism on the street corners, and in the big meeting halls of the large cities. Was the king in sympathy with them, or indeed, was he in league with the German National Socialists themselves?

It is part of the mythology of the Abdication Story, trotted out with every new book on the subject.

This is one of those areas where supreme acts of historical imagination are required if one is not to sail off into fantasy. We look at the 1930s through the dark glass of the Second World War and its aftermath, so that sympathy with, or actual membership of fascist organizations is inevitably, and rightly, linked in our minds with the millions who died in the conflict, and with the systematic murder by the Nazis of 6 million Jews. It is a poor sort of memory which only works backwards, as the White Queen says to Alice, and the 'fascist' sympathies of King Edward VIII did not extend to condoning any of the National Socialist programme – though the Nazis were very keen indeed to exploit his name in their propaganda.

One has to recognize a climate in which the horrors perpetrated by socialism in Russia led quite reasonable people to fear that milder forms of socialism would inevitably lead to the same kind of mayhem and loss of life. In a debate in the House of Lords in 1934, Viscount Esher said: 'The prosperous middle classes of this country will defend themselves, just as they did in the General Strike. On the other hand, it ought to be made clear to them, too, that the rise of Sir Oswald Mosley is nothing more than a reply to the policy of Sir Stafford Cripps [i.e. of the Labour party]. If they want to destroy Sir Oswald Mosley they can only do it by repudiating Sir Stafford Cripps. There is no other way of doing it. There are innumerable quiet people in this country who, hating both these gentlemen, will if they are forced to choose between them, I am glad to say, choose Sir Oswald Mosley.'[23]

The old King George V would probably have gone along with that, and there is no secret about the fact that when the new King Edward VIII was living in exile as the Duke of Windsor, he made friends with Sir Oswald and his wife, enjoying long conversations in which they set the world to rights. Twelve years after the war, Sir Oswald's acerbic sister-in-law Nancy Mitford wrote to a friend from Paris: 'The Mosleys . . . and the Windsors are literally never apart. They want us all to be governed by the kind, clever, rich Germans and be happy ever after. I wish I knew why they all live in France and not outre-Rhin.'[24]

It was disastrous to his historical reputation that after the abdication the Duke of Windsor and his new bride Wallis visited Germany and were photographed smiling and bowing to Hitler. By then it was perfectly clear what sort of regime Hitler had brought into being. The Nuremberg laws were fully enforced, and principled persons such as Harold Nicolson refused to go to the place. Others, however, such as Edward VIII's friend Chips Channon, were bowled over by the magnificence of Nazi ceremonial, and while having no interest whatever in athletics, were held in thrall by those parts of the 1936 Olympic Games which contained pageantry, salutes to the Führer and so forth. When presented to Hitler, Chips had felt 'more excited than when I met Mussolini in Perugia, and more stimulated, I am sorry to say, than when I was blessed by the Pope in 1920'.[25]

It is probably true to say that Edward VIII was pro-German but not especially pro-fascist, not by the standards of the age. He is not recorded as having any especially anti-Semitic feelings; unlike his brother, the moronic Duke of Gloucester, who surprised an officers' mess at the beginning of the war by remarking airily: 'You can say what you like about this Hitler Johnny, but he knows how to treat the Nosey Brigade.' Nor did Edward VIII show any more fondness for the odious new German ambassador in London, Joachim von Ribbentrop, than, say, his brother the Duke of Kent, who was very much part of the Ribbentrop 'set'. Harold Nicolson wrote, disapprovingly, of the 'champagne-like influence of Ribbentrop'.[26] It was one of the Nazis' fantasies that Edward VIII was more than halfway to being of their political persuasion, which is why so many who wanted to ingratiate themselves with the upper ranks of the party, and with Hitler himself, implied or openly stated that the king, either before or after his abdication, had expressed actual Nazi opinions as opposed to the package of fellow-travelling beliefs which many perfectly nice people (wrongly) held at the time: belief that the Nazis had brought full employment and peace and a bloodless revolution, that the Nazis had no territorial ambitions beyond the lands of which the Versailles treaty had deprived the Fatherland, and so on. It certainly suited Baldwin's purposes, and those of the new king and queen after 1936, to play up the rumours that David and Wallis were Nazis, or would be the puppet-king and queen in the event of a Nazi takeover of Britain.

The idea that Nazi Germany in general, Hitler in particular, could be attractive to foreign visitors is a disturbing one. One does not need to excuse those who were enraptured by the Führer, any more than one needs to excuse those, like George Bernard Shaw, who loved Mussolini and went to the Soviet Union during the Stalinist purges and thought that it was an earthly paradise. The truth is, however, that all but the most acute and inquisitive foreign visitors to a country see either what they are shown or what they wish to see.

Many things were obscure to foreigners, however intelligent they may have been in other areas of life, which were obvious to the natives. The diaries of Friedrich Reck-Malleczewen, translated as *Diary of a Man in Despair*, depict the real Germany to which figures such as Chips Channon and many others from Britain and America were blind. One obvious thing, which these foreign visitors missed, was that the Nazis were gangsters. Reck-Malleczewen, a lofty North German liberal aristocrat with lands in Bavaria, seeing a picture in the *Berliner Illustrierte Zeitung* of Göring with his lady, noted: 'They stood in front of an immense Gobelins tapestry which had been part of the Wittelsbach private collection which had been stolen.'

Reck-Malleczewen was a snob, undoubtedly. The commonness of the Nazis offended his aristocratic sensibility; but his diary is one of the documents which undoubtedly give snobbery a good name. For he believes that the old idea, still retained in England, of a governing aristocracy, of a class which is set apart by birth and education to govern fairly and decently, was a better system than the one in which the Germans had entrapped themselves. He recalls a moment in 1920 when staying with a friend called Clemens von Franckenstein (good name!). Someone who, according to the butler, had gatecrashed the party 'wearing gaiters, floppy wide-brimmed hat and carrying a riding-whip', and accompanied by a collie-dog, began to harangue the other guests. It was Hitler. 'The effect, among the Gobelin tapestries and cool marble walls, was something akin to a cowboy's sitting down on the steps of a baroque altar in leather breeches, spurs, and with a Colt at his side.' Reck found him to be 'the stereotype of a head waiter', and was unimpressed by the rant – 'he went on at us like a chaplain in the army'. When he eventually left, the host stood up and opened one of the huge windows. 'It was not that our grim guest had been unclean, and had fouled the room in the way that so often happens in a Bavarian village. But the fresh air helped to dispel the feeling of oppression.'[27] When he saw Hitler glide past in a car in 1936, only five days after Chips Channon had felt that meeting the Führer was better than being blessed by the Pope, Reck observed: 'so sad, so utterly insignificant, so basically misbegotten is this countenance that only thirty years ago, in the darkest days of Wilhelmism, such a face of an official would have been impossible. Appearing in a chair of a minister, an apparition with a face like this would have been disobeyed as soon as its mouth spoke an order – and not merely by the higher officials in the ministry: no, by the doorman, by the cleaning women!'[28]

Reck saw that what had happened to Germany was not merely a socio-political change. It was something metaphysical. 'I am neither an occult nor a mystic. I am a child of my time despite all forebodings, and I hold strictly to what I see. But there is a frightful riddle here, and I come back again and again to what appears to me the only answer to it: What I saw gliding past, behind the face of his mameluke, like the Prince of Darkness himself, was no human being.'[29]

From a completely different perspective, that of a Jewish academic, Viktor Klemperer, who, astonishingly, lived through the whole of the Third Reich, there is the same tangible sense of things having gone mad, of a Germany taken over by gangsterism, and by the entirely new and twentieth-century idea of the mass media. 'Religious madness and advertising madness,' Klemperer calls it. 'And always the lies that accompany everything.'[30]

It is hardly surprising that Edward VIII should have been caught up in this drama, becoming king as he did at precisely the moment when the Nazi propaganda machine was working so hard to persuade the British that it was in their interest not to resist their expansionism or to be caught up by treaty in anything which would limit Hitler's quasi-imperial ambitions. Leopold von Hoesch, Ribbentrop's predecessor in London, dispatched to his masters in Berlin the view that 'I am convinced that his [King Edward's] friendly attitude towards Germany might in time come to exercise a certain amount of influence in the shaping of British foreign policy.'[31]

Memos of this sort are adduced by some biographers to suggest that the British government was right to be wary of Edward VIII. If the Germans' estimate had been true, it is odd that so many of the professional politicians who were of 'the King's party' – Duff Cooper, Colonel Wedgwood, Winston Churchill – were actually those who were most anti-appeasement, and anti-German. These men by 1936 were urgently reminding the British people, and the world, of the dangers of Nazi expansion; they were arguing for rearmament. Is it likely they would have backed a king who was pro-Nazi? It remains the case, however, that the old men who decided to sack the king, come what may, sniffed out in him that kind of cheap populism which Reck-Malleczewen found so detestable in Nazism. Reck rightly saw Nazism as a product of an entirely new phenomenon, popular culture. Mass-man, he called the result of such manipulation – 'stupefied mass-man, and the conversion of human societies into heaps of termites!'[31] It was a particular cause of resentment by David and Wallis, after their abdication, that the Old Men banned by law the sale of gramophone records of his one and only wireless broadcast to his people, explaining why he had given up the throne.[32] They were determined to control the 'mass media' of their day and to make them as unpopulist and as unpolitical as possible.

Luckily for the Old Men, they did not need to conspire against the king. They did not need, until they had pushed him out, to exaggerate his (in fact quite mild) fascistic leanings. The king whom they so much disliked can only with a small part of himself have wanted to be king. With another part of his nature, he must have needed, very deeply, to wound his mother and insult the memory of his father by doing the unthinkable thing of renouncing the throne. Baldwin and Cosmo Gordon Lang did not need to do anything except stand firm on a simple religious point of principle. This principle is that the national Church – founded in order to facilitate a royal annulment (Henry VIII) and rescued from Roman Catholic obliteration by the maritally irregular Elector of Hanover (George I) – forbade the remarriage of divorced persons in church. The British constitution is an unwritten phenomenon which is made up on the hoof. Had Baldwin and the Dominion prime ministers so desired, it would probably have been possible to do as the King's Party desired and allow the king his crown and his wife. They did not want this, so they offered him a *fait accompli*. Wallis always denied, with vehemence, that her marital status was the sole reason for the Old Men sacking her husband, and she had some evidence on her side.

In her memoirs, *The Heart Has Its Reasons*, Wallis describes her shock upon the story breaking in the Press. 'The dam was broken; I felt unnerved; self-reproach flooded through me . . . through my mind ran the question: Why? *Why? Why? Why didn't you follow your first instinct? Why didn't you go when you first knew that was the only thing to do?*'

She said to the King: 'Dearest David, I am sorry I've done this to you.' His reply was: 'What's done is done. We've got things to do right now.'³³

These things included spiriting Wallis abroad – to France – in her Buick with the king's lord-in-waiting 'Perry' Brownlow and Brownlow's chauffeur at the wheel. From the Villa Lou Vieie near Cannes she attempted to keep in touch with the king by a crackling telephone line, and to persuade him to stay on the throne, if necessary to give her up. Theodore Goddard, her solicitor, was dispatched to France to persuade her to withdraw divorce proceedings against Ernest Simpson. Lord Brownlow, in her presence, told the lawyer that if the king did abdicate, which he was close to doing, he would do so in order to marry, so that scrapping divorce proceedings would solve nothing.

Wallis became convinced at this stage of things however that Mr Baldwin would force the king to abdicate whether she remained in the picture or not. The implications of her letters to Sibyl Colefax are not given sufficient weight by all commentators. On 18 December, after the abdication, she wrote to Lady Colefax:

I still can't write about it all because I am afraid of not conveying the true facts – as brain is so very tired from the struggle – of the past two weeks – the screaming of a thousand plans to London, to pleading to lead him and not to force him. I know him so well. I wanted them to take my advice but no driving in they went headed for this tragedy – if only they had said – Let's drop the idea now and in the autumn we'll discuss it again – and Sibyl darling in the autumn I could have been so very far away – I had already escaped – some day if we ever meet I shall tell you all. The little faith I have tried to cling on to has been taken from me when I saw England turn on a man that couldn't defend himself and had never been anything *but* straight with his country.³⁴

What this letter shows is that at the height of the crisis Wallis had wanted to get shot not merely of England but of the King. Chips had surely been right, that all she had envisaged was to be the King's mistress: to reap fun and social advantage of this, not to be with him for ever. Two tragic ingredients conspired against such a light-hearted scheme. One was that the King was in love with her, and stubbornly determined to marry her, partly to show what he thought of Baldwin and the 'Old Gang'.

Another letter, written a few days later in December 1936, makes it clear not only that *she* had been planning to drop the King, but that *he* had been prepared to drop, or at least postpone, marriage to avert a constitutional crisis:

> It is a cruel world and honesty doesn't seem To [sic] be the quality that gets you the longest way. Naturally you knew the King need never have gone – *he* offered to drop the subject of marriage for the present. It was turned down by the powers that be. What does one read into that? I did all in my power and succeeded rather well with the King. But you know I had no power with the Government – remember my dear only one side of their case is known to the world at present and it has been presented almost too cleverly.[35]

There is no evidence that Mrs Simpson was here lying to her friend Lady Colefax. It surely, therefore, constitutes proof that Baldwin sacked the King even if the younger man agreed not to force the government's hand over the royal marriage. So if the King was not forced to abdicate because of his desire for marriage, what was the reason? It is easy to see why the conspiracy theories sometimes come to the surface – as that the King was sacked for having fascistic leanings.

When he had gone, the Archbishop of Canterbury felt constrained to rub a little salt in his wounds. Broadcasting to the nation on Sunday, 13 December, he said: 'What pathos, nay what tragedy, surrounds the central figure of these swiftly moving scenes! On the 11th of December, 248 years ago, King James II fled from Whitehall. By a strange coincidence, on the 11th day of December last week, King Edward VIII, after speaking his last words to his people, left Windsor Castle, the scene of all the splendid traditions of his ancestors and his Throne, and went out an exile. In the darkness, he left these shores.'

The Archbishop's broadcast caused very great offence, even among those who broadly speaking felt it had been right for the king to go. In particular, the humbug tone of the Archbishop's moralizing was felt to strike the wrong note. 'Even more strange and sad it is that he should have sought his happiness in a manner inconsistent with the Christian principles of marriage, and within a social circle whose standards and ways of life are alien to all the best instincts and traditions of his people.' A wag responded: 'My Lord Archbishop what a scold you are!/And when your man is down, how bold you are!/Of Christian charity how scant you are!/And auld Lang swine, how full of cant you are!'[36]

Though the broadcast made the Archbishop disliked, it was to have a deadly influence with the one family who should have ignored it: the royal family themselves. One can imagine how robustly either George IV or Edward VII would have responded to the impertinence of an unmarried old gentleman of over seventy commenting upon his choice of friends or his sexual morals. George VI, who did not have a social circle of any kind, never mind one whose standards were alien to the traditions of the British people, could hardly have been affected by the words. But his wife was, and ensured that her daughters surrounded themselves until they were grown up with the stuffiest old Scottish aristocrats and a few hand-picked homosexuals, such as Osbert Sitwell and Noël Coward. Nemesis, however, never forgot the Archbishop Lang broadcast. Princess Margaret Rose, sister of Queen Elizabeth II, was the first casualty, giving up the man she loved because he was divorced and going on to mix with a strangely rackety 'set' who would not have passed muster with Cosmo Gordon Lang. Her sister, both as Princess Elizabeth and as Queen Elizabeth II, was as blameless as her father, but she achieved the remarkable hat trick of seeing three out of her four children contract marriages that ended in divorce.

Poor Little Dook, as his friends in exile called him. You can see why Baldwin wanted to ban his last broadcast. It is electrifying: the slightly cockney, already slightly Americanized voice. The passion. He had no idea when he gave it that thirty-five years stretched ahead in which he was not to be allowed back to reside in Britain. During the war years, they kept him out of harm's way by making him the Governor of the Bahamas. They could indulge the malice of the new Queen-Empress, Elizabeth, by denying Wallis the privilege, which she strangely enough craved, of calling herself Her Royal Highness The Duchess of Windsor. Otherwise, it was a thirty-five-year stretch of golf, shopping trips to New York, dinners with the Mosleys, Daisy Fellowes, and others.

'At long last I am able to say a few words of my own' – that is one of the best sentences ever broadcast. Some would think it was the first distant cry, decades too early, of the me-generation; others would see it as the gentlest of reproofs to intolerably interfering politicians.

You all know the reasons which have impelled me to renounce the throne. But I want you to understand that in making up my mind I did not forget the country or the Empire which as Prince of Wales, and lately as King, I have for twenty-five years tried to serve. But you must believe me when I tell you that I have found it impossible to carry the heavy burden of responsibility and to discharge my duties as King as I would wish to do without the help and support of the woman I love.[37]

After he had delivered the broadcast, he went to Royal Lodge to say goodbye to his family. As well as being grief-stricken, Queen Mary was stiff with rage[38] at the 'humiliation of it all'. It was a moment which might have been invented by the man who won the Nobel Prize for literature that year, Eugene O'Neill, that brilliant chronicler of the hatred and power struggles which are interwoven in the love between sons and mothers. With a bowler hat on his head and a West Highland terrier tucked under one elbow, the king went aboard the Royal Naval vessel HMS *Fury*, which conveyed him by night to France.

When, less than two weeks before, on 30 November 1936, the Crystal Palace, outward and visible sign of buoyant economic liberalism, was destroyed by fire, it must have seemed to many as if the Victorian Age was now decisively over. The building which, when it was erected, had embodied so many Victorian causes for self-congratulation now buckled and melted in a prodigious conflagration visible for miles around. And yet in the closing scenes of the Abdication, Britain, and most especially England, seemed to be enacting a rather different story. The Victorian Establishment, the privately educated parliamentarians, the civil servants who knew the Odes of Horace by heart, and the House of Lords continued unshaken. The young man with soft collars and a fondness for jazz records was sent packing by a septuagenarian Archbishop and Prime Minister. In place at Windsor were a royal family whose gentle and retiring habits would have won the approval of Prince Albert himself. Although younger in years than his brother, the new King George VI, in his attitudes and habits, was about a hundred years older. Age had defeated Youth; Conservatism had vanquished Progressivism; Religion of a distinctly stiff-corseted kind had cast out Secularism; Perfect Fear had cast out Love.

Those who paint a purely political picture of the abdication get it wrong. So do conspiracy theorists. It was, however, a drama which convulsed the nation, obsessing even those who would normally consider themselves too sophisticated to be interested in the royal family.

On that 10 December, Malcolm Muggeridge wrote in his Diary:

In the evening we sat listening to the wireless broadcasting the news of the King's abdication. I had the feeling that the affair somehow symbolized the whole horror of life, the struggle between Man's noblest, richest impulses, and the shoddy fabric of Time. Hughie [Kingsmill, writer and wit] described how he had once visited in Brittany the ruins of an ancient sacrificial Temple, and how there he had first realized what sacrifice meant – the offering up of Youth by Age, a spiking of young blood by withered arms, paying Life as a tribute to Death . . . We drove Hughie back. Blackshirts were selling their papers in the streets surrounded by a circle of admiring girls. Kit [Muggeridge, his wife] keeps saying to me: 'Everything's going to be all right, isn't it?' and I nod without conviction.[39]

25

The European Crisis

Between July 1936 and 1 April 1939, Spain was involved in a civil war which not only involved its own citizens in ferocious bloodletting, but which also gripped the imagination, and engaged the political conscience, of all the other major European powers. Because of the direct intervention, with economic aid, arms and troops, on one side of the Soviet Union, on the other side of Germany and Italy, the Spanish Civil War has seemed to many to be a dress rehearsal for the world war which followed.

Yet there are many paradoxes about viewing it in this way. The war was won by the Right. The generals who had rebelled against the elected leftist government in 1936 achieved their objective. General Franco became a dictator who held power until his death in 1975. Tens of thousands of republicans, after the civil war, were shot, or given prison-sentences of over twenty years. But estimates for the numbers actually killed in the war 'have dropped and dropped' according to the historian Hugh Thomas,[1] who also believes that 'it would be perfectly admissible to argue that Spain lost fewer people dead in acts of violence than any other major European nation in [the twentieth] century'.[2]

At the time, the unimaginable numbers of twentieth-century dead were either in the future, or had been concealed. Very few believed those, such as Malcolm Muggeridge, who spoke of the organized famines in the Ukraine, killing perhaps over 10 million. And the massacre of 6 million Jews, or the killing of over 200,000 Japanese civilians before the dropping of nuclear bombs, or the bombing of German cities, killing hundreds of thousands of civilians, these and comparable war crimes lay in the future. The bombing of the Basque town of Guernica, therefore, killing a few hundred, seemed, quite rightly, to be an act of terrible savagery. Strangely enough, it is those nations, Britain and America, who killed civilian numbers of this order roughly every hour of the last year of the Second World War who make most of a cult of Picasso's famous painting evoking Guernica's tragedy.

We are almost still too close to the Second World War, and to the Spanish War which was its overture, to speak or write about it rationally. But perhaps we are approaching the era when such a rationality might become at least a possibility? In which case, what do we make of the fact that General Franco, an autocratic military leader who won his victory with the help of German Nazis and Italian fascists, and who was prepared to exercise a murderous autocracy for about eight years after his victory, went on to lead a modern European state deep into our own lifetimes, and did so peaceably, prosperously and seamlessly? He achieved, without any Marshall Aid or outside help, an economic revolution in the 1960s, and he handed over his regime into the hands of a constitutional monarch, Juan Carlos, who must rank as one of the most enlightened of modern world leaders. Meanwhile, in Eastern Europe, the Soviet Union which had sent aid to the elected government of Spain throughout the civil war, and which was to become the ally of the Western powers during the Second World War, is now seen to be without any rival as the most murderous, repressive and tyrannous system of human enslavement ever to exercise dominion over the human race.

It is very understandable why people on both sides of the political divide saw Spain as the stage on which their ideological conflicts were being enacted. And the policy of the British government throughout the Spanish Civil War, of broad sympathy for Franco while maintaining the non-interventionist position, seems in retrospect to be coherent. The broad interests of the British people, and the broad political allegiance of the governing party, both seem to have been met by this position.

And yet, the figure who is to emerge as the most important in the British and indeed Western political landscape, Winston Churchill, takes a different view.

When the civil war broke out, Churchill was in favour of Franco, but he changed. In August 1938, interviewed by a Buenos Aires newspaper, *La Nación*, he said: 'Franco has all the right on his side because he loves his country. Also Franco is defending Europe against the Communist danger – if you wish to put it in those terms. But I – I am English, and I prefer the triumph of the wrong cause. I prefer that the other side wins, because Franco could be an upset or a threat to British interests and the others not.'[3]

If you were approaching this matter from even a partially rational point of view, this would be hard to understand. Churchill had been, since the first emergence of socialism as a viable political force in the politics of Britain and of the world, its most belligerent opponent, as he would continue to be after the Second World War. He hated Bolshevism, he hated communism, and he could see that Franco was defending not merely Spain, but Western Europe, from the possibility of being taken over by communism.

The tragedy of the twentieth century is that in order to defeat Hitler, Churchill believed it was not merely necessary but desirable to ally himself to Stalin. It is very easy, from our comfortable twenty-first-century armchairs, to take positions. We can rewrite history as imaginatively as we choose. We can say: 'But – Franco saved Europe! If it had not been for Franco's victory, Blum, the Socialist Prime Minister of France, would have allowed France to become communist, and then the sinister hand of Stalin would have held sway from Siberia to Dieppe.' Or we can think the other way, and we can say that it would have somehow been possible for Britain to stand neutral, as, no doubt, many Conservatives in Baldwin's cabinet and backbenchers wished. Hitler and Mussolini could have behaved in their monstrous way, but it did not directly concern the British Empire, so why should it have mattered whether Czechoslovakia, or Poland, or Austria was governed by this power or that?

In the end, such armchair history is rather tasteless. Millions upon millions died as a result of the Second World War. There is something unseemly about being wise after the event. History is the story of what happened, and not of what did not happen. We can fantasize about what might have happened had the Second World War been averted. Millions of lives might have been saved. The Shoah, the slaughter of the Jews, would probably have been impossible in peacetime. Hitler, rather than Stalinist Russia, might have dominated Czechoslovakia, Poland, Hungary . . . In time, Hitler might have been overthrown by a decent group of Germans, or the German economy would have imploded, and Hitler would have fallen from grace in the eyes of the electorate; or Hitler would have been like Franco – horrific in his early years in peacetime power but latterly gentler, more in tune with the modern world. And so, millions upon millions of lives might have been saved. But history is the story of what was, not of what might have been. And whatever judgement we pass upon Churchill, and whatever view we take of the British, French and American politicians who directed the course and ultimately the victory of the Second World War, we have to say that one at least of the things which directed them was a sense of decency.

Reck-Malleczewen, in his diaries, railed against the nations of the world 'standing by and watching' while Hitler triumphed. 'You have broken our internal resistance through political lethargy.' As he writes in his diaries, Luftwaffe bombers fly overhead, and he adds: 'For a whole hour the drone has gone on above, as though these planes were flying against a world power. I am a German. I encircle this land in which I live with all my love . . . I know that this land is the living, beating heart of the world. I will go on believing in this heartbeat, despite all the covering layers of blood and dirt. But I know also that the thing up there that rumbles and thunders is the denial of right and justice, of truth and faith and everything that makes life worth living.' In 1938, on 20 March, he wrote: 'If five years ago, at the time of the so-called Power-Grab

[*Machtergreifung*, the word the Nazis used for their assumption of power], the European nations had drown the sword – everything would have ended with a police raid, with the gang being hustled off to jail by the collars.' Further, on 22 September 1939, when war had finally broken out between Britain and Germany, he wrote: 'Germany has been sinking deeper and deeper into unreality . . . It is now completely drugged on its own lies. The cure will be more awful than anything ever seen before in history. One must hate Germany now, truly and bitterly, in order once again, if only for the sake of its glorious past, to be able later to enfold it in all of one's love – like a parent with his misguided and unfortunate child.'

These are extraordinary words for a man to write about his own country.

Valentin Berzhkov, who worked as an interpreter for Stalin's regime, was in Berlin during the spring and summer of 1940 as part of a commission monitoring deliveries of German technology to the Soviet Union under the terms of the Molotov–Ribbentrop Pact signed between the two dictatorships in August 1939 arranging for the partition of Poland. He found 'how much there is in common' . . . 'The same idolization of the "leader", the same mass rallies and parades . . . Very similar, ostentatious architecture, heroic themes depicted in art much like our socialist realism . . . massive ideological brainwashing'.[5]

Both régimes encouraged their citizens to spy on each other and denounce one another to the authorities. One of the marked contrasts between the Italian fascist regime and the German Nazis was that ordinary citizens willingly collaborated, in Germany, with informing on foreign workers, Jews, criminals and others they deemed undesirable. The psychology of this kind of 'good citizenship' weakened the strength of resistance movements in Germany and softened up the 'ordinary' Germans, so that they were prepared, when the killing started in earnest, that is after 1941, to condone or even to participate in the most monstrous acts. That such acts would happen, intelligent German observers, such as Bonhoeffer or Reck-Malleczewen, could not doubt, from quite an early stage. But it is worth while to note the differences, as well as the similarities, between the Germany of Hitler and the Soviet Union of Stalin, not in order to exonerate anyone from blame, but in order to explain: to explain how the Germans could have behaved as they did, and how those outside Germany could have believed themselves to be doing right either in condoning Hitler's regime, or appeasing it, or collaborating with it.

One very simple difference between Germany and the Soviet Union was that Germans, with a few very obvious exceptions, were allowed to own property. The Nazi leadership had a gangster mentality, looting and stealing what they chose from the palaces of the Wittelsbachs in Bavaria, for example, as well as purloining the assets of Jews. They were certainly not respecters of property in the conventional sense. But their politics were inspired by fantasies of race rather than by Marxist notions of capital. The factory owner, the businessman, the shopkeeper, provided he was of Aryan stock, and provided he was prepared to go along with the government, could continue his independent life. Many prospered, and not just the owners themselves. In the apparent 'economic miracle' which Hitler had worked, tens of thousands of Germans, who had been out of work during the Weimar days, or who had lost their savings, felt their prosperity return. In November 1936, Viktor Klemperer saw a young man in the crowded Berlin street – 'a complete stranger'. He 'half turns and says with a beaming face, "I've got work – the first time in three years – and good work – at Renner's – they pay well! – for four weeks".' There was a heady atmosphere of joy about those early National Socialist days for many people, such as the young man Klemperer saw. They could see the autobahns being constructed, and every family, in a People's Car, a Volkswagen, could dream of driving about like lords of all they surveyed. This last dream, which continued to cheer Germans up until the outbreak of war, was, like many of the Führer's promises, not as reliable as his admirers believed. Whereas by 1939 over 200,000 Germans had handed over the 1,000 Reichsmark purchase price, only 50 cars had been manufactured. (Compare the Morris factory in Oxford, producing 20,000 cars a year.) The point is, the people believed the Nazi propaganda about their being prosperous and efficient industrialists, and it made them happy. When the invasions of the Sudetenland, and the rest of Czechoslovakia were under way, it was very largely in order to bolster German industry, and to keep the factories supplied with necessary minerals and raw materials.[6]

Robert Gellately in his book *Defending Hitler* reiterates the fact – difficult to credit given all our post-dated hindsight, all our knowledge of the atrocities perpetrated post-1940 – that up to the outbreak of the Second World War, the Nazi regime was plausible to many people, Germans and non-Germans.

The concentration camps, for example, were not, as is sometimes imagined, kept as a secret from the populace, or indeed from the world.* When a concentration camp was started at the small town of Dachau, near Munich, the local Press hailed it as bringing 'new hope for the

---

* By contrast with the extermination camps which were set up after the outbreak of war, outside Germany.

Dachau business world'. It was 'an economic turning point', the 'beginning of happier days'. On 23 May 1933, one newspaper crowed that Dachau was 'Germany's most famous place', a 'model concentration camp'. By 1936, some of the local councillors of Dachau (town population 8,234) were having their doubts about its reputation as 'KZ city' (that is *Konzentrationslager*). But the visitors who were allowed into the camp saw only lines of singing workers, marching in rhythm and working in a disciplined way. They imagined that the sole purpose of concentration camps was to discipline errant souls such as communists and to bring them into a better frame of mind. The concentration camps were 'civilized', 'educative', even 'healing'. Bishop Hermann Wilhelm Berning, the Catholic bishop of Osnabrück, paid an official visit to the Emsland camps. 'Those who doubt the constructive work of the Third Reich should be led here,' he was quoted as saying. He saw Emsland as a Sleeping Beauty whose prince had been 'our Führer Adolf Hitler'.

In July 1933 the numbers held in 'protective custody' in such places was put at 26,789. At Dachau, some 600 prisoners were released each month after 're-education' or a short sharp shock. The fact that many detainees were tortured was kept secret, but very few, by the standards of General Franco, let us say, were killed in the first six years, the prewar period of the Third Reich. Later, of course, the killings in Nazi prisons and camps turned into slaughter of horrific scale. In the little prison camp at Flossenbürg where Bonhoeffer was hanged, over 30,000 were killed. But when such 'useful idiots' as the bishop of Canabrück were making their visits to camps, they were not the death-factories they would become. They were boot-camps, of the kind which many conservative-minded people in Britain and America today wholeheartedly approve. The Nazis were much better at propaganda than twenty-first-century democratic governments. They had complete power over a censored Press, and they had a population who, in the first few years of their regime, grew more slavishly grateful to them for bringing jobs, prosperity and a sense of national pride. In the years 1934 and 1935, the populations of the concentration camps declined, many prisoners were released, and it was perfectly possible for Germans to be persuaded that, cruel as the remedy had been, it had been both non-murderous and efficacious in its battle against communism.[7] By 1936, when the triumphant Olympic Games were so impressing Chips Channon, together with millions of others, the Germans had full employment, a system of public works which seemed to guarantee further employment, and a vigorous foreign policy in which their government was sticking up for their interests against the injustices of the Versailles treaty. Of course, they were, very many of them, happy.

The 1930s were a period of desperate social and economic hardship for the working class. Men are seen here queuing outside the Labour Exchange in Stepney, East London.

The Jarrow Hunger March in October 1936 brought attention to the more prosperous southerners to the plight of the unemployed and their families

Extreme conditions called forth extreme politics. Adolf Hitler before the micro-phones in 1935.

The dictators Benito Mussolini and Adolf Hitler viewing columns of German troops in Munich in 1935. Hitler's 'economic miracle' in restoring Germany to full employment was posited on militarism, a fact to which the rest of the world tried to blind itself.

Ezra Pound, greatest of modernist poets, spent much of the 1930s studying economics and denouncing Usury. His views led him to support the fascists, and his wartime broadcasts in favour of Mussolini caused outrage.

Sir Oswald Mosley moved from being a Conservative, to the rising hope of the Labour Party, before becoming an aspirant Fascist leader in Britain. His movement provided good theatre, and plenty of street fights, but his party the British Union of Fascists did not win a single parliamentary seat in an election.

John Cowper Powys (1872–1963) is surely the greatest English novelist of his generation

Stanley Spencer, seen here sketching as an official war artist in Clydeside, has a visionary picture of England which in some ways complements that of John Cowper Powys and his brothers

Cosmo Gordon Lang, Archbishop of Canterbury, stands on the steps of St Paul's Cathedral in London after a Maundy Thursday service in the late 1930s. His vitriolic denunciation of King Edward VIII after the Abdication was shocking to many.

King Edward VIII was a hugely popular King, dismissed by a highly unpopular *coup d'etat* by the Establishment. Here he is depicted with his chic American wife Wallis in September 1939.

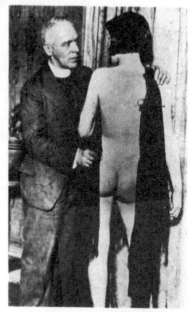

The Rector of Stiffkey, when put on trial for conduct unbecoming a clerk in Holy Orders, claimed, 'I do not know what the buttock is.' He is seen here with a young friend.

The disastrous Teheran conference at which Churchill finally began to realize that the price of defeating Hitler had been to hand the world into the power of Stalin and the Americans

Stan Laurel, English born, and Oliver Hardy made innumerable comic films which unconsciously echoed the 'Special Relationship' between the two great Western democracies

Lord Louis Mountbatten with his wife Edwina depicted with Pandit Jawaharal Nehru and Dr Radhakrishnan. Mountbatten, or Mountbottom as he was privately known, was given the task by the new Labour Government of disposing of the Indian Empire as soon as possible. The speed with which partition with Pakistan was accomplished led to hundreds of thousands of avoidable deaths.

Riots in Calcutta in 1946. This riot alone cost the lives of over 2,000 – with 4,000 injured.

The radiant beauty of Princess Elizabeth, heir to the throne, consoled many for the drabness of post-war Britain. Here she is seen with her sister Princess Margaret visiting South Africa in 1947 and sounding the whistle of the Beyer-Garratt locomotive.

It was the new Queen's decision to insist upon her Coronation being televised and viewed by millions across the world. This row of movie-cameras focussed on the royal pageant is emblematic of the life which the twentieth-century royal family had to live, beneath the constant surveillance of the camera.

James Watson and Francis Crick, the inspired young scientists who cracked the code of DNA and established beyond question the hereditary basis of life

After the war, Britain had lost its empire and its place in the world. The desire to conquer the globe was set aside in favour of more modest aspirations – a house, a family, a car.

Bonhoeffer, from a position of moral intelligence and deep piety, Reck-Malleczewen, with his saving snobbery – seeing the fantastical commonness of figures such as Göring – were able to see through the regime. And there were hundreds of thousands of Germans who did so, too. But it is very difficult to budge a totalitarian régime, and, as Reck said in his journals, the cowardice of foreign régimes weakened the resolve of any potential resistance in Germany before the war.

The historians who, in the postwar period, began to try to make sense of what had happened, to plumb its unfathomable blackened depths, tended at first to fall into two categories, whom one could call the ideologues and the diplomats. For the ideologues, the Spanish Civil War was the beginning, properly speaking, of the great European War. On the one hand there were the forces of the soft, or liberal, Left, the elected government of the Spanish Republic, represented by the president, Manuel Azaña, and Dr Juan Negrín, an internationally esteemed professor and psychologist from the university of Madrid. For many of all shades of leftish opinion, ranged from the Liberal party in Britain to the extreme anarchists and communists, their fight was seen to be with the forces of fascism, as represented by Mussolini, and its more sinister Hitlerite manifestations in Germany. Behind the Republic – if you were against it – you could see the blood-curdling faces who had so alarmed Burke when he reflected upon the French Revolution 140 years earlier, figures such as the lovely Dolores la Sardinera, a great orator and Stalinist, said to have cut a priest's throat with her own teeth.[8] Behind these people were the actual armaments of the Soviet Union. Stalin saw the civil war as a chance not only to spread communism, but to win allies in the field against Germany, should that conflict come.[9] Russia sent over 75,000 tons of oil to Spain between August and October 1935; it sent fighter planes – the I-15 biplane known as the 'Chato' or 'snubnose' and the Mosca; as well as machine guns, bombers, faster than and technically superior to the German ones sent to the rebels. On the other side, the ideologues saw Franco as the defender of Old Europe against communism. He united the swashbuckling, appallingly brutal Carlist mainly northern forces, who supported one branch of the deposed royal family, with the fascist Falangists, and to do his brutal work he enlisted the help of Italian and German troops, aircraft and armaments. Anthony Powell, destined to chronicle English upper-class Bohemia in this period in his unforgettable novel sequence *A Dance to the Music of Time*, well summed up the all but apolitical right-wing position at the time: 'My position on the Spanish War was that people should mind their own business. Much against my taste I should have been for Franco in preference to a Left [Government] dominated by Communists. It seems now clear [he was writing in April 1992] that had

Franco not won, the Communists would have dominated Spain, there would have been a Europe "Red at each end", in 1939 Spain, like Russia, would have come in on the Nazi side and we should have been in a very ticklish situation.'[10]

For those more ideologically engaged than Powell, Spain was the chance to go and fight for an idea: an idea of how the human race in Europe should be governed. It was the closest thing since the Thirty Years War to an all-out ideological conflict. Some 40,000 non-Spanish nationals fought for the Republic, never more than 18,000 at any one time.[11] Most of them were French, but there were some 5,000 German leftists, fewer than 3,000 Americans and some 2,000 from Britain, of whom 500 were killed and 1,200 wounded.[11] General Franco also had his ideological supporters – White Russians, the Romanian Iron Guard, or the 670-strong Irish Brigade, mainly drawn from rural Ireland and West Belfast, some but not all members of the Irish fascist organization the Blueshirts. Their contribution was not always as useful to Franco as he might have hoped when he laid on the cardinal primate of Spain to greet their arrival. On the station platform at Salamanca, in whose town hall they had been entertained perhaps too lavishly, the band struck up the Irish national anthem. One Irish soldier, 'drunk as a coot', leant out of a window of the train and vomited down the neck of a general who remained ramrod straight and unmoving throughout.[13] Other English-speaking Franco-ites included Peter Kemp, a twenty-year-old Cambridge graduate, whose motives seem to have been a mixture of anarchism, toryism, and wanting an adventure. In spite of being a Protestant ('I shit on Englishmen', his first commander told him bluntly), he found the Foreign Legion to be full of superb soldiers. The brutality of the Carlists disgusted him; he was wounded badly in the jaw, but went on to have a 'good' Second World War, being parachuted into France for the British Special Operations Executive (SOE), as well as organizing anti-fascist partisans in Albania and fighting with the Polish home army. Another Second World War hero, Frank Thomas, who was wounded at Tobruk, was the son of a food wholesaler in Cardiff. A convinced fascist, he fought in most of the major battles around Madrid. He saw appallingly brutal behaviour on both sides, but hated the Falangists. The brutality of the republicans he considered even worse. Franco, he said, 'put many captured members of the International Brigade safely over the French frontier with a new suit of clothes and five pounds in their pockets'.[14]

The difficulty for the historians who interpret the Second World War as a pure continuation of ideological battles first fought out in Spain is that none of the major controllers of Europe's 'destiny' neatly fit the pigeon-holes of their ideological followers. If the Second World War was fought 'against fascism', then the ambivalence of the Soviet Union, and of its fellow travellers in France and Britain, makes no sense, since once Hitler and Stalin had formed their Axis, for purely cynical and non-ideological reasons, the whole war against fascism ideals collapsed. Franco, whether you abominate his memory, idolize him, or wish, like Anthony Powell, to keep out of the conflict, manifestly was fighting for a set of ideas – namely Catholic conservatism, enforced by military dictatorship. This was rather different in many respects from fascism proper, not least in its overt desire to submit to the authority of the Church rather than, as Mussolini and Hitler did, hide from the Church's followers the full extent of their profound hostility to the Christian idea.

So, the Second World War cannot be said to have started for ideological reasons.

Yet Hitler's anti-Semitism surely did play a part in the change of British public perception of the whole European situation. Many of the 70,000 of those Jews (55,000[15] of whom settled permanently) who came to Britain as a result of Hitler's persecutions were to become household names, like Karl Popper, Nikolaus Pevsner, Georg Solti, Geoffrey Elton. Others were household names already. When Sigmund Freud arrived, all the rules were bent, and he was made a British citizen the very next day.[16] Apart from enriching life in innumerable ways for the British, their very presence prompted the questions in the mind which would lead to something much deeper than questions of mere national interest. What kind of a world would it be, if it were controlled by a régime that wanted to expunge Albert Einstein and Yehudi Menuhin? Those who came often did so shyly, aware of their German-ness more than their Jewishness.

'Where are you from?' Eva Neurach was asked shortly after arriving in England.

'Berlin,' she told the lady who had enquired.

'Ah, well, never mind,' was the reply.[17]

The more Hitler triumphed, taking over first one territory then another, the more he and his henchmen dared to increase their persecution of the Jews. Between April and November 1938 alone 4,000 businesses were simply appropriated from their Jewish owners. At about the same time, 500 Jews were sent to Buchenwald, and were packed into a sheep barn so tightly that within two months 150 of them were dead. In Hamburg there were public auctions of stolen Jewish property, at which patriots were encouraged to come along and 'buy' pillaged property. There was frequent talk now from Goebbels, Göring, Hitler and Himmler of expelling all the Jews from Germany, and to speed them on their way they were forbidden to attend concerts, theatres, cinemas. In November

1938 the Gestapo planned a further 'sharp measure'. Instructions were given to the police in all areas that there was to be a violent strike against Jewish property. They must not attempt in any area of Germany to prevent Jewish houses or properties being destroyed. Synagogues were to be torched. Between 20,000 and 30,000 Jews were to be arrested and paraded through the streets, following the night known as *Kristallnacht*, Crystal Night. The next morning, newspapers instructed by Dr Goebbels proudly announced that 'not a hair was touched of a Jew's head' – totally untrue – in the night of destruction, designed to make Jews simply want to leave their country.[18]

The British Consul-General in Frankfurt am Main wrote:

Recent events have revealed to me a facet of the German character which I had not suspected. They seemed to me to have no cruelty in their make-up. They are habitually kind to animals, to children, to the aged and the infirm. The explanation of the outbreak of sadistic cruelty may be that sexual perversion, and in particular homosexuality, are very prevalent in Germany. It seems to me that mass sexual perversity may offer an explanation for this otherwise inexplicable outbreak. I am persuaded that, if the Government of Germany depended on the suffrage of the people, those in power and responsible for those outrages would be swept away by a storm of indignation if not put up against a wall and shot.[19]

This is not as naive as it seems. The majority of Germans almost certainly did abhor the Nazi atrocities against the Jews, even when they remained (compared with the horrors which were to come) at the comparatively unmurderous level of bullying, theft, arson and intimidation. Very many Germans by this date realized that they had been duped by the National Socialists, but it took a particular kind of courage to stand up against them, and without international support, what would such 'standing up' have done? Only the army could ever have conducted an internal putsch against Hitler, and that did not happen until later.

While it is right, then, to say that when war came it was not a crusade waged on behalf of the Jews, it was nevertheless true that the organized thuggery, the state-sponsored criminality of the Third Reich did shock the world. It undoubtedly played its role in changing British resolves, in startling the British public out of one state of mind – ecstatic gratitude in autumn 1938 that war had been averted – into a grim knowledge, by September 1939, that Hitler must be got rid of. One psephological statistic and one anecdote would confirm this generalized impression. The statistic: the British Union of Fascists was not by definition an anti-Semitic organization, and its leadership always claimed to repudiate personal antipathy to Jews. But this was casuistry. The rank and file liked to tramp through the East End of London chanting: 'The Yids, the Yids, we've got to get rid of the Yids.' They killed no Jews, but they created terror in poorer Jewish districts. They exchanged with one another the valediction 'P.J.' or 'Perish Judah!'[20] The more anti-Semitic they became, the lower their percentage of the vote when it came to local elections. Unlike the Communists, who at least won four parliamentary seats, the Fascists never won any seat in the House of Commons, and by 1939 their share of votes in local elections had fallen even in parts of London where they were popular. This in spite of the earlier popularity of Mosley. A generalized feeling of disgust at the thuggery of the Mosleyites, and in particular distaste for their overt anti-Semitism, surely played a part in this.

Secondly, an anecdote. Before an English person narrates such a story, it is perhaps worth saying that, of course, the whole climate of opinion has altered in the years since the Second World War. What is now called 'political correctness' was unknown, as was the Race Relations industry. Throughout the British Empire, an effectual apartheid operated which was social as much as racial. (Indian and Malay princes were treated like white men.) Ordinary 'natives', whether Indian, Malay or Chinese, or African, were not educated at the same schools, or entertained at the same restaurants and clubs as Europeans. In the United States, blacks and whites were still segregated in all the southern states, and for social purposes in the northern ones too. These things, to those who live in a post-Nazi era, strike us as bizarre, as well as distasteful. I repeat my anecdote in the consciousness that it will sound smug, but I am sure it is true. It was told me by one of the soldiers in the prisoner-of-war camp where it happened, and I am sure that every one of those soldiers – certainly the one who told it me – would have been 'politically incorrect', made jokes which would sound to us racist, or very likely raised an eyebrow if an Indian was offered a drink at the bar, or a Jew proposed for the golf club. I tell the story not to suggest that the British were saints and the Germans all sinners, but to suggest that there was a strong sense of decency in these men; and they were aware, long before the Holocaust began, and long before the full extent of the atrocities had been revealed, that Hitler had crossed the bounds of decency.

When the young John Buxton, a minor poet, was taken prisoner by the Germans in 1940, he found himself in a PoW camp with several hundred other British troops. On their first evening, the British sergeant-major was called to be interviewed by the camp commandant, who turned out to be a polite army officer, not SS, not a criminal. The German commandant apologized, in civilized tones, for the nature of his request, but he wanted the British to tell him the number of Jews in their unit. He suggested that the following morning when the men were lined up on parade, the sergeant-major should ask the Jews present to take three paces forward. Nothing would happen to the Jews, the German promised. It was purely for administrative purposes that the authorities wished to know.

The next morning, several hundred British PoWs lined up in the yard of the camp. The RSM bellowed: 'All those who are Jews, three paces forward.' Every British man present stepped forward.[21] Innumerable instances of British anti-Semitism can be adduced before, during and after the Second World War, but this story suggests a generalized horror at the meanness inherent in racialism or religious prejudice, and which certainly made most British people respond with steel resolve when the call to arms eventually came.

As with Churchill's conversion to the Republican cause in Spain ('I am English, and I prefer the triumph of the wrong cause'), the diplomatic and political reasons for the inexorable progress towards war were incoherent, even self-contradictory. Of course, the revisionist historians have much right on their side when they argue that it was not 'in British interests' to stop Hitler invading this or that patch of earth far from home. And they were right to say that the Second World War broke Britain, destroyed it more surely than it destroyed her enemies, broke, by its 'finest hour', the very core of the mother country and of its Empire. But there was a fittingness in the incoherence, a rightness in the wrongness which was deeper and ultimately more satisfactory than any coherent strategy could have been. The sad, dangerous and well-calculated situation changed and became tragic, and thereby human.

The League of Nations, which had been started at the behest of an American president, but never joined by the United States, was powerless against the Japanese when they invaded Manchuria in 1931, powerless against Italy when it attacked Abyssinia, powerless against Germany in its territorial expansionist triumphs. As soon as Hitler came to power in 1933, he withdrew from the League. Japan left it the same year. Italy followed suit in 1937. The only 'policemen' left in the world to stand up to those nations who were abusing their power, and threatening other nations' borders, were other great powers: the USSR, France, Great Britain and the United States. In History-as-Mythology, the mid-to-late Thirties have left a legacy in the minds of right-wing thinkers, in the early twenty-first century, in Britain and America. Today, for all its manifold weaknesses and faults, there is an organization called the United Nations which is in every way more powerful than its feeble ancestor the League. For one thing, it can raise peace-keeping forces. For another, it contains the great powers, especially the United States. Nations can be called to account in its chambers, and its Security Council can summon warring, or potentially warring partners, to discuss peace. Of course, there have been continual wars since its foundation, as those who would see it as a feeble continuation of the League delight to indicate. Thus it is that America and Britain can use the failure of appeasement as a policy against Hitler as an argument for sidetracking the UN, and exercising force – for example in the invasion of Iraq – as a way of eliminating 'tyranny'. The implication is that, had Britain and France gone to war sooner with Hitler, the devastation and loss of life during 1939–45 might have been reduced or averted. This is a very questionable proposition, as we have seen, since the pro-appeaser version of history has at least this strength of argument on its side: how could anyone have been in a position to mass armies on the German border in order to topple its elected government? Previous to the dismemberment of Poland in 1939, Germany and the USSR did not even possess a common border. France and Germany did.

The pathos, not to say distastefulness, of the appeasing position, either at the time, in the minds of the politicians, or later in the writings of the historians, is that it demands a piece of mental gymnastics which is as foolish as it is pointless: namely believing Hitler, believing one of the most proven liars in diplomatic history. 'I got the impression that here was a man who could be relied upon when he had given his word,' said Neville Chamberlain in a private letter on 19 September 1938 after his first meeting with Hitler, not realizing that Hitler proudly saw himself as a warlord who had been on the warpath since 1933.[22] No wonder Hitler despised the 'men of Munich'. 'I always knew that Neville [Chamberlain] was the lowest (I can't spell it) flatest[sic]-footed creature that creeps. But will the country follow him in his appeasement policy?' asked Maynard Keynes in a letter of February 1938, and the answer is that not only would the country follow him, but so would Keynes.[23]

Stanley Baldwin's policy with the European dictators had been to 'keep them guessing'. Chamberlain's was to offer the 'brigand powers', to use Keynes's good phrase, 'better relations' with France and Britain. 1938 was Hitler's greatest year. He had already, in 1936, occupied, or reoccupied, the demilitarized Rhineland, territory to which most reasonable people believed Germany to be entitled. In the spring of 1938 he remarked to the Austrian Chancellor, Kurt Schuschnigg: 'Perhaps I'll appear some time overnight in Vienna; like a spring storm.' On 11 March, German troops entered Austria and Grossdeutschland was born, the union of the two great German-speaking nations. Viewed with dread from abroad, the development was welcomed by most Austrians, who idolized Hitler then, just as most of them still do.

The question of Czechoslovakia was very different. The 3 million Germans living in the Sudetenland, the part of 'Czechoslovakia' which had been cobbled together during the Versailles Peace Conference, wanted their 'national self-determination'. This meant that they wanted to be absorbed into the greater Germany, the Third Reich. President Wilson's principle of 'self-determination' was not to be more sharply tried than over this issue. Why shouldn't they be Germans, if that was what they wanted to be? The answer is that Versailles had destroyed the empires which created 'umbrellas' for such peoples as the Sudeten Germans, and the League of Nations was no substitute for the Austro-Hungarian Empire when it came to holding disparate peoples together in peace.

Pan-Germanism had begun to show the violence which had been inherent in Hitler's schemes from the beginning. It was not like self-determination for the Welsh, or even for the Irish. Hitler in the Sudetenland had the perfect launch-pad for the fulfilment of those dreams which he spelled out in such lurid detail in *Mein Kampf*: vengeance upon his Slavic neighbours for the brutality they had meted out to the East Prussians at the end of the First World War; the destruction of the Eastern Barbarian. Stalin would see this, which is why he so brilliantly pursued his own version of the 'appeasement' policy: signing up to an actual non-aggression pact with Hitler in August 1939, with the eager expectation that they would be able to carve up Poland between them.

The Sudetenland had been occupied by Germany in 1938. Where did this leave the body from which the great Sudeten limb had been amputated, Czechoslovakia? This, the former region of Bohemia, now focused the minds of all the statesmen in the West. From the point of view of the democrats, Czechoslovakia was one of the great success stories of Versailles. It was an extremely prosperous democracy, it had efficient industry, mineral resources, a large and well-trained army. Any Western power that wanted to put a limit on Hitler's expansionist powers, or to restrain his murderous activities at home by some resolute sabre-rattling, would have been well-advised to keep Czechoslovakia united, and strong.

By handing over Czechoslovakia to Hitler, Britain neutered 36 Czech divisions, fully equipped, trained and armed, waiting on the German border. Such an army could not have fought Germany unaided, but with the help of France's 80 divisions, and with British aircraft now rolling off the production lines at 240 a month, a formidable opposition could have been offered to Hitler – especially when we remember that this was before the Russians signed their pact with him; they could easily have been persuaded, as they later were, to fight on the side of Britain.

Opinions differ about whether Hitler really believed that he could get away with taking Czechoslovakia without a fight, or whether he was playing a game of poker. His whole strategy, from 1936 onwards, was based on the belief that he could win short strikes, and this worked until he invaded Russia. Had he thought he could take Prague within a couple of weeks, he would probably have done so, even with armed opposition; but we shall never know. He, and Chamberlain, and Edward Daladier, who had taken over from Blum as the premier of France in April 1938, all realized that if they went to war over Czechoslovakia it would mean a general war, another European bloodbath in which millions of people would get killed. No one wanted that. Those who had argued against appeasement since it began to emerge as the foreign policy of Great Britain were not, most of them, arguing for a war; they believed that rearmaments and threats to Hitler would make him retreat or back down. This in itself is questionable. So, while seeing that the appeasers got it wrong, we also have to acknowledge that Churchill and his friends would probably have 'got it wrong' too had they been in charge of things in the early to mid-1930s. Building more British aeroplanes or tanks would probably not have stopped Hitler's almost preternaturally easy path of total power. Nor would it have stopped him annexing Austria. But it might have had an effect in negotiating with Hitler over the Czechs.

In July 1938, Chamberlain sent Walter Runciman, formerly a Liberal MP, and now a viscount and Lord President of the Council, to Prague to persuade President Benes that it was vain to resist Hitler. His role was the distasteful one of having, in effect, to tell Benes that he was a betrayed Czech. The earlier suggestions, urged by the French, that the Allies would unite to protect Czechoslovakia, were withdrawn.

At home, in London, the government gave orders for trenches to be dug in the London parks. Thirty-eight million gas-masks were distributed. The message was clear: do you want to be gassed and bombed, or do you want to let your politicians betray a little country in the middle of Europe about which none of you really care? The Foreign Office was, by September, playing a game of brinkmanship. 'If German attack is made upon Czechoslovakia . . . France will be bound to come to her assistance, and Great Britain and Russia will certainly stand by France.'²⁴

On 15 September, Chamberlain had flown to Berchtesgaden and met Hitler in his mountain retreat. Chamberlain was not a poker player. He arrived with all his cards visible. He offered Hitler the Sudetenland if he left the remainder of Czechoslovakia alone. It was a ridiculous, as well as disgraceful thing to have done, thereby destroying any hope for the rest of Czechoslovakia to survive as an independent political entity. It made war look, for a week or two, more rather than less likely. But there were behind-the-scenes negotiations with Mussolini. The British public had been terrified by the trenches and the gas-masks ploy. They had been psyched up now to yearn for any solution of the crisis, however disgraceful.

Harold Nicolson, who had abandoned his flirtation with Mosley's New Party and become an anti-appeaser and pro-Churchill, records on 15 September that his wife Vita 'takes the line that the Sudeten Germans are justified in claiming self-determination and the Czechs would be happier without them in any case. But if we give way on this, then the Hungarians and the Poles will also claim self-determination, and the result will be that Czechoslovakia will cease to exist as an independent State. Vita says that if it was as artificial as all that, then it should never have been created.' Yet Nicolson reaches the nub of these strange times when he adds: 'Hitler has all the arguments on his side, but essentially they are false arguments. And we, who have right on our side, cannot say that our real right is to resist German hegemony. That is "imperialistic".'[25] We are back in the mysterious moral territory entered by Churchill when he said, of Spain: 'I am English and I prefer the triumph of the wrong cause.'

On 18 September, Daladier, the French Prime Minister, and Bonnet, his Foreign Minister, visited London to draw up a plan by which all areas of Czechoslovakia with a more than 50 per cent German population should be handed over to Hitler. But when, on the 22nd, Chamberlain flew back to meet Hitler at Godesberg to present him with these craven concessions, he was told they were not enough. The Hitler whom Chamberlain now met was not the smiling, friendly fellow he had met the previous week – 'a man who could be relied upon'. He would not even listen to the Anglo-French plans, and when Sir Horace Wilson patiently began to go through the proposals, Hitler went into one of his rages. He jumped to his feet and shouted: 'There is no point in negotiating further!' The interpreter had never seen Hitler so incandescent. 'If France and England want to strike,' he shouted, 'that is entirely indifferent to me!' (*Mir ist das vollständig gleichgültig.*) He gave the Czechs until 28 September to accept his terms for negotiating the Sudetenland, otherwise Germany would occupy the territory by force. In the huge Sportspalast in Godesberg that evening Hitler did one of his set-piece shouting-acts to an audience of 20,000. The American journalist William Shirer thought him 'in the worst state of excitement I've ever seen him in'. In Dr Goebbels's view the speech was a 'psychological masterpiece'.[26]

No doubt it was, for it sent the leaders of the Free World scuttling

back to their parliaments, terrified that they might have led their countries to the brink of war and determined to do anything they could to
negotiate themselves out of the difficulty. By the end of September the
public were prepared for the worst. On the 28th, Parliament was recalled
and Chamberlain was able to produce a last-minute reprieve. It was, he
said, 'horrible, fantastic, incredible that we should be digging ditches and
trying on gas masks here because of a quarrel in a far-away country
between people of whom we know nothing'. Mussolini had persuaded
Hitler to hold a four-power conference at Munich the next day. Peace
remained a possibility. 'Herr Hitler has just agreed to postpone his mobil-
isation for twenty-four hours and meet me in conference with Signor
Mussolini and Signor [why not Monsieur?] Daladier at Munich.' Harold
Nicolson thought it was one of the most dramatic moments he had ever
witnessed. For a while there was silence and then the whole House of
Commons broke into ecstatic cheering and sobbing. Churchill went up
to Chamberlain and said to him, sourly: 'I congratulate you on your good
fortune. You were very lucky.'[27]

Chamberlain flew back to Germany the next day to meet Hitler at
Munich. It was in effect an advertisement to the whole world that, whatever the terms Britain thought it could dictate or suggest, Hitler would
override them. He promised peace if all he took was the Sudetenland,
but it was perfectly obvious to all that he would eventually do what he
did in March 1939, that is occupy the rest of Bohemia. The craven way
in which Chamberlain gave in to Hitler at Munich only increased the
German leader's cocksure certainty that he could do as he liked. 'Our
enemies are small worms,' he would tell his generals in August 1939. 'I
saw them at Munich.'[28]

The news of Chamberlain's caving in to Hitler at Munich meant no
war – yet. It was therefore greeted with ecstatic joy. 'No conqueror
returning from the battlefield has come home adorned with nobler
laurels,' said *The Times*. Chamberlain appeared on the balcony of
Buckingham Palace with the King and Queen to a crowd of adoring and
happy people. When he had arrived at the airport, the king's message
was waiting for him – 'Come straight to Buckingham Palace so that I
can express to you personally my most heartfelt congratulations on the
success of your visit to Munich.'[29] Forty thousand letters congratulating
Chamberlain came to Number 10 Downing Street, 4,000 tulips were sent
from Holland. There were telegrams from the King of Norway and the
King of the Belgians.

Yet even as he did it, Chamberlain, and his Foreign Secretary Lord
Halifax, knew that the peace could not hold, and that honour had been
lost. Maynard Keynes, listening to the wireless news that night, must

have been expressing what many felt even in the midst of their relief. 'Tremendous relief' . . . but 'his [Chamberlain's] sympathies are distasteful. If he gets us out of the hole, it was he (and *The Times*) who got us into it by leading the Nazis into the belief that the English ruling class were with them . . . We are not out of the trouble yet . . . but we *shall* be, if only the PM can bring himself to be just a little harsh to the Führer.'[30]

Harold Nicolson felt gloomy. 'Even Winston seemed to have lost his fighting spirit,' he noted on 29 September 1938. The Church of England responded very largely as if the men of Munich had been guided by Almighty God. 'You have been enabled to do a great thing in a great way at a time of almost unexampled crisis. I thank God for it,' wrote Cosmo Lang to Chamberlain.[31] There were services of thanksgiving in all the churches and cathedrals of England on the next Sunday. In Lincoln Cathedral, the dean held the congregation spellbound 'by ascribing the turn of events to God's wonderful providence'.[32]

One young man, however, a theological student, ran from the cathedral 'feeling sick to the point of convulsion'. He was twenty-five years old. He had been born in 1913, in Berlin, into a scholarly family. The Bonhoeffer family were neighbours and friends, and as a boy, this child, named Ulrich Simon, had played the triangle in their family orchestra while Dietrich, future theologue and martyr, 'very fair and beautiful and manifestly kind . . . who shone like a star', played in the strings as they performed the Toy Symphony, which was at that date still attributed to Haydn. At school during a period of hardship in Berlin, when he had to pay 840,000 marks for a packet of cotton wool when sent on an errand by his mother, he had a peculiar Scripture master who had ranted to the eleven-year-old about the inequity of the Sermon on the Mount. If only Abraham had sacrificed Isaac, said this teacher, we should not be in the hands of the profiteers, the racketeers, the usurers and money-grubbers. This man was later to be executed as an Obergruppenführer of the SS, having massacred thousands of Poles and Jews. Ulrich Simon, until exposed to this sort of thing at school, had no idea that he was Jewish. His parents did not practise a religion. By an extraordinary geographical and imaginative journey, he found himself in Lincoln Cathedral aged twenty-five, a naturalized Englishman just in time before the war, and training to become an Anglican clergyman. At the Armistice service in 1938 he preached from St Paul's text: 'Are they Hebrews? So am I.'[33] His short book *Sitting in Judgement, an Interpretation of History 1913–1963* is the best account I know of what was really going on in the late 1930s, and the significance of Munich, appeasement and all.

A fortnight after Hitler occupied Prague and took over the rest of

Czechoslovakia, Britain and France signed an agreement that they would go to war if he marched into Poland. Much of the credit for this must go to Halifax, who realized that the policy of appeasement had failed, and run its course. In common with Churchill, Halifax believed passionately in the British Empire. It was to preserve that Empire from involvement in another European apocalypse, which would almost certainly spell its downfall, that he had supported appeasement. Now, something stirred inside this tall, gaunt 'holy fox'. Britain, which had been rearming now for two years, scarcely felt itself ready for war, but something happened in the year following Munich.

War was declared on 3 September 1939. The change which took place in the public mind, from ecstatic joy over the Munich disaster in September 1938 to a recognition of what had to be done after Hitler had (inevitably) invaded Poland in September 1939, was something which had been taxing the minds of theologians for the last few years. That is, was it possible to be a good person in a bad world, without getting your hands dirty? In India, Gandhi was having a remarkable success at dismantling the British Empire by the means of Tolstoyan pacificism. But this was surely because, for all the immense gulfs between Gandhi and the imperialists, there was at some deep core a shared value, a belief in freedom and decency which made the British feel that such things as the massacre at Amritsar in 1919 had been an aberration, a departure from the civilized values that they sought to promote. Halifax saw the British Empire as 'a rallying point of sanity for a mad civilisation'.[34] The centre of his life was religion. He took his chaplain with him on honeymoon. If you stayed at his Yorkshire house, Hickleton Hall – later converted into a hospital for the insane – the butler could greet you in the morning with the alternative: 'Tea or Eucharist, sir?'[35] You can hardly imagine a government composed of such men as this treating Gandhi and the Indian rebels as Hitler or Stalin treated their dissidents.

For the Nazis, a massacre such as Amritsar would not be an aberration, it would be the norm. The first six years of Hitler's regime in Germany could leave no one in any doubt that the very values on which European civilization had been thought to be based were now quite disregarded.

A pessimistic Spenglerian vision of things would have thought that there was an inevitability about this. The age of Christianity was over, and it was now the time of Yeats's 'rough beast, its hour come round at last'. Such an attitude of pessimism surely informed the peoples of the world who thought that Munich was a cause for celebration. But a year's reflection made it quite clear that it was no such thing. Nor could virtue of the kind preached by Tolstoy or practised by Gandhi be quite enough when confronting so committed an overturn of the Judaeo-Christian inheritance as formed part of Hitler's programme. Moral man had to defend himself against an immoral society, an anti-moral system. That was how Reinhold Niebuhr (1892–1971) defined the dilemma. Today he is best known as the author of 'The Serenity Prayer' read at meetings of Alcoholics Anonymous. From the moment of his arriving in the United States in 1928 as a professor at Union Theological College in New York, he had a profound effect on the public awareness of what issues were involved in the politics of Europe. As Ulrich Simon says, 'He believed in freedom, reason and love – the very qualities which were now ridiculed and about to be stamped out by the totalitarian states.'[36]

In August 1939, Dietrich Bonhoeffer wired to John Baillie in Edinburgh that he had decided upon the theme of the Croall lectures that he was due to give in Edinburgh: 'Death in the Christian Message'. As Ulrich Simon says, 'They were never to be given except in blood.'[37]

Bonhoeffer had moved a very long way from the Liberal Protestantism of his master Adolf Harnack. He and his fellow Christians in Germany were at the very front line, living out the new thoughts developed by Niebuhr. Bonhoeffer's *Ethics* is one of the great books of the twentieth century, written almost in blood, and confronting the question, how good people – and Christian good people at that – can respond to evil on the scale which had overcome first Germany, now so much of Europe. In individual cases, he knew that it was a call to martyrdom. But in generalized terms, he saw it as a stage to that 'religionless Christianity' which would surely come to pass after the Inferno. There must be a preparedness, in defence of the highest good, to forsake one's own moral purity and to fight.

After the invasion of Poland, there followed the so-called Phoney War, in which the reality of what was being proposed on both sides had failed to sink in. A Heinkel bomber crashed in Clacton-on-Sea, Essex, in April 1940 causing not only great damage on the ground, but also the deaths of all four of its German crew. The four young men were carried to the local cemetery with full RAF honours. Local women wept. 'The gallant foe were laid to rest amidst numerous floral tributes, their coffins being covered with wreaths of lilies, irises and other spring flowers.'[38]

At the beginning of November 1939, Evelyn Waugh noted in his diary: 'They are saying, "The generals learned their lesson in the last war. There are going to be no wholesale slaughters." I ask how is victory possible except by wholesale slaughters?'[39] In fact, the really immense casualties of war did not begin until Hitler authorized the invasion of Russia in 1941. Certainly during the Phoney War any death was still regarded as something notable. The amateurism on the part of the British, verging on the downright incompetent, was terrifying.

The British attempt to invade Norway inflicted great losses on the German navy – three cruisers and ten destroyers were sunk. But German air power made it impossible for an invading force to land in the fjords and the venture which began in the middle of April led to an ignominious retreat two weeks later. The failure of the Norwegian campaign in spring 1940 could very well have been seen as primarily the responsibility of the First Lord of the Admiralty, Churchill himself. And yet it was the debate about this fiasco, and the vote of confidence in Chamberlain in the House of Commons (the government's majority of 240 fell to 81), which, by an extraordinary sequence of events, led to the resignation of Chamberlain as Prime Minister. There was now a choice for him. He could recommend to the king that he make Lord Halifax prime minister, or he could recommend Churchill.

Quintin Hogg, one of the men of Munich, looked back on that strange summer and said this: 'Cardinal Newman used to say that he looked in vain for the finger of God in history. It was like looking in a mirror, expecting to see his own face, and seeing nothing. The one case in which I think I can see the finger of God in contemporary history, is Churchill's arrival at the Premiership at that precise moment in 1940.'[40]

But another perspective is that of Chips Channon, who had been an arch-appeaser, a friend of Ribbentrop's, and who disliked Churchill heartily. He sneered: 'We might as well have Macaulay or even Caruso as Prime Minister.'[41] This is meant to be damaging, but it is sort of right. The question of the future of Europe, and the future of the British Empire, and perhaps the future of civilized values themselves, could no longer be reduced to a question of diplomatic niceties, or treaties, or even to a question of common sense. It was precisely because Churchill, in his extraordinary hybrid rhetoric, saw life as a tuppence-coloured history drama, or even, to extend Channon's metaphor, to an opera, that he was right. But civilization could not afford many more blunders like Norway. And Britain, as everyone knew, could not really sustain a campaign against Germany without the help of America. A decade earlier, in an undated letter, Clementine Churchill had written to her husband hoping he might rise further in the Conservative party, perhaps even replacing that 'animated cardboard marionette Austen Chamberlain' as leader. She added, however, with what seems an extraordinary judgement in the light of his subsequent life: 'I am afraid your known hostility for America might stand in the way.'[42]

26

The Special Relationship I

Laurel and Hardy first appeared together in a silent film called *A Lucky Dog* (1917),[1] but it was far from being an instant partnership. When Churchill met Roosevelt in Newfoundland in 1941, he made a gracious speech about how delighted he was to be encountering the President for the first time. Roosevelt replied that they had actually met before in 1918, at Gray's Inn, in London. Roosevelt was too gracious to point out that the meeting had not been a success. 'He acted like a stinker at a dinner I attended, lording it over us,' Roosevelt recalled in a conversation with Joseph Kennedy.[2]

The 'special relationship' between Churchill and Roosevelt began in Newfoundland twenty years after their actual first meeting, and the film partnership between Laurel and Hardy began in earnest a whole decade after *A Lucky Dog*, being sponsored by the inspired midwifery of the Hal Roach studios from the mid- to late Twenties onwards. Both Laurel and Hardy brought very different gifts to the partnership. The magic of the films is drawn from more than one source, which is surely why they are so much funnier than the monochrome mimetic Chaplin – whom Stan Laurel had understudied in his twenties when working for the Fred Karno Performers. Oliver Hardy (1892–1957) had been born in Harlem, Georgia, and studied at the Atlanta Conservatory of Music. He was in part a serious person, and much of his seriousness is retained in the films; his exasperation with Stan Laurel stems in part from an eternal optimism, a wish that life could be better. The themes of their best films are the stuff of which many dramatists make not farce but tragedy – the inability of human beings to transcend their fate, whether they are a fat man and a thin man trying to carry a piano up a very long flight of stone steps (*The Music Box*, 1932 – the only one of their films to win an Oscar), or just two honest men trying to better themselves by converting a thriving wet fish business into a disastrous venture by which they catch, as well as sell, their own fish (*Towed in a Hole*, also 1932). Written by Arthur Miller, the same story would reduce audiences to the depth of despondency.

Sons of the Desert (1933) saw Ollie and Stan as childishly naughty husbands momentarily escaping the domestic tyranny of two termagant wives, and two suburban houses so identical that one man can walk in on the wrong one and not know he's done so. Nothing in fact demonstrates their infantilism so vividly as this boys' away-trip in *Sons of the Desert* to the quasi-Masonic convention in Chicago. (Ollie's ashes, incidentally, were interred in 1957 in the Masonic Garden of Valhalla Memorial Park in North Hollywood.) But although in that famous film they are depicted as errant husbands, in nearly all the rows and scrapes which embroil them, Laurel and Hardy are emblems of the impossibility of two human beings doing the simplest thing together without having a row: and to that extent they are paradigms not of grown-up chums but of childhood siblings or married partners. In *Sons of the Desert* they are supposedly middle-class, but in most of the best films they are bums, hoodlums, victims of the Depression, unable to find employment, and when they do so – as in the surreally brilliant *Busy Bodies* (1933), in which, as saw-mill operatives, they end up sawing their own car in half and driving away with it in two – always bringing mayhem.

Deadly as it might be to explain humour, one of the ingredients of the success is that both Laurel and Hardy are stooges. There is not one straight man and one funny man with comedic or the closely related demagogic power. They are both straight men at variance, not with a comic partner but with comedic fates. If Ollie, with the semi-tragic dignity of the very fat, came from the American South, and from an aspiration to make serious music, Laurel, whose real name was Arthur Stanley Jefferson (1890–1965), came from the almost Dickensian world of English music hall. He had been born in Ulverston, in the north of England, and his father was an actor-manager. One sees this background emerging in one of the most delightful scenes in the history of cinema, in *Way Out West* (1937), when the two friends, employed as messengers by an Eastern law firm, go to Brushwood Gulch, a one-horse town in the West, to tell an innocent young woman that she has inherited a gold mine. Mary Roberts, the innocent, is working as a drudge in a sleazy saloon, where the squint-eyed villain James Finlayson is the proprietor and the magnificent Sharon Lynne his flamboyantly tarty and unscrupulous wife Lola. Such practical questions as why the lawyer has chosen two such chumps to deliver an important message, or why he hasn't paid them their railfare, do not matter. They emerge on the road as two timeless wanderers with a pony, who could be travelling clowns in the age of Shakespeare or picaresque eccentrics encountered by Don Quixote and Sancho Panza. The innocents abroad manage to offend the sheriff of the place before they have arrived – accused preposterously of trying to touch up his ample wife in the stagecoach which squeezes them in for a lift on their last leg into town. Then they walk into a group of cowboys sitting on the steps of the saloon and singing, 'Commence yer dancin', commence yer prancin'.' Suddenly these two men, one thin, fey, not of this world, the other enormously stout with patches on his trousers, both wearing bowler hats, break into dance. It is not symbolic of anything. It isn't an expression, as it would be if it happened in a film nowadays, of homosexual love. Like a song sequence in a Shakespearean comedy or like such interludes in the music halls it is simply a piece of exuberant nonsense. Stan Laurel in this sequence is visibly the heir of Dan Leno (1860–1904), the surreal, manic genius of the late Victorian music halls in London. Within minutes, the chumps have entered the bar and blabbed the secret about Mary's rightful ownership of a gold mine; within a few more highly satisfactory minutes, everyone is running round in frenzied circles, as Sharon Lynne nabs the deed of ownership, squint-eyed Finlayson reaches for his gun, and Stan and Ollie hurl pillows and feathers. When they've escaped, Mary Roberts and Ollie discover they are both from the South. Stan surprises his friend by claiming the same. 'You're not from the South,' says Ollie indignantly. 'Sure I am. The South of London.'

It was only three years later that Laurel and Hardy made a very different film, in its way no less memorable, but the only film in the oeuvre, as far as I am aware, in which the English origins of Stanley are made much of, and having bubbled to the surface, destroy the dream. Beneath some good comic moments, *A Chump at Oxford* (1940) contains an explicit theme which isn't really funny, merely embarrassing. By abandoning in early career his real name, which was that of one of the most famous American presidents, Stan had paradoxically ceased to be English and become an American evergreen. In 1940 the American chump discovers that he is actually an English lord, Lord Paddington, and the minute he makes the discovery he starts acting, as Churchill had done to Roosevelt in 1918, like a stinker.

A Chump at Oxford (directed by Alfred Goulding) was originally produced as a 'streamlined feature' to run for 42 minutes for the American market. A 20-minute prologue was added for the European market so that the film could be shown as a full-length feature. The prologue is classic Depression comedy of the kind Laurel and Hardy did best. Entering the employment agency, they say:

'We'd like a job.'

'Anything you've got missis. We're down to our last six bucks, aren't we, Ollie?'

In the employment agency they sit between a man with a cloth cap and a thin man in a bowler hat who looks like Lord Halifax, who became British ambassador to Washington in the year the film was released, 1940. While they are sitting around waiting they hear a rich woman ring up in despair in need of a maid and a butler. It is a rare (unique?) moment when in the next sequence the butler and maid arrive at the rich man's house and we see Stanley in drag; he is the maid in a frilly wig. Ollie makes a good butler from the visual point of view but his irrepressible friendliness diminishes the dignity of the dinner. 'There's everything from soup to nuts, folks – come 'n get it.'

'What kind'v a joint is this?' asks Stan. 'He wants me to serve the salad undressed.'

It ends with the apoplectic and squinting employer, James Finlayson of course, taking a gun to them as their clumsiness wrecks the dinner party. It is familiar Laurel and Hardy territory. But then the mood shifts.

'Well, here we are at last,' says Ollie, 'right down in the gutter.'

'You know what the trouble is, we've never had no education. We're not illiterate enough.' (Stan).

They are reduced to sweeping the streets, but it is in so doing that just for once they meet a smiling Fortune. Chucking a banana skin away during his lunch break, Stan manages to trip up an escaping bank robber, and the chairman of the bank, as a reward, offers the two friends 'the finest education money can buy'.

('Whaddya mean, 3 Rs?'

'Reading, writin' and figurin'.')

The rich man exports them from America to Oxford. ('Well, it'll save us the trouble of goin' to night school.') It is there that by a series of wildly improbable sequences it turns out that Stanley is really the long-lost Lord Paddington, who knocked his head on the window-lintel and thereby lost his memory. When the doltish innocent Stan knocks his head again, he turns into the lofty aristo, full of scorn for poor Ollie, whom he starts calling Fatty and forces to work as his valet. The foppish, cruel English students, a youthful Peter Cushing among them, having tormented the two American dolts on their arrival, turn into a really nasty mob chanting:

> Fee, fi, fo, fum,
> We want the blood of an American.
> We'll chew them up like chewing gum,
> Fee, fi, fo, fum,
> And chase them back where they came from! Etc.

A heart-broken Ollie turns to his friend – 'Why, Stan, don't you know me? Don't you remember – we used to sweep the streets together?'

'Meredith,' replies Lord Paddington to his other servant, 'show this common person the egress.' Stan is by now sporting a chequered smoking jacket, an eyeglass and a cigarette holder. The dean of the college comes grovellingly to Lord Paddington, who has already won all the sporting events, to announce: 'Professor Einstein's just arrived from Princeton, and he's just a bit confused about his Theory. He wondered if you could straighten him out?'

'Einstein!' exclaims Ollie. 'If it wasn't for that bump on the head he wouldn't know the difference between Einstein and a Beer-Stain.' Paranoia grows in self-hatred. One of the fascinating things about the film is that while resenting, it rather appears to endorse the anti-American prejudices of the British which undoubtedly existed at the time. It is truly paranoid, hinting that in his brief period as Lord Paddington, Stanley is not merely claiming superiority but doing so with justice. He really is a sporting genius who can correct little Einstein in his spare time. ('My husband', remarked Mrs Sumner, wife of the Warden of All Souls College, Oxford, when introduced to Lindemann ('the Prof'), 'my husband always says that with a First in Greats you can get up science in a fortnight.')

When Ollie's temper cracks under Lord Paddington's intolerable patronage the languid aristo says: 'Only trying to help you out, old dear.' Ollie's reaction is the understandable one of 'Back to America for me!' The film breathes the isolationist sense that dear, friendly, doltish old America, embodied in the obese, clumsy Ollie, is better off not getting mixed up in camp, devious, cruel, effete Europe. To this extent, different as it is in atmosphere and treatment, *A Chump at Oxford* is very much a rerun of the old Henry James themes.

Luckily, devious, lofty Lord Paddington hits his head on the window once again and turns back into the American dolt with whom we all feel at home. The film ends with the two old friends united once more, and clasped in deep embrace. Funnily enough, after this film Laurel and Hardy lost their touch, and although they continued to work together for a decade, something had gone out of the magic.

In September 1940, the House speaker, William Bankhead, died and the presidential train left Washington DC for the funeral, held in Bankhead's home town of Jasper, Alabama. The train contained Franklin Delano Roosevelt and many members of his cabinet. When they reached Jasper, temperatures were in the nineties. Sixty-five thousand people attended the funeral, and as soon as it was over the presidential entourage returned to the capital.

Among those on the train was the Undersecretary of State, Sumner Welles, who, aged twelve, had been a page at FDR's wedding to cousin Eleanor Roosevelt. Welles, like FDR, had been educated at Groton and Harvard. He balanced snobbery and Anglophilia in personal style with a political distrust of British governments and institutions. Thus, while clothing his tall frame in Savile Row suits tailored for him in London, and his long feet in polished shoes made to measure at Lobb's, he did almost more damage to Anglo-American political relations than the profoundly anti-English ambassador in Britain, Joe Kennedy. He was a good linguist, and a close adviser of the President's on international affairs. Welles had been the pioneer of the Good Neighbor policy with Latin America. (He was largely responsible for establishing Fulgencio Batista's long tyranny in Cuba.) He was, a little reluctantly but in the end decisively, a Zionist. And he had been used by Roosevelt as a sounding-board on European affairs. Many spoke of him as an obvious successor to the ailing Secretary of State Cordell Hull, if the President was able to win a third term in the November 1940 elections.

It could be said that this presidential election was one of the decisive political events of the twentieth century. Franklin D. Roosevelt was not merely an ideological liberal, but far less isolationist than his Republican opponents. The American public would need some persuading of the importance of interesting themselves in the European tragedy which was unfolding on the other side of the Atlantic. And of course we can say that, once Pearl Harbor had been bombed on 7 December 1941 by the Japanese, any American president, Democrat or Republican, would have been involved in the world war. But Roosevelt's sympathy for the anti-Nazi cause in Europe, though he approached the whole matter with agonizing caution and slowness as far as Britain was concerned, and not without ambiguity, was certainly closer to support for the Allies Britain and France than anything which would have been offered either by the Republicans or by the members of his own Democratic cabinet.

Undersecretary of State Welles, on the swelteringly hot train, could very easily have caused a scandal which would have secured a Republican victory in the polls had his behaviour that night come to public notice. Welles was a drunk, and a secret bisexual, addicted to his work and trapped in a miserable marriage. In a desperate letter, found among his papers after his death, his wife pointed out that she saw him 'exactly ten minutes each day at breakfast, or passing upstairs to your bath'. She begged him not to drink or work so hard. 'Oh Sumner, for you in your position, it will get you yet, my dear. I can't help you. It's you I care for, not the Under-Secretary of State. God help us both, but there is no God. Just you and me and this unhappy life and struggle.'[3]

As the train rattled back to Washington on that sultry September night, Welles stayed up drinking. All but two of his cabinet colleagues had gone to bed. Welles sat with Roosevelt's electoral running-mate as Vice President, Henry Wallace, and Federal Works Administrator John M. Carmody. His theme of themes, as the alcohol coursed through his blood and as the train clacked and swayed, was the European tour on which the President had sent him in the spring of that year, 1940.

Roosevelt had decided to send Welles to Europe 'on impulse'.[4] He also dispatched James D. Mooney, chief of General Motors' overseas division, to visit Germany, where GM had substantial investments, to sound out the Nazi leadership and report back on the situation there. What FDR was trying to find out at first hand was whether there was a chance, in those first months of the war between European powers, to broker a peace.

This was very definitely not what the British wanted the Americans to be doing. Hitler, having occupied the Sudetenland, then Austria, and taken Czechoslovakia, had finally invaded Poland. The British had at long last decided that enough was enough and they had declared war, as had France. But there had then ensued the 'Phoney War' in which both sides perhaps contemplated the enormity of their situation; and there were certainly those in all countries who hoped, even at this late stage, for a negotiated peace.

Mooney, who was the recipient of the Order of Merit of the German Eagle as well as being a decorated American veteran of the last war, came home to tell his President that he should not get involved in European affairs. The highly lucrative American trade with Nazi Germany should continue.

This, incidentally, had been the view of the great American aviator Colonel Charles A. Lindbergh Jr, who had flown the Atlantic single-handed in 1927. Married to the heiress Anne Morrow, daughter of a Wall Street millionaire, in 1932 he had suffered the appalling fate of having his baby kidnapped and murdered. When this prominent American hero had visited Germany, Göring himself had pinned the Service Cross of the German Eagle to his chest. He had been hugely impressed when Göring showed him the Messerschmitt Bf 109, the basic fighter aircraft of the Luftwaffe.[5]

Unlike Mooney or Lindbergh, Sumner Welles was not an instinctive isolationist, but his European tour had left him convinced that America should avoid war with Germany. His mission to Europe as he himself called it[6] was primarily contrived to persuade Italy to remain neutral, but it was also a publicity exercise directed at an American Congress and still more an American public, that did not want to become involved in another European war. As such, the 'mission' achieved enormous publicity throughout the world and was seen by the dismayed British as an indication that if any countries were to defeat Hitler, it was to be Britain and France together without American help.

Welles sailed on the Italian liner *Rex* on 17 February. Whatever his chances of persuading the European belligerents to speak peace, his departure caused rage in American diplomatic circles, with the ambassador to France, Welles's arch enemy William Christian Bullitt, especially furious that Welles should have so high-profile, if essentially meaningless, a role at this juncture of world history. For what exactly was he meant to be doing on this 'mission'? There was a value in having the 'total situation surveyed by one mind',[7] but this was pretty nebulous. The Americans, concluded Sir Robert Vansittart of the British Foreign Office, 'are a strange people and pursue strange methods'.[8]

Welles was greeted by a red carpet as he disembarked at Naples. Italy's foreign minister, Count Ciano, a chubby smiling figure, thought the toweringly tall American a 'gentleman', altogether preferable to the German officials who were 'presumptuous barbarians'. The next day Ciano introduced Welles to his father-in-law, the Duce himself. It is perhaps not surprising that Welles, the diplomat who established Fulgencio Batista in Cuba, should have concluded that Mussolini was a 'genius'. Ciano felt the meeting at the Palazzo Venezia in Rome was glacial; Welles felt it had been cordial, but Ciano was perhaps not used to Welles's formality of manner. Mussolini chatted to him about tennis, which he had lately begun to play.[9] He did not let on that he was about to have a decisive meeting with Hitler which would force Italy into the war against France and Britain. Instead Welles had been able to draft a report to FDR from Zurich that if the Duce could only meet the President, Italy would be persuaded to remain neutral.

Welles could not at once visit Paris, where he would be guaranteed a hostile reception by Ambassador Bullitt, so he took the train to Berlin. There both Ribbentrop and Hitler insisted that the keystone of their foreign policy had been to make peace with England. Instead, the British had declared war and clearly wished to destroy the Third Reich. Evidently forgetting the fact that he had just invaded Czechoslovakia, Austria and Poland and was on the verge of invading Scandinavia, Hitler, who had been planning a war since he wrote the first page of *Mein Kampf* in 1924, confided in Welles: 'I did not want this war. It has been forced upon me against my will. It is a waste of my time.'[10]

Mein Kampf rises to its foaming, semi-literate peroration by invoking ancestral Teutonic voices and prophesying war. 'Just as our ancestors did not receive the soil on which we live today as a gift from Heaven, but had to fight for it at the risk of their lives, in the future no folkish grace will win soil for us and hence life for our people, but only the might of a victorious sword.'[11] The entire *raison d'être* of Hitler's political and economic programme, its huge increase of armament manufacture, its promise of conquest to east and to west, its military parades, the language and music of its rallies, was posited on overt warmongering. He himself said that war was the 'ultimate goal of politics'.[12] 'Every generation needs it own war and I shall take care that this generation gets its war,' Hitler had said on 9 November 1937 to Captain Wiedemann, his company commander in the First World War.[13] It is true that by a propaganda feat of dazzling audacity the National Socialists had persuaded the German people that the wars, like the revolutions, could be all but bloodless; and that on the day war was declared against Poland, Hitler was disappointed to see no cheering crowds in the streets of Berlin. The American journalist William Shirer in Berlin noted that, unlike the crowds in 1914 who cheered the announcement of war, the people of Berlin heard the news of Britain's declaration of war in 'shocked silence'.[14]

For a thoughtful foreign observer to believe the Führer's protestations of peace in the spring of 1940 is somewhat surprising. Believe them, however, Sumner Welles did. It is yet another tribute to Hitler's phenomenal plausibility when he wished to impress foreign visitors. One reason for this was that Hitler, like many lesser politicians, had a chameleon quality: in intimate tête-à-têtes he could become the person that his interlocutor wished him to be – witness his convincing Ramsay MacDonald's first ecclesiastical appointee, Dean Duncan-Jones of Chichester, a perfectly intelligent, liberal man with fluent German and no glimmering of Nazi sympathy, who visited the Reichs Chancellery in April 1934, that the German churches were safe in National Socialist hands.* Welles believed him. In his descriptions, incidentally, Sumner Welles had a vivid eye for the physical appearance of the gangsters at that time in charge of Europe. Mussolini seemed 'fifteen years older than his actual age of fifty-six. He was ponderous and static rather than vital' . . . 'He was heavy for his height and his face in repose fell in rolls of flesh. His close-cropped hair was snow-white. During our long and rapid interchange of views he kept his eyes shut a considerable part of the time.'[15] Hitler by contrast was taller than Welles had expected, while Göring's 'thighs and arms were tremendous'.[16]

Presumably, it was with such reminiscences that Welles regaled his cabinet colleagues on that sweltering night train to Washington. Somewhere near 4 am when the last of his friends had retired, Welles, by now extremely intoxicated, summoned the steward, a black man called John Stone, and offered him money for sex. Stone said no. Welles then began summoning other porters and made such a nuisance of himself that Luther Thomas, Southern Railways' special assistant for security,

---

* Duncan-Jones quickly saw that he had been hoodwinked by the Führer and penned *The Struggle for Religious Freedom in Germany*, Gollancz, 1938.

made complaints to Dale Whiteside, the chief of the President's Secret Service.

They were just seven weeks away from the election. Roosevelt hushed the matter up. Ambassador Bullitt continued to pursue the case, until his own fall from grace – when he urged the US government, after the fall of France, to side with Pétain's Vichy government against the Free French.

Roosevelt's personal liberalism was not in question, nor his commitment to decency in public life. But how far could he wear such credentials on his sleeve without exacerbating the hostility of the American electorate? His reaction to Crystal Night had been on one level uncompromising, on another a demonstration of the powerlessness even of a great nation such as the United States when another country chose to behave savagely towards its own citizens. FDR ordered the American ambassador home, and publicly denounced the outrages. 'The news of the past few days from Germany has deeply shocked public opinion in the United States . . . I myself could scarcely believe that such things could occur in a twentieth century civilization.'[17] But the American government, short of invading Germany and replacing its government, could not stop the Nazis from persecuting the Jews, and the American public objected to accepting Jewish refugees. In 1939, 67 per cent of Americans opposed the admission of 10,000 European refugee children (religion unspecified) to the United States. As late as 1946, when the extent of the death-camps was known, 72 per cent of Americans were against allowing in more Jews.[18] Millions of Americans tuned in to listen to the inflammatory broadcasts of Father Charles Coughlin, the son of an Irish-American mother and an Irish-Canadian father, whose wireless talks and articles in his periodical Social Justice were stridently anti-Semitic. Roosevelt in Coughlin's view was simply an instrument of the Jews, the British, the East Coast bankers. 'I oppose the Jew bankers – what's wrong with that?' he asked.[19]

Coughlin's broadcasts and journalistic activities built him up assets of over half a million dollars. There were millions of Americans, Irish or German in origin, who enthusiastically tuned in to hear him denounce the Jews. He predicted that Washington DC would be renamed Washingtonski and there were politicians such as the right-wing congressman for New York, Hamilton Firth, who rallied to Coughlin's support. Roosevelt, according to Coughlin, was 'a power-mad dictator who would place upon his own brow the crown of World Messiah'. The only people, according to this point of view, who wanted America mixed up in a war were the Jews, or those in their pocket. Social Justice archly pointed out that 70 per cent of those who wanted war came from the eastern states and 45 per cent from New York, 'which used to be an Irish town'.[20] Lest it should be thought that such views belonged entirely with the lunatic fringe of American life – such as the Daughter of the American Revolution, Mrs Schuyler, who revealed to the public that Pope Pius XI had been a Jew controlled by international bankers[21] – it is worth while to note the popularity of General George Van Horn Moseley, who believed that the Jews were responsible for plotting to bring America into the war. This man's views were indistinguishable from those of the European fascists. He believed that the dear old America of his youth had been destroyed by the New Deal, the Jews and the trade unions, as well as by Big Business. He 'continued to enjoy the respect' of former President Hoover, though Hoover drew the line at Moseley's suggestion that all Polish Jews should be sterilized.[22]

It was against the background of extreme antiwar feeling among the American public that the 1940 election was fought. Both sides exploited war terror. Wendell Wilkie, the Republican candidate, accused FDR of being like the European dictators. Former President Hoover thought that war would lead inevitably to the expansion of world communism, which in turn would mean that 'our country must be mobilized into practically a Fascist government'.[23] The Democrats were not above a few dirty tricks. They put it about that Wendell Wilkie was really Wendelle Wilcke – this German surname had been found on a gravestone in the Wilkie family burial plot. It was said that Wilkie's sister, in fact married to a US naval attaché stationed in Berlin, was the wife of a Nazi naval officer.[24]

Throughout that year, Roosevelt, as President, was having to discover the right way forward by a means of positively Hegelian thesis and antithesis. On the one hand was to be weighed his visceral hatred of Nazism, on the other his distrust of England, and his understandable dismay at the incompetence with which they appeared to be waging the opening stages of their war. 'The thing that made me hopping mad', he told Treasury Secretary Henry Morgenthau Jr, 'is where were the British Fleet when the Germans went up to Bergen and Oslo?' The First Lord of the Admiralty, that stinker Churchill – discovered very drunk on whisky by the by no means sober Sumner Welles during his spring visit to London – was the master intelligence behind the Dardanelles-style fiasco in Norway. By one of the major paradoxes in history, it was through the failure of this Churchill-inspired operation that the British Prime Minister, Neville Chamberlain, was forced by a collapse of parliamentary confidence to resign. Churchill became his successor.

Apart from having unpleasant memories of Churchill personally, and no reason to admire his performance as first lord of the Admiralty, Roosevelt was bounded by concerns which were both smaller and larger, during the middle and closing months of 1940, than the immediate ones of the American alliance with Britain.

The smaller concern – but in political terms the most immediate – was how he could sell himself to the electorate for a third term, and how he could quell the war fears being whipped up by the Republicans. Roosevelt was a consummate politician and a realist. There was no use his being an anti-Nazi in opposition. If he was to make a difference to the world scene, then he could do so only as President; and he could not be elected as a warmonger. It was not just Wilkie and the Republicans who were against the war. John L. Lewis, labour leader and chief of the United Mine Workers, had radio audiences of over 30 million Americans. In the light of Roosevelt's preparedness to send American destroyers to the assistance of the British, Lewis ranted: 'You, who may be about to die in a foreign war, created at the whim of an international meddler, should you salute your Caesar? May I hope that on election day [the mothers of the nation] with the sacred ballot [will] lead the revolt against the candidate who plays at a game that may make cannon fodder of your sons?'[25] In spite of this alarming talk from his many opponents, Roosevelt won the election, becoming the first in American history to be President for a third term in succession.

He had been wrestling, as well, not merely with the immediate, the parochial – if one can use such a word of so vast a political entity as the American public – issue of the election, but also with the much greater conundrum, What was America's role to be, not merely in the war now being waged on a world scale, but in the postwar world?

In the most famous of all his informal radio talks known as Fireside Chats, the one delivered on 29 December 1940, the newly elected President asserted that America was to be the 'arsenal of democracy'. He still hedged his bets over the question whether any American should actually be required to fight, but he was uncompromising about appeasement. 'A tiger could not be tamed into a kitten by stroking it. There can be no appeasement with ruthlessness.' If Britain were to be defeated, 'all of us in the Americas would be living at the point of a gun'.

It was clear from this Fireside Chat, which made an enormous and cheering impression in Britain as well as in the United States, that the American moment of History had arrived. But quite what the Fates had in their store was concealed even from the major figures in the drama – from Churchill, from Roosevelt, from Hitler, Mussolini and Stalin.

History viewed from the Malthusian or Darwinian point of view would perhaps see wars less as ideological struggles than as great culls. The overpopulated world, its economies in turmoil, turns to the one form of activity which 'solves' all the problems of the 1930s – hunger, idleness and overpopulation. The world war, with all its requirements of huge armament manufacture, could provide a boost to the American economy such as Hitler had apparently achieved in Germany. The dole queues could be put in uniform. The hungry could be filled, not with good things, but with bullets.

No one is suggesting that Roosevelt or Churchill were so cynical as to see the war in these terms. But war obviated the need for ideology – or even for explanation. The Thirties had seen the great impersonal movements of history as phenomena only to be resolved in terms of ideology. Ideology believed that the solution, like that of a mystery story or a crossword, could be found if worried at hard enough. Suddenly war, in its crude basic way, swept ideology away, allowing a solution through mechanics, through technology, through movement, through bloodletting.

If the great Hegelian moment of historical change had come, if America was about to emerge not merely as a big country with a huge economy but as a world power involved profoundly in the affairs of Europe and Asia, then inevitably there was to be no room on the same rung of the ladder for Britain. Even as he gave his Fireside Chats and saw Britain as holding the pass, Roosevelt was beginning to see what had been apparent to many of his entourage for years, that whatever happened to Germany, the factor which stood in the way of American hegemony was British imperialism. Luck, or Destiny, more than devious Machiavellianism, presented this state of things to the American President. By alliance, or quasi-alliance, to Britain, America could kill two birds, not one. They could hope to rid Europe of a dangerous German dictatorship, but in so doing they could also reduce British power to negligible levels. The Stinker could get his comeuppance. 'Fatty' could have his revenge on Lord Paddington.

27

Churchill in 1940

It was a Victorian funeral, held in a post-Victorian world. Everyone who remembers that January day in 1965 will know that as the world said its farewell to Winston Churchill, Britain finally closed an imperial story-book. The child of the celebrated Victorian statesman, roué and cad had outlived John F. Kennedy. The young subaltern who had taken part in the cavalry charge at the Battle of Omdurman, and said: 'My faith in our race and blood was much strengthened' had lived into the era of the Beatles. The First Lord of the Admiralty, who sent so many thousands to avoidable death at Gallipoli, had lived to be the contemporary of Vietnam draft-dodgers. The Chancellor of the Exchequer who helped to crush the General Strike was destined to die during the Labour government of Harold Wilson. The man who spent the 1930s in the political wilderness because he could not persuade Baldwin and Chamberlain to rattle their sabres against the European dictatorships lived to see Germany and Japan become two of the most vibrant economies of the modern age, and the European Economic Community one of the most successful economic and political success stories. So those who watched the coffin being borne on its gun-carriage through the streets of London, and saw it drifting on its barge up the River Thames, were watching the history of the early twentieth century being laid to rest. Above all, the world watched this funeral, this hero's funeral, because he was seen to be the man who would be remembered, above all his other achievements, his failures and his triumphs, as the person who saved his country, and the values of Western democracy from Adolf Hitler. Millions of human individuals had been engaged in that conflict which had called forth in the human race such conspicuous examples of bestial wickedness and super-human virtue. But there was a more than emblematic truth which saw that war, at any rate, during the crucial months of the summer of 1940 after the Fall of France, as a form of single combat between two individuals, two representatives of entirely incompatible and irreconcilable viewpoints. Both were painters. The one was a boozy, brave, historically obsessed old man, half aristocrat, half American, whose history-writing was as splodged with bright patches of unrealistic colour as were his sunny amateur oil paintings. The other was a teetotalling fanatic, of lower-middle-class Austrian origin, obsessed by race, and by the idea of the Greater Germany, whose essential dullness of spirit was evinced in the postcard-sized eerily normal architectural drawings and watercolours with which he had eked out an idle existence in his Viennese young manhood. Both believed in their race and their blood. Both believed in political systems which, when the devastating war between them was over, were in ruins: on the one hand, the British Empire, spread across the globe; on the other the Third Reich, dominating Europe for a few blood-soaked, hideous years. Both were natural autocrats, though with the essential difference that Churchill gave more than lip-service to democracy, and believed he had been fighting, among other things, for individual liberty. The world of 1965, excitedly discovering freedom like a teenager, believed it owed many of its freedoms to the old man who was being conveyed down the Thames, and hymned in St Paul's Cathedral, as best of the old world, and saviour of the new. Peace and Love, the hippy luxuries, would not have been much in evidence if Hitler had won the conflict. But nor were they in evidence in those unfortunate European countries dominated by the Soviet Union, the country upon whose alliance Churchill had ultimately relied to defeat the Nazis.

The year 1940 did, in the opinion of Isaiah Berlin, 'turn a large number of inhabitants of the British Isles out of their normal selves and, by dramatising their lives and making them seem to themselves and to each other clad in the fabulous garments appropriate to a great historic moment, transformed cowards into brave men, and so fulfilled the purpose of shining armour'.[1] That was how it felt to a fluent and able political philosopher in 1949. His Churchill was 'the saviour of his country, a mythical hero who belongs to legend as much as to reality, the largest human being of our time'.[2]

To write about Churchill is to find oneself in territory highly comparable to that occupied by writers on the subjects of Shakespeare and Jesus. On the one hand, there is the body of accepted factual evidence. In Churchill's case, this constitutes mountains of written, oral, cinematic and other material. But there is also the huge potency of the collective attitude to the hero. This encourages some sparkier, perhaps attention-seeking historians to poke fun at the myth, to be iconoclastic, to suggest that Churchill was not such a successful war leader, or that he could have done things differently; even, if revisionism wants to attract real obloquy to itself, that the whole war, the deaths of the countless millions, could have been played differently, or avoided altogether. So the revisionists have their little day, and are succeeded once more by the even more bestselling counter-revisionists, asserting that, for all the mistakes made, the cult of the Last Great Englishman is still valid.

Central to the potency of the 1940 myth, however, for the British, is the tragic knowledge that the Finest Hour was lived through at a price, and that the Saving Hero was a figure like Samson among the Philistine lords at Gaza. He could defy them, but in the world conflict which followed the Finest Hour he was obliged to pull down the pillars of the enemy on himself in a great act of self-destruction. All the phenomena in which he believed – British world-domination, through its Empire; and at home, the survival and political usefulness of the Whig aristocratic order – were left, just as surely as was the Third Reich, in a heap of rubble by the time the noise and smoke of battle had subsided.

The fineness of the Finest Hour, when it made its first appearance in 1940 in the Grand Rhetoricaster's speech, derived from its moral purity, its courage, its rash gamble for victory, its glorious claim that even if victory was not achieved, the fight would go on and on until the heroic end. Upon becoming Prime Minister, on 13 May, he said to the Commons: 'You ask, What is our aim? I can answer in one word: Victory – victory at all costs, victory in spite of all terror; victory, however long and hard the road may be; for without victory, there is no survival. Let that be realized; no survival for the British Empire; no survival for all that the British Empire has stood for . . .'

To have made this speech in May 1940, and to have ended, 'Come then, let us go forward together with our united strength', was to give new meaning to all the qualities and pastimes for which Churchill was famous: it was fighting talk, it was gambling talk, it was valorous to the point of heroic fantasy. The German army had marched through, and vanquished, all the countries of Northern Europe – Belgium, the Netherlands, Luxembourg. France was on the verge of falling. The British Expeditionary Force in Europe was surrounded by the German army and no one yet knew that Hitler would order his panzers to hold back from all-out victory, so that the German infantry had time to catch up with the panzers. Had General Franz Halder's urging been accepted, the entire British army would have been surrounded and defeated in that very week that Churchill spoke his words. He made his 'victory at all costs' speech before the Germans made their mistake (or tactical error if you believe that Hitler deliberately spared the British army in hope of a negotiated peace).

The 'myth' of Churchill's saving courage is a myth in the sense that it is a story by which a nation tells itself a story about itself. But it certainly happened, and Churchill was a hero in an almost superhuman mould during those weeks. When Stalin toasted Churchill after dinner at Yalta on 9 February 1945, he said something which everyone present believed to be true:

Without the Prime Minister's guts – the interpreter didn't say guts, but this is what he meant – England could not have stood up to Hitler.

She was alone; the rest of Europe was grovelling before Hitler. Do you know what Stalin said? He said that he could think of no other instance in history where the future of the world depended on the courage of one man.[3]

By the time Stalin made that speech, nearly five years after the 'Finest Hour', Russia was preparing to take over Eastern Europe, America was insisting that India be given its independence, Britain was economically destroyed, and the world was in ruins. The next especially famous speech Churchill made, first in the House of Commons on 18 June 1940 and then as a broadcast on the BBC, was delivered after the near-miraculous retreat from Dunkirk. By then, he claimed, 1,250,000 men were under arms in Britain. It would certainly have made life harder for any invading force than if General Halder had taken the entire BEF captive three weeks earlier. 'Let us therefore brace ourselves to our duty,' Churchill said, 'and so bear ourselves that, if the British Commonwealth and its Empire lasts for a thousand years, men will still say. "This was their finest hour."'[4]

This glorious sentence contains within it the least convincing conditional since Hitler had proclaimed the one-thousand-year duration of the Third Reich. It is some if. Within twenty months, the Japanese would occupy Hong Kong and Singapore and demonstrate to the world the essential indefensibility of British colonial outposts. President Roosevelt made it clear to Churchill whenever they met that he believed India should be given its independence even before the war ended; while his secretary of the Treasury, Henry Morgenthau, laid down in all his economic discussions with John Maynard Keynes that as far as America was concerned, the removal of Imperial Preference, tariffs and any economic protection of the Empire was a condition of American aid. Churchill from the very beginning had known that Britain could not stand alone for very long against so formidable a force as the as yet unconquered Third Reich. It would need, as he said in another of those glorious 1940 speeches, the one of 4 June, a continued struggle in which 'our Empire beyond the seas, armed and guarded by the British fleet, would carry out the struggle until in God's good time the New World, with all its power and might, steps forth to the rescue and the liberation of the old'. But only on the New World's own conditions, only on condition that Britain surrendered any claim to be a world power and handed that role to the Americans. That was what Churchill, great gambler that he was, could not have fully foreseen in 1940. He saw it clearly enough by 1945, and the British, nearly sixty years later, see it more clearly than ever. The British Empire had been shaky at the time, even though it was so dear to Churchill's heart. Within seven years of his making the speech about the Empire lasting a thousand years, India had gone; within twenty years, the Empire itself no longer existed. In terms of Britain's Victorian economic ascendancy in the world, that was on the wane by 1929, and the Finest Hour determined that Britain would be not merely economically ruined, but also politically. This might have been in the long term an inevitability. It was not an accident, if by accident one means something which comes about by mere chance or by impersonal forces. It was quite clearly decided by the US Treasury and by the US State Department that if support was given to President Roosevelt's desire to help Britain and France in the war, there should be a price exacted. And that price was, and should be, the effective dismantling of Britain as a first-rank world economic power.

Hitler told foreign observers, and anyone who would listen, that he had hoped and supposed that Britain would keep out of the European war and retain its Empire. Not many believed that he would allow this to happen. The Anglophile Dean Acheson, Assistant Secretary of State 1941–45, and Secretary of State 1949–53, complained that the US Treasury during the Second World War was 'envisaging a victory where both enemies and allies were prostrate – enemies by military action and allies by bankruptcy'. They succeeded as triumphantly in this as did the Russians in their territorial and political victory over the countries of Eastern Europe. That is the screen of events through which the British of today see the historical palimpsest of the Finest Hour; and whether they are nostalgic for their old Empire, or embarrassed by its very existence, the Finest Hour has a particular poignancy. Nothing since has matched its glory.

Nor, it need hardly be said, has any British Prime Minister, before or since, ever matched Churchill for colour, exuberance, eccentricity, sheer strength. Alec Douglas-Home (Lord Dunglass as he was at the time of Munich, when he helped Chamberlain carry his briefcase to that sorry episode) once remarked that what he discovered, having been Foreign Secretary and then briefly in the early 1960s Prime Minister, was that prime ministers have very little to do. In peacetime this is true, which is why they have often seemed nondescript characters; none more so than those who were unprepared to admit the fact that for many weeks of the year there was nothing which needed to be done, and who therefore made themselves bustling parodies of a leader, like Chaucer's Man of Law, who 'seemed busier than he was'.

In wartime, things are very different, especially if, as Churchill did, the Prime Minister upon taking office pulls off a one-man *coup d'état* and makes himself into a virtual dictator. Without seeking parliamentary authority, he made himself Minister of Defence and took charge of directing personally all the military activities of the war. He excluded the three service ministers from the war cabinet. He was the warlord by air, sea and land.

Even if he had not been the very forceful and commanding character that he was, he would by this very act alone have been in a stronger position than any of his predecessors to leave his mark on events. Hitler, someone once said to Churchill, does not just want to plan the general policy of the war, he even plans the details. 'Yes,' answered Churchill with a smile, 'that's just what I do.'[5]

But of course it was his character which shaped his actions, and which made him into something which no previous prime minister, with the exception of Lloyd George, had even tried to be: that is a leader, a national leader. For all his courtly deference towards the Crown, and towards the great institutions of state, Churchill enjoyed something like absolute power for the five and more years that he held office for the first time as Prime Minister.

When it was all over in 1945, defeated in the polls and crushed in spirits, he went on a painting holiday in a borrowed villa on the shores of Lake Como. His daughter Sarah, his doctor Charles Wilson (who had become Lord Moran in 1943) and various others were of the party. Churchill's spirits began to rise as he got into his stride once again. (He had painted only one canvas during the war, a landscape in Morocco when he was recovering from pneumonia.) On the walls of the Italian villa, or rather let into the walls, there was a dull landscape representing a lake and a wooded shore. It caught Churchill's eye during dinner and he said there was no light in it; he could, he said, improve it. Major Ogier, a young officer of the 4th Hussars, saw the chance for the sort of jollities which might enliven a regimental mess, and rose to gouge the picture out of its place in the wall, thereby dislodging quite a bit of plaster. Churchill removed the glass and triumphantly bore off the canvas to his bedroom where, in spite of his daughter's protests, he proceeded to add a gaudy sunset, using some new paints the young people had found for him in Milan. Later, he sheepishly undid his work with turpentine.

It is impossible to think of any other prime minister who would have played such a prank, and it seems entirely emblematic of his place in the prime ministerial gallery. Arthur Balfour and Herbert Asquith had been men of cleverness; Lloyd George had possessed qualities of greatness as a leader in war and peace. But on the whole, the prime ministers of the twentieth century constitute a procession of dullness from Campbell Bannerman to Bonar Law, from Ramsay MacDonald and Baldwin to Chamberlain. Then, the lightless canvas is roughly hacked from its place in the wall and a bright sunset is proudly splodged upon the leaden lake.

Churchill was sixty-five years old when he became Prime Minister. He was even more out of touch with the way 'ordinary' people lived than had been Lord Curzon, about whom the apocryphal story was told that he had ordered an omnibus driver to take him directly to his front door in Carlton House Terrace. 'He knows nothing of the life of ordinary people,' said his wife, 'he's never been in a bus, and only once on the Underground. That was during the General Strike, when I deposited him at South Kensington. He went round and round, not knowing how to get out, and had to be rescued eventually. Winston is selfish; he doesn't mean to be; he's just built that way. He's an egoist, I suppose, like Napoleon. You see, he always had the ability and force to live his life exactly as he wanted.' Thinking that he should express concern for the lives of the ordinary people, when rationing was introduced he asked for some rations to be presented to him on a tray. He was pleasantly surprised and said that he just about could imagine living on what was spread out before him. It was then pointed out that what he had believed to be enough for a day was actually intended to feed an individual for a week.

One of the many paradoxes about Churchill's relationship with The People during the war was that this noisy, colourful man should have presided over a period of unprecedented drabness in the personal lives of British subjects; and that so self-indulgent and Falstaffian an advocate of excess in matters of food and drink should have been the national leader during a time of tightening belts and food shortages. The great Victorian Libertarian presided over the birth of the Nanny State, where politicians felt it was their business to supervise national eating-habits, and to censor jokes.

The paradox is markedly brought home in Churchill's correspondence with his Minister of Food, the retailer Lord Woolton. This Northern-educated, socially conscious figure was hardly Churchill's type of man. He had spent his young manhood as an assistant to a Congregationalist minister, helping out at youth clubs while teaching mathematics at Burnley Grammar School. Later he went into the retail trade, eventually joining forces with David Lewis in his department stores in Manchester, Birmingham and Liverpool (no connection with the John Lewis shops in and around London).

When meat supplies ran low in the first years of the war, it was Woolton's task to try to persuade a largely carnivorous people to enjoy a tasteless pasty of root vegetables that came to be known as the Woolton Pie. Churchill airily assumed that there would always be plenty of meat, and nagged Woolton to make sure that no one ran short of bread or tea.

I am glad you do not set too much store by the reports of the Scientific Committee. Almost all the food faddists I have ever known have died young after a long period of senile decay. The British soldier is far more likely to be right than the scientists. All he cares about is beef. I do not understand why there should be these serious difficulties about food, considering the tonnages . . . we are importing. The way to lose the war is to try to force the British public into a diet of milk, oatmeal, potatoes, etc, washed down on gala occasions with a little lime juice.[6]

While the bureaucrats and puritans dreamed up their bossy wartime slogans – 'Wage War on Waste', 'Start a Rag Bag!', 'Dr Carrot Guards Your Health'[7] – Churchill's brandy-sodden rhetoric and high colour gave different messages to the public. Hitler could dismiss him as 'a super-annuated drunkard supported by Jewish gold';[8] Roosevelt's first question to his Republican rival Wendell Wilkie, when he returned from a visit to England in February 1941, was to ask (about Churchill): 'Is he a drunk?' (Amusingly, when they met, Churchill himself was a little taken aback by the President's method of making a Martini with sweet and dry vermouth added to lashings of gin.)

It was Hitler's sobriety, in the circumstances, which seemed so eerie and Churchill's drunkenness which was natural in the heightened terror of the times. The London pubs were full during the war. Even so high-minded a foreign visitor as the philosopher Simone Weil, working for the Free French, commented upon the comradely boozy atmosphere of the pubs, and kept a bottle of vodka in her bed-sit. The front page of the *Evening Standard* for 30 December 1940 had the headline SEVEN LONDON CHURCHES HIT IN FIERCEST LONDON RAID, while a box in the upper right-hand corner of the same page proclaimed 'NICHOLSON'S GIN It's Clear, It's Good'.[9]

Robert Bruce Lockhart, civil servant, records: 'I am drinking far too much – like most people in Whitehall these days. The Ministers are no better; Dalton [Minister of Economic Warfare] has a strong head, drinks hard and has a particular liking for brandy. Brendan [Bracken, Minister of Information] is rarely completely sober after 11 pm, and even Eden takes a man's full share in the evening. War's effects on the nerves, I suppose.'[10] Churchill, who drank very weak whisky and water throughout the day, on top of the drinks he consumed during and after meals, was an apt figurehead for this gruesome period when the gods of war borrowed the attributes of Bacchus, and the grapes of wrath made mortals drunk.

In his dress-sense as in much else, Churchill was *sui generis*, or one could say pre-First World War Bohemian. The Canadian newspapers seemed surprised in 1943 when he arrived in Quebec wearing an unbleached linen suit. Domestically, especially when working late, he wore his self-invented crimson boiler suits, which emphasized that baby appearance on which all remarked. He loved uniforms, and could appear, apparently at whim, in naval caps, or wearing the uniform of any of the armed forces. At Teheran, where Stalin appeared wearing a brand-new and clearly newly designed mustard-coloured uniform with huge epaulettes, Churchill dressed as an Air Commodore. At Potsdam, Churchill was arrayed as a colonel. (In Hansard 1916–18 he is always referred to as 'Colonel Churchill'.) The scornful remark of Chips Channon, that they might as well have made Caruso the Prime Minister, had a back-firing truth in it; for an operatic, colourful, and inspiring figurehead was precisely what the hour required, rather than a grey career-politician.

It was also an essential part of Churchill's character that he was a Victorian. At Bristol University, of which he was Chancellor, he wore the robes which his father Lord Randolph had worn as Queen Victoria's Chancellor of the Exchequer. On all formal occasions, he wore not a cutaway morning coat but a full frock-coat and tall silk hat, and looked every inch the contemporary of Mr Gladstone or Lord Salisbury. His eating and drinking habits – grouse for breakfast, champagne to drink with dinner, followed by lashings of port and brandy – had little to do with the austere twentieth century. 'I have always tried to understand the point of austerity' – a broad grin appeared – 'though I cannot claim to have seriously practised it' was his remark upon visiting the shattered monastery of Monte Cassino in 1944. Victorian too were his religious unbelief and his views of the East. 'He spoke of himself as a link with Queen Victoria,' his doctor remembered.[11] And Isaiah Berlin, who neither unpatronizingly nor inaccurately saw Churchill's vision of history as 'vivid historical images – something between Victorian illustrations in a child's book of history and the great procession painted by Benozzo Gozzoli in the Riccardi Palace',[12] was precisely right when he saw Churchill as a nineteenth-century figure. He saw Roosevelt as a figure whose whole political career, and whose vision of his country and its destiny were based upon a confidence about the future; Churchill, by contrast, in Berlin's view, was still inhabiting the brightly coloured illustrations of his child's history book. Both men, Roosevelt and Churchill, had an 'uncommon love of life'. The difference between them is best summarized in terms of era. 'Mr Roosevelt was a typical child of the twentieth century and of the New World; while Mr Churchill for all his unquenchable appetite for new knowledge, his sense of the technological possibilities of our time, and the restless roaming of his fancy in considering how they might be most imaginatively applied, despite his enthusiasm for basic English, or the siren suit which so upset his hosts in Moscow – despite all this, Churchill remains a European of the nineteenth century.'[13] More than half a century after Berlin wrote those words, you could go further and change the 'despites' to 'withs'

In point of fact, Churchill was the nineteenth century's revenge on the scoffing generation which produced Bertrand Russell's sceptical philosophy, Lytton Strachey's anti-heroic essays on Victorian icons, and E. M. Forster's sub-Wildean belief that it was better to betray your country than your friend. Churchill was not a Christian, and certainly not a believer in a personal deity, but he believed in a sort of Destiny, which was highly comparable to Carlyle's views of history, rescuing decadent societies by the arrival of a great man – an Odin, a Cromwell, a Mahomet. Churchill saw himself as such a figure in 1940, and most others in Europe shared his view: that was his triumph. He made others share the vision. He meant it when he said, 'we entered the war for honour',[14] and honour was what he not merely maintained, but summoned up in others.

In his book *The World Crisis*, he wrote up his impressions of Clemenceau. The words were penned in 1920, when he was forty-six, but he could have been describing himself as he took office as Prime Minister and steered Britain through the dramas of 1940. 'Clemenceau embodied and expressed France; as much as any single human being, miraculously magnified, can ever be a nation, he was France . . . he left me with the impression of a terrible engine of mental and physical power, burning and throbbing in that aged frame.'[15]

Churchill's was not merely going to be the political comeback of a failed Edwardian politician who had made a mess of most of his previous jobs and wanted one last stab at the top job. Nor was it even to be the resistance of one small Northern European power to the advances of a large one. It was the return of the Victorians. He brought back into British life a rhetoric of optimism, a haughtiness of temper, and a humour which had not truly been known since the days of Palmerston and Disraeli. His very language about Hitler – 'bloodthirsty guttersnipe' – was that of a Victorian aristocrat whose temper has been tried too far and who now reaches for his riding-crop to deal with the upstart.

But it was also a moral stand, and that was Victorian too. He combined the colourful speech and eccentric clothes of Disraeli with the fervour of that Gladstone who had hated the Bulgarian atrocities and called for the British people to defend the Christian civilization which had been violated.

Of the King and Queen, Churchill said: 'They have the rare talent of being able to make a mass of people realize, in a flash, that they are good.'[16] From the beginning, Churchill's grounds for opposing National

Socialism transcended politics or strategy. His speeches enabled people to see the fundamental contrast between the decent values of Christian civilization, as embodied in the King and Queen, and the sheer brutality of Nazism, with its contempt for the human individual and its lack of concern for freedom. So the old Victorian, with his old Victorian values, returned to fight the Last Battle. The revisionist historians are no doubt right to say that, at various points during 1940 or 1941, the British could have made peace with Germany. For all that we know, had they done so, Hitler might have lived out his days like some Teutonic General Franco, and his successor might have handed over Germany to a more liberalizing or democratic regime some time in the 1950s or 1960s.

Such a fantasy is impossible, however, because it is not what happened. There is such a thing as the mood of an hour. Churchill both awakened it and rode it like a surfer on the ultimate ocean roller. He enlisted the British Commonwealth and Empire for a struggle which would wound it mortally. Far from surviving a thousand years, it lasted barely a hundred weeks after Hitler's death.* The victory was achieved at the cost of alliances with Soviet communism and modern America, which would be the everlasting undoing of the Victorian world. Yet the battle was one of honour. However incapacitating it is today for the British to live with the mythology of 1940, however much it holds them in the past, it is understandable why they cling to it. There was a genuine glory and a dignity to the story of the old hero returning to slay some dragons before, bloodied and weakened, he and his Victorian world sank into the regions of twilight.

* India anyway. The African Empire lasted until the 1960s.

28

From the Battle of Britain to Pearl Harbor

Hitler knows that he will have to break us in this island or lose the war. If we can stand up to him all Europe may be free and the life of the world may move forward into broad, sunlit uplands; but if we fail then the whole world . . . will sink into the abyss of a new Dark Age . . .

This was the extraordinary alternative which Winston Churchill placed before the British people, and the world, in June 1940. Hitler and his régime provided the sticking point, as the 'brigand power', with which to compromise would be disaster. That other brigand power, Mussolini's, had impressed Churchill when they met in 1927, and he was happy for Britain to do deals with the Italian dictator during the 1930s. He sided at first with General Franco in Spain. He developed a warm affection for the mass-murderer Stalin. As for Japan – in his first few weeks in office as Chancellor of the Exchequer, Churchill had opposed any notion that Japan represented a threat to British imperial interests. 'A war with Japan!' he had exclaimed with incredulity. 'But why should there be a war with Japan? I do not believe there is the slightest chance of it in our lifetime . . . Japan is at the other end of the world. She cannot menace our security in any way.'[1] Most British people in 1940, and most Europeans since 1945, have shared Churchill's instinctual belief that there was something uniquely horrible, even by the standards of other twentieth-century brigands, about the National Socialists; and this was before the wholesale massacre of the Jews had begun. (Not, of course, before their anti-Semitic policy was in practice.)

Hitler saw England, as he always called Great Britain (most Germans do), as an essentially imperial power. 'The basic reason for English pride is India. Four hundred years ago the English did not have this pride.'[2] He was sure that eventually the English and the Germans would become allies. Even in 1941, after the evacuation of Dunkirk, the Battle of Britain, and the exchange of bombing raids between English and German cities in the previous year, he still spoke of the two countries as essential allies. 'It is quite certain that in future England's Empire won't be able to exist without the support of Germany.'[3] As he saw matters, the existence of the British Empire, the support for which was the very core of Churchill's politics, and the politics of almost all English Tories, was incompatible with an American alliance. 'England and America will one day have a war with one another, which will be waged with the greatest hatred imaginable,' he predicted, adding with what some would consider prescience: 'One of the two countries will have to disappear.'[4]

The declaration of war by Britain therefore had taken Hitler by surprise. In May 1940 the German army had repeated its victories of 1870: in the earlier war they surrounded the French at Sedan; in 1940 they bypassed the French line. The French were more or less certain to be defeated in the field – if they had stomach for the fight. Within five days, the Germans took Amiens and reached the sea at Abbeville. Paul Reynaud, who in March 1940 had taken over as Prime Minister of France after the defeatist Edouard Daladier, appealed to the new British Prime Minister, Churchill, for help from the air. Passionately Francophile, and caught up in the emotional fervour of the situation, Churchill convened a cabinet meeting at which he asked the C-in-C of Fighter Command, Sir Hugh Dowding, to be present.

It would be difficult to find two men more different from one another than Churchill and Dowding. The one, small, fat, flamboyantly exhibitionist, wearing his emotions on his sleeve, bullying, impulsive, loquacious; the other tall, lean, diffident, intense, pessimistic, introverted. They were both men of iron stubbornness, and the cabinet meeting in May 1940 was perhaps the most crucial that has ever taken place in the history of Britain.

Dowding was shown into the Cabinet Room which also served as the Prime Minister's office. Churchill was seated in the middle with other members of the war cabinet and representatives of the services seated around him at the table. There was the Secretary of State for air, Sir Archibald Sinclair, an old friend of Churchill: they had served together on the Western Front in 1915 after Churchill, to escape the bad publicity of Gallipoli, had resigned from the cabinet and commanded the 6th Royal Scots Fusiliers as a Lieutenant Colonel. There was the Chief of the Air Staff, Sir Cyril Newall. Churchill was in a state of very high tension. When he was like this, his temper, like Hitler's, could be explosive, and it was a bold man who checked him. That very morning, Holland had caved in to the Germans, and the Dutch Queen Wilhelmina, with a gas-mask slung over her shoulder, had escaped on a Royal Navy vessel and come to continue the government of the Netherlands from a London hotel. The French premier had just been on the telephone, begging for planes. A menacing atmosphere of defeat was hovering in the air. Apart from the future of Europe, the future of Churchill hung in the balance. He had been waiting all his life for this moment of destiny. Only a few military blunders on his part, or a failure of nerve by his colleagues, or by the British people, or a little more audacity by the Germans, and his finest hour would have lasted about three weeks. No one in that room was brave enough to seem to be snatching it from him. Sinclair, the leader of the Liberal party, was Churchill's friend, and as such wary of his temper. 'The abuse and insults Winston heaped upon [Sinclair] were unbelievable,' a colleague recalled. Newall had tried to point out the unrealism of the French request and been snapped at by Churchill. He had sunk into an obedient silence when Dowding entered the room. While Churchill spoke of the planes he was proposing to send to aid the French, the two senior ministers representing the air force remained cravenly silent.

The previous day, Dowding had prepared a graph of the Hurricane fighter planes which had already been lost over France.

> I got to my feet and taking my graph with me, I walked round to the seat occupied by the Prime Minister. I leant forward and laid the graph on the table in front of him, and I said, 'If the present rate of wastage continues another fortnight, we shall not have a single Hurricane left in France or in this country'. I laid particular emphasis on 'or in this country'.[5]

Dowding returned to his seat. There was complete silence as Churchill glanced at the graph in front of him. The Air Ministry representatives said nothing in Dowding's support. It was entirely Hugh Dowding who prevented Churchill, in one of his characteristic rash blunders, from destroying what was left of the Royal Air Force, and thereby guaranteeing certain defeat by the Germans that summer.

Dowding did not, as is sometimes stated, threaten to resign. He merely presented Churchill with the sobering facts. When Churchill had had time to absorb the message of the graph, Dowding spoke, distinctly and with his own quiet eloquence, of the vital need for more supplies, more aeroplanes and more pilots in the defence of Britain – above all, for more pilots. In his own recollections of this momentous cabinet session, Churchill makes no reference to his being checked by Dowding. He merely wrote: 'The Cabinet gave me authority to move four more squadrons to France.' Dowding's comment, when he read Churchill's memoirs, was: 'You couldn't very well expect him to admit that he came within a hair's breadth of wrecking Fighter Command before the Battle ever started.'[6]

Authority was given immediately for a major production of fighter planes – Hurricanes and Spitfires. Such was the speed with which aircraft technology was advancing during the 1930s and early 1940s that the British had done well out of their last-minute approach. Even the latest

Messerschmitt fighter plane, the Me 109E, was not nearly as fast as the Spitfire, and many of the Messerschmitts which had been in production since 1936 or 1937 were already way behind the British models. Spitfires at 18,000 feet could fly at 354 miles per hour versus the Messerschmitt's 334. The Ju 87B 'Stuka' bomber was already slow by 1940 speeds and the Germans had not yet mastered sufficient fuel technology to be able to keep these magnificent machines in the air for a very long time. By the time they had flown to England most Stukas could only last ten minutes before having to fly home. The fighter planes could last a little longer – maybe half an hour – but they were at a distinct disadvantage against the British fighters, which could land and refuel in mid-battle when fighting over British soil.

The next month, after Dowding's confrontation with Churchill in the Cabinet Office, was decisive. French defeat had now become inevitable. Lord Gort, C-in-C of the British Expeditionary Force, had the choice of watching his troops be marooned in enemy-occupied France, or organizing a tactical retreat. He was faced with the need to evacuate an army of over 360,000 men from the beaches of Dunkirk. Around 5,000 British soldiers were killed in the operation, but the rest of the army was rescued, chiefly by the Royal Navy, but with the assistance of the 'little boats', pleasure steamers, fishing craft and the like, which volunteered to make the cross-Channel journey. Many arrived in the ports and seaside resorts of the English South Coast, their funnels splintered with bullet-holes, only to turn round when their passengers had disembarked, and return to France to pick up more.

The weather was preternaturally calm and bright; the result, many averred, of prayer. All the non-portable equipment was lost, every heavy gun, every tank. Many men had even lost their rifles. The RAF was vital in warding off the attacks by Stuka bombers. They lost 474 planes in the fight, and the Royal Navy lost six destroyers, but the bulk of the army, thanks to Gort, was rescued. In total, over half a million men were transported across the Channel, 18,246 of whom were French, 24,352 Polish, 4,938 Czech and 163 Belgian.[7] It meant that, if the Germans did try to invade Britain, they would find, by September 1940, 16 divisions amassed in the South East. The disadvantage, from the British point of view, is that the Germans would have found them more or less unarmed.

> Could you please oblige us with a bren gun,
> Or failing that, a hand grenade would do,

trilled Noël Coward.

We've got some ammunition
In a rather damp condition,
And Major Huss
Has an arquebus
Which was used at Waterloo.

The German High Command was divided about the best method of putting their invasion plan – Sea Lion – into operation. The army wanted to enter Britain in September, landing in Kent, but Reichsmarschall Göring believed that the Luftwaffe alone could defeat Britain. Not all his officers agreed. Adolf Galland, a squadron commodore in the Luftwaffe, said: 'In my opinion the plan' – to invade Britain – 'was not serious. Our preparations were ridiculous. The air force was not trained to conduct an independent air war over England.' That would seem to have been the case. So long as the German air force was used as back-up to its, to date, unbeaten army, with the support of its navy, it would probably have been unbeatable. Against Dowding and his fighter pilots, it was a different story.

It was partly the courage and ingenuity of the pilots, partly the superiority of the aircraft design, but above all it was the technological ingenuity of the boffins, which helped win the Battle of Britain. Radio direction finding, RDF, had been pioneered in 1935 by Robert Watson-Watt, who initially developed it as an instrument of meteorology and immediately saw its defence potential. By 1938, Watson-Watt had supervised the building of the first CH (chain, home) radar station on the east coast; a second chain (CHL) could provide low cover on 1.5 metres wavelength for aircraft flying beneath the detection zones of the CH stations. Similar devices were available for ships at sea. By the beginning of the war, Watson-Watt was the director of communications at the Air Ministry with special responsibility for radar. The system he created could rightly be described as 'one of the greatest combined feats of science, engineering, and organization in the annals of human achievement'.[8] Max Aitken, Beaverbrook's son and a squadron leader in 1940, said: 'Radar won the Battle.'[9]

By the time Göring sent his Luftwaffe, Watson-Watt had organized a chain of radar stations round the coast looking out as far as 100 miles and feeding all the information instantaneously to Fighter Command. Dowding could therefore decide how to deploy his fighters, many of whom were desperately undertrained, to the best advantage. The first attacks by the Germans were bombing raids by the Stukas on merchant convoys and harbours. Dover was badly hit. Such tactics gave Dowding valuable time to plan, and to retrench. On 13 August, Göring suddenly changed his tack and ordered an attack on the radar stations. For the next fortnight, in the summer-holiday sky, the fighter pilots of England and Germany confronted one another. It was almost like a return to the single combat of medieval warfare. The fate of Britain hung on the fighting skills of about 1,400 men, some of whom were barely out of school. The Luftwaffe bombed airfields with serious, but never devastating, results.

It was at the end of the month of August, after two weeks of particularly heavy losses of aircraft on the ground and sustained fighting in the air, that the pilots experienced what they called 'the miracle'. Instead of attacking airfields, on 7 September the German bombers bombed the London docks. By the time the next major Luftwaffe daylight attack occurred, on 15 September, the RAF was waiting for them, with Spitfires and Hurricanes regrouped skilfully by Dowding. On 15 September, 56 German planes were shot down. Britain had maintained control of the air by day. The German planes remained a droning presence of malice and doom over the night skies of British cities, but by day the air was clear. The RAF had won the Battle of Britain. No invasion would be possible until the following spring.

Dowding had been due for retirement when the Battle of Britain began. On 25 November 1940 he was replaced at Fighter Command by Deputy Chief of Staff Air Vice-Marshal Sholto Douglas. Thereafter, Dowding was sidelined. He was difficult to work for, the men in the Air Ministry did not like him, and Churchill could not quite forgive him for having been right in May 1940. The Prime Minister eagerly hogged the glory of the Battle of Britain with his 'Never in the field of human conflict has so much been owed by so many to so few'; but he would have preferred the actual victor, a man who is surely the Second World War equivalent of Lord Nelson, to have been dropped from the cast list of heroes. Dowding was sent to America to ask for supplies on behalf of the Air Ministry; the visit was not a success: the Americans did not like 'Stuffy' Dowding, nor he them. The Air Ministry asked him to write a short book about the Battle of Britain. He wrote the book, and sent a typescript to Churchill, asking him to read it, and saying that if he did so, the Prime Minister might understand why Dowding did not wish to stay in the air force with the job of overseeing possible economies. The book ended with a heartfelt wish that in future the world might learn to solve its differences by peaceable means.

He was summoned to dine and sleep at Chequers, the Prime Minister's official country residence. The dinner was something which Dowding, habitually abstemious, found deeply uncongenial. There was much shouted conversation between Brendan Bracken and Churchill, then the showing of a Russian film, which Dowding thought crude. Very late at night Churchill got round to talking with Dowding. The book contained a passage about a balance of power in the world. Churchill did not like it. He believed it would be quoted 'by our enemies'. Dowding was then astounded to hear Churchill say that he 'did not believe in world harmony'. He compared it with mixing together all the colours in a child's paintbox. Dowding formed the impression that Churchill 'didn't seem to believe in working for peace'. He apparently thought – or 'thought', for it was late at night – 'that an atmosphere of struggle was necessary to avoid decadence. "I said it was all very well in the old days when all that was necessary was for men to keep their bodies fit and their weapons handy". But Churchill was drunk, and it was not an occasion "for serious or sensible discussion".'[10]

After the war, Dowding, who had been for many years a widower, remarried – in 1951. He lived until February 1970, increasingly lean and bright-eyed. 'His vision was intense but narrow,' wrote E. B. Haslam.[11] Dowding was a spiritualist who wrote a number of books about his certainty of a future life. He gave up shooting and became a vegetarian. When a grandchild developed a passion for collecting butterflies, Dowding expressed disapproval. The idea of pinioning these silent, colourful creatures with their outstretched wings shocked the gentle soul of a man who had directed aerial warfare with more acuity than anyone else in history.[12] When he was approached, yet again, by an historical researcher who wanted help with a book about the Battle of Britain, he replied: 'If you ever "did" the Aeneid at school, you may remember one of the opening lines: "Infandum regina jubes renovare dolorem", "You ask me, O Queen, to resuscitate an intolerable grief".'[13]

Britain, during the winter of bombing in 1940–41, dug itself in for the long haul. There was no hope of achieving victory against the Germans in France, even if there had been the technical possibility of landing a British army on the Normandy beaches in 1941. Churchill's policy was to concentrate on dominating the Mediterranean. The Australians had notable success in capturing the Libyan port of Bardia from the Italians in January 1941, and taking 45,000 prisoners. (James Joyce died a week later in Zurich.) Under the overall command of the gentle, one-eyed (he lost an eye at Ypres) General Sir Archibald Wavell, the British drove the Italians back in the desert, with fighting of prodigious tenacity led by Lieutenant-General Richard O'Connor, 'the little Irish terrier' who fought with his troops in the front line, and, in the week that the Italians captured Bardia, took Tobruk from the Italians. There was then an ill-fated attempt to occupy Greece. The German army was simply too much for the opposition in the Balkans. Yugoslavia was smashed into submission; Belgrade was flattened with German bombs; the Allies retreated ignominiously from Athens in April; and in May there was a hellish week of fighting in Crete – Australian, New Zealand and British troops, as well as Greeks and Cretans – followed by the evacuation from the island, after a German airborne invasion. When General Rommel landed with his Afrika Korps in North Africa, he had little difficulty in regaining most of the Italian losses. By June 1942, Tobruk had fallen to the Germans, with over 30,000 Allied prisoners taken. All the gains by Wavell and O'Connor in 1940–41 were thrown away by the folly of the Greek and Cretan campaigns.

By 1941, Churchill had 'peaked' as a war leader. His great achievement was standing firm in 1940, and steadying national morale. Thereafter, there was a very great deal of hit and miss; alcohol, age and illness clouded his judgement. Sir Alan Brooke, who was chief of the Imperial General Staff from 1942, wrote after the war: 'The President [Roosevelt] had no great military knowledge and was aware of this fact and consequently relied on Marshall and listened to Marshall's advice . . . My position was very different. Winston never had the slightest doubt that he had inherited all the military genius of his great ancestor, Marlborough . . . To wean him away from his wilder plans required superhuman efforts.'[14] As F. E. Smith, one of Churchill's closest friends in the early days of his political life, used to say, 'Winston was often right, but when he was wrong, well, my God.'[15]

Had Hitler wished to use the concerted expertise and fighting strength of his army, navy and air force to invade Britain in the spring of 1941, he might well have conquered. It might well have brought the war to an end, and ushered in, if not the thousand years of which he dreamed, a very long time in which Europe was ruled by murderous gangsters. Instead, as anyone knew who had studied his overblown account of his world view in *Mein Kampf*, he wanted to conquer Russia. 'What India was for England, the territories of Russia will be for us!' he mused in August 1941. 'If only I could make the German people understand what this space means for our future.'[16]

The Germans invaded the Soviet Union on 22 June 1941. It does not make sense to compare one sort of suffering with another, and yet it is hard to believe that any soldiers in other parts of the world were as sorely tried in battle as the Wehrmacht and the Red Army, locked in the vast, mechanized Iliad of suffering which was Operation Barbarossa. The Nazi-Soviet Axis, which had posed such a sinister threat to the West, was now turned into a deadly struggle between two monster tyrannies, fought out by their brilliantly trained and courageous soldiers. The Russian citizens themselves, above all in the besieged cities of Stalingrad and Leningrad, endured great hardship. More than 20 million Soviet citizens died during the war, and perhaps 11 million Soviet soldiers.[17]

The advance of the German army also led to a general increase in barbarity, some of it planned. Vyacheslav Molotov, in November, protested against the German treatment of Soviet prisoners of war. In one day alone, in the Chernukhinsk camp in the Ukraine, 95 prisoners were shot. Far greater numbers of Jews were now being rounded up and killed – by November, for example, over 18,000 at Sachsenhausen concentration camp alone. In Berlin at the end of July, Göring directed Reinhard Heydrich, head of the Reich Chief Security Office (*Reichssicherheitshauptamt* or RSHA): 'I commission you to carry out all organizational, material and financial preparations for a total solution of the Jewish question in the German sphere of influence in Europe.' Already, by the end of September, at Babi Yar, members of *Einsatzgruppe* C, led by Otto Rasch, had murdered 33,771 Jews in two days. They were thrown down a ravine on the outskirts of the city of Kiev. The SS men machine-gunned the adults, but hurled the children off the edge alive. Most of these atrocities came to light only after the end of hostilities, but when they did they surely confirmed Churchill's instinct that, if Europe were not purged of Nazism, the Dark Ages would indeed have come again.

While these dreadful events were in preparation, on the night of 10 May 1941 Hitler's deputy, Rudolf Hess, jumped by parachute from a Messerschmitt 110, having flown the plane from Germany to Scotland. In his hand he clutched a briefcase, believed to contain an offer of peace from the Führer. One of Hitler's supposed conditions was that the Churchill government should resign; if so, it is hardly surprising that the matter was not given very serious consideration in cabinet. Hess had come to meet the Duke of Hamilton, whom he claimed to have got to know during the 1936 Olympic Games in Berlin. 'This is one of those cases,' Churchill told the Commons, 'where imagination is somewhat baffled by the facts as they present themselves.' But quite what the facts are, or were, remains a mystery. One theory is that the Duke of Kent was posing as a potential Quisling or double-agent and waiting to meet a representative of the Führer in Scotland, but Hess got hopelessly lost and the plot was abandoned. Hess was imprisoned after the war and kept under a four-power guard in Spandau gaol until, at the age of ninety-three, he was strangled in his cell. What discussions, if any, he had with senior British politicians, and how realistic the chance of a negotiated peace would have been, will remain a mystery until papers in the Churchill archive, if they exist, throw light on the matter. The dismissal of the peace offer, if it was serious, was probably in accord with the general will, but we shall never know the truth of that either. By May 1941, Churchill enjoyed all but absolute power.

Tom Jones, deputy Secretary to the Cabinet, is reported to have said: 'If Winston Churchill had been born ten years later he would, in the 1930s, have made England a fascist state, ranged with the other fascist powers; but . . . he was too old a man with roots too firmly rooted in the Victorian aristocratic traditions to adopt so alien a philosophy.'[18] Clementine Churchill reminded her husband that 'except for the King, the Archbishop of Canterbury, & the Speaker, you can sack anyone & everyone'.[19]

Yet the paradox of this is that Churchill suffered almost more than any character in British history from watching his most decisive acts have the very opposite effect of the one intended. He who so deplored communism saw Eastern Europe go communist; he who loved the British Empire lost the Empire; and he who throughout his peacetime political career had lambasted socialism presided over an administration which was in many ways the most socialist government Britain ever had. While Churchill directed the war he left domestic policy to his socialist colleagues Attlee and Bevin. The controlled wartime economy, rationing, propaganda newsreels, austere 'British restaurants' for food, and the tightest government control over what could be bought, sold, said, published, worn, produced what A. J. P. Taylor called 'a country more fully socialist than anything achieved by the conscious planners of Soviet Russia'.[20]

The newsreels, delivered invariably in the strangulated vowels of BBC English, kept up a relentless facetiousness which might have had the sole purpose of cheering people up, but which also tried to infantilize them. 'The one-time footsloggers have turned kickstart pushers,' says the commentary to one of them, as the black and white screen shows a lot of men on motorbikes more festooned with foliage camouflage than Malcolm's soldiers marching through Dunsinane at the end of Macbeth. 'The left right, left right folks have got both feet off the ground at the same time. They are part of Britain's mighty mobile mountain. All keen welcomers of Adolf when he drops in for a cup of tea and a cream bun.' Watching the motorbikes swoop down into a ditch and judder upwards over some heathland, the cinema audiences are rib-nudgingly told: 'Up and down they go but unlike the Hun they are always on the level.'[21]

Many of the gestures called for by government had emblematic rather than practical significance. The handsome railings outside London parks, or the areas of houses, were torn out, supposedly for armament, in fact for scrap. Beaverbrook, when he became Minister of Aircraft Production on 4 February 1942, asked for the population to hand in saucepans and frying-pans. The fantasy that aluminium pots could be melted down and transformed into Lancaster bombers was never believed by anyone in government. It was merely assumed that such pointless gestures of sacrifice would improve morale. The saucepans were all thrown away.

It is no accident that the Second World War was approached by so many in a spirit of grim irony. The mawkish patriotism of so much propaganda and attempts at poetry during the First World War was not something the 1940s generation, whether in or out of uniform, could really echo. 'Who the hell dies for King and Country any more? That crap went out in the first world war,' said one Canadian soldier who spoke for almost everyone.[22]

There are 'serious' war poets of the Second World War, but they are not even in the same league as the good–bad poems of Brooke, Owen, Sassoon from the First. One of the best-loved British poems to come out of the Second World War is a comic poem, Henry Reed's 'Naming of Parts': its contrast between the impassible and beautiful world of nature and the dull absurdity of army training evokes the tone of the early Forties as well as any of the patriotic stuff:

> This is the lower sling swivel. And this
> Is the upper sling swivel, whose use you will see,
> When you are given your slings. And this is the piling swivel,
> Which in your case you have not got. The branches
> Hold in the gardens their silent, eloquent gestures,
> Which in our case we have not got.

As 1941 drew to its close, there was not much for British people to cheer about. It was now over two years since anyone in Britain had eaten a Camembert, or a banana. Eggs were luxuries, sugar in short supply. The radio blared nonsense about carrots helping pilots see in the dark. True, Britain had conquered Ethiopia, Eritrea, Somaliland, Syria and (for about the third time) Iraq. The war news, though, was generally bleak: Crete, the Balkans – the North Sea, where one of the fastest warships afloat in the world, the battle cruiser HMS *Hood*, was sunk by the *Bismarck*. The year 1940 had demonstrated Churchill's pluck, and the collective courage and resilience of the British people. The year 1941 had demonstrated their patchy military skill, and their essential powerlessness. They could temporarily resist conquest, but they could not themselves be European conquerors. Whatever happened at the end of the appalling conflict being waged in Russia, it could not wholly be to Britain's advantage. In the Far East, Japan, which Churchill believed would never make war, was sniffing hungrily around Malaya;

who knows but that that ingenious empire might not train its sights on India itself?

As the dismal Christmas approached, many would have agreed with Martin Bormann's verdict, though not perhaps when he delivered it (in 1945): 'Britain should have made peace in 1941. We had each of us triumphed over a Latin race. In the skies over London she had proved her valour. Now she needed to protect her Empire, and concern herself with the Global balance of power, not the narrow European one. Pitt would have seen this – Churchill did not.'[23] Bormann was not a noted historian, so we do not know to which Pitt he referred, the Pitt who sent a supportive army to Germany in 1758 or the one who did likewise in 1805. Still, Britain remained 'alone against the rest of the world'. The Americans were not entering the conflict directly.

Then, everything altered. On 7 December, over the Hawaiian island of Oahu where the US fleet lay in Pearl Harbor, 184 Japanese aircraft appeared in the early morning sky. Eighty-six warships lay beneath them, of which nineteen were sunk or disabled. One hundred and eighty-eight military aircraft were destroyed, another 159 badly damaged, and 2,403 Americans died that morning. It was hardly good news, especially when to this triumph the Japanese could add the occupation of the Philippines and northern Malaya. On Christmas Day Hong Kong surrendered to the seemingly unconquerable imperial power. But Churchill, together with most of his fellow countrymen, felt enormous relief. American declared war on Japan on the day of Pearl Harbor. With Russia in bloody chaos (on Christmas Day in Leningrad, 37,000 people died of starvation), the whole world was now caught up in a global struggle. For a man who had told Dowding that he did not believe in world harmony, Churchill could not but be stimulated. Speaking to the US Congress on 26 December, having spent Christmas with the Roosevelts in the White House, Churchill gave his famous two-fingered V sign, and asked – of the Germans and the Japanese – 'What kind of people do they think we are? Is it possible they do not realize we shall never cease to persevere against them until they have been taught a lesson which they and the world will never forget?' It was fighting talk, and fighting days lay ahead.

29

Bombers and the Bombed

In July 2004, a charming elderly gentleman, Willy Schludecker, aged eighty-two, bespectacled, tweed-clad, paid a visit to Northumberland in the far north-east of England. His appearance is that of a retired Lutheran bishop, or perhaps the headmaster of a gentle, but studious *Gymnasium*.

He was coming to see the village of Bolam, near Morpeth. A memorial window in the church there carries the inscription: 'This window marks the place where, on 1st May 1942, a bomb dropped from a German aircraft entered the Church but did not explode'. Willy Schludecker had been the bomber pilot flying a Dornier 217 from Holland with the intention of bombing Sunderland, then one of the great shipbuilding areas of Britain. Coming under attack from British fighters, the young Schludecker took a split-second decision to jettison his explosive load. One of the four 1,100-lb bombs bounced through a side-wall of the Saxon church before sliding across the tiled floor.

Joy Scott, four years older than the bomber pilot, was in the village when the explosives fell. 'It was terrifying. The place shook for five minutes when the bombs dropped. The first bombs blew in the windows of the vicarage. The vicar had got out of bed and the window frame ended up framing him on the bed. The bomber came so low it clipped the trees, which is probably why the bomb that hit the church did not go off.'

A local historian, investigating the night of the bombing, discovered that Herr Schludecker was still alive. When contact had been made, the former pilot wanted to come to the village. 'He was mortified and decided that he would like to come over and tell the people there that it was not his intention to bomb their church.' The newspaper, on the morning of 13 July 2004, showed the photograph of old Willy Schludecker holding the arm of Joy Scott outside the sturdy little Saxon church.[1]

Schludecker's own nearest city of Cologne on the Rhine was the scene of one of Sir Arthur Harris's set-piece bombing raids in which Bomber Command proudly flew 1,000 Lancasters over in a single night. The gentleness of the two old people in the July 2004 photograph made it seem totally unimaginable that sophisticated nations should ever have thought to solve their political differences by spending huge sums of money in constructing aeroplanes and explosives for the single purpose of bombing human beings of all ages, and destroying their docks, their

406

factories, their houses, their schools, their hospitals, their altars and their shrines. There had been sieges in the past, from the legendary times of Troy to the horrible Siege of Paris in 1870 when civilians had been caught up in 'dolorous war', as Homer calls it. Such atrocities had always been incidental to war's main business, which was battle between combatants by sea and land. The invention of the aeroplane changed all that. In 1922, the British cabinet had approved the policy of establishing 'Air Control' in Iraq. Charles Portal, Arthur Harris and Edward Ellington, the officers who oversaw this policy of cowing the Iraqi population by bombs from the air, were senior officers in the RAF during the run-up to the Second World War. There was an added poignancy in the story of the old Luftwaffe pilot revisiting the English village which he had inadvertently bombed, since, on the day that his visit was reported on the middle pages of the English newspapers, the front pages contained stories of allied air raids on Iraq. Those selfsame targets selected by Portal and Harris in 1922 were still being pounded by expensive Western explosives in the summer of 2004. The policy described sardonically by Field Marshal Wilson as 'appearing from God knows where, dropping their bombs on God knows what, and going off again God knows where'[2] was always going to be popular with politicians, since it could be done with comparatively few casualties – certainly fewer than using infantry to subdue a populace.

Bombing of civilian targets in the First World War had been frequent. The Germans bombed the suburbs of Paris on 14 August 1914. Hitler's invasion of Russia fell on the twenty-fifth anniversary of the French scoring a direct hit on a circus at Karlsruhe, during a performance: 110, mainly children, were killed. It is not surprising then that in 1939, at the outbreak of war, all British intelligence, and most of the pundits, assumed that Hitler would direct a bombing campaign against London. Sir John Anderson, Home Secretary and chairman of the Committee of Imperial Defence (a pompous man later to give his name to a semi-effective cheap form of air-raid shelter which people could construct in their back gardens), calculated that 2,000 bombs would fall on London in the first twenty-four hours of war. They worked out that 28,000 would be killed by bombing in the first month. Bertrand Russell in *Which Way Peace?* envisaged the mayhem: 'London would be one vast raving bedlam, the hospitals will be stormed, traffic will cease, the homeless shriek for peace, the city will be pandemonium.'

In fact no British civilian was killed by aerial bombardment until a stray bomb, aiming for the battleships in Scapa Flow – where the old German fleet was scuppered at the end of the First World War – accidentally hit a house and killed James Isbistern, aged twenty-seven, in the village of Waithe Bridge in Loch of Stenness. In the fight between Britain and Germany the policy of bombing civilians was pursued by the British, who mounted their first raid on 11 May 1940. It aimed at targets along the Ruhr the day after Churchill became Prime Minister. The RAF continued, without cessation or interruption, to bomb German civilian targets until the end of the war. It was Churchill who as Secretary for War (combined with air) had directed the first civilian bombings in Iraq in 1922.

The Germans, of course, had taken part in savage aerial attacks on European cities, including Guernica during the Spanish Civil War, and on Rotterdam, The Hague, and such French towns as Nancy during their conquest of Northern Europe during the summer of 1940. It was Britain from which their bombers were held back, for as long as Hitler entertained any hope of a negotiated peace based on the loose general scheme of Germany running Europe and Britain the rest of the world.

Whoever fights monsters, decreed Nietzsche in his prophetic text *Beyond Good and Evil*, 'should see to it that in the process he does not become a monster; when you look into the abyss, the abyss looks into you'.[3] The fear of being bombed, and the knowledge that both sides were prepared to bomb, if necessary upon a limitless scale, changed the whole rhetoric of warfare, and the way in which it was conceived by governments and populace alike. The First World War, with its Angels of Mons, its hymns of knightly valour, its need to dignify the muddied, bloodied battlefields with chivalric glow, had been consciously archaic in its way of selling itself to the people. Hence the appalling and shocking contrast, in the more popular songs, as in the war poets, between the florid calls to war by generals and bishops and the reality of shell-shock, amputated limbs, gas and mechanized slaughter. Techniques of slaughter had improved since 1919. Governments would now in 1939 be capable of effective acts of genocide with greater speed and efficiency than previous generations had dreamed of. The Young Turks, killing their million Armenians, had needed to employ armies, with bayonets, rifles, swords. Such grisly means would still be in use during the 1939–45 war. But the invention of the bomber could distance governments and war leaders imaginatively from what they were doing, and in such circumstances, Homeric or Arthurian metaphor came to be displaced by cosier, chummier injunctions to sing along together in the air-raid shelters as the fire-bombs rained down; to take the medicine, to continue business as usual.

One of the ways in which the peoples of the twentieth century made tolerable for themselves the scale of mass slaughter was by invoking the language of heroism. The Heroic Age, as perceived through the litera-

ture of Epic and Romance, had been one in which weaponry was primitive and the grim business of battle was dignified by focusing upon the
deeds of individual combatants. While the mayhem, the casual and
painful deaths of Trojans, Greeks, Persians, Spartans, Geats, Arthurian
Celts or Brythons, could be attributed to pitiless Fate or capricious deities,
the whole grisly business was redeemed by the personal courage of Hector,
Patroclus, Lancelot. At a time when modern warfare became a Malthusian
slaughter programme; when tanks, advanced artillery, machine guns could
mow down tens of thousands by the day, herding together human beings
like animals in a highly mechanized slaughterhouse; when sophisticated
explosives could wipe out thousands, regardless of their skills as fighters
or their moral fortitude, the linguistic convention was revived that anyone
who died in war was a hero. The brave became the valiant. Tens of thousands of mutilated young corpses became the slain. Their unwitting and
involuntary deaths were described as sacrifice, even as a Calvary.

Language from Malory's *Morte d'Arthur* or Andrew Lang's Homer
tried to hide from the governed and the governors, the generals and the
foot soldiers, the fact of which the dictators were all too aware: that
human life had become cheap, expendable: that the old metaphysical
beliefs in soul or human individuality had all been replaced by various
forms of materialism and determinism which made it possible to eliminate human beings on a prodigious scale without any strong underlying
intellectual challenge. War was bound to become a projection of
Darwinian Fitness rivalry. In the First World War, there were some 'victories' and 'defeats' in the field, but very few decisive battles. After both
sides had demonstrated their willingness to sacrifice tens, hundreds of
thousands of young lives month in, month out, the contest became a
question of who could bring the winning combination of most active
troops and most military hardware. The arrival of over a million
Americans in Europe simply crushed the morale of German leadership.

After the First World War, and the resolve of Western leaders that no
such wasteful fighting should be repeated on Western soil, there developed the view that science and technology had in any case made obsolete
such methods of war as had carved up France and the Low Countries.
The few bombs dropped on European cities by the rivals of the Great
War left the statesmen in the ensuing two decades convinced that the
power that controlled the air would ultimately win the war. Radar, and
anti-aircraft technology, had not been pioneered when Stanley Baldwin
told the House of Commons in November 1932: 'the bomber will always
get through'.[4]

If the land battles, however mechanized, could be seen as re-enactments
of medieval chivalry, air battles could certainly be seen as tournaments.

The Battle of Britain had stopped the German advance, made impossible the Nazi invasion of Kent, and created if not the inevitable outcome of an Allied victory, at least a stay of execution. Dowding's 'Few' of Fighter Command had done something which no land battle could have achieved: brought about a decisive change in the destiny of nations with losses in the low thousands, not the tens of thousands of Mons, Ypres or Passchendaele. Those on both sides who engaged as fighter pilots were heroes in the Homeric mould, individuals who actually made a difference.

Another branch of the Royal Air Force, Bomber Command, called for no less courage on the part of pilots and their crews, but when the war was over, the politicians were sheepish about their achievement. Arthur Harris, C-in-C of Bomber Command, was offered no employment by the RAF in 1945 and left for South Africa. He was not made a peer but offered the minor reward of a baronetcy. No Campaign Medal was struck for the men who took part in the destruction, not only of Germany but of many cities in Holland, France, Italy and Central Europe. The language of heroism could be stretched to include the unfortunates caught up in battles between uniformed combatants in the deserts of North Africa or the beaches of France. But what was heroic about dropping tons of high explosives on medieval churches, on hospitals, on heavily populated and ill-defended towns and cities?

In the trials of the vanquished German leadership at Nuremberg in 1945, it was brazenly taken for granted by the Allies that the bombardment of civilian targets was a war crime. 'Was not your purpose in this attack to secure a strategic advantage by terrorization of the people of Rotterdam?' asked Sir David Maxwell Fyfe of General Albert Kesselring, indicted for his part in the defeat of Holland in 1940. Göring, mastermind of the aerial bombardment of Britain in the same year and onwards, admitted: 'I decided on Coventry because there the most targets could be hit within the smallest area.'[5] While the men who directed the bombing of Rotterdam (civilian losses about 840) or Coventry (568 killed during the worst raid, in November 1940, when the cathedral was destroyed; 1,253 killed by air raids during the entire war)[6] could be put on trial for their lives, it was perhaps as well that Harris was conveniently in South Africa lest against the British and Dutch losses be placed the 600,000 German civilians who lost their lives, the 3.5 million German homes which were destroyed, the 7.5 million Germans left homeless. By then a variety of justifications had been adduced by the Allied leadership, American as well as British, for the policy of civilian bombing. These justifications included strategic necessity, the shortening of the war, the need to sap enemy morale. None of these reasons could quite stand exposure to the light of common day, once the Army of Occupation moved across Europe and began to see for themselves what Arthur Harris's Lancasters, Mosquito Mk IVs, Halifax Mk IIIs and other ingenious planes, together with American B17 Fortress Mk IIIs, had wrought on people and places. Those who had flown in Bomber Command on dangerous raids through the night in the latter years of the war, and survived, saw themselves as the lucky ones, but also as the heroes of the war. Half the boys who had flown with them in Bomber Command had died. But their senior officers, and above all Harris himself, had assured them that their courageous flights over enemy territory were a vital, perhaps the vital contribution to Allied victory. The men of Bomber Command were kept isolated from others in the air force and by the very nature of their service – cooped up either in planes or back on the ground with their squadron – they had never mingled with the army or navy.

When the fighting was over one small group of bomber pilots in their RAF uniform were sitting in the rubble of some building they had destroyed, smoking a quiet cigarette. The small town or village they had wrecked seemed miles from anywhere and everything was still. It had never occurred to any of these very young men that what they had been asked to do, at such personal risk, was anything but brave, virtuous and necessary. In the distance, they saw, and heard, the arrival of a small army jeep coming up a dusty road. When it reached them, an officer, an English public schoolboy, leaned over his rolled-down window and addressed the little group. His arm took in the devastation, the ruined buildings, the teetering masonry.

'Did you do this?' he asked.

The class thing kicked in. These working-class Lincolnshire boys, brought up to habits of deference but resentful of the drawling superiority of the voice which questioned them, said:

'Yes, sir.'

They expected congratulations – some school slang from a Biggles book or a *Magnet* magazine which they could snigger about but which would confirm their sense of self-worth.

'You bastards!' exclaimed the officer and drove off at speed.[7]

It was their first indication that the world did not necessarily regard their war work in the same light that they did.

Before war broke out, it was assumed that the German air force would set out to bomb London flat. In fact, severe as the German bombardment of British cities was to become, it was months after the outbreak of war before Germany bombed any civilian targets in Britain. By contrast bombing German cities was part of British policy from the moment Neville Chamberlain lost control of the government. 'Whatever be the lengths to which others may go, His Majesty's Government will never resort to the deliberate attack on women and children, and other civilians for purposes of mere terrorism,' he promised the Commons at the beginning of the war.[8] While Churchill approved constant bombing of German civilian targets, German attacks on Britain were always more sporadic, less concentrated.[9]

By the time the war was at its height and Churchill with his scientific advisers was weighing up the rival merits of different varieties of poison gas to be dropped on German cities, he was able to express in a memo the wish 'that this matter in the meanwhile will be thought through cold-bloodedly by rational people, and not by these psalm-singing uniformed spoilsports who always encroach on the territory of others'.[10] The uniformed psalm-singers were those chiefs of general staff who doubted not merely the morality but the efficacy of civilian bombing.

Blitzkrieg, lightning war, was, in the German language, that deployment of quick strike which had secured such easy victory over all the European countries invaded by their armies. For the British, however, 'the Blitz' meant bombing. Since the German air force had no plane which could last longer than 30 minutes over England without running out of fuel, and most German planes had about ten minutes, either to fight or to bomb, before turning for home with even a faint hope of survival, the policy of aerial bombardment was haphazard.

An early, and emblematic, victim of German bombing was the Warwickshire city of Coventry. The place was a palimpsest through which appeared the history of England. On the borders of this West Midland manufacturing town was the large Triumph Motor-cycle Works and the smaller Lee Francis Cycle Works. But Coventry was not one of those nondescript villages such as Manchester or Birmingham which were purely the creation of the Industrial Revolution. There had been a human settlement at 'Coffa's Tree' in the seventh century. The Benedictine abbey had been founded in 1043 by Earl Leofric, and his wife, the Countess Godiva, entered legend by her celebrated naked ride through the city to 'free the town of Coventry from heavy bondage and servitude'. (The first chronicle to mention the event, more than a century later, speaks of the horse, not the rider, being 'naked', that is, saddle-less; but why spoil a good story?)[11] The thriving market town swelled to eminence as a meeting-place for trade guilds in the fifteenth century. Shakespeare probably came here from nearby Stratford to see the miracle plays and to hear the Coventry Carol, a Christmas song from those plays. (The great medieval abbey church became a cathedral – the new diocese was carved out of that of Worcester – in 1918.) Between the 1860s and 1914 Coventry became 'the bicycle capital of the world'. In the post-First World War era, Courtaulds established a vast modern factory manufacturing synthetic fibres. In addition the Gauge and Tool Company was established here by the mid-1930s. The factories were on the outskirts of what remained a charming old town with a Georgian coaching inn, medieval houses, and modern housing developments for its 280,000 inhabitants.

It could be seen as a miniature version of modern England, an individual complex built around a settlement which stretched back through Tudor merchants and medieval monks to Saxon times. The factories were being put to war use even before September 1939. Courtaulds nylon works was producing parachutes. Alfred Herbert Ltd, since Munich, had been working shifts night and day to produce tools for weapons. Aircraft components were being manufactured in Coventry from March 1940. The first German bombs in the area fell on the nearby Ansty aerodrome in June 1940.

The first German bombs on London were dropped by accident on 25 August 1940, when a German pilot released explosives on a civilian target, which had been meant for oil tanks at Thameshaven.[12] On 8 November 1940 the RAF bombed Munich. The raid achieved nothing, but it so influenced Hitler that he insisted there should be retaliation.

The German squadron leader gave the following instructions to his men, for the so-called Operation Moonlight Sonata:

> Comrades, you are acquainted with the nature and essentials of tonight's operation. Our task is, with other squadrons, to repay the attack on Munich by the English during the night of 8 November. We shall not repay it in the same manner by smashing up harmless dwelling houses, but we shall do it in such a way that those over there will be completely stunned.

The aim, their squadron leader assured them, was to smash the factories making engine parts, including the Rolls-Royce aero-engine works.[13]

The 14th of November 1940, a Thursday, was early-closing day in Coventry. The boys of King Henry VIII school played their usual game of rugger. The clergy of St Thomas, and of the cathedral of St Michael, said Evensong. Over high tea the citizens read the *Midland Daily Telegraph* or listened to Children's Hour, episode five of *Forgotten Island* by J. D. Strange. It was shortly after 7 pm that the bombers arrived and dropped about 100 incendiary bombs over the city. Mingled with the incendiaries were a few high explosives.

'Strangely persistent this raid tonight, Kenneth,' remarked the vicar of Holy Trinity Church to his curate.[14] By nine o'clock many of the factories on the outskirts of town were ablaze – Alfred Herbert Ltd, and the

Daimler works in Sandy Lane. The Coventry and Warwickshire Hospital glowed with incendiary bombs. It was at about eight that the first of the incendiaries struck the cathedral. Clergy and people rescued a few treasures – cross, candlesticks, the colours of the 7th Battalion, the Royal Warwickshire Regiment – but by 11 o'clock that night it was clear that the fire-fighters could not rescue the cathedral itself.

Those who saw the raid from afar – Birmingham is eighteen miles away – felt they were witnessing 'a gigantic sunset'. The next day there was drizzle in the air. It looked, and felt, as if the whole city had been destroyed, even though by the standards of other bombarded cities later in the war, remarkably few people were killed or injured.

There survives an extraordinary recording of the provost and choir of Coventry Cathedral singing the medieval Coventry Carol in the ruins, on Christmas Day 1940. The world heard Provost Howard say: 'I am speaking from the ruins of Coventry Cathedral . . . Last Christmas we had our wonderful carol services in the glorious building of pink sandstone . . . with its wide arches and spacious windows, every stone of it loved and treasured by twenty generations of Coventry people. Six weeks ago the enemy came and hurled down fire and destruction upon our city all through the long night . . . Early this morning, here under these ruins in the lovely little stone chapel built six hundred years ago we began the day as usual with our Christmas communion, worshipping the Christ, believe me, as joyfully as ever before . . .'

But for all the brave and pious words, more than the sum of 568 lives, a cathedral, a lot of houses and factories and streets and gardens, had been destroyed. The past had gone. In some European cities which suffered similar fates, it was decided, when peace came, to reconstruct an ersatz version of the old building. In Coventry in the 1950s there was a brave attempt to build a new cathedral (Sir Basil Spence, architect) surrounded by the honest but predictable hideousness of a postwar town. In both cases, the past, that accumulation of masonry and memories which accrues its patina through generations, could not be recovered. The Luftwaffe had destroyed old Coventry – Cuffa's, Godiva's, Shakespeare's – as surely as the RAF would remove the life, the guts of German history. Lübeck, Rostock, Cologne, Hamburg, Dresden, Frankfurt am Main and many other towns were punitively and thoroughly incinerated. Berlin, the Prussian capital and symbol since Bismarck of German unity, was wrecked.

Bombing with intelligent tactical purpose was not really of interest to Harris. In February 1943, for example, he enlisted the help of his old colleague, now Chief of Air Staff, Sir Charles Portal to resist the conversion of thirty Lancaster bombers to carry a new spinning bomb devised by the scientist Barnes Wallis.[15] The bouncing bomb, if it worked, would burst the Ruhr dams and flood the industrial heartland of Germany. The ingenuity, the sheer brilliance, of Wallis must have been one of the things which repelled Harris's very crude personality. He dismissed Wallis's invention as 'just about the maddest proposition as a weapon that we have yet come across'.[16] 'My boys' lives are too precious to be wasted on your crazy notions.'[17] He was eventually converted. The damage inflicted upon two of the Ruhr dams on the night of 16/17 May 1943 was substantial but the third dam was not breached. The Dam Busters had not quite succeeded in wiping out the bulk of the German mining and manufacturing strength in one audacious raid. But this sort of precision bombing, focusing on single achievable objectives, never appealed to Harris. When asked to consider targeting the rubber factories of Hanover, for example, he said: 'I distrust experts and specialists on "panacea" commodities . . . for example a fortnight after we were told Germany was nearly on the rocks for oil she staged the biggest campaign in history [Russia] using billions of gallons.' He preferred to ignore the 'panacea merchants'[18] and concentrate on huge destructive plans of what came to be known as 'area bombing'.

As early as his appointment in 1942 Harris was telling readers of the *Daily Express*: 'If I could send 1,000 bombers to Germany every night, it would end the war by the autumn. We are going to bomb Germany incessantly . . . the day is coming when the USA and ourselves will put over such a force that the Germans will scream for mercy.'[19] He had learnt in Iraq that Arab villages could be bombed into submission. The examples of the courage and fortitude of people in Glasgow, Coventry, Plymouth, Liverpool and hosts of other British towns, including London, with its defiant photographic self-image of St Paul's surviving the smoke and flames, gave him no pause. He began with medieval towns, not because they had the smallest strategic importance but because, being built of wood, they burnt well. Lübeck and Rostock went up like matchsticks. Over Cologne in May 1942 Harris had his dream fulfilled – 1,000 bombers in one raid.

Workers in the Ruhr had chanted the song:

> Tommy, please don't drop that bomb;
> All we are is miners, Tom.
> Berlin's where you want to drop it,
> They said 'Yes' so let them cop it.

Harris in August 1943 was telling Portal: 'we are on the verge of a final showdown in the bombing war', but after nearly two years more of his bombing raids, Germany had still not caved in. By the end of the war, Harris had ordered 14,562 sorties over Berlin. He dropped more bombs on the German capital alone, 33,390 tons, than were dropped on the whole of Britain throughout the war. The suffering of the people of Hamburg, Dresden and ultimately Berlin was on a scale unseen in any British city, since the devastation was so much more widespread, the havoc and destruction more absolute, the casualties so hugely greater. One reason for this in Berlin was that the city was filling up with foreign workers – as many as 800,000 had arrived by 1943 – to replace factory workers who were now dying, in uniform, at the Russian Front. Many of these workers were slaves, and the Gestapo made sure that none of them came near an air-raid shelter. Tens of thousands died in RAF raids.[20]

Although Berlin was on fire for much of the time in the closing months of the war it never reached the stage of the total inferno which engulfed, for example, Hamburg. One witness recollected, nevertheless: 'the air-raids kept on getting worse. Sometimes the whole city was on fire. At times, you could not differentiate between night and day. When you went outside you had to have a wet cloth over your face because there was so much dust and dirt in the air that it was impossible to breathe . . . incendiary bombs fell by the thousands every day.'[21]

The bombing of London in the closing weeks of 1940 and the beginning of 1941 had an extraordinary effect upon its population. Naturally, there was some panic, and much distress, but the universal mayhem predicted by the Anderson Committee simply did not happen. People huddled in the Underground stations. The authorities forbade them to do so, but the authorities were defied. 'We was always singin',' one woman told the Thames Television *World at War* programme, 'always happy, just like there was no war at all, I remember one night when the big guns started . . .'

The tension of the atmosphere, and the fires themselves, created an extraordinary collective response. In one of the most remarkable novels to come out of the Second World War, Elizabeth Bowen's *The Heat of the Day*, the author evokes the atmosphere of the blacked-out streets, the smell of burning and death . . . 'From the moment of waking you tasted the sweet autumn not less because of the acridity on the tongue and nostrils; and as the singed dust settled and smoke diluted you felt more and more called upon to observe the daytime as a pure and curious holiday from fear.' Shops had BUSINESS AS USUAL defiantly posted outside them when they had been bombed. Bombed-out civil servants dictated to their secretaries, typewriters perched on their knees, on benches in St James's Park. 'The very soil of the city', wrote Bowen, 'seemed to generate more strength: in parks and the outsize dahlias, velvet and wine, and the trees on which each vein in each yellow leaf stretched out perfect against the sun emblazoned the idea of the finest hour.'[22]

London was bombed on seventy-six nights in succession during that autumn and over 40,000 people were killed. There were more than 1,500 fires burning in and around the Square Mile in December 1940. The heart of the City was destroyed, but St Paul's survived.

Churchill visited the East End to inspect the damage, for, as always happened in bombed cities, it was the poorer areas, with the most densely and cheaply built housing, closer to factories and docks, which were most easily destroyed. 'I can remember,' one woman recalled, 'just off of Green Street and there were crowds of women there trying to get their bits and pieces out of houses . . . Churchill called out, "We can take it!" and the women told him what he could take in no uncertain terms.'[23]

In Germany, open defiance of authority such as this would have been punished by instant arrest. But as in England, the bombing strengthened the desire to carry on as normal. 'Noble, patient, deep pious and solid Germany', as Thomas Carlyle had called it,[24] continued in its virtue and piety. For example, when the RAF bombers destroyed the Treasury in Berlin, and with it every Berliner's tax documents, they continued to pay their taxes.[25]

On the night of Harris's thousand-bomber onslaught on Cologne, the morale of the people was terribly shaken. A hospital doctor recalled: 'We were all shaking with fear, many of the patients were crying, many people actually caught fire and were running round like live torches.' Amazingly, however, the survivors doggedly went on with life, just as Londoners did. The summer raid over Hamburg in July 1943, conducted in extreme heat, led in effect to a tornado of fire which took possession of the whole city. Ben Witter, a Hamburg journalist who witnessed the raid, recollected: 'The water by the docks was on fire. It is difficult to explain why the water was burning, there were many ships more in the canals. They had exploded; burning oil was on the water and the people who were themselves on fire jumped into it; they burned and swam, burnt and went under.' A Hamburg fire officer, Hans Brunswig, said: 'Most people were killed by the fierce heat: the temperature in some places reached 1,000 degrees centigrade.'[26] Over a million and a quarter people fled from Hamburg. On 20 August 1943 Friedrich Reck-Malleczewen, the Man in Despair, saw a group of such refugees trying to force their way on to a train in Upper Bavaria. As they do so a cardboard suitcase bursts open 'and spills its contents. Toys, a manicure case, singed underwear. And last of all, the roasted corpse of a child, shrunk like a mummy, which its half-deranged mother has been carrying about with her, the relic of a past that was still intact a few days ago.'[27]

Thirty thousand people died during that raid in Hamburg. Albert Speer believed at the time that six more such raids would finish the war. But there were many more such raids across Germany, and Germany did not cave in, even after American bombers joined the RAF, and, in the words of one US pilot, 'England was just an airport really.'[28] Only when the Red Army reached Berlin was it actually defeated.

By March 1945, when the beautiful city of Dresden had been destroyed by Harris with the scarcely calculated loss of between 30,000 and 100,000 human lives, many of them refugees, even Churchill was concluding: 'The moment has come when the question of the bombing of German cities simply for the sake of increasing the terror . . . should be revised . . . The destruction of Dresden remains a serious query against the conduct of Allied bombing.' Harris remained impertinent and uncomprehending. 'In Bomber Command we have always worked on the assumption that bombing anything in Germany is better than bombing nothing.'[29]

How could such a lunatic idea have been allowed to prevail? Given that this was Harris's viewpoint, how come he was not arrested as a murderer? One reason was that he was personally a frightening man. In January 1945, when told to abandon 'area bombing' and concentrate his attacks on oil targets, he simply refused, challenging Portal to dismiss him. Portal did not dare.

The second reason is that the bombing of Germany has to be understood in the general context of the war campaign. Germany had been set on a course of outright victory and conquest until Dowding in the summer of 1940 held off the fighter pilots of the Luftwaffe, and granted Britain a stay of execution. No invasion of Britain could take place until the spring of 1941, and by then Hitler had conceived his plan, executed on 22 June, of invading Russia.

The British options, when it came to fighting Germany in the years following Dunkirk, were distinctly limited. Even after the United States entered the war, even after Stalin's Russia joined the Alliance, the invasion of France, or other territories occupied by Hitler, on a Second Front (i.e. second to the Eastern Front where the *Wehrmacht* and the Red Army fought it out) was not deemed by Churchill to be a practical possibility. Hence his doggedly wise refusal to open up a Second Front until the summer of 1944 and his insistence that the war be pursued first in North Africa, then in the Mediterranean and then, with painful slowness, in Italy. The German army, on the traditional battlefields of Northern Europe, could not be reached by British troops since they had been sent home in fishing skips and pleasure steamers from Dunkirk. This frustrating fact is part of the reason for the decision to attack the comparatively easy targets of German cities by air. One says 'compara-

tively' since, as has already been emphasized, the men of Bomber
Command were required to take terrible risks. Their losses, out of the
125,000 who served, were 59,423 killed and missing, a mortality rate of
47.5 per cent. The strategic air offensive of 1940–41 killed many members
of the RAF, and in 1941 the RAF lost a bomber for every 25 tons of
bombs dropped.

The arrival of Harris as C-in-C boosted morale not only in Bomber
Command in 1942 but in a Britain where, after three years of fighting,
disaster had followed disaster. The church bells rang in England on 15
November 1942 to celebrate the victory of General Sir Bernard
Montgomery and the Eighth Army at El Alamein. It was a victory born
of the patient accumulation of huge superiority in the numbers of British
troops, tanks and guns. Up to that moment in the desert, the brilliant
Rommel, the Desert Fox, had reversed all the earlier victories over the
Italians. Tobruk had fallen on 20 June – 33,000 British troops surren-
dered. The Germans had conquered Greece in early April 1941. On 27
May, after some of the bloodiest fighting of the war, Crete was lost.

Against this background, the attempts of Bomber Command to subdue
Nazi Germany could be seen as welcome. English cinema audiences
cheered the bombing of Cologne, just as Irish cinema audiences had
cheered the bombing of Coventry. Such was the frenzied and desperate
condition into which the war had excited the human race, that bombing
was seen by some as liberation. The Man in Despair, Reck-Malleczewen,
said to his diary: 'Is it not the absolute height of tragedy, simply incon-
ceivable shame, that just those Germans who are left of the best of them,
who have been prisoners of this herd of evil-tempered apes for twelve
years, should wish and pray for the defeat of their own country, for the
sake of that same country?'[30]

And Joe Horn, once a concentration-camp prisoner, later a businessman in New Jersey, recalled: 'The first time I saw bombers in the sky, I
was a kid in Buchenwald, dressed in a striped suit and completely demor-
alized. The bombers gave us hope and led to the realization that this
unrelenting nightmare could end sometime.'[31]

30

In the Broadcast

On 18 August 1976, the tarmac was removed from the prison yard in Wandsworth Prison in London, and the remains of a hanged corpse exhumed from plot number 87 at the dead of night. The remains were transported to an Aer Lingus plane and flown to Galway. On a dazzlingly warm August day, the coffin was laid to rest in the Protestant section of the Bohermore cemetery, for this was a man who, despite pleadings from the prison chaplain in London, had chosen to die in his mother's faith – that of the Anglican Church of Ireland. His name was William Joyce. Ludovic Kennedy summed up the strangeness of his life and fate by saying: 'The man who was born an American, lived a German, and died a British traitor will at the end become what he really was all along – an Irishman from Connemara.'[1] His family had some difficulty in persuading the local authorities in Galway to rebury this man in Irish soil. Finton Coogan, a member of the Dail, pointed out that as a young man, William Joyce had associated with British soldiers in Galway during the Troubles. He had been opposed to Irish Republicanism, on the grounds that it was Bolshevik. But charity prevailed and the mayor of Galway, Mary Byrne, believed that since Joyce's daughter Heather wanted her father to be given a decent burial, it was only right that she should be allowed to do so. Heather remembered her father as a good man, a fine Latinist, and a good teacher. Once his very brief phase of collaboration with the British had been overlooked, Joyce could be reburied with full Irish honours which included, in spite of his specific wish to die an Anglican, a full Tridentine Latin mass, celebrated by Father Padraic O'Laoi. (Heather thought her father would at least have enjoyed the Latin, though if he was as keen a classicist as his biographer suggests, he might have winced a little at the 'dog Latin' of the Mass.)

Thus was laid to rest the man who in his lifetime became one of the most notorious broadcasters in history: Lord Haw-Haw. It did not appear to worry the Galway council that the man to whom they accorded such funerary pomp was an eloquent exponent of National Socialism and a propagandist for German victory in the Second World War. The only blot on his escutcheon was his willingness to offer succour to the enemy, that is the British, during the Troubles.

As Mary Kenny shows in her truly remarkable reconstruction of William Joyce's life, such attitudes might be offensive to some English people, but they should be understandable, given the strange and troubled history of Anglo-Irish and indeed of German–Irish relations. Sir Roger Casement was reburied with a state funeral, so why not a ceremonial burial for Lord Haw-Haw?

William Joyce was born in New York. (In 1933, applying for a British passport under false pretences, he claimed to have been born in Galway, and it was this little lie which led to his being hanged twelve years later.) His father had been born on a farm in the west of Ireland, and emigrated to the United States in 1888. By this date, 40 per cent of New Yorkers were of Irish extraction. Michael Joyce became an American citizen, worked as a builder, and acquired an American accent. He married an Englishwoman. Their son William was born at 1377 Herkeimer Street, Brooklyn, on 24 April 1906. They left America in 1909, and ran a pub in Westport, County Mayo. William was educated by the Jesuits in Galway. He joined the Royal Worcester Regiment in 1921; when it was discovered that he had lied about his age, he was discharged. By then he was living with relations in the North of England, where he was able to witness the effects of Indian nationalism on the Lancashire cotton trade; then he moved to London, where he continued his studies at the Battersea Polytechnic. The speeches of the Communist MP Shapurji Saklatvala (see chapter 24) only exacerbated Joyce's feeling that the British Empire was finished. He began to dabble with the politics of the extreme Right, and became associated with the group known as the English Fascisti, founded by the feminist Rotha Linton-Orman, daughter of a military family, who looked a little like Radclyffe Hall. In 1922 he campaigned against Saklatvala on behalf of the Conservative party, and it was during the fisticuffs of an election meeting that he received the livid scar which stretched across his face from ear to mouth.

In 1923 he enrolled at Birkbeck College, of the university of London, which catered for mature students. In fact he was only seventeen, and was not good at mixing with his contemporaries who were all much older. He worked very hard, and got a First Class degree. He married a dentist's daughter called Hazel Barr. When a child was on the way, William tried to get a regular job, working at the Foreign Office. He had good languages, and a good degree, but his reference from the Principal of Battersea Polytechnic damned his chances, with its revelation that he held 'extreme views and upheld the use of violence in political action'.

Joyce joined Mosley's British Union of Fascists in 1933, while working on a PhD on educational psychology at King's College in the Strand. He knew he had it in him to be a good speaker, and he soon came to be known as the Mighty Atom – short and thickset, with a dramatic platform presence which rivalled that of the leader, Sir Oswald himself. (Joyce disliked Mosley personally and nicknamed him The Bleeder.) Mosley hired Joyce as his propaganda director with the salary of £300 a year, at a time when MPs received £400 and an office clerk around £77. The writer Cecil Roberts described the effect of hearing Joyce speak in 1936:

> Never in any country, had I met a personality so terrifying in its dynamic force, so vituperative, so vitriolic. The words poured forth from him in a corrosive spate. He ridiculed our political system. He scarified our leading politicians, seizing upon their vulnerable points with a destructive analysis that left them bereft of merit or morality. We listened in a kind of frozen hypnotism . . . when he invoked the rising wrath of his colleagues against the festering scum that by cowardice and sloth had reduced the British Empire to a moribund thing, in peril of annihilation.[2]

Mosley sacked Joyce, largely because the BUF, despite receiving funds from Mussolini, was running out of money, and losing followers by 1937. Only a small section of the public had been attracted to Fascism. In spite of the huge crowds who came to hear Mosley and a few of the star turns speak, no Fascist candidate in a British election ever came anywhere near winning a parliamentary seat. There was more than a suggestion that Mosley felt that Joyce was a little bit too eloquent; but also a liability, with his nakedly anti-Semitic views. Joyce became involved with the setting up of a rival organization called the National Socialist League, with headquarters in the Vauxhall Bridge Road, but his heart was already in the land he had come to refer to habitually as the Heimat. Like Hitler, Joyce believed that Germany should rule Europe, while Britain revived its Empire and ruled the rest of the world. His first marriage had broken down and he had married a fellow fascist and fellow boozer called Margaret Collins, who worked on Mosley's Blackshirt newspaper *Action!*. They emigrated to Germany in 1939.

It was the wireless critic of the *Daily Express*, Cyril Carr Dalmaine, who wrote under the name 'Jonah Barrington', who first identified and nicknamed Haw-Haw. His proprietor, Lord Beaverbrook, set particular store by the wireless as a means of propaganda, and so he got his critic, 'Barrington', to analyse the various propaganda broadcasts coming down the airwaves from Berlin. There was 'Winnie the Whopper' and 'Ursula the Pooh' and 'Auntie Gush', but the most interesting, speaking as early as 14 September 1939, was 'Lord Haw-Haw'. 'A gent I'd like to meet is moaning periodically from Zeesen. He speaks English of the haw-haw, damn-it-get-out-of-my-way variety, and his strong suit is gentlemanly indignation.' There followed a frenzy of speculation about 'Haw-Haw's'

identity. Such questions were discussed as whether Haw-Haw's aristocratic drawl was truly upper-class, or whether behind it could be detected
a hint of Irish. As early as December 1939, in an interview with the
Sunday Pictorial, Joyce's first wife Hazel identified the voice, though it
was not until 1941 that the authorities officially recognized this.

In the first year of the war, the BBC was lacklustre. There was no television. Hardly anyone had a receiving set; but in any event, the television
service closed during the showing of a Mickey Mouse film on 1 September
1939, and remained closed for the next seven years.[3] It was to be a wireless war, with the wireless the sole means of spoken mass communication
throughout the hostilities. In the opening months of the Phoney War,
when the worst horrors had not yet been unleashed, Haw-Haw provided
entertainment for many listeners. Entire satirical shows were invented
around this unknown personality. There was a comedy review at the
Holborn Empire music hall in London entitled simply *Haw-Haw*. Many
other music halls had Haw-Haw turns. Arthur Askey did one. Formal
banquets in the City of London were entertained by Haw-Haw imper-
sonators, who would lisp out of loathing for the 'spoilt darlings of
Mayfair'.

The government and the military did not find him so funny. 'The BBC
news bulletins were extremely dull,' said a secret military report to the
BBC in 1940, 'but when someone tunes in to Lord Haw-Haw the whole
room gets up and gathers round the wireless.'

Lord Haw-Haw asked some awkward questions:

Where else in Europe will you find a privileged class comparable with
the upper nation in England? Look around anywhere in Britain and
you will understand what I mean. Go to the slums and there you will
find the lowest stratum of the lower nation huddled together in inde-
scribable filth and poverty. Here you will find the permanent underdogs
of the capitalist system; recruits for Borstal, Barnardo's hospitals, jails
and brothels. Yet it is from the great majority of decent and honest
slum-dwellers and the frugal, industrious working classes that the
upper nation expects to draw recruits from the army to fight and die
for King and country. For a country that has confined them to the
slums.

Or again:

It is an unforgettable experience to watch the entrance to a London
theatre in the evening: pre-war of course. Limousine after limousine
with extravagantly clad women and their male companions stepping

out of cars like condescending gods and goddesses, whilst the dull and silent crowd composed of the members of the lower nation looks at this brazen display of wealth and leisure. The sight almost reminds one of the conditions in the declining Roman Empire, and one is at a loss to say whether the impudence of the upper classes or the meek tractability of the lower classes is the more astonishing. The upper nation of the Mayfair type of snob feeds on the lower nation whom it robs. How long is it going to last?[4]

Home intelligence agents circulated in pubs, offices and factories, picking up what people were saying in Britain in the early months and years of the war. These reports would suggest that much of what Haw-Haw had to say would be well received by the British public. Behind their humorous response, there was a belief in many quarters that the war was unnecessary, or that any form of government, even one led by one of Hitler's quislings, could only be an improvement on what the British had endured in the last decade from Baldwin and Chamberlain. David Lloyd George, the 'man who won the war' last time round, was now leading a Peace Party, a group of thirty or more MPs calling for a negotiated settlement with Germany. Not all of these MPs shared Lloyd George's belief that Hitler was 'the German George Washington'. Nor would they, as late as autumn 1940, as Lloyd George did, number Hitler as 'among the greatest leaders of men in history'. But they did believe that Churchill's government might be a short-lived thing and many – including the military strategist Basil Liddell Hart, the future Tory Home Secretary and Master of Trinity, Rab Butler, and an unlikely alliance of pacifists, communists and fascists – were in favour of making peace. Home intelligence suggested that after the fall of France the mood in Britain was one of 'gloomy apprehension'. In mid-June one report stated that 'Many workers say about Hitler: he won't hurt us; it's the bosses he's after: we'll probably be better off when he comes.'[5] These people might well have been tuned in to Lord Haw-Haw when he informed listeners that in Germany: 'There are no unemployed outcasts as in England . . . I should like you to contrast the friendly and sympathetic attitude of the party members of the National Socialist welfare with the methods of public assistance offered in England. You would be very sorry you ever condemned National Socialism.'[6] Unlike the politicians, Haw-Haw seemed to understand the plight of the workers, and of ordinary people; he knew the price of a loaf of bread; he knew about pensions. Many soldiers' wives listened in to him because 'he seemed to be the only person interested in them'.[7]

Moreover, once the bombing began, and civilian lives were in continual danger, Haw-Haw could torment the population with punctiliously accurate predictions of what would be hit next: Fry's factory in Surrey, Bradford Grammar School – specific towns and individual buildings would be mentioned in his lilting, perhaps psychic tones, as targets for aerial destruction. Chairmany Calling! Chairmany Calling! He moved from being joke-object to a figure who was feared; feared, because believed.

If the National Socialists in Germany were happy to make use of William Joyce's very considerable rhetorical and persuasive skills, the Italian Fascists were less certain that their cause would be helped by the backing of Ezra Pound. He went to Rome to ask the minister of popular culture, Alessandro Pavolini, the supremo of all propaganda activity, to allow him to broadcast to America. 'Well the Ministro looked at me careful [sic] and said in perlite [sic] words to the effect that: Ez, or probably he said "Mio caro Signore", if you think you can use OUR air to monkey in America's INTERNAL politics you got another one comin'.' Later, he would say: 'It took me, I think it was, TWO years, insistence and wangling etc to GET HOLD of their microphone.'[8]

What the Italians saw in the 55-year-old Pound was probably what his fellow students at the University of Pennsylvania saw when they threw 'Lily Pound' in the Frog Pond, or what pre-First World War editors and hostesses in 'Deah Ole Lunnon' saw when he swanked about in his bright green trousers made from billiards-table cloth: namely a buffoon who might, or might not, be a genius. Severer critics might suggest that a movement which revered Mussolini as a revival of the Caesars would not be too fussy about an element of buffoonery entering public rhetoric, but even the Italian Fascists drew the line somewhere; and the quality of Pound's broadcasts, when he was eventually allowed to make them, suggested that Alessandro Pavolini's initial impulse to refuse Ole Ezra a slot on the airwaves was the right one. His attacks on 'Jewry, all Jewry, and nothing but Jewry', and on the president of his country as 'Stinkie Roosenstein' or 'Franklin D. Frankfurter Jewsfeld', are among the most puerile rants of anti-Semitism ever aired. For years now, he had been brooding on the evils of Usury. The broadcasts gave him the opportunity to share some of his economic ideas with the Americans as well as to praise such figures as 'Ole Pete Pétain'. Luigi Viullari of the Institute of Overseas Cultural Relations opined, two months after Pound's first broadcast, that he was insane.[9] 'EUROPE CALLING! EZRA POUND SPEAKING!' he would bellow, and then he would clown about, putting on an extraordinary, exaggerated accent – 'Mebbe in time the Amurrican cawledge boys will git roun' t' readin' me or Céline, or some of the livin' authors . . .' He would tell the would-be soldiers of 'Mister Rooo-se-velt's dee-term-in-ation to starve the French in unoccupied France'. There were routine insults to 'clever kikes runnin' ALL our communication system'; there was the assertion that Britain had become a 'Jew-owned deer-park with tea-rooms', whereas the Nazis had 'wiped out bad manners in Germany'.

When he was arrested and accused of treason, Pound claimed that he had never incited US troops, once America had entered the war, to mutiny or revolt. He also claimed, probably accurately, that he knew nothing of the fate of the Jews in Eastern Europe. But though he did not openly incite the troops to mutiny, it cannot have done much for an American serviceman to hear complaints 'that any Jew in the White House should send American kids to die for the private interests of the scum of the English earth and the still lower dregs of the Levantine' (19 February 1942), nor, a few weeks later: 'For the United States to be making war on Italy and on Europe is just plain damn nonsense, and every native-born American of American stock knows that it is plain downright damn nonsense. And for this state of things Franklin Roosevelt is more than any other man responsible.'[10]

Pound and Haw-Haw represent the political extremes; but they also serve as demonstrations of the extraordinary reversals which are occasioned by wars. Who, meeting the young Ezra Pound in the company of Yeats or Gaudier-Brzeska or Henry James in Edwardian London could ever have predicted that in a coarser and more violent time, thirty years hence, he would be spouting such vulgarities, such violence, such cruelty, down the airwaves to his fellow Americans? Then again, who, having heard the broadcasts, and witnessed his buffooneries, could have believed him capable of the extraordinary poems which came from him after his arrest? But this lies in the future.

There was another Edwardian literary survival lured most unwisely to the radio-mike during the Second World War. In a postwar preface to *Joy in the Morning*, the novel he began in Le Touquet before the Germans invaded France, and completed during his internment by the Nazis, P. G. Wodehouse had some very interesting things to say about the contrast between the universe of his own sun-filled Edwardian imagination and the world into which he, and his creations, so incongruously survived. 'I suppose one thing that makes these drones of mine seem creatures of a dead past is that with the exception of Oofy Prosser, the club millionaire, they are genial and good-tempered, friends of all the world.' This was P. G. Wodehouse's own sin, when he was arrested by the Germans. 'All that happened as far as I was concerned, was that I was strolling on the lawn with my wife one morning, when she lowered her voice and said, "Don't look now, but here comes the German army". And there they were, a fine body of men, carrying machine guns.'[11] After a year in an internment camp, the former lunatic asylum at Tost, Wodehouse was released, and taken to Berlin, where his wife Ethel and Wonder, a favourite Pekinese, were waiting for him at the Adlon, the grandest hotel. Wodehouse was not released on condition that he broadcast from a German radio station: his release came as a result of well-intentioned petitions by Americans resident in Germany before the United States was at war with that country and pointing out that he was nearly sixty years of age, when he would have been released anyway. Asked by the German authorities to deliver some broadcasts to his American fans, Wodehouse was gullible enough to accept the offer, and to give utterance to jolly paragraphs like the one just quoted about the Nazis being a fine body of men.

Humourless people have scoured Wodehouse's works for evidence of Nazi sympathy. It is only a little less heavy-handed to defend him by describing his ludicrous Sir Roderick Spode and the Black Shorts as a 'satire' on Mosley's Blackshirts. The skilful propagandists in Berlin knew that the value of Wodehouse to them was precisely that he was not polit-ical. 'If old P.G. can make jokes about the Third Reich, then perhaps the Allied Propagandists had been making too much of the innate evil of the Hitlerite regime?' That was the corrupting power of Wodehouse's broadcasts. The fact that he only did them for a week suggests that their essential good nature was as baffling to the Germans as to the Americans, British and French who allowed themselves to be worked up into parox-ysms of hate against this innocent and agreeable man. Malcolm Muggeridge, the intelligence officer sent to investigate Wodehouse in Paris in 1944, wisely noted that 'he is a man singularly ill-fitted to live in a time of ideological conflict, having no feeling of hatred about anyone, and no very strong views about anything. In the behaviour of his fellow-humans, whoever they may be, he detects nothing more pernicious than a kind of sublime idiocy.'[12] At the time of the broadcasts, the minister of information in London, Duff Cooper, had considered the possibility of Wodehouse being apprehended after the war and even hanged. The *Daily Mirror*'s columnist 'Cassandra', William Connor, had broadcast a denuciation – 'honour pawned to the Nazis . . . thirty pieces of silver' – which Dorothy L. Sayers rightly said 'was as ugly a thing as ever was made in Germany'.[13] A. A. Milne, John Buchan and others all clamoured their hatred of poor Wodehouse. With patriotism was a good admixture of envy in these writers as they denounced an author whose books sold so many more than theirs.

When Duff Cooper arrived in Paris at the end of the war to become ambassador, Muggeridge tried to make him see that there were differing levels of reality. 'Could we be sure, for instance, that Hitler's ravings and Churchill's rhetoric and Roosevelt's Four Freedoms would seem more real to posterity than Blandings Castle? I rather doubted it.'[14] Such talk, at such a date, suggests a mind peculiarly able to rise above the weird fever of hatred and mass hysteria into which wars drag even rational beings. The most interesting thing about the affair of the Wodehouse broadcasts is the extent to which it revealed so many of Wodehouse's fellow Britons as peevish, vindictive, bloodthirsty (the calls for his death from such supposedly intelligent lawyers as Quintin Hogg were quite serious) and utterly humourless. All these qualities are ones which some British people like to assume are the special faults of Germans or Russians. Some people meditating upon the 1940s like to speculate about how the British would have behaved in the event of a Nazi victory: which British politicians would have collaborated with the Nazis, and so on. The Wodehouse affair shows something much less pleasant than that somehow half-comforting fantasy (half-comforting because the German victory did not take place, and buried inside the speculation is the smug belief that most British people would not have behaved as so many Belgians, Dutch, French and Austrians did when their countries were overrun). What the Wodehouse story shows is that you did not have to be a Nazi to be down-right nasty.

The war had begun, as far as almost everyone in Britain was concerned, by listening in.

I am speaking to you from the Cabinet Room at Number Ten Downing Street. This morning the British Ambassador in Berlin handed the German Government a final note, stating that, unless the British Government heard from them by 11 o'clock that they were prepared to withdraw their troops from Poland, a state of war would exist between us. I have to tell you now that no such undertaking has been received and that consequently this country is at war with Germany . . .

Chamberlain's words must be the flattest announcement in the history of the world of so highly dramatic an event. After the conquest of Norway by the Germans, paper shortages in Britain made newspaper production very difficult. Broadsheets were reduced to four pages, and much the best way of keeping up with world events was by listening to the news on the wireless. It was on the wireless, in the first Christmas of the war, that the king was heard quoting from a poem called 'God Knows' which he had found in a commonplace book: 'I said to the man who stood at the Gate of the Year: "Give me a light that I may tread safely into the unknown." And he replied: "Go out into the darkness and put your hand into the Hand of God. That shall be to you better than light and safer than a known way."'

Because of his stammer, the king could hardly finish the lines, and they came over as 'Anona Way' – somehow it is all the more affecting for that. The hitherto unknown author of the poem, Minnie Louise Haskins, a retired university lecturer, suddenly found her poems being reprinted, and they sold 43,000 copies.

Listening to the news on the wireless became a national ritual. Godfrey Talbot, a news sub-editor at the BBC who went on to become a household name as a war correspondent, recollected that 'in public houses people didn't order a drink, or take a drink, but huddled to the end of the bar where the loudspeaker was. In millions of homes up and down these islands, and elsewhere too, nothing happened. The records of water companies, telephone companies, gas suppliers, electricity suppliers show the demand going down, down to nothing. Nobody went to spend a penny, nobody put the kettle on, nobody did anything but listen to this man who was so confident that his confidence somehow oozed out of the loudspeakers.'[15]

Churchill's attitude to the BBC had always been hostile. The Corporation had defied Baldwin and Churchill during the General Strike of 1926 by carrying statements from the strike leaders; they had only asked Churchill to speak four times during his 'wilderness years' in the 1930s. The Director General, Sir John Reith, loathed him. When Churchill became Prime Minister, he sacked Reith (Old Wuthering Heights as he called him) as a Minister of Information and made him into a Minister of Works and Public Buildings. He told Reith that he saw the BBC as 'the enemy within the gates, doing more harm than good'. This was because the BBC had refused to compromise in its principle of telling the truth on the news, whether that news was good or bad. 'It seems to me', said R. T. Clark, the Home Service's news editor, 'that the only way to strengthen the morale of the people whose morale is worth strengthening is to tell them the truth, and nothing but the truth, even if the truth is horrible.'[16] Later, Churchill referred to the BBC as 'one of the major neutrals'. In his early days as Prime Minister he had tried to abolish the Corporation's independence by making it a branch of the Ministry of Information presided over by the figure of Duff Cooper. The M of I, model for Orwell's Newspeak in 1984, was a national joke. Cooper had been responsible for Cassandra's radio denunciation of P. G. Wodehouse, insisting against the wishes of the Corporation (whose lawyers considered it libellous)[17] that it should go ahead; and it was after this moral fiasco that Cooper was replaced by Churchill's PPS Brendan Bracken.

Little as Churchill approved of the BBC, his broadcast voice was, in the memory of millions of men and women, a phenomenon of prodigious power. The speeches were all the more powerful for being only occasional. On 9 February 1941, for example, listeners heard him say: 'Five months have passed since I spoke to the British nation and Empire in the broadcast.' His voice, when it came, was heard after the nine o'clock news. The highly imitable distinctiveness of its half-slurred, defiant, aristocratic tones was never forgotten by the generation who heard them in those circumstances. In silenced pubs or blacked-out rooms, men and women hung on every one of Churchill's words. In July 1940, for instance: 'Here in this City a refuge which enshrines the title deeds of human progress and is of deep consequence to Christian civilization; here, girt about by the seas and oceans where the Navy reigns; shielded from above by the prowess and devotion of our airmen – we await undismayed the impending assault . . . We shall seek no terms, we shall tolerate no parley, we may show mercy – we shall ask for none.'[18] Or in 1941, having visited the bombed cities of Liverpool, Manchester, Cardiff, Bristol and Swansea:

The British nation is stirred and moved as it has never been at any time in its long eventful, famous history, and it is no hackneyed trope of speech to say that they mean to conquer or die. What a triumph the life of these battered cities is, over the worst that fire and bomb can do. What a vindication of the civilized and decent way of living we have been trying to work for and work towards in our Island. What a proof of the virtues of free institutions. What a test of the quality of our local authorities, and of institutions and customs so steadily built. This ordeal by fire has even in a certain sense exhilarated the manhood and womanhood of Britain. The sublime but also terrible and sombre experiences and emotions of the battlefield which for centuries has been reserved for the soldiers and sailors, are now shared, for good or ill, by the entire population. All are proud to be under the fire of the enemy. Old men, little children, the crippled veterans of former wars, the ordinary hard-pressed citizen or subject of the King, as he likes to call himself, the sturdy workmen who swing the hammers or load the ships; skilful craftsmen; the members of every kind of ARP service, are proud to feel that they stand in line together with our fighting men, when one of the greatest of causes is being fought out, as fought out it will be, to the end. This is indeed the grand heroic period of our history, and the light of glory shines on all.[19]

The power of the spoken word was demonstrated in a different way by the Yorkshire novelist J. B. Priestley, whose voice first became familiar to people reading his novel *Let the People Sing*, and who subsequently broadcast talks. His description of the Dunkirk evacuation was something which stayed in many memories – 'Yes, those *Brighton Belles* and *Brighton Queens* left that innocent foolish world of theirs to sail into the inferno, to defy bombs, shells, magnetic mines, torpedoes, machine-gun fire, to rescue our soldiers.' Apart from the words, which many found impressive, there was novelty in the accent. Until the war, there had been a strict rule at the BBC that the only people allowed to broadcast with regional accents were comedians.[20] The BBC had an advisory panel to guide its wireless announcers in the mysteries of English pronunciation. When consulted about the word sausage, for example, one panel-member, Rose Macaulay, was insistent that the correct pronunciation was Sorsidge. (Well, how else would one pronounce it?)

J. B. Priestley did not merely say Soss-ij; he said Bath not Bahth and Castle not Cahstle. The government complained about the contents of his talks, which, in his Yorkshire accent, appeared to be advocating left-wing politics. After the second series of talks, entitled *Postscript*, Priestley, at the insistence of the Ministry of Information, was confined to the overseas service. It was at Priestley's suggestion that the BBC hired the Yorkshire character actor Wilfred Pickles to join the team of newsreaders on 17 November 1941.[21] Heard today, Priestley sounds positively patrician, and even Wilfred Pickles sounds much more BBC than he sounds Yorkshire. But a small revolution had occurred. In order to win the war, the country must unite. Churchill himself in his first broadcast as Prime Minister had said: 'I have formed an administration of men and women of every party, and from every point of view. We have differed and quarrelled in the past, but now one bond unites us all: to wage war until victory is won and never to surrender ourselves to servitude and shame, whatever the cost and the agony may be.'

In time, even Churchill was recognizing over the airwaves that after the war Britain must change. Postwar Britain would need to draw her leaders 'from every type of school and wearing every type of tie . . .' Tradition must play its part, but 'broader systems must now rule'.[22]

The politicization of the electorate inevitably happened, partly as a result of classes mixing in the armed forces; partly because of their rubbing shoulders in food queues, makeshift air-raid shelters and the like; but also through the common experience of listening in. Such programmes as *The Brains Trust* were widely listened to. The diary of a worker in a chemical factory in November 1941 recorded 'Favourite topic on Mondays seems to be the previous day's *Brains Trust* session. Hardly anyone confesses that he didn't hear it, or if they do, take care to give adequate reasons for so doing'[23] It was a discussion programme between five people: usually C. E. M. Joad, head of the Philosophy Department at Birkbeck College, Julian Huxley, secretary of the Zoological Society, and Commander A. B. Campbell of the Merchant Navy, who represented the Voice of No Nonsense and Common Sense. There would then be a variable group of people from whom the other two members of the team were selected – Kenneth Clark, Gilbert Murray, Jennie Lee, Anna Neagle, Malcolm Sargent. Strict questions of religion and politics were avoided, but the general themes of religion and politics as they affected ordinary discourse could not be entirely sidestepped.

Archbishop Lang complained that the discussions showed 'an irreverent disregard for revealed truths in the Holy Scriptures'. Early questions included quite simple ones such as 'What are the Seven Wonders of the World?', but by 1943 they were being asked such questions as 'What are the causes of anti-Semitism?' and 'What is the difference between a Liberal, a Socialist and a Conservative?'

Many people found such discussions stimulating, and continued them in their own homes or workplaces. There was also the phenomenon of shared humour. The military passion for initials and acronyms spread even into radio comedy titles. The most famous of the comedy shows was *ITMA*, mainly written by Ted Kavanagh. It had an array of comic characters played by Dorothy Summers, Tommy Handley and Jack Train. Summers played a charlady called Mrs Mopp – 'Can I do yer now, sir?' Catch phrases from the programme entered the common language. 'Ta-ta for now, or TTFN.' 'I don't mind if I do', when offered a drink. 'After you, Claude.' 'No, after you, Cecil.'[24] Few of the jokes, if written down, seem remotely funny now. But then, things were different. Priestley's description of the little boats now seems mawkish. Churchill's full-blown rhetorical flights embarrassed sophisticated listeners even at the time. But in all these cases, one has to remember the heightened tension of the war, and the sense of a common danger threatening all. Irony did not work on the radio. When Noël Coward first sang 'Don't Let's Be Beastly to the Germans' at a party in 1943 Churchill thought it was so funny that he demanded several encores. 'Though they've been a little naughty/To the Czechs and Poles and Dutch/I don't suppose those countries really minded very much.' But when he sang it on the wireless there were complaints by those who thought Coward was advocating conciliation with the enemy, and the BBC eventually decided to ban the song. United in a simpler form of laughter at the jokes of Tommy Handley, or in the new-found sense, inspired by Churchill, that they were all capable of rising to heroism, the wireless worked an alchemy on the spirit.

Above all, perhaps, it was as a purveyor of music that the wireless made most impact. As a character remarks in one of Coward's plays, *Private Lives*, it is funny how potent cheap music is. 'Lili Marlene' was popular with both sides, whether sung by Marlene Dietrich in America or by Anne Shelton in England. Vera Lynn was a plumber's daughter from East Hackney. Her very strong voice ('a gallery voice; she didn't need a microphone to reach the gallery', said Charlie Chester)[25] had a megaphone obviousness which matched the mood of the age. There was certainly something erotic in the way her voice broke and caught, but like Churchill she did not mind pulling out the vox humana stops, and she was equally unafraid of obviousness.

It is not surprising when you hear 'We'll Meet Again' that she was the Forces' Sweetheart for singing this song, or 'White Cliffs of Dover', 'Wish Me Luck', 'It's a Lovely Day Tomorrow' – one of the saddest songs ever sung – and others to troops some of whose chances of meeting anyone again were as slender as those of their loved ones surviving aerial bombardment at home. It was the wireless which made Lynn's voice so famous, just as it was the wireless which popularized jazz and Big Bands. B. E. Nicholls, the Reithian controller of programmes, implored the Variety Department to play 'waltzes, marches and cheerful music' rather than jazz. Reith shared Hitler's hatred of jazz, though probably not for Hitler's racialist reasons. But simple waltzes were not what people wanted to hear when they could be listening to Jack Payne, Geraldo, Joe Loss, Harry Roy, Victor Silvester, Billy Cotton, or the phenomenally popular Glenn Miller, who sacrificed a lucrative career to serve in the US army and who was lost, mysteriously, in a small plane just before the war ended. The hectic tones of Miller's trombones and sax make even the stiffest and the shyest listener want to roll up the carpet and dance. But also, perhaps, it is possible to hear in the music a strength, a vigour, which is emblematic of the land from which it came, and the global power which the war was delivering into American hands.

31

The Special Relationship II

King George V is said to have replied, when asked if he wanted to see a film, that he would see 'anything except that damned Mouse'. Yet two years after his death, when the new American ambassador was having luncheon at Windsor Castle with the new King and Queen, George V's granddaughter, Princess Elizabeth, was thrilled to hear that Mr Joe Kennedy had once worked in the movie business. She told him how much she liked Snow White, and especially the Seven Dwarfs.[1] Her fondness for Walt Disney, and for American films in general, reflected that of her future subjects. George V, as in so many respects, harked back to a vanished past.

One of the most abidingly successful films of all time, which emerged from the MGM studios in the year that Britain went to war with Germany, was *The Wizard of Oz*. When Dorothy Gale emerges from the old black and white existence which she had inhabited before the tornado swept through her Aunt Em's farm, she steps, clutching her faithful dog Toto, into a brightly lit, *coloured* world of Munchkins, yellow and red brick roads, witches, strange castles, a Technicolor Brothers Grimm world, a Europe gone mad, it may be thought. She stares around her, and she remarks to her little dog: 'Something tells me we're not in Kansas any more.' Did anyone at the time see the film as allegorical – the innocent from a world which combined American Gothic and folksy rural ranch-life finding herself cast by the Munchkins as their deliverer because the farmhouse which had landed from the star called Kansas had inadvertently squashed the Wicked Witch of the East? There was one further battle to wage, the defeat of the Wicked Witch of the West, and the good American country girl must enlist some strange allies, a tin man, a straw man, and a cowardly lion, as she dances down the Yellow Brick Road to complete her adventures.

Kipling had urged the United States, when it took possession of the Philippines, to Take Up the White Man's Burden, but this, in the sense of becoming a colonialist power such as Britain, Belgium, Holland, Germany and France were, America always resolutely refused to do. It wanted to be a world power, and Roosevelt and his closest colleagues – Henry Morgenthau at the US Treasury, and Cordell Hull, Secretary of State, did their best to foster that power. But in some ways it could be said that power came to it automatically, through the defeat of Germany and the bankruptcy of Britain. That defeat and that bankruptcy were partly America's doing, but they were partly self-inflicted. No one, after all, had asked Hitler to invade Poland and so provoke the war with Britain. No one asked him to take on both Britain and Russia, and to declare war on the United States. Thereafter, his defeat was all but inevitable. Britain's bankruptcy was less inevitable, perhaps, but given the way the Americans wished to play things, it became unavoidable.

By the end of the war, Technicolor, which in *The Wizard of Oz* had seemed such an innovation, was commonplace. Princess Elizabeth had grown up, served in the ATS, fallen in love with a distant cousin, Prince Philip of Greece. 'Their song' was not some English lullaby, but a number from *Oklahoma* – 'People Will Say We're in Love'. 'The Surrey with the Fringe on Top,' 'Oh, What a Beautiful Morning' – the songs poured out of Richard Rodgers and Oscar Hammerstein II, who were undoubtedly the liveliest and most exciting duo in the golden age of musicals. *South Pacific*, of 1949, was the favourite of Princess Elizabeth's sister, Princess Margaret Rose. There were no lyrics to match 'Some Enchanted Evening', 'There Is Nothing Like a Dame', 'You've Gotta Have a Dream' and 'I'm Gonna Wash that Man Right Outa my Hair'. That particular musical reflected the postwar exuberance of an America almost innocently triumphant in its power, and, the Korean and Cold Wars notwithstanding, ecstatic at the coming of peace. As Secretary of State from 1947 to 1949, George Catlett Marshall instituted a plan of genuine liberality for which he was awarded the Nobel Peace Prize. Rodgers and Hammerstein musicals reflect the joyousness, the energy, the self-love of the United States at this period. 'Everthin's up to date in Kansas City – They've gone about as far as they can go' was a jokey piece. Everyone who sang along to it knew that the USA could go a whole lot further – to the Moon and back one day. These musicals are much the best thing which the twentieth century produced in the way of light music, easily as good, in their own way, as the operettas of Gilbert and Sullivan. But whereas Gilbert and Sullivan throve on poking mild fun at British institutions such as the Law, the House of Lords, the Police Force and the Royal Navy, Rodgers and Hammerstein are basically celebrations of America both at home in Oklahoma and abroad in the South Pacific. Their popularity in Britain reflected the way in which British culture had become subsumed to American, a process which has continued inexorably in the years since the Second World War.

For most Britons and Americans, the relationship between the two countries has been friendly, but tinged with envy and suspicion. The GIs who came over to Europe did so to help liberate the Continent from Nazism, yes. But they also came, with dollars, nylons and cigarettes, to seduce our women and drive out our older way of doing things. And the jury is still out as to how far General Eisenhower brought blessing or disaster to Europe in his management of the final stages of the campaign to conquer and subdue the Germans.

During the world crisis over Iraq in 2004, when President George W. Bush and Prime Minister Tony Blair formed an alliance against a ruthless dictator, somewhat to the sceptical alarm of France and Germany, some sixty-year-old themes were replayed, sixty-year-old wounds reopened, sixty-year-old myths rehearsed. And once again, as in my chapter of 1940, it is perhaps necessary to stress that I am using the word 'myth' to connote a self-defining story told by a nation or group to itself, about itself. Secretary of State Donald Rumsfeld, and his supporters in the British Press, saw the caution of the French government in particular as a repetition of the moral collapse of France, accepting a Nazi victory: the creation of a collaborationist regime in Vichy under the leadership of Marshal Pétain and eventually Laval. The Americans and the British, it seemed, were the only ones prepared to stand up to tyranny, whether the date was 1941 or 2004. What was written by the *New York Times* at the beginning of the 1991 Gulf War, but could have been said by Winston Churchill in 1941, once again became the motto of the hawks in 2004: 'The war has breathed new life into the "special relationship" between the United States and Britain.'[2]

According to this version of events, old Europe was liberated from a great tyranny by the combined courage and altruism of the United States and the United Kingdom. The refusal of France and Germany to join in the war against Saddam Hussein in 2004 was seen on the one hand as an expression of 'ingratitude' for the precious gift of democracy, returned to the Western Europeans by the thousands of American GIs prepared to give their lives on the Second Front after 1944; and also as an example of the incorrigible 'weakness', which Henry James's heroines saw in Europeans as far back as the 1880s – moral ambivalence, shiftiness. Consequently, French fries became Freedom fries for patriotic Americans. The extent to which such stereotypes were rehearsed by politicians and serious journalists was remarkable, given the fact that what was being discussed was a highly controversial and contentious campaign, involving the possibility of great civilian loss of life in Iraq in 2004, and having no obvious bearing on the dramatic, tragic state of Europe in 1941–4.

Behind such thoughts as the pro-war party were expressing was a very strong unwillingness to engage with one of the central political questions of the Second World War. 'At the root of that hypnotic spell', wrote Warren F. Kimball, editor of the Churchill–Roosevelt correspondence, and professor at Rutgers University, 'is a perception of the conflict as an unambiguous, just war against evident evil. That patriotic, idealized romantic image makes American students and the general public recoil, even half a century later, from evidence of selfish American war aims or even Anglo-American discord or competition for wartime glory and post-war advantage.'[3]

Among the more uncritical supporters of the Special Relationship in our own day is an unpreparedness to see the devastating truth of Dean Acheson's judgement, in his speech at the Military Academy, West Point, on 5 December 1962, which enraged Churchill so much, that after the war Great Britain had lost an empire and not yet found a role. Even in his extreme old age, Churchill would show profound resentment of Dean Acheson's *aperçu*, obvious though the truth of it was. Indeed, it must be the obviousness of the truth which makes for the resentment. Churchill hated the idea of Britain playing only a 'tame and minor role in the world'.[4] This has led, over the last twenty years or so, to a division of opinion among right-wing commentary in Britain, over the whole question of the Anglo-American relationship. On the one hand, there have been those who saw Churchill's alliance with the Americans as essentially destructive of British power and interest. More recently, there has been a tendency, particularly among Conservative-minded journalists, to read the Special Relationship in 1941–4 as a template of what is best in modern Anglo-American relations. For them, therefore, Churchill's testiness with Acheson is forgotten, or played down. The undoubted truth of the Allied Victory is insisted upon as the thing which matters. Britain's continued friendship with America is seen less as a pathetic piece of toadyism than a demonstration that Britain does indeed still have a 'role' in the world, alongside America and outside the inner circle of the European Union, defending such values as democracy and the free market. It is difficult, entirely, to rid oneself of present perceptions about the place of America in the twenty-first century when considering what she was doing, politically, in the early 1940s, sixty years ago. Because America is today the great superpower of the world, it is quite hard to reconstruct the extent, for example, of American isolationism in 1940. Equally, it would be a mistake to emphasize this to the exclusion of recognizing that many American politicians and strategists saw the entry of their country into the war as a moment of decisive change, the moment when isolationism became impossible, and the United States became in inescapable deed what President Wilson had tried to make it in theory in 1917–18, the leading nation of the West, supplanting Britain for better or worse.

The US Senate was by no means in favour of America entering the war in 1940: only Pearl Harbor changed the political and national mood about that. Roosevelt's cabinet was not wholly pro-war even then, and certainly not entirely pro-British. What almost united it was a sense that, if America had to be involved in a European war, it could at least seize the opportunity to neuter British power in the process, so that in the postwar world the dominant Western democracy would be, not the British Empire, but the United States. The Special Relationship during the 1940s was in part, like a lot of outwardly successful marriages, an abusive relationship, in which Britain was quite decidedly the junior partner. Lord Halifax recalled, after the war, his appointment in 1940 as the British ambassador in Washington. He remembered being asked to dinner by a group of Republican senators to whom he was to make a short address. One of them said: 'Before you speak, Mr Ambassador, I want you to know that everyone in this room regards Mr Roosevelt as a bigger dictator than Hitler or Mussolini. We believe he is taking this country to hell as quickly as he can.'[5]

In such a land, Halifax was able to see, Churchill 'seemed to them a museum piece, a rare relic. When he told them that he had not become First Minister of the Crown in order to preside over the liquidation of the British Empire, they felt they were listening to a voice out of the eighteenth century.'[6]

The truth is, Britain could not have won the war without American help, but this help inevitably led the larger and richer of the two nations to emerge from the war stronger, and the smaller, poorer nation to emerge with its power irrecoverably reduced. Two vivid examples of the process are found in the scientific–technological aspects of the alliance, as forged by the Tizard Mission in 1940; and by the economic terms of Anglo-American friendship.

Henry Tizard (1885–1959)[7] combined the gifts of an imaginative research scientist with those of a patient administrator. He had been a key figure in the election of Frederick Lindemann, later Lord Cherwell, to the leadership of the Clarendon Laboratory in Oxford. During the First World War he had been both a scientist, developing research into aeronautics, and a courageous test pilot. In the 1920s he had been a pioneer of research into aircraft fuel, originating the term 'toluene number' to express the detonation characteristics of each fuel, gauging what we would call octane numbers, and assessing, basically, what fuel would enable a plane to stay in the air for the longest distance.

As well as being a research scientist, Tizard was also passionately concerned to create more British scientists and engineers, and it was with this evangelical mission that he went to the Department of Scientific and Industrial Research, first as assistant permanent secretary, then as permanent secretary. He was largely responsible for establishing the Chemical Research Laboratory at Teddington (later the National Chemical Laboratory) and as rector of Imperial College from 1929 to 1942 he did more than anyone of his generation to foster scientific education, including schemes for entrance scholarships for children – boys, almost invariably – who had not specialized in science at school.

Tizard, though only fifteen years old when Queen Victoria died, was, in other words, yet another of those dutiful, high-minded Victorians who believed in bettering the human race by means of institutions and education. With his pince-nez and formal clothes he was almost as much a throwback to the nineteenth century as Churchill himself.

The nature of his intellectual interests, however, was very far from antiquated. From early manhood he had been interested in aircraft, and engines, and defence. During the 1930s, two great areas of hostility opened up for Tizard. On the one hand he was concerned with the possibility of a Continental war, and saw the vital role that science would play in it. On the other hand, he managed to offend Lindemann, and the two had one of those feuds which academic life seems to foster with particular ease. Harry Wimperis, at the Air Ministry, asked Tizard to chair a small committee to encourage technical advance in air warfare. Lindemann, when he wrote to the Air Minister in December 1934 suggesting the creation of just such a committee, was furious to discover that it had already been formed, with Tizard in its chair; he persisted in believing that the Air Ministry and Tizard were involved in a plot to circumvent him. It was a very important committee, and it gave encouragement to such vital work as Frank Whittle's pioneering of the jet engine, and Robert Watson-Watt's development of radar.

As early as January 1935, Watson-Watt had told Tizard's committee that it might be possible to detect the presence of aircraft by radio beam. In other words, Baldwin's ominous prophecy of November 1932, that 'the bomber will always get through', was not necessarily true. By the late 1930s, Lindemann's plottings had led to Tizard's resignation from the committee. Lindemann had, among other things, arranged for a meeting between Watson-Watt and Churchill, who was then still in the political wilderness, and anxious to use for political ends Watson-Watt's view that not enough was being spent on air defence.

The importance of Watson-Watt's development of radar is something we have already noted in our description of the Battle of Britain. By the summer of 1940, Tizard was convinced that Britain could not develop its inventions fast enough, or in sufficient quantity, to withstand German assault. One of the great technical miracles that changed the course of the war was the invention by John Randall and Henry Boot, at the university of Birmingham, of a copper disc capable of generating high power, 10 kilowatts, and a very short wavelength, 10 centimetres. This was the cavity magnetron, and it revolutionized radar. Randall and Boot had a prototype ready by November 1939. It was not the basis for static radar installations, and efficient airborne radar for night fighters could be made without using it, as the Germans showed to British cost on many a night-time raid when the bombing began. Its real, and revolutionary, value was that it could distinguish buildings from ordinary ground; it could scan the Earth's surface, not just the sky. It was the most efficient tool developed for locating cities by night, so that they could be bombed. If Watson-Watt's development of radar was the primary tool in British defence against airborne attack, Randall and Boot's cavity magnetron was a vital tool of aggression.

It was an invention which could establish British superiority in a coming air war, but only if the 'resonant magnetron' could be produced and developed on an industrial scale. When tested the magnetron delivered 400 watts on a 9-cm wavelength. The magnetron was passed to the research department of General Electric, who increased its power to 10 kw.

Watson-Watt was sure that Britain could do it alone, without American help. Tizard disagreed. By the summer of 1940, Churchill was Prime Minister and Tizard's arch-enemy Lindemann was the chief scientific and technological adviser to the government. Lindemann happily acquiesced in the idea of sending Tizard to America with a group of six men. What came to be known as the Tizard Mission consisted of Brigadier F. C. Wallace, a distinguished army officer who had been in charge of anti-aircraft defences at Dunkirk; Captain H. W. Falkner, Royal Navy, and Group Captain F. L. Pierce, Royal Air Force. There were two scientists: John Cockcroft, the Cambridge physicist, and Edward (Taffy) Bowen, one of the youngest of those working on radar. Arthur Woodward-Nutt, a civil servant from the Air Ministry, came as secretary. The mission was composed of men at the top of their military and scientific fields, but they might as well have been mendicant monks with begging bowls.

Tizard had the statutory interview with Roosevelt, being ushered in at the back door so as not to attract the attention of the Press. In some ways more crucial, however, was the encounter he had with Alfred Lee Loomis, the Wall Street tycoon and amateur scientist whose laboratory in Tuxedo Park, a guarded enclave of rich men's houses in the foothills of the Ramapo Mountains some forty miles northwest of New York City, was made available for scientific war work.

Loomis (1887–1975) was first cousin to Henry Stimson, the Army Secretary in Roosevelt's administration, and one of the most pro-British and most anti-isolationist of American statesmen. Loomis's lab at Tuxedo Park was not just a rich man's plaything. He had been gathering round himself pioneers of the atomic bomb, though of course during the late 1930s American research in this respect lagged far behind that of the British, the Danish, the French and the exiles from Germany. Loomis had the money and the political influence to make things happen. It was in his house that Taffy Bowen and John Cockcroft produced a rough wooden box, and showed their American hosts the coppery disc which was the prize of their many scientific secrets. 'The atmosphere was electric,' Bowen recalled. 'They found it hard to believe that such a small device could produce so much power and that what lay on the table in front of us might prove to be the salvation of the Allied cause.'[8] Within days of Tizard's departure from the United States, Loomis had placed a production order with the Bell Telephone Company for an exact copy of the magnetron.[9]

What the Tizard Mission did was very simple. With the authority of Churchill, it put at the disposal of the Americans every single patented and secret device which had been pioneered by British scientists and engineers. The pattern was established which came to be known as the Brain Drain, of British technological and scientific expertise being drawn inexorably towards the magnet of superior American resources.

There can be no doubt that technology allied to American industrial muscle won the Second World War for the Allies. The pooling of Anglo-American skills won the war in the air. It was also vital in the war at sea. The detection of U-boats, thanks to largely British technological skill developed in the United States, led to a decisive victory in the Atlantic; and the failure of the Japanese to develop anti-submarine weapons or tactics led to the slower, but no less inexorable victory in the Pacific, with 4,859,634 tons of Japanese shipping sunk for the loss of 44 American submarines.[10]

Without American help – which included the political good will of Roosevelt, Stimson and others, as well as scientific expertise and industrial resources – the technological victories over Japan and Germany would not have been possible. But the victory was exacted at a price, namely the loss of British scientific pre-eminence.

Tizard's Mission with his scientists is matched and mirrored by John Maynard Keynes's wartime journeys to America to negotiate the future economic relations between the two allies.

Churchill owed his very existence on this planet to the widespread aristocratic belief that when an Englishman was living beyond his means, the simplest solution to his liquidity problems was to marry an American. As an extravagant young subaltern in the 4th Hussars, he had shamelessly spent more than his income. When his army pay and his allowance ran out, he would write to his American mother for more.[11] The habit of mind remained with him, as did the optimistic belief that it would always be possible to increase income rather than reduce spending. His personal life had been conducted on that basis since his days as a young Victorian spendthrift, and it was the way he chose to conduct the war economy. His earliest statement as Prime Minister had looked forward to the moment when 'the new world, with all its power and might, steps forth to the liberation of the old'.[12] He could have added, with all its dollars, just as when in his famous imprecation to the Americans he asked for the tools, he really meant 'Give us the money and we'll finish the job.' Not everyone in the US Treasury saw the exchange in quite such one-sided terms.

The Americans in fact got a good deal out of Lend Lease, the scheme by which they provided money in exchange for deferred payments, services, construction work, especially the building of American bases in Australia, India and Britain, military stores and petrol. Some parts of the Empire – New Zealand, for instance – actually supplied more aid to the US than they got back. All the tyres and inner tubes used by the US forces in the South Pacific were manufactured in Australia with rubber from Ceylon. So it was by no means entirely a question of Americans supplying the British with hardware in exchange for loaned cash in the case of tanks, transport aircraft and landing craft. The overall budget was $30,073 billion of American aid to the British Empire, with $7,567 billion being paid back.[13]

By the time the Battle of Britain had been won, and Roosevelt re-elected – that is, by the end of 1940 – British gold and dollar reserves were in danger not merely of running low, but of running out altogether. The Secretary to the US Treasury, Henry Morgenthau, was warned by the British ambassador – still Lord Lothian: Halifax had not yet arrived – of the situation. Morgenthau's view that was 'the longer we keep them going' (i.e. the British) 'that much longer we stay out of this war'.[14] Morgenthau could also see, however, that the faster the gold and dollar reserves ran out in London, the stronger was Washington's position to bring about the financial ruin of Britain and the dismantlement of that British Empire which he and Roosevelt so much detested. Morgenthau told the British ambassador that Britain could place orders 'for anything they wanted if they said they had money to pay for it'; a policy interpreted by Kimball thus: 'Roosevelt gave the green light to Great Britain to make commitments they could not meet.'[15]

Morgenthau put pressure on the British to sell off their big American companies – Shell Oil, Lever Brothers, Williamson Tobacco. John

Maynard Keynes was dispatched to negotiate with Morgenthau. The two men did not get along; their first meeting was a disaster. 'I have seldom struck anything stickier than my first interview,' Keynes said, and, on his return to London, he confided: 'I always regard a visit to the USA as in the nature of serious illness to be followed by convalescence.'[16]

The negotiations between Keynes and the US Treasury, most notably with Treasury adviser Harry Dexter White, have been described as 'one of the grand political duels of the Second World War'.[17] White and Morgenthau continually had their eyes fixed on the postwar world order. They envisaged, and brought about, an end to Imperial Preference, that is preferential tariffs within the trading area of the British Empire, and an extension of American economic influence beyond the two Americas into Europe and Asia. Unknown either to Keynes or to Morgenthau was the fact that White was a Soviet agent, passing all the private information he negotiated with Keynes back to his communist masters.[18] Keynes was not by any means an extreme imperialist, but he felt it was crazy for Britain to promise, in advance of an unknown postwar situation, to abolish any system of economic or trading controls. This, however, was the price exacted, in his long and frequent negotiations with them, by the Americans. Even the mustachioed, tweedy Anglophile Dean Acheson was adamant about this, though he could see that the terms imposed by Morgenthau at the Treasury would be as ruinous to America's European allies as to their enemies.

When Morgenthau, after a visit to England in 1944, told the President that England was broke, Roosevelt replied: 'Very interesting. I had no idea that England was broke. I will go over there and make a couple of talks and take over the British Empire.'[19] Of course it was a joke, but there was more to it than mere verbal tomfoolery.

It is not simply the revisionist historians who see the British alliance with the United States during the war as self-defeating. Many complained at the time that Churchill was getting too close to Roosevelt. Few went as far as one intelligence adviser with an office next to Churchill's Cabinet Room who said that the Prime Minister's devotion to the President was 'almost homosexual' and that it had blinded him to Roosevelt's wish to 'overthrow the British Empire'.[20] Yet many objectors noted the emotional intensity of Churchill's response to diplomatic encounters. Before the American entry into the war, Roosevelt sent his close colleague Harry Hopkins to sound out Churchill, get his measure. After four or five weeks of getting the measure of wartime Britain, Hopkins gave a dinner for Churchill at the North British Hotel in Glasgow. (He had been to Clydeside to inspect the shipyards.) He ended his speech with a quotation from the Book of Ruth: 'Whither thou goest, I will go; and where thou lodgest I will lodge. Thy people will be my people and thy God my God'. Even before Hopkins had completed the quotation with 'even unto the end', Churchill was weeping copiously.

When he finally got to know Roosevelt, the two men got on well enough, and the President said: 'It is fun to be in the same decade with you' on his sixtieth birthday. But Roosevelt was jealous of Churchill's personal charisma, and found him, much of the time, extremely tiresome.

Those who see Churchill as having sold out British interests to the Americans disregard the very wide number of issues about which he and Roosevelt, and the governments of the two countries, disagreed, often noisily. The Tizard Mission gave every British technological and scientific secret to the Americans, and the tough bargaining of Keynes could not bend Morgenthau's will to bankrupt the British after the war. But in the matter of foreign policy and war strategy, Churchill was a highly effective disputant with his American allies. Roosevelt's, and after him Truman's, hostility to the idea of the British Empire no doubt played some small part in loosening the ties between Britain and India, but the final dissolution of the Raj can hardly be laid at America's door. In the question of other British colonial interests in the East, Roosevelt was adamant that Britain should hand back Hong Kong to China and give Malaya independence when the Japanese were defeated. Churchill successfully resisted both – Hong Kong did not become Chinese until 1997, and there were many Hong Kong Chinese residents who wished it had not, just as many residents of Singapore pine for the days of the British Empire.

Over the conduct of the war itself, Churchill resisted every pressure from the Americans, and later from the Russians, to open up a Second Front against the Germans in France. He saw the possibility of a repetition of the First World War, with enormous casualties and indecisive battles. The Americans wanted to fight the Germans where they were – in France, Holland, Belgium. Churchill was prepared for the long slog, first by defeating them in North Africa and dominating the Mediterranean, then by moving slowly and inexorably through Sicily and up into Italy until the Third Reich was weakened, and the Allies had amassed sufficient forces and landing craft to make possible the Normandy landings of the summer of 1944.

It was an achingly slow war, and historians sixty years on can indulge in the luxury of wondering whether Churchill's policy was vindicated.

Some idea of what might have happened had the Americans had their way, and Operation Overlord (the invasion of the Normandy coast) been attempted before the summer of 1944, could be derived from reading what happened to the force of 6,100 British, Canadians and Free French who attempted a beach landing on an eleven-mile stretch near the French port of Dieppe on 19 August 1942. The Germans were ready for them. Landing craft – which Churchill always saw to be the key to a successful landing on the French beaches – were inadequate. The Canadians bore the brunt of the attack, with 907 dead and 1,496 taken prisoner.

The painful incident raised two questions, one tactical, the other strategic. The tactical question was how this war was ever going to be won. Landing an army on the French coast was a stupendously difficult task, however much Roosevelt, and later Stalin, might clamour for it, and to do so too soon, and without sufficient fire power or defence from the air, would simply be suicidal. The second, and in a way even more taxing question facing the Allies, now that they were indeed comrades in arms, was what was the aim of the war? Churchill had said at the beginning that it was Victory at all costs. But was Victory at all costs for the Allies the same as outright defeat, or unconditional surrender, for the Germans?

Herein lies one of the central questions governing the story of the Special Relationship between Britain and the United States. If Germany had changed its government, if, for the sake of argument, some anti-Nazi group had seized power from Hitler, would it have been in a position to negotiate with the British and American governments? The British position was always a little vague about this, since, after all, the likelihood of such a coup or putsch succeeding was slight. However, the German resistance movement would have been greatly strengthened if the Allies had signalled a willingness to cooperate with it. And this cooperation, or the remotest likelihood of it, was destroyed when America entered the war.

On 9 January 1940, Clement Attlee, leader of the Labour party and destined to become the Deputy Prime Minister in Churchill's war cabinet, made a wireless address to the German nation.

> We are opposed to any attempt from outside to break up Germany. We do not seek the humiliation or dismemberment of your country. We wholeheartedly desire to welcome you without delay into the peaceful collaboration of civilised nations. We must warn you, however, that Hitler and his system prepared and started this war. He could not continue if you ceased supporting him. Until this accursed Nazi regime is overthrown there is no hope of peace between us. If you establish a Government willing that Germany should be a good neighbour and a good European, there shall be no humiliation or revenge.[21]

This was an important broadcast, since it set out very clearly that, in spite of the invasion of Poland – the immediate casus belli – the British would be perfectly prepared for a negotiated peace with a decent German government. The Americans, however, had a different policy. Roosevelt had pressed for the unconditional surrender of Germany. That is, he would not negotiate with any German, until Germany had been completely destroyed by military force.

When the war was over, and Attlee had become the Prime Minister, the House of Commons was discussing the rebuilding of Germany. The Labour Foreign Secretary, Ernest Bevin, said that as a result of the policy of unconditional surrender 'it left us with a Germany without law, without a constitution, without a single person with whom we could deal, without a single institution to grapple with the situation, and we had to build right from the bottom with nothing at all. We had to build a State which has over 20 million displaced persons scattered about it, and we had to build it while something like five million people were driven out of one part of the country into the other.'[21]

All this, said Bevin, had come to pass as a result of the policy of unconditional surrender, 'on which neither the British Cabinet nor any other Cabinet had a chance to say a word'.

The young Michael Foot, future leader of the Labour party, rose to his feet and asked for confirmation of this extraordinary statement. He asked Bevin if he really meant that the British cabinet had never heard of the policy of unconditional surrender. Bevin replied: 'The first we heard about it was in the Press.' Churchill rose to confirm: 'The first time I heard the phrase was from the lips of President Roosevelt.' Bevin added: 'I say that I never heard of that phrase until I saw it in the Press, and that if it had been put to me, as a member of the British Cabinet, *I would never have agreed to it.*'

The full import of this has not been understood by all historians, especially by present-day enthusiasts for the Special Relationship.

The occasion to which Churchill referred, when he heard of the policy of unconditional surrender on the lips of Roosevelt, was the Casablanca Conference, when the two men met from 14 to 23 January 1943. President and Prime Minister had strolled across the lawn in the January sunshine to greet the amazed journalists who had not even been aware that they, together with the deadly French rivals Generals Giraud and de Gaulle, were locked in conference in the hotel. In the spontaneous Press conference which ensued, Roosevelt announced that 'Some of you Britishers know the story – we had a General called U. S. Grant. His name was Ulysses Simpson Grant, but in my, and the Prime Minister's early days, he was called "Unconditional Surrender" Grant. The elimination of

German, Japanese and Italian war power means the unconditional surrender by Germany, Italy and Japan . . .'

When Roosevelt spoke these words Churchill's Chief of Staff, General Sir Hastings Ismay, noticed a startled look pass over the Prime Minister's face. Later that day Averell Harriman, the American millionaire turned diplomat, had never seen Churchill so upset. He was 'offended that Roosevelt should have made such a momentous announcement without consultation'.

This was not just a question of words. It had the profoundest possible effect on the strategy and conduct of the war. And it led, ultimately, to General Eisenhower's slow, clumsy advance across Europe, and the failure of the British and American forces to reach Berlin, or Czechoslovakia, or Poland, before those strongholds had been captured by the Red Army. Sir Bernard Montgomery (Monty), Eisenhower's subordinate, spoke for almost the entire British army, as well as for the peoples of Eastern Europe, when he denounced this policy as a 'tragic mistake'.[22]

The extent to which Churchill had lost control of the conduct of the war was only made clear to him at the end of 1943, at the point described by the Russians as the Turning Point, the Teheran Conference. It was at this crucial summit, held at the end of November 1943, that Roosevelt met Stalin for the first time. Churchill had wanted it to be the world summit which would decide the foreign policy of the Great Powers after the war. Some weeks earlier, he had accordingly dispatched his Foreign Secretary, Anthony Eden, to Moscow to have preliminary talks with the Russians. Churchill was furious that, without his being consulted, Roosevelt had made the Teheran Summit a four-part affair, with the Chinese Nationalist leader Chiang Kai-shek forming the fourth member of the Quadrumvirate. Churchill deplored Chiang Kai-shek's hostility to the British Empire and resented the fact he had not been told, let alone asked, about the Chinese presence at Teheran. When Stalin arrived, it was as if all Anthony Eden's carefully worked out Foreign Office briefings about the new postwar France, Germany or Poland had never been discussed. The delegates were surprised, at what they had all supposed was a *diplomatic* conference concerned with postwar world order, that Stalin ignored the agenda and said he had only one item to discuss – 'Measures to Shorten the War'. He urged the Western Allies to bring forward the cross-Channel attacks on the French coast.[23]

Eden and Churchill then tried to interest Stalin and Roosevelt in making sure that Poland should be guaranteed its independence. After all, the invasion of Poland had been the very reason for the British declaration of war in 1939. Stalin paid the idea no attention. Soviet troops were poised to occupy Poland from the east, and everyone at the conference knew that Britain and America lacked either the power or the will to stop them.

Roosevelt sided with Stalin in his belief that when Operation Overlord began, the British should effectively abandon their Mediterranean campaign. Roosevelt sided with Chiang Kai-shek against Churchill's view of operations in the Far East – the Americans and the Chinese believing that all the war effort should be devoted to defeating Japan in the Pacific, ignoring, for example, the British campaign against the Japanese in Burma. (And this came after long days at an earlier Cairo conference in which the Americans had agreed to support the so-called 'Buccaneer' British campaign in Burma.)[24]

All Churchill's cherished war plans – to guard and fight for the Eastern Mediterranean, to protect the British Empire by land in the Far East, to liberate Poland, and above all to establish a strong and united postwar Europe – were swept aside at Teheran by Roosevelt and Stalin. For all de Gaulle's posturing, Stalin and Roosevelt agreed. The 'real' France was that of Pétain and the collaborationists. Churchill's idea that France could ever again be a great power in the world was wishful thinking.[25]

One of the most painful moments of the conference, perhaps of Churchill's career to date, occurred at dinner on 29 November. Stalin was the host and he genially discoursed upon his view that 'really effective measures were necessary, or Germany would rise again in fifteen to twenty years'. He proposed the liquidation of the entire German general staff – the execution of 50,000, perhaps as many as 100,000 officers. Churchill heatedly replied that he could never agree to cold-blooded murder or to 'barbarous acts' on such a scale. Roosevelt tried to rescue the situation with a bad joke to the effect that perhaps 49,000 would do.

The truth was not that Roosevelt and Stalin were the two brutes in the presence of an English Tory aristocrat. It was much more complicated. Teheran shows Roosevelt at his most mercurial. Was he a good witch, a bad witch, or not a witch at all? Roosevelt let Eastern Europe go to Stalin because he saw no hope of establishing American influence there. He got what he very much wanted: a position of power both in the Pacific and as the principal military controller of Operation Overlord. His rarefied and basically civilized soul lacked the imaginative equipment with which to comprehend Stalin. Churchill, who was half a benign Victorian liberal, half a bruiser, a man who had admired Hitler and Mussolini in the early days, who had rejoiced in the Siege of Sidney Street, in bashing the workers during the General Strike, in clapping Gandhi in irons, understood the bruiser who was Stalin. A part of Churchill even liked Stalin. At Teheran, however, he saw with crystal clarity the nature of the man. Roosevelt thought that when Marshal Stalin spoke about liquidating 100,000 officers he was having his little joke. Churchill knew the sort of people the Bolsheviks were. He was the only one of the three who had known action at first hand. He himself, far more than Roosevelt, had been a hands-on warlord. In the bunker where he sometimes slept in London next to the War Cabinet Rooms the visitor can still see the array of weaponry he kept by the bed – a sub-machine gun and a revolver. There is no doubt he would have used them on any would-be assailant. He had authorized some bloody campaigns and he had sent many men to their deaths.

At Teheran, Churchill saw that power, because of the war for which he had been so doughty an enthusiast, had slipped from British hands. Thanks to Teheran, Czechoslovakia and Poland and the other countries of Eastern Europe would be 'liberated' not by American troops but by the Red Army, and the peoples of Eastern Europe who had been enslaved by Hitler for six or seven years would endure another thirty years and more of enslavement by the Soviet Union.[26]

32

Prisoners

European wars, historically, offered a variation of life for the criminal classes, since it was from the scouring of prisons that there came the cannon-fodder of battlefields. Enlistment in army or navy provided the convict with a chance of reprieve from the confinement and degradation of gaol. The Second World War was different, as in so many other respects, from other wars. If previous wars allowed criminals out to fight, this war saw to it that thousands, tens of thousands, eventually millions of human beings who had committed no crime against anyone would be herded up and punished in a manner that was utterly degrading and terrible to victims and to perpetrators.

The opening chords of this war's music were a reverse of the great scene in Beethoven's *Fidelio* when the prisoners come out of their dungeon. The years 1939 and 1940 bring the clank of chains, the sound of bolts being shot, locks fastened, and gates barred. The panic atmosphere of war in Britain led to very many people being quite unnecessarily incarcerated. It was understandable that genuine Nazi sympathizers were interned, figures such as 'Putzi' Hanfstaengl, Hitler's former Press secretary. (He was taken to Butlin's holiday camp at Clacton which had been requisitioned by the army.) But the great majority of the non-British nationals who found themselves in Britain at the beginning of the war were no threat at all to security. Refugees from the Spanish Civil War, who had arrived without luggage or passport; Jews escaping Nazi Germany; Italian ice-cream vendors: all were detained as enemy aliens. Also imprisoned were harmless British cranks who had joined the Blackshirt movement in the 1930s, who found themselves apprehended under the notorious provision 18B, which suspended Habeas Corpus and allowed for persons to be interned indefinitely without trial. 1,769 British subjects were interned, of whom 764 had been members of the British Union of Fascists, whose leader had urged his supporters to fight the Germans and who had tried to rejoin his old regiment before himself being imprisoned in Pentonville; 1,106 were later released, and the others were kept locked up for the duration, or at least for most of the war.

'I didn't know there were so many Jews among the Nazis,' said the commander of the Huyton internment camp as he watched the new batch arriving. The future publisher, Hungarian-born André Deutsch, recalled friendly treatment from his camp commander on the Isle of Man: he

A Battery Shelled by Percy Wyndham Lewis.
The Vorticist depiction of modern warfare shows human beings as automata in a mechanized fate.

Stanley Spencer's picture of travoys
of wounded at a dressing station in
Smol, Macedonia, retains a poignant
sense of human tragedy

Paul Nash's work of 1918 has the ironic title,
We are making a New World

FORWARD!

(*Left*) 'Forward! Forward to Victory, Enlist now'

(*Below*) The soldier welcoming his civilian comrade across the channel gives no indication of the bloodshed and mayhem which awaits him in the trenches

COME LAD
SLIP ACROSS AND HELP

Forward to Victory
ENLIST NOW

This poster by contrast emphasizes the dangers of war and appeals to the spirit of adventure in the boys whom it urges to enlist

Will they *never* come?

REPRINTED FROM
"THE WEEKLY DISPATCH"

Spencer's post-war religious paintings, such as this suburban depiction of the Garden of Gethsemane and Judas kissing Christ, owes much to his memories of the war

The timeless simplicity of William Nicholson's still lives hid his greatness from many contemporaries, though we see it now

The twentieth-century transformed domestic life by the invention of gadgets

(*Left*) Here is a gas cooker of 1923

(*Below*) A German hair-dryer of 1925

(*Bottom right*) An American washing-machine, 1929

(*Bottom left*) An electric mixer, also American, of 1918

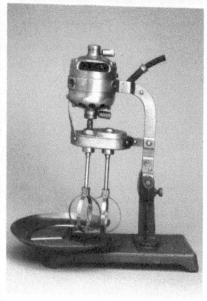

BRITISH EMPIRE EXHIBITION 1924
SCENES OF EMPIRE
SERIES · · No. P.30
APRIL — OCTOBER
SCENES OF EMPIRE
SERIES · · No. P.30

These posters for the British Empire Exhibition at Wembley reflect the exoticism of the occasion. (*Above*) This colour lithograph by Gerald Spencer Pryse shows Africans. (*Right*) Here Pryse creates the equivalent of a Kipling short-story with his splash of Indian light and colour.

The Spanish Civil War was seen by many not only as a national tragedy but as an international response to the rivalries between Communism and Fascism. The bombing of the Spanish city of Guernica by German aircraft helped to insure Franco's victory. Picasso's canvas of the event became totemic.

This recruiting poster shows the struggle in its political colours, with the Popular Front of international socialists united against the Church and the Fascists

FESTIVAL OF BRITAIN

1951
MAY 3 - SEPTEMBER 30

(*Right*) Some of the most charming poster-art in the post-war decade was inspired by the Festival of Britain in 1951. (*Below*) This poster by Robin Day advertises a celebration of British scientific achievement which coincided with the Festival of Britain.

FESTIVAL OF BRITAIN
EXHIBITION OF SCIENCE
EXHIBITION RD SOUTH KENSINGTON
MAY 3-SEPTEMBER 30   ADMISSION 2/-(4/-TUESDAYS)
CHILDREN AGED 5-16 HALF PRICE - UNDER 5 NOT ADMITTED

(*Above*) The Festival had some innovatory architecture on the South Bank of the Thames including this fine weather vane with an optimistic sunny face looking forward to the 1950s

For all the positive achievements of science and democracy, the post-war era was dominated by the now universal knowledge that science had developed the capacity for the human race to destroy itself. This mushroom cloud from Ivy Mike, one of the largest nuclear explosions ever, was photographed on November 1, 1952. The blast completely destroyed Elugelab Island.

turned out not merely to be half Hungarian, but also the son of Baroness Orczy, the creator of the Scarlet Pimpernel.[1]

Jews interned on the Isle of Man felt terror, as Hitler's advance across Europe headed the news, that the British had 'done Hitler's work for him', and that when the invasion came the Germans would find the Jews rounded up already in the camps. Some figures of great distinction were dispatched there, especially in the sphere of music. Three-quarters of what would become the Amadeus Quartet were interned, as were Hans Gal, Egon Wellesz, Franz Reizenstein and Hans Keller. The future controller of Radio Three, Stephen Hearst, the future warden of Wadham College, Oxford, Claus Moser, and his father, with the journalist Sebastian Haffner and the Dada artist Kurt Schwitters, together with many physicists, publishers, photographers, classicists and other scholars, found themselves detained.[2]

Naturally, when a war breaks out, there is fear for national security. Rumours abounded that Hitler had planted spies among the Jewish and other German émigrés. Fifth columnists were suspected everywhere in the early months of the Phoney War, and with hindsight, most internees saw the reasons for their uncomfortable detainment. Of course, by the standards of prisons and camps run by the Japanese Empire, or the Third Reich, or Stalin's Soviet Union, the restrictions in Britain at the beginning of the war were benign. They were still sufficiently a departure from such principles of prewar freedom as justice, and the right to a trial before condemnation, that they provoked intense dismay at the time, not only among the internees and their families, but among those who cared about the principles of a free society.

Primo Levi, in one of his accounts of life in Auschwitz, tells the story of Chaim Rumkowski, a merchant of the Lodz ghetto who became almost literally its king. He was useful to the Germans, and they allowed him to mint his own coinage, bearing his head, and to tyrannize over the inmates of the ghetto. In the end, of course, he perished, together with most other Polish Jews. What was so shocking about his story was that he came to ape the tyrannical ways of his bullying enemies. 'He's not a monster,' says Levi, 'but he isn't like other men either; he is like many, like the many frustrated men who taste power and are intoxicated by it.' And Levi adds: 'It is typical of regimes in which all power rains down from above and no criticism can rise from below, to weaken and confound people's capacity for judgement, to create a vast zone of grey consciences that stands between the great men of evil and the pure victims.'[3]

That this should happen in lands where Hitler stood at the top of the pyramid, we can believe that we understand. The whole world, however, became authoritarian after 1939. Churchill made himself a dictator, as did FDR at the beginning of America's involvement in the war. They were comparatively benign dictators, whereas Hitler and Stalin and Mussolini were the reverse of benign. Roosevelt and Churchill fully intended, no doubt, to lay down their office when the democratic process required it of them. While they held sway, however, it was absolute. And one symptom of this in Britain was not merely the imprisonment of men and women *against whom no charges were ever brought* but their gross maltreatment when in custody. There was Bathsheba, a Jew, put in the so-called 'Black' cell at Holloway, London's prison for women, for three days and three nights in her nightgown. The cell contained no bedding, or other equipment. Sanitary towels were refused her even though she was menstruating. Dorothy was suffering from hysteria, and an allergic reaction called urticaria, which caused huge painful blotches to form all over her body. Doctors were called only when another prisoner, Alice, threatened to inform the Home Office. Alice herself suffered from boils in her ears. She had a skin disease which, untreated, made her bald. She had about eighty boils over her body, and the pain was so intense for eight months that only when she threatened suicide was she given proper medical attention. Frances, a Polish subject, had a long and protracted labour in Holloway and gave birth when she was unconscious. Gaby, a Spaniard, knew no English. She was not allowed to write to her husband, and her distress became so acute that she was eventually deemed to be insane and locked in a padded cell. She, together with other inmates of Holloway, had come to Britain as a refugee, and been forced at gunpoint from a foreign ship apprehended in the Channel.[4] All these things happened in what Churchill called 'this City of refuge which enshrines the title deeds of human progress'.[5] The brutality, and the disregard for the humanity of the detainees, alerts us to what war does to the human psyche, how it dehumanizes those in authority.

This phenomenon of imprisonment, and dehumanizing brutality, was replicated across the globe for the duration of the conflict. Each nation and human group carries about its own memories – often too appalling to be articulated until the next generation.

Of all the great nations, Japan had most successfully contrived to embrace the twentieth century while holding fast to its cultural traditions. One of the most celebrated English works of fiction to emerge from the Second World War was Evelyn Waugh's trilogy *Sword of Honour*. It begins with a devout man, Guy Crouchback, the descendant of an ancient and religious family of warriors, feeling an awakening at the moment of the Nazi–Soviet Axis. 'The enemy at last was plain in view, huge and hateful. All disguise cast off. It was the Modern Age in arms.' Many a Japanese must have felt this as he saw the Far East ruled over by clumsy red-faced British merchants, swigging their gin-slings in Singapore or Shanghai; or when they contemplated the culture of the United States, its Mickey Mouse films, and its seeming lack of any sense of, let alone reverence for, the past, extending its commercial tentacles throughout the Pacific during the 1930s. Since 1904, when it defeated the Russians in Manchuria, the Japanese Empire had shown itself equal to, and militarily superior to, one of the great Western Powers. In 1931, while Great Britain's economy cascaded as its leaders were forced to abandon the Gold Standard, Japan invaded Manchuria. China, by appealing to the League of Nations, gave an early indication, long before Hitler became Chancellor, of that body's essential impotence. From that date onwards, Japan, this archipelago of a mere 72 or 73 million inhabitants, was essentially the overlord of the East, combining all the efficiency of a modern state with the ancient tradition of the ancestor-worshipping Shinto religion. Their emperor was a Divinity, descended from Amaterasu, the goddess of the Sun.

Between December 1941 and February 1942, Japan brought off two victories of audacious brilliance. First, five minutes before eight o'clock on the morning of Sunday 7 December 1941, Hawaii time, 184 Japanese bombers attacked the American fleet in Pearl Harbor. A second wave arrived an hour later. Four American battleships were sunk or blown up; four were damaged; eleven other warships were sunk or disabled. The Japanese pilots also destroyed 188 American aircraft on the ground. A total of 2,330 Americans were dead or dying, with 1,177 killed on the battleship *Arizona*. It was a major traumatizing event for the Americans. Both the leaders in the European conflict rejoiced, and for the same reason. 'Now it is impossible for us to lose the war,' Hitler said. 'We now have an ally who has never been vanquished in three thousand years.'[6] Churchill felt the same. What months of cajoling, and speaking to the president on the telephone, had failed quite to achieve, was brought to pass by one bombing raid. The United States had entered the war. 'We are no longer alone,' said Churchill. Germany declared war on the United States on 11 December. The war was now truly global, and Japan would ultimately pay the most terrible price for its boldness.

Three days after Pearl Harbor, Japanese bombers and torpedo planes sank the British battleship *Prince of Wales* and the battle cruiser *Repulse* off the coast of Malaya, with heavy loss of life (840 officers and men were drowned). The British position in Malaya now had no defence. By colossal oversight, the British had supposed that they could hold Singapore by the sea alone, so that when, on 8–9 February 1942, the Japanese army crossed the Johore Strait to land on Singapore Island, the British and Commonwealth defenders had no hope. They surrendered on

15 February; 32,000 Indians, 16,000 British and 14,000 Australian soldiers were taken prisoner.

It was less than a century since Japan's forced opening to the West. By the code of bushido, the Japanese warrior tradition, to be taken prisoner was shameful even for a civilian, but for a soldier it was ultimately disgraceful, a denial of what he was called to be, namely a fearless fighter, happy to wage war for his emperor, and to sacrifice his spirit on behalf of his ancestors. That British soldiers did not do this on behalf of their king and their ancestors filled the Japanese with a bewildered contempt. Another factor, understandable to all the peoples of the East, even those who viewed the Japanese victories with dread, was a desire to crush the face of European imperialism in Asia.

There were so many taken prisoner in Singapore that no pre-existent camp or prison could hold them. They were herded into Changi barracks on Singapore Island, and it was from here that many British, Australian, New Zealand, Canadian and other prisoners of war were taken as slave labour to work on the Burma–Thailand railway and other projects. They were beaten, starved, tortured. The brutality was something which no cultural conditioning or difference, even when mentioned and taken into account, can excuse or explain.[7] While they endured terrible suffering, such experiences – brutal prison guards, physical and psychological degradation of all kinds, the killing of innocent prisoners either by calculated acts of violence or by maltreatment, failure to treat disease or starvation – was being replicated in Europe.

At the heart of the National Socialist experiment was the Concentration Camp. That was its defining institution, the ultimate expression of contempt for individuals. On 21 March 1933, in his capacity as police chief of Munich, Heinrich Himmler had announced the opening of the prototype camp at Dachau, 15 kilometres northwest of Munich on the road to Ingolstadt. The Nazis advertised the fact that the concentration camps were needed to restore law and order and to re-educate Communists and other subversives. On 23 May 1933 a local newspaper boasted that the 'model concentration camp . . . makes Dachau known well beyond the borders of the Fatherland',[8] a grisly accolade which was to be truer than the sycophantic journalist could have guessed. In the face of protests by the Church, and with the 1936 Olympics in prospect, Dachau and other camps did release very many prisoners. By 1937 the SS had ordered a vast complex of buildings to expand Dachau so that the camp became in effect a small town with its own *Lagerstrasse,* camp streets, a large gravel area called the *Appellplatz,* where roll-calls and punishment parades could take place, a canteen, a library, day-rooms, workshops, stores . . . By 1943, to discourage homosexuality, Himmler ordered the setting up of brothels in the *Sonderbau* (Special Building). The 'staff' came from the all-female Ravensbrück camp, and were promised their freedom after working six months in Dachau.[9] By the time it had expanded, Dachau, this camp which had begun with the supposed aim of re-educating a few hundred Communists, contained some forty to fifty thousand men: 'politicals' – Communists to start with, but soon all manner of social democrats, liberals and persons of whom the regime disapproved; 'racials', including Jews of all ages from children to old men of over eighty, and gypsies; criminals, who included those who had done time in regular prisons and yet were still considered dangerous and professional criminals, the *Berufsverbrecher*. Then there were the 'antisocials' – beggars, hawkers, tramps; the *Bibelforscher*, Jehovah's Witnesses; and the homosexuals, forced to wear special pink stars, and whose numbers included men who were not homosexuals but had been denounced as such by vindictive neighbours or colleagues. It has been calculated that 228,300 people passed through Dachau.[10]

Tortures included such as the *Baum* (tree) and the *Pfahl* (pole). To inflict the latter, the victim was tied to the eight-foot pole with his hands behind his back, attached to the pole by the wrists. After climbing on to a stool which was then kicked away, the man remained suspended with his feet off the ground for anything up to two hours. Victims could often not use their arms for weeks afterwards. Beatings were frequent. Work was unrelenting – the hardest of it in the nearby sand quarry. The guards were brutes, selected SS thugs. Executions were frequent. Medical experiments conducted by such figures as Professor Klaus Schilling included deliberately infecting over a thousand prisoners (the largest group Polish clergy) with tropical diseases. Others were locked in pressurized cabins to simulate high altitude, often dying horribly as pressure and oxygen were reduced. Other crazy acts of cruelty worthy of an H. G. Wells fantasy included 'super-cooling' in which human beings were in effect frozen; others who had to be killed were given blood coagulants to test their efficacy; others suffered bone transplants. Overcrowding and disease were endemic. With the Allied advance on Dachau, it did not prove practicable for the SS to gas all their prisoners and so prevent them from telling their story, but there were attempts at mass poisoning, shooting, and extermination by the oldest and cheapest method of all: starvation. The mass graves and crematoria did their work, but when the Americans arrived to liberate the camp, they still found a grisly sight, with thousands of half-starved inmates and corpses piled high.[11]

Dachau was technically a *Konzentrationslager*, concentration camp, and not what historians now designate a *Vernichtungslager*, extermination camp. The first such camp, where Jews could be eliminated by carbon monoxide gas, was established near the Polish village of Chelmno about 45 miles from the Lodz ghetto. It began operating in December 1941. Death factories established in Belzec and Sobibor, with stationary gas chambers fuelled by diesel exhaust, started work in March 1942. Three months later Treblinka, a murder factory near Warsaw, was established. Cyanide gas, Zyklon B, was widely used at Auschwitz, near Cracow, and at Maidanek, on the outskirts of Lublin in eastern Poland. The mass gassings were fully under way by 1942, and by 1943 the majority of Polish Jews had been killed. In Dachau the death toll was smaller than in the extermination camps but the increase is striking. In 1940-3 it was between 1,000 and 3,000 prisoners. In 1944, it had risen to 403 in one month, 997 in the next, 1,915 in December. In the first months of 1945 it ranged from 2,625 to 3,977 *per month*.[12] By the last year of the war, the numbers become unthinkable; Chelmno, 150,000; Belzec, 600,000; Treblinka, 700,000, Auschwitz perhaps a million and a half.

As the Allies advanced, and entered the camps, there came the war correspondents. In April 1945, from Belsen, Richard Dimbleby gave one of the most memorable of early pictures of what the Third Reich in its dying fall had accomplished.

One woman, distraught to the point of madness, flung herself at a British soldier who was on guard at the camp on the night that it was reached by the Eleventh Armoured Division; she begged him to give her some milk for the tiny baby she held in her arms. She laid the mite on the ground and threw herself at the sentry's feet and kissed his boots. And when in his distress, he asked her to get up, she put the baby in his arms and ran off crying that it would find milk because there was no milk in her breast. And when the soldier opened the bundle of rags to look at the child, he found that it had been dead for days.

Here in Belsen we are seeing people, many of them lawyers and doctors and chemists, musicians, authors, who'd long since ceased to care about the conventions and customs of normal life. There had been no privacy of any kind. Women stood naked at the side of the track, washing in cupfuls of water from British army water trucks. Others squatted while they searched themselves for lice, and examined each other's hair . . . Just a few held out their withered hands to us as we passed by, and blessed the doctor whom they knew had become the camp commander in place of the brutal Kramer.

We were on our way down to the crematorium where the Germans had burned thousands of men and women in a single fire. The furnace was in a hut about the size of a single garage. A little Pole whose prison number was tattooed on the inside of his forearm, as it was on all the others, told me how they burned the people. They brought them into the stockade, led them in, and then an SS guard hit them on the back of the neck with a club and stunned them. And then they were fed straight into the fire, three at a time, two men, one woman. The opening was not big enough for three men and that I verified by measuring it.

Those officers and men who have seen these things have gone back to the Second Army moved to an anger such as I have never seen before.[13]

The anger was purgative, but useless. It all came too late. All over Europe, as the war came to an end, men and women waited behind bars and barbed wire, some prisoners of war, some in refugee camps. Some would be released from these prisons but none would be released from their memories and mental scars.

In the Age of Faith, men and women had sustained themselves by contemplating the composure and courage of the martyrs as they endured torture, imprisonment and death. The twentieth century made martyrs of millions, and if martyr is a Greek word meaning witness, then they were witnesses to the sheer wickedness to which politicians will put the use of unbridled power, the murderous savagery of human beings driven by fear and hate.

The Germans who resisted Hitler also did so too late and in too disorganized a way to make any appreciable difference. Not only was Hitler quite extraordinarily lucky in escaping assassination attempts, but also, his enemies within the Germany army, Church and liberal political circles failed signally to group themselves together in such a way as to convince the British Prime Minister or the American President that they were in a position to negotiate with the free world on behalf of a non-Nazi Germany.

The last serious attempt on Hitler's life had been that of Colonel Claus Schenk von Stauffenberg, a South German aristocrat who collected around himself a substantial number of disaffected and well-intentioned Germans. As chief of staff to General Friedrich Fromm, he was able to get near Hitler and offered himself as the assassin. He did so by planting a bomb under a conference table at Rastenburg. The Führer was leaning over the table looking at a map when the blast occurred. There was a deafening crash, and it blew the great leader's trousers off in a manner which, had it occurred in a Laurel and Hardy film, would have been farcical. Hitler displayed the tattered trousers as emblems of his 'miraculous rescue'.

The first retaliatory executions, including that of Stauffenberg himself, were by shooting, at Fromm's orders, on the evening the coup failed. The remaining conspirators were put on trial. Ghoulishly anxious to make the punishment fit the crime, Hitler ordered that the first batch should be executed in Plötzensee prison. They were led into a room where butcher's hooks were suspended from the ceiling. A rope was passed round their necks, and their bodies bared to the hips. They were then hoisted to the hooks and slowly strangled while a guard removed their trousers. Hitler had film made of the proceedings, and enjoyed watching them.[14]

Thousands of Germans were arrested after the Stauffenberg bomb plot, among them the young pastor Dietrich Bonhoeffer. This serene young man had evolved in his prison cell the concept of 'religionless Christianity'. 'It is not with the beyond that we are concerned, but with this world as created and preserved, subjected to laws, reconciled and restored. What is above this world is, in the gospel, intended to exist *for* this world.'[15]

In his death, as in his luminous writings and his innocent but unpriggish life, Bonhoeffer embodied the decency and goodness for which civilized Christian Germany (and Europe) had always stood, and which the twelve-year nightmare of Nazi rule, both clownish and bestial to the extremest degree, was unable completely to extinguish. Taken to the concentration camp at Flossenbürg to be executed, Bonhoeffer had found a freedom which Hitler, imprisoned in his own ego and in his Berlin bunker, could not dream of. The camp doctor described that morning, towards the very end of the war, the grey dawn of 9 April 1945.

On the morning of that day between five and six o'clock the prisoners, among them Admiral Canaris, General Oster . . . and *Reichsgerichtsarzt* (barrister) Sack were taken from their cells, and the verdicts of the court martial read out to them. Through the half open door in one of the huts I saw Pastor Bonhoeffer, before taking off his prison garb, kneeling on the floor praying fervently to his God. I was most deeply moved by the way this lovable man prayed, so devout, and so certain that God heard his prayer. At the place of execution, he again said a short prayer and then climbed the steps to the gallows, brave and composed. His death ensued after a few seconds. In the almost fifty years that I worked as a doctor, I have hardly ever seen a man die so entirely submissive to the will of God.[16]

Reck-Malleczewen says: 'A miserable hysteric may play Alexander the Great before the world for a while. But sooner or later, history comes along and tears the mask off his face.'[17] The man who had preserved his early authority by sending his political opponents to prison; whose armies had taken millions of prisoners of war; whose concentration camps had exploited slave labour and killed millions of his supposed enemies through the processes of disease and hard labour, while extermination camps ensured sheer coldly devised massacres by means of gas, was to end his days as a prisoner of his own making.

As the tide of war turned, and the Allies advanced upon Berlin, Adolf Hitler grandly opined: 'I am beginning to doubt whether the German people is worthy of my great ideals.'[18]

At fifty-five, Hitler was now too sick to speak in anything louder than a whisper. His limbs shook. He was ashen-pale, and feeble. Since the rounding up of the plotters, and the killing of Stauffenberg and the others, Hitler trusted almost no one except Blondi, his dog, and Eva Braun, who became his wife in a short private ceremony held in the bunker the day before he died. For months he had been both too afraid and too ill to emerge from the six rooms in the Führerbunker, from which he still believed himself to be directing the Reich. Hitler was described now by one of his entourage as 'a cake-gobbling human wreck'.[19] Another visitor, an elderly General Staff officer, said: 'he presented a dreadful sight. He dragged himself about painfully and clumsily, throwing his torso forward and dragging his legs after him from his living-room to the conference room of his bunker. He had lost his sense of balance; if he were detained on the brief journey (seventy-five to a hundred feet) he had to sit down on one of the benches that had been placed along either wall for the purpose or even cling to the person he was talking to.' Most of the time he was completely torpid, talking only of his need for chocolate and cake. The great imprisoner was himself imprisoned. The man who had taken Germany into the most reckless war in its history for Living Space could hardly stagger around his own air-raid shelter. He shot the body in which he had become a prisoner in the afternoon of 30 April, giving instructions that his underlings should incinerate it with petrol. In the same afternoon, two Soviet sergeants hoisted the Red Flag on the dome of the Reichstag.[20]

With Allied victory in Europe, many of those who had been prisoners of the Third Reich simply became automatically prisoners of the Soviet Union. Stalin's Empire now stretched from Prussia to Siberia, taking in Poland, Czechoslovakia, Hungary, Romania, Bulgaria and, effectively, Yugoslavia. The *Glavnoe Upravlenie Lagerei*, Main Camp Administration or *Gulag*, now had more inmates than ever in its history. 'According to the official statistics, on 1 January 1950, the Gulag contained 2,561,351 prisoners in the camps and colonies of its system – a million more than there had been five years earlier, in 1945.'[21]

One of the great transformations effected by the English political reformers of the early nineteenth century had been the move from systems of corporal and capital punishment to ones of control. Jeremy Bentham, the father of Philosophic Radicalism, built a model of a prison in his house, a construction of circular device, with a central Panopticon, that is a device which could see everything. Pitt the Younger and Dundas came to see Bentham in his house to inspect the Panopticon in 1793.[22] Victorian liberals looked back to this moment as a humane advance, away from the culture in which there were over 200 crimes on the statute book for which a man could be hanged to one in which criminals, having paid their debt to society, could return, sobered and righteous, to useful work.

To Pitt, to Bentham, even to their contemporary Napoleon, such nightmare phenomena as the Nazi death-camps and the slave camps of the Gulag would have been unimaginable. Yet, once the principle had been admitted that states had power over persons to the extent of being able to look at them all day long through a Panopticon, some fundamental ingredient of freedom had gone, and when populations had swollen sufficiently, and economic conditions become sufficiently unfavourable, great nations could find themselves submitting to tyrannies from which extrication could not easily be had, even at the cost of world wars and millions upon millions of deaths.

Victorian economic liberalism was a long way from National Socialism or Soviet Russia, but with its increased preoccupation with the way that the swelling population behaved – its sexual morality, its drinking habits – it was laying the foundations for twentieth-century systems of control. No Western state can be absolved from the charge of abusing its prisons and prison camps during the twentieth century. The atrocities which took place under the cover of war can be rehearsed endlessly, and should never be allowed to be forgotten; but the imagination can still fail to absorb the sheer enormity of it all: not merely the numbers of dead, nor even just the disgusting things done, sometimes for the sake of casual sadism. What shocks, almost more than anything, is that at the end of the Second World War, a war which historians still speak of as one of liberation, so many more millions of human beings should have remained imprisoned and enslaved than at its beginning.

33

If God Wearied of Mankind

Edward Gibbon's *Decline and Fall of the Roman Empire* caused dismay to eighteenth-century churchmen with its controversial and primary contention: that European civilization was undermined, less by the advance of the barbarian hordes without, than by the growth of Christianity within, its borders. What was it about Christianity, according to this diagnosis, which was so corrosive to the civilized idea? It was, surely, that the fanatical early Christians, zealous for a holy death, and fervently credulous about the greater reality of the life beyond than the life before it, made civilization itself seem superfluous. What use are the skills of statesmanship, of civil planning, of architecture, of laws, if at any moment, as the early Church taught and believed, the very edifice of worldly existence was going to be wound up, if the Maker was to bring the pageant of human history to a close, taking to Himself His few chosen ones in robes of white to sing perpetual hymnody before His throne, and hurling the rest, the huge majority, into pits and lakes of everlasting fire and destruction?

Gibbon's book is one of the most eloquent works, not merely of history, but of apology for what is called the Enlightenment, that phase of European self-consciousness which on the one hand challenged the received dogmas of Christianity as they had never been challenged for a thousand years, and, in the writings of Rousseau and Voltaire, laid the foundations for a new political order. The American Revolution was the stateliest, the French Revolution the bloodiest expression of the new idea that human societies could order themselves not upon aristocratic privilege and the superstitions of religious monarchy, but upon reason, and law and justice. Out of such political innovations sprang the modern political settlements of the nineteenth and twentieth centuries. Of course, there are no hard-and-fast beginnings and endings in political history. Long before Voltaire, the British had a civil war in which they disposed of the absolutism of monarchy and, in their settlement of 1689, established a principle of oligarchic or aristocratic government which in some ways continued until the mid-twentieth century. This settlement, based on ideas of law and reason, paid lip-service to Christianity. But it did so lightly. The early Christian conviction that this world was on the point of dissolution did not figure largely in the political thinking of John Locke. Those late seventeenth-century, early eighteenth-century English rationalists wrote with an eye to the future, with a belief which is central to political stability, a belief that the future exists.

The development of nuclear weapons, first the atom bomb and then the hydrogen bomb, brought about a fundamental change in human consciousness which was comparable to the conversion of the Roman Empire to Apocalyptic Christianity. In both cases, in the generation of Constantine and that of Harry S. Truman, the curtain of material being seemed as if it could be imminently ripped apart. In such circumstances, the institutions of law and peace, painstakingly and wisely tried over generations, themselves seemed insubstantial. Queen – Parliament – Lords and Commons – Empire; Senate – Congress – President; they still continued, just as the Roman senate and the Roman emperors continued for hundreds of years after Constantine saw the illumination of his Saviour's Cross in the visionary sky before his victory at the Milvian Bridge. But life was never to be the same.

The Victorians were, some of them – though in decreasing numbers – nominal Christians, but very nominal. The New Testament taught that *Here we have no abiding city*. The generations which had established Britain as the greatest free-trading nation believed that their city would abide on Earth for ever. Free trade and the Great Exhibition of 1851 paid deferential tribute to the Almighty as a family might arise to toast a decrepit and no longer powerful grandsire before reinvesting and tripling his capital. The great industrial cities of Britain, its shipyards in Glasgow and Belfast and Newcastle; its manufacturing towns of Birmingham and Manchester, Bradford and Leeds; its imperial and manufacturing capital of London; its ever-burgeoning Empire, had all seemed to signify a power which might endure a thousand years.

It is symptomatic, and probably an essential part of his world-vision, that Churchill did not believe in life after death. Here was an abiding City. Here was a City which could be expanded, threatened, fought over, strengthened, but which was all that there was.

The devastations and revolutions of the First World War and its aftermath might have shaken such confidence, especially when it was followed by the great crises of capitalism of the late 1920s and early 1930s, with all their grotesque political consequences. It was still possible to build, and rebuild the world, to hope for the future, to sing, 'It's a lovely day tomorrow'.

The Bomb changed this. Churchill saw it – 'nothing so menacing to our civilization since the Mongols'. That was a private observation. In his public discourse, the old Victorian agnostic used the language of biblical apocalypse. 'Which way shall we turn to save our lives and the future of the world? It does not so much matter to old people; they are going soon anyway, but I find it poignant to look at youth in all its activity and ardour and, most of all, to watch little children playing their merry games, and wonder what would lie before them if God wearied of mankind.'[1]

The development of nuclear physics was the collective achievement of physicists in the West before the Second World War. Rutherford had been the pioneer, and as early as 1928 he had exclaimed to the gentleman-amateur physicist Alfred L. Loomis: 'You damned American millionaires. Why can't you give me a million volts and I will split the atom.'[2] Dr Otto Hahn, director of the Kaiser Wilhelm Institute for Chemistry in Berlin, had split in two the nucleus of the uranium atom a few days before Christmas 1938. His assistant, Lise Meitner from Vienna, was able to confirm that when the uranium isotope 235 was bombarded with neutrons it split into two lighter elements with a loss in mass and an enormous release of energy. The Italian physicist Enrico Fermi and the Dane Niels Bohr were both in America for the Fifth Conference on Theoretical Physics when they heard the news.

Plainly, in the context of the war, the possibility of nuclear fission was of far greater than theoretical interest. The struggle for the power which these experiments demonstrated now took on Wagnerian dimensions. Just as in the case of radar, the scientific expertise came from Europe; it was 'you damned American millionaires' who had the means to develop the idea.

It was generally believed among world physicists, especially by those physicists who had fled Hitler for their lives, that the Germans would stop at nothing to develop nuclear power as a weapon. Then, as they saw it, the forces of darkness would hold the world to ransom. As it happens, even allowing for the fact that the Germans dealt themselves a self-inflicted wound through their insane anti-Semitic policies – which guaranteed that many of their best physicists went into exile – they held back from developing the Bomb. Why so, has been a subject of endless debate. A recent book on *Hitler's Scientists* gives credence to Albert Speer's testimony that Hitler himself considered the idea of nuclear weapons immoral.[3]

Whatever the reasons, it was the enemies of Germany who raced ahead with the vital research; undoubtedly the thought of Hitler with control over a nuclear bomb, even if such a policy filled even his destructive mind with revulsion, was a spur to action. The potential of nuclear fission as a source of energy had been known to scientists ever since Rutherford's experiments in 1919. Professor Meitner had demonstrated its possibility on the very eve of war in Berlin. One of the earliest refugees from Hitler,

Leo Szilard, as early as 1933, had realized, in a sort of daydream while crossing the road near the British Museum in London, that when a neutron bombarded a nucleus it would release more energy than the neutron itself supplied: he had seen, in effect, the truly explosive and destructive quality of this phenomenon.

But none of this meant anything unless the energy could be harnessed; unless a device could be invented, that is a nuclear bomb, which could contain the necessary equipment to set off such a chain reaction. Many physicists at the beginning of the war believed that the notion of nuclear warheads was the stuff of science fiction. Szilard admitted himself that he owed as much to H. G. Wells's late novel *The Shape of Things to Come* as he did to Einstein or Rutherford for his insight. Sir George Thomson, son of the great Edwardian physicist 'J.J.', and professor at the Imperial College of Science and Technology, was one of those who believed that it was technically impossible to harness a uranium chain reaction for military purposes. 'There were two stages in the military application of such a thing,' he wrote later.

> The first would be the establishment of an endless chain reaction, releasing energy in large and (perhaps) controllable amounts as a source of power; the second possibility was to make the process so rapid that an appreciable fraction of the available energy would be released before the whole contrivance was blown to the four winds and ceased to work . . . By the outbreak of war we had established that an endless chain was not possible using uranium oxide and ordinary water or paraffin as the second constituent. It seemed likely that it could be done by using heavy water, but this was not available in Britain in large amounts, and the military value of the first stage alone seemed too remote to justify further work in wartime. The second stage seemed nearly impossible, and if this conclusion now seems disgraceful blindness I can only plead that to the end of the war the most distinguished physicist in Germany thought the same.[4]

It was therefore more or less inevitable, from an economic, scientific and political viewpoint, that the perfection of this deadly thing would happen in the United States. Two vital developments in the story, however, occurred in Britain. It was in Britain that scientists discovered the importance of fast neutrons. And it was in Britain that the actual possibility of building a nuclear weapon was demonstrated. A key figure in this was Rudolf Peierls, pronounced Piles, who, like Franz Simon, Nicolas Kurti, Max Born, Otto Frisch and Leo Szilard, found himself in England because of the German anti-Jewish laws. It prompts the thought that, were it not for its anti-Semitism, the Third Reich would have mastered the world.

Peierls was a young Berliner who left Germany aged thirty-two, migrated on a Rockefeller Fellowship to Cambridge, worked for a time in Manchester, and for a time at the Mond Laboratory in Cambridge, where he worked with John Cockcroft, before moving to the university of Birmingham as the professor of Mathematical Physics. His work ran parallel with Lise Meitner and her nephew Otto Frisch. In June 1939, in a paper to the Cambridge Philosophical Society, he investigated the question of how to measure the critical mass of a block of pure uranium. To anyone listening, it must have seemed in the first half of his paper as if he were interested in the conundrum from a purely academic point of view, but by the end it was clear what Peierls was asking himself. He was the first physicist to address in purely practical terms how large a mass of uranium would be required to manufacture a nuclear bomb. He concluded at this stage that it would be so large that it could not fit into any aeroplane. He was thinking of something the size of a Windscale reactor. Had he realized that he was on the verge of providing a solution to his own problem, he said that he would never have allowed the paper, 'Critical Conditions in Neutron Multiplication', to be published.[5]

James Chadwick, professor of Physics at Liverpool, and a pupil of Rutherford's, a dark-haired, ivory-faced, smiling Buddha of a man, and his colleague, the Pole Dr Joseph Rotblat, were working on the same problem. Bohr's theory – that uranium isotope 235 (U235) could be smashed at a rate 10,000 times faster than U238 atoms – was demonstrated by Chadwick with his invention of the cyclotron.

In February 1940, Peierls's naturalization papers came through; he was officially an Englishman, and could settle down in his Georgian house in Edgbaston with his friend Otto Frisch and work out the implications of the new discoveries. They were not doing so in the idle isolation of academic peacetime. They sat, literally scribbling on the backs of envelopes, two German Jews, in an English house, in February 1940. They were trying to work out the proportion of U235 in uranium that would be required to produce a radioactive super-bomb. As they scribbled, Peierls realized that his calculation in the Cambridge paper the previous summer had been wildly inaccurate. They had hugely overestimated the size of the proportion; what he had been weighing in tons of hundredweights could be measured in pounds. 'In fact,' Peierls said, 'our first calculation gave a critical mass of less than one pound.'[6]

They were thunderstruck by what they had worked out on the backs of their envelopes. What they saw with these new calculations was that a few pounds of uranium could produce millions of degrees of heat, and an explosion of almost unimaginable destructiveness. They were aliens in a foreign land; and a land at war. To whom could they turn? Peierls consulted his colleague Sir Marcus Oliphant, an Australian who had been working in secret on radar for the Admiralty under cover as a research physicist at Birmingham. 'Write to Tizard' was his advice.

There was the usual red tape and palaver. This was Chamberlain's Britain. A committee was set up, under the chairmanship of Sir George Thomson, whose confession that he did not believe in the possibility of nuclear weapons has already been quoted. In the course of the spring and early summer of 1940, while Hitler's panzers advanced over Europe and conquered France, Peierls and his associates in Birmingham – he got a very young man called Klaus Fuchs out of his internment camp to help him with his mathematical calculations – had taken the investigation one stage further. The matter was so vital to national security that Tizard was worried that those who were technically aliens should be working on it; and there was for a period the absurd possibility that 'classified information' might be forming itself inside the brains of Frisch, Fuchs and others before it was even committed to paper. Much of the material was so dangerous that Peierls typed it up himself, and after the Fall of France, knowing his own certain fate (and that of so many of his colleagues) if Hitler were to stage a successful invasion that summer, he went to see Churchill's scientific adviser Professor Lindemann. Peierls was by now completely desperate. He had in his hands sealed envelopes with the results of the research he and his colleagues had perfected at Birmingham. He wanted 'the Prof' to assure him that, in the event of a German invasion, these documents would be sent to America.

Lindemann, with his German name and ancestry, was more English than the English, bowler-hatted, immaculately clad, and never happier than when staying in the grander country houses. He treated the geekish Peierls, with his risible accent and hyperanxiety, with the loftiest disdain. The thought of Hitler invading, let alone conquering, Britain was dismissed as improbable; and Lindemann let Peierls know that he thought it highly unlikely that a uranium bomb, even if developed, would have an effect on the current war.[7]

The physicists in America were equally concerned to alert their government, not just to the possibility of the Germans developing a nuclear weapon, but to the advantages of the United States doing so first. Leo Szilard had not advanced as fast as Rudolf Peierls in his calculations; he and Enrico Fermi, however, had discovered enough in experiments with carbon and uranium to know that the possibility of a chain reaction was almost within their grasp. By May 1939, Szilard was personally touting his idea round the US military trying to raise capital to construct some kind of enormous bomb. Together with Edward Teller, now teaching physics at Columbia University, Eugene Wigner at Princeton, and eventually Albert Einstein himself, they alerted the President. Einstein had been amazed when Szilard told him of his and Fermi's experiments, with secondary neutrons leading to chain reaction. *Daran habe ich gar nicht gedacht* – I never thought of that! he exclaimed. Einstein had the idea of telling, of all people, the Queen of Belgium as a way of alerting the Allied powers. It was eventually Dr Alexander Sachs, Vice President of the Lehman Corporation, who was deputed to go to the White House with a letter, signed by Einstein, telling President Roosevelt of the magnitude of the scientific discovery.

Roosevelt grasped the significance of what had happened in that first conversation. 'Alex,' he said to Sachs, 'what you're after is to see that the Nazis don't blow us up.'[8] Einstein's letter still envisaged an enormous lump of uranium, too large to fit into an aeroplane, being used as an offensive weapon. 'This new phenomenon,' he wrote, 'could also lead to the construction of bombs, and it is conceivable – though much less certain – that extremely powerful bombs of a new type may thus be constructed. A single bomb of this type, carried by boat and exploded in a port, might well destroy the whole port together with some of the surrounding territory. However, such bombs might very well prove to be too heavy for transportation by air.'[9]

So it was that the Americans set up the Uranium Advisory Committee, eventually subsumed by the National Defense Research Committee.[10] After America entered the war, the President of Harvard, Professor James B. Conant, arrived in London to set up a London office of this committee. The Tizard Mission had already established the principle that the British would hand over to the Americans all their scientific insights. It was only a matter of time before British scientists were revealing how far they had advanced towards the potential creation of a nuclear bomb. Under the anodyne name of Tube Alloys, the British were very close to possessing their own Ring of Power. As the theoretical work at Birmingham and Liverpool continued, industrial plants were being constructed. An isotope separation plant was built near Mold in North Wales at Rhydymwyn to refine pure uranium. Similar work was being done at the Clarendon Lab in Oxford. Niels Bohr had escaped from Denmark and was having conversations with Lord Cherwell (as Lindemann had become) and Churchill not only about the technical progress which had been made, but about its moral and political significance. He wrote to Roosevelt in July 1944: 'The fact of immediate preponderance is, however, that a weapon of unparalleled power is being created which will completely change all future conditions of warfare.'[11] It was only a matter of time before Bohr was lured across the Atlantic by the 'damned American millionaires'. Thanks to the agreement made in Quebec in September 1944, Churchill handed over to the Americans all the results of British nuclear research, and most of the scientists who had been involved in the project. Under the directorship of Robert Oppenheimer, a boys' school thirty-five miles northwest of Sante Fe on the western slope of the Jemez Mountains was selected as the ideal site for the secret laboratory. It was here that the nuclear bomb would eventually be built and perfected. The name of the school was Los Alamos.

Oppenheimer, professor of Physics at Berkeley, was in his late thirties when he took over the directorship of Los Alamos. A thin, chain-smoking, tormented man, he was a strange mixture of social confidence and self-doubt. His father, who had left Hanau in Germany in 1898, made a fortune in ready-made suits. He and his delicate wife Ella, whose unformed right hand was always hidden in a prosthetic glove, were clever people, and Robert, who was born on 22 April 1904, grew up in a spacious apartment on Riverside Drive, with a summer house at Bay Shore in Long Island. His parents were liberals, artistic in their interests. The Oppenheimers frequently took summer vacations in Europe. Robert was a widely cultivated man, feeling, when he went to Harvard as an undergraduate, like a 'Goth coming to Rome'. He looted the place intellectually. He majored in chemistry but also took classes in physics, French literature, philosophy, mathematics and other languages. He also found time to sail a 27-foot sloop his father had given him.

Later he went to England and worked at the Cavendish Laboratory in Cambridge. He was intensely miserable, and visited a psychiatrist in London. A friend at the time recalled Oppenheimer saying that this 'guy was too stupid to follow him and that he knew more about his troubles than [the doctor] did'. The psychiatrist diagnosed dementia praecox, today called schizophrenia.

Oppenheimer arrived at Los Alamos in 1943, and he spent the next year assembling literally thousands of scientists to work on the project. At some stage in the next two years almost all the big names in the nuclear project would pass through Los Alamos: Edward Teller, George Kistiakowsky, Rudolf Peierls, the British hydrodynamicist Geoffrey Taylor, Leo Szilard. Oppenheimer was a driven force overseeing every aspect of work at this immense and highly complex factory of human destructiveness. 'Oppie knew in detail what was going on in every part of the laboratory,' Teller fondly recalled.[12]

Throughout 1944, while the Americans fought their slow and bloody war in the Pacific, with huge casualties on both sides, and while British,

American, Australian and other Allied troops suffered terrible maltreatment in the Japanese prison camps, and on the Burmese railway, the scientists at Los Alamos continued their work. By 26 September 1944 the largest atomic pile yet assembled on Earth was ready.[13]

The crude cylinders, packed with deadly five-kilogram loads of plutonium, were being made to a number of rival designs, each with crudely whimsical nicknames – Fat Man for the implosion bomb, Little Boy and Thin Man. While the engineers were constructing these world-changing engines of obliteration, the politicians were too distracted by the fast-moving events of the war, and by their own personal illness, to give more than cursory attention to the seriousness of what was happening in New Mexico. For example, when Niels Bohr tried to alert Churchill to the extreme dangers of making or using nuclear bombs, it was three months before he even had an answer to his letter. This was not surprising, since he wrote in May 1944, on the eve of the D-Day landings, the occupation of France and the conquest of Germany on European soil – the event to which the Americans and Russians had been urging Churchill since they entered the war. Bohr's speculations about what might happen if nuclear weapons were to proliferate simply did not register with Churchill; in so far as they did, he, in common with the Americans, felt that any aggressive threat against Japan was to be welcomed. 'It has just come in time to save the world' was his view.[14]

Churchill was by now seventy years old. He was drinking heavily. He had suffered, since the war began, a minor heart attack and three bouts of pneumonia. Roosevelt, though much younger – sixty-two – was mortally sick, had weakened dramatically during 1944 and was doomed to die in April 1945. Almost as worrying to him as the progress of the D-Day landings, and the conquest of Europe under the overall command of General Eisenhower, was the persistent briefing that he received from his ambassador in Moscow, W. Averell Harriman, that Stalin was not to be trusted, and intended to keep none of the agreements he made with Britain and America with regard to Eastern Europe. On 12 April, while sitting for his portrait, the President suffered a cerebral haemorrhage from which he died at 3.35 pm that day. Two days afterwards, Otto Frisch delivered to Robert Oppenheimer his report on the first experimental determination of the critical mass of pure $U235$. On 16 July 1945 at Alamogordo, New Mexico, the first atomic bomb was exploded.

Oppenheimer said:

When it went off, in the New Mexico dawn, that first atomic bomb, we thought of Alfred Nobel, and his hope, his vain hope, that dynamite would put an end to wars. We thought of the legend of

Prometheus, of that deep sense of guilt in man's new powers, that reflects his recognition of evil, and his long knowledge of it. We knew that it was a new world, but even more we knew that novelty itself was a very old thing in human life, that all our ways are rooted in it.[15]

Whether or not it changed the human perception of evil, the bomb certainly put a spring in the step of the newly promoted Vice President, now President, Harry S. Truman. Negotiations with the Russians took a suddenly aggressive turn. The conference at Yalta in the Crimea between the Big Three in February 1945 had airily agreed that after the war there would be a 'new Government' in Poland. The bespectacled lawyer from Missouri was something of an unknown quantity on the international stage. Molotov, upon meeting him in April 1945, was astounded by his aggressiveness when talking of such questions as Eastern Europe, and the Russian attempts to muscle in on the war with Japan. 'I have never been talked to like that in my life,' declared the thunderstruck Soviet Foreign Minister. 'Carry out your agreements and you won't get talked to like that,' said the man from Independence, Missouri. Something had given him new confidence in dealing with the United States' only serious rival for world domination.[16]

Roosevelt's death in April 1945 coincided with crucial turning points in Europe, in the Far East and in Los Alamos. America now had the Bomb. Russia was advancing into Manchuria. Germany was on the point of surrender. These were the crucial political facts of the world as President Harry S. Truman took office and – perhaps even more importantly – James Byrnes succeeded Edward R. Stettinius as secretary of state.

Opinion is divided about Roosevelt's views on the deployment of nuclear weapons. There is some spotty evidence that Roosevelt was mulling the possibility of using the bomb only as a warning, or as a demonstration in territory from which human and animal life, after prior warning, had been moved. There is very definite evidence that Stettinius favoured a negotiated peace with the Japanese, giving them assurances that they would not lose their emperor if they laid down their arms. After Byrnes took over as Secretary of State, things altered. Byrnes was determined, before the Allies met at the Potsdam Conference, that America should already have tried out the nuclear bomb. For this reason, unbeknown to the Russians, the conference was postponed. Byrnes and Truman wanted to use the bomb as a demonstration to the Russians: a demonstration of what? Of their own ruthlessness. A demonstration that they would, if necessary, use this weapon – at that stage of history uniquely the weapon of the United States – on civilian targets if they did not get their way.

Many theories have been advanced as to why Truman should have been prepared to bomb not one, but two, Japanese cities, at so brief an interval. After all, over a quarter of a million Japanese civilians had already been killed by aerial bombardment from conventional explosives. We now know that Japan, for all its fighting rhetoric, was on the verge of surrender; and had Britain, Russia and America guaranteed the safety of the emperor, the war might have well ended before July 1945. In May, the first of the war crimes tribunals had begun in Germany, and there was talk of hanging the Japanese emperor. This rumour undoubtedly encouraged many Japanese troops to continue fighting. It was Byrnes, at the Potsdam Conference of 17 July to 2 August 1945, who insisted upon removing any assurance about the future of the emperor. After the Russians invaded Manchuria, the Japanese knew that their war was over, and they privately approached the Russians, asking for a negotiated peace. This was rejected by America. Byrnes was effectually the architect of the Cold War. He wanted no cooperation with Russia. And he did not want a messy negotiation with Japan which could lead to Versailles-style repercussions. An outright Japanese surrender, without condition; a Russian government left in no doubt that America was if necessary prepared to kill tens, hundreds of thousands of civilians if it did not get its way. This was the lure for Truman and Byrnes as they reached their decision.[17]

In the light of all that we now know about the decision, we can safely lay aside the myth fed to, and believed in by, generations of Americans and British: namely that the Bombs were dropped on Hiroshima and Nagasaki in order to shorten the war (it was more or less over anyway); to save the lives of American troops; or to force the Japanese warriors to lay down their arms. (If that argument is used, why was it necessary to bomb two cities, and add the incinerated and radiated corpses of 70,000[18] more people, those of the citizens of Nagasaki, to the obscene death figures of the Second World War?)

There is a strong element of racialism in the beliefs of many of those involved in the decision-making process, a sense that the Japanese were somehow 'different' from Americans or Europeans; or that their culture made them impermeable to reason. This perhaps flavoured the atmosphere of the crucial meeting at the Pentagon on 31 May 1945 when Secretary of State Byrnes – did ever a politician have a more horribly apt 'Happy Families' nomenclature? – met Robert Oppenheimer, James B. Conant and Secretary for War Henry Stimson, and they all agreed, having heard the scientific evidence, that 'we could not give the Japanese any warning'.[19]

Albert Einstein, as early as 1946, stated the true reason for dropping the Bomb, namely that it was 'precipitated by a desire to end the war in the Pacific by any means before Russia's participation. I am sure that if President Roosevelt had still been there, none of that would have been possible.'[20]

Many of the scientists who had been pioneers of nuclear weaponry were disgusted by the use to which it had been put. After the demonstration in Alamogordo, there was no need, as far as the war with Japan was concerned, to use the bombs at all. Honourable old Secretary of War Stimson expressed horror at the 'appalling lack of conscience that the war had brought about . . . the complacency, the indifference, and the silence with which we greeted the mass bombings in Europe and above all, Japan'.[21] Oppenheimer remembered the old man saying it, but such sentiments did not get into Stimson's published memoirs, and he died of heart failure not long after the war. Leo Szilard was vociferously opposed to the use of the bomb other than as a threat.

> I told Oppenheimer that I thought it would be a very serious mistake to use the bomb against the cities of Japan. Oppenheimer didn't share my view. He surprised me by saying 'The atomic bomb is shit'. 'What do you mean by that?' I asked him. He said, 'Well, this is a weapon which has no military significance. It will make a big bang – a very big bang – but it is not a weapon which is useful in war'. He thought it would be important however, to inform the Russians that we had an atomic bomb and that we intended to use it against the cities of Japan rather than taking them by surprise.[22]

Oppenheimer, diagnosed as a schizophrenic by that 'stupid' psychiatrist in his youth, moved from two quite extreme positions about the Bomb. Asked by a *Time* journalist if the atomic bomb had any limitations, he quipped: 'The limitations lie in the fact that you don't want to be on the receiving end of one. If you ask, "Can we make them more terrible?" the answer is yes. If you ask, "Can we make a lot of them?" the answer is yes. "Can we make them terribly more terrible?" the answer is probably.' But after the war he suffered agonies of remorse, and was even investigated, when he had gone back to academic life, for un-American thoughts and activities such as wanting to de-escalate the Cold War and to make peace with the Russians.[23]

Of course the overwhelming view of those who actually knew about the atomic bomb, and its effects upon human lives, was that its use was an obscenity. Niels Bohr, Albert Einstein, Szilard were all utterly opposed. It took tremendous lies, of a Goebbelsesque scale of magnitude, to persuade two or three generations that instead of being acts of gratuitous mass murder, the bombardments of Hiroshima and Nagasaki were almost benign – first, because they avoided the supposed deaths of half a million American troops (the estimated numbers of casualties had America conquered Japan by an invasion of infantry – a pretext utterly ruled out by the brevity of the time lapse between the dropping of the two weapons); and second, because it was better the weapon should be in the hands of Good Guys rather than truly wicked people such as Hitler or Stalin. Both these views, enlivened with a dash of Bible Christianity, helped to put the President's mind at rest as he meditated upon it all in his diary. 'We have discovered the most terrible bomb in the history of the world. It may be the fire destruction prophesied in the Euphrates Valley Era, after Noah and his fabulous Ark . . .' Truman then states, for his own peace of mind, or for that of posterity, that it is not (early August 1945) intended to drop the Bomb on Tokyo.

Even if the Japs are savages, ruthless, merciless and fanatic, we as the leader of the world for the common welfare cannot drop this terrible bomb on the old Capital or the new. He (that is Stalin) and I are in accord. The target will be a purely military one and we will issue a warning statement asking the Japs to surrender and save lives. I'm sure they will not do that, but we will have given them the chance. It is certainly a good thing for the world that Hitler's crowd or Stalin's did not discover the atomic bomb. It seems to be the most terrible thing to have discovered, but it can be made the most useful.[24]

Little Boy, weighing in at 9,700 pounds, resembled 'an elongated trash can with fins'.[25] He was finally complete by the end of July, and it was now agreed that they should drop him on 6 August, the Feast of the Transfiguration, when Jesus went up the mountain with his disciples, and was transformed, his whole being filled with blinding light and his clothes becoming 'white and glistering'.[26] The crew of the B29 bomber *Enola Gay* (named for the 509th commander's mother) ate a breakfast of ham and eggs and pineapple fritters. As they loaded Little Boy into the plane, the Protestant pastor prayed to the Almighty Father 'to be with those who brave the heights of Thy heaven and who carry the battle to our enemies'.

And then they were off. By 0552 they approached Iwo Jima and could see below the green islands of the Japanese archipelago. At 0730, Deke Parsons, the officer who had been working on radar development since the beginning of the war, bald as an egg, entered the unheated bomb bay with Morris Jephson, an ordnance expert, and they inserted four sections of cordite one at a time into Little Boy. They monitored the circuitry. Everything was going according to plan. The plane crossed the Ota River in central Hiroshima. The bomb-bay doors were opened, and the bomb dropped. The plane bounced. There was a noise like a piece of sheet metal snapping. As *Enola Gay* turned, dived, circled and made for home they could see smoke and fire climbing all over the city, a natural amphitheatre. One man on board said it looked like a pot of boiling black oil.

The prewar population of Hiroshima was something like 400,000 but it had sunk to 290,000. Thousands of soldiers, bare to the waist, were exercising in the parade ground at Hiroshima Castle. Eight thousand schoolgirls were already up, at 7.30 their time, clearing rubble and debris from bombsites wrecked by conventional weapons. The blinding flash of light in the sky was accompanied by instantaneous scorching heat. Within 4,000 yards of the hypercentre of the fallen bomb, flammable objects spontaneously combusted. The people who ran through the streets were already scarcely recognizable as human beings. A child, its face swollen like a purple balloon, uttered inchoate groans as it moved between the flames with curious jerking motions. An old man muttered prayers as the skin on his face unpeeled like that of an over-baked potato. A woman with her jaw missing and her tongue dangling staggered through what seemed to be raining pitch. A policeman stood rooted to the spot, stark naked save for a few shreds of trouser-uniform clinging to his scorched body. The seven rivers of the city were soon drifting with scorched pieces of human flesh, dismembered people. Those on the banks who watched had burned skin hanging off them like loose kimonos. The lucky ones had died instantly, like the charcoaled figure of a man, glimpsed sitting bolt upright on a bicycle leaning against an all but molten railing. Those who survived all felt the effect of the blast, even if they were not actually turned, like those near the centre, into flayed red torture-victims. Boils, ulcerated throats and extreme skin discomfort were felt even by those miles away, or those who had the unlucky experience of surviving and feeling themselves, as one fifth-grade schoolboy said afterwards, 'left behind in an uncanny world of the dead'. In 1986, the number of identified victims was given on the Cenotaph at Hiroshima as 138,890, but people were still suffering horribly, and dying, from the effects of radiation for decades to come.

The President found the thought of wiping out another 100,000 people 'too horrible'. He did not like the idea of killing 'all those kids'; or so he told his diary.[27] Nevertheless, Fat Man was ready to go and was dropped on Nagasaki on 9 August 1945. It caused less immediate damage than Little Boy, but it is reckoned that 70,000 had died in Nagasaki by the end of 1945, with probably 140,000 altogether over the next five years.

On 14 August a thousand Japanese soldiers stormed the Imperial Palace in Tokyo to try to prevent their emperor from humiliating himself by announcing the surrender of the Empire to the United States. They did not realize that he had already recorded his wireless announcement. On 15 August, the Japanese radio announcer told listeners that they were about to hear something which, at the beginning of the war, would have been quite unimaginable: the ineffable voice of their Divine Emperor. Almost more than the surrender itself, there was an indignity in this preparedness of a Divinity to take the stage, alongside Vera Lynn and Lord Haw-Haw, Tommy Handley and Churchill, in the twentieth-century Vaudeville. It was in 660 BC, according to Japanese tradition, that the sun goddess Amaterasu gave birth to the first Japanese emperor, Jimmu Tenno. Hirohito was the 124th in descent, the Tenno Heika, Son of Heaven. Hirohito is the name given him by Westerners. To the Japanese he is the Showa ('Enlightened Peace') Emperor. The Bomb had made the very question of whether this dynasty survived a matter for the say-so of a poor boy from Missouri.

In a high, ancient voice, as strange as the voice of the elves in *The Lord of the Rings*, the emperor spoke to his people:

> Despite the best that has been done by everyone . . . the war situation has developed not necessarily to Japan's advantage, while the general trends of the world have all turned against her interest. Moreover, the enemy has begun to employ a new and most cruel bomb, the power of which to do damage is indeed incalculable, taking the toll of many innocent lives . . . This is the reason why We have ordered the accept-ance of the provisions of the Joint Declaration of the Powers . . .

As the hieratic incantation called for his 'entire nation to continue as one family from generation to generation', the rest of the world knew that the Second World War had come to an end.[28]

34

Retributions

The man in the cage shouted 'Cat Piss and Porcupines!' at his neighbour. Guards were forbidden to speak to the man who shouted out. His neighbour, in another cage, was about to be hanged, so he did not take much notice. Nevertheless, American soldiers in the Disciplinary Training Camp made detours across the parade ground to glimpse this prize exhibit. He was a fellow American, not an Italian or a German prisoner. The cage, which measured six by six and one-half feet and was ten feet high, was reinforced with the steel mats used in airport runways. It contained no bedding, only a bucket for lavatory facilities, and was open to the weather all the time. By night it was lit by relentless blue acetylene torches. All the other cages contained a murderer or rapist. This cage contained a poet, Ezra Pound, and he was about to write some of the most extraordinary lines ever penned, the so-called *Pisan Cantos*.[1]

Pound, as long ago as 1910, had begun to fashion his poetic utterance in Cantos. In Paris, from one of the bookstalls on the *quai* there, he had picked up a Renaissance Latin version of Homer's *Odyssey*, and he had begun his great work with a translation:

> And then went down to the ship,
> Set keel to breakers, forth on the godly sea, and
> We set up mast and sail on that swart ship,
> Bore sheep aboard her, and our bodies also
> Heavy with weeping . . .[2]

James Joyce used the story of the wanderings of Odysseus as the template by which to tell the story of Leopold Bloom and Stephen Dedalus, and much else besides in *Ulysses*. Pound's ambition had always been much more diffuse. He had drawn on Chinese philosophy and poetry and, increasingly, as the twentieth-century tragedy unfolded, he had become preoccupied by economics, by theories of usury, by admiration for Mussolini and the Italian Fascists. These interests are all reflected in *The Cantos*, which provide the most extraordinary palimpsest in literature. We begin by looking at the Greek epic through a Latin translation, rendered into an English which is heavily redolent of Pound the man of the Nineties, Pound the Dandy. It is not so very different, with its 'swart' ship, from those late Victorian Hellenic renditions by Andrew Lang which are beloved of Le Bas, the schoolmaster in Anthony Powell's *A Dance to the Music of Time*.

Now, the Italian Fascist dictator had been overthrown, the Germans had invaded Italy, the Jews had been transported to their fates, the British and the American soldiers had fought their terrible campaign from Sicily northwards, the Allies were triumphant. The retributive killing had started. Tito, the Communist fighter, soon to be dictator of Yugoslavia, and his followers, slaughtered 15,000 Italians in northeast Italy and the Italian partisans killed another 35,000 people without trial. Four days before Pound was taken into custody by the Americans, Mussolini was killed by the Italian partisans, with his mistress Claretta Petacci, the daughter of a Rome doctor. For two hours after they had been shot in Milan, the partisans kicked, spat at and urinated on the corpses in the Piazzale Loreto. Then someone had the idea of hanging the corpses upside down from a girder over a petrol station. When Mussolini was strung up there was a great cheer. When Petacci was hung by her feet, the crowd fell silent. She had on expensive suspenders and stockings, but no knickers. It was the quality of the stockings which held the attention of the war-tired women who watched. 'There's not a single ladder on them,' one of them murmured.[3]

'Manes! Manes!' exclaimed Pound in his cage, recalling the leader of the Zoroastrians who had been killed by the Persians.

> Thus Ben and la Clara *a Milano*
> by the heels at Milano
> That maggots shd/eat the dead bullock
> DIGONOS, Δίγοvος,* but the twice crucified
> where in history will you find it?[4]

He is talking about Dionysus, the twice-born god.

T. S. Eliot had imagined, in *The Hollow Men* of 1925, that the world would end not with a bang but a whimper, but 1945 was no whimper . . .

'With a bang not with a whimper,' Pound replies to his old friend, Possum. 'To build the city of Dioce whose terraces are the colour of stars.' The city of Dioce was an ideal city, the capital of the Medes mentioned in Herodotus.

Any reader whose head is by now spinning can be forgiven. But Pound wants to send his readers' heads spinning. Was he by now mad, as his defence lawyers claimed, in order to spare him charges of treason? The doctor who was closest to him, in the hospital of St Elizabeth in

*i.e. Twice-born

Washington, DC, where Pound was confined, was definitely of the view that Pound was not mad.[5] However you define madness, the *Pisan Cantos* are unquestionably the great work of literature in the English language to come out of the Second World War. And the section begins with 'The enormous tragedy of the dream in the peasant's bent shoulders'. The war was a Pyrrhic victory for the British, who had stood firm in 1940 and could now watch Germany be partitioned, half of its ruined, scarred and pitted surface given over to slavery under a puppet of Marshal Stalin, and the other regions revivified by a combination of independent German resourcefulness and American money with Marshall Aid. The British were bankrupted by the war; they had lost their Empire and their position in the world. The war was a defeat for Hitler, and for Mussolini, and to some extent for the Japanese. But the real losers, apart from the millions of dead soldiers and civilians, were those who would continue to live under Soviet oppression in those very territories, of Czechoslovakia and Poland, as well as in the Baltic states and in the Balkans, which the Allies had supposedly fought to 'liberate'.

'Over wide areas, a vast quivering mass of tormented, hungry, care-worn and bewildered human beings gape at the ruin of their cities and their homes and scan the dark horizons for the approach of some new peril, tyranny or terror' – thus Churchill in Zurich on 19 September 1946. 'That is all that Europeans . . . have got by tearing each other to pieces and spreading havoc far and wide.'[6]

Things would have been even worse if Hitler had been triumphant, that is obvious. But much had been lost, and lost irreparably. To read the 74th Canto, the first of the *Pisan Cantos*, is to be stumbling around in the ruins of European culture. The central phrase could be said to be that extremely 1890s utterance near the end – 'Beauty is difficult'. When a war is being fought, largely by young men, torn between terror of death and fear of their commanding officers, there is not much time for contemplating beauty. That is one of the unnatural things about war, which gouges out beautiful landscapes and makes them charred mud heaps, which kills and maims young, beautiful people, and which knows that the thing to do with a medieval cathedral is to smash it to smithereens. From the cage, the so-called madman saw it all.

> Old Ez folded his blankets
> Neither Eos nor Hesperus has suffered wrong at my hands.[7]

Most wars in history have ended with peace, but the Second World War was unlike this. It had shaken the whole world, and no one anywhere was going to start all over again just as they had been in 1939. Something profound had happened to the world, it had altered for ever. Already, on 12 May 1945, Churchill was expressing his anxiety to President Truman that the Russians would draw down 'an Iron Curtain upon their Soviet front'. He famously used the phrase again in Fulton, Missouri, in the spring of 1946 when he said that the Iron Curtain stretched across the continent of Europe 'from Stettin in the Baltic to Trieste in the Adriatic', and that as long as it existed, peace and democracy could no longer be sustained by the three great powers of the wartime alliance. He did not think that the Russians wanted outright war, but their desire was 'for the fruits of war and the indefinite expansion of their power and doctrines'.

The postwar world, even before it was a postwar world, was perceived to be one of conflict. Men had set out, clutching their secular texts with the fervour of the most superstitious sectaries in the religious wars of the seventeenth century, and they had tried to build the city whose terraces are the colour of stars. With *Mein Kampf* as their handbook, or Lenin's interpretations of *Das Kapital*, they had justified to themselves the most deadly crimes ever perpetrated in human history; with the aid of modern technology, they had managed to destroy and ruin million of human lives.

The victors could no longer claim total moral purity. The bombing raids on civilian cities in Europe went far beyond any strategic need; and the use of the atomic bomb on Japanese cities was a crime against humanity. Yet it would be a perverse reading of history, either at the time or with our comfortable hindsight, not to see that the Western Allies, who made many blunders, including moral blunders, were attempting to fight for a set of principles and political ideals which included freedom and justice. They had been driven by the terrible circumstances of the time to forget their aims on many occasions and to promote brutal and destructive policies. When it was all over, however, they wanted their own people, and those within their control, to be free. Had Hitler won the war, this would not have been so.

There was an understandable desire for revenge on the part of those who eventually succeeded in beating the Nazis. In those countries which had been occupied by the Germans, the revenges exacted, both against Germans and against those nations of any country who had collaborated with them, were often terrible. In France, the reprisals were on an extraordinary scale, with many murders going undetected which could only have had the loosest, if any, political motive. Thousands of murders took place in Paris and its environs after the liberation.

How was it possible for the Allies to express, not only to themselves but to the country they had conquered; to convey, not only to the Germans but to the world; to state unequivocally, not only to the world but to posterity, that the Third Reich had been a colossal inversion of all the values held sacred by the human race for thousands of years? In the face of so much destruction, so much despair, so many deaths, so many displaced persons and so many ruined human lives, what gesture could be adequate? In Auschwitz, the rabbis had gone so far as to put God Himself on trial. They found Him guilty and then went to their evening prayers. The times were so extreme and the suffering and devastation so total that just such mad gestures seemed called for.

Whereas the rabbis in Auschwitz had uttered a metaphysical howl of anguish as loud as the Book of Job, such rhetoric would not pass on the stage of international politics and diplomacy. Something needed to happen in Europe which would demonstrate unequivocally that the rule of law had once more been established; and indeed that it had never been suspended; that the guilty men of Germany must be put on trial and answer for their crimes.

The place selected for this demonstration of justice was itself a physical and architectural embodiment of what Pound was writing about in the *Pisan Cantos*. Nuremberg, the medieval town which stood at the crossroads of European commerce from the times of Dante and Chaucer to the 1930s, had been flattened. The Nuremberg of Albrecht Dürer, gentlest and most meticulous of artists, his gentleness and his attention to detail so quintessentially German, was now a burnt-out, pitted, sewage-infested ruin. Modern Nuremberg, with its hideous Nazi stadium, scene of so many of Hitler's rallies, and immortalized by the cinematic choreography of Leni Riefenstahl, survived the air raids. At the time of writing (2005) it still stands, deserted and ghostly, as empty as the appalling rhetoric which once blared through its loud speakers into the ears of spellbound multitudes.

There will always be those who see something absurd about the Nuremberg trials. Those who favour rough justice as the appropriate end of war felt at the time, and no doubt feel now, that such figures as Keitel, Streicher, and the thugs in the Nazi high command did not deserve the platform of a courtroom in which they were given the chance to defend their disgusting actions. A wall and a firing squad was all they needed. Others, more cynical, felt that 'great events of international politics were not really a fit subject for judicial decision'.[8]

There were several reasons why the Nuremberg trials, for all the unsatisfactoriness of the procedure, were defensible, difficult as it was to distinguish between individual depravity and the overall policy of a nation caught up in crisis and war. (The defence, that the Nazis were 'only obeying orders', became a sick joke, and a cliché, from the beginnings of the trial, and it does, surely, beg all kinds of questions about the nature of civil obedience, and the point at which private conscience should or should not defy the higher authority of government or military command.)

The justifications for the Nuremberg trial were these. First, the government of the Third Reich had flagrantly broken an international law agreed upon by the Charter of the League of Nations, the Hague Convention on Land Warfare of 24 September 1927, which stated that aggressive war was itself a crime. As we have already observed, the whole programme of National Socialism, from before it took power, was posited on the idea of aggressive war, and this is what appeasers at the time, and revisionist historians since, did not recognize. Second, the regime had perpetrated, both within Germany and in the lands it occupied, such terrible crimes against humanity, such abuses of freedom, such mass murder, torture, humiliation and degradation of people, on so great a scale, that the perpetrators simply had to be brought to justice.

Some of those who opposed the trial regretted giving these human monsters the chance to defend themselves. But it was in this very act of justice, for six months in the Nuremberg courtroom, that the Third Reich really condemned itself. The only defendant who put up a good showing – indeed a brilliant one – was Göring, and he in the end eluded the hangman's noose by taking poison hours before his execution. Göring, too, was almost the only one of the wretched crew who showed any spirit or courage, continuing to wear uniform, though stripped of its ludicrous insignia, and speaking with as much eloquence as dishonesty. He denied knowing anything about the wholesale slaughter of the Jews, which was a preposterous claim, only matched by the claim that Hitler had not known anything about it either.[9] On the other hand he was probably telling the truth when he said that he had had a flaming row with Hitler about the illegal execution of captured RAF pilots, one of the crimes for which he was indicted, and there was a crazy brio in his rhetorical self-defence. 'In the struggle of life and death, there is no legality,' he quoted Churchill as saying, though he did so not in defence of some act of valour in the field but in order to slither out of the fact that he was, among his other dubious accomplishments, a thief on the grand scale who had stolen vast sums, including furniture, jewels, paintings and treasures, from Jews, German aristocrats and invaded French families. 'I did not want a war, nor did I bring it about. I did everything to prevent it by negotiation. After it had broken out I did everything to assure victory . . . The only motive which guided me was my ardent love of my people, its fortunes, its freedoms, its life. And for this I call upon Almighty God and the German people as my witness.' Everyone agreed that Sir David Maxwell-Fyfe, a star prosecutor with some of the other Nazis, had allowed Göring to get the better of him.

Churchill had said in 1944, when people were speaking of what reparation to extract from Germany: 'I agree with Burke. You cannot indict a whole nation.'[10] That is why the trials were so helpful. The chief villains who had led Germany into the Nazi abyss were the ones who were indicted, allowing for the possibility that Germany might rejoin the civilized world in the 'sunlit uplands'. If one says that the value of the Nuremberg trials was in their theatre, one does not mean to diminish the appalling seriousness of what was being discussed. Heinrich Himmler had poisoned himself by swallowing a cyanide capsule after his capture by the British at Lüneburg, but the trial could hear repeated his words, proudly spoken to the SS generals at Posen in October 1942, and which many of his colleagues had helped to carry out.

I want to talk to you, quite frankly, on a very grave matter . . . I mean the clearing out of the Jews, the extermination of the Jewish race. It's one of those things it is easy to talk about – 'The Jewish race is being exterminated', says one party member, 'that's quite clear, it's in our programme – elimination of the Jews, and we're doing it, exterminating them'. And then they come, 80 million worthy Germans, and each one has a decent Jew. Not one of all those who talk this way has witnessed it, not one of them has been through it. Most of you know what it means when 100 corpses are lying side by side, or 500 or 1000. To have stuck it out and at the same time – apart from exceptions caused by human weakness – to have remained decent fellows, this is what has made us hard. This is a page of glory in our history which has never been written and is never to be written.

Himmler was wrong there. The Nuremberg trials of the twenty-two surviving movers in the Third Reich made it clear, beyond any doubt, that this was a regime founded upon the idea of aggressive war, sustained by banditry, theft and the abolition of morality and justice, and glutted like some blood-feeding ogre on mass murder. The catalogue of crimes, the abuses of science by doctors, the systematic use of slave labour, and the detailed programme to eliminate the Jews, could not, after the trials, be in any doubt. Those who were acquitted only got away on technicalities. It was unfortunate that Franz von Papen was acquitted – he lived on until 1969, incredibly. A special indictment should have been devised for this centrist career politician, since it was his weakness, his preparedness to sup with the devil, which had persuaded General Hindenburg in 1933 to suppress the Prussian socialist government and to form a coalition with the National Socialists – thereby not merely allowing Hitler in, but more or less legalizing him.

Papen could be said to have done more damage to the human race than many who were subsequently hanged, since he was the great midwife, the enabler of the hideous regime which ruined not merely Germany but the whole of old Europe.

What I mean by using the word theatre is that nothing, of course, could undo the crimes which these Nazi leaders had unleashed upon the world. Some satisfaction could be derived from the fact that Ribbentrop, Ernst Kaltenbrunner, Julius Streicher, Wilhelm Frick, Hans Frank, Wilhelm Keitel and the other horrors were hanged, but would be a gruesome sort of satisfaction. The stronger aspect to the 'theatre' of the trial was that these appalling individuals, with their list of shabby, inexcusable and undeniable crimes, were confronted, not by a firing squad, not by a court martial, but by the trappings of an old-fashioned trial, a courtroom, a judge, advocates prosecuting and defending. Against the brutal, amoral nightmare which they had knowingly created, the old world of order and morality was posited, embodied by the trial judge, Lord Justice Lawrence (Sir Geoffrey Lawrence). He was a Pickwickian in appearance, but firm, gentlemanlike, serious with occasional flashes of humour. 'His rare smile was a joy,' wrote one witness, 'so humanly kind that you found yourself smiling with him, and looking over to the long dock and its strained, sombre men you saw that some of them were smiling too.'[11]

The first stage of the trials, then, the hearings about the twenty-two chief Nazis, was a purgative experience, for Germany, for the Allies, and for the world. The trial tried to set the precedent, alas too optimistic, that any future tyrant would know that one day he would stand answerable for his crimes before the bar of justice and the law.

Clearly, when it came to dealing with all the tens of thousands of underlings who had done the dirty work in the Third Reich, and, even more complicated, with the numberless thousands who had somehow or another colluded in the crimes while not actually perpetrating murder or theft, what was to be done? For several years after the war, many of the nastier individuals involved in labour and death camp atrocities and so on had escaped to South America. Most of them escaped justice altogether. On 15 January 1951, Ilse Koch was sentenced to prison in West Germany. In 1947 she had been imprisoned for four years for her activities in Buchenwald as wife of the sadistic commandant Karl Koch, whom the SS had themselves hanged for corruption in 1945. She received a life sentence and committed suicide after sixteen years. Yet three weeks after her sentence, the American High Commissioner in Germany, John J. McCloy, issued a general amnesty to all those industrialists who were on trial for using slave labour. All the remaining generals awaiting trial were also given an amnesty. Among the industrialists released was Alfried

Krupp von Bohlen, whose factories had depended on the unscrupulous and vast use of slave labour. Henry Morgenthau Jnr, US Treasury secretary, had drawn up a plan during the war which would have forbidden Germany to be an industrial power. It would have been an entirely agrarian economy. If one thinks of it as a return to the rural duchies of the eighteenth century, each with its Ruritarian schloss, its harpsichord-playing grand duke, and its gambolling beer-fed peasants, it might have been quite charming, like the world of the fat duke and his sinister toymaker in *Chitty Chitty Bang Bang*. One would quite like to have lived in Morgenthau's Germany, sitting in the castle library of some prince bishop, reading a volume of Kant as one watched the Brueghelesque figures in the cornfields hunched over their scythes. Morgenthau's ideas, farfetched as they might seem today, were seriously entertained for a while. By the time of the 1950s, however, America needed not revenge but a rebuilt and revivified West Germany in its Cold War against Russia. German industry depended upon the most successful German industrialists, and if that required the help of a few slave-drivers and Nazi fellow travellers, so be it. Thus were the loftier ideals which led to the setting up of the Nuremberg trials reduced to moral absurdity.

Retribution is always visited, at the end of wars, by the victors upon the defeated. But here, as in so many other respects, the Second World War was unusual. The true victors suffered as well as the defeated.

Winston Churchill had three major claims on the gratitude of the British people. First, by his rhetoric in 1940 he had stiffened their resolve, and the gamble had paid off. He had stood up to Hitler, and from that autumn and winter of resistance had been made possible the ultimate victory of the Allies over the Third Reich. The many blunders Churchill made as a strategist do not take away from this fundamental fact. It is true that if Dowding had not prevented him from making the ultimate blunder – that of sacrificing the RAF to the defence of France in May 1940 – the resolve and bloody-minded courage of late 1940 might have had to confront a Nazi invasion of Britain. But his willingness to climb down and accept Dowding's judgement (albeit something he played down in his own account of the matter) is part of his greatness.

The second thing for which the British had to be grateful to Churchill was that he refused the pressures from Stalin and Roosevelt to open up a Second Front, and invade France from the shore before 1944. The cataclysm of the Dieppe raid in August 1942, when so many young Canadians were simply massacred by the Germans, showed that without proper landing craft, and without a severe weakening of the German position in France and Eastern Europe, as well as Allied mastery of North Africa and the Mediterranean, the victory would be uncertain. This slow haul was, once again, full of mistakes and blunders by all concerned, but the overall strategy, insisted upon so doggedly and bravely by Churchill, was right. Without it, British troops might once again, even if or when they managed to land in France, have found themselves involved in the sort of costly military stalemate which had wiped out millions of young lives in the First World War.

The third thing for which the British had to be grateful to Churchill was that he had formed what was in effect the first working socialist government in English history. 'Except for you and me,' he remarked to Anthony Eden when the chancellor of the exchequer, Kingsley Wood, died in 1943, 'this is the worst Government England ever had.' But the wartime government had prepared for peace very responsibly. Rab Butler had drawn up, and implemented, his educational reforms. Churchill had been frequently driven to exasperation by some of the Labour MPs whom he had invited to join his cabinet, but there was a side of him which was always a good old Edwardian liberal.

'Oh to be in England now that Winston's out,' crowed Pound.[12]

A major reason for Churchill's losing the election of 1945 – though it did not feel like this to him at the time – was in fact the small-c conservatism of the electorate. They voted for what they had been having already. They voted for the continuation of a state-controlled system of ration-books, housing provision, and so forth, to which they had become accustomed from Ernest Bevin, Clem Attlee, Stafford Cripps and others who had all been in office for the previous four or five years. Churchill could mock his Labour colleagues. Of Sir Stafford Cripps he said that 'there but for the grace of God, goes God'; he also said that Cripps had 'all the virtues I dislike and none of the vices I admire'.

Once the war in Europe was over, the Labour members of Churchill's government withdrew their support. He wanted them to stay on to form a Government of National Unity at least until the war with Japan was thoroughly finished. The truth was that, as Churchill's remarks to Eden, just quoted, show, there was little or no sympathy between Churchill and his cabinet. The Labour party could not forget the prewar years of poverty and unemployment and were determined that the postwar years should not be a repetition. So the king accepted Churchill's resignation, and the old man formed a caretaker government until the General Election.

Harold Nicolson, standing as a Conservative in West Leicester, wrote to his son Nigel: 'people feel, in a vague and muddled way, that all the sacrifices to which they have been exposed and their separation from family life during four or five years, are all the fault of "them" – namely the authority or the Government. By a totally illogical process of reasoning, they believe that "they" mean the upper classes or the Conservatives, and that in some manner all that went ill was due to Churchill.'[13]

Churchill did not help his own cause. He rejected the Beveridge Report, which proposed the establishment of the modern Welfare State and which had a 90 per cent public approval rating. In his radio election broadcasts he could have been conciliatory, speaking to One Nation as the grand old man who was all but above party politics. Instead, he gave them a taste of the old prewar, unreasonable, cantankerous Churchill:

> No Socialist government conducting the entire life and industry of the country could afford to allow free, sharp, or violently worded expressions of public discontent. They would have to fall back on some sort of Gestapo, no doubt very humanely directed in the first instance. And this would nip opinion in the bud; it would stop criticism as it reared its head, and it would gather all the power to the supreme party leaders, rising like stately pinnacles above their vast bureaucracies of Civil Servants, no longer servants and no longer civil.[14]

It was a singularly inept speech, coming from the one British Prime Minister (except perhaps Lloyd George) who ever had wielded something very like absolute power and who had, as Tory Home Secretary, made numerous attempts to censor the press and the BBC.

So it was that Britain, in common with its vanquished foes and its exhausted liberal allies, changed its government. Of all the prewar leaders in Europe, Stalin alone remained in place at the end of the war. Hitler had shot himself to avoid the fate of Mussolini. Laval, Pétain's deputy, was executed, together with innumerable French collaborators. Pétain was arraigned for treason, and locked up for life, dying in captivity in 1951. Winston Churchill, subsequently seen as the Greatest Englishman, and the Saviour of his Nation, was, at the first chance given to the electorate, voted decisively out of office. Instead of the orator, with his boozy, polychromatic phrases, his courage, and the sense he gave that life was an adventure, the British voted in as Prime Minister the 'sheep in sheep's clothing', as Churchill had called him: Clement Attlee, a pipe-smoking, bald figure who looked like the respectable headmaster of a small private school somewhere on the South Coast. Why did the nation turn against their saviour? Attlee himself said: 'They didn't turn against him, they turned against the Tories.'[15] It did not feel like that to Churchill himself. Clementine tried to tell Winston Churchill that perhaps the election defeat might be a blessing in disguise. If so, he replied, 'at the moment it's certainly very well disguised'.[16] There was not even domestic comfort to console either of them. 'I cannot explain how it is,' Clementine wrote to her daughter Mary, 'but in our misery we seem, instead of clinging to each other to be always having scenes. I'm sure it's all my fault, but I'm finding life more than I can bear. He is so unhappy & that makes him very difficult . . . I can't see any future.'[17] In fact, being in Opposition allowed Churchill some much-needed rest. It also stung him into some of his best jokes and sallies, as when he accused an MP called Bossom of 'being neither one thing nor the other'; or as in his response to Air Vice Marshal Bennett standing as a Liberal candidate at Croydon – it was 'the first time he had ever heard of a rat actually swimming out to join a sinking ship'.[18] When Clementine Churchill expressed such despondency in 1945, neither she nor Churchill could know how short-lived, nor how unpopular, Attlee's benign attempt at state socialism was going to be.

35

The End of the British Empire –
India and Palestine

Astrologers had deemed 14 August to be an unlucky day for Hindus, and so India was born as a nation at midnight between the two days of 14 and 15 August 1947. Jawaharlal Nehru's speech to the Constituent Assembly was a splendid piece of rhetoric:

> Long years ago we made a tryst with destiny, and now the time comes when we shall redeem our pledge, not wholly or in full measure, but very substantially. At the stroke of the midnight hour, when the world sleeps, India will awake to life and freedom. A moment comes, which comes but rarely in history, when we step out from the old to the new, when an age ends, and when the soul of a nation, long suppressed, finds utterance. It is fitting that at this solemn moment we take the pledge of dedication to the service of India and her people and to the larger cause of humanity.[1]

An age had indeed ended. Churchill, now leader of the Conservative Opposition, was despondent. 'In handing over the Government of India to those so-called political classes, we are handing over to men of straw of whom in a few years no trace will remain . . . Many have defended Britain against her foes, none can defend her against herself.'[2] Earlier, he had petulantly told the Americans that he had not become the King's First Minister to preside over the dissolution of the British Empire. But that dissolution was the ineluctable consequence of the war Churchill had waged, so bravely and so defiantly, against Hitler. His doctor, Lord Moran, travelling with him in America in 1952, when the old man had once again become the Prime Minister, sensed that Churchill had begun to understand this. Bowling along on the train from Washington to New York, Churchill allowed his mind to wander back to his youth, to dinners with Joe Chamberlain in 1895, to his absorption of Kipling, in whose writings, he said, he could have sat an examination, and to the attitude of mind which these imperialists had instilled in him. 'When you learn to think of a race as inferior beings it is difficult to get rid of that way of thinking; when I was a subaltern the Indian did not seem to me equal to the white man.' There was an unspoken 'but, now . . .' hovering after this paragraph. 'Was he too', asked the doctor, 'having second thoughts? Was the India of his youth, Kipling's India, a mistake after all? Had he been wrong about the Empire?'[3]

Moran leaves the question in the air. The wistful moment in the American railroad carriage, however, suggests that within five years of India having its independence, even the doughtiest defender of the British Empire had come to see its dissolution as an inevitability. Interestingly, Churchill focuses upon its racialism as the core of why it was unworkable, and that, surely, historically, is right. The India of Clive, and of the East India Company making a whole series of alliances with local princes, was the beginning of the Empire; but it had not begun with an imperialistic idea. It was trade which had led the British to India, and those who went there, absorbing Indian customs, very often falling in love with India's language, philosophies, religions, women, did not in the first instance come with the sense that European culture was superior to Indian, still less white faces superior to brown. These things developed as the deadly combination of Benthamite economists and Christian missionaries enforced in the British a sense of Indian barbarism. The Indians, like the poor at home in Britain, needed to be improved. That was when the trouble started. After the tragic events of 1857–9, the so-called Indian Mutiny, the East India Company was wound up and the British governor became a viceroy. Eighteen years later the queen became the empress of India, and the whole aberration of the 'British Empire' was enforced. It lasted, as far as India was concerned, just ninety years, a very short period in the lives both of Britain and of India.

One thing was certain: the British could not continue to govern India against its will. Another certainty was that the British incursion into India, which had begun as a profit-making enterprise for merchants, had become a drain on British resources. The war in the Far East had demonstrated that it took very little to make a British stronghold such as Singapore collapse. Throughout the war years, India had seethed with discontent, and the problems of the subcontinent were never going to be resolved until independence was achieved. The dilemma was: what sort of polity would be acceptable to the multitudinous peoples of this vast land mass, which had never been a united nation? Mahatma Gandhi had been its prophet, its Moses, or its Garibaldi leading it into its promise. Jawaharlal Nehru needed to be its Saviour, the modernizing liberal statesman who had to moderate the fervour of the early revolutionary nationalist sentiments of his followers in order to hold together the opposing factions of the new nation. The nub of the difficulty was actually a reworking of a problem which the British themselves, with the best of intentions, had brought to India in the first place. Lord Macaulay, as early as his years as legal adviser to the Supreme Council of India, 1834-8, had made English the official language of Indian law, schools and professions. Those Indians who had absorbed Victorian liberalism were those who were anxious to bring India up to date, and this in time included independence. But their very liberalism was a threat to the ancient religions and customs of the subcontinent. That was what had provoked the 'Mutiny' of 1857-9: the fear of the traditionally minded Indian soldiers, the sepoys, that they were being made to defile themselves by biting cartridges which were greased with impure animal-fat. Behind the casual, thoughtless British insistence that such matters were trivial was the much bigger thought that whole Indian ways of living and thinking should be modernized, brought up to nineteenth-century European levels of cleanliness, efficiency, common sense. In time, this meant intrusions by secular liberalism into the Indian home, the Indian marriage bed, even into the Indian funeral pyre.

Gandhi, by adopting the loincloth and the begging bowl, had tried to reverse this trend and to emphasize that he was at one with the Indian peasant. But the very fact that he was, as Churchill never tired of mockingly reminding the world, a Middle Temple lawyer, lay behind the device; and in his war on the caste system, even he had a touch of the improving Victorian liberal.

The Old Harrovian Nehru was a modernizer and a would-be democrat. And as soon as you brought democracy to a society as diverse as India's, you invited a tyranny by the majority. For this reason, the Muslims dreaded a democratic election after British withdrawal, and this was the problem which faced the Attlee government as soon as they had decided upon a speedy and immediate departure from India after the war, a war in which well over 2 million Indian troops had served and over 100,000 had been killed or wounded.

Since at least Curzon's time, Bengal had seen itself as separate from its Hindu neighbours. The Punjab had only been brought into the union with the rest of India, as far as modern times were concerned, after the wars of the late 1840s. When Dalhousie had arrived as the youngest (aged thirty-five) Governor-General in history (1847-56), he regarded the Sikhs there as little better than savages. He soon discovered them to be honourable warriors, with a fine religious tradition which respected the equality of men and women rather more than Christianity did. The Sikhs and the Muslims in the Punjab, after Dalhousie's settlements, had come to an uneasy truce. 'The modern spirit had come to the Punjab with all its material benefits and spiritual unrest.'[4] The idea of asking them, a century later, to submit to a government by Hindus was not so much a pipedream as an impossibility. To this Gandhi tried to blind himself, but it was probably always going to be the case.

Muhammad Ali Jinnah, originally an ally of Gandhi in the fight for Indian independence, had struck out on his own for Muslim independence from the Hindus. In the great city of Lahore, where little Kim had sat astride the cannon outside the museum in Kipling's great tale, Jinnah had made his revolutionary proclamation. He had left India for England in 1930 an all but forgotten figure in Indian politics, and returned in 1934. Somehow he got elected as the President of the Muslim League. And in the Lahore declaration of March 1940: 'If the British Government are really earnest and sincere to secure peace and happiness of the people of this sub-continent, the only course open to us all is to allow the major nations separate homelands by dividing India into autonomous national states.'[5]

It was an inflammatory and unstoppable idea which complicated the question of Indian independence immeasurably. Not only did it fly in the face of Gandhi's (and at first the British government's) idea of a united India, in which peoples of different ethnicities and languages and creeds formed a common polity. It also posed questions of the greatest difficulty about precise borders of any autonomous state. What, for example, would be the fate of the Sikhs in any independent Punjab? What about Hyderabad, hundreds of miles south of Jinnah's political stamping grounds in the northwest; a state which was primarily Hindu, ruled over by a Muslim Nizam who said he would prefer to be part of an independent Muslim state under the protection of Jinnah's Pakistan than to be part of Nehru's India? What about Kashmir? – a tragic question this, which rages to this very hour. What about Bengal? Jinnah assumed he would be able to take Calcutta into his Muslim state. Terrible violence erupted in that huge city, once the capital of the British Raj, on 16 August 1946, with 5,000 dead, over 15,000 injured and more than 100,000 rendered homeless in only four days of fighting, when the Hindus rose up to demonstrate what they thought of the Muslims taking their city.

When Clement Attlee became Prime Minister in 1945, he knew that the likelihood of Labour surviving more than one term in office was slight. (In fact they scraped in a second time in 1950, to be thrown out in 1951.) He had a huge political programme to push through – the nationalization of the major industries and the setting up of a welfare state at home, and the solution of the Indian problem abroad, as well as many other imperial and post-imperial problems which included the future of Palestine.

Since 1927, when he had sat on the Simon Commission to discuss the future of India, Attlee had favoured self-government for India, and he believed that 'but for the violent and obstructive opposition' of 'Winston Churchill and his friends we might perhaps have got an all-India solution to the Indian problem before the Second World War'.[6] He decided that the only way, in the circumstances, to solve the Indian question was to set a deadline and to tell the various parties, including Jinnah, Gandhi, Nehru and the other leaders, that after a certain date they would be responsible for the future of their country.

With peremptory lack of grace, Attlee recalled Lord Wavell, who was Viceroy. He made him no gracious speech of thanks upon his arrival in London, nor did he reveal to him the name of his successor, the man selected by the Labour government to become the last Viceroy, charged with the responsibility of handing over power in summer 1947.[7] Given the egalitarian nature of the times, and the socialist complexion of Attlee's government, it was perhaps surprising that his candidate was Lord Louis Mountbatten, by now Viscount Mountbatten of Burma (1900–1979), who took up his appointment as Viceroy on 23 March 1947.

Dickie Mountbatten, who was destined to be blown up in a fishing boat off the coast of County Sligo on 27 August 1979, by a bomb planted by the IRA, was one of the most colourful members of the royal family. His extraordinary popinjay arrogance and self-conceit were marked even in his boyhood when he joined the naval training college at Osborne House in 1913, twelve years after the death of his great-grandmother, Queen Victoria.[8] But he was an energetic and courageous naval officer. As captain of the destroyer HMS *Kelly*, he displayed extraordinary heroism trying to evacuate British troops from Crete during the disastrous engagement there in May 1941. The *Kelly* was sunk with the loss of half the crew. Mountbatten had to swim out from under the ship when it turned turtle. Noël Coward, a friend, perhaps lover, of Mountbatten's, acted the role in a film, *In Which We Serve*, which moved cinema audiences in wartime by its demonstration of simple heroism, even though viewed today it seems screamingly camp.

Even after he had left active service, Mountbatten maintained his links with the navy. When an employee of *Burke's Peerage and Baronetage* called on the war hero in his small mews house in Belgravia shortly before his assassination, he found the place 'awash with young, muscular and suspiciously good-looking Naval ratings, bustling about the place to no apparent purpose'.[9] The young genealogist found Mountbatten abuzz with one of his obsessions, namely that the royal family should take his surname. Although he had never met the 25-year-old Hugh Montgomery-Massingberd, who had only called on him to discuss the possibility of his writing a foreword to a *Guide to the Royal Family*, Mountbatten poured out indiscreet talk about the quarrels which had erupted in the family ever since Princess Elizabeth married Philip Mountbatten in 1947. When the cabinet refused to allow the new Royal House to take the name Mountbatten, '"That old drunk Churchill backed up by that crooked swine Beaverbrook (who paid off all Churchill's debts) objected to this and forced the Queen to announce that 'the House of Windsor' would continue as before. My nephew was furious as you can imagine. 'It makes me into an amoeba', he said, 'a bloody amoeba'. Have you ever wondered why there was a ten-year gap between the births of Princess Anne (1950) and Prince Andrew (1960)"?'[10] This vignette of Mountbatten in old age ('Mountbottom' as old friends knew him) gives an unforgettable picture of his impulsiveness, his indiscretion, his bustling desire to change, reform, interfere. He was destined to be the power behind Queen Elizabeth II's throne, an eminence less *grise* than *cerise* perhaps.

In his very early twenties he had married Edwina Ashley, granddaughter of Edward VII's hugely wealthy financial adviser Sir Ernest Cassel, and descended via her mother from the great Victorian statesman Palmerston and collaterally related to the philanthropist Earl of Shaftesbury. Broadlands, Palmerston's estate near Romsey, became the Mountbattens' through inheritance (together with £2.3 million, in 1923) from Cassel, and it was here that Philip Mountbatten and Princess Elizabeth spent their honeymoon.

The marriage of Edwina and Louis Mountbatten was, to put it mildly, stormy, and there were many affairs. Whether or not it was true, there was an inevitability about the claim that both Mountbattens, having arrived in India in 1947, conducted love affairs with Jawaharlal Nehru. Nehru's most recent biographer points out that the war had liberated Edwina Mountbatten to escape the somewhat stultifying world of a 1930s heiress and society flapper and to do something 'in her own right' with the International Red Cross. She loved India, and was determined to assist her husband in making the transition from British rule to independence as successful as possible. It was after independence, when Mountbatten stayed on as governor-general for a short period, that Edwina's relationship with Nehru deepened. The extent to which the relationship between them was 'in any way physical . . . pales into insignificance beside the fact that two lonely and complex individuals, both driven personalities, found in each other in middle life a source of inspiration, fun, solace and strength'.[11]

Whatever else was going on between Edwina Mountbatten, Nehru and Dickie Mountbatten, it was clearly all very different from what had happened when Lord Dalhousie had gone out to bring British rule to the Punjab a hundred years before. It is difficult to agree with the assessment that the extent of physicality of the relationship was irrelevant.

There is the world of difference between highly charged flirtations and love affairs proper. The latter dredge up, irrespective of the lovers' wishes, all kinds of uncontrollable feelings which in the former case may be kept under control. The highly charged, brittle and almost manic relationship which both Mountbattens had with Nehru seems to the eyes of hindsight to be much more explicable in terms of a non-consummated sexual –emotional passion.

It is against this background that we read the extraordinary and tragic events of the Partition.

By the time the Mountbattens arrived, the pressure from Jinnah and the Muslim League to establish an independent Pakistan was already all but irresistible. Mountbatten and Attlee shared a Pontius Pilate-like desire not to be held responsible for any of the ensuing violence, so that the British line, until the last possible minute, was to press for a united independent India. The dissension and subsequent bloodshed was to be seen as the responsibility of the Indians alone. In Mountbatten's case there was also an òbsessive desire to get the Indian business finished before his nephew Philip's wedding to Princess Elizabeth, a ceremony in which he had every intention of playing a major role, as in the subsequent marriage.

One of the most grotesque things about the rush to independence, and the British acceptance of Partition as an idea, was the way they eventually decided on the boundaries of the new states. They brought in a clever Inner Temple lawyer (Haileybury, like the Prime Minister, and New College, Oxford) by the name of Sir Cyril Radcliffe, who had never been to India in his life. He was given a house on the viceregal estate in early July 1947, just weeks before independence, and, with a pile of maps of a country he had never visited, he was asked to devise the boundaries. Judges sitting in Calcutta and Lahore submitted to him further evidence to help him in his deliberations. He had to make a hasty pronouncement about the tremendously complicated question of which territories in the Punjab should be given to the Sikhs and which to the Muslims. On 17 August East Punjab was deemed to contain the whole of the Jullundur and Ambala divisions, and the Amritsar district of the Lahore division. The East Punjab gained control of three of the five rivers (Punjab means Five Rivers), the Beas, the Sutlej, and the upper waters of the Ravi – a decision with devastating consequences for tens of thousands of people whose irrigation was now in the hands of those they considered their enemies. West Punjab, however, was granted, by a stroke of Radcliffe's pen, 62 per cent of the area and 55 per cent of the population. For the Sikhs, the loss to Pakistan of Lahore as well as the canal colonies of Shekhupura, Lyallpur (now Faisalabad) and Montgomery (now Sahiwal) was grievous; the Muslims resented not getting the whole of the Lahore division.

No sooner had he made his decision than Radcliffe skedaddled. 'People sometimes ask me whether I would like to go back and see India as it really is. God forbid. Not even if they asked me. I suspect they'd shoot me out of hand – both sides.'[12] Within days of his boundaries decision, one of the greatest migrations in human history overtook the Punjab. A sea of humanity broke across the steamy plains. Massacres on both sides were of appalling savagery. Muslims set fire not only to Sikh homes but to Sikh beards, even though being bearded was something which the men of both religions had in common. No one has ever calculated the exact numbers killed in the Punjab, but probably half a million is about right.[13] The tryst with destiny which Nehru envisaged was to be a bloody one. They had stepped out of the old world, in which a few hundred people being massacred in Amritsar by General Dyer was rightly regarded as an intolerable outrage, into a world where Amritsar and Lahore had become scenes of unspeakable butchery, where whole villages were put to fire and sword, and where religious and racial hatred was allowed to rage unchecked. They had made their tryst with a new world in which Islam would be perpetually at war with its neighbours and rival religions, ever more paranoid, ever more violent, ever more detested and feared, its noble intellectual and moral traditions less and less highly regarded.

Much of the blame for the way that Partition was handled – its brusque haste, its insufficient policing, the genocidal carelessness with which the fine print and the borders were decided – must be laid at the door of Louis Mountbatten, whose government awarded him an earldom in October 1947. By his superficial haste, his sheer arrogance, his inattention to vital detail, and his unwillingness to provide the huge peace-keeping forces which could have protected migrant populations, Mountbatten was responsible for as many deaths as some of those who were hanged after the Nuremberg trials.

On 21 July 1947, President Harry S. Truman wrote in his diary: 'Had ten minutes conversation with Henry Morgenthau about Jewish ship in Palistine [sic]. Told him I would talk to Gen[eral George] Marshall about it.'[14] That day, the world had heard that the ship Exodus, containing 4,500 Jewish refugees, had tried to land at Haifa, and been seized by British troops. These displaced persons, as they were called in those days, were moved on to three other vessels and taken to Cyprus for detention. The homeless families, who included 1,000 children, were kept in cages on board. The aim was to return them to Europe, where they had come from.

The United States had refused any more Jewish refugees. The British, whose job it was to keep the peace in the Mandated territory of Palestine, believed that any more Jewish immigrants would exacerbate an already explosive situation in which Jews and Arabs were killing one another. On 22 July 1946 Jewish terrorists led by Menachem Begin, a future Israeli Prime Minister and Nobel Peace Prize winner, blew up the British HQ in the King David Hotel in Jerusalem, killing 91 people. Twenty British servicemen were killed in that year. A year later the same group captured two British army sergeants and hanged them in retaliation for three of their own members having been executed.[15] One hundred thousand British personnel – 80,000 troops and 20,000 special police – were trying to keep peace between the Jews, desperate for somewhere to live free of persecution, and the Palestinian Arabs who saw Jewish arrivals as a threat to their freedom.

President Truman was the first world leader to recognize the state of Israel when it was finally proclaimed on 14 May 1948. It therefore came as a shock to many when his diary entries about the telephone call with Henry Morgenthau came to light in 2003. Morgenthau, who had been US Treasury secretary under FDR, was chairman of the United Jewish Appeal. Truman went into a tirade to his diary. 'He'd no business whatever to call me,' wrote the President. 'The Jews have no sense of proportion, nor do they have any judgement on world affairs. Henry brought a thousand Jews to New York on a supposedly temporary basis and they stayed.' Warming to his theme, Truman made a statement which, written in only the second year after the world had discovered the horrors of Auschwitz and the other death camps, is quite startling. 'The Jews I find are very, very selfish. They care not how many Estonians, Latvians, Finns, Poles, Yugoslavs or Greeks get murdered or mistreated as Displaced Persons as long as Jews get special treatment. Yet when they have power, physical, financial or political neither Hitler nor Stalin has anything on them for cruelty or mistreatment to the under dog.'[16]

In a letter to Eleanor Roosevelt, the late President's widow, Truman wrote: 'Jews are like all underdogs. When they get on top they are just as intolerant and as cruel as the people were to them when they were underneath.'[17] The director of the US Holocaust Memorial Museum is quoted as saying that such remarks are 'typical of a sort of cultural anti-Semitism that was common at the time'.

Since this was President Truman's view, it is not surprising that Ernest Bevin, the British Foreign Secretary, told a Labour party conference that the Americans were pushing for a Jewish state in Palestine because 'they did not want too many Jews in New York'.[18] Interestingly enough, identical views were entertained by other members of the British government at the time, but these led Clement Attlee and Bevin to oppose the setting up of a Jewish state. When Labour came in Chaim Weizmann assumed that they would be sympathetic to the Zionist cause, but the burly figure of Bevin, who was once described by Churchill as a working-class John Bull, consulted with the Foreign Office and then waddled across Whitehall to consult the Prime Minister. 'Clem,' he said, 'about Palestine. According to my boys, we've got it wrong. We've got to think again.'[19] Attlee like Truman possessed the flaw of 'cultural anti-Semitism'. When his Chancellor Hugh Dalton suggested Ian Mikardo and Austen Albu as potential junior ministers in the government, Attlee replied that 'they both belonged to the Chosen people and he didn't think he wanted any more of them'.[20]

The decision to allow a Jewish homeland was an admission by the British that they were unable to control the situation in Palestine. They did not do so willingly. They did so because they had no other option. Just as their method of abandoning India left the subcontinent with problems which persist into our own day, the abandonment of the British mandate in Palestine before any international agreement had been formed about the political future of the Arabs in the region, or any plan for relief and aid to the inevitable multitude of new refugees caused by the setting up of the state of Israel, must be seen as another current world problem[21] which has the 'Made in England' label stamped indelibly upon it.

After hundreds of thousands of needless deaths in India, there was one, in Delhi, on 30 January 1948 which rounded the story in the most tragic way. Throughout the disturbances, Mahatma Gandhi had prayed and fasted for peace. The emaciated lawyer, turned political agitator, turned holy man, was seventy-eight years old, but by now he could really have been any age. He had become like the statue of a saint. The skinny figure in its loincloth symbolized an ideal which was never, it would seem, to be accomplished, a time when religious hatred and the rivalries between political and creedal factions would cease, and the human race unite in the love of God. Tolstoy, Gandhi's great mentor, had essentially been a man of the Enlightenment. Distrustful as he was of science, technological progress, wealth-creation and so many of the achievements of which the capitalistic nineteenth century had been so proud, and in love as Tolstoy was with his idea of peasants and peasantry, he remained, to his core, a believer in the power of human reason. Gandhi carried into his peace campaigns something of his Master's belief in reasonableness. It appeared, after all, to have worked. The British, so long stubbornly holding on to an Empire which had only grown up, as one of the Victorians had observed, in a fit of absence of mind, were eventually persuaded that a vast land mass such as India could not be governed by a few white men from far away. Though Africa, where Gandhi's political awakening had occurred, still remained part of the Empire, it would as surely go the way of India and Palestine–Israel.

When an assassin tried to kill him with a bomb, Gandhi replied: 'This is not the way to save Hinduism. Hinduism can only be saved by my method.'[22] But just as Tolstoy's reasonable Christianity had depended upon removing many of that faith's core elements – such as a belief in the miraculous, the Resurrection and so on – so for many Hindus, the Mahatma, with his wish to do away with the caste system and to pray with Muslims, Sikhs and Christians, was anathema. Figures such as Madan Lal and Nathuram Vinayak Godse, Hindu refugees from the Punjab, were incensed by Gandhi's willingness to have the Koran read at Hindu prayer meetings and by his urging upon the newly formed government of Nehru a policy of conciliation with the Pakistanis who had murdered or dispossessed so many of their co-religionists. Godse later testified: 'I sat brooding on the atrocities perpetrated on Hinduism and its dark and deadly failure if left to face Islam outside and Gandhi inside.'[23] Godse was facing up to a challenge which still haunts the world: what is the appropriate response to Islam in its militant and aggressive form? In common with many Western politicians today, he believed that Gandhi's policy of conciliation was essentially impossible. He said at his trial that he bore Gandhi no ill will. He took a small pistol, and waited for Gandhi to emerge, in the early morning of 30 January 1948, from his joint prayer meeting. He bowed to the Mahatma because he felt genuine reverence for a man who was visibly holy, and trying to do right. Then he fired. Gandhi's last word was Rama, one of the incarnations of the Hindu god Vishnu.

The funeral of the holy man attracted over a million people. Hindus, Muslims, Sikhs, Parsees assembled, with many British, by the banks of the Jumna river to witness the burning of the cortege. They cried out 'Mahatma Gandi ki jai' – Long Live Mahatma Gandhi. To keep the peace among the peace-lovers, the commander in chief of the Indian army (an Englishman, General Roy Bucher, who had served in India since 1918, had been appointed to the role by Nehru) deployed four thousand soldiers, a thousand airmen and a thousand policemen. Three Dakota aircraft incongruously did a fly-past over the burning pyre whose flames rose into the sky for fourteen hours as the entire text of the *Gita* was chanted.

Nehru began his panegyric by saying that a light had gone out and then corrected himself – 'For the light that shone in this country was no ordinary light. The light that has illumined this country for these many years will illumine this country for many more years . . .' And so on.[24]

The pious Sir Stafford Cripps, a devout Christian Socialist, wrote: 'I know no other man of any time or indeed in recent history who so forcefully and convincingly demonstrated the power of spirit over material things.'[25]

Certainly there are few human beings of the twentieth century more impressive than Gandhi. But half a century after his death, his desire that religious fanaticism should give place to a spiritual calm, and his wish that we should settle our differences by prayer and not with guns, seems as impracticable as it did in 1948. And the word which came so aptly to his dying lips, that of the ineffable, all-holy and ever-merciful Rama, remains, like Allah, or Yahweh, as difficult to understand.

36

Widmerpool's Britain

The Victorians were now dying off, and so was their England. William Nicholson (1872–1949) was one of the most impressive painters of his time, easy to undervalue because, as his son the modernist painter Ben remarked, all William had ever wanted to do was merely to paint. His portraits – of the Earl of Harewood, George VI's brother-in-law, or of Arthur Quiller-Couch (editor of that volume of all but Biblical status, *The Oxford Book of English Verse*), or of Sidney and Beatrice Webb beside their austere bricky chimneypiece, captured many of the key figures of his time. Unlike Augustus John, this painter has not (in any sense) imposed himself upon the sitters. His landscapes, especially of the Wiltshire Downs, his interiors – whether of City Dinners or of ballrooms suddenly emptied by an air-raid – are both rich, painterly works of art and records of a passing age. Perhaps most eloquent of all are his still lives, pale English light glowing on newly burnished pewter, gold or silver. In 1949, it probably felt as if a merely minor painter had died. Now, seeing his work as a whole, we probably rank William Nicholson with the giants. And like all great artists, however private their concerns, we see that he reflected the age in which he lived with complete sureness.

In the post-war world which he just lived long enough to see, they looked to the future, and yet so much, in spite of bombing and war, survived of the world not just of pre-1939 but of pre-1914. Especially was this true of the railways.

If we had travelled about in Victorian England we should almost certainly not have imitated John Ruskin, who was rich and old-fashioned enough to go everywhere in his own privately designed horse-drawn coach. We should have gone by train. The hiss of steam, the clank of coupling, the rattle of girders, the vast tenders heaped with glistening Welsh coal, and the smell, on every station, of coal; the gas-lit platforms of the Victorian rail networks survived deep into the twentieth century. Until the 1950s, at least, Britons travelled in much the same way as Sherlock Holmes and Mr Gladstone had done. That magnificent old steam locomotive the Stanier 'Pacific' *City of Birmingham* was still puffing its way up Shap, drawing the 'Night Scot' from London to Glasgow, as late as 1964. But it already looked like an anachronism;[1] it was at one with such great, lost, majestic locomotives as the 1938 *Flying Scotsman*, an 'A4' Pacific No. 4498, designed by Sir Nigel Gresley; or

Liddesdale's North British 'Atlantic' No. 9877, or the superb engines which ran on the Great Western with the names of Welsh castles, such as Abergavenny and Caerphilly. In these railway engines, and the lines on which they ran, a century and more of Britain's past was carried in a rattling rhythm and a steam-filled cloud of romance never to be recaptured. The beginnings of change came with the new Labour government.

The nationalization of the railways took effect from 1 January 1948. The Big Four railway companies – LMS (London, Midland and Scottish), the LNER (London and North Eastern Railway), the Southern and the Great Western – were now absorbed into British Railways. These four companies had themselves, in the course of time, absorbed innumerable smaller Victorian railroad companies, many with picturesque and distinctive engines and carriages: the Brighton and South Coast Railway, the Dingwall and Skye, the Settle and Carlisle, the London, Chatham and Dover, the South Devon and many another.

The war had put great pressure on the railways. The Southern Railway was alone in seeing a fall in passenger numbers (361 million in 1938 down to 347 million in 1944); this was owing to the all but complete collapse of holiday traffic. All the other railways, which had been used both for troop movements and for freight traffic, including the transport of munitions, had a huge increase; there was also a rise in the number of 'passenger specials' – there were 24,241 special trains commissioned by the government to move troops in 1940 alone. Imports, and rail transport from the docks, a traditional source of rail income, fell, and not much money was spent on infrastructure, so that by 1948 most of the railways were in a poor state of repair. 'This railway system of ours is a very poor bag of assets,' complained the Chancellor of the Exchequer Hugh Dalton. 'The railways are a disgrace to the country.'[2] It was inevitable perhaps that coal-dependent steam trains would eventually be phased out. Americans during the war had begun to interest British railway engineers with the change in some US railroads from steam to diesel traction.[3] Inevitable, too, once nationalization had gone ahead, would be the eventual arrival upon the scene of a figure such as Dr Richard Beeching, the Widmerpool of the railways, who in the early 1960s under a Conservative government began his merciless closure of branch lines. Had the railways not been nationalized, some of the old steam trains would probably have survived.

Although in the early days of steam, some landowners had protested at the new-fangled railway innovation, steam trains had quickly become part of the British landscape. There was no more romantic way to travel through the West Highlands, or the Lake District, or across the expanses of Suffolk and Norfolk, than by train; the movement and smell, the gushes of steam, though all the consequences of engineering skill, had an almost organic quality which made the steam trains part of nature in a way that diesel and electric never could be. As with the mists of nature, in dawn or autumn, there was always a hint of melancholy about the steam trains. Their banshee warning-shrieks had something about them, especially when heard at night, of the uncanny. Almost no writer in English conveys the romance of rail travel so well as the crime writer Michael Innes, whose *The Journeying Boy* or *Appleby's End* describe railway journeys which have not been possible since Beeching, and which would entirely lack poetry without their steam accompaniment.

Typical of the British habit of coming in at the end of things and therefore creating almost instantaneous nostalgia was the Rev. W. Awdry's decision, in the late Forties, to write a series of children's stories about Thomas the Tank Engine on a small branch line. Within a very few years of Awdry's series beginning, the Fat Controller, one of the old private railway bosses, would in fact have been sent packing by the new British Railways apparatchiks; and Thomas's friends, Gordon the Big Engine, Henry the Green Engine, and so on, would only have survived in museums or those slightly sad small stretches of track on which enthusiasts still run steam trains. In the world of children's literature, however, these steam trains with their Fat Controller appear to be as immortal as the fairies or the gods, impervious to any changes on the Earth, let alone changes of government or transport ownership. Children who have hardly travelled on a train, still less a passenger steam train, find these stories endlessly re-readable. In part this is surely because of the illustrations by C. Reginald Dalby which evoke – witness the marvellous snow scenes in the story called 'The Flying Kipper' – a vanished Britain, though not always one which is sin or crime-free. (In a later story in that volume, 'Henry's Sneeze', some boys throw stones from a railway bridge and leave the Fireman concussed.)

The Labour victory came as no surprise to those who had heard the way men spoke while on active service about their hopes for postwar Britain. Few, if any, wanted a return to the high unemployment, the poverty, the social divisions of the 1930s. Most people in Britain, though obviously not all, attributed these ills to the Conservatives.

A Mass Observation Poll was conducted at the height of the Blitz to determine the answer to a number of deep political questions: would postwar Britain have less class distinction? More state control? A reform of the educational system? A levelling of incomes? An increase in social services? A dictatorship, possibly along fascistic lines?

Mass Observation was not an opinion poll to which people knew they were contributing. The observation was *by* busybodies *of* the Masses. Obviously, it was rough and ready, but the results of this particular report, drawn up by a panel of observers who had moved among a cross-section of society in pubs, factories and other work-places, were as follows: 29 per cent thought there would be less class distinction; 21 per cent more state control; 19 per cent educational reforms; 15 per cent a levelling of incomes; 14 per cent increased social services; while 13 per cent believed that there would be a fascist state after the war. If by fascist they meant absolutist, or interventionist on lines undreamt-of in former ages, this was hardly surprising given the conditions of wartime, in which Habeas Corpus had been suspended, the press and broadcasting were heavily censored, a high proportion of the male population was in uniform, and, it seemed, the state was suddenly in unstoppable control.[4]

It is interesting that 71 per cent therefore believed that class distinction would continue after the war more or less as it had before; and that a thundering 81 per cent thought there would be no real educational reform. These people were broadly speaking right. The trivial details of class distinction would perhaps become less important in the immediate postwar years; and by the 1960s, deference, and debutante presentations at Court, and the sillier outward trappings of the class system had been laid aside. But as late as 1962, in his *Anatomy of Britain*, for example, Anthony Sampson could observe that while the Civil Service 'lean over backwards to avoid favouring public schoolboys', between 1948 and 1956, 50 per cent of recruits to the Senior Civil Service were from Oxford, and 30 per cent from Cambridge, and the great majority of those educated at the older universities were still from public schools.[5]

The existence of private schools, and in particular those private boarding schools called public schools, Eton, Harrow, Winchester and the rest, was one of the most socially divisive, and deliberately socially divisive, features of Victorian Britain. Although many of these schools went back to the sixteenth, and some as far as the fifteenth (Eton) or fourteenth (Winchester) century, the constitution of the public schools, their ethos and their place in the scheme of things were essentially Victorian. Moreover, it had been the policy of the Victorians, as they founded and built new schools, and gradually provided education for all, to do so on strictly stratified lines. Funds which had been laid aside by philanthropists of an earlier age were often simply plundered for the middle classes. For example at Sutton Coldfield, where a charitable fund existed to educate the poor, £15,000 was taken by the Victorians to provide a 'high school for well-to-do children'. In the older public schools, which had all been founded to educate the poor, money was taken by the nineteenth-century reformers to build new schools for the lower orders.

For example, one of Thomas Arnold's first acts when becoming head-master of Rugby was to close the free class for town boys, and to make his school exclusively the preserve of 'gentlemen'. The Lawrence Sheriff School was started in Rugby town for the more plebeian customers. Canon Woodard, founder of High Church boarding schools for boys and for girls, did so with clear ideas, in each case, about the social position of the parents. Lancing was meant to be a sort of nouveau riche equivalent of Eton, preparing boys for the university or the army, whereas Ellesmere, Denston or Ardingly, some of the canon's other creations, were for 'respectable tradesfolk'.[6]

By the close of the nineteenth century, there were many good schools in England, but as well as imparting knowledge they were reinforcing the fairly recently devised social hierarchies. 1945 would have been an obvious moment to abolish private education altogether, and to force the British to draw, for their Civil Service, their better universities, their professions and skilled jobs, from as wide a pool as possible, regardless of wealth or levels of gentility. When it came to it, however, the likes of C. R. Attlee (Haileybury), Sir Stafford Cripps (Winchester), Viscount Stansgate (Westminster) and Hugh Dalton (Eton) funked the abolition of their old schools.

The Fleming Committee,[7] which sat from 1942 to 1944, and was set up to review the position of independent schools and direct grant schools,* recommended that after the war, society should no longer tolerate the social divisiveness of the old public school system. A minimum of 25 per cent public schoolboys, in the first instance, should be chosen from state primary schools. This proposal was dropped in the Conservative Rab Butler's Education Act of 1944, which merely increased the opportunity for clever boys and girls to go to grammar schools. Butler had been in favour, personally, of abolishing the fee-paying element of direct grant schools, and he was an agnostic about the question of whether the private schools should be abolished.[8] Butler, however, was a Man of Munich, a compromiser. Half his name was given to the phenomenon of consensus politics which governed Britain until the 1970s – Butskellism (an amalgam of the names Butler and Hugh Gaitskell, Social Democrat leader of the Labour party after Attlee). His autobiography was entitled *The Art of the Possible*. He had to be able to sell the generous, and on the whole liberal, flavour of his educational reforms to the diehards on the Tory backbenches and to the House of Lords. Moreover, since the funding for education passed largely from central government to local government, the overall question of whether powerful private schools

---

* Direct grant schools depended in part on government funding and in part on private fees charged at the school's discretion.

should continue to exercise their overwhelming bias in favour of particular groups and classes was simply allowed to drop.

So, most astoundingly, it may be said with hindsight, was much of an
attempt to counteract the essentially aristocratic method by which Britain
was governed. Just before he became Home Secretary and when he was
still the president of the Board of Trade, in 1910, Winston Churchill had
said: 'The time has come for the total abolition of the House of Lords
. . . Many Conservatives have frankly abandoned the hereditary principle. Scarcely a voice in any party is raised on behalf of the existing
institution. We as a Liberal Party stand outside this spontaneous repu-
diation of hereditary and aristocratic privilege.'[9]

As leader of the Opposition in the postwar period, however, Churchill
took a rather different view. The question of the abolition of the House
of Lords might have been dear to the heart of a few firebrands on the
left of the Labour party. All the Tory Opposition found themselves
opposing, however, was some very mild tinkering with the Parliament
Act, shortening the time in which the House of Lords could delay legislation which was passed to it for approval from the Commons. The Lords
were careful not to antagonize the new Labour government, the 5th
Marquess of Salisbury (leader of the Tories in the Upper House) taking
the view that it was not peers' job to stifle the mandate of an elected
government.[10]

Churchill, with his love of building up the Labour party as a swarm
of anti-democratic demons, represented the new legislation as 'class
tyranny'. What Labour wanted, he claimed, was 'virtually single Chamber
Government'.[11] He now defended the Lords, which in 1910 he had wanted
abolished, on democratic grounds. The constitutional aim was 'that the
persistent resolve of the people shall prevail without throwing the community into convulsion and disorder by rash or violent, irreparable action
and to restrain and prevent a group or sect or faction assuming dictatorial power'.[12]

In fact, House of Lords reform did not loom large in the 1945
Parliament because the Attlee government had so much else on its agenda.
The only reason the Labour government wished to shorten the veto was
in order to speed through iron and steel nationalization, which the Tories
in the Lords were questioning. It was very much as an expedient parliamentary measure that this check on the Lords' power was proposed and
not per se as an attack on the hereditary principle, such as the Liberals
had made in 1909–10. By leaving alone the private schools, and the House
of Lords, the Attlee government revealed that it was not attempting to
turn Britain into one of the northern European socialist states such as
Finland or Sweden. Its social engineering took a back place behind its

belief in centralized, government-owned industries – coal, steel, iron – government-owned railways, and government-sponsored welfare, especially in the field of pensions, and with the creation of the first National Health Service in the world where treatment was free at the point of entry.

One of the first acts of nationalization was more in the nature of a symbolic act than anything else: the Bank of England. 'Make me Chancellor of the Exchequer and give me a good Labour majority in Parliament and I will undertake the nationalization of the Bank of England over a dinner party,' said Hugh Dalton. In fact he did not even need a dinner party. He 'nationalized' the Bank over a cup of tea with his friend, the governor of the Bank of England, Lord Catto. All that happened was that the Court of the Bank was reduced in number, and restricted to technical experts. The superfluous merchant bankers resigned. Nicholas Davenport, who knew the City well in those days, wrote in his memoirs: 'What Dalton did was really a non-event. First, he asked . . . Lord Catto of Morgan Grenfell to stay on because he was such a nice friendly chap who had risen from the ranks. Then he reduced the Court from twenty-four to sixteen and took power to appoint only four of them each year. He retained the prominent directors who had been associated with the worst disasters of Montagu Norman' – that is, the deflationist governor who had presided over the financial disasters of the between-war years.[13]

Times were hard in these austere war years. Men were coming back from the armed services to a bomb-scarred, bankrupted country. Housing was desperately short. 'We DEMAND a Home, not the WORKHOUSE. EX-SERVICEMEN demand Justice for our wives and kids' read the notice outside one Islington squat in a council-owned building. Tiny little prefabricated houses – prefabs – sprang up all over the place as a temporary solution to the problem; but it was only temporary, and the Conservative government, when it was returned in 1951, was faced with a massive rebuilding programme.

There was a run on the pound from almost the moment Labour took office, and the financial situation in the exchequer was dire, with tax income at an all-time low, and no help from the Americans at first on offer to a socialist party. Barbara Castle was a new Labour MP in 1945 – later a minister in the Labour governments of 1966 onwards. She recalled that the attitude of the Truman administration to Britain changed automatically with the election. 'Even ships which were crossing the Atlantic changed their nature' as they became conveyors of goods which had to be paid for on docking rather than of a contribution from one ally to another.[14]

The British economy had never faced graver difficulties. There were accumulated foreign debts of £4,000 million. Foreign assets were hugely reduced. Exports had shrunk to about 40 per cent of their 1939 levels. There was a calamitous shortage of raw materials.[15] A low point was reached in 1947 when, on top of food shortages (even bread was rationed), fuel shortages and money shortage, the worst winter on record immobilized the country under mounds of snow and ice. 'Snow fell, east winds blew, pipes froze, the water main (located next door in a house bombed out and long deserted) passed beyond insulation or control. The public supply of electricity broke down. Baths became a fabled luxury of the past. Humps and cavities of frozen snow, superimposed on the pavement, formed an almost impassable barrier of sooty heaps at the gutters of every crossing, in the network of arctic rails,' as Anthony Powell powerfully evoked that time.[16] Hugh Dalton, the somewhat clerical (his father had been a canon of Windsor) Chancellor of the Exchequer, leaked the contents of an emergency budget in November 1947 to a lobby journalist. In the twenty-first century, British lobby journalists are told the contents of the chancellors' budgets before they are announced to the Commons, but in those days the House of Commons was still considered to have a serious political function, and Dalton honourably resigned. He was replaced as Chancellor by Sir Stafford Cripps, an austere bespectacled Wykehamist, rumoured to subsist upon mustard and cress grown from the blotting paper on his desk. His nickname was Austerity Cripps. Briefly a member of the war cabinet, when he had been a persistent critic of Churchill and his policies, his own Puritanism and zest for self-denial matched the necessary leanness of the times. Major W. H. Lewis, the brother of C. S. Lewis, the Oxford don and literary scholar, gloomily told his diary in November 1947: 'Potatoes are put "on rations" on a scale of 3 lbs per week for the bourgeois. And so the last "filler" food disappears from the diet, and the days of real hunger come upon us. It's extraordinary how one is conditioned by a secure past: even now I can't grasp the fact that I, WHL, will go to bed hungry and get up hungry; these, I say, are things that happen to nations one reads about in the papers, not to me.'[17]

Cripps was a much more effective Chancellor than Dalton, rising betimes and getting through the equivalent of a day's work before most of his Treasury colleagues had had their breakfast. Thanks largely to American aid in the Marshall Plan from 1948 onwards, and to his encouragement of collaboration between the unions, government and management in the newly nationalized industry, the postwar economy began to recover. It exacted a very great personal cost. He resigned through ill health on 20 October 1950, and six months later, three days short of his sixty-third birthday, Cripps was dead.

Cripps's economic and political ideas were left-wing, in so far as they assumed the desirability of state ownership of the transport system and the coal, iron and steel industries. But Ruskin's *Unto This Last* more than Marx's *Capital* was the inspiration for his belief in a mixed economy. Even more Victorian was the philanthropic inspiration of the welfare state, which was the Attlee government's lasting legacy to the British people. The guiding spirit and founding father of the welfare state was not a socialist but William Beveridge, who was born in Rangpur, Bengal, on 5 March 1879, the son of a judge in the Indian Civil Service. After Charterhouse and Balliol, he worked at Toynbee Hall, the Oxford settlement in the East End of London, and throughout his life, as a civil servant, academic (he was for a while Master of University College, Oxford) and politician (briefly Liberal MP for Berwick-upon-Tweed, 1944–5), he was a classic Victorian liberal who believed not in a nanny state nor in a dependency culture, but in self-betterment. He never liked the phrase welfare state. His persistent belief was that society existed for the individual, and it was this belief which inspired his famous Report of 1944 in which he set out a programme to wage war on the five giants who stood across the path of national reconstruction: Want, Disease, Ignorance, Squalor and Idleness.

With the advent of Margaret Thatcher on to the political scene in Britain in the late 1970s it became fashionable to belittle the achievements of the Attlee government and to question the very notion of welfare. Churchill's words of 1909 were forgotten – 'I do not agree with those who say that every man must look after himself, and that intervention by the state . . . will be fatal to his self-reliance, his foresight and his thrift . . . It is a mistake to suppose that thrift is caused only by fear: it springs from hope as well as fear. Where there is no hope, there will be no thrift'.

Beveridge, and those whom he inspired, who included not merely members of the Labour party, but all who wished to build a decent society after the war, can hardly be blamed for any of the problems facing an under-funded, badly managed welfare service in the Britain of the twenty-first century. What the Report, and the Labour government that had the courage to put it into practice, brought to pass was the chance of a decent schooling for every child; the chance of decent housing for all – it was no longer left to the likes of Basil Jellicoe to build habitable dwellings for the less well-off; the chance of full employment – through those Keynesian methods encouraged by Oswald Mosley in 1931 and finally adopted by his old party in 1945; and the provision of health care, which included dental care, for all, regardless of their income. What Beveridge was recommending, and what Attlee's government was putting into practice, was a programme almost identical to that of Mosley's New Party in 1931. In 1931, it had been regarded as 'extreme'. By 1945, it was seen as no more than the people of Britain, after six years of war, and a much longer history of being shafted by the capitalist system, deserved.

Any who now feel called to mock the Beveridge Plan, or its extraordinarily faithful execution in the period of 1945–50, should ask themselves – would they rather live in the slums of one of the big British cities before or after the Second World War? Would they rather be a poor person in 1933 or in 1953? Would they rather be sick in 1933 or 1953? Would they rather be an old person in the workhouses which still survived until the Second World War, or living on the, albeit modest, pension provided by the Labour government of 1945?

It was not merely the health service of which the Attlee government was rightly proud, it was the whole achievement. In economic circumstances of unprecedented exigency, these so-easily mockable men in their three-piece suits, with their pipes and their trilby hats, did the decent thing. It would have been intolerable to leave things as they had been before the war, with children suffering from rickets in mushroom-infested slum-dwellings, with the pensionless old dying destitute, with health care available only to those who could afford to pay for it. Of course, decent-minded doctors in general practice had always cared for patients regardless of whether they could pay or not. But the National Health Service was one of the most stupendous British inventions. As soon as it was started, it was in a state of 'crisis', and it has been in a state of crisis ever since. It could have been better run from the beginning. No doubt wiseacres know ways of making it better. The simple and magnificent thing about it cannot be diminished. You no longer needed, before you had your appendix removed, or your teeth fixed, or your weak heart, kidney or stomach attended to, to produce a chequebook. It was the great Ruskinian corrective to the Darwinian relentlessness of capitalist necessity.

Undoubtedly the boldest cabinet appointment of Attlee's was to make Aneurin Bevan ('Nye') the Minister of Health. He was far to the left of the party; indeed, during the 1930s he had advocated the Popular Front, an alliance of left-wing parties with the Communists, and an 'English Revolution'. Not that there was anything English about this brilliant Welshman. Born in 1897 in Tredegar, Monmouthshire, he was the son and grandson of coal miners. He himself went down the pits at the age of thirteen. He spoke in childhood with a stammer, and his vast reading, like his later legendary eloquence, was the combination of energetic self-improvement and inborn genius. From the beginnings of his political self-education, he was a reader of, and believer in, Marx. In 1931 he had been attracted to Mosley's New Party, but he never really wavered in his belief that in practical terms, the British Labour party was the only institution which could bring to pass the socialist society in which he believed. Throughout the war he was a vociferous critic of Churchill, who repaid the compliment by describing him as 'a squalid nuisance'.[18]

The importance of personal charm in history is sometimes forgotten. Chaim Weizmann had it in abundance, and this largely explains Arthur Balfour's 1917 Declaration. Churchill had it, and could woo the most unlikely political opponents. When Nye Bevan arrived at the Ministry of Health, Sir William Douglas, a natural Conservative, had been appointed his Permanent Secretary. Douglas made it clear to friends that he did not intend to stay long. Bevan, he said, was 'a terrible fellow. I'll never forgive him for all those attacks on Churchill during the war. I made it clear that I would carry on only for three months until they got someone else.' A few weeks later, a colleague asked Douglas how he was managing under Bevan. 'What are you driving at?' Douglas asked. 'He's the best Minister I ever worked for. I've made it clear that while Bevan's there, I'll stay.'[19]

Of all the professions, the British medical profession was perhaps the most conservative in all senses. On 26 July 1945, while the election results were being announced, the British Medical Association was holding its annual meeting in its headquarters in Tavistock Square. This was a building where clerical staff, as late as the 1930s, were instructed that they must vacate the lift, rather than share it with the frock-coated, top-hatted consultants who had arrived from Harley Street to conduct business. Deference towards doctors in the great hospitals rivalled the reverence shown towards the higher clergy in Rome. When the BMA heard that Beveridge had lost his parliamentary seat in the election, they interrupted their meeting and burst into a loud round of applause. One Harley Street consultant said: 'I have spent a lot of time seeing doctors with bleeding duodenal ulcers caused by worry about being under the State.'[20]

Butler in 1944 had allowed schools to be under the spending control of local government authorities, which still accounts for the current state of muddle in British education. Bevan made sure that spending for the health service was nationalized and centralized, the responsibility of central government: and that probably accounts for the current state of chaos in the health service. The truth is, that with an organization on such a scale, however it is funded, and whoever is doing the funding, some measure of chaos is inevitable. Butler's aim was to give grammar school-quality education to all, all who would benefit from it, regardless of their wealth and of where they lived. He broadly achieved his aim, until the educationalists themselves introduced the dogma that it was socially divisive for schools to distinguish between clever pupils and stupid ones. In health, the fundamental aims were always more rational, even if in an expanding population, with limited resources, and a medical profession ever growing in skill and knowledge, the aims were unaffordable: namely health care, free of charge, for all.

This had been the aim of the Labour party for a very long time, at least since 1909, when Beatrice Webb, in her report to the Royal Commission on the Poor Law, wanted a 'state medical service'. By 1930, such was the chronic state of health in the big cities, the BMA itself was suggesting 'a general medical service for the nation'. Beveridge recommended a comprehensive health service. The question which faced the incoming Labour health minister in 1945 was how to implement it.

Hospital care in Britain, very much like education, had grown up in a haphazard way, with a mixture of old foundations, and more recent ones established by Victorian philanthropists. There were 1,334 voluntary hospitals. These included nearly all the great teaching hospitals, as well as specialist research hospitals such as the Great Ormond Street Hospital for Sick Children. By the end of the 1930s most of these voluntary hospitals were desperately strapped for cash, with most of their investments reduced in value. (In 1891, 88 per cent of their income came from investment; in 1938 only 33 per cent.) As for the municipal hospitals, many of them had grown up as workhouse infirmaries. They were run by local councils with money from the rates and most of them were awful. Bevan's genius was to see that the health service could only be made to work by nationalizing the hospitals, and putting them all under one central authority with government funding. To make it work, he had to persuade the Royal Colleges of Surgeons, Physicians, and Obstetricians. And he enlisted the help of 'Corkscrew Charlie', Lord Moran. Conversations such as this took place:

BEVAN: I find the efficiency of the hospitals varies enormously. How can that be put right?

MORAN: You will only get one standard of excellence when every hospital has a first-rate consultant staff. At present the consultants are all crowded together in the large centres of population. You've got to decentralize them.

BEVAN: That's all very well, but how are you going to get a man to leave his teaching hospital and go into the periphery? [He grinned] You wouldn't like it if I began to direct labour.

MORAN: Oh, they'll go if they get an interesting job and if their financial future is secured by a proper salary.

BEVAN: (after a long pause) Only the State could pay those salaries. This would mean the nationalization of the hospitals.[21]

Bevan made some concessions which must have upset him; they certainly upset his leftist colleagues. He allowed the doctors in hospitals to continue their private practice, which effectively meant that many of the best consultants were only offering part of their time to the new health service. But some time was better than none. The profession which had collectively cheered when Beveridge was booted out of Parliament in 1945 formed a determination, by 1950, to make the new health service work. By and large, they, with the nursing profession, succeeded in doing so. The failures to fund or administer the unwieldy health service in the last thirty years have led to hospitals in many parts of Britain being reduced to a state which Bevan, Moran and Beveridge would find completely incredible if they were to return to Britain in the twenty-first century. It does not diminish Bevan's achievement. Apart from his eloquence, and his wit, which inspired so many who heard his oratory both on the hustings and in the House of Commons, he was that very, very rare thing in the history of politics, a man whose decisions on behalf of those he served brought about human betterment. This book has been a catalogue of mistakes by politicians, moral and practical disasters which led to wars, enslavement and human wretchedness on a scale which no previous age could have dreaded or dreamed of. The National Health Service, which inspired so many other countries in the world to imitate it, did what it set out to do, and with all its many mistakes and short-comings, it still does so: it provides free medicine, free advice, free surgery, free nursing to everyone, regardless of their income. Others could have bungled things at the outset as, one must candidly say, Butler bungled education by not abolishing private education. Bevan's bold and patient nationalization programme of the hospitals, together with his drawing into the national fold the general practitioners and the dentists, was a formidably skilful achievement. He deserves the laurel crown as the British politician who did least harm and most good.

Three weeks before the general election which returned Churchill to power as Prime Minister in the autumn of 1951, Clem Attlee addressed the Labour party:

I am proud of our achievement. There is an immense amount more to do. Let us go forward in this fight in the spirit of William Blake:

I will not cease from mental strife,
Nor shall my sword sleep in my hand
Till we have built Jerusalem
In England's green and pleasant land.[22]

Labour lost the election largely because of national mood. England was not a green or pleasant land, and nor were the other parts of the United Kingdom. Housing was a problem which the government has still not solved. Many of the bombsites were not cleared until the 1960s. It was the Britain captured in Rose Macaulay's beautiful novel *The World My Wilderness*, a story of the London bombsites. 'The squalor of ruin . . . was a symbol of loathsome things, war, destruction, savagery; an earnest, perhaps, of the universal doom that stalked, sombre and menacing, on its way.'[23]

The films and literature of the period reflect the sense of drabness, greyness and bureaucracy threatening people's lives. George Orwell's telling political satire, *Animal Farm*, was the most devastating possible analysis of Communist Revolution. He followed it up with the much sourer *1984*, a book which foresees a world in which thought police and totalitarian interference into personal life in effect destroy humanity. As with *Animal Farm*, he had in his sights the Soviet Union, but the drabness of his invented world surely owed much to the actuality of Attlee's Britain.

Passport to Pimlico was the first of the famous comedies to emerge from the Ealing Studios. Pimlico in those days was a melancholy district of London which had known more prosperous days. The eruption of an unexploded bomb makes a crater in which the local grocer, played by Stanley Holloway, discovers hidden treasure, belonging to a medieval duke of Burgundy. The researches of the learned Professor Hatton-Jones (Margaret Rutherford) establish beyond doubt that Pimlico was actually on Burgundian soil. (The starting point for the original joke was that the government of Canada officially made a hotel room in Ottawa a part of the Netherlands so that Princess Juliana could bear the heir to the Dutch throne on Dutch soil.)

Wearied by the bureaucracy of the Labour government, and by the austerity of rationing, the people of Pimlico declare their independence of Britain. In the pub, they all tear up their ration books; it must have been a wonderfully liberating fantasy to watch in 1949. As well as being a film which expresses exasperation with the dreary state of things in Britain, it is also a gentle expression of consensus politics. After extensive negotiations, the little London area is reabsorbed into the United Kingdom in return for assurances that it will have many of the social amenities which became commonplace in the 1950s. The bomb crater, for example, becomes a public lido where the children can bathe. Although Tory in its anti-bureaucratic instincts, the film has embraced the centralized public service ethos of Attlee's government, and which would remain a characteristic of all subsequent Westminster governments, however right-wing or radical they wished to appear to their fans.

The gallant little Burgundians of Pimlico also reflect the insularity of Britain in its relation to Europe. The European Coal and Steel Community began in 1950 with France and Germany agreeing to pool their production of resources. Britain's attitude to Europe was well summed up by the Foreign Secretary, Ernest Bevin's, remark to Christopher Mayhew in 1948: 'Well you know, Chris, we've got to give them something and I think we'll give them this talking shop in Strasbourg – the Council of Europe – we'll give them this talking shop.'[24] Bevin as Foreign Secretary and Stafford Cripps as Chancellor both resented deeply the Marshall Plan for Europe, and the American desire that Britain should get involved with the origins of the Common Market with Konrad Adenauer of Germany, the Christian Democrat leader, with Jean Monnet, the effective architect of the Common Market, and with the French foreign minister Robert Schuman. Attlee's government wanted nothing to do with it. Britain, like Pimlico in the film, was to go it alone. And this spirit was reflected also in the Festival of Britain of 1951. Whereas the 1851 exhibition in Hyde Park had reflected Britain's cosmopolitan place in the world, the Festival of Britain was in part a celebration of her natural history and cultural heritage of an unashamedly insular kind, in part a hopeful looking-forward to the new nation which would emerge from the war. Much of the exhibition space was devoted to housing, to domestic and industrial design. Those looking round the exhibition must have felt, surveying the clean lines of the Scandinavian-inspired furniture and architecture, that a new world had come into being.

Sir Hartley Shawcross, after the Labour victory, had announced: 'We are the masters at the moment.' But who were the 'we' in this sentence?

The most eloquent answer to this question in art is found in Anthony Powell's comic masterpiece *A Dance to the Music of Time*, the first volume of which, *A Question of Upbringing*, was published in 1951. The story begins in the year 1921 at an unnamed boarding school, obviously Eton, as the hero, Nick Jenkins, ambles idly through the winter mist to have tea with his chums. As he makes his way back to the house he passes a very different sort of boy – it is Widmerpool, who forces himself to have a run each afternoon. Widmerpool appears to be no more than a figure of fun in the school section of the book, but even in this early glimpse of him, the narrator and his readers become aware that he is a figure who lives by the will, in some mysterious sense more in tune with his times than the languid, bohemian Nick, who wishes to live by the imagination.

Powell was a close friend of Malcom Muggeridge at this date, and the two men would often walk round Regent's Park together discussing the fundamental clash on which the emergent novel was to feed, namely the war between the will and the imagination. Power mania had been an obsession of Muggeridge's since his Marxist days: what draws men and women to power, how they become addicted to it, how it takes over from other appetites. One of Muggeridge's beliefs was that power addicts were often dyspeptic, and he rather cruelly attributed Stafford Cripps's dyspepsia to power addiction. When Widmerpool grows up, he too is a dyspeptic. There is a memorably funny Sunday lunch when Widmerpool gives the narrator a meal in his club, washing down cold tongue with a glass of water.[25] By the time the narrative has reached the postwar period, it is no surprise to find that Widmerpool, a fellow-traveller with the Communists, who has rather dubious associations in Eastern Europe, is an MP in the Labour interest. He has achieved what he wanted from the very beginning, on that run through the winter mists in the Thames Valley: the free exercise of power. Widmerpool is a manager, a wheeler-dealer. He judges people by how they have got on; he has no sense of England's past, no feeling for people (at quite a late stage of the sequence, he forgets the narrator's Christian name). Much of Powell's somewhat peppery Toryism goes into the creation, no doubt, but the novel contains a really acute perception of what had happened to England during the war. It had not been taken over by Bolsheviks or by the working class. Widmerpool is an efficient, ruthless staff officer, a paper pusher. He could easily have said, after the 1945 election: 'We are the masters.' He would have meant that the managerial class, previously all but non-existent, had taken over. The growth of bureaucracy in Britain in the postwar years, the filling up of political, Civil Service and professional posts with colour-less, pushing people controlling others for the sake of control, was to be a feature of life from then onwards. Widmerpool was a man of his time, and a man of the future.

37

The Hereditary Principle

In 1953, two young men came into the Eagle pub in Cambridge at lunchtime. One was an American called James Watson, aged twenty-five, who had studied zoology at the university of Chicago before moving to Europe for a period of study. The other, an Englishman called Francis Crick, was thirty-seven years old. He was a physics graduate who had spent the war working on mines for the Admiralty. Both were now working on cell biology. They owed much to the work of other scientists, especially to M. H. F. Watkins, Rosalind Franklin and Erwin Chargaff. But it was Watson and Crick who finally worked out the double-helical structure of deoxyribonucleic acid, or DNA. Hence Crick's famous announcement in the pub – that together they had discovered the secret of life. 'I have never seen Francis Crick in a modest mood,' Watson wrote later.[1]

The science of genetics was grounded in the papers on inheritance in peas by the Austrian monk Gregor Mendel in 1865. Since then, scientists had known that, but not how, the principle of heredity worked. Crick was one of those scientists who see their work as in direct opposition to mysterious or religious interpretations of phenomena. His mission was to explain things in terms of physics and chemistry. DNA is the substance in every living cell, or almost every living cell, which is the repository of hereditary information that determines the characteristics of the organism. Eventually, science would be able to translate the language of the DNA code, to read the signature of each and every organism, thereby seeing that we human beings, no more or less than other living beings in the universe, are the products of our genes.

'How do genes replicate, and how do they carry information?' These were the two questions to which Watson and Crick had provided seemingly irrefutable answers.

The discovery revolutionized the study of biology, and in time it would revolutionize many other studies too, including forensic science. Henceforth, the old-fashioned detective story or whodunit was redundant. Such questions as had exercised the minds of Hercule Poirot or Miss Marple – motive, opportunity for murder, and so forth – were hardly going to bother a scientist who could identify the murderer by the smallest particle of hair or fingernail left on the body of the victim; the tiniest smear of sweat from the palm of the criminal's hand left on the doorknob.

The exact structure of DNA, the Double Helix, was a discovery, but it was in one sense the confirmation of a hunch which the human race had always had. Why else does all old poetry, from the Book of Numbers to the *Iliad* and to the fragments of the Norse Edda, consist of rehearsing the names of supposed ancestors? The hereditary principle was as old as European civilization itself, and probably all other pre-twentieth-century civilizations also. Proust, in one of the later volumes of his great sequence, *The Captive (La Prisonnière)*, notices, as he grows older, how he is coming to resemble all his relations – his mother, his grandmother, his father, and even his reclusive aunt Léonie, who at the beginning of the book sees all life from her bedroom window at Combray, just as the novel itself is coming to us only because the narrator has retreated to his own bizarre bedroom solitude to meditate upon the past.

When we have passed a certain age, the soul of the child that we were and the souls of the dead from which we sprang come and shower upon us their riches and spells, asking to be allowed to contribute to the new emotions which we feel and in which, erasing their former image, we recast them in an original creation. Thus my whole past from my earliest years, and beyond these, the past of my parents and relations, blended with my impure love for Albertine the tender charm of an affection at once filial and maternal. We have to give hospitality, at a certain stage in our lives, to all our relatives who have journeyed so far and gathered round us.[2]

The ideologies which tore the twentieth century apart had been assertions of the will. Fascism, according to Mussolini, had replaced 'the century of the individual', that is the nineteenth century, with 'the collective century, the century of the State'.[3] Hitler would have approved this idea. So would Stalin, and the various exponents of state Bolshevism or Communism who had moved in to take over so many of Hitler's conquered peoples in Eastern Europe. Mao Zedong in China would expound a similarly impersonal and collectivist creed.

Yet in every single country such views flew in the face of the simple experience enunciated by Proust, and eventually demonstrated by Watson and Crick, that we are not cogs in a machine, nor building blocks in a dictatorial state, even if dictators choose to so regard us. We are, more than anything, members of a family. We are the sum of our parents, grandparents, cousins, aunts, uncles, even if we resent or dislike the idea. C. S. Lewis, in his book *Studies in Words*, points out that for the Greeks the word 'philos' meaning friend or beloved also means 'our own'. We love what is our own; it is our own because it is beloved.

It is this, surely, much more than any feelings of superficial snobbery, which underpins the idea of an aristocratic society. Mysteriously, when all the other Continental countries, during the nineteenth century, abandoned the aristocratic principle of government, the British adapted it. Victorian society was enriched by commerce, industry, capitalism. But it always modelled itself on the old Whig agreement of 1689, that the country should be run by landed grandees. Those who enriched themselves, whether in professional or commercial life in the Victorian age, ended up, very often, joining the peerage. Everything was determined by pedigree, adopted or otherwise.

Such a bizarre phenomenon could hardly be expected to survive in the second half of the twentieth century, but strangely enough, in some respects, it did. Only in twenty-first-century Britain did the hereditary peers cease to sit, as of right, in the second parliamentary chamber.

In spite of the state socialism of Attlee's government, the House of Lords went on, the huge bulk of land in Britain continued to be owned by the old landed classes, and the hereditary principle remained intact. Some people suppose that the hereditary principle is limited to the upper class. This is not true, as a visit to any part of Britain would have shown you in the years immediately after the Second World War. The local factory, unless one of the huge conglomerates such as ICI, would almost certainly be called Someone or Another and Sons. Most of the manufacturing base of Britain, until the growth of corporate and conglomerate firms in the 1960s, consisted of family businesses – the brewers, the bakers, the potters, the shoemakers were X and Sons. Most farms were handed down from father to son through the generations, and this continued well into the 1950s and beyond. Even professional firms – banks, law firms, accountants, publishers – tended to be family-run, with one or another of the sons taking over the business when father grew too old or died. The vast majority of the clergy of the Church of England, until the 1950s, were sons of the clergy. Most doctors were doctors' children. The same was true of almost all the shops in any British high street. The hereditary principle was the basic structure of British life, and it was much more fundamental, or durable, than any political system or set of ideologies. It was, in short, what Francis Crick called 'the secret of life'.

Life was austere in the years immediately following the war. Meat continued to be rationed until 1954. Sugar was rationed. There was not much variety in the diet. Housing was scarce. Few people, compared with today, owned a motor car. Television was rare. Foreign holidays were for the few, and severely limited by the amount of currency you were allowed to take out of the country. Luxuries were scarce. But there was a collective sense of relief in Britain that the country had come through the war, and that it had done so, whatever you may think of individual blots on the record such as the bombing of civilians in Germany and Japan, without fundamental moral disgrace. It had also done so with a quite astounding lack of disruption to the basic structure of life. All sorts of things had changed for ever, of course. There was no servant class any more – only the very rich or the very old-fashioned had butlers, and few in the middle class even had maids. Quite different attitudes to sex, marriage, class, politics either had been, or would be, adopted with the new postwar generation. Religion, in its organized forms, was on the verge of near-extinction. A vast change was preparing itself for British society which would only fully become clear in the 1960s.

But politically no fundamental revolution had occurred. Fascism and communism had never been tried. State socialism of the Attlee/Stafford Cripps variety did not wish to intrude upon the basic structure of British life which was that privacy based on the family, and family life based upon privacy. The true monstrousness of the brigand states was that they had barged in upon the sacred hearth of the household gods. Children had been urged to spy upon parents. Casual remarks made at breakfast were repeated at school by zealous children. In the hateful and stupid doctrines of National Socialism the state even had the right to tell you whom you should and should not love or marry.

For the Victorians, family became a nightmare. After the Victorians, it could be seen as a salvation. The rebellions against the family staged by such figures as Samuel Butler in *The Way of All Flesh*, or as Sigmund Freud, had been daring, even liberating, when first proposed. After Hitler and Stalin, the family, however tyrannical, seemed a less unpleasant form of autocracy than the state.

Porius, published in 1951, but begun ten years earlier, is the last great, though by no means the last, production of John Cowper Powys's pen. It made something of a sensation when it was published, though there would be many to echo his remote cousin Rose Macaulay's reaction: 'I found it rather confused and confusing, to say the truth.'[4] It is a huge book, well over 600 closely printed pages in its first published state (the publisher insisted upon heavy cuts) and nigh on 1,000 pages in its fuller version. It is subtitled 'A Romance of the Dark Ages' and it is the story of that transitional period of British history when the Roman Empire was unravelling, the Germanic tribes were preparing to take over not merely Europe, but Britain, and when King Arthur stands alone to hold the pass against their incursion. Even if one did not know that the book was begun at the time of Dunkirk, or thereabouts, the historical parallels between the time written and the time written about would be obvious. But the book is in no sense an allegory about the Second World

War. It is, rather, a huge, albeit flawed, masterpiece about the British past, about the actual physical being of the island, its rocks, mountains, forests, animals; it is about its peoples – Pictish, Celtic, Romano-British and others. It is about religion and the part it plays both in the individual consciousness of people, and in their collective self-awareness. And it is, which makes it so timely a book, about what happens when civilizations go through huge changes; what survives, and what is disrupted, when empires fall and when whole peoples lose or change their faiths. In a period when Bonhoeffer's religionless Christianity had failed to materialize – most people had simply become religionless, and the flourishing forms of Christianity seemed to be the fundamentalism of Billy Graham and of Pope Pius XII (who in 1950 declared infallibly that the Virgin Mary had ascended bodily into the sky like her Son) – these matters were timely; just as they were before, during and after the last tragic upsurge of Germanic tribal power; as they were when many in Britain felt their old ways of life being changed and threatened by the future. All these thoughts and preoccupations hover beneath the strange surface of *Porius*, which is also, like all Powys's books, deeply concerned with the part played in human lives by sex.

Though often associated with Nietzsche (Powys went to Germany to meet the philosopher's villainous sister), John Cowper Powys was really most influenced, philosophically, by the nineteenth-century German philosopher Max Stirner (pseudonym of Johann Kaspar Schmidt). Stirner asserted that in a world of power struggles between classes and nations, the only true reality was the self, the individual ego with all its mysterious consciousness and 'take' on the world. The logical conclusion to be drawn from his work is that of anarchism. Powys is never more Stirnerish than when in *Porius*, he makes Merlin (Myrddin Wylt) have the following conversation with the strange little bisexual pageboy, Neb.

'Listen, child. Do you think obedience is a good thing?'
   'Am I to say the truth?'
   'Of course'.
   And Neb, the son of Digon, boldly shook his impish head. 'No master, I don't. It's what cruel people do to children and animals'.

Neb goes on to ask Merlin what it is which turns a god into a devil. He receives the answer which is really Powys's *Credo*:

'Power, my son. Nobody in the world, nobody beyond the world, can be trusted with power, unless perhaps it be our mother the earth: but I doubt whether even she can. The Golden Age can never come again till governments and rulers and kings and emperors and priests and druids and gods and devils learn to un-make themselves as I did, and leave men and women to themselves! And don't you be deceived, little one, by this new religion [i.e. Christianity's] talk of "love". I tell you wherever there is what they call love there is hatred too and a lust for obedience! What the world wants is more common-sense, more kindness, more indulgence, more leaving people alone. But let them talk! This new Three-in-One with its prisons and its love and its lies will only last two thousand years.'[5]

An Anglophile such as Simone Weil (1909–1943), who died of tuberculosis and starvation in Ashford, Kent, during the war, believed that England had been exceptional among European powers in maintaining 'a centuries-old tradition of liberty guaranteed by the authorities'.[6] When she came to London to work for the Free French she was struck by the fact that in the British constitution the chief power is vested in one who is all but powerless, the monarch. She found connections between this and the fact that Britain maintained traditions of liberty while Germany, Russia, France and other countries who had lost their monarchs had also lost freedom.

If there was any truth in this very spiritual view of the constitutional monarchy, King George VI was a good representative of it. He was slight in figure. He could barely speak without a debilitating stammer. The film footage of him addressing the Fleet and being hardly able to get the words out was thought so damaging that it was not shown to the British public for four decades after his death. He was an edgy, bad-tempered and in many ways weak man, though passionately dutiful, a kind husband and father, and a devout Christian. He was also like so many of his subjects at this date a heavy cigarette-smoker, and it was obvious to his doctors that he was not to have a long life. The 2nd Lord Hardinge of Penshurst, a devoted courtier, revealed very touchingly the habit of mind which sees everything done by royal personages as heroic when he told his son: 'As a result of the stress he was under the King used to stay up too late and smoked too many cigarettes – he literally died for England.'[7] No one else who developed lung cancer as a result of smoking too much could be described as doing so 'for England', but there probably was a sense in which for the King it was true. Everything he did was for England; everything his daughter and heir, Princess Elizabeth, did, and has done, has been 'for England', or as we should say now for Britain and the Commonwealth. The peculiar emblematic existence of the royal family, the iconic role to which their political impotence has assigned them, makes the rhetoric true, for them, and it was certainly true in the 1950s for the huge majority of their subjects. In the reign of George VI this was especially true, since nationalistic feelings, and fear about the possibility of defeat at the hands of the Nazis, had been focused with the scorch of sunbeam through magnified glass on the little family – the King, with his haggard, perpetually worried expression, his unflappable round-faced wife, and the two little girls, one serious, pensive and dutiful, the other sometimes suppressing, sometimes not, the giggles.

The little family alone against the world was a potent image for many Britons who had survived the war, and who now came together to share the austerity years, sometimes in a prefab, sometimes in a not very adequate flat, with rations still making diet meagre, and with all provisions scarce. One of the most brilliant evocations of those times is in Mary Norton's novel for children *The Borrowers*, published in 1952. The Borrowers are little people who survive behind the wainscoting in a large old house. If you have ever wondered why you lose gloves, safety-pins, old corks, handkerchiefs, the answer could be that they have been 'borrowed' by these strange beings, who are the same shape as human beings, and indeed have all the human characteristics except size. The house in the story used to be heavily populated with these Little People – the Harpsichords, who gave themselves airs, the Overmantels, the Sinks, the Rainpipes and the Broom-Cupboard Boys. But that was in the old days. Then, the Human Beans upstairs got a cat. Cousin Eggletina was seen no more. And little by little, the other Borrowers departed for other domiciles, leaving only the Clocks, the very limited Pod and Homily, and their daughter Arrietty. There is even the hint that the Borrowers used to be much bigger, but that by living so limited an existence they have shrunk, and that they might even now have reached the end of the line. Eventually Arrietty has an outburst – 'Oh, I know papa is a wonderful Borrower. I know we've managed to stay when all the others have gone. But what has it done for us in the end? I don't think it's so clever to live alone, for ever and ever, in a great big, half-empty house; under the floor with no one to talk to, no one to play with, nothing to see but dust and passages . . .'[8]

Of course, it is not intended as a piece of political allegory, though the ingenious way in which Pod and Homily 'make do' with the cast-offs of the Human Beans surely does reflect the resourcefulness of British families during the austerity years, and the terrible moment at the end when Mrs Driver, the cook, rips up the floor and gets the rat-catcher to smoke the Borrowers out owes much to the British experience of losing houses and possessions through aerial bombardment. Many readers in 1952, however, the year of the book's publication and of King George VI's death, must have seen some parallel between Arrietty, last of her strange race and guardian of the Borrowers' future, and the figure of Princess Elizabeth. George VI and Queen Elizabeth, partly at the government's insistence, had kept their daughters as virtual prisoners in Windsor Castle during the war. Much of the time the princesses were underground, like the Borrowers, for fear of kidnap or death by enemy bombs, though later in the war Princess Elizabeth served in the ATS. Pod had even disapproved of a female taking over his role as chief Borrower. 'The way I look at it,' said Homily, 'and it's only now it's come to me: if you had a son, you'd take him borrowing, now wouldn't you? Well, you haven't got no son – only Arrietty.' Then Pod accedes to his wife's demands. 'As she followed her father down the passage Arrietty's heart began to beat faster. Now the moment had come at last when she found it almost too much to bear. She felt light and trembly, and hollow with excitement.'[9]

By the closing months of 1951, the king was visibly weakening. Princess Elizabeth, aged twenty-five, was taking on more and more public roles. In October she and her husband Prince Philip went to Washington and stayed in the White House as the guests of President Truman. While they were there, the Labour government was defeated back home in a general election, so Truman was able to break the glad tidings to the princess: 'Honey, your father's been re-elected.' He meant Churchill.

'When I was a boy,' Truman said later, 'I read about a fairy princess, and there she is.'[10]

They returned to an England with the first Conservative government since 1929. Elizabeth and Philip agreed to go to Kenya after Christmas, to stay at a farm which had been given to the couple by the colonial government as a wedding present – Sagana Lodge. There was a royal family Christmas at Sandringham. Though the king, aged fifty-six, had recently been operated upon, he did not know what his doctors knew. He spoke of reorganizing the estate, and there was some shooting. At the end of January he came back to London with Philip and Elizabeth, and the family went together to see *South Pacific*, the new Rodgers and Hammerstein musical at the Theatre Royal, Drury Lane. The next day, looking like death, he went to the airport to wave his daughter goodbye, and returned to Sandringham.

The pheasant shooting season was now over, so that the last day of his life was spent shooting hare. It was 5 February, a 'Keepers' Day', the sort of occasion which he preferred to grand shooting parties. The twenty guns included policemen, estate tenants and gamekeepers. The King caught a hare at top speed, killing it instantly and painlessly. Before going back to the house he stared at the row of furry corpses which he and his friends had dispatched. He went to bed at 10.30 that night, and was still awake at midnight, for a watchman in the garden saw him fiddling with the window catch in his room. When his valet, James MacDonald, carried in his morning cup of tea at 7.30 am, he found him dead.[11]

His daughter Elizabeth had, at the moment he died, climbed a tree near Sagana Lodge to reach a lookout point over the jungle. The sun was rising, as they looked down at the baboons. Over their heads, an eagle soared, as if from nowhere, and hovered for a while before flapping off into the sky.[12]

Those close to the Queen have suggested that beneath the stiffness and reserve there lurks a well of humour. She is, we are told, a brilliant mimic. 'After all the guests had left, the door would shut. Then the eyes would brighten and the face light up – flashing with feline humour at the expense of those who had just paid her court.'[13] If this is true, it is hard to find it a very attractive combination. If extreme reserve and quietness are combined with ebullient humour in a public figure, one would surely hope that the smiles and japes, at least occasionally, might come out in public.

The truth is that the Queen is, was, and probably always ever shall be a completely mysterious character. The closest and most vivid portrait of her is contained in *The Little Princesses* by Marion Crawford. 'Crawfie', as she was known to the children, was engaged as the governess to Elizabeth and Margaret just before the elder child's seventh birthday. She remained with them fourteen years, until 1947, just before Princess Elizabeth married Philip Mountbatten, a remote cousin. In 1950, Crawfie asked her former charges' permission to publish an account of their childhood. Queen Elizabeth – that is, the wife of King George VI – was even sent proofs of *The Little Princesses*, and no objection appears to have been raised. But when serialization of the book began in the American *Ladies' Home Journal*, the reaction from the royal household was intense. Stronger expressions of disapproval could hardly have been expressed at some serious breach of state security, or at a piece of deliberate blasphemy. Perhaps in the eyes of the royal family *The Little Princesses* was both. It is written in an extraordinarily mawkish style, saturated with reverence and love for the king and queen and for both their daughters. Yet, like the artful blabbing of a child to strangers about the strange home life of its parents, it is much more revealing than many of the later treatments by grown-ups of the life and personality of Queen Elizabeth II.

Marion Crawford's charges, known as Lilibet and Margaret Rose, are instantly recognizable portraits. Aged ten, Lilibet is self-contained, obsessively neat – at one point Crawfie found the little girl getting up in the middle of the night to tidy her shoes – and with a piety and sense of duty which would not have been out of place in a medieval or seventeenth-century monarch. When George V died, for example, Margaret Rose, too young to know what was happening, remained absorbed in her toys, but Lilibet looked up from grooming one of her toy horses and asked: 'Oh Crawfie, ought we to play?'[14] Aged ten, 'If I am ever Queen,' said Lilibet firmly, 'I shall make a law that there must be no riding on Sundays. Horses should have a rest too. And I shan't let anyone dock their pony's tail.'[15] The royal family probably resented Crawfie's intolerable breach of manners in writing the book at all, and for letting slip such facts as that Margaret had tantrums and Lilibet bit her nails. But throughout the wondrous childhood related by Crawfie there is not a single instance of the child allowing her guard to drop. She is always royal. Typical is the scene during the war when the little princesses are immured in Windsor Castle and there is an air raid. Crawfie runs to the nurseries and calls for Alah, the princesses' nurse. The Governor of the Castle and the various officials have all rushed down to the air-raid shelter, where in terrible anxiety they await their royal highnesses. But all that Lilibet will say through her bedroom door is: 'We're dressing, Crawfie. We must dress.'[16] Louis Quatorze would have approved.

No wonder the book published in 1950 was an instant success. Poor Crawfie was banished from royal favour for having written it, but as the nation prepared itself for the coronation, *The Little Princesses* was an invaluable and authentic glimpse into the personality of the new sovereign.

Rose Macaulay in her subsequently published *Letters* protested to friends and family at the excesses of royal-worship at the time of the king's death and, some eighteen months later, his daughter's coronation. She described February 1952 as 'this present desert of royal funerals, royal accession proclamations, lauding of the late monarch and the new one, mournful valedictory music and words on the radio, official assumption that all other interests are in abeyance. Most people are now very tired of it; out of no disrespect to the good king dead or the new queen enthroned, for there is a great feeling for both, but the feeling is inflated and blown up of out proportion by our publicists.'[17] She describes how, during the two minutes' silence for the King's funeral, two absent-minded people continued to walk down Fleet Street, and were pursued by 'the mob . . . shouting "Throw him under a bus!" "Put him in the Thames" . . .' This robust Victorian liberal, daughter of Lord Macaulay's nephew, saw that 'royalty has a hypnotising effect on our nation',[18] and was relieved to be abroad for the coronation ceremony itself.

Few people in the British Commonwealth were able to take so detached or so sophisticated an attitude. For those, now an ageing breed, who recollect it, the coronation is their first experience of television. Those few who owned television sets could invite their friends and neighbours to gather round the wood-encased, flickering grey cathode ray tube to witness the mystery, the shy, smiling woman in her coronet, riding in a state coach to the abbey through driving rain and cheering crowds, her Ruritanian prince in cocked hat and golden epaulettes seated beside her; the royal family awaiting her – the Queen Mother and Princess Margaret in coronets, little Prince Charles in court dress. The television showed, too, the peerage, en masse, living embodiments of the Watson and Crick demonstration that genes are all. Perhaps some of their ermine was a little moth-eaten, their coronets a little tarnished, but there they all were, after a half-century of democracy, still possessed of their titles, their voting rights in the Second Chamber, and many of them still among the richest in the land. The young Duke of Devonshire, though all but bankrupted by death duties, was still the heir to one of the greatest estates in England. Together with Lord Wilton, thirty-two, he chartered a launch to glide down the Thames that night. 'It's mainly to give the children a chance to see the fireworks,' the duchess, formerly the Hon. Deborah Mitford, told reporters. Television viewers, too, could see the bishops of the Church in their copes, escorting the young monarch to her throne. In her right hand was placed the sceptre and cross, ensign of power and justice; in her left, the rod with the dove, a sign that equity and mercy would temper that power. She was anointed with the oil of chrism on her head and on her chest by the former headmaster of Repton, Dr Geoffrey Fisher, archbishop of Canterbury, a crossword fanatic and firm disciplinarian who, while headmaster, had caned the schoolboy Michael Ramsey, who now stood beside the throne as bishop of Durham. British life, in other words, in all its old-fashioned oddity, was much as it had always been. And here came the crowned heads of other lands, driving through the rain in their landaus – the big, jolly, laughing queen of Tonga, and opposite her the diminutive sultan of Johore. (Who was that? 'Her lunch,' replied Noël Coward.) And here is the Prime Minister, Sir Winston Churchill, dressed as Warden of the Cinque Ports, stiff with gold braid, and golden buttons, and medals and old glory, his smiling Clementine, tiara'd and bejewelled, beside him, in the mantle and collar of the GBE.

'Have you your camera with you to-day?' asked the London *Evening Standard*. 'Then catch the mood of Gay London and enter your snapshot in the *Evening Standard*'s Gay London contest.'[19] They simply meant that London was a jolly place that day: they were not asking for photographs of particularly attractive guardsmen or police officers.

Coronation Day gave the British, and the Empire, a chance to relive VE and VJ Day. The atmosphere was 'Look, we have come through!'

They had conquered the brigand states, they had conquered the poverty and wretchedness of the 1920s and 1930s, they could afford to be self-congratulatory and optimistic. All their patriotic joy could be focused on the young woman who, with such dignity and grace, gave herself up to these arcane and centuries-old rituals. After the coronation, and before the fireworks, the Home Service of the BBC broadcast Jennifer Vyvyan (soprano), accompanied by the BBC Symphony Orchestra conducted by Sir Malcolm Sargent, singing 'Land of Hope and Glory'. Much had happened in the years since Dame Clara Butt first sang the song in public in the Royal Opera House in 1902 at the time of Edward VII's (delayed) coronation. In those days, it still made sense to believe that the bounds of the Empire would be set 'wider still and wider'. Now, with India gone, the Middle East in turmoil, and Africa merely waiting for independence, the imperial pomp of the British seemed merely unrealistic.

We began this book in the snows of the Himalayas, with Younghusband's invasion of Tibet. Since early spring 1953, forty-two-year-old Colonel John Hunt had been leading a team of British and New Zealand mountaineers, together with Nepalese Sherpas, with the aim of climbing Everest. On Coronation Day, at 8 am, a New Zealander called Edmund Hillary and a Sherpa named Tenzing, with their oxygen supplies running low, reached the peak of the highest mountain in the world and placed there a tiny Union Jack.[20] The mountaineering feat was described in military language as a 'conquest', though the British were not on this occasion taking possession of the mountain, nor had they met any resistance, except from the elements.

The *Evening Standard* probably represented quite widely and seriously held opinion when it said:

Let the mind travel far from the Coronation route to the snow of Everest. There, on this day of Elizabeth's crowning, the Union Jack flies proud, defiant and challenging on a place where no man has been before.

Is this achievement the product of an Empire that has seen its finest hour and can look forward only to increasing decrepitude and senility? Or is it an omen designed to show that with the Crowning of Elizabeth a new age begins? An age in which if they only have the courage and faith to seize it, there can be for the British people in the years to come greater glory and greater power than they have ever known before?

Much significance was read by the newspaper into the fact that the man who planted the flag was a New Zealander 'working and fighting in partnership and fellowship with other men of the Empire'. (The *Standard* was still a Beaverbrook newspaper.) 'Does not the lesson of Everest stand out clear that while collectively and acting in unity the men of the Empire can conquer everything, singly they can conquer nothing?'

Such sentiments, when read today, can produce smiles of nostalgia or derision depending upon temperament. They were written in an intelligent newspaper and in 1953 they were believed by the great majority of British people. Vestiges of the creed, imaginatively adapted, survive in Queen Elizabeth II's unswerving belief in the British Commonwealth of nations. Her coronation service was in part a splendid piece of religio-patriotic pageantry to celebrate great things which deserved celebration: peace, freedom, prosperity. In part, however, it can now be seen as a consoling piece of theatre, designed to disguise from themselves the fact that the British had indeed, as Dean Acheson so accurately remarked nearly a decade later, lost an empire and failed to find a role.

Notes

1 Oedipus Rex, Oedipus Kaiser

1   Sigmund Freud, p. 202.
2   ibid., p. 203.
3   *Dearest Mama*, ed. Roger Fulford, p. 30.
4   ibid., p. 55.
5   His collar bore the legend, 'I belong to the King', Hibbert, p. 231.
6   Edel (ed.) (1984), p. 184.
7   ibid., p. 181.
8   ibid.
9   Both quoted Hibbert, p. 299.
10 Thomas A. Kohut, 'Kaiser Wilhelm II and his parents', in Rohl & Sombart, pp. 70–1.
11 Pakula, pp. 362–3.
12 Kohut, 'Kaiser Wilhelm II and his parents'.
13 Lamar Cecil, 'History as family chronicle', in Rohl & Sombart, p. 106.
14 ibid., p. 105.
15 *Manchester Guardian*, 6 January 1896, Reinermann (2001), p. 165.
16 ibid., p. 188.
17 *Daily Chronicle*, 20 November 1899, Reinermann, p. 191.
18 *Daily Telegraph*, 5 February 1901.
19 St Aubyn, p. 344.
20 Topham, p. 141.
21 Van der Kiste, p. 127.
22 *Daily Mail*, 5 February 1901.
23 Van der Kiste, p 127.
24 Ensor, p. 377.
25 Steed, p. 283.
26 Fortescue, p. 369.
27 St Aubyn, p. 325.
28 ibid., p. 354.
29 ibid., p. 359.
30 Lee, vol. II, p. 676.
31 Hibbert, p. 219.

2 Rupees and Virgins

1 *Encyclopaedia Britannica*, 13th edn (1926), 'Sir Hiram Stevens Maxim'.
2 ibid., 'Machine-Gun'.
3 Morris, p. 134.
4 Patrick French, p. 221.
5 ibid., p. 224.
6 Younghusband Collection. Oriental and India Office, Mss. Eur F/197/80.
7 Verrier, p. 146.
8 Alastair Lamb, Introduction to Younghusband (1985), p.v.
9 OIOC, Younghusband Collection, Mss. Eur F/197/80.
10 Verrier, p. 199.
11 ibid.
12 Younghusband Collection, Mss. Eur F/197/80.
13 Patrick French, p. 242.
14 Carrington, p. 235.
15 ibid., p. 240.
16 Kipling (2002), p. 257.
17 *Bombay Gazette*, 10 December 1904.
18 Nicolson, p. 59.
19 Gilmour, p. 118.
20 OIOC Mss. Eur F 306/12.
21 Brown & Louis, p. 7.
22 Dilks (1970), vol. I, p. 177.
23 ibid., I, p. 170.
24 Ronald Hyam, 'The British Empire in the Edwardian Era', Brown & Louis, p. 50.
25 Symonds, p. 37.
26 Kipling (2002), p. 239.
27 Nanda, p. 43.
28 ibid., p. 67.
29 Hansard Parliamentary Debates, House of Lords, 5th series, vol. I, col. 132.
30 'The Killing Fields', *New Statesman*, 26 January 2004, p. 18.
31 Owen, p. vii.
32 Wells, p. 268.

3 The Land

1 Jaeger, p. 118.
2 Marsh, p. 195.
3 Michael Kennedy, p. 172.

4 Moore (1984), p. 84.
5 Michael Kennedy, p. 172.
6 Newsome (1980), p. 105.
7 Marsh, p. 71.
8 Christopher Taylor (1975), p. 161.
9 Ridley, p. 143.
10 Brown (1982), pp. 26–7.
11 Ridley, p. 57.
12 Brown (1996), pp. 26–5.
13 Galsworthy, p. 51.
14 ibid., p. 52.
15 Darwin, p. 35.
16 Marsh, p. 83.
17 Camplin, p. 30.
18 ibid., p. 30.
19 Horn, p. 217.
20 ibid., p. 224.
21 Camplin, p. 253.
22 *Encyclopaedia Britannica*, 15th edn, vol. 19, 'Macropaedia', p. 573.
23 MacNeil, pp. 210–12.
23 ibid., p. 212.
24 ibid., p. 367.
25 ibid., p. 361.
26 ibid., p. 131.
27 Statistics in *Encyclopaedia Britannica*, 15th edn, vol. 19, 'Macropaedia', p. 577.
28 Robert Blake, p. 282.
29 ibid., p. 283.
30 A. N. Wilson (2002), p. 586.
31 Crook (1997), p. 239.

4 The Accursed Power

1 Butler & Freeman, p. 122.
2 Jenkins (1964), pp. 179–80.
3 Ensor, p. 390.
4 McCarthy, pp. 102–3.
5 ibid., p. 103.
6 Camplin p. 61.
7 McCarthy, p. 109.
8 *OED*.
9 Ensor, p. 375.

10 Donald Read (ed.) p. 59.
11 Camplin, p. 74.
12 Randolph S. Churchill, vol. II, pp. 89–90.
13 Money, p. 39.
14 Donald Read (ed.), p. 16.
15 Randolph S. Churchill, vol. II, p. 31.
16 ibid., p. 113.
17 Belloc (1991), p. 115.
18 *DNB* (1922–1930), p. 298.
19 Eustace et al., p. 61.
20 Webb (1971), p. 353.
21 Webb (1983), p. 57 (5 November 1906).
22 ibid., p. 27 (1 March 1906).
23 ibid.
24 ibid., p. 39 (15 July 1906).
25 ibid., p. 40.
26 ibid., p. 122 ('Early August').
27 ibid., p. 163.
28 ibid., p. 81.
29 Carey, p. 125.

5 Love in the Suburbs

1 Jenkins (2001), p. 8.
2 Aronson, p. 213.
3 Webb (1984), p. 54.
4 ibid., p. 402.
5 Maddox, p. 95.
6 ibid., p. 113.
7 D. H. Lawrence (1981), p. 217.
8 Corke, p. 41.
9 Arnold Bennett, p. 321.
10 Ridley.
11 ibid., p. 120.
12 ibid., p. 168.
13 ibid., p. 247.
14 Filson Young, p. 211.
15 Hesketh Pearson, p. 124.
16 Cullen (1977), p. 140.
17 ibid., p. 59.
18 ibid., p. 218.
19 ibid., p. 132.
20 ibid., p. 221.

6 God – and the Americans

1   Anson, p. 282.
2   Falkner, p. 393.
3   Vidler, p. 49.
4   Loisy, vol. I, p. 41.
5   ibid., p. 72.
6   Carpenter, p. 102.
7   ibid., p. 124.
8   Kenner, p. 5.
9   William James, pp. 506–7.
10 Edel (1972), pp. 373–4.
11 Chesterton, p. 53.
12 Stewart, pp. 107–8.
13 Edel (1972), p. 539.

7 Nationalisms

1   *The Annual Register*, p. 137.
2   ibid.
3   Morgan (1981), p. 183. Morgan (1966), pp. 28–30.
4   Grigg (1978), p. 51.
5   ibid., p. 35.
6   Morgan (1966), p. 25.
7   Morgan (1981), p. 5.
8   ibid., p. 184.
9   Lord Robert Cecil's preface to Ormsby-Gore, p. 10.
10 The Rev. John Owen, quoted Ballinger, p. 61.
11 ibid., p. 15.
12 D. H. Lawrence (1930), pp. 190, 184.
13 Hyam, p. 87.
14 Powell (1995), p. 6.
15 ibid.
16 *British Medical Journal* 1907, p. 1412.
17 Hyam, p. 76.
18 ibid.
19 Quoted Hamilton (2004), p. 5.
20 ibid, p. 87.
21 Geoffrey Alderman, 'The Anti-Jewish Riots of August 1911 in South Wales', *The Welsh History Review*, vol. 6, December 1971, no. 2, p. 191.
22 ibid., p. 197.
23 Garrard, p. 213.
24 Norman Rose, p. 47.

25   ibid., p. 50.
26   Litvinoff (ed.), p. 55.
27   Isaiah Berlin, quoted Halpern, p. 9.
28   Norman Rose, p. 102.
29   ibid., p. 137.
30   ibid., p. 144.
31   Litvinoff (ed.), p. 11.
32   ibid., p. 17.
33   ibid., p. 19.
34   ibid., p. 20.
35   Noam Chomsky, *Guardian*, 11 May 2002.
36   Kee, p. 182 and *passim*.
37   ibid., p. 191.
38   ibid., p. 219.
39   Foster (1989), p. 471.
40   Kee, p. 195.
41   Dudgeon, p. 180.
42   ibid., p. 153.
43   ibid., p. 416.
44   ibid., p. 448.
45   Doerries, p. 20.
46   Kee, p. 271.
47   Foster (1989), p. 483. Kee, p. 274, has 64 rebels killed during the week's fighting, 220 civilians, and 600 Crown forces wounded. 134 Crown forces were killed or died of wounds.
48   From 'Easter 1916', Yeats, p. 180.
49   Kee, p. 4, and for much of the above, pp. 1–15.
50   Yeats, p. 182.
51   ibid., p. 7.
52   Dudgeon, p. 12.
53   ibid., p. 614.
54   ibid, p. 491.
55   ibid., p. 18.

8 Shipwreck
1   Behrmann, p. 82.
2   Kenneth Rose, p. 321.
3   ibid., p. 226.
4   ibid.
5   Pope-Hennessy, p. 100.
6   ibid.
7   Boyd Carpenter Papers, BL Add. 46722, f 70.

8   Topham, p. 237.

9   Pope-Hennessy, p. 80.

10 Ensor, p. 422.

11 *The Annual Register*, 1909, p. 168.

12 Jenkins (1954), p. 74.

13 Spengler, vol. II, p. 464.

14 Cannadine (1990), p. 308.

15 ibid., p. 316.

16 Belloc (1991), p. 219.

17 Robert Rhodes James (1978), pp. 270–2.

18 Cannadine, p. 334.

19 Ensor, pp. 440–3.

20 Rumbelow, p. 41.

21 ibid., p. 75.

22 *The Annual Register*, 1911, p. 3.

23 Randolph S. Churchill, vol. II, p. 85.

24 ibid., p. 410.

25 ibid., p. 355.

26 For developments of this theme see Howells (1999); Biel (1996); Heyer (1995).

27 Walter Lord, p. 73.

28 Howells, p. 141.

29 Lord, p. 13.

30 Howells, p. 92.

31 ibid., p. 121.

32 ibid., p. 150.

33 Biel (1990), p. 108.

34 ibid., p. 99.

35 ibid., pp. 41–78.

36 ibid., p. 69.

37 ibid., p. 133.

38 ibid., pp. 136–7.

39 *Encyclopaedia Britannica* (1911), vol. XXIV, p. 885.

40 Biel (1990), p. 134.

41 Heyer, p. 162.

9 An Asiatic Power

1   Kenneth Rose, p. 133.

2   ibid., p. 163.

3   Pope-Hennessy, p. 448.

4   ibid., p. 101.

5   Kenneth Rose, p. 136.

6   Smith, p. 777.
7   ibid.
8   ibid., p. 122.
9   Brown & Louis, p. 122.
10 Smith, p. 778.
11 Brown & Louis, p. 428.
12 Shaw & Shaw, vol. II, p. 262.
13 ibid., p. 273.
14 ibid., p. 316.
15 Lang, p. 289.
16 A. J. P. Taylor (1965), p. 25.
17 Winston S. Churchill (1938), vol. I, pp. 101, 136.
18 Jastrow, p. 97.
19 ibid., p. 84.
20 ibid., p. 120.
21 Hansard, 4th Series, vol. CXX, p. 1371.
22 13 July 1912, P2724 f193.
23 The article is filed with 'Political and Secret Papers' in the India
    Office Records, so evidently the Foreign Office did not expect peace-
    time *Telegraph* readers to notice foreign news.
24 Hansard, 5th series, vol. LXIV, p. 118.
25 Jastrow, p. 89.
26 ibid., pp. 114–15.
27 Sir Llewellyn Woodward (1967), p. 65.
28 Moorehead, p. 71.
29 ibid., p. 362.
30 ibid., p. 151.
31 Winston S. Churchill (1938), vol. III, p. 845.
32 Robert Rhodes James (1965), p. 348.
33 Raymond (1922), p. 179.
34 Michael Hastings, p. 210.
35 ibid., p. 39.
36 Moorehead, p. 112.
37 Lawrence James (1990), p. 269.
38 Lawrence James (1993), p. 154.
39 ibid., p. 169.
40 T. E. Lawrence (1964), p. 97.
41 Lawrence James (1990), p. 141.
42 ibid., p. 154.
43 T. E. Lawrence (1935), p. 76.
44 Lawrence James (1964), p. 162.
45 T. E. Lawrence (1935), p. 434.

46 ibid., p. 436.
47 Kenner, p. 301.

10 Barbarous Kings

1 Lawrence James (2001), p. 401.
2 Clark (1961), p. 11.
3 Callwell, I, p. 102.
4 ibid., p. 95.
5 ibid., p. 159.
6 Mann, p. 291.
7 Woodward (1967), p. 7.
8 Strachan, p. 11.
9 ibid., p. 15.
10 Mann, p. 295.
11 Bülow's *Memoirs*, quoted ibid., p. 295.
12 Clark (1961), p. 17.
13 Alastair Horne pointed out the statistics. He is quoted in Gilbert (1994), p. 123.
14 A. J. P. Taylor (1965) p. 12.
15 Gilbert (1994), p. 117.
16 ibid., p. 118.
17 Kenneth Rose, p. 317.
18 Cork, p. 17.
19 ibid., p. 21.
20 ibid., pp. 467–87.
21 Massie, p. 125.
22 Cork, p. 251.
23 Lawrence James (2001), p. 407.
24 Charles Taylor, p. 130.
25 Gilbert (1994), p. 265.
26 Howard, p. 79.
27 Massie, p. 530.
28 Gilbert (1994), p. 300.
29 Cork, p. 100.
30 ibid.
31 Pound (1916), p. 21.
32 Kenner, p. 202.
33 Ezra Pound, 'Lament of the Frontier Guard', *Personae*, p. 136.
34 Guy Davenport, quoted Kenner, p. 249.

11 Revolutions

1 Seton-Watson, pp. 723–7.

2   Edmund Wilson, p. 462.
3   Hitler (2001), p. 13. The author presented a handsome leather-bound copy of this work to his old teacher; Dr Pötsch presented it to a monastery library.
4   Monk (1990), p. 33.
5   See, for example, Anthony Quinton, *From Wodehouse to Wittgenstein*, which questions the influence of the early (*Tractatus*) Wittgenstein on the Vienna Circle and the logical positivists; and which doubts the intelligibility or coherence of the later (*Philosophical Investigations*) Wittgenstein's explorations into analytical or linguistic philosophy.
6   Russell (1967), p. 56.
7   ibid., p. 36.
8   Monk (1990), pp. 39, 47.
9   ibid., p. 56.
10 Russell (1967), p. 148.
11 ibid., p. 19.
12 ibid., p. 80.
13 Monk (1996), p. 528.
14 Monk (2002), p. 459.
15 Russell (1967), p. 18.
16 ibid., p. 99.
17 Kragh, p. 93, and Heilbron (ed.) (2003), *passim*.
18 French (ed.) (1979), p. 6.

12 Chief
1   Pound & Harmsworth, p. 407.
2   BL Add. MS 62201 f. 133.
3   A. P. Ryan, p. 11.
4   Tom Clarke, p. 51.
5   BL Add. MS 62201 f. 81.
6   ibid., f. 98.
7   A. P. Ryan, p. 145.
8   BL Add. MS 62201 f. 89.
9   Tom Clarke, p. 105.
10 S. J. Taylor, p. 178.
11 A. P. Ryan, p. 21.
12 S. J. Taylor, p. 30.
13 Tom Clarke, p. 100.
14 BL Dept. 3890. *Northcliffe Papers*, vol. 49, 19 May 1909.
15 Tom Clarke, p. 65.
16 Pound & Harmsworth, p. 253.

17   ibid., p. 257.
18   Clifford, p. 228.
19   ibid., p. 229.
20   ibid., p. 279.
21   Tom Clarke, p. 74.
22   ibid., p. 79.
23   A. J. P. Taylor (1965), p. 69.
24   A. J. P. Taylor (1972), p. 71.
25   ibid., p. 81.
26   ibid., p. 109.
27   ibid., p. 101.
28   ibid., p. 99.
29   Tom Clarke, p. 102.
30   Pound & Harmsworth, p. 479.
31   Both views quoted Margaret MacMillan, p. 14.
32   Gilbert (1994), p. 303.
33   Woodward (1967), p. 241.
34   Gilbert (1994), p. 318.
35   David R. Woodward, 'Trial By Friendship: Anglo-American Relations, 1917–18', p. 20, quoted Grigg (2002), p. 73.
36   Pound & Harmsworth, p. 531.
37   The phrase is that of *The Times* Washington correspondent.
38   Arthur Willert, quoted Pound & Harmsworth, p. 532.
39   Grigg (2002), p. 124.
40   S. J. Taylor, p. 184.
41   Pound & Harmsworth, p. 540.
42   BL Add. MS 62164, f. 85.
43   ibid., f. 96.
44   ibid., f.106.
45   Grigg (2002), p. 256.
46   Tom Clarke, p. 117.
47   ibid., p. 25.
48   S. J. Taylor, p. 219.
49   ibid., p. 218.

13 Peace

1   Brittain, p. 186.
2   Grigg (2002), p. 640.
3   A. J. P. Taylor (1965), p. 97.
4   Margaret MacMillan, p. 388.
5   Robert Skidelsky, *New Statesman*, 26 January 2004, p. 20.

6   Margaret MacMillan, p. 2 and *passim*, for all the information on the previous two pages.

7   Edel (1972), p. 508.

8   Henry James (1987), pp. 582–3.

9   Henry James (1999), p. 497.

10   Gilbert (1994), p. 522.

11   Rohan Butler, 'The Peace Settlement of Versailles', in *The New Cambridge Modern History*, vol. XII, p. 445.

12   ibid., p. 465.

13   Gordon, p. 20.

14   Richard Ellmann, 'Thomas Stearns Eliot', entry in *Dictionary of National Biography 1961–1970*.

15   Betjeman (1960), p. 30.

16   Gordon, p. 43.

17   ibid., p. 55.

18   ibid., p. 67.

19   ibid., p. 68.

14 Protons – Massacres – Bombs. Ireland and Iraq

1   Heilbron (ed.), p. 703.

2   Francis Robinson, 'The British Empire and the Muslim World', in Brown & Louis, p. 406.

3   ibid., p. 408.

4   Porter, p. 484.

5   All the above in Draper.

6   ibid., p. 216.

7   Deirdre McMahon, 'Ireland and the Empire-Commonwealth 1900–1948', in Brown & Louis, p. 146.

8   Richard Bennett, p. 57.

9   Calwell, vol. II, p. 281.

10   Jeffrey (1984), p. 82.

11   Richard Bennett, p. 190.

12   Wilson to Arnold Robertson, 30 March 1921, in Jeffrey (ed.) (1985), p. 250.

13   Glubb (1959), p. 124.

14   Lawrence James (1990), p. 377.

15   W. H. Gallaher to Miss Marcelene Fisher, 2 August 1920, in Sir A. T. Wilson Papers. BL Add. MS 52459A, f. 113.

16   Hoepli, p. 121.

17   Sir A. T. Wilson Papers. BL Add. MS 52455A-B, f. 100.

18   Omissi, p. 160.

19 Martin Gilbert, *Winston S. Churchill*, vol. IV, p. 557.
20 Budiansky, p. 141.
21 Liddell Hart (1932), p. 147.
22 Martin Gilbert, vol. IV, p. 481.
23 ibid., p. 802.
24 ibid., p. 805.
25 ibid., p. 810.
26 J. A. Chamier, 'The Use of Air Force for Replacing Military Garrisons', *Journal of the Royal United Service Institution*, 66, 1921, pp. 205–16.
27 Budiansky, p. 147.
28 ibid., p. 143.
29 Martin Gilbert, vol. IV, p. 812.
30 ibid., p. 817.

15 Communists and Fascism – The Allure of Violence

1   Isabel Hull, p. 266.
2   Rohl, p. 207.
3   Victoria Louise, p. 127.
4   Rohl, p. 213.
5   Heinrich Mann, p. 146.
6   Anne Applebaum, 'Why the Red Flagged', *The Daily Telegraph*, 28 June 2003, p. 4.
7   Brogan, p. 154.
8   ibid., p. 164.
9   ibid., p. 173.
10 ibid., p. 176.
11 ibid., p. 188.
12 Welch, p. 86.
13 Figes, p. 640.
14 ibid., pp. 641–2.
15 ibid., p. 81.
16 Robert Rhodes James (1998), p. 60.
17 Van der Kiste, p. 199.
18 ibid., p. 203.
19 ibid.
20 Royal Archives GV o 2570/37, quoted Robert Rhodes James (1998), p. 50.
21 Kenneth Rose, p. 238.
22 ibid., p. 239.
23 Belloc (1928), p. 164.

24   Gilbert (1989), pp. 456–7.
25   Collier, p. 92, from which all the examples are cited.

16 The Silly Generation – From Oswald Spengler to Noël Coward
 1   Coward, p. 47.
 2   John Montgomery, pp. 279–81 (with a few additions of my own).
 3   ibid., p. 105.
 4   ibid., p. 111.
 5   Coward, p. 129.
 6   John Montgomery, p. 22.
 7   ibid., p. 281.
 8   Letter from Logan Pearsall Smith to Lytton Strachey, 1 December 1928, BL Strachey Papers Add. MS 60699 f. 30.
 9   Acton, p. 112.
10   Green, p. 115.
11   Acton, p. 113.
12   Sitwell, p. 201.
13   Horne, p. 31.
14   John Pearson, p. 19.
15   Powell (1978), p. 165.
16   Glendinning, p. 9.
17   Acton, p. 76.
18   Glendinning, p. 81.
19   Lesley, p. 88.
20   ibid., p. 94.
21   Coward, p. 99.
22   ibid., p. 108.

17 The Means of Grace and the Hope of Glory
 1   A. J. P. Taylor (1965), p. 73.
 2   A. J. P. Taylor (1972), p. 167.
 3   ibid., p. 252.
 4   ibid., p. 198.
 5   Gilmour, p. 583.
 6   Alan Clark (1998), p. 23.
 7   Gilmour, p. 464. It was of this popular novelist, author of *Three Weeks, Halcyone* (*sic*) and other sensationalist tales, that they spoke the lines: 'Would you like to sin with Elinor Glyn on a tiger skin? Or would you prefer to err with her on some other fur?'
 8   A. J. P. Taylor (1965), p. 205.
 9   Muggeridge (1940), p. 47.
10   Wedgwood, p. 238.

11   Lloyd, vol. II, p. 117.
12   ibid., p. 131.
13   ibid., p. 115.
14   Cole, p. 164.
15   A. N. Wilson (2002), p. 508.
16   A. J. P. Taylor (1965), p. 238.
17   Skidelsky, p. 344.
18   ibid., p. 351.
19   A. J. P. Taylor (1965), p. 239.
20   ibid., p. 245.
21   Jenkins (2001), p. 409.
22   A. J. P. Taylor (1965), p. 248.
23   Kenneth Rose, p. 343.
24   Cole, p. 193.
25   A. N. Wilson (1984), p. 296.

18 The Secrets of a Woman's Heart – Marie Stopes, Radclyffe Hall

1   Grigg (1980), p. 97, my source for the next two pages until note 2.
2   Rowbotham, p. 61.
3   Hall, p. 307.
4   ibid., p. 12.
5   Stopes Papers, BL Add. MS 59848.
6   Ruth Hall, *Observer Magazine*, 15 July 1973.
7   Stopes Papers, BL Add. MS 59848 f. 11.
8   ibid., 58483, f. 49.
9   June Rose, p. 141.
10   ibid., p. 115.
11   John Montgomery, p. 162.
12   *Good Housekeeping*, March 1924.
13   McKibbin, p. 314.
14   ibid., p. 314.
15   Rowbotham, p. 43.
16   Galton, p. 43.
17   Hall, p. 302.
18   Rowbotham, p. 25.
19   ibid., p. 48.
20   ibid., p. 43.
21   Stopes Papers, BL Add. MS 58638 f. 37.
22   Hansard, Parliamentary Debates, Fifth series, vol. XC, 804.
23   ibid, 826.
24   Inge, p. 72.
25   Hansard, Fifth Series, vol. XV, 818.

26 Baker, p. 233.
27 Hall, p. 285.
28 Master, p. 168.

19 For the Benefit of Empire

1 John Montgomery, p. 117.
2 Kenneth Rose, p. 393.
3 Posters in British Library collection.
4 John Montgomery, p. 119, Kenneth Rose, p. 392.
5 John Montgomery, pp. 118–19.
6 *The Story of the Building of the Greatest Stadium in the World*, Sir Robert McAlpine and Sons, 1923.
7 Craig, pp. 35–6, quoting Nietzsche, 'On the Utility and Disadvantage of History for Life' ('Vom Nutzen und Nachteil der Historie für das Leben'), the second of his *Untimely Meditations (Unzeitgemässe Betrachtungen)*.
8 British Empire Exhibition 1925. Opening Ceremony by HM the King accompanied by HM the Queen, Wembley, 9 May 1925.
9 John W. Chell, 'Colonial Rule', in Brown & Louis, pp. 233–43.
10 *Spectator*, 26 April 1924.
11 John M. Mackenzie, p. 111.
12 John M. Mackenzie, 'The Popular Culture of Empire in Britain', in Brown & Louis, p. 216.
13 Judith Brown (2003), p. 117.
14 Muggeridge (1940), p. 95.
15 ibid.

20 The ABC of Economics

1 Eliot, p. 46.
2 Pound (1953), p. 71.
3 A. N. Wilson (1984), p. 295.
4 *DNB (1922–1930)*, p. 604.
5 Micklethwait & Wooldridge, p. 84.
6 ibid., pp. 165–6.
7 ibid., p. 81.
8 Cole, p. 231.
9 ibid., p. 229.
10 ibid., p. 235.
11 Skidelsky, p. 268.
12 ibid., p. 357.
13 ibid., p. 359.

21 Puzzles and Pastoral

1 *The Times*, 18 January 1934.
2 Woods & Bishop, pp. 243ff.
3 Dawson had two phases of editorship, from 1912 to 1919 and then again from 1923, after the Astor purchase, until 1941.
4 *The Times*, 31 July 1970.
5 Millington, p. 19.
6 ibid., p. 21.
7 ibid.
8 ibid., p. 61.
9 *The Times,* 1 March 1934.
10 ibid., 15 August 1934.
11 ibid., 17 August 1934.
12 ibid., 21 August 1934.
13 Fitzgerald, p. 201.
14 ibid., p. 202.
15 ibid., p. 192.
16 Waugh (1959), p. 189.
17 ibid., p. 224.
18 Christopher Hollis to the author.
19 Knox & Lunn, p. 130.
20 ibid., p. 220.
21 Fitzgerald, p. 214.
22 Christie (1934), p. 112.
23 Symons, p. 122.
24 Auden, p. 158, 'The Guilty Vicarage'.
25 Rahn (ed.), p. 29.
26 Christie (1938), p. 220.
27 Auden, p. 151.
28 Jenkins & Spalding, p. 37.
29 Betjeman (1979), p. 162.

22 Two Thousand Whispered Voices

1 Iremonger, p. 379.
2 ibid., p. 525.
3 ibid., p. 378.
4 Hansard, 5th series, vol. 218, p. 1267.
5 ibid., p. 1107.
6 ibid., p. 1212.
7 ibid., p. 1210.
8 ibid., p. 1201.
9 Lloyd, vol. I, p. 393.

10   ibid., p. 402.

11   ibid., p. 394.

12   *The Times* obituary of 14 December 1974 is particularly unfair to Maufe.

13   Bethge, p. 209.

14   Dom Philip Jebb, OSB, Monk of Downside, to the author.

15   Wykeham-George & Mathew, p. 72.

16   Valentine, p. 48.

17   Private information. *The Mind and Heart of Love* was d'Arcy's most celebrated book.

18   Adrian Hastings, p. 265.

19   Blythe, p. 134; Cullen (1975), *passim*.

23 Politics

1   *DNB (1931–1940)*, p. 822.

2   Cole, p. 20.

3   ibid., pp. 234–5.

4   Oswald Mosley, p. 237.

5   ibid., p. 241.

6   *New Statesman*, 27 October 1961.

7   Webb (1985), p. 217.

8   ibid., p. 240.

9   Nicholas Mosley, p. 191.

10   Webb (1985), p. 240.

11   ibid., p. 244.

12   Harold Nicolson (1966), p. 83.

13   ibid., p. 91.

14   Hicks, p. 225.

15   Galbraith, p. 89.

16   Hoover, vol. II, p. 209.

17   Tindall, p. 1052.

18   Zinn, p. 382.

19   Cabinet Papers (Public Record Office), Minutes and Memoranda of the Committee on Preparations for the League of Nations Disarmament Conference 1931–2.

20   Barnett, p. 297.

21   McKibbin, p. 113.

22   Orwell, *The Road to Wigan Pier* (Complete Works, vol. Five), p. 62.

23   ibid., p. 165. One of the more absurd things about Chesterton's literary beeriness was that it was an affectation limited to the page. When the truly beery Henry Slesser, a judge who lived in the Thames Valley, initiated something called the Fraternity of St Ambularis

devoted to 'fresh air, blue skies and wayside inns', he and his friends enlisted Chesterton from nearby Beaconsfield. G.K. was compelled to do penance when he was discovered to prefer cocoa to beer (Pople, p. 193).

24 Orwell, vol. Five, p. 215.
25 Diana Mosley in conversation with the author.

24 The Abdication

1 Annual Register 1936, p. 7.
2 ibid., pp. 179 and 27.
3 Burleigh, p. 294.
4 Saklatvala, p. 480.
5 His mother's brother J. N. Tata owned the largest commercial empire in India – see Squires, p. 1.
6 ibid., p. 91.
7 ibid., p. 205.
8 Saklatvala, p. 481.
9 Muggeridge (1940), p. 75.
10 Lycett, p. 585.
11 Betjeman (1979), p. 110.
12 F. Watson, 'The Death of George V', History Today (December 1986), p. 28.
13 Kenneth Rose, pp. 401–2.
14 ibid., p. 403.
15 Donaldson, p. 69.
16 Channon, p. 89 (3 December 1936).
17 Donaldson, p. 40.
18 Harold Nicolson, p. 244.
19 Channon, p. 33.
20 ibid., p. 71.
21 Donaldson, p. 106.
22 ibid., p. 139.
23 Hansard, Parliamentary Debates, Fifth Series, Column XC, p. 1014, 28 February 1934.
24 Harrod Papers, BL Add. MS 71186 f. 61, letter dated 8 October 1957.
25 Channon, p. 106, 6 August 1936.
26 Harold Nicolson (1966), p. 273.
27 Reck-Malleczewen, p. 36.
28 ibid., p. 34.
29 ibid.
30 Klemperer, 9 November 1935, p. 133.
31 Donaldson, p. 197.

32 Reck-Malleczewen, p. 204.
33 The Duchess of Windsor, p. 261.
34 Colefax Papers, Bodleian MS Eng C. 3272.
35 ibid.
36 Lockhart, pp. 405–6. Archbishops of Canterbury sign themselves 'Cantuar'.
37 Donaldson, p. 295.
38 Pope-Hennessy, p. 578.
39 Muggeridge (1981), pp. 155–6.

25 The European Crisis
1   Thomas, p. xx.
2   ibid.
3   ibid., p. 847.
4   Reck–Malleczewen, p. 55.
5   V. M. Berzhkov, *At Stalin's Side*, New York, 1994, pp. 7, 72, 117, quoted Overy (2005), pp. 635ff.
6   Harvey, p. 534.
7   All the details come from Gellately.
8   Thomas, p. 9.
9   Jackson, p. 60.
10 Quoted Barber, p. 112.
11 Thomas, p. 982.
12 ibid., p. 983.
13 Keene, p. 121.
14 ibid., p. 102.
15 Snowman, p. 85.
16 A. J. P. Taylor (1965), p. 420.
17 Snowman, p. 59.
18 Gellately, pp. 123–9.
19 Harvey, p. 515.
20 Grundy, p. 72 and *passim*.
21 Told to the author by John Buxton, who was present.
22 Kershaw (1998), p. 60.
23 Skidelsky, p. 564.
24 Harold Nicolson (1966), p. 359.
25 ibid., p. 130.
26 Kershaw (1998), p. 117.
27 Harold Nicolson (1966), p. 371.
28 Kershaw (2000), p. 123.
29 Macleod, p. 268.
30 Skidelsky, p. 576.

31   Macleod, p. 270.
32   Simon, p. 63.
33   ibid., p. 64.
34   Roberts, p. 306.
35   Stephenson, p. 81.
36   Simon, p. 67.
37   ibid., p. 72.
38   Johnson, p. 94.
39   Waugh (1979), p. 449.
40   Roberts, p. 308.
41   Harvey, p. 742.
42   Jenkins (2001), p. 419.

26 The Special Relationship I

1   All biographical and other information derives from the website www.laurel-and-hardy.com.
2   Stafford, p. xvi.
3   Benjamin Welles, p. 278.
4   ibid., p. 243.
5   Herzstein, p. 228.
6   Sumner Welles, p. 61.
7   Benjamin Welles, p. 245.
8   ibid., p. 245.
9   Sumner Welles, p. 73.
10   ibid., p. 88.
11   Hitler (2001), p. 597.
12   Fest, p. 607.
13   Bethge, p. 531.
14   Shirer (1970), p. 150.
15   ibid., p. 70.
16   ibid., p. 92.
17   Black, p. 490.
18   ibid., p. 492.
19   Herzstein, p. 259.
20   ibid., p. 260.
21   ibid., p. 224.
22   ibid., p. 269.
23   ibid., p. 224.
24   Abbott, pp. 172–3.
25   Black, p. 589.

27 Churchill in 1940

1   Berlin, p. 29.
2   ibid., p. 39.
3   Moran, p. 244.
4   Hansard, 5th Series, vol. 363, cols. 51–61.
5   Moran, p. 170.
6   Jenkins (2001), p. 268.
7   Fussell (1989), p. 255.
8   ibid., p. 102.
9   ibid.
10 Lockhart, vol. II, p. 130.
11 Moran, p. 614.
12 Berlin, p. 32.
13 ibid., p. 12.
14 Moran, p. 351.
15 ibid., p. 352.
16 ibid., p. 397.

28 From the Battle of Britain to Pearl Harbor

1   Robert O'Neill, 'Churchill, Japan and British security in the Pacific, 1904–1942' in Blake & Louis, p. 278.
2   Hitler (1958), p. 23.
3   ibid., p. 12.
4   ibid., p. 14.
5   Wright, p. 104.
6   ibid., p. 107.
7   Blaxland, p. 387.
8   H. V. Jones, 'Sir Robert Alexander Watson-Watt', in *DNB 1971–1980*.
9   'Alone in Britain', written by Laurence Thompson, *The World at War*, Episode 4. *The World at War* was a 26-episode televised history of the Second World War, broadcast 1973–4 by Thames Television.
10 Wright, p. 268.
11 E. B. Haslam, 'Hugh Dowding', *DNB 1961–1970*.
12 Private information.
13 Wright, p. 5.
14 A. D. Harvey, p. 741.
15 Moran, p. 835.
16 Hitler (1958), p. 24.
17 Gilbert (1989), p. 746.
18 Harvey, p. 738. The quote is from John Colville, *The Fringes of Power*, p. 131.

19 Gilbert, *Winston S. Churchill*, vol. VI, p. 588.
20 A. J. P. Taylor (1965), p. 507.
21 *The World at War*, Episode 4. (See note 9 above.)
22 Fussell (1989), p. 131.
23 Alan Clark (1998), p. 206.

29 Bombers and the Bombed

1 *Daily Telegraph*, Tuesday 13 July 2004, p. 7.
2 Budiansky, p. 147.
3 The Nietzsche quote is cited by Robin Niellands, p. 72.
4 A. J. P. Taylor (1965), p. 364.
5 Max Hastings (1979), p. 346.
6 Longmate, p. 254.
7 Told to author by one of the men present.
8 A. J. P. Taylor (1965), p. 454.
9 Kurowski, p. 8.
10 PRO Prime Minister 3/89, quoted Kurowski, p. 17.
11 Longmate, p. 72.
12 Richie, p. 495.
13 Longmate, p. 4.
14 ibid., p. 84.
15 Probert, p. 221.
16 ibid.
17 ibid., p. 254.
18 ibid., p. 257.
19 ibid., p. 185.
20 Richie, p. 533.
21 'Whirlwind', written by Charles Douglas-Home. *World at War*, Episode 10.
22 Bowen, chapter 5, p. 86.
23 'Alone in Britain', written by Lawrence Thompson, *The World at War*.
24 *The Times*, 1870, A. N. Wilson (2002), p. 345.
25 Richie, p. 534.
26 'Whirlwind', see note 21 above.
27 Reck-Malleczewen, p. 269.
28 'Whirlwind'.
29 ibid.
30 Reck-Malleczewen, p. 225.
31 *Moral Issues and the Bomber War*, p. 399.

30 In the Broadcast

1   Kenny, p. 243.
2   ibid., p. 109.
3   McKibbin, p. 468.
4   Kenny, p. 153.
5   Overy (2000), pp. 12–14.
6   Kenny, p. 153.
7   ibid., p. 154.
8   Carpenter, p. 568.
9   ibid., p. 585.
10 Torrey, p. 162.
11 McCrum, p. 211.
12 Muggeridge (1973), p. 235.
13 McCrum, p. 308.
14 Muggeridge (1973), p. 230.
15 Hickman, p. 31.
16 ibid., p. 21.
17 Briggs, p. 205.
18 Gilbert, vol. VI, *Finest Hour*, p. 664.
19 Winston Churchill (1989), p. 216.
20 Briggs, p. 68.
21 Hickman, p. 39.
22 ibid., p. 47.
23 Briggs, p. 215.
24 Hickman, p. 88.
25 ibid., p. 90.

31 The Special Relationship II

1   Renehan, p. 44.
2   Warren F. Kimball, 'Wheel Within a Wheel: Churchill, Roosevelt and the Special Relationship' in Blake & Louis, p. 291.
3   ibid., p. 292.
4   Larres, p. 190.
5   Charmley (1993), p. 215.
6   Moran, p. 792.
7   Biographical details from Harold Hartley's entry in *DNB 1951–1960*.
8   Conant, p. 191.
9   ibid., p. 194.
10 Harvey, p. 583.
11 Jenkins (2001), p. 27.

12 ibid., p. 417.
13 Harvey, pp. 566–7.
14 Skidelsky, p. 617.
15 Kimball (1969), p. 104.
16 Skidelsky, p. 620.
17 ibid., p. 628.
18 ibid., p. 696.
19 Charmley (1995), p. 121.
20 His name was Major Desmond Morton, quoted in Stafford, pp. 238–9.
21 Toughill, p. 149.
22 ibid., p. 169.
23 Sainsbury, p. 171.
24 ibid., p. 283.
25 ibid., p. 226.
26 See Härtle, p. 290 and *passim*.

32 Prisoners

1 Snowman, p. 109.
2 ibid., p. 107.
3 Levi, p. 171.
4 *Persecuted Women in Britain Today*, The 18B Publicity Council, 1941.
5 Gilbert, vol. VI, *Finest Hour*, p. 664.
6 Gilbert (1989), p. 274.
7 See such heartrending accounts as Roy Whitecross, *Slaves of the Son of Heaven*, or Reginald Burton, *Railway of Hell*.
8 Gellately, p. 52.
9 Berben, p. 7.
10 ibid., p. 19.
11 ibid., p. 195.
12 Marcuse, p. 45.
13 Hickman, p. 191.
14 Fest, p. 712.
15 Bethge, p. 777.
16 ibid., p. 831.
17 Reck-Malleczewen, p. 193.
18 Trevor-Roper (1950), p. 35.
19 Fest, p. 732.
20 ibid., p. 748.
21 Applebaum, p. 416.
22 Halévy, p. 252.

33 If God Wearied of Mankind

1   Moran, pp. 673, 675.
2   Conant, p. 135.
3   Cornwell, p. 26.
4   Ronald W. Clark, p. 37.
5   ibid., p. 43.
6   ibid., p. 51.
7   ibid., p. 94.
8   Rhodes, p. 275.
9   Ronald W. Clark, p. 31.
10 Black, p. 539.
11 Ronald W. Clark, p. 179.
12 Rhodes, p. 539.
13 ibid., p. 557.
14 Moran, p. 301.
15 Rhodes, p. 676.
16 Barton J. Bernstein, 'Roosevelt, Truman and the Atomic Bomb', *Political Science Quarterly*, vol. 90, Issue 1, Spring 1975, pp. 23–69.
17 Most of the information for this part of the chapter is derived from Gar Alperovitz, *The Decision to Use the Atomic Bomb*.
18 Gilbert (1989), p. 715.
19 ibid., p. 696.
20 Alperovitz, p. 663.
21 Rhodes, p. 647.
22 ibid., p. 642.
23 ibid., p. 691.
24 ibid., p. 701.
25 ibid., p. 724.
26 Luke 9: 29.
27 Rhodes, p. 724.
28 ibid., p. 743.

34 Retributions

1   Kenner, p. 420.
2   Pound (1964), Canto I, p. 7.
3   Farrell, p. 474.
4   Pound (1964), Canto LXXIV, p. 451.
5   Torrey, pp. 76–85.
6   Sauter, p. 101.
7   Pound (1964), Canto LXXIX, p. 521.
8   David Maxwell-Fyfe, one of the prosecutors, reviewing the case

against holding the trial in a preface to R. W. Cooper, *The Nuremberg Trial.*

9   Cooper, p. 203.
10 Moran, p. 190.
11 Cooper, p. 28.
12 Pound (1964), Canto LXXX, p. 549.
13 Harold Nicolson (1967), p. 465.
14 Winston Churchill (1989), pp. 270–71.
15 Attlee, *The Granada Historical Records Interview*, Granada, 1967, p. 27.
16 Soames, p. 382.
17 ibid., p. 391.
18 Muggeridge (1981), p. 244.

35 The End of the British Empire – India and Palestine

1   Judith M. Brown (2003), p. 175.
2   Das, p. 25.
3   Moran, p. 395.
4   Smith, p. 619.
5   Das, p. 63.
6   ibid., p. 28.
7   ibid., p. 29.
8   Captain Bob Shaw, Royal Navy (Mountbatten's contemporary at Osborne), to the author.
9   Massinberd, p. 147.
10 ibid., p. 148.
11 Judith M. Brown (2003), p. 171.
12 Das, p. 184.
13 Lawrence James (1994), p. 554.
14 The Truman Diaries are in the Truman Library, Independence, Mo. I am quoting from the *New York Times*, 14 July 2003, which had extensive treatment of the recently discovered diary entry.
15 Hennessy, p. 241.
16 Quoted *New York Times*, 14 July 2003.
17 ibid.
18 Hennessy, p. 239.
19 ibid.
20 Dalton, 20 February 1951, p. 508.
21 Together with the problems of Zimbabwe, Northern Ireland, Egypt, Iraq, etc., etc.
22 Fischer, p. 624.

23   ibid., p. 625.
24   ibid., p. 19.
25   ibid., p. 22.

36 Widmerpool's Britain

1   Nock (1966), p. 248.
2   Wragg, p. 113.
3   Nock (1966), p. 218.
4   Hennessy, p. 77.
5   Sampson, p. 225.
6   A. N. Wilson (2002), p. 281.
7   Timmins, p. 87.
8   Gosden, p. 256.
9   Gilbert, Companion vol. II, Pt 2, p. 914.
10 Kevin Theakston, 'Winston Churchill and the British Constitution', in Blake & Louis, p. 54.
11 ibid., p. 55.
12 Gilbert (1983–6), vol. VI, p. 62.
13 Davenport, p. 161.
14 Rt Hon Barbara Castle, television interview, BBC 1, 28 September 1989.
15 Harling, p. 165.
16 Powell (1971), p. 141.
17 Lewis, p. 232.
18 Harold Macmillan, p. 65.
19 Michael Foot (1973), vol. II, p. 134.
20 Timmins, p. 103.
21 Michael Foot (1973), vol. II, p. 132.
22 Timmins, p. 160.
23 Macaulay (1950), p. 252.
24 Hennessy, p. 340.
25 Powell (1968), chapter 2.

37 The Hereditary Principle

1   Watson, p. 19. *The Times* obituary of Francis Crick, 30 July 2004, p. 38.
2   Proust, vol. III, p. 564.
3   Mussolini, 'Political and Social Doctrine', quoted Zeev Sternhell, 'Fascist ideology', in Laqueur, p. 355.
4   Macaulay (1961), p. 211.
5   Powys (1951), p. 276.
6   'The Need for Roots', in Weil, p. 218.

7   Bradford, p. 449.
8   Norton, p. 46.
9   ibid., p. 52.
10 Pimlott, p. 172.
11 Bradford, p. 459.
12 Pimlott, p. 175.
13 ibid., p. 580.
14 Crawford, p. 32.
15 ibid., p. 17.
16 ibid., p. 71.
17 Macaulay (1961), p. 266.
18 Macaulay (1962), p. 92.
19 *Evening Standard*, Tuesday 2 June 1953.
20 Hunt, p. 178.

Bibliography

Abbott, Philip, *The Exemplary Presidency*, The University of Massachusetts Press, Amherst, 1990

Acheson, Dean, *Present at the Creation: My Years in the State Department*, New York, Norton, 1969

Acton, Harold, *Memoirs of an Aesthete*, Methuen, 1948

Alderman, Geoffrey, 'The Anti-Jewish Riots of August 1911 in South Wales', *The Welsh History Review*, vol. 6, December 1972, Number 2

Aldington, Richard, *D. H. Lawrence*, Chatto & Windus, 1930

—— *Portrait of a Genius, But . . .*, William Heinemann, 1950

Ali, Tariq, *The Nehrus and the Gandhis. An Indian Dynasty*, Picador, 1985

Allen, Frederick Lewis, *Only Yesterday*, Harper and Brothers, New York, 1931

Allen, Kevin, *Elgar the Cyclist in Worcester and Hereford. A Creative Odyssey*, Aldine Press Ltd, Malvern, 1997

Allfrey, Anthony, *Edward VII and his Jewish Court*, Weidenfeld & Nicolson, 1991

Alperovitz, Gar, *The Decision to Use the Atomic Bomb*, HarperCollins, 1995

Anson, Peter, *Fashions in Church Furnishings*, The Faith Press, 1960

Applebaum, Anne, *Gulag: a history of the Soviet Camps*, Allen Lane, 2003

Armstrong, Anne, *Unconditional Surrender*, Rutgers University Press, New Brunswick, 1961

Aronson, Theo, *The King in Love: Edward VII's Mistresses*, John Murray, 1988

Ashton, J. Norman, *Only Birds and Fools,* Airlife, Shrewsbury, 2000

Auden, W. H., *The Dyer's Hand*, Random House, New York, 1962

Baciu, Nicolas, *Sell-out to Stalin. The Tragic Errors of Churchill and Roosevelt*, Vantage Press, New York, etc., 1984

Baker, Michael, *Our Three Selves. A Life of Radclyffe Hall*, Hamish Hamilton, 1985

Ballinger, C. & J., *The Bible in Wales*, Henry Sotheran & Co., 1906

Barnett, Corelli, *The Collapse of British Power*, Eyre Methuen, 1972

Behrmann, S. N., *Conversations with Max*, Hamish Hamilton, 1960

Belloc, Hilaire, *The Cruise of the Nona*, Constable, 1928

—— *Complete Verse*, Pimlico, 1991

Bennett, Arnold, *The Journals of Arnold Bennett*, Cassell, 1932

Bennett, Daphne, *Vicky: Princess Royal of England and German Empress*, Constable, 1983

Bennett, Richard, *The Black and Tans*, Severn House Publishers, 1976

Berben, Paul, *Dachau 1933–1945. The Official History*, The Norfolk Press, 1975 (Bruxelles, 1968)

Berlin, Isaiah, *Mr Churchill in 1940*, John Murray, 1949

Bernstein, Barton J., 'Roosevelt, Truman, and the Atomic Bomb, 1941–1945: A Reinterpretation', *Political Science Quartely*, Spring 1975, vol. 90, Issue 1, pp. 23–69

Bethge, Eberhard, *Dietrich Bonhoeffer*, Kaiser, München, 1967

Betjeman, John, *Summoned By Bells*, John Murray, 1960

—— *Collected Poems*, John Murray, 1979

Biel, Steven (ed.), *Titanica. The Disaster of the Century in Poetry, Song and Prose*, W. W. Norton, New York, 1990

—— *Down with the Old Canoe. A Cultural History of the Titanic Disaster*, W. W. Norton, New York and London, 1996

Blake, Conrad, *Franklin Delano Roosevelt*, Weidenfeld & Nicolson, 2003

Blake, Robert, *Disraeli*, Eyre and Spottiswoode, 1966

Blake, Robert, & Louis, Wm. Roger, *Churchill*, Oxford University Press, 1993

Blaxland, Gregory, *Destination Dunkirk. The Story of Gort's Army*, William Kimber, 1973

Blumberg, H. M., *Weizmann, His Life and Times*, St Martin's Press, New York, 1975

Blythe, Ronald, *The Age of Illusion: England in the Twenties and Thirties*, Hamish Hamilton, 1963

Bolitho, Henry Hector, *A Penguin in the Eyrie. An R.A.F. Diary*, Hutchinson, 1955

Boulton, James J. (ed.), *The Letters of D. H. Lawrence*, vol. I, September 1901–May 1913, Cambridge University Press, Cambridge, 1979

Bowen, Elizabeth, *The Heat of the Day*, Jonathan Cape, 1949

Bradford, Sarah, *King George VI*, Weidenfeld & Nicolson, 1989

Branson, Noreen, *Britain in the Nineteen Twenties*, Weidenfeld & Nicolson, 1975

Briggs, Asa, *The BBC: The First Fifty Years*, Oxford University Press, Oxford and New York, 1985

Brittain, Vera, *Testament of Youth*, Jonathan Cape, 1933

Brogan, Hugh, *The Life of Arthur Ransome*, Jonathan Cape, 1984

Brooke, Rupert, *The Letters of Rupert Brooke*, ed. Geoffrey Keynes, Faber & Faber, 1968

Brown, Jane, *Gardens of a Golden Afternoon*, Penguin Books, 1982

—— *Lutyens and the Edwardians*, Viking, 1996

Brown, Judith M., *Nehru. A Political Life*, Yale University Press, New Haven and London, 2003

Brown, Judith M., & Louis, William Roger, *The Twentieth Century* (vol. IV of *The Oxford History of the British Empire*), Oxford University Press, Oxford, 1999

Buchan, John, *Prester John*, Thomas Nelson & Sons, 1910

Budiansky, Stephen, *Air Power*, Viking, 2003

Bullock, Alan, *Hitler and Stalin: Parallel Lives*, HarperCollins, 1991

—— *Hitler. A Study in Tyranny*, Odhams Press, 1952

Burmeister, Hans Wilhelm, *Prince Philipp Eulenberg-Hertefeld (1847–1921)*, Franz Steiner Verlag GmbH, Wiesbaden, 1981

Burns, James Macgregor, *Roosevelt: The Lion and the Fox*, Secker & Warburg, 1953

—— *Roosevelt: The Soldier of Freedom*, Harcourt Brace Jovanovich, New York, 1970

Burton, H., 'Annie Kenney' entry in *Dictionary of National Biography, 1951–1960*

Burton, Reginald, *Railway of Hell*, Leo Cooper, Barnsley, 2002

Butler, David, & Freeman, Jennie, *British Political Facts 1900–1960*, Macmillan, 1963

Calvocoressi, Peter, Wint, Guy, & Pritchard, John, *Total War: The Causes and Courses of the Second World War*, Allen Lane, 1972

Callwell, Major-General Sir C. E., *Field Marshal Sir Henry Wilson. His Life and Diaries*, 2 vols, Cassell & Company, 1927

Camplin, Jamie, *The Rise of the Plutocrats. Wealth and Power in Edwardian England*, Constable, 1978

Cannadine, David, *Aspects of Aristocracy*, Yale University Press, New Haven and London, 1994

—— *The Decline and Fall of the British Aristocracy*, Yale University Press, New Haven and London, 1990

Carey, John, *The Intellectuals and the Masses*, Faber & Faber, 1992

Carpenter, Humphrey, *A Serious Character: The Life of Ezra Pound*, Faber, 1988

Carrington, Charles, *Rudyard Kipling, His Life and Work*, Penguin Books in association with Macmillan, 1986

Casement, Roger, *The Crime Against Europe*, introduced by Brendan Clifford, Athol Books, Belfast, 2002

Cathcart, Brian, *The Fly in the Cathedral*, Viking, 2004

Cashman, Sean Dennis, *America, Roosevelt and World War II*, New York University Press, New York, 1989

Cave Brown, Anthony, *Bodyguard of Lies*, Harper & Row, New York, 1975

—— *The Last Hero: Wild Bill Donovan*, New York, Times Books, 1982

—— *The Secret Servant*, Michael Joseph, 1987

Channon, Henry, *Chips: The Diaries of Sir Henry Channon*, ed. Robert Rhodes James, Weidenfeld and Nicolson, 1967

Charmley, John, *Churchill: The End of Glory*, Hodder & Stoughton, 1993

—— *Churchill's Grand Alliance*, Hodder & Stoughton, 1995

Chesterton, G. K., *Heretics*, Bodley Head, 1905

Christie, Agatha, *Murder in Mesopotamia*, Collins, 1936

—— *Murder on the Orient Express*, Collins, 1934

Churchill, Randolph S., *Winston S. Churchill* (2 vols, Heinemann, 1966–7), continued in a further six volumes by Martin Gilbert (Heinemann, 1971–88)

Churchill, Sir Winston, *The Second World War*, vols I–VI, Cassell, 1948–54

—— *The World Crisis 1911–1918*, 4 vols, Odhams Press Ltd, 1938

—— *Blood, Toil, Tears and Sweat: Winston Churchill's famous speeches*, ed. David Cannadine, Cassell, 1989

Clark, Alan, *Suicide of the Empires*, Library of the 20th Century, 1971

—— *The Donkeys*, Hutchinson, 1961

—— *The Tories*, Weidenfeld & Nicolson, 1998

Clark, Ronald W., *The Birth of the Bomb*, Phoenix House, 1961

Clarke, Peter, *Hope and Glory*, Allen Lane, 1996

Clarke, Tom, *My Northcliffe Diary*, Victor Gollancz, 1931

Clayton, G. D., *Britain and the Eastern Question: Missolonghi to Gallipoli*, Lion Library, 1971

Clifford, Colin, *The Asquiths*, John Murray, 2002

Cole, G. D. H., *A History of the Labour Party from 1914*, Routledge & Kegan Paul, 1948

Collier, Richard, *The Rise and Fall of Benito Mussolini*, Collins, 1971

Colville, John, *The Fringes of Power. Downing Street Diaries, 1939–1955*, Hodder & Stoughton, 1985

Conant, Jennet, *Tuxedo Park*, Simon & Schuster, 2003

Coogan, Tim Pat, *De Valera, Long Fellow, Long Shadow*, Hutchinson, 1993

Cooper, R. W., *The Nuremberg Trial*, Penguin, Harmondsworth, 1947

Cork, Richard, *Vorticism and Abstract Art in the First Machine Age*, Gordon Fraser, 1976

Corke, Helen, *D. H. Lawrence. The Croydon Years*, University of Texas Press, Austin, 1965

Cornwell, John, *Hitler's Scientists*, Viking, 2003

Coward, Noël, *The Lyrics*, Methuen, 1965

Craig, Gordon Alexander, *Germany 1866–1945*, Clarendon Press, Oxford, 1978

Crawford, Marion, *The Little Princesses*, Cassell & Co., 1950

Crook, J. Mordaunt, *The Rise of the Nouveaux Riches*, John Murray, 1997

Cullen, Tom, *Crippen. The Mild Murderer*, The Bodley Head, 1977

—— *The Prostitutes' Padre*, Bodley Head, 1975

Dallek, Robert, *Franklin D. Roosevelt and American Foreign Policy, 1932–1945*, New York, Oxford University Press, 1979

Dalton, Hugh, *The Political Diary of Hugh Dalton, 1918–40, 1945–60*, ed. Ben Pimlott, Cape in association with the London School of Economics and Political Science, 1986

Dangerfield, George, *The Strange Death of Liberal England*, Harrison Smith and Robert Haas, New York, 1935, Serif, 1997

Darwin, Bernard, *Fifty Years of Country Life*, Country Life Ltd, 1947

Das, Manmath Nath, *Partition and Independence of India*, Vision Books, New Delhi, 1982

Davenport, Nicholas, *Memoirs of a City Radical*, Weidenfeld & Nicolson, 1974

Davie, Michael, *The Titanic. The Full Story of a Tragedy* [1986], Grafton Books, 1987

Davis, Arthur N., *The Kaiser I Knew*, Hodder, 1918

Dilks, D., *Curzon in India*, 2 vols, Rupert Hart-Davis, 1970

—— (ed.), *The Diaries of Sir Alexander Cadogan 1938–45*, Cassell, 1971

Dodds, E. R., *Missing Persons. An Autobiography*, Clarendon Press, Oxford, 1977

Doerries, Reinhard, *Prelude to the Easter Rising. Sir Roger Casement in Imperial Germany*, Frank Cass, Portland, OR, and London, 2000

Donaldson, Frances, *Edward VIII: The Road to Abdication*, Weidenfeld & Nicolson, 1974

Dönitz, Karl, *Ten Years and Twenty Days*, Weidenfeld & Nicolson, 1959

Draper, Alfred, *Amritsar. The Massacre that Ended the Raj*, Cassell, 1981

Dudgeon, Jeffrey, *Roger Casement. The Black Diaries with a Study of his Background, Sexuality and Irish Political Life*, Balfour Press, Belfast, 2002

Duncan-Jones, A.S., *The Struggle for Religious Freedom in Germany*, Gollancz, 1938

Eaton, John P., & Haas, Charles A., *Titanic Destination Disaster*, Patrick Stephens, Wellingborough, 1987

Edel, Leon, *Henry James: The Master, 1901–1916*, Rupert Hart-Davis, 1972

—— (ed.), *Henry James's Letters*, vol. IV, *1895–1916*, The Belknap Press of Harvard University Press, Cambridge, Massachusetts, 1984

Eliot, T. S., *Collected Poems, 1909–1962*, Faber, 1974

Ensor, R. C. K., *England, 1870–1914*, Oxford at the Clarendon Press, 1936

Eustace, Claire (ed.), Ryan, Joan, & Ugolini, Laura, *A Suffrage Reader. Charting Directions in British Suffrage History*, Leicester University Press, London and New York, 2000

Eve, A. S., *Rutherford*, Cambridge University Press, Cambridge, 1939

Falkner, John Meade, *The Nebuly Coat*, Edward Arnold, 1903

Farcigny-Lucinge, Princess F. de, *Lord Curzon aux Indes*, Ernest Flammarion, Paris, 1906

Farrell, Nicholas, *Mussolini. A New Life*, Weidenfeld & Nicolson, 2003

Feiling, Keith, *The Life of Neville Chamberlain*, Macmillan, 1970

Ferguson, Robert, *The Short, Sharp Life of T. E. Hulme*, Allen Lane/Penguin, 2002

Fest, Joachim, *Hitler, eine Biographie*, Propyläen, Frankfurt, 1974

Figes, Orlando, *A People's Tragedy*, Jonathan Cape, 1996

Findlater, Richard, *Lilian Baylis. The Lady of the Old Vic*, Allen Lane, 1975

Fischer, Louis, *The Life of Mahatma Gandhi*, Jonathan Cape, 1951

Fitzgerald, Penelope, *The Knox Brothers*, Macmillan, 1977

Florence, Arnold, *Queen Victoria at Osborne*, English Heritage, 1987

Foot, M. R. D., *British Foreign Policy since 1898*, Hutchinson's University Library, 1956

Foot, Michael, *Aneurin Bevan*, 2 vols, Davis-Poynter, 1973

—— *H. G. The History of Mr Wells*, Black Swan, 1996 (Doubleday, 1995)

Fortescue, Seymour, *Looking Back*, Longmans Green & Co., 1920

Foster, R. F., *Modern Ireland 1600–1972* [1988], Penguin Books, 1989

—— *W. B. Yeats: A Life. 1. The Apprentice Mage. 1865–1914*, Oxford University Press, Oxford and New York, 1997

Frankland, Noble, *Prince Henry, Duke of Gloucester*, Weidenfeld & Nicolson, 1980

Freidel, Frank, *Roosevelt: A Rendezvous with Destiny*, Little, Brown, Boston, 1990

French, A. P. (ed.), *Einstein. A Centenary Volume*, Heinemann, 1979

French, Patrick, *Younghusband. The Last Great Imperial Adventurer*, HarperCollins, 1994

Freud, Andrea, *Loathsome Jews and Engulfing Women (Wyndham Lewis, Charles Williams and Graham Greene*, New York University Press, 1995

Freud, Sigmund, *The Interpretation of Dreams* [1900], ed. Joyce Crick, Oxford University Press, Oxford, 1999

Fulford, Roger, 'Christabel Pankhurst' entry in *Dictionary of National Biography*, 1951–1960

—— (ed.), *Dearest Mama. Letters between Queen Victoria and the Crown Princess of Prussia, 1861–1864*, Evans Brothers Ltd, 1968

Fussell, Paul, *The Great War and Modern Memory*, Oxford University Press, New York and London, 1975

—— *Wartime*, Oxford University Press, New York, 1989

Galbraith, J. K., *The Great Crash, 1929*, Penguin Books, Harmondsworth, 1961

Galsworthy, John, *The Forsyte Saga* [1922], Heinemann, 1960

Galton, Francis, *Inquiries into Human Faculty and its Development*, Macmillan, London, 1883

Garnett, David, *Great Friends*, Macmillan, 1979

Garrard, John A., *The English and Immigration, 1880–1910*, Oxford University Press, 1971

Gellately, Robert, *Backing Hitler*, Oxford University Press, 2001

Gilbert, Martin, *The First World War*, Weidenfeld & Nicolson, 1994

—— *Winston S. Churchill*, vols VI–VII, Heinemann, 1983–86

—— *The Second World War*, Weidenfeld & Nicolson, 1989

Gilmour, David, *Curzon*, John Murray, 1994

Glendinning, Victoria, *Edith Sitwell. A Unicorn Among Lions*, Weidenfeld & Nicolson, 1981

Glubb, Sir John Bagot, *Britain and the Arabs. A Study of Fifty Years 1908 to 1958*, Hodder & Stoughton, 1959

—— *War in the Desert. An R.A.F. Frontier Campaign*, Hodder & Stoughton, 1960

Goldman, C.S. (and others), *The Empire and the Century*, John Murray, 1905

Gordon, Lyndall, *Eliot's Early Years*, Chatto & Windus, 1979

Gosden, P. H. J. H., *Education in the Second World War*, Methuen, 1976

Green, Martin, *Children of the Sun*, Constable, 1977

Gregory, Alexis, *The Gilded Age. The Super-rich of the Edwardian Era*, Cassell, 1993

Gribbin, John, *Science and the Making of the Modern World*, Heinemann, 1983

Griffiths, Percival, *Modern India*, Ernest Benn Ltd, 1965

Grigg, John, *The Young Lloyd George*, Eyre Methuen, 1973

—— *Lloyd George: The People's Champion, 1901–1911*, Eyre Methuen, 1978

—— *Nancy Astor. Portrait of a Pioneer*, Sidgwick and Jackson, 1980

—— *Lloyd George: From Peace to War 1912–1916*, Methuen, 1985

—— *Lloyd George War Leader*, Allen Lane, 2002

Grundy, Trevor, *Memoir of a Fascist Childhood*, Arrow, 2000

Guderian, Heinz, *Panzer Leader*, Michael Joseph, 1952

Guttsman, W. L. (ed.), *The English Ruling Class*, Weidenfeld & Nicolson, 1969

Halévy, Elie, *The Growth of Philosophic Radicalism*, Faber, 1928

Hall, Radclyffe, *The Well of Loneliness*, Jonathan Cape, 1928

Hall, Ruth, *Marie Stopes. A Biography*, André Deutsch, 1977

Halpern, Ben, *A Clash of Heroes. Brandeis, Weizmann and American Zionism*, Oxford University Press, New York and Oxford, 1987

Hamilton, Jill, *First to Damascus. The Great Ride and Lawrence of Arabia*, Kangaroo Press, East Roseville, NSW

—— *God, Guns and Israel*, Sutton Publishing, 2004

Harling, Philip, *The Modern British State*, Blackwell, 2001

Harré, Horace Romuno (ed.), *Scientific Thought 1900–1960. A Selective Survey*, Clarendon Press, Oxford, 1969

Harriman, W. A., *Special Envoy to Churchill and Stalin, 1941–6*, Random House, New York, 1975

Härtle, Heinrich, *Die Kriegsschuld der Sieger*, Verlag K.W. Schütz, Oldendorf, 1971

Harvey, A. D, *Collision of Empires*, Hambledon, 1992

Hastings, Adrian, *A History of English Christianity 1920–1985*, Collins, 1986

Hastings, Max, *Bomber Command*, Michael Joseph, 1979

—— *Overlord*, Michael Joseph, 1984

Hastings, Michael, *The Handsomest Young Man in England*, Michael Joseph, 1967

Heilbron, J. L., *The Dilemmas of an Upright Man: Max Planck as Spokesman for German Science*, 2nd ed., Harvard University Press, 1999

—— (editor-in-chief), *The Oxford Companion to the History of Modern Science*, Oxford University Press, 2003

Hennessy, Peter, *Never Again*, Jonathan Cape, 1992

Herre, Franz, *Kaiser Wilhelm II: Monarch zwischen den Zeiten*, Kiepenheuer & Witsch, Köln, 1993

Herzstein, Robert Edwin, *Roosevelt and Hitler: Prelude to War*, John Wiley & Sons Inc., New York, etc., 1994

Heyer, Paul, *Titanic Legacy. Disaster as Media Event and Myth*, Praeger, Westport, Connecticut and London, 1995

Hibbert, Christopher, *Edward VII*, Allen Lane, 1976, Penguin, 1982

Hickman, Tom, *What Did You Do in the War, Auntie?*, BBC Books, 1995

Hicks, John Donald, *Republican Ascendancy*, Hamish Hamilton, 1960

Hill, J. R. (ed.), *A New History of Ireland VII. Ireland, 1921–84*, Oxford University Press, Oxford, 2003

Hitler, Adolf, *Mein Kampf* [1925–6], ed. Ralph Manheim, Pimlico, 2001
—— *Hitler's Table Talk 1941–44*, Oxford University Press, 1958

Hodson, H. V., *The Great Divide. Britain-India-Pakistan*, Hutchinson, 1969

Hoepli, Henry U., *England im Nahen Osten*, Verlag von Palm und Enke in Erlangen, 1931

Hoover, Herbert Clark, *The Memoirs of Herbert Hoover*, 2 vols, Hollis & Carter, 1952

Horn, Pamela, *The Changing Countryside*, The Athlone Press and Fairleigh Dickinson University Press, 1984

Horne, Alastair, *Macmillan 1894–1956*, Macmillan, 1987

Howard, Michael, *The First World War*, Oxford University Press, 2002

Howells, Richard, *The Myth of the Titanic*, Macmillan, Basingstoke, 1999

Hull, Cordell, *The Memoirs of Cordell Hull*, Hodder & Stoughton, 1948

Hull, Isabel V., *The Entourage of Kaiser Wilhelm II 1888–1918*, Cambridge University Press, Cambridge, 1982

Hunt, John, *The Ascent of Everest* [1953], Hodder & Stoughton, 1993

Hyam, Ronald, *Empire and Sexuality. The British Experience*, Manchester University Press, 1990

Ickes, Harold L., *The Secret Diary of Harold L. Ickes*, Weidenfeld & Nicolson, 1955

Inge, William Ralph, *Vale*, Longmans, Green, 1934

Iremonger, F. A., *William Temple, Archbishop of Canterbury*, Oxford University Press, 1948

Irish Times, *Eamon de Valera, 1881–1975. The Controversial Giant of Modern Ireland*, The Irish Times Ltd, Dublin, 1976

Irving, David, *Hitler's War*, Hodder and Stoughton, 1977

Jackson, Gabriel, *A Concise History of the Spanish Civil War*, Thames & Hudson, 1974

Jaeger, Gustav, *Dr Jaeger's Essays on Health Culture*, Waterlow & Sons, 1887

James, Henry, *The Complete Notebooks of Henry James*, Oxford University Press, New York, 1987
—— (ed. Philip Horne), *A Life in Letters*, Allen Lane, 1999

James, Lawrence, *Imperial Warrior. The Life and Times of Field Marshal Viscount Allenby, 1861–1936*, Weidenfeld & Nicolson, 1993
—— *The Golden Warrior. The Life and Legend of Lawrence of Arabia*, Weidenfeld & Nicolson, 1990

—— *The Rise and Fall of the British Empire*, Little, Brown, 1994

—— *Warrior Race*, Little, Brown, 2001

James, Robert Rhodes, *Gallipoli*, Batsford, 1965

—— *The British Revolution. British Politics, 1880–1939*, Methuen & Co. Ltd, 1978 (as one-volume paperback, vol. 1 [1976], vol. 2 [1977])

—— *A Spirit Undaunted. The Political Role of George VI*, Little, Brown, 1998

James, William, *The Varieties of Religious Experience*, Longmans, 1902

Jardine, Lisa, *Ingenious Pursuits*, Little Brown, 1999

Jastrow, Morris, *The War and the Bagdad Railway*, J. B. Lippincott & Co., Philadelphia and London, 1918

Jeffrey, Keith, *The British Army and the Crisis of Empire, 1918–1922*, Manchester University Press, Manchester, 1984

Jenkins, David Fraser, & Spalding, Frances, *John Piper in the 1930s*, Merrell, 2003

Jenkins, Roy, *Mr Balfour's Poodle*, William Heinemann Ltd, 1954

—— *Asquith*, Collins, 1964

—— *Churchill*, Macmillan, 2001

Johnson, Derek, *East Anglia at War*, Jarrold, Norwich, 1992

Jones, Thomas, *A Diary with Letters 1931–1950*, Oxford University Press, 1954

Kee, Robert, *Ireland, A History*, Weidenfeld & Nicolson, 1980

Keegan, John, *Six Armies in Normandy*, Jonathan Cape, 1982

—— *The Second World War*, Hutchinson, 1989

Keene, Judith, *Fighting for Franco*, Leicester University Press, 2001

Kennedy, Michael, *Portrait of Elgar*, 2nd edn, Oxford University Press, 1982

Kennedy, Paul, *The Rise and Fall of the Great Powers*, Unwin Hyman, 1988

Kenner, Hugh, *The Pound Era*, Faber & Faber, 1972

Kenny, Mary, *Germany Calling*, New Island, Dublin, 2003

Keppel, Sonia, *Edwardian Daughter*, Hamish Hamilton, 1958

Kershaw, Ian, *Hitler, 1889–1936. Hubris*, Allen Lane, 1998

—— *Hitler, 1936–1945. Nemesis*, Allen Lane, 2000

Kimball, Warren F., *The Most Unsordid Act*, Johns Hopkins Press, Baltimore, 1969.

—— *The Juggler: Franklin Roosevelt as Wartime Statesman*, Princeton University Press, 1991

—— (ed.) *America Unbound. World War II and the Making of a Superpower*, St Martin's Press, New York, 1992

—— *Forged in War: Churchill, Roosevelt and the Second World War*, W. Morrow, New York, 1997

Kipling, Rudyard, *Kim*, Macmillan, 1908

—— *The Complete Verse*, Kyle Cathie Ltd, 2002

Klemperer, Victor, *The Diaries of Victor Klemperer 1933–1945*, Phoenix, 2000

Knox, Ronald, & Lunn, Arnold, *Difficulties*, Eyre & Spottiswoode, 1932

Kragh, Helge, *Quantum Generations. A History of Physics in the Twentieth Century*, Princeton University Press, Princeton, NJ, 1999

Krockow, Christian Graf von, *Kaiser Wilhelm II und seine Zeit*, Siedler, Berlin, 1999

Kurowski, Franz, *Bomben über Dresden*, Tosa, Wien, 2001

Lamb, Andrew, *Jerome Kern in Edwardian London*, printed by the author, Littlehampton, W. Sussex, England, 1981

Lamb, Richard, *The Ghosts of Peace, 1935–1945*, Michael Russell, Salisbury, Wilts., 1987

—— *Churchill as War Leader – Right or Wrong*, Bloomsbury, 1991

Lambton, Anthony, *The Mountbattens*, Constable, 1989

Lang, David Marshall, *Armenia, Cradle of Civilization*, George Allen & Unwin, 1970

Langer, W. L., & Gleason, S. Everett, *The World Crisis and American Foreign Policy*, Royal Institute of International Affairs, 1952–3

Langer, William, *In and Out of the Ivory Tower*, Neale Watson, New York, 1977

Laqueur, Walter (ed.), *Fascism. A Reader's Guide*, Penguin Books, Harmondsworth, 1979

Lash, Joseph P., *Roosevelt and Churchill 1939–41*, Norton, New York, 1976

Lawrence, D. H., *Assorted Articles*, Alfred A. Knopf, New York, 1930

—— *Letters*, vol. 1, ed. James T. Boulton, Cambridge University Press, Cambridge, 1979

—— *Letters*, vol. 2, ed. George J. Zytaruk & James T. Boulton, Cambridge University Press, Cambridge, 1981

Lawrence, T. E., *The Seven Pillars of Wisdom: a Triumph*, Jonathan Cape, 1935

—— *The Letters of T.E. Lawrence* [1938], Spring Books, 1964

—— *The Mint*, Penguin Books, Harmondsworth, 1978

Leahy, William D., *I Was There*, Victor Gollancz, 1950

Leavis, F. R., *D. H. Lawrence, Novelist* [Chatto & Windus, 1955], Penguin, Harmondsworth, 1973

Lee, Sir Sidney, *King Edward VII. A Biography*, 2 vols, Macmillan & Co. Ltd, 1927

Lees-Milne, James, *The Enigmatic Edwardian. The Life of Reginald, 2nd Viscount Esher*, Sidgwick & Jackson, 1986

Lesley, Cole, *The Life of Noel Coward*, Jonathan Cape, 1976 (Penguin, 1978)

Levi, Primo, *Moments of Reprieve*, trans. Ruth Feldman, Summit Books, New York, 1986

Leutze, James (ed.), *The London Observer: The Journal of Raymond E. Lee 1940–41*, Hutchinson, 1972

Lewis, W. H., *Brothers and Friends*, Harper & Row, San Francisco, 1982

Liddell Hart, Basil, *When Britain Goes to War*, Faber, 1932

—— *The Other Side of the Hill, Germany's Generals*, Cassell, 1948
Memoirs, 2 vols, Cassell, 1965

—— *History of the Second World War*, Cassell, 1970

Linklater, André, *An Unhusbanded Life: Charlotte Despard, Suffragette, Socialist and Sinn Feiner*, Hutchinson, 1980

Litvinoff, Barnet, ed., *The Essential Chaim Weizmann*, Weidenfeld & Nicolson, 1982

Lloyd, Roger, *The Church of England in the Twentieth Century*, 2 vols, Longmans, Green, 1946

Lockhart, J. G., *Cosmo Gordon Lang*, Hodder & Stoughton Ltd, 1949

Lockhart, Robert Bruce, *The Diaries of Sir Robert Bruce Lockhart*, 2 vols, Macmillan, 1980

Loiperdinger, Martin, et al., *Führerbilder. Hitler, Mussolini, Roosevelt, Stalin in Fotografie und Film*, Piper, München, 1995

Loisy, Alfred, *Mémoires pour servir à l'histoire réligieuse de notre temps*, E. Nourry, Paris, 1930

Longmate, Norman, *Air Raid*, Arrow Books, 1979

Lord, Walter, *A Night to Remember* [1956], Penguin Books, Harmondsworth, 1978

Lycett, Andrew, *Rudyard Kipling*, Weidenfeld & Nicolson, 1999

Macaulay, Rose, *The World My Wilderness*, Collins, 1950

—— *Letters to a Friend 1950–1952*, Collins, 1961

—— *Last Letters to a Friend*, Collins, 1962

—— *Letters to a Sister*, Collins, 1964

MacKenzie, John M., *Propaganda and Empire: the manipulation of British public opinion, 1880–1960*, Manchester University Press, Manchester, 1984

MacKenzie, Norman & Jean, *The Time Traveller: The Life of H. G. Wells*, Weidenfeld & Nicolson, 1973

Macleod, Iain, *Neville Chamberlain*, Frederick Muller Limited, 1961

Macmillan, Harold, *Tides of Fortune*, Macmillan, 1969

MacMillan, Margaret, *Peacemakers*, John Murray, 2001

Maddox, Brenda, *The Married Man*, Sinclair-Stevenson, 1994

Mann, Golo, *The History of Germany since 1789*, Chatto & Windus, 1968

Mann, Heinrich, *Man of Straw (Der Untertan)*, Hutchinson, 1947

Marcus, Geoffrey, *The Maiden Voyage* [1969], Unwin Paperbacks, 1988

Marcuse, Harold, *Legacies of Dachau*, Cambridge University Press, Cambridge, 2001

Marsh, Jan, *Back to the Land. The Pastoral Impulse in England from 1880 to 1914*, Quartet Books, 1982

Massie, Robert K., *Castles of Steel. Britain, Germany and the Winning of the Great War at Sea*, Jonathan Cape, 2003

Massingberd, Hugh, *Daydream Believer*, Macmillan, 2001

Master, Anthony, *Nancy Astor. A Life*, Weidenfeld & Nicolson, 1981

Matheson, P. E., *The Life of Hastings Rashdall, D.D.*, Oxford University Press, London, 1928

Matson, John, *Dear Osborne*, Hamish Hamilton, 1978

McCarthy, John P., *Hilaire Belloc: Edwardian Radical*, Liberty Press, Indianapolis, 1978

McCormick, T. J., *America's Half Century*, Johns Hopkins University Press, Baltimore, 1989

McKibbin, Ross, *Classes and Cultures, England 1918–1951*, Oxford University Press, Oxford, 1998

McNeil, Ian, *An Encyclopaedia of the History of Technology*, Routledge, 1990

McVeagh, Diana, 'Edward Elgar', in *Twentieth Century English Masters*, The New Grove, Macmillan, 1986

Mehta, V., *Mahatma Gandhi and His Apostles*, Andre Deutsch, 1977

Micklethwait, John, & Wooldridge, Alan, *The Company*, Modern Library, New York, 2003

Miller, Douglas, *You Can't do Business with Hitler*, Hutchinson, 1941
—— *Via Diplomatic Pouch*, Didier, New York, 1945

Millington, Roger, *The Strange World of the Crossword*, M. & J. Hobbs, Walton on Thames, 1974

Money, L. G. Chiozza, *Riches and Poverty*, Methuen, 1905

Monk, Ray, *Ludwig Wittgenstein. The Duty of Genius*, The Free Press, New York, 1990
—— *Bertrand Russell. The Spirit of Solitude*, Jonathan Cape, 1996
—— *Bertrand Russell. The Ghost of Madness*, Jonathan Cape, 2002

Montgomery Hyde, H., *The Quiet Canadian*, Constable, 1962
—— *Baldwin. The Unexpected Prime Minister*, Hart-Davis, MacGibbon, 1973

Montgomery, John, *The Twenties. An Informal Social History*, George Allen & Unwin, 1957

Montgomery of Alamein, *The Memoirs of Field Marshal Montgomery*, Collins, 1960

Moore, Jerrold Worthrop, *Spirit of England. Edward Elgar in his World*, Heinemann, 1984

—— *Edward Elgar. A Creative Life*, Oxford University Press, 1987

Moorehead, Alan, *Gallipoli*, Hamish Hamilton, 1956

Moran, Lord, *Churchill: The Struggle for Survival*, Constable, 1966

Morgan, Kenneth O., *Freedom or Sacrilege*, Church in Wales Publications, 1966

—— *Rebirth of a Nation: Wales, 1880–1980*, Oxford University Press, 1981

Morley, John, 'Carlyle'. *Critical Miscellanies* (1886)

Morris, James (later Jan), *Farewell the Trumpets*, Penguin, Harmondsworth, 1979

Mosley, Nicholas, *Rules of the Game*, Secker & Warburg, 1982

Mosley, Oswald, *My Life*, Nelson, 1968

Mowrer, Edgar Ansel, *This American World*, Faber & Gwyer, 1928

—— *Triumph and Turmoil: A Personal History of our Time*, New York, 1968

Muggeridge, Malcolm, *The Thirties*, Hamish Hamilton, 1940

—— *The Green Stick*, Collins, 1972

—— *The Infernal Grove*, Collins, 1973

—— *Like it Was*, Collins, 1981

Nanda, B. R., *Mahatma Gandhi. A Biography*, Oxford University Press, Delhi, 1989

Newsome, David, *On the Edge of Paradise: A. C. Benson the Diarist*, John Murray, 1980

—— (ed.), *Edwardian Excursions: From the Diaries of A. C. Benson, 1898–1904*, John Murray, 1981

Nicolson, Harold, *Diaries and Letters, 1930–39, 1939–45, 1945–62*, 3 vols, Collins, 1966, 1967, 1968

Nicolson, Nigel, *Mary Curzon*, Weidenfeld & Nicolson, 1977

Niellands, Robin, *The Bomber War. Arthur Harris and the Allied Bomber Offensive*, Oxford, 1986

Nisbet, Robert, *Roosevelt and Stalin: The Failed Courtship*, Regency Gateway, New York, 1988

Nock, O. S., *The Railways of Britain, Past and Present*, B. T. Batsford Ltd, 1949

—— *Steam Railways in Retrospect*, Adam and Charles Black, 1966

Norton, Mary, *The Borrowers*, Puffin, 1992 (1952)

O'Donnell, James P., *The Berlin Blunder*, Dent, 1979

O'Keefe, Paul, *Gaudier-Brzeska. An Absolute Case of Genius*, Allen Lane, Penguin, 2004

Omissi, David E., *Air Power and Colonial Control: The Royal Air Force 1919–1939*, Manchester University Press, 1990

Ormsby Gore, W. G. A., *Welsh Disestablishment and Disendowment*, West Strand Publishing Co. Ltd, 1912

Orwell, George, *The Complete Works of George Orwell*, Secker & Warburg, 1986

Overy, Richard, *The Battle of Britain*, Penguin, 2000

—— *The Dictators*, Allen Lane, 2004

Owen, Roger, *Lord Cromer*, Oxford University Press, Oxford, 2004

Pakula, Hannah, *An Uncommon Woman. The Empress Frederick*, Weidenfeld & Nicolson, 1996

Panter-Downes, Mollie, *At the Pines*, Hamish Hamilton, 1971

Pearson, Hesketh, *Gilbert and Sullivan. A Biography*, Hamish Hamilton, 1935

Pearson, John, *Façades*, Macmillan, 1978

Peel, Robert A. (ed.), *Marie Stopes, Eugenics and The English Birth Control Movement*, published by The Galton Institute, 1997

Philips, C.H., & Wainwright, Mary Doreen (eds), *The Partition of India, Policies and Perspectives 1935–1947*, George Allen & Unwin, 1970

Pimlott, Ben, *The Queen,* HarperCollins, 1996

Pope-Hennessy, James, *Queen Mary 1867–1953,* George Allen & Unwin Ltd, 1959

Pople, Kenneth, *Stanley Spencer: a biography*, Collins, 1991

Porter, Bernard, *Critics of Empire*, Macmillan, 1968

Porter, Roy, *The Greatest Benefit to Mankind. A Medical History of Humanity from Antiquity to the Present*, HarperCollins, 1997

Pound, Ezra, *Gaudier-Brzeska. A Memoir*, Lane, 1916

—— *ABC of Economics*, Norfolk, Connecticut, 1953

—— *The Cantos of Ezra Pound*, Faber & Faber, 1964

Pound, Reginald, & Harmsworth, Geoffrey, *Northcliffe*, Cassell, 1959

Powell, Anthony, *At Lady Molly's*, Heinemann, 1968

—— *Books Do Furnish A Room*, Heinemann, 1971

—— *Messengers of Day*, Heinemann, 1978

—— *Journals, 1982–1986*, Heinemann, 1995

Powys, John Cooper, *Autobiography*, John Lane, The Bodley Head, 1934

—— *Porius* [1951], Village Press, 1974

Prange, Gordon, W., *At Dawn We Slept*, McGraw-Hill, New York, 1981

—— *Pearl Harbor: The Verdict of History*, McGraw-Hill, New York, 1986

Pratten, John D., *Social Stratification in Edwardian England*, Crewe-Alsager College of Higher Education, 1985

Probert, Henry, *Bomber Harris. His Life and Times*, Greenhill Books, London, Stackpole Books, Mechanicsburg, Pennsylvania, 2001

Proust, Marcel, *In Search of Lost Time*, 4 vols, trans. C. K. Scott

Moncrieff and Terence Kilmartin, revised by D. J. Enright, Everyman Library, 2001

Pugh, Martin, *Women and the Women's Movement in Britain 1914–1959*, Macmillan, 1992

—— *The March of Women*, Oxford University Press, Oxford, 2000

Quinton, Anthony, *From Wodehouse to Wittgenstein*, Carcanet, 1998

Rahn, B. J. (ed.), *Ngaio Marsh. The Woman and Her Work*, Scarecrow, 1995

Raymond, Ernest, *Tell England*, Cassell, 1922

—— *The Story of My Days. An Autobiography 1888–1922*, Cassell, 1968

Read, Anthony Fisher David, *The Fall of Berlin*, Hutchinson, 1992

Read, Donald (ed.), *Edwardian England*, Croom Helm, 1982

Reck-Malleczewen, Friedrich Percyval, *Tagebuch eines Verzweifelten*, J. H. W Dietz Nachf., Berlin, 1981 (English translation © Stephen Hill, *Diary of a Man in Despair*, Duckworth, 2000)

Reid, B. L., *The Lives of Roger Casement*, Yale University Press, New Haven and London, 1976

Reinermann, Lothar, *Der Kaiser in England*, Ferdinand Schöningh, Padergorn – München – Wien – Zürich, 2001

Renehan, Edward, *The Kennedys at War*, Doubleday, New York, 2002

Retallack, James, *Germany in the Age of Kaiser Wilhelm II*, Macmillan, 1996, St Martin's Press, NY, 1996

Rhodes, Richard, *The Making of the Atomic Bomb*, Simon & Schuster, New York, 1986

Ribbentrop, Joachim von, *The Ribbentrop Memoirs* (Zwischen und Moskan), English translation Weidenfeld & Nicolson, 1954

Richie, Alexandra, *Faust's Metropolis*, HarperCollins, 1999

Ridley, Jane, *The Architect and His Wife*, Chatto & Windus, 2002

Roberts, Andrew, *The Holy Fox*, Weidenfeld & Nicolson, 1991

Rohl, John C. G., *The Kaiser and His Court*, Cambridge University Press, Cambridge, 1994

Rohl, John C. G., & Sombart, Nicolaus, *Kaiser Wilhelm II. New Interpretations*, Cambridge University Press, Cambridge, 1982

Roosevelt, Elliott, *As He Saw It*, New York, 1946

Rose, June, *Marie Stopes and the Sexual Revolution*, Faber, 1992

Rose, Kenneth, *King George V*, Weidenfeld & Nicolson, 1983

Rose, Norman, *Chaim Weizmann: A Biography*, Weidenfeld & Nicolson, 1986

Rowbotham, Sheila, *A New World for Women. Stella Browne: Socialist Feminist*, Pluto Press, 1977

Rowse, A. L., *All Souls and Appeasement*, Macmillan, 1961

—— *A Man of the Thirties*, Weidenfeld & Nicolson, 1979

Rumbelow, Donald, *The Houndsditch Murders and the Siege of Sidney Street*, W. H. Allen, 1988

Russell, Bertrand, *The Autobiography 1871–1914*, George Allen & Unwin, 1967

—— *The Autobiography of Bertrand Russell*, vol. II, *1914–1944*, George Allen & Unwin, 1968

—— *The Selected Letters of Bertrand Russell*, vol. I, *The Private Years (1884–1914)*, Allen Lane, 1992

Ryan, A. P., *Lord Northcliffe*, Collins, 1953

Ryan, Cornelius, *The Last Battle*, Collins, 1966

Sainsbury, Keith, *The Turning Point*, Oxford University Press, Oxford, 1986

St Aubyn, Giles, *Edward VII Prince & King*, Collins, 1979

Saklatvala, Sehri, *The Fifth Commandment. A Biography of Sharpurji Saklatvala*, Miranda Press, Salford, 1991

Sampson, Anthony, *Anatomy of Britain*, Hodder & Stoughton, 1962

Sauter, Max, *Churchills Schweizer Besuch 1946 und die Zürcher Rede*, Schläpfer, Herisau, 1976

Sebald, W. G., *On the Natural History of Destruction*, Hamish Hamilton, 2003

Seil, William, *Sherlock Holmes and the Titanic Tragedy*, Breese Books, 1996

Seton-Watson, Hugh, *The Russian Empire, 1801–1917*, Oxford at the Clarendon Press, 1967

Shaw, Stanford, J., & Shaw, Ezel Kural, *History of the Ottoman Empire and Modern Turkey*, Cambridge University Press, Cambridge, 1977

Sherwood, Robert E., *The White House Papers of Harry Hopkins, September 1939–May 1945*, 2 vols, Eyre & Spottiswoode, 1948–9

—— *Roosevelt and Hopkins*, Enigma Books, New York, 2001

Shirer, William L., *The Rise and Fall of the Third Reich*, Secker and Warburg, 1960

—— *Berlin Diary*, Sphere, 1970, incorporating *Berlin Diary* (1942) and *End of a Berlin Diary* (1947)

Simon, Ulrich, *Sitting in Judgement, 1913–1963*, SPCK, 1978

Sitwell, Osbert, *Left Hand Right Hand*, Macmillan, 1945

Skidelsky, Robert, *John Maynard Keynes 1883–1946. Economist, Philosopher, Statesman*, Macmillan, 2003

Smith, Vincent, *The Oxford History of India,* ed. Percival Spear, 4th impression, Oxford University Press, Delhi, 1985

Snowman, Daniel, *The Hitler Emigrés*, Chatto & Windus, 2002

Soames, Mary, *Clementine Churchill*, Cassell, 1979

Spengler, Oswald, *The Decline of the West*, 2 vols, Allen & Unwin, 1922

Squires, Michael, & Talbot, Lynn K., *Living at the Edge. A Biography of D. H. Lawrence and Frieda Von Richthofen*, Robert Hale, 2002

Squires, Mike, *Saklatvala: A Political Biography*, Lawrence & Wishart, 1990

Stafford, David, *Roosevelt and Churchill, Men of Secrets*, Little, Brown, 1999

Steed, Henry Wickham, *Through Thirty Years, 1892–1922*, Heinemann, 1924

Stephenson, Colin, *Merrily on High*, Darton, Longman & Todd, 1972

Stevenson, William, *A Man Called Intrepid*, Macmillan, 1976

Stewart, J. I. M., *Eight Modern Writers*, Clarendon Press, Oxford, 1963

Strachan, Hew, *The First World War. A New Illustrated History*, Simon & Schuster, London and New York, 2003

Strachey, Ray, 'Emmeline Pankhurst', entry in *Dictionary of National Biography, 1922–1930*

—— 'Millicent Fawcett', entry in *Dictionary of National Biography, 1951–1960*

Symonds, Richard, *Oxford and Empire. The Last Lost Cause*, Macmillan, 1986

Symons, Julian, *Bloody Murder*, Viking, 1985

Taton, René, *Science in the Twentieth Century*, Thames & Hudson, 1966

Taylor, A. J. P., *English History 1914–1945*, Oxford at the Clarendon Press, 1965

—— *Beaverbrook*, Hamish Hamilton, 1972

Taylor, Charles, *The Life of Admiral Mahan*, John Murray, 1920

Taylor, Christopher, *Fields in the English Landscape*, Dent, 1975

Taylor, Fred (ed.), *The Goebbels Diaries 1939–41*, Secker & Warburg, 1978

Taylor, S. J., *The Great Outsiders. Northcliffe, Rothermere and The Daily Mail*, Weidenfeld & Nicolson, 1996

Tebbel, John, *An American Dynasty: The Story of the McCormicks, Medills and Pattersons*, Doubleday and Co., New York, 1947

The Dictionary of National Biography, Oxford University Press

Thomas, Hugh, *The Spanish Civil War*, Penguin, 2003

Timmins, Nicholas, *The Five Giants*, HarperCollins, 1995

Tindall, George Brown, *America, A Narrative History*, W. W. Norton, New York, 1984

Toland, John, *Adolf Hitler*, Doubleday, New York, 1976

—— *Infamy: Pearl Harbor and Its Aftermath*, Doubleday, New York, 1982

Topham, Anne, *A Distant Thunder: Intimate Recollections of the Kaiser's Court*, New York, New Chapter Press, 1992

Torrey, E. Fuller, *The Roots of Treason*, McGraw-Hill Book Company, New York, etc. 1984

Toughill, Thomas, *A World to Gain*, Cal Cal, Gibraltar, 1999

Trefusis, Violet, *Don't Look Round*, Hutchinson, 1952

Trevelyan, Humphrey, *The India We Left*, Macmillan, 1972

Trevor-Roper, H. R., *The Last Days of Hitler*, Macmillan, 1950

—— (ed.), *Hitler's War Directives, 1939–45*, Sidgwick & Jackson, 1964

Usher, Roland, *Pan Germanism*, Houghton Mifflin Company, Boston, 1913

—— *Pan Americanism*, The Century Co., New York, 1915

Valentine, Ferdinand, *Father Vincent McNabb O. P.*, Burns & Oates, 1955

Van der Kiste, John, *Kaiser Wilhelm II. Germany's Last Emperor*, Sutton Publishing, Stroud, 1999

Vaughan, W. E. (ed.), *A New History of Ireland VI. Ireland Under the Union II, 1870–1921*, Clarendon Press, Oxford, 1996

Venkataramani, M. S., & Shrivastava, B. K., *Roosevelt, Gandhi, Churchill*, Radiant Publishers, New Delhi, 1983

Verrier, Anthony, *Francis Younghusband and the Great Game*, Jonathan Cape, 1991

Victoria Louise, Duchess of Brunswick, *The Kaiser's Daughter*, ed. R. Vacha, W. H. Allen, 1977

Vidler, Alec, *A Variety of Catholic Modernists*, Cambridge University Press, 1970

Watson, James D. *The Double Helix*, Weidenfeld & Nicolson, 1968, revised 1997

Waugh, Evelyn, *The Life of Ronald Knox*, Chapman & Hall, 1959

—— *The Diaries of Evelyn Waugh*, Penguin, Harmondsworth, 1979

Webb, Beatrice, *My Apprenticeship* (first published Longmans, Green & Co., 1926), Penguin, Harmondsworth, 1971

—— *The Diary of Beatrice Webb*, ed. Norman & Jean MacKenzie, vol. 1, *1873–1892*, *Glitter Around and Darkness Within*, Virago in association with the London School of Economics and Political Science, 1982; vol. 2, *1892–1905*, *All the Good Things of Life*, Virago in association will the LSE, etc., 1983; vol. 3, *1905–1924*, *The Power to Alter Things*, same publishers, 1984; vol. 4, *1924–1943*, *The Wheel of Life*, same publishers, 1985

Webb, Sidney & Beatrice, *A Constitution for the Socialist Commonwealth of Great Britain* (with an introduction by Samuel H. Beer), London School of Economics and Political Science, Cambridge University Press, 1975

Wedgwood, Josiah, *Essays and Adventures of a Labour MP*, Allen & Unwin, 1924

Weil, Simone, *The Simone Weil Reader*, ed. George A. Panichas, David McKay Company Inc., New York, 1977

Weinberg, Gerhard L., *Germany, Hitler and World War II*, Cambridge University Press, Cambridge, 1995

Weizsäcker, Ernst von, *The Memoirs of Ernst von Weizsäcker*, Victor Gollancz, 1951

Welch, Frances, *The Romanovs and Mr Gibbes*, Short, 2002.

Welles, Benjamin, *Sumner Welles – FDR's General Strategist*, Macmillan, Basingstoke, 1997

Welles, Sumner, *The Time for Decision*, Hamish Hamilton, 1944

Wells, H. G., *The New Machiavelli* [1911], Penguin, Harmondsworth, 1985

Wheeler, Burton K., *Yankee from the West*, Doubleday, New York, 1962

Whitecross, Roy, *Slaves of the Son of Heaven*, Kangaroo Press, East Roseville NSW, 2000

Williams, Charles, *He Came Down From Heaven*, William Heinemann, 1938

Williams, Trevor I., *A Short History of Twentieth Century Technology, c. 1900–1950*, Clarendon Press, Oxford, Oxford University Press, New York, 1982

Wilmot, Chester, *The Struggle for Europe*, Collins, 1952

Wilson, A. N., *Hilaire Belloc*, Hamish Hamilton, 1984

—— *The Victorians*, Hutchinson, 2002

Wilson, Edmund, *To the Finland Station*, Secker & Warburg, 1941

Wilson, John, *CB. A Life of Sir Henry Campbell-Bannerman*, Constable, 1973

Wilson, Sir Henry, *The Military Correspondence of Field Marshal Sir Henry Wilson*, ed. Keith Jeffery, Bodley Head for the Army Records Society, 1985

Windsor, The Duchess of, *The Heart Has Its Reasons* [Michael Joseph, 1956], Sphere Books, 1980

Woods, Oliver, & Bishop, James, *The Story of the Times*, Michael Joseph, 1983

Woodward, Sir Llewellyn, *Great Britain and the War of 1914–18*, Methuen & Co. Ltd, 1967

—— *British Foreign Policy in the Second World War*, HMSO, 1972

Wragg, David, *Signal Failure: Politics and Britain's Railways*, Sutton Publishing, Stroud, 2004

Wright, Robert, *Dowding and the Battle of Britain*, Macdonald, 1969

Wykeham-George, Kenneth, & Mathew, Gervase, *Bede Jarrett*, Blackfriars Press, 1941

Yeats, W. B., *The Poems*, revised, ed. Richard J. Finnerman, Macmillan, 1989

Young, Desmond, *Rommel*, Collins, 1950

Young, Filson, *The Trial of Hawley Harvey Crippen*, William Hodge & Company Ltd, 1920

Young, Kenneth, *Arthur James Balfour*, G. Bell & Sons Ltd, 1963

Younghusband, Francis, *Among the Celestial*, John Murray, 1898

—— *India and Tibet* [John Murray, 1910], Oxford University Press, Oxford, Hong Kong, New York, Melbourne, 1985

—— *The Epic of Mount Everest* [Edward Arnold, 1926], Pan Books, 2000 (Mallory's expeditions)

Ziegler, Philip, *Osbert Sitwell*, Chatto & Windus, 1998

Zinn, Howard, *A People's History of the United States*, Longman, 1980

Index

Abdication crisis (1936), 331, 338–9, 343–7

Abdulhamit II, Ottoman Sultan, 132–3

Abdullah I, King of Jordan, 217

Abyssinia: Italy invades, 330, 360

Acheson, Dean, 437, 443, 528

Action française, L' (newspaper), 158

Acton, Sir Harold, 236, 238, 241

Adenauer, Konrad, 514

Admiralty Arch, London, 47

adultery, 70–1

Afghanistan: bombed by British, 218

Afrika Korps (German), 401

Aga Khan, 240

agriculture: decline, 42

Ahmed, Selim ('Dahoum'), 143

Aiken, Conrad, 203

aircraft: developed, 44

Aitken, Max (Beaverbrook's son), 398

al-Afghani, Jamaluddin, 207

Alamogordo, New Mexico, 469, 472

Albert, Prince Consort, 4–5, 8, 47, 347

Albu, Austen, 497

Alexandra, Queen of Edward VII, 5, 57, 116

Alexis, Tsarevich of Russia, 224–5

Aliens Act (1911), 123

Aliens Bill (1904), 122

Allenby, General Edmund Henry Hynman (*later* 1st Viscount), 140–1, 144, 146, 193

Allingham, Helen (*née* Paterson), 38

Allingham, Margery, 298

Alsace-Lorraine, 200

Altrincham, Edward Grigg, 1st Baron, 228

Amadeus Quartet, 451

American Revolution, 461

Amiens, 194

Amritsar massacre (1919), 31, 208–10, 213, 367, 495

anarchists, 121–2

Anastasia, Grand Duchess of Russia, 225

Anderson, Elizabeth Garrett, 58

Anderson, Sir John, 407, 416

Andrew, Prince, 493

Anglicanism *see* Church of England

Anne, Princess Royal, 493

Anschluss, 3

anti-Semitism, 102, 357–60, 379–80, 425, 463

Anzacs: at Gallipoli, 137–8

appeasement policy, 360–1, 365–6

Arabs
  in First World War, 140–1
  and Jewish homeland, 150
  T.E. Lawrence romanticizes, 143

architecture, 39–40

aristocracy
  adapted, 518
  and education, 505
  as ruling class, 45–6, 48, 117–18, 249
  as stabilizing force in Edwardian Britain, 7
  system, 319

Armageddon, Battle of (1918), 140

579

INDEX

ALSO AVAILABLE IN ARROW

The Victorians

A.N. Wilson

People, not abstract ideas, make history, and nowhere is this more revealed than in A.N. Wilson's superb portrait of the Victorians, in which hundreds of different lives have been pieced together to tell a story – one which is still unfinished in our own day. The 'global village' is a Victorian village and many of the ideas we take for granted, for good or ill, originated with these extraordinary, self-confident people. What really animated their spirit, and how did they remake the world in their view? In an entertaining and often dramatic narrative, A. N. Wilson shows us remarkable people in the very act of creating the Victorian age.

'Rarely have author and subject been found in such deep and contented harmony . . . Wilson's tour de force'
Robert McCrum, 'Books of the Year', *Observer*

'The best single-volume work on the Victorian age yet written'
Andrew Roberts, *Evening Standard*

'A masterpiece of popular history'
Frank McLynn, 'Books of the Year', *Independent*

arrow books